International Interplay

International Interplay: The Future of Expropriation Across International Dispute Settlement

By

Riddhi Dasgupta

Foreword by Martin Hunter

CAMBRIDGE SCHOLARS

PUBLISHING

International Interplay:
The Future of Expropriation Across International Dispute Settlement,
by Riddhi Dasgupta

This book first published 2013

Cambridge Scholars Publishing

12 Back Chapman Street, Newcastle upon Tyne, NE6 2XX, UK

British Library Cataloguing in Publication Data
A catalogue record for this book is available from the British Library

ISBN (10): 1-4438-4597-3, ISBN (13): 978-1-4438-4597-7

For
My Beloved Grandmother

CONTENTS

FOREWORD

Many academic supervisors instruct, or persuade, their doctoral students to define their thesis topics much more narrowly than they propose initially. I have to admit that I do also. The reason is that a doctoral thesis should be innovative and 'add to the science'. Wide topics tend to lead to comprehensively researched compilations of the science that has been developed previously, with an associated commentary. Whilst such work can be useful, only exceptionally can it add to the science.

Similarly, many post-graduate doctoral students – having eliminated much of their formative initial research – understandably do not have the stamina to revisit their doctoral theses and rewrite or expand large chunks of their work for the purposes of preparing a book for separate publication.

Mr (now 'Dr', I am pleased to report) Dasgupta first discussed his plans with me about two years ago. He told me that, after he had defended his thesis, he was thinking of spending approximately another year revisiting his earlier, wider, research and converting his 'examined text' into a book with a wider scope for possible publication. I expressed admiration for his stamina, and was very pleased when he achieved this goal.

The result is impressive, and provides his readers with a well-constructed and organised analysis of the ways in which modern international arbitration tribunals have 'moved with the times', in tackling the expropriation-related issues placed before them for decision.

The introductory chapter demonstrates the importance of expropriation in international law, with facts and figures. The author reflects on the co-extensive evolution of international tribunals with respect to expropriation and property rights and establishes that *'each has been the others' access point to growth'*. Also, when defining the term *'expropriation'* he explains that its scope is treated in its broadest sense in that it covers both direct and indirect expropriations.

The author examines the current expropriation-related standards, new trends and future challenges. This book thus fills an obvious need for a systematic account on this topic because the ever-broadening scope of the meaning and effect of expropriation has shown to be an elastic concept.

In Chapter 3, Dr Dasgupta deals with 'attribution' and 'causation'. This chapter is mainly concerned with the ethos and predispositions of international tribunals. He explains that:

> *. . . . it is about really entering the minds of the international tribunals empowered to decide if an expropriation has taken place and, if so, what compensation is to be paid.*

There have been many conceptual changes since the time of the famous *ex parte* Libyan oil concession arbitrations of the 1970s and, later, the more liberal approach of the *Aminoil v Kuwait* tribunal in the early 1980s. This Chapter discusses how modern tribunals think, what criteria they apply when they decide whether a respondent state is responsible ('attribution'), and what degree of *nexus* amounts to proximate causation. He notes that:

> *. . . . there is a constant tug of war between investors and property owners, who typically want to make it easier to show attribution and state responsibility, and governments, who usually do not.*

Chapter 4 addresses, first, the exhaustion of local remedies and, secondly, continuous nationality standards in international law. Chapter 5 deals with concepts such as non-discrimination, national treatment, and the application of most favoured nation principles. Chapter 6 explores other substantive issues: fair and equitable treatment, due process, minimum standard of treatment, and compensation, explaining that the 'Chapter 6 standards' are absolute, unlike those described in Chapter 5, such as non-discrimination, legitimate expectations and *force majeure*.

In the context of future developments Dr Dasgupta also discusses a number of thus far intractable problems such as the appellate mechanism that exists in the ICSID system, as to which he makes a proposal that deserves consideration by the appropriate authorities.

The work finishes with some helpful and provocative conclusions which pull together many of the strands that run through the work. The concluding chapter is of particular interest as it contains Riddhi Dasgupta's well thought-out predictions for future developments, and the dialogues and debates that will lead to them. I am happy to recommend the book most warmly to readers interested in the study of international law of expropriation and property rights.

—Professor J. Martin Hunter
London, United Kingdom
December 2012

Preface and Acknowledgements

I was counselled to retain rather a *res ipsa* approach to the task of writing prefatory remarks. The well-intentioned suggestion was, "The monograph should speak for itself, so keep the preface Spartan." Moreover, I cannot be so presumptuous as to add very much to the comments and analyses of Professor Martin Hunter, the esteemed writer of the *Foreword*, and academic-practitioner-arbitrator-innovator *par excellence*. I will just reinforce three simple notions undergirding this monograph. In this, I beg your patience.

First, I should say that in international law, which by nature needs to reach a wide and diverse audience, there is a preferred form of delivery and it matters. It is encapsulated by one word: Simplicity. After all, the point is to have an impact, meaning that the message must reach people who do not ordinarily live in this orbit. Second, while there are risks in comparative analysis, it would be tantamount to throwing the baby out with the bathwater if we did not consider the analytical possibilities which only a comparative and multi-linear process can give us. If you do not know what is out there, you do not know what your comparators or your potential sources of inspiration are. Not only might the premises and assumptions resulting from a one-dimensional process be cramped and narrow but so might our deductions. Third and lastly, the intellectual process is not offended — rather it is vindicated — when we directly engage with the notion that ideas come from people who have lives which are composed of both biology and experiences. The legal profession is rendered stimulating as well as valuable because of diversity. Life experiences empower lawyers with a diverse set of perspectives to dissect important questions of rules and justice.

Along those lines, it is crucially important to focus not only on the people upon whose ideas this book is built but also those people who have been instrumental in making this book see the light of day — in short, the people important to me. I must thank my grandmother, my parents, my aunt Ranu Basu, the rest of our family, and friends and well-wishers who have been there for me. I do not wish to leave anyone out but some other people just *had* to be named for their constant support, help and inspiration: Rahul Mediratta, Amrita Basu Somani, Chris Thompson, Kingdar Prussien, Jacob Marty and Marissa Cope, Darleny Cepin, Anaïs Menard, Lourdes

Madagisekera, Laura Ertmer, Gustavo Barros de Carvalho, Mark O'Flynn, Thierry Maldonado, Apurba Khatiwada, Shira Goldstein, Daniel Brusser, Daniel Barton, Madjdy Fawzy, Laura Bolton, Caroline Hull, Sebastian Robins, Rebecca Hadgett, Xiaolu Zhang-Coenen and Peter Coenen, Albert Monroe, Norma Weir, Rosemary Luff, Asif Khan, Daniel Baker, Alice Dub, Adam Samarillo, Paul Syers, Joshua Parker, Christian Perrone, Ryan Rogers, Pascal Knoll, Christoph Trautrims, Sean Bhattacharya, Mark Stadnyk, Ruvi Ziegler, Jan-Fabian Meis, Claudia Buitkamp, David Chait, Fotis Vergis, Tom Hamilton, Matthew Morton, Sam and Anna Littlejohns, Samuel Dahan, Kenneth Burns and the Burns family, Yu Zhang, Christian Brink, Nicholas Crawford, Michael Walker, Vess Popov, Michael Campbell, Besim Hatinoglu, Christina Brittain, Benjamin Watts, Joshua Poritz, Aashika Damodar, Alex Cocavessis, Bethan Saunders, Ola Janusz, Ana Lise Feliciano Hansen, Shalina Daved, Siddarth Mitroo, Simon Gray, Rohan Shekhar, Esther Widmann, Jeremy Richardson, Paula Koelemeijer, Sayan Chaki, Christian Capasso, Jay Orenduff, Daniele Mercadente, Alex Mills, Maximilian Bulinski, Mariano Beguerisse, Luka Krsljanin, Shane Kelly, Brad Hiller, Kevin Morgan, Ramona Meyricke, Isabella Wanderley Vitali, Aditi Chokshi, Dwayne Menezes, David Adelsberg and Jocelyn London, David Gordon, Joana Borlido, Roberta Wells, Sir Martin and Lady Barbara Harris, Irene Hills, Karolis Stašinskas, Tadas Jucikas, Kristina Jucikaitė, Marianna Zaslavsky, Sebastian Pender, Graham Wheeler, Adam Nagorski, Andrew Simpson, Laura Mckoy, Nitish Upadhyaya, John Niland, Govert Coppens, David Hostert, Laurence Groot Bruinderink, Michael Chalk, Michael Waibel, Alexander Rodney, Charles Justin Henck, Jonathan Kamler, Ben Taylor, Nabil Wilf, Eric Koskinen, Damian Eads, Artūras Ratkus, Sid Misra, Rebecca Hiner, Mariela Aguirre Sanchez, Maribel Butler, Alexander Kaus, Roland Saam, Christian Winzer, Justin Kempley, Sabena Panesar, Christian Capasso, Elan Gada, David Goldin, Terence Zaleski, Brian Kauffman, Scott Keller, David Greenhouse, Emily Jordan, Gwen McDougal, Jason Parsont, Brandon Walsh, Charmaine Jelbert, Cedric Vanleenhove, George Bangham, Daniel Ham, Kunaal Sharma, Daniel Silovitz, Alex Grow, Trisha Garbe, Simon and Sophie Leimbacher, Rahim Moloo, Todd Weiler, Evianne Van Gijn, Bill Asquith and Mario, Erin and André Faure.

My Ph.D. supervisor Professor Martin Dixon was superbly patient with me throughout this process, and whatever this book is it is so because of him. I am grateful to Professor Sara Seck and the University of Western Ontario's Faculty of Law for sponsoring my research during the summer of 2010. I am beholden to Dr. Markus Gehring and Dr. Kate Miles for being incredibly conscientious about assessing my Ph.D. thesis and for making helpful suggestions. These suggestions I have done my best to incorporate into this publication. I am grateful to Professor James Crawford, Dr. Tom Grant, Professor Roger O'Keefe, Dr. Michael Waibel and the entire Lauterpacht Centre family at Cambridge University for their doctrinal entrepreneurship in general and help to me in particular. I also thank from the very bottom of my heart Judge David Faber and Mrs. Debbie Faber for their unceasing friendship, understanding, and courage. They have demonstrated to the world that new frontiers are a lifelong aspiration, and attainable too. They have shown me kindnesses that one day I wish to pass on to "youth, whose feet must pass this way." May we all learn from their valour and enterprise. I am grateful to Professor Tom Ginsburg at the University of Chicago Law School for his personal help and theoretical contributions alike. Judge Charles Brower and Chief of the Investment Arbitration at the United States Department of State, Mr. Jeremy Sharpe, assisted me immensely in clarifying issues, lending their assistance and backing me up. Their enchanting, courtly and modest manners made me feel instantly at ease when interacting with these giants of the law. I am also grateful to my editor for her vigilance and care. I can say nothing that will do justice to what my parents have done for me.

In giving of themselves to my growth, each person has demonstrated the value of looking beyond formal datasets and credentials which tell only a narrow (and frequently misleading) part of the story. By taking up qualitative assessment, the process is made slightly more difficult, to be sure, but it is also made better. I have benefited significantly, especially in difficult times, from their courage. Lastly, some judicial personages and legal advisors gave me extensive help but did not want to be identified publicly (frequently because of a lengthy clearance process required in order to give on-the-record interviews). They know who they are, and they have my warm and heartfelt gratitude.

There is an awe-inspiring amount of talent around me reposed in gifted lawyers and other innovators. Their curse is their imagination which some sterile checklists cannot capture and with which the latter simply cannot cope. This tragedy has cost these innovators, and the rest of us, the prospect of coveted roles through which they might have made great strides for all of us. By subconsciously or perhaps consciously choosing some paths of least resistance we might have done ourselves a grave disservice. May we all become a little wiser, and may we all appreciate those who did give us their time as well as chances when things looked bleak for us.

I have been blessed with excellent, supportive people in my life. Each of these top-drawer dignitaries imparted to me the message that what counts in life is the wholesome composite of resilience, generosity, solidarity, diligence, courage, imagination, perseverance and kindness. During the most challenging days of churning this product out as well as responding to several other wildfires, I was at first stunned and impressed, and eventually deeply moved, by the iconic performances of the differently-abled athletes in the 2012 London Paralympics. Their countless disappointments earlier in life are said to have paved the way to these remarkable moments in the summer of 2012. Each of the aforementioned traits — imperatives, really — was embodied in their performances. They must have been told a million times, as we all have, that our gifts are no gifts at all. They combined their aptitudes with perseverance and imagination to redefine the very notion of "talent."

Being on the losing side of an advantage, even if it is something that others in your environment take for granted, need not be a disqualifying feature. In my own small way, then, I drew tremendous inspiration to soldier on and complete the book. Thus the process and the craft have been ever so meaningful, for in *its* own way this book beseeches the international law community to think imaginatively about the weighty and sensitive questions facing us in the coming years. The well-trodden path is a time-tested path and merits reverence. But we should not be above paying ourselves the greatest reverence of all, which is constant introspection and active efforts to adapt and improve. No more fulsome a tribute is even possible.

The errors are mine alone. I request the reader to pardon my Dickensian, Greek tragedies, and other cultural (both popular and esoteric) fascinations. This book imparts legal strategy and observations to putative and current practitioners, judges and academics. But there is no reason that strategic observations may not also be entertaining or relatable. My prose-style happens to be a hybrid of practitioner manuals, cultural anthologies and theoretical texts. Above all, this book attempts to be useful, clear and memorable. These articles of faith simply help the writing and, I can only hope, reading processes — and they make the subject come to life.

Cambridge, United Kingdom
December 2012

CHAPTER ONE

INTRODUCTION: EXPROPRIATION IN INTERNATIONAL LAW

Aim of the Enterprise

Enthusiastically, this book sets out to determine how to maximise the advantages and minimise the disadvantages in the international law of expropriation. Some of this book is prescriptive, some descriptive, all riveting. We consider past as well as potential transfers of knowledge among international tribunals[1] that have been duly constituted and those which strive to protect the rights of the parties to have their claims properly heard, with due deliberation, to have a process free of fraud and corruption, and to have a prompt and "reasoned judgment in accordance with the applicable law."[2]

In that venture, this book adopts a comparative approach and assumes a healthful, impartial dose of scepticism. This endeavour has been aided by the fact that, to the extent I am aware, I have no axe to grind.[3] This book is no ideological jeremiad, unless of course "ideology" encompasses legal pragmatism and wholesome, constructive and usually-unifying

---

[1] There is some controversy as to what an "international tribunal" is or does and what the "ideal-type" attributes of an international tribunal are. International tribunals might be described as judicial or at least judicial-like institutions "created by inter-governmental agreement (including agreements made within, or by, inter-governmental organizations), or by agreement between a national government and a foreign private entity, where the court is legally situated either fully or partly outside the national juridical and governmental system of any state." B. Kingsbury, "International Courts: Uneven Judicialization in Global Order," *in* CAMBRIDGE COMPANION TO INTERNATIONAL LAW 38 (James Crawford and Martti Koskenniemi, eds., Cambridge University Press, 2012).

[2] V.S Mani, INTERNATIONAL ADJUDICATION, PROCEDURAL ASPECTS 23 (Martinus Nijhoff, 1980).

[3] Of course, a good commentator, like a good judge, must be open-minded enough to question her or his unobvious prejudices at every point. Ignoring a problem cannot be the answer.

common sense. There are strong arguments on both sides, and one is tempted to ask the critical follow-up question: What do the *details* indicate? The proverbial Devil often dwells in the details. This book strives to spell out imaginative strategies of advocacy, including counterarguments, for the next generation of investment and property disputes in international law. Contained herein are innovative theories which rest on the shoulders of giants.

International lawyers might appreciate that with respect to expropriation and property rights, international tribunals themselves have been changed, sometimes absentmindedly, and of course the tribunals have altered the field of property rights. Each has been the others' access point to growth. This coextensive evolution is the book's narrative.

§ 1.1—Undertaking this Monograph

Public international law is often seen as a mammoth *gestalt*. When we do somehow dissect its anatomy, its distinct compartments (to mean tribunal types and legal standards) begin to reveal themselves to us. This book deduces the interactive lessons on international expropriation law to be learned from the different compartments for their mutual benefit and for the benefit of emerging international law systems. Unifying or even adequately comprehending the international legal order in its totality, including specific jurisdictional and merits doctrines, entails a nuanced understanding of international human rights.

We trace where the various expropriation-related standards currently are and where the trends of these force-fields are headed. Such a book has not ever been shared with the world. It is high time that this is done because expropriation law's ever-broadening scope has shown itself to be highly elastic. It is not that there are no relentless efforts to slow the tide but the overall trend decidedly and definitely is in the expansive direction. When Indonesia tries to ban open-pit mining in its forests, Canada tries to introduce public auto insurance options—had the "public option" component of the recent Patient Protection and Affordable Care Act (PPACA) in the United States been enacted, might we have witnessed a similar NAFTA or other IIA request for arbitration challenging the provision? Quite likely[4]—or Costa Rica nullifies erstwhile-active concessions to an investor now seeking off-shore oil exploration, another

[4] This angle was not given much coverage during the pre-PPACA enactment debates in Congress, on-line or over the airwaves.

creative (though not necessarily illegitimate) expropriation claim is docketed.

Right now there is a genuine hunger within the international law community to brainstorm about the way forward by merging the different subject-matter and tribunal-type compartments. This is unsurprising because the flow of foreign direct investment (FDI)[5] into developing and transitional economies has been steadily growing,[6] and in 2011 reached the peak of $776.562 billion.[7] The global FDI in-flow reached $1524.422 billion, thus deriving by subtraction the amount of FDI in-flow for developed countries: $747.86 billion.[8]

Some might say this has been the inevitable consequence of the "unbundling of global production"[9] since the fall of the Berlin Wall (and the end of the Cold War it signalled), the intensity of globalisation, and the mushrooming international character of investment projects that even half a generation ago might have been unthinkable. With the steady progressions have come higher stakes and more complex contentions. Complexity has become a genuine concern due to the tangible FDI-related differences

---

[5] See N. Bajpai & N. Dasgupta, "Multinational Companies and Foreign Direct Investment in India and China," Columbia India Program, Columbia University, January 2004, at 3, n. 1, available at
<www.earth.columbia.edu/cgsdOLD/documents/bajpai_mncs_china_india_001.pdf> ("FDI can be defined as a financial stake a foreign company acquires in a domestic company. FDI is the category of international investment that reflects the objective of a resident entity in one economy ('direct investor' or parent enterprise) obtaining a 'lasting interest' and control in an enterprise resident in another economy ('direct investment enterprise') (International Monetary Fund (IMF) Balance of Payments Manual, Fifth Edition, 1993)").

[6] It must be remembered that FDI out-flow is not necessarily the same as an "expansion of productive capacity, as it . . . [might be] due in large part to cross-border acquisitions and increased amounts of cash reserves kept in foreign affiliates rather than the much-needed direct investment in new productive assets through . . . [various] investment projects or capital expenditures in existing foreign affiliates." See UNCTAD: "Global FDI Outflows Continued to Rise in 2011 Despite Economic Uncertainties; However Prospects Remain Guarded," Global Investment Trends Monitor, April 2012, available at
<http://unctad.org/en/PublicationsLibrary/webdiaeia2012d19_en.pdf>.

[7] See "Inward and Outward Foreign Direct Investment Flows, Annual, 1970-2011," United Nations Conference on Trade and Development (UNCTAD), available at <http://unctadstat.unctad.org/TableViewer/tableView.aspx>.

[8] *Id.*

[9] Baldwin R. (2006), *Globalization: The Great Unbundling(s)*, Prime Minister's Office, Economic Council of Finland.

among developing nations,[10] and also because the erstwhile order of the day—FDI out-flow *from* developed *to* developing nations—has been turned on its head in several cases.[11] The economics of BITs, particularly a nation's marginal benefit of entering one, is also telling: it has been argued that "[a]s more countries sign BITs, the benefit of BITs to any one country falls, but because the benefit of staying out also falls, more and more countries sign up. . . ."[12] Furthermore, "although the marginal value to a

---

[10] See, *e.g.*, N. Bajpai & N. Dasgupta, "Multinational Companies and Foreign Direct Investment in India and China," Columbia India Program, Columbia University, January 2004, at 1, *available at* <www.earth.columbia.edu/cgsdOLD/documents/bajpai_mncs_china_india_001.pdf>. (articulating that "the yawning gap between China and India in attracting the non-debt creating FDI flows raises some important fundamental questions about its actual FDI potentials. What could be the possible reasons behind China's success in attracting FDI inflows? Has the Chinese FDI been said to take place at least partially, at India's expense? Can India possibly become an FDI destination as attractive as China? Who are the target groups of foreign investors for India? What lessons can India possibly derive from China to attract these investors?"); N. Bajpai & N. Dasgupta, "FDI to China and India: The Definitional Differences" prepared jointly with Dr. Nirupam Bajpai, Senior Development Advisor and Director of the South Asia Program at the Center for Globalization and Sustainable Development (CGSD), Columbia University, Business Line, May 15, 2004. The issue is especially central for emerging markets (and Brazil-Russia-India-China, the BRIC countries), and the differences therein.

[11] See generally N. Dasgupta, "Examining the Long Run Effects of Export, Import and FDI Inflows on the FDI Outflows from India: A Causality Analysis," Journal of International Business and Economy (JIBE) (2009); N. Dasgupta, "Indian Companies Investing in USA: An Enquiry into the Recent Pattern and Trends to the US-Bound Indian FDI", in Sauvant, K. P. and J.P. Pradhan, with A. Chatterjee and B. Harley (2010), (eds.), THE RISE OF INDIAN MULTINATIONALS: PERSPECTIVES ON INDIAN OUTWARD FOREIGN DIRECT INVESTMENT, New York: Palgrave Macmillan (2010); UNCTAD: "Global FDI Outflows Continued to Rise in 2011 Despite Economic Uncertainties; However Prospects Remain Guarded," Global Investment Trends Monitor, April 2012, *available at* <http://unctad.org/en/PublicationsLibrary/webdiaeia2012d19_en.pdf> ("FDI outflows from developing countries fell by 7 per cent mainly due to significant declines in outward FDI from Latin American and the Caribbean and a slow down in growth of investments from developing Asia.").

[12] J. Tobin & S. Rose-Ackerman, *When BITs Have Some Bite: The Political-Economic Environment for Bilateral Investment Treaties*, Yale Law School Working Paper (2006), pp. 11-12 [J. Tobin & S. Rose-Ackerman, *When BITs Have Some Bite*].

country of signing an extra BIT will be positive, the size of that marginal effect falls as the global coverage of BITs increases."[13]

The graphs to illustrate these data are provided below. The first three graphs concern the FDI in-flow of developing economies; the fourth concerns transitional economies; the fifth concerns developed economies; the sixth concerns the global economy; and finally the seventh graph concerns emerging economies. Each graph's *x*-axis denotes years and *y*-axis denotes the FDI in-flow in millions of U.S. Dollars ($).

Graph I
African Developing Economies' FDI In-Flow (1980-2011)

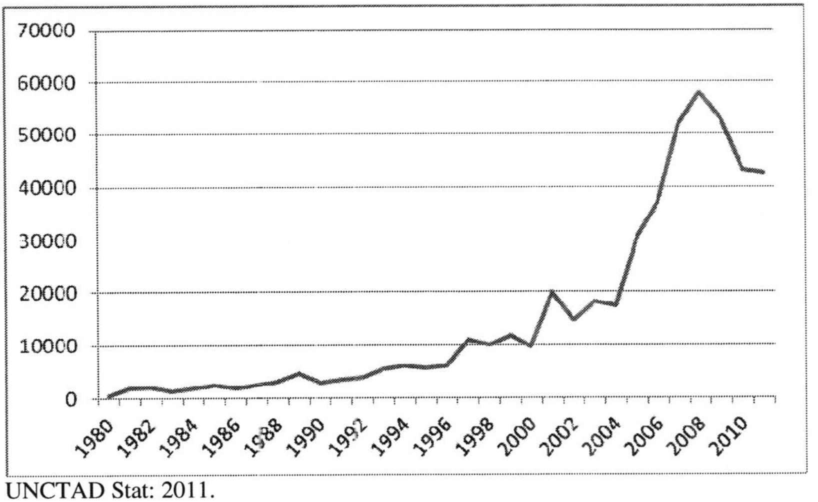

UNCTAD Stat: 2011.

[13] *Id.*

Graph II
North and South American Developing Economies' FDI In-Flow (1980-2011)

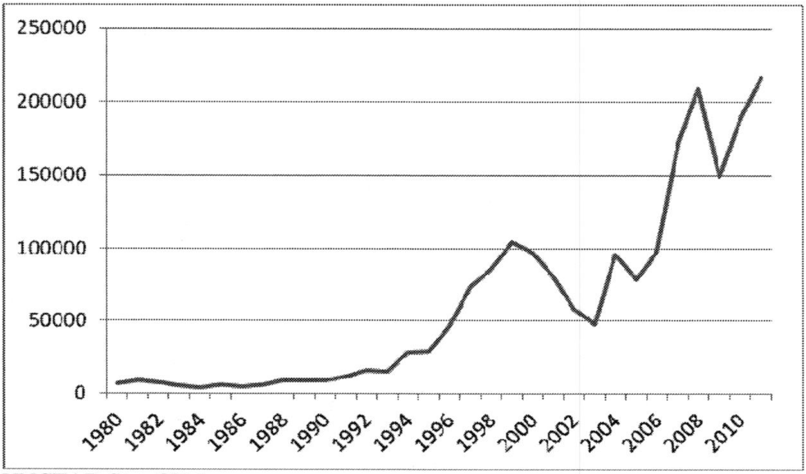

UNCTAD Stat: 2011.

Graph III
Asian Developing Economies' FDI In-Flow (1980-2011)

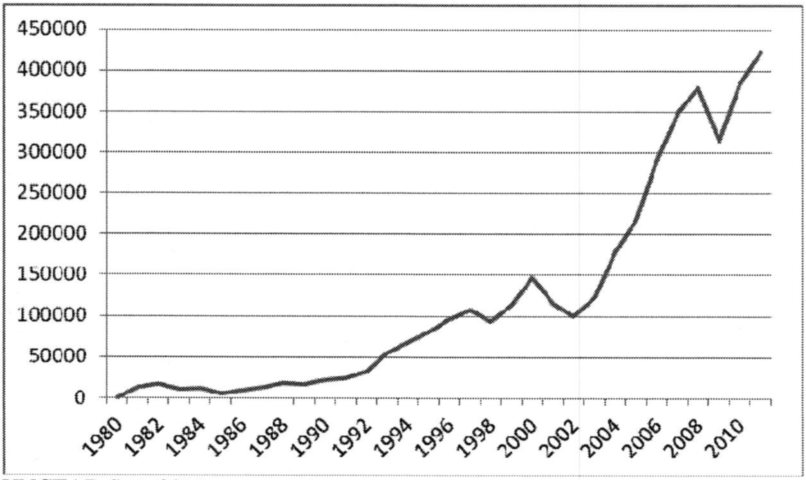

UNCTAD Stat: 2011.

Graph IV
Transitional Economies' FDI In-Flow (1980-2011)

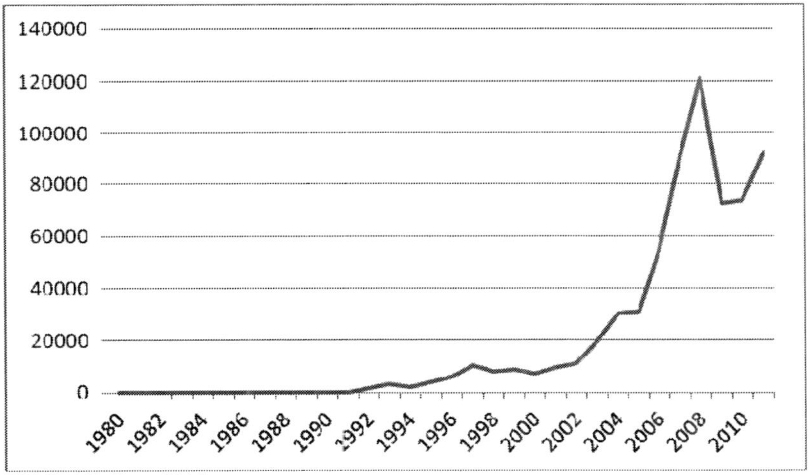

UNCTAD Stat: 2011.

Graph V
Developed Economies' FDI In-Flow (1980-2011)

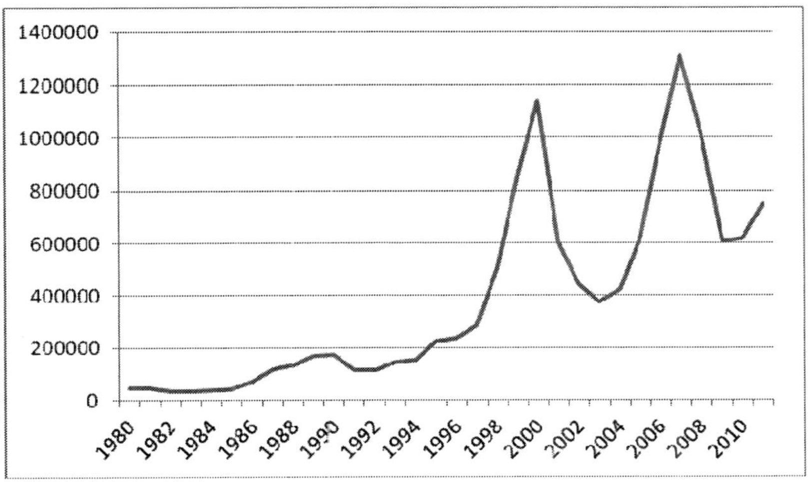

UNCTAD Stat: 2011.

Graph VI
Global Economy FDI In-Flow (1980-2011)

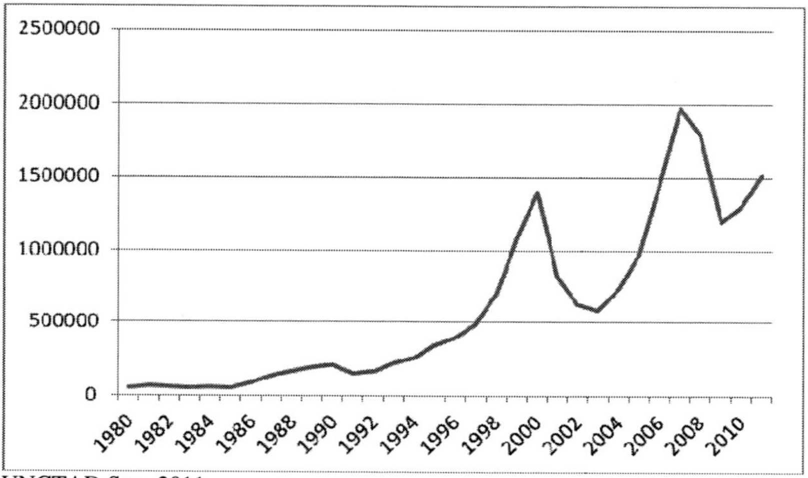

UNCTAD Stat: 2011.

Graph VII
Emerging Economies' FDI In-Flow (1980-2011)

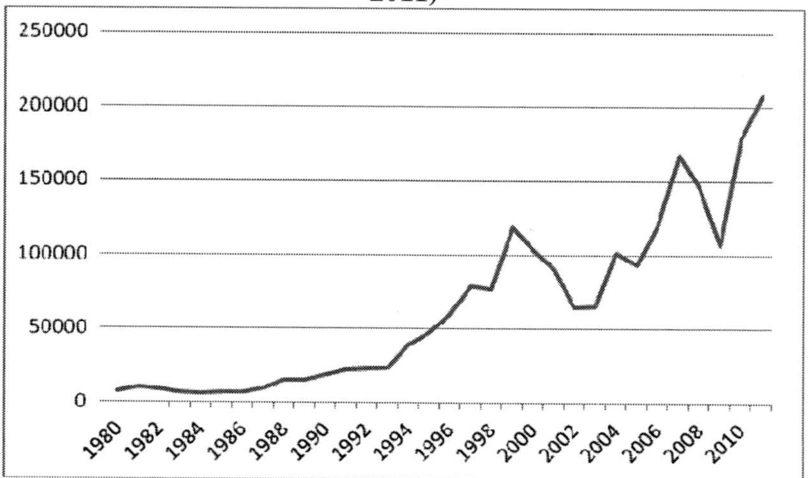

UNCTAD Stat: 2011.

Presently expropriation law is receptive to creative idea-generation and ingenious lawyering. Did this come from an insightful *eureka* experience? Perhaps. Talking over with some involved lawyers the possibility that maybe the Republic of Uruguay would, in a particular case, be best served in claiming cogently the "national security" secondary defence, I began to experiment with the idea of a book about how to think most effectively like a public international lawyer in practice or academia.

Consider the unenviable position in which the Republic of Uruguay finds itself. Uruguay has its task cut out: To salvage[14] its 2009 cigarette packaging law—the new law mandates that 80 percent of each side of cigarette boxes be covered by graphic images of the possible pernicious health effects of smoking—which has been challenged by the tobacco giant Philip Morris International. The State's defence: national security. Surely, at least the law blogs would have something interesting to churn out and discuss in droves. Its starting proposition might be that all throughout history, and especially recent history, the magic words "national security" have been claimed by States as a sort of malleable shibboleth to achieve almost anything they wanted. Danger lurked.

The reasoning went this way: Since smoking can and does cause cancer to persons not suspicious or aware of the risks is such a grave problem, the State is entitled to protect its national security interests by requiring such packaging. After all, for whom and by whom will the Nation's borders be defended if a significant population of the country and, if true, its military forces are cancer-prone or -stricken? Uruguay may yet advance this argument in its Memorial sometime in the near future. Imaginative still was Uruguay's *expressio unius est exclusio alterius* argument in its Memorial on Jurisdiction, stating that an express and rare "public security and order, public health or morality, as well as activities which by law are reserved to their own investors" exception,[15] though not clearly vindicating the government position, is by reason of its very

[14] Of course, the statute cannot be invalidated or its enforcement proscribed by an international investment tribunal. But the tribunal *may* find a violation of an international obligation and issue an award of damages which has the *de facto* effect of leading to the statute's repeal or non-enforcement. Moreover, in future treaty negotiations the losing sovereign is likely to have less leverage than if the tribunal had not found a violation.

[15] Art. 2(1), Switzerland-Uruguay BIT ("The Contracting Parties recognize each other's right not to allow economic activities for reasons of public security and order, public health or morality, as well as activities which by law are reserved to their own investors.").

presence a significant help to Uruguay.[16] Potentially effective, with a surface plausibility.

Most importantly perhaps, this book lays out the challenges and benefits over the arc of the future: the next one to two decades (perhaps even longer). I did not start out by articulating the differences between the international and domestic orders. But it became increasingly clear to me that shaping the book's thesis will have proved to be a fool's errand had I glossed over this important set of differences. It constitutes the centrepiece of the book's unifying argument in several respects, especially as it justifies the consent function (coming up in the ensuing chapters).[17]

There is also another reason for embarking on this project *now*. We live on the cusp of great changes in the fundamental idea and mechanics of property rights internationally. For instance, there is an emerging recognition that investment protection rather than developmental objectives is the main purpose behind modern IIA's.[18] Bilateral investment treaties,

---

[16] *Philip Morris Brands Sàrl, Philip Morris Products S.A., and Abal Hermanos S.A. v. Republic of Uruguay*, ICSID Case No. ARB/10/7 (2011), Memorial on Jurisdiction, at ¶ 7 ("This language is unique among BITs and is significantly stronger than the more typical "non-precluded measures" clauses litigated in prior cases. . . . [B]y mutually underscoring, at the very outset of the BIT, their mutual sovereign rights to prohibit economic activities for reasons of public health, Switzerland and Uruguay manifested their clear intent to exclude public health measures from the protections otherwise afforded to investors in the subsequent provisions of the Treaty, including the dispute resolution clause. Any other reading of Article 2 would render it meaningless, in violation of basic precepts of treaty interpretation. The conclusion is strengthened further by the structure of the BIT as a whole considered in light of its object and purpose.").

[17] Whoever undertakes this sort of book, I realised, must be both the proverbial poet as well as the historian — speaking as the descriptor explaining how the state of the law is and will develop to be (the historian's role) and how it should, if that path is a different one (the poet). The erudite Sampson states: "It is one thing to write like a poet, another like a historian. A poet can say or sing things not as they were, but as they should have been. The historian should write them down not as they should have been, but as they were, without adding or omitting anything." ("Pero uno es escribir como poeta, y otro como historiador: el poeta puede contar o cantar las cosas, no como fueron, sino como debı´an ser; y el historiador las ha de escribir, no como debı´an ser, sino como fueron, sin an˜ adir ni quitar a la verdad cosa alguna."). Miguel de Cervantes, *Don Quijote de la Mancha, Segunda Parte Del Ingenioso Caballero*, Capı´tulo III (1605 and 1615), Edicio´n del IV Centenario (2004).

[18] See, *e.g.*, L. Petersen, BILATERAL INVESTMENT TREATIES AND DEVELOPMENT POLICYMAKING 8 (International Institute of Sustainable Development, 2004) ("While BITs can, in theory, be written with an eye towards flexibility for

or BIT's ("foundational elements of international investment law"), have been characterised succinctly as "agreements between two states designed to provide investors with recourse when the foreign state in which they invest harms or discriminates against their investment."[19]

On the other hand, developing countries and sustainable development advocates are calling for a more level playing field, as the expression goes, along with "special and differentiated treatment" for their goals.[20] The nascent but growing sustainable development movement in the law is calling for "the need to clarify and strengthen the relationship between existing international instruments or agreements in the field of environment and relevant social and economic agreements or instruments, taking into account the special needs of developing countries."[21]

The debate before international tribunals, sometimes subliminally, inquires whether and to what extent this reconfiguration in *specific* cases might displace default principles of international law. Tribunals must also ask if, more generally speaking, older default principles of international law should yield to newer ones. When the older rule is quite simply obsolete and dysfunctional and/or might even contain the serious and probable risk of being counterproductive, its reevaluation is warranted.

Is there such a notion as too many fissures in international law? Can we capitalize on this state of affairs? An age fraught with tense scenarios such as the Arab Spring, Latin American and Eurozone financial crises is also an age of opportunity for international law to show its value, notably to disabuse laypeople and lawyers alike of the too-fragmented-to-be-effective (an inverse of too-big-to-fail perhaps) myths surrounding modern international law. Several strands and various degrees of precedent applicable to international law are said to cause fragmentation.

However, fragmentation can also generate diversity in the marketplace of effective ideas and thereby result in tremendous solidarity and might help mediate this conflict. In my view, it is preferable that the stakeholders, namely the international tribunals, practitioners, academics, and of course laypeople, should know the facts rather than speculate about

---

development purposes, it appears uncommon for them to have been crafted in such a manner. Rather, BITs tend to be *highly* reciprocal, narrowly focused on investment protection (rather than development or other policy goals), and garnished with few exceptions.").

[19] K. Claussen, *Comment: The Casualty of Investor Protection in Times of Economic Crisis*, 118 YALE L. J. 1545, 1545, n. 3 (2009).

[20] Agenda 21, 1992 Report of the UNCED, I (1992) UN Doc. A/CONF.151/26/Rev.1, (1992) 31 I.L.M. 874 Chapter 38.

[21] *Id.*

the correctness of some allegations directed at this area of international law.[22] That is part of the reason this monograph must be delivered at this time.

Through the prism of property rights and to better analyse property rights, various international fora can learn from each other. This can be achieved through an important sequence: functionalism, expressivism, assemblage, and paragon-building. In the international law process of "law-perfection," this metamorphosis cannot guarantee durability of the legal instrument, though it makes that prospect likelier, but it can guarantee solidarity both within a country and among countries.

Even though international law is classed as a species different from comparative law, comparative law is inextricably connected to international law. Indeed, the two are internecine to one another. To inform or improve the effectiveness of a given mechanism in international law, comparative law and other sources of international law are necessary. A chief technique of law-building in the aftermath of chaos is to seek a wholesale substitute elsewhere that could serve as a model, the rationale being that piecemeal assemblage is too experimentally delicate. Debates attending the adoption of the African Charter on Human and Peoples' Rights, for example, found no *one* document that "fit Africa's needs." After more than a decade of human rights dominance by the quasi-judicial body African Commission on Human and Peoples' Rights (AComHPR), modeled on the United Nations Human Rights Committee and lacking binding authority, in 1998 full powers were invested in the African Court on Human and Peoples' Rights (ACtHPR).

The next stage is *expressivism*—to identify certain consistent instrumental and revelatory public purposes that are faithful to the history and goals of the regime in question. International investment agreements concerned with the energy sector trying to follow the multilateral North American Free Trade Agreement (NAFTA) and Energy Charter Treaty (ECT) models faced these limitations early.[23] The deficiencies of functionalism

[22] There is something of an "image problem," particularly concerning international arbitration, that has become too vociferous not to go unaddressed any longer. See, *e.g.*, P. Eberhardt & C. Olivet, "Profiting from injustice: How law firms, arbitrators and financiers are fuelling an investment arbitration boom" (Corporate Europe Observatory and the Transnational Institute, 2012), *available at* <www.tni.org/sites/www.tni.org/files/download/profitingfrominjustice_0.pdf>.

[23] J. M. Marlles, *Public Purpose, Private Losses: Regulatory Expropriation and Environmental Regulation in International Investment Law*, 16 J. OF TRANSNAT'L L. & POL'Y 275, 277 (2006) ("NAFTA, the [Energy Charter Treaty (ECT)], and almost all BITs are united in requiring governments to pay compensation to

thus reveal themselves, and necessitate clearer thinking about principles as well as behaviourally-based rules.

Assemblage (or what Professor Mark Tushnet has called *bricolage*)[24] from various effective sources now comes into play, demonstrating that both a system of values and a system of black-letter rules are essential. I would modify Tushnet's axiom slightly and call it *ordered bricolage* because this stage need not necessarily be haphazard, disorganized, and succeeded by buyer's remorse. Legitimacy is prime among the values that the rules attempt to create and sustain; otherwise even some *exclusively* retrospective international tribunals not have clearly demarcated *lex specialis* and *lex generalis*. The prerequisites to legitimacy are following others as well as giving others a roadmap to follow you. The importance of this template creation cannot be overstated. Other values that the book will explore are democracy, rights of the vulnerable, separation of powers, and federalism. Despite this gradual metamorphosis towards law-perfection, both international law instruments and domestic constitutions may prove to be ineffective or unsustainable.

Nonetheless, the *paragon-building* that has been achieved might lead to solidarity and cohesion among the populations. Therefore, if this legal instrument or even this regime disintegrates (and they might for infinite reasons), the solidarity generated within a population or among populations of various nations will push them to keep trying. The scent of success will have proved to be too alluring. Moreover, the disintegration may or may not be attributable to the frailties in the instrument. The elephant in the room, the real reason at work on some level, is the civic spirit (or lack thereof). Measured and cautious solidarity, then, might be the end achieved by various means interstitial to (and inter-locking with) the law-building metamorphosis.

---

foreign investors when direct governmental expropriation occurs which resembles a physical taking. Article 1110 of NAFTA, Article 13 of the ECT, and Article 6 of the U.S. Model BIT all use similar language in requiring compensation for actions constituting expropriation or measures equivalent to expropriation.").

[24] M. Tushnet, *The Possibilities of Comparative Constitutional Law,* 108 YALE L.J. 1225, 1286 (1999); M. Tushnet, *The Bricoleur at the Center*, Book Review of THE PARTIAL CONSTITUTION by Cass R. Sunstein (1993) 60 U. CHICAGO L. REV. 1071; Claude Lévi-Strauss, THE SAVAGE MIND (University of Chicago Press, 1966) at 17-36 (coining the term "bricolage" to generally mean borrowing whatever is readily at hand). One of the great exports through the "third wave" of constitutionalism is judicial review. See T. Ginsburg, JUDICIAL REVIEW IN NEW DEMOCRACIES 6-9 (Cambridge University Press, 2003) (containing a list of countries and designating them as having created legislation and policy review by a special body, by courts, and scope of review or level of access).

This complex and multi-layered interrelationship among domestic, international and comparative law may lead to a respectful conversation among nations and their people, a conversation whose centerpieces are comity as well as respect for autonomy and rights of all recognised entities. Private and public parties are a consequential part of this dialogue. Ultimately this might be *the* Holy Grail, of which expropriation is an important component.

Adding Value through this Endeavour

Various international courts tend to differ with regard to the extent to which they depend "on consent of (or delegation from) the affected states or legal persons," with regard to the "independence (*vel non*) of judicial appointments and judicial decisions from those actors," with regard to "their levels of independent agency as actors over time," with regard to the degree of these courts' effect on tangible results, including policy changes, "or on political actors or on legal norms or on values such as individual or collective freedom or responsibility or self-determination," with regard to the reasons they courts themselves were created and the purposive functions they are expected to discharge, and with regard to "their sustained activity or inactivity" over a period of time.[25] But to limit the differences between international tribunals to this laundry list is to ignore the point of origination for any analysis: the text and relevant proviso called into examination in any case or arbitration.

Diplomacy was never taken off the table but since the late nineteenth century nations have shown themselves to be more open to international adjudication and arbitration. The arbitrations of claims where public law remedies were sought for losses suffered by private individuals in relation to the Britain-United States Treaty of 1794 (Jay Treaty), and of inter-state claims of the *United States v. Britain (Alabama Arbitration)* (1872),[26] were by this time thought to be representative of the growing possibilities, even if not yet realities, of bilateral as well as multilateral arbitration. At the time, "[i]nternational law was . . . concerned principally with the protection of . . . [foreign-owned tangible] property . . . [and financial interests in investments] against seizure and the right of creditors to collect

---

[25] B. Kingsbury, "International Courts: Uneven Judicialization in Global Order," in CAMBRIDGE COMPANION TO INTERNATIONAL LAW 37 (James Crawford and Martti Koskenniemi, ed., Cambridge University Press, 2012) [B. Kingsbury, "International Courts"]; see also M. J. Dixon, INTERNATIONAL LAW 54 (Oxford University Press, 2005).

[26] Moore, 1 Int. Arb. 495.

debts."[27] Several treaties were therefore negotiated to "protec[t] foreign property, such as merchandise and vessels, against expropriation"[28] and these treaties gave rise to awards.[29]

The 1899 Hague Peace Conference, for its part, established the Permanent Court of Arbitration (the PCA), which as a structure continues to facilitate arbitration by *ad hoc* panels. After many cases in its first few decades, the PCA suddenly was lacking in business from 1935 until a powerful surge starting around the mid-1990s. When the twentieth century came around, three fundamental kinds of international arbitration were in existence and they have remained so: Inter-Governmental Claims Commissions, such as the Iran-United States Claims Tribunal and the Eritrea-Ethiopia Claims Commission; *Ad hoc* Inter-State Arbitration; and Inter-State Arbitration Embedded in Pre-Existing Legal Institutional Structures.

In 1929, the first proposal to protect investors was created by the International Chamber of Commerce (ICC) and the League of Nations: Draft Convention on the Treatment of Foreigners.[30] "Not only" did it apply "to the exercise of all economic activity," but also "to civil and legal rights, to the acquisition, preservation and transmission of property by foreigners and to fiscal charges both exceptional and normal"—in short, the Full Protection and Security (FPS) standard.[31] The proposal froze the investors out by focusing on the relationship among the States, thereby

---

[27] *Scope and Definition*, UNCTAD Series on Issues in International Investment Agreements II, 2011, p. 8 [*Scope and Definition*, UNCTAD Series 2011].

[28] See, *e.g.*, Article 10, General Convention of Peace, Amity, Navigation and Commerce, United States-Colombia, 3 October 1824 in United States Treaty Series, No. 52.

[29] *Scope and Definition*, UNCTAD Series 2011, *supra*, at 8 (citing *Petroleum Development Limited v. Sheikh of Abu Dhabi*, Judgement (International Law Reports, 1951, Vol. 18, pp. 144-164); *Sapphire International Petroleum Limited v. National Iranian Oil Company*, Judgement (International Law Reports, 1967, Vol. 27, pp. 117-233); *Ruler of Qatar v. International Marine Oil Company Limited*, Judgement (International Law Reports, 1953, Vol. 20, pp. 534-547); *Saudi Arabia v. Arabian American Oil Company (ARAMCO)*, Judgement (International Law Reports, 1963, Vol. 27, pp. 117-233)).

[30] League of Nations, "Responsibility of States for Damage Caused in Their Territory to the Person or Property of Foreigners," Conference for the Codification of International Law, Bases of Discussion, vol III, LN Doc C.75.M.69.1929.V (1929).

[31] A.K. Kuhn, *The International Conference on the Treatment of Foreigners,* 24 A.J.I.L. 570 (1930).

creating a diplomatic protection regime, but its sweeping NT protections for investor rights led to the proposal's rejection by States.

It is not that international amity is not a significant tribunal motive; it is, as was evinced by the United Nations' International Tribunal for the Law of the Sea's (ITLOS) December 2012 decision in the *ARA Libertad (Ghana v. Argentina) Case*.[32] A brief recitation of the case is in order. The American hedge-funder Paul Singer owns the Cayman Islands-based hedge fund NML Capital, also known pejoratively as a "vulture fund," had purchased Argentine bonds at fire sale rates and was now seeking full repayment of principal plus interest in the amount approximately of U.S. $1.6 billion. Argentina's 2001-02 had forced a rapid and escalating devaluation of its currency and had led Argentina effectively to default on Singer's bonds.

In the wake of the default a decade ago, Argentina signed agreements with most creditors to pay back a fixed sum over a period of several years. The creditors who rejected this deal, such as NML Capital, are called "holdouts," who are not receiving debt repayments from Argentina. Singer used Ghanaian authorities to detain the Argentine ship for recovery of Argentina's obligations. Holding that the frigate ARA Libertad's detention might serve as "a source of conflict that may endanger friendly relations among states,"[33] especially since the Libertad was "a warship belonging to the Argentine Navy"[34] (a strong national security defence supersedes a commercial argument perhaps), the ITLOS panel ordered the Libertad's "release" in a manner that was both "forthwith and unconditiona[l]."[35]

Surely, the Ghanaian seizure seemed to the tribunal to be disproportionately excessive since the ship's detention also meant the detention of the Commander and the crew who must be "able to leave the port of Tema and the maritime areas under the jurisdiction of Ghana."[36] Even though the ITLOS left it unspoken, present were the seeds of a competing FPS claim (based in customary law) from innocent third-parties. The ITLOS recognised, of course, that international arbitration avenues were open but maintained that the frigate's detention was simply

[32] Order, ITLOS Case No. 20, December 15, 2012, *available at* <www.itlos.org/fileadmin/itlos/documents/cases/case_no.20/C20_Order_15_12_2012.pdf>.

[33] *Id.*, at ¶ 97.

[34] *Id.*, at ¶ 98 (stating that the warship had the right to "discharge[e] its mission and duties [, which] affect the immunity enjoyed by this warship under general international law.").

[35] *Id.*, at ¶ 108.

[36] *Id.*

contrary to the applicable law.[37] The seething acrimony from this episode had the chance to negatively affect other facets to diplomatic relations.[38] It is incontrovertible that the ITLOS was simply trying to ward off long-term conflict by proceeding expeditiously. To what extent it succeeded remains to be seen.

Standing international courts such as the Permanent Court of International Justice (PCIJ), the International Court of Justice (ICJ), and various international criminal tribunals have also been created. The last international tribunal type to have been created before the end of the 1920's were international administrative tribunals, such as those used by the International Labour Organization (ILOAT) and the United Nations (UN). The ITLOS is just such a U.N. tribunal. International tribunals created in the post-1945 innovative era are the European Court of Human Rights (ECtHR), the European Court of Justice (ECJ), panels operated under General Agreement on Tariffs and Trade (GATT) of 1947 (later transformed into the World Trade Organization (WTO)) and certain other trade agreements, and finally tribunals in which foreign investors may sue host States to remedy the allegedly violations inflicted by the host State.

Those fora include the International Settlement for the Settlement of Investment Disputes (ICSID), the United Nations Commission on

---

[37] Article 32, UNCLOS; Article 3 of the 1926 Convention for the Unification of Certain Rules concerning the Immunity of State-owned Vessels.

[38] See, *e.g.*, "UN court orders immediate release of Argentine ship seized by hedge funder Paul Singer over unpaid debt," *N.Y. Post*, December 15, 2012 ("Argentine Economy Minister Hernan Lorenzino hailed the court's decision and vowed to continue fighting what President Cristina Fernandez has called 'vulture funds,' with whom the country is locked in a series of legal battles. 'Argentina will continue to defend itself from the financial pirates,' Lorenzino said via Twitter on Saturday. 'Vultures, you won't succeed, with the ship nor with the debt.'"); L. Ford, "Maritime tribunal orders Ghana to set Argentina's Libertad frigate free," *The Guardian*, December 17, 2012 ("Nick Dearden, director of Jubilee Debt Campaign, welcomed the ruling. He said: "We are delighted that Argentina has won this case. It is a disgrace that a group of speculators can seize the property of a sovereign nation in this way and points to the need for a fundamental change in the international debt system. Hopefully the ARA Libertad will now be promptly released. . . . the UN independent expert on foreign debt and human rights, Cephas Lumina, said: 'Vulture funds, such as NML Capital, should not be allowed to purchase debts of distressed companies or sovereign states on the secondary market, for a sum far less than the face value of the debt obligation, and then seek repayment of the nominal full face value of the debt together with interest, penalties and legal costs or impound assets of heavily indebted countries in an attempt to force repayment.'").

International Trade Law (UNCITRAL), and the Stockholm Chamber of Arbitration (SCC). This last category is known as international investment arbitration (IIA). It is generally acknowledged that a main "objectiv[e] of providing" this kind of "dispute resolution [is] that" it must "ai[d]—rather than disrup[t]—international investment flows intended to eliminate poverty," thus the tribunal "must prove worthy of trust and provide effective and independent dispute resolution services."[39] The bottom-line goal is "foster[ing] fairness, efficiency, and institutional integrity."[40]

These tribunals—each tribunal is a "self-contained unit"[41]—operate under varying jurisdictional and substantive rules. Nor is the scope or subject-matter jurisdiction always identical. Nor are the remedies identical or even equivalent. Some tribunals are empowered only to issue advisory opinions while the awards by some others are binding. Some of the tribunals may order pecuniary relief but no injunctive relief and some

---

[39] S. D. Franck, *The ICSID Effect?*, *supra*, at 832 (citing I.F.I. Shihata, LEGAL TREATMENT OF FOREIGN INVESTMENT: THE WORLD BANK GUIDELINES 97 n.68 (1993) ("The World Bank sponsored the establishment of ICSID in the belief that the availability of a dispute settlement machinery of this kind could help to promote increased flows of international investment."); S. A. Hipsher, "Creating Market Size: Regional Strategies for Use in the Least Developed Areas of the World," in INNOVATIVE APPROACHES TO REDUCING GLOBAL POVERTY 153, 154–57 (James A.F. Stoner & Charles Wankel eds., 2007)); *id.*, n. 17 (connecting the ICSID's stated aims with the Bretton Woods Agreement (from the 1944 Conference) aims of "recognize[ing] the rights of foreign investors and to move beyond diplomatic protection for foreign investment, it took two decades to establish ICSID to address these concerns."). But see See K. P. Gallagher & E. Shrestha, *Investment Treaty Arbitration and Developing Countries: A Re-Appraisal*, GLOBAL DEVELOPMENT AND ENVIRONMENT INSTITUTE WORKING PAPER, May 2011, *available at* <www.ase.tufts.edu/gdae/Pubs/wp/11-01TreatyArbitration Reappraisal.pdf>, at p. 3 ("We . . . recommend caution when relying on Franck's work to argue that investor-state arbitration is neutral toward developing countries").

[40] *Id.*

[41] Decision on Appeal of pre-trial Judge's Order Regarding Jurisdiction and Standing, Special Tribunal for Lebanon, Appeals Chamber, 10 November 2010, at ¶ 41 (stating, moreover, that in the international legal order, "[t]here is neither a horizontal link between the various tribunals, nor, a fortiori, a vertical hierarchy."). See also *Prosecutor v Tadić*, Appeals Chamber, Decision on the Defence Motion for Interlocutory Appeal on Jurisdiction, 2 October 1995, at ¶ 11; *Prosecutor v Zejnil Delalic et al.*, Case No: IT-96-21-A, ICTY, Appeals Chamber, 20 February 2001, at ¶ 24; *The Right to Information on Consular Assistance: In the Framework of the Guarantees of the Due Process of Law*, IACHR., Advisory Opinion OC-16/99 of 1 October 1999, Series A No 16, at ¶ 61.

others *vice versa*. Some commercial arbitration awards from international tribunals and domestic systems exercise some sphere of influence; they are relevant to and susceptible of further dissection but they are not necessarily controlling.[42] From domestic law and private international law, there must be "much adaptation for the purposes of the new international institution."[43]

Finally, an important deduction is that the international human rights tribunals, the inter-governmental claims commissions, and the IIA fora are the only international adjudicative bodies which entertain expropriation-related claims by a private party against a State by eliminating the mandatory litigant role of the home State. This breakthrough and break-away from the era of diplomatic espousals (also known as "diplomatic protection") arguably has been the greatest procedural development in twentieth-century international law.

Practitioners, tribunals and students of international investment arbitration (IIA), international human rights (especially the ECtHR but also the Inter-American Court of Human Rights (IACtHR), and the African Court on Human Rights (ACtHPR)) and other dispute settlement bodies will derive use from this book. The book has chosen the Iran-United States Claims Tribunal (IUCT) as the third prototype of an inter-governmental claims commission; it is such a unique international tribunal deciding expropriation-related issues under a special mandate borne of diplomatic, political and economic crises. The IUCT also has the least *textually*-limited mandate, making it a closer mirror of the "general principles of law" than most other international tribunals.[44] Finally, the

---

[42] The caveat comes from *International Status of South-West Africa* (Advisory Opinion) [1950] ICJ Reports 128 at 148 (Sir Arnold McNair) ("The way in which international law borrows from … [Article 38 (1)(c) of the Statute of the International Court of Justice, which stipulates the sources of international law,] is not by means of importing private law institutions 'lock, stock and barrel', ready-made and fully equipped with a set of rules. It would be difficult to reconcile such a process with the application of 'the general principles of law'. In my opinion, the true view of the duty of international tribunals in this matter is to regard any features or terminology which are reminiscent of the rules and institutions of private law as an indication of policy and principles rather than as directly importing these rules and institutions.").

[43] *Id.*; see also *Rex v. Christian*, South African Law Reports [1924], Appellate Division, 101, 112.

[44] Special Report by Sir Gerald Fitzmaurice, "The Future of Public International Law and of the International Legal System in the Circumstances of Today" *in* LIVRE DU CENTENAIRE 251, Institut de droit International 1873–1973 ("[A]lthough on the domestic plane there may still remain uncertainty as to what the law is (for

label "prototype" refers to the most effective lens of looking at a particular area of international dispute settlement. The number and importance (to mean their immediate and conceptual stakes) of the claims in each prototype have steadily skyrocketed.

There are serious textual differences among the prototypes. The ECtHR, for instance, protects the "peaceful enjoyment" of property rights by "legal and natural persons" so long as it does not interfere with "the right of a State to enforce such laws as it deems necessary to control the use of property in accordance with the general interest" whereas the North American Free Trade Agreement (NAFTA) simply forbids its signatories from "nationali[sing] or expropriat[ing] an investment of an investor of another Party in its territory or tak[ing] a measure tantamount to nationalization or expropriation" unless it is for a "public purpose," is "non-discriminatory," is consistent with the "due process of law" and pays compensation.

There have been some concerns out there that international arbitration has strayed from its original purpose of being a truth-seeking enterprise, which it must be in order to survive.[45] For its part, the Claims Settlement Declaration (CSD) governing the IUCT simply provides that "property shall not be taken except for a public purpose, nor shall it be taken without the prompt payment of just compensation."

These instruments allow or compel adherence to the general principles of international law though the CSD, in addition to this, allows the IUCT to decide on "choice of law." The so-called general principles of international law are instrumental *only* as to the process of gap-filling where the text and purpose of the specific instrument are ambiguous. Equity cannot be implemented *contra legem*.[46] Institutional features of

statutes, judicial decisions, etc., have to be interpreted and applied) there is never any uncertainty as to what is law. On the international plane there may be uncertainty under both heads.").

[45] W. W. Park, *Arbitrators and Accuracy,* 1 J. OF INT'L DISP. SETT'MENT 25 (2010) ("Evidentiary tools in [international] arbitration should balance sensitivity towards cost and delay against the parties' interest in due process and correct decisions. If arbitration loses its moorings as a truth-seeking process, nostalgia for a golden age of simplicity will yield to a clarion call for reinvention of an adjudicatory process aimed at discovering what happened, finding relevant legal norms and properly construing contract language. Though not so jealous as to exclude all rivals, truth does insist on being first among equals.") [W. W. Park, *Arbitrators and Accuracy*].

[46] *Case Concerning the Frontier Dispute (Burkina Faso v Republic of Mali)* (Judgment) [1986] ICJ Reports 554 at 567–8; *North Sea Continental Shelf Cases (Federal Republic of Germany v Denmark; Federal Republic of Germany v Netherlands)* [1969] ICJ Reports 4 at 46-50.

international tribunals is informative about a specific adjudicative body: its decisions, its express or tacit motivations in various cases, and its legal methods (including whose opinions it values, especially in cases where no preconceived inclination exists and in cases where there is a preconceived inclination, the opinions and sources might have an effect on prospective cases).[47]

At the same time, however, it is far too easy to say that if the instrument does not provide a specific protection or well-defined class of protections (or coverage), that is evidence enough that coverage does not exist. Means of interpretation such as *ejusdem generis, in pari materia, noscitur a sociis or generalia specialibus non derogant* can help only so much because they too run into the now-familiar *cul-de-sac*: the "class" depends on how one elects to slice it, and the adjudicator has rather a discretionary hand in shaping that taxonomy. For instance, 10-year-long environmental permits concerning nuclear waste might be classed as a short-duration permit, a long-duration permit, a public health concern, and even a contract of sorts (or several of these choices). Each choice, none any less valid than the others, might nonetheless produce vastly different monetary, practical and doctrinal implications.

What, then, are the general principles of international law? Benedict Kingsbury bluntly states it is merely an "international law myth that there is one unified approach to interpretation that is embodied in the Vienna Convention on the Law of Treaties [(VCLT)] and shared among all tribunals."[48] There might be some pillars in this approach ("unified" or not),[49] however. To Immanuel Kant in *Perpetual Peace*, the most fundamental among these "definitive articles" are that, first, the basic structure of the

---

[47] Increased role of treaties and institutional interactions between and among States may have led to the diminished importance of these "general principles." However, the notions of *estoppel* and *equity* retain a prominent place in international dispute settlement. See *North Sea Continental Shelf cases, (Federal Republic of Germany v Denmark; Federal Republic of Germany v Netherlands)* [1969] ICJ Reports 4 at 26; *Case Concerning the Temple of Preah Vihear (Cambodia v Thailand) (Merits)* [1962] ICJ Reports 6 at 32–3.

[48] *Id.*, at 38 ("Tribunals develop their own hermeneutics connected with many of these institutional factors – thus the [World Trade Organization] Appellate Body purports to adhere closely to the underlying treaty texts, while the [European Court of Justice] may be more expressly teleological in aiming to achieve the purposes of the [European Union] treaty."); K. Claussen, *Comment: The Casualty of Investor Protection in Times of Economic Crisis*, 118 YALE L. J. 1545, 1546 (2009) (referring to the VCLT as "the codified authority on treaty interpretation in international law.").

[49] Probably not, at least in the main.

states be republican; second, it must be a federation of free states that forms the basis for international law; and third, each legal person be entitled to hospitality by other states.[50]

The first and second pillars give rise to the controversy regarding the validity of international agreements signed with undemocratic regimes, treated as the "Dictator Paradox" in Chapter V (NON-DISCRIMINATION) of this book. The last pillar serves as the premise for protection of the property of foreign investors. What the third "definitive article" does not explicitly cover is the enforcement mechanism: both jurisdictional and substantive. In Chapter IV (EXHAUSTION OF LOCAL REMEDIES AND CONTINUOUS NATIONALITY), we tackle perhaps the most sensitive jurisdictional question: exhaustion of local remedies. If Kant were amongst us today and he could survey the field of international law, he would probably divine a fourth definitive article: good faith. The ICJ, for its part, has referred to good faith as "[o]ne of the basic principles governing the creation and performance of legal obligations."[51]

The next section of this Chapter does for a brief moment return to the classroom. Moreover, the book makes a determined effort to speak in plain language so that the ideas can reach a wide readership. That readership is most interested in transferability of knowledge. The transferability narrative needs to wake up to the all-too-real legitimacy crisis in some international tribunals: "lack of consistency in outcome," "loss of risk-free exercise of domestic policy space," "the purported failure to support development objectives," and the tribunals' inability to "incorporate[e] . . . norms related to corporate social responsibility, the environment, or human rights."[52] The allegation out there is that these deficiencies cause, or accelerate, the race to the bottom. But experience also hints darkly that

---

[50] C. Layne, *Kant or Can't: The Myth of Democratic Peace* in INTERNATIONAL SECURITY, 19 (1994), pp. 5-49; I. Kant, POLITICAL WRITINGS 93-108, ed. H. Reiss (Cambridge University Press, 1991).

[51] *Nuclear Tests Cases (Australia v France; New Zealand v France)* [1974] ICJ Reports 253 at 268. We also know the important role of equity from cases such as *River Meuse Case (Netherlands v Belgium)* PCIJ Reports Series A/B No 70, 76 (Judge Hudson).

[52] S. D. Franck, *The ICSID Effect? Considering Potential Variations in Arbitration Awards*, 51 VA. J. INT'L L. 825, 843-4 (2011) (internal citations and footnotes omitted) [S. D. Franck, *The ICSID Effect?*]; M. Sornarajah, *Power and Justice: Third World Resistance in International Law*, 10 SING. Y.B. INT'L L. 19, 32 (2006) (arguing that there is no evidence that international law systems raise the quality of development or living standards, and in any case they are not worth it because of the sovereignty that is abdicated).

there is another consideration that might cause this deficiency: insufficiently meaningful and candid politician-judge discourses.[53]

Statistical inferences suggest that foreign direct investment (FDI) inflow—typically advanced (or at least sold to the public) as the primary argument in favour of generous property rights protections to foreigners—is not significantly determined by investment agreements. Still, many governments, especially of less developed countries (oft-reluctant host States), do not seem to have given up hope. In addition to the fact that the revenue or rights relinquished by tax incentives and other subsidies cannot be easily determined, tracking the number of jobs or FDI is also difficult on a domestic level.[54]

Empirical information does demonstrate, however, that GDP and the legal, political and economic cultures (denoted as United Nations indices) to some extent determine FDI probabilities. The benefits and limitations of the methodology, as well as these inferences have been analysed in Chapter VI (OTHER SUBSTANTIVE STANDARDS: EXPROPRIATION, FAIR AND EQUITABLE TREATMENT, MINIMUM STANDARD OF TREATMENT, AND COMPENSATION). It is far likelier that well-informed stochastic analysis, rather than "chance alone, unrepresentative experience, or unfounded intuition,"[55] should and will inform the expected future behaviour of firms, governments and tribunals.[56]

---

[53] Some commentators might believe the flaw is that this discourse has not been prolific enough. But whether or not something is prolific is a function of volume, and volume is not the same thing as substance.

[54] L. Story, *As Companies Seek Tax Deals, Governments Pay High Price*, N.Y. Times, December 1, 2012 ("[S]tates, counties and cities are giving up more than $80 billion each year to companies. The beneficiaries come from virtually every corner of the corporate world, encompassing oil and coal conglomerates, technology and entertainment companies, banks and big-box retail chains. The cost of the awards is certainly far higher. A full accounting . . . is not possible because the incentives are granted by thousands of government agencies and officials, and many do not know the value of all their awards. Nor do they know if the money was worth it because they rarely track how many jobs are created. Even where officials do track incentives, they acknowledge that it is impossible to know whether the jobs would have been created without the aid.") [L. Story, *As Companies Seek Tax Deals*].

[55] S. D. Franck, *The ICSID Effect? Considering Potential Variations in Arbitration Awards*, 51 VA. J. INT'L L. 825, 832, n. 15 (2011).

[56] G. King et al., DESIGNING SOCIAL INQUIRY: SCIENTIFIC INFERENCE IN QUALITATIVE RESEARCH 6 (1994) ("[N]othing in our set of rules implies that we must . . . collect all relevant data before we can make valid social scientific inferences. An important topic is worth studying even if very little information is

Cross-pollination across various international law areas and fora already is taking place in many respects but there are areas that could be fertilised better and more effectively. Of course, there are areas that could be fertilised *worse*, which is a cautionary point. This book deals with both the good and the space for improvement because it is important to know what is being done correctly (and should be amped up) and what to reduce. The cross-pollination is justified, even enhanced by the fact that while the text of a particular international instrument controls the outcome, the background legal culture also influences the construction.

What informs this "legal culture" mix? That legal culture is a composite of the aims and goals of the judicial institutions engaging in the decision-making, the backgrounds and personalities of the decision-makers, the times and the climate in which the tribunals are operating, their sense of what common sense and "justice" requires, and, perhaps their most important consideration, their perceived methods of seeking legitimacy. Beyond the traditional and shared canons of interpretation, the legal, political and economic cultures are indeed significant determinants.

The book commences with a bird's-eye view of public international law itself and gradually delves further into expropriation. To understand expropriation's mechanics, we need to situate the issue within the larger international law system. Expropriation and related standards cut across the entire international law spectrum. The international law rules, processes and institutions engaging with expropriation are manifold and they have a variety of objectives in mind. Their first and primary (perhaps primal too) objective is to survive; this book addresses why survival of an international tribunal for its own sake is not reason enough. If a decision is issued against a particular factual scenario containing unique challenges, *e.g.*, *force majeure* or environmental protections, then the goal is to observe the reasoning and limitations of that decision and apply them to the other judicial institutions.

---

available. The result of applying any research design in this situation will be relatively uncertain conclusions, but so long as we honestly report our uncertainty, this kind of study can be very useful. Limited information is often a necessary feature of social inquiry."); R. S. Pindyk & D. L. Rubinfeld, ECONOMETRIC MODELS AND ECONOMIC FORECASTS, at xiv–xv (4th ed. 1998) ("[E]ven an intuitive forecaster constructs some type of model, perhaps without being aware of doing so. . . . [T]here are several advantages to working with models explicitly. Model building forces the individual to think clearly about, and account for, all of the important interrelationships involved in a problem. The reliance on intuition can be dangerous at times because of the possibility that important relationships will be ignored or improperly used.").

The book seems to me important, necessary even, at this juncture as the culmination of years of study because of certain slow but decisive trends in international law: money, hegemony, and predictability. Shrewd investors want, more than anything else, clarity and stability. Certain examples are warranted. Previously it was rather like hornbook law that international tribunals could order money damages but not enjoin the enforcement of certain government actions. But this has begun to change in international investment arbitration and might bring a radical shift across international law.

A second point is that tribunals are determining the importance of following and creating precedent if not just for the sake of making its command in a given case easier to understand or follow but rather for the preservation of its own legitimacy. This legitimacy consideration is the underpinning of the entire book and pervades its premises, principles and most of its assumptions.

Third, the fact remains that most, if not all, judicial and scholarly literature in the field focuses on international tribunal introspection—how the tribunals and scholars operate in the expropriation world—rather than how the interplay between the arbitral-political spheres functions or should function. Special attention will be given to the developing-developed world interrelationships, especially through the Chapter III (ATTRIBUTION AND CAUSATION: "FOR WANT OF A NAIL . . . THE KINGDOM WAS LOST") and Chapter VI (OTHER SUBSTANTIVE STANDARDS) statistical analyses.

§ 1.2—Parameterising "Expropriation" and Back to Basics

The whole business of international law started with the State's acknowledged need, driven by a *quid pro quo* mindset, to protect a foreigner's property and person. This was really the birth of the school of thought which prized solidarity, tolerance and peacefully strategic means over more pugnacious, arbitrary ones.[57] Roughly, this phenomenon is

[57] See, *e.g.*, J.D. Haskell, *Hugo Grotius in the Contemporary Memory of International Law: Secularism, Liberalism, and the Politics of Restatement and Denial*, 25 EMORY INT'L L. J. 269, 270 (1986) (stating that the original "efforts [of international law jurists] are remembered to spark the political aspiration, implied to be at the core of international law itself, towards a more liberal tolerance of difference and a sentiment of restraint towards over-aggrandizing political agendas.") [J. D. Haskell, *Hugo Grotius in the Contemporary Memory of International Law*]. More than just giving international law separate recognition, this process also had the effect of giving political imperatives a separate and

today codified in international agreements as full protection and security (FPS) in the positive rights dimension. The other side of the coin, in the negative rights sense, is that the State may not invade a foreigner's property rights in certain situations.

What is the scope of "expropriation"? Even though pinning down one universal definition or "magic formula" is difficult (and perhaps misguided as well),[58] identifying several handy features is not as coruscatingly elusive an endeavour as one might at first surmise. The book handles both direct and indirect expropriations. *Direct* expropriations are straightforward takings of real property "on the basis of an executive or legislative act [often] for the purpose of transferring property or interests into the public domain."[59] These are often called *nationalisations* (even if the expropriation is conducted by a state or local government). Direct expropriations also

---

"emancipated" identity distinct from theological imperatives. See, *e.g.*, *id.*, at 270, n. 6; A. Nussbaum, A CONCISE HISTORY OF THE LAW OF NATIONS 105 (1947) ("[Grotius] made an important step toward the emancipation of international law from theology by his famous pronouncement [about] the law of nature."); Josef L. Kunz, *Natural-Law Thinking in the Modern Science of International Law*, 55 AM. J. INT'L L. 951, 951–52 (1961) ("The Protestant Grotius, who wrote the first treatise on international law, was still strongly influenced by the traditional natural law, but he secularized it by stating that natural law would be valid even if there were no God. This secularization profoundly changed the character of natural law. . . . [T]he Catholic natural law is . . . discovered by man's *recta ratio* — a term stemming from the Stoics; yet . . . it necessarily presupposes the Christian faith in the Creator . . . . [W]ith Grotius this right reason becomes the basis of natural law."); A. Nussbaum, *Just War—A Legal Concept?*, 42 MICH. L. REV. 453, 466 (1943) ("[Grotius] claimed in earnest that the law of nations and international law derived therefrom could subsist without a divine foundation."); R. Pound, *Grotius in the Science of Law*, 19 AM. J. INT'L L. 685, 686 (1925) (contending that Grotius helped separate theological pursuits from jurisprudence).

[58] *Arkansas Game & Fish Commission v. United States*, 2012 U.S. LEXIS 9409 (2012).

[59] "INDIRECT EXPROPRIATION" AND THE "RIGHT TO REGULATE" IN INTERNATIONAL INVESTMENT LAW, OECD Working Papers, Number 2004/4, September 2004, p. 3, n. 4 ["INDIRECT EXPROPRIATION," OECD Working Papers 2004]; see also R. Dolzer & M. Stevens, "Bilateral Investment Treaties," ICSID 1995 at 98. Nonetheless, some treaties and agreements refer to expropriation and nationalisation as discrete violations. See, *e.g.*, Clause 9, Agreement Between the Government of the Republic of Italy and the Government of the People's Republic of Bangladesh on the Promotion and Protection of Investments of 1990 (providing for dispute-settlement and subsequently "compensation for expropriation, nationalization, requisition or similar measures including disputes relating to the amount of the relevant payments.").

include situations where the government takes the property from Private Entity *A* and gives it to Private Entity *B*, and when the government just makes the property unusable.[60]

On the other hand, *indirect* or *regulatory* expropriations are "individual measures taken for a public purpose"[61] and which diminish the value of the property—"even if the title of the property is still vested in the owner."[62] *Indirect* expropriation, as that term is used here, covers "creeping expropriations," viz. expropriations that incrementally encroach on property rights, as well. The most common forms of indirect expropriation are: denying the owner the right to manage or control the property or to enjoy its profits; cancelling or refusing to issue licenses and permits; and excessive taxation intended specifically to cause hardship to the owner or her class without any rational state interest.[63]

The book does not address intellectual property rights but it does branch beyond real property: like international tribunals, the book addresses market share and access rights conferred by a specific legal instrument. The corresponding legal instrument might be an international investment agreement (IIA), including bilateral (BIT) or multilateral investment treaties (MAI). Across international dispute settlement, the

---

[60] Whether "taking" is the right word for these instances is a good question. Most scholarship uses "taking" and "expropriation" interchangeably.

[61] "INDIRECT EXPROPRIATION," OECD Working Papers 2004, p. 3.

[62] R. Moloo and J. Chao, *International Investment Law and Sustainable Development: Bridging the Divide*, p. 9 (2011) (unpublished paper on file with the author) (citing in n. 35: *Starrett Housing Corp. v. Islamic Republic of Iran*, Award No. ITL-32-24-1 (19 Dec. 1983), reprinted in 4 Iran-US Claims Tribunal Rep. 122, 154; see also Jan Paulsson & Zachary Douglas, 'Indirect Expropriations in Investment Treaty Arbitrations', in N. Horn & S. Kröll, (eds), *Arbitrating Foreign Investment Disputes: Procedural and Substantive Legal Aspects* (004) 152; Fortier & Stephen L. Drymer, 'Indirect Expropriation in the Law of International Investment: I Know It When I See It, or Caveat Investor' (2004) 19 ICSID Review – Foreign Investment Law Journal, 293, 297; Rudolf Dolzer, 'Indirect Expropriations: New Developments?' (2002) 11 N.Y.U. Environmental Law Journal 64; Thomas Waelde & Abba Kolo, 'Environmental Regulation, Investment Protection and "Regulatory Taking" in International Law' (2001) 50 ICLQ 811, 833; Andrew Newcombe, 'The Boundaries of Regulatory Expropriation in International Law' (2005) 20 ICSID Review – Foreign Investment Law Journal, 1; Catherine Yannaca-Small, '"Indirect Expropriation" and the "Right to Regulate" in International Investment Law', (2004) OECD Working Papers on International Investment, No. 2004/4 <http://www.oecd.org/dataoecd/22/54/ 33776546.pdf> accessed 22 February 2012.) [R. Moloo and J. Chao, *Bridging the Divide*].

[63] G.C. Christie, *What Constitutes a Taking Under International Law*, 33 B.Y.I.L 307, 309 (1962) [G.C. Christie, *What Constitutes a Taking*].

tribunals have in common the most important procedural (Exhaustion of Local Remedies and Continuous Nationality) and substantive (Non-Discrimination (National Treatment (NT) and Most-Favoured-Nation Treatment (MFN)),[64] Due Process (DP), Fair and Equitable Treatment (FET), Minimum Standards of Treatment (MST), and Compensation) standards of international expropriation law.

This standards group has been selected from the larger pool of "standards of treatment"[65] because they directly measure the quality of treatment and its impact on awards.[66] There is significant overlap among some of the standards.

Dispute Settlement in Public International Law

Before we address the crux of this book, we have to ask what public international law *is*. Public international law may not satisfy John Austin's narrow definition of "law"—command of a sovereign enforced by a sanction, also known as *positive morality*—or a recalibration of what law is. We do not re-enter in any great detail the existential debates attending the philosophy of international law. For the sake of argument, I assume (without necessarily agreeing with) the "realist" response that international law is *ultimately* an expression of power even with the garb of the formal equality of States.[67] This particular garb is maintained by the United Nations Charter itself.[68] But the rights guarantees were difficult to invoke

---

[64] Chapter V (*Non-Discrimination*) also discusses domestic discrimination (relevant, among our tribunals, for the international human rights systems), *i.e.*, instances where the State discriminates amongst its own nationals, citizens, and people who live there.

[65] Fair and Equitable Treatment, Full Protection and Security, Access to Justice, Fair Procedure and Denial of Justice, Emergency, Necessity, Armed Conflicts and *Force Majeure*, Arbitrary or Discriminatory Measures, National Treatment, Most Favoured Nation Treatment, Transfer of Funds, and Continuous Nationality. Continuous Nationality and its relationship to diplomatic espousal was a tempting choice but its impact is narrower than the ones chosen in this dissertation.

[66] W. W. Burke-White, *The Argentine Financial Crisis: State Liability Under BITs and the Legitimacy of the ICSID System*, 3 ASIAN J. WTO & INT'L HEALTH L. & POL'Y 199, 222 (2008) (arguing that international arbitration's legitimacy comes, in part, from its standards of treatment).

[67] The "realist" argument tends to be that this purported formal equality is just decoy that conceals and enables the actual inequality to grow.

[68] See Art. II, ¶ 1 of the U.N. Charter.

and access.[69] The Universal Declaration of Human Rights (the UDHR), the International Covenant of Civil and Political Rights (the ICCPR), and the International Covenant of Economic and Social Rights (the ICESCR) have sought to rectify the enforcement deficiencies.[70]

Public international law is also an expression of rules, supported by the pragmatic sanction of incentives and disincentives. We should not mistake actual or active rules for enforcement. In fact, "law without courts" or the judicialisation of international law was the approach familiar to Hugo Grotius when he authored *Law of War and Peace* in 1625. Pretty much the only significant deviation was Alberico Gentili's *Law of War*, published in 1598, which addressed arbitration among sovereigns. But no mechanism of private claimant-sovereign adjudication or arbitration was on the scene at the time.[71]

We start from four public international law postulates: (*i*) Formal Equality of States; (*ii*) Reciprocity; (*iii*) Consent and Sovereignty; and (*iv*) Coexistence in the Community of Nations. The importance of reciprocity, consent and coexistence seem all the more pronounced in light of public international law's ordinarily decentralised enforcement and expropriation's incentive-based foundations. Host states, especially concerned with their lagging sectors, wish to attract foreign investment and they cede part of their judicial sovereignty in submitting to the jurisdiction of the international investment tribunals.

Nations also wish to belong to the community of nations on human rights questions; they consent to the jurisdiction of supranational human

---

[69] T. Buergenthal, *The Evolving International Human Rights System*, 100 A.J.I.L. 783, 786 (2006) (maintaining that the UN Charter was left intentionally obscure on the issue of human rights obligations).

[70] Universal Declaration of Human Rights, Dec. 10, 1948, U.N. Doc. A/810; International Covenant on Civil and Political Rights, Dec. 16, 1966, U.N. Doc. A/6316; International Covenant on Economic, Social, and Cultural Rights, Dec. 16, 1966, UN Doc. A/6316.

[71] The reader might be tempted to think that international "law" was uncontested in the late sixteenth and early seventeenth centuries. I have been advised that "[a]s early as 1710, a dissertation was written to demonstrate the inexistence of international law." See F. Zarbiyev, *Judicial Activism in International Law—A Conceptual Framework for Analysis*, J. OF INTERNATIONAL DISPUTE SETTLEMENT, (2012), 1, 22, n. 121 [F. Zarbiyev, *Judicial Activism in International Law*] (citing Arnold Rotgers, *Dissertatio qua demonstrator jus gentium non dari*, cited in Ernest Nys, *Le droit international* (Albert Fontemoins 1904) 250)). There always is (at least) that one dissenting hold-out.

rights and international criminal tribunals.[72] Consent plays a broodingly omnipresent role in these questions. The issue becomes more complex for host States when the very protection of citizens' human rights (sometimes allegedly invaded by investors, with the host State's own machinery's complicity) clashes with investor rights. Lastly, diplomatic, commercial and *ad hoc* international dispute settlement issues necessitate the creation of this third umbrella category of tribunals.

Consent and sovereignty constitute a running thread throughout this book, as it is throughout international law. The case arguably is stronger in international law than in domestic law. Even though domestic and international law on expropriation share some doctrines, international law undeniably is different from domestic law for five fundamental reasons. Those reasons should be articulated.

First is the democratic pedigree argument: "international law is not generated within the institutional framework of liberal constitutional democracy and does not allow for a central role for electoral supervision."[73] Features present in domestic law but mainly absent from international law are separation of powers, inherent judicial power (also known as compulsory jurisdiction), legislation, judicial review, accountability, basic human rights, and centralised military or enforcement power.

Second, consent—it certainly possesses some similarities with the doctrine of sovereign immunity[74]—means that nations may stop participating

---

[72] In the 1990s, the United Nations Security Council adopted binding resolutions creating the International Criminal Tribunal for Former Yugoslavia (ICTY, 1993-) and subsequently the International Criminal Tribunal for Rwanda (ICTR, 1995-). In fact, the Rome Statute of the International Criminal Court (ICC), a treaty adopted in 1998 and later entered into force in 2000, established a criminal tribunal invested to try international defendants — but only those whose countries of nationality have ratified the treaty or those who allegedly have committed these acts in the territory of a signatory state, consent being key here — for certain particularly heinous offences, provided the states with jurisdiction somehow fail to pursue prosecution. A "third generation" of courts concerning international criminal justice has developed: Crimes Panels of the District Court of Dili, East Timor; "Regulation 64" Panels in the Courts of Kosovo; the Special Court for Sierra Leone, and the Extraordinary Chambers in the Courts of Cambodia.

[73] M. Kumm, *The Legitimacy of International Law: A Constitutionalist Framework of Analysis*, 15 E.J.I.L. 907, 915 (2004).

[74] J. P. Stevens, "Henry IV Comes to America" (Lecture), Chicago Inn of Court Luncheon Meeting, October 4, 2012, *available at* <www.supremecourt.gov/publicinfo/speeches/JPS%20Speech(Chicago)_10-04-2012.pdf> ("That rule of law - known as the doctrine of sovereign immunity - was supported by two reasons, first, a belief that the King could do no wrong, and

in an international compact (or as a prominent international jurist put it to me colloquially, "smash their own club to bits"), generally at their pleasure. If the threat is a credible one, the tribunals must take notice.[75] Non-compliance could imperil the reputation of the nation and of the tribunal.[76] The possibility of the "exit option" being exercised by certain dissatisfied States is not sufficient to automatically trigger a judgment in their favour. Indeed, no court worthy of its salt would do so. But this factor does make it more likely, and in some cases *significantly* more likely, that the corresponding international tribunal will bend over backwards to propose a remedy that is functionally acceptable to all sides.[77]

---

second, the fact that the architect of a legal system has the power to decide whether judges should entertain such suits.") [J. P. Stevens, "Henry IV Comes to America"].

[75] It is Game Theory 101 that if the threat is *not* a credible one, it does not follow that the signatories will not retaliate against the compact or the structure if the deterrence effort fails. They might do so in a less drastic but still unravelling manner. In no absolute sense is the threatened party necessarily "home-free."

[76] F. Zarbiyev, *Judicial Activism in International Law—A Conceptual Framework for Analysis*, J. OF INTERNATIONAL DISPUTE SETTLEMENT, (2012), 1, 18 [F. Zarbiyev, *Judicial Activism in International Law*] (stating that non-compliance "may be costly not only in material terms, as in the case of the WTO, but also in terms of reputation. Political culture can make the option unattractive as well: contesting judicial decisions is not 'something that is done' in societies in which the ideal of the rule of law is taken seriously.").

Outright disobedience would be even worse for the losing State under a "utilitarian" cost-benefit analysis, both short and long-run perspectives (especially the later). See, *e.g.*, R. Brewster, *Unpacking the State's Reputation*, 50 HARV. INT'L L. J. 231, 231-32 (2009) ("Rationalist scholars formalize reputational concerns as a repeated prisoner's dilemma game while non-rationalists rely on more intuitive notions of reputation . . . . A state that cheats develops a bad reputation, which leads other states to exclude that state from future opportunities to cooperate. The costs of such a boycott may lead government leaders to comply with international law, even where the short-term costs of the compliance are high and there are no centralized means of enforcing compliance. In cost-benefit terms, states will comply with international law when the boycott costs outweigh the immediate compliance costs.").

[77] But see *id.* ("[E]ven when jurisdiction is subject to an optional recognition which could be withdrawn by the states, it does not automatically follow that international judges would be sensitive to the threat of exit. Consider, for instance, the examples of France in the context of the *Nuclear Tests* cases[, ICJ Reports 1974, 253, 457], and the United States in relation with the . . . [*Military and Paramilitary Activities in and against Nicaragua*, ICJ Reports 1986, 14; *LaGrand*, ICJ Reports 2001, 466; *Avena and Other Mexican Nationals*, ICJ Reports 2004, 12] cases before the ICJ. In neither case did the ICJ subscribe to the core position

Notably, Bolivia, Venezuela, Ecuador and Nicaragua have either withdrawn or publicly admonished that they are tempted to withdraw from the World Bank's International Center for the Settlement of Disputes (ICSID). India as well as Norway and certain other developed nations have either refused to enter into IIA's due to perceived losses of sovereignty and "public polarization," respectively.[78] The cause was their apparent dissatisfaction at the jet-age use of international arbitration by private investors and their preference for domestic avenues of investment dispute resolution.[79] Strikingly, Australia announced in 2011that "it would no longer include in its investment agreements any provision enabling an investor to submit its disputes with the government to an arbitral tribunal."[80]

Some experts suspect that Argentina's time, given its nationalisations and crises since the early 2000s, will come soon.[81] In international law, the States's specific intention is extremely important. Thus purpose and intent occupy a more privileged position in relation to various forms of textually strict interpretations, both as to jurisdiction and merits, than is sometimes the case in domestic law.[82] From an international tribunal's perspective,

---

of the defendant states."). Distinguished scholar though Fuad Zarbiyev is, his cited cases do not really address the argument that a credible threat concerning the exercise of the "exit option" might make international tribunals somewhat more responsive to the needs and imperatives of the potential "exit" candidates.

[78] J. W. Yackee, *Controlling the International Investment Law Agency*, 53 HARV. INT'L L. J. 391, 394-95, n. 14 (2012) [J. W. Yackee, *Controlling the IIL*] ("India . . has cited the Philip Morris lawsuits as one of the reasons behind its rejection of investor-state arbitration in a proposed European Union-India Free Trade Agreement. . . . Even developed countries are rethinking their commitment to [IIA]. Norway, for instance, has informally shelved its IIA program in the face of public polarization. Much more significantly, the European Union is actively considering whether to eliminate intra-[European Union] IIAs.") (internal citations omitted).

[79] See, *e.g.*, "Threats to withdraw from Bank's investment tribunal," Bretton Woods Project, July 2, 2007, available at <www.brettonwoodsproject.org/art-554233>.

[80] F. Zarbiyev, *Judicial Activism in International Law, supra,* at 19 (citing Jürgen Kurtz, *The Australian Trade Policy Statement on Investor-State Dispute Settlement* (2011) 15 (22) ASIL Insights.). There is fear of a domino effect here. *Id.* ("If such a movement were followed by a relatively significant number of states, it would be unlikely for investment tribunals to remain insensitive to the charges levelled against them.").

[81] See, *e.g.*, W. Burke-White, *The Argentine Financial Crisis: State Liability Under BITs and the Legitimacy of the ICSID System*, Scholarship at Penn Law, Paper 202 (2008).

[82] See, *e.g.*, *Tokios Tokelés v. Ukraine,* ICSID Case No. ARB/02/18, Decision on Jurisdiction (2004), at ¶ 36 ("An international tribunal of defined jurisdiction

preservation and promotion of its "external image" must be balanced with the tribunal's "obvious interest in not losing its 'clientele.'"[83]

In international law, of course, the domestic sovereign is hardly the architect of the international legal system (at least strictly speaking). However, a Hobbesian justification for the consent basis is that the sovereign has the ultimate duty to protect and secure the lives of its subjects, so frankly perhaps they all owe him or her a "compensation-based" exemption from the indignity, problem, risk and cost of defending his or her actions in court, regardless whose court it is—provided the sovereign is making a serious, fundamental and good-faith effort to protect the entities within its borders.

This is not necessarily my view but it is a possible contention that might be advanced as yet another rationale supporting the consent pillar of international law. I call this the "Hobbesian security compensation" thesis. It could have the result of strengthening the presumptive status according consent. The point becomes clearer in Chapter V (NON-DISCRIMINATION)'s analysis of the *dictator paradox*.

Why, then, would a sovereign ever abrogate its own authority? To attract investment, to promote human rights around the world (at least around their region) and/or to create a sustainable culture of respect for the rule of law. If the nation defaults on the terms of the compact or evades an award or judgment against it, future business partners will be less likely to trade with the nation. In this respect, Argentina's series of nationalisations and subsequent ICSID experience is a cautionary tale.[84] Once an international

---

should not reach out to exercise a jurisdiction beyond the borders of the definition. But equally an international tribunal should exercise, and indeed is bound to exercise, the measure of jurisdiction with which it is endowed."); *Compañia de Aguas del Aconquija S.A. and Vivendi Universal v. Argentina*, Decision on Annulment, ICSID Case No. ARB/97/3 (2002), at ¶ 112 ("In the Committee's view, the Tribunal, faced with such a claim and having validly held that it had jurisdiction, was obliged to consider and to decide it."); at ¶ 115 ("[T]he Committee concludes that the Tribunal exceeded its powers in the sense of Article 52(1)(b), in that the Tribunal, having jurisdiction over the Tucumán claims, failed to decide those claims.").

[83] F. Zarbiyev, *Judicial Activism in International Law, supra,* at 18 (some tribunals wish especially to demonstrate that "no special treatment is reserved for powerful states when it comes to the settlement of disputes on the basis of international law.").

[84] "Repsol files int'l complaint on Argentina YPF takeover," Reuters, December 3, 2012 ("Argentina has a poor record at the ICSID. In March [2012], U.S. President Barack Obama said he would suspend trade benefits for Argentina because it has failed to pay more than $300 million in compensation awards in two disputes

tribunal is confronted with a case or arbitration, it is engaged in a juggling act of these two often-competing and sometimes difficult-to-reconcile sets of priorities.

Third, and on a related note, an international compact is valid and honoured in international law *only* because enough nations so regard and submit themselves to adhere to this compact[85]—and to the judicial authority such a compact creates for enforcement purposes. While an IIA or a human rights system technically requires just two consenting nations, even the jurisprudence of such a regime is informed by other international compacts within and beyond their prototypes.

It is also the case that legitimacy borne of customary law status will not attach unless other international compacts do so; if the regime's very character is *sui generis*, of course, that is a different question altogether. But here too in order for time-honoured legitimacy to develop, even if other compacts and cases do not expressly adopt the doctrine they must not at the very least repudiate it unanimously and roundly. If the doctrine is and remains discredited, it is very difficult for the doctrine to shed its permanently-dissenting status.

Fourth, any international tribunal exists mainly for problem-solving purposes and is sorely dependent on the will of the signatories. Therefore, it must compete with other tribunals for business. One scholar has even argued that "rigid rule[s] of judicial harmoni[s]ation (e.g. according *stare decisis* to first-in-time judgments) might sterilize potential jurisprudential discourse and entrench conservative positions."[86] I am not entirely sure what "conservative" in this context means, though I agree that cutting off the experimentation at this nascent stage would likely be premature. After

---

handled by ICSID. [Argentine President Cristina] Fernandez's takeover of YPF drew strong criticism from the European Union and several other key trade partners already irked by Argentina's import curbs and other unorthodox policies aimed at boosting the trade surplus.").

[85] Slightly more flexible is the development of international doctrine, as this Chapter and other chapters articulate.

[86] Y. Shany, THE COMPETING JURISDICTIONS OF INTERNATIONAL COURTS AND TRIBUNALS 123 (Cambridge University Press, 2003); *id.*, at 122-23 (giving the example of the King's Bench's declining business in the fifteenth century to explain that the "deterioration of judicial relations, in the short run, might inspire, in the long run, a radical solution to the problem of inter-for a relations, such as the reallocation of competences or the introduction of clearer jurisdiction-regulating standards, which will take care of the problem of jurisdictional competition once and for all.") [Y. Shany, COMPETING JURISDICTIONS OF INTERNATIONAL COURTS]. This is not an insignificant point but it should turn out to be more of an exception than a rule.

all, a wrong-headed decision could assume the character of a diabolical demiurge in the law.

Moreover, while the risk of a forced "judicial harmoni[s]ation" (harmonising, as better put perhaps) is strong, it need not be inevitable. The reason is simply that the percolation of cogent dissenting ideas often has a strong gravitational pull, which resists concepts that might systematically freeze out change. It should be remembered that the great benefit of being a (persuasive) pariah, whether an idea, a movement or even a person, is that it sets you free — and perhaps sets you up to eventually assume the prevailing position on your *own terms*, not terms scripted by an obsolete order. There is no cogent reason for automatic *stare decisis* value to be attributed to "first-in-time judgments." Awaiting a consensus before embarking on harmonisation on the point appears to be a superior option.[87]

Furthermore, international tribunals have not just an abstract need to harmonise rules. Rather they need to harmonise awards against the same claimant and/or the same respondent on a similar set of facts and textual instruments in a variety of cases arising from a variety of fora. The counsel in *Renta 4 S.V.S.A. v. Russian Federation* (2009)[88] counsel for the Claimants openly observed that "[t]his important case" concerns "more than the few million dollars that are at stake for the Claimants in this case."[89] Why? It is so because "owners of about [USD] $10 million in losses reside in countries that have [BITs] with Russia, and the large majority of those live in countries that have [BITs] with Russia that are similar to the [United Kingdom] treaty [at issue in *RosInvestCo v. Russia*] and the Spanish treaty."[90]

Fifth and finally, it must be remembered that not only does consent function differently across the different areas of international law, occasionally consent functions differently even *within* a category. Consider that whereas under the European Convention on Human Rights (ECHR), and specifically its and its protocols' 1950 ratification, States' implicitly have consented to the jurisdiction of the European Court of

---

[87] *Saipem v. The People's Republic of Bangladesh*, ICSID Case No. ARB/05/7, Award, at ¶ 67 (2009) ("subject to the specifics of a given treaty and of the circumstances of the actual case, [the Tribunal] has a duty to seek to contribute to the harmonious development of investment law and thereby to meet the legitimate expectations of the community of States and investors towards certainty of the rule of law.") (footnote omitted).

[88] SCC, Mar. 29, 2009.

[89] *Id.*, at 1, n. 1 (Separate Opinion of Judge Charles Brower) (citing T:377).

[90] *Id.* (citing T:378).

Human Rights (ECtHR), it is not so under the American Convention on Human Rights (1969) and its organ Inter-American Court of Human Rights (IACtHR). With respect to the latter, consent must be given—it might be on an unconditional basis or in exchange for reciprocity—for a particular period of time or for certain specific disputes.[91]

Now, the other side of the coin concerning commonalities between international law and domestic law: Assumption of risk is an important method of highlighting international-domestic law similarities. As indicated earlier, investors necessarily assume some risks and recognise concessions, and host governments do the same. Both know that awards in the immediate case where they have failed to meet some obligation are important but also important are their respective track records that might make other parties correspondingly likely to enter into a future contract or business arrangement with them. Imagine, then, what emerging markets and volatile States must do to attract investments from abroad.[92] "The need for effective [IIA] protection has been felt more keenly in light of recent nationalizations and asset seizures in parts of Latin America, Africa and the former Soviet Bloc."[93]

In June 2009, the President of Venezuela Hugo Chavez proclaimed that "land is for the people," and that particular pieces of real estate within his country could now be nationalised. He has engaged in voracious nationalisation of the oil, electricity, telecommunications and infrastructure sectors within Venezuela. Bolivia too has conducted similar acts of expropriation. The collateral impact of this chain of events, the execution

---

[91] This can be accomplished via a declaration presented to the Secretary General of the Organization of American States (OAS).

[92] T. G. Nelson, P. Mitchard, K. Nairn & D. Kavanagh, "New Arbitral Ruling in Yukos Case Exposes Possible Gaps in Bilateral Investment Treaty (BIT) Coverage for Managed Investment Funds," Skadden Arps Newsletter, p. 1, June 2009, *available at* <www.skadden.com/sites/default/files/publications/Publications1841_0.pdf> [T. G. Nelson, et al, "Possible Gaps in Bilateral Investment Treaty (BIT) Coverage for Managed Investment Funds"] ("Investors in emerging markets or volatile foreign jurisdictions are increasingly focusing on the legal protections that may be available to them under applicable bilateral investment treaties (BITs) or free trade agreements (FTAs), should their investments be subjected to expropriation or other hostile host government action. BIT or FTA protections typically feature the right to pursue investor/state arbitration claims before an international forum . . ., plus the right to claim damages equal to the market value of an expropriated investment.").

[93] *Id.*; see also I. A. Vincentelli, *The Uncertain Future of ICSID in Latin America*, 16 LAW & BUS. REV. AM. 409, 410 (2010).

of domino theory, is that other emerging States (and certainly so-called "failed States" that nonetheless retain features of investment hospitality) will be forced to respond to the market's doubts and make larger-than-otherwise concessions to investors. They will have to do so in order to "insure" the investors or simply convince them of the security of their investments.

The reciprocity in international law that is a consequence of the earlier premises merits comment. International law seeks to regulate as well as to provide the means for power to be expressed in diverse and often long-term ways. Examples abound: Monroe Doctrine (1823), Hull Rule (1942), Marshall Plan (1948), Geneva Continental Shelf Convention (1958), and various other United Nations Conventions. If the reader considers the Truman Proclamation (1945), just as an example, the Proclamation intrinsically did not constitute international law; what did "make" it part of international law was the acceptance of its implications by States generally in a durable process lasting up to 8 years and culminating in the universal acceptance of the continental shelf as a legal institution. Same with ostensibly formal-sounding "rules" and "doctrines" which began to accumulate force and substance due to economic and geopolitical circumstances and the variable equation of power. Their sustaining or losing force (or evolving) depends also on these factors.

This is not to say that peremptory norms or other important international law values have no serious influence. The international community, whose main components are States (193 United Nations members, the Vatican, and doubtful candidates such as Kosovo and Taiwan), international organisations, and approximately 20 international courts and tribunals at any time, is governed by a decentralised body of legal rules, created by treaty and international agreement, through practice and sometimes by international organisations and courts. There is a growing body of international law *principles* around which a consensus has been or is being formed. Nonetheless these principles tend to be guideposts which may be qualified or even completely abrogated by a specific textual provision. What is remarkably interesting is that certain arbitrators are accused of "*rewrit[ing]* treaty provisions in light of what they consider to be an inherent rule of general international law."[94]

[94] F. Zarbiyev, *Judicial Activism in International Law, supra,* at 26-27 (emphasis added) (citing in n. 153: "The decision in the case of *Víctor Pey Casado and President Allende Foundation v Republic of Chile* (Decision on Provisional Measures, ICSID Case No ARB/98/2, 25 September 2001), is a good example. . . . [T]he Tribunal concluded that provisional measures indicated by ICSID tribunals

This book relies on and calibrates those principles in the expropriation context. Working within the *jus gentium* tradition, Hugo Grotius, Samuel von Pufendorf, Emerich de Vattel and Christian Wolff, among others, helped to develop the fundamental system of principles for international law.[95] Primarily European in origin, this system was transplanted to the Americas, Africa, Asia and Australasia by commerce and colonisation. Given Jerome Frank's world divided into rule-sceptics and fact-sceptics,[96] it can safely be said that international expropriation law contains elements of both. International expropriation law is skewed towards rule-sceptics representing their views as fact-based or interpretive disagreements rather than intrinsic and somewhat-philosophical disagreements about the rule itself. Perhaps we have license enough to characterise them as "Masquerading Rule Sceptics."

In a common law regime where *stare decisis* holds sway, the fecund existence of masquerading rule-sceptics makes much intuitive sense. Such a regime is, after all, a "hard precedent" regime. But in civil law regimes or IIA regimes where there is no system of precedent and disputes are resolved as they arise in an individual arbitration ("soft precedent" regimes), this is harder to fathom. The explanation, borne out by earnest tribunal language seeking legitimacy and scholarship by arbitrators and judges, is that tribunals are more confident providing a pedigree for their

---

were binding even though the ICSID Convention grants the ICSID Tribunals only a recommendatory power in this regard (art 47).").

95 S. Ratnapala, JURISPRUDENCE 146-54 (Cambridge University Press, 2009) (discussing Grotius and von Pufendorf); R. P. Anand, INTERNATIONAL LAW AND THE DEVELOPING COUNTRIES: CONFRONTATION OR COOPERATION? 15 (Martinus Nijhoff Publishers, 1987) (discussing Wolff); E. de Vattel, THE LAW OF NATIONS: OR, PRINCIPLES OF THE LAW OF NATURE APPLIED TO THE CONDUCT AND AFFAIRS OF NATIONS AND SOVEREIGNS (G.G. and J. Robinson, 1797). See also B. Kingsbury & B. Straumann, "State of Nature versus Commerical Sociability as the Basis of International Law" 1, 3 in *Philosophy of International Law* (Samantha Besson and John Tasioulas, ed., Oxford University Press, 2010) [B. Kingsbury & B. Straumann, "State of Nature versus Commercial Sociability"] (stating that although "Grotius, Hobbes and Pufendorf each took distinctive approaches to the problems of whether and how there could be any legal or moral norms between these states in their emerging forms," "[e]ach was acutely interested, for biographical as well as intellectual reasons, in the emergence of modern states as means to overcome civil war and religious strife. We believe it is fair to see some commonality in the engagement of each author, albeit in different ways, with the *salus populi* and reason of state.").

96 J. Frank, COURTS ON TRIAL: MYTH AND REALITY IN AMERICAN JUSTICE viii-ix (Princeton University Press, 1949).

ideas—especially if they are rejecting or distinguishing away a prevailing position in international law.

What this book also points out throughout, and others would help themselves by providing, a roadmap for future tribunals to follow their holdings and logic (if not their presuppositions). From a tribunal perspective, this objective is at least as important as justifying the legitimacy of the decision based on prior case-law. Legitimacy depends both on past adherence to certain shared international law understandings and what scholars have called the "enmeshment of norms" *as well as* the decision-trees that future tribunals are to follow.[97]

Apart from the consistency question, we also must ask if it is "legitimate for international courts . . . to interpret international treaty law in light of human rights" and *vice versa* "even if the contracting parties have deliberately not [so] incorporated . . . into the [relevant compact]."[98] Moreover, the conversation to be had here is also by teaching and learning from political actors in charge of creating those tribunals.

Apart from precedent (both "hard" and "soft"), classically legal ideas organising themselves around international expropriation law are sovereignty, territory, formal and informal equality (for State and non-State parties), attribution and responsibility, sovereignty, consent and self-determination. The extra-legal organising ideas are hegemony, balance of power, sphere of influence, coercion, and subliminal ("pheromonal" and between-the-lines)[99] reasoning by tribunals. This is not to say that subjective assumptions and premises necessarily outweigh the textual proviso but it is only to say that the adjudicator might not even see those assumptions and premises as illegitimately subjective because the adjudicator sees those assumptions and premises as the *only* acceptable method of deriving an answer.

This last idea occupies a prominent place in this book because it is a prominent thread running across international tribunal life. It runs across all of domestic law too, especially in common law systems where precedent is binding, especially on lower courts *within* a system ("vertical

[97] J. Brunnée & S. Toope, LEGITIMACY AND LEGALITY IN INTERNATIONAL LAW: AN INTERACTIONAL ACCOUNT 101 (Cambridge University Press, 2010) [J. Brunnée & S. Toope, LEGITIMACY].

[98] E. U. Petersmann, *Human Rights and International Economic Law in the 21st Century: The Need to Clarify their Interrelationships*, J. INT'L ECON. L. (2001), at 7.

[99] Congenital or experiential factors make perfectly reasonable adjudicators and arbitrators arrive at different resolutions. The causes for the discrepancy typically are different premises and assumptions, sometimes underlying and lurking ones. This issue is discussed further in Chapter III.

stare decisis"). Horizontal *stare decisis*, of course, is usually an advisory affair. This latter scenario usually applies to international tribunals, which act parallel to each other.[100] As will curiously emerge, most horizontal tribunals, both international and domestic, prefer to "distinguish" away an unhelpful and non-binding case rather than repudiate it overtly. The unspoken need for comity and the fact that the legitimacy of the international tribunals is interdependent makes it so.

Moreover, since expropriation is a consistent staple in an international tribunal's diet, subliminal reasoning in judicial literature and submissions is very important indeed, as Chapter III seeks to demonstrate. The importance of what is left unsaid cannot be overstated. Its determinants tend to be contextual and value judgments, usually legitimate ones such as purpose, objective, structure, and so on. It might become illegitimate when the mooring for a specific factor or decision is nothing more than the subjective predilection of a judge. The line between the two categories can sometimes be indistinct, made all the more so by the occasionally obfuscating static and noise in the public sphere.

On various occasions, the book argues that the difficulty of these projects is a genuine one that should be embraced and acknowledged by the tribunals. A return to rigor, in this sense, is long overdue. Direction in which these organising ideas are currently developing has given rise to a debate between those who regard the standards as still obtaining and those who see them as flaws in international organisation requiring rectification by becoming more like domestic models.

Still, *whom* do these organising principles govern? The primary actors in international law have always been States. A cogent definition is "collective territorial entities having certain characteristics of separateness and independence from other States." Historically, this resulted from the weakening or disappearance of "supra-state" actors such as the Holy Roman Empire, the development of nationalism, the consolidation of several minor city-states into nations, the expansion of European colonial empires, and the suppression or conversion into suzerains of various indigenous peoples. Many of these developments occurred in the latter half of the twentieth century. To give the reader an idea of this expansion of the number of nations, in 1945 51 states were members of the United Nations while now in 2012 there are 193.

---

[100] Of course, even when international tribunals are stratified, a lower-ranked tribunal of one system is not bound by the decisions of any tribunal of a different system. The latter's decisions have the same horizontal *stare decisis* effect on the former's decisions as they would on the former's reviewing tribunal(s).

The change has not just been reflected in numbers. It has also made serious, lasting and significant doctrinal and categorical difference to international law. Consider that in 1905 the legendary positivist L. F. L. Oppenheim confidently declared the prevailing wisdom of his age: "States only and exclusively are subjects of international law." It was not until the *Reparations Case* (1949) that the International Court of Justice (ICJ) rejected the notion that only States could be possess legal personalities.

The Court also preferred the "objective" view of what a legal person was, rejecting the more "subjective" argument that the entity had to be officially recognised by the State in order to count as a legal person. The United Nations, it was held in the *Reparations Case*, retains "objective" legal personality which could be relied upon as distinct from a third party's non-personality. The ICJ did not resolve in the *Reparations Case* whether the "objective" legal personality label was limited to major multinational organisations or whether it applied to public international organisations broadly. In some cases, international organisations such as the Security Council or the European Union wield power over States which States often perceive as a type of delegation.[101]

An inseparable implication of the Oppenheim era understanding above was that non-State entities such as indigenous groups or international organisations were ignored, devalued or excluded. While much is now made of the development that allows complainants to circumvent the State and seek relief directly in international tribunal or court in a specific situation, it is only *with the consent* of the complainant's State that there even is a relevant international law instrument that is the font of relief. The primary rules of international law revolve around the State as an organising idea and indeed disputes over whether an entity is, should be, or should be recognised as a State cause significant friction and instability. These debates trigger basic questions about state responsibility and attribution. These questions become even more pronounced in Chapter III.

A State is nothing if its sovereignty is not accompanied by self-determination and the right to consent or to withhold that consent from international compacts. This particular point of international law is a direct source of much controversy discussed later in this book, both as to procedural as well as substantive standards in expropriation-related claims.

The self-determination principle was applied to mandated territories under the League of Nations Covenant, and more broadly to colonial territories under Chapters XI and XII of the United Nations Charter.

---

[101] A recent example is the dispute attending the Maastricht Treaty in the United Kingdom and Germany, and more recently the European Court of Justice's decision in *Kadi I* (2008), confirmed by the General Court in *Kadi II* (2010).

Arguably its most consequential impact lies in speeding up the grant of independence to colonial territories in the 1960s. In cases like Southern Rhodesia (now Zimbabwe), the self-determination principle has also affected the very incidence of statehood. Nonetheless, self-determination remains a limited and limiting principle, and it must be exercised within established international boundaries and must be balanced against respect for those boundaries (what commonly is known as *uti possidetis*).[102]

What about recognition and attribution? How are they connected to each other and why is their connection important? A contentious debate brews about the role of recognition concerning statehood, with most participants choosing either the "constitutive" or the "declaratory" school of thought. State recognition is highly consequential from a political as well as legal standpoint. While international law obligates no State to maintain diplomatic relations (formal or informal), it does *allow* a State to do so. Use of force, international responsibility and other weighty questions often turn on this precise issue.

Non-recognition often is used as a weapon in the international community's arsenal. It is sometimes employed as a policy of hostility to a new entity. Nevertheless, *unilateral* non-recognition is rarely effective in the long run, unless it is coordinated by a systematic policy of non-recognition via established international law organs. General non-recognition ordinarily is considered powerful evidence as to the status of an entity. Generalisations are, or should generally be, avoided in such situations. Some guideposts and necessary (and less likely, sufficient) factors are appropriate but, beyond this, it is a case-by-case approach that prevails.

On the "statehood" question, there remains a crucial distinction between the legal personality, the State and its government. Changes in the *government* of a State do not ordinarily affect the identity, rights or obligations of the State itself. We should not gloss over the significant connections that exist between the two concepts. In order for an entity to become a "State" in the first place, its government must have general control of its territory. However, an important caveat is that this precept is something of a one-way ratchet; a State's temporary lack of a government does not somehow cause it to lose its statehood. The *de facto* policy for many governments is not to extend formal recognition in such situations.

The importance of "democracy" as a rule of law value was stated cogently in Article XXV of the International Covenant on Civil and

[102] See, *e.g.*, *Reference concerning the Secession of Quebec* [1998] 2 S.C.R. 217, at ¶ 61-3 (Supreme Court of Canada); *Kosovo UDI Advisory Opinion* (ICJ, 2010, at ¶ 80-3).

Political Rights (ICCPR): everyone has the right to participate in "genuine periodic elections . . . guaranteeing the free expression of the will of the electors." Something of an irony, and yet somehow understandable because of international law's value system, is that a regime's undemocratic character traditionally has not imperilled its competence to act on behalf of the State. But in the recent Haitian situation the Security Council did treat President-elect Jean-Bertrand Aristide's government, who had not been able to assume his office due to a military coup, as "legitimate,"[103] whereas the military regime under Lieutenant General Raoul Cédras the Security Council called the "the *de facto* authorities in Haiti."[104]

Democracy and democracy-deficit considerations affect not just our interpretation of international law but also comparative law analysis *within* domestic tribunals. Say a domestic tribunal is hard at work trying to decipher what its national constitution's (the ultimate trump card's) "equal protection" or "due process of law" guarantee means. For an education, it might look to its sister supreme courts in jurisdictions that share its fundamental values. Would such a comparative process, even if it merely "confirms" its own inclinations based on its constitution—again, an ace which is difficult to amend—undervalue or devalue the democratic choices of its own people?

We have already discussed briefly the techniques, such as functionalism (potentially "consider[ing] whether . . . [a domestic] constitutional system could use a mechanism developed elsewhere to perform a specific function, to improve the way in which that function is performed here"), expressivism ("learning from experience elsewhere in an expressivist mood") and *bricolage* ("assembly of something new from whatever materials the constructor discovered"), which underlie comparative constitutionalism.[105] Of course, on the international plane a similar argument could be made. This brings us to the point of justifying the comparative nature of this book and the attending extrapolations.

First, the reason that the democracy-deficit argument is weaker in an international law forum is that most textual instruments explicitly require or allow such tribunals to consider the "general principles of law" for purposes of gap-filling.[106] Many national constitutions do not.

[103] SC Res. 841 (1993).

[104] SC Res. 940 (1994).

[105] M. Tushnet, *The Possibilities of Comparative Constitutional Law*, 108 YALE L.J. 1225, 1229 (1999).

[106] If there is an elephant in the room, it is sometimes necessary to acknowledge the elephant's presence so that others may not be trampled by it. Similarly, it might

Comparativists could argue that constitutional doctrine within a nation *already and inevitably* develops, overtly or unsaid, in response to developments in other nations. A vivid and tragic example come from terrorism and security check cases in the immediate aftermath of the terrorist attacks on September 11, 2001.

To this claim, a sound anti-comparativist response is that constitutional doctrine within a nation might develop in light of those developments but that the nation has a monopoly on its own judicial responses to those developments. Another strong anti-comparativist point (this time, on the offensive) could be that the "general principles of law" do not expressly undermine democracy as a value and yet dictatorial regimes receive the same deference as non-dictatorial or democratic ones. This "Dictatorial Paradox" is explained in greater detail in Chapter V (NON-DISCRIMINATION).

Controlling for the differences among international investment arbitration, human rights or other scenarios, comparative doctrinal analysis is possible. Gap-filling is necessary only to the extent that "clear definition and the specific regime established by the terms of the [legal instrument]" are unavailable; otherwise an "illegitimate revision" of the instrument might be at work.[107] Context is important, but context encompasses more than prototype. Prototype alone is a misleading indicator for context. Certainly there is the institutional factor, whereby the textual remit of a particular prototype of a tribunal is enough to assure a similar tribunal that its decision is not illegitimate, even if its reasoning might be suspect. One could argue that it is categorically different when tribunals engage in *cross*-prototypical borrowing. That line of thinking, not to be rejected out of hand, merits some comment and treatment.

That situation is analogous to one where prototypes matter very little indeed, and the pressure point of the case is instead a different factor. Possible examples are environmental considerations, corruption, delay in administrative processing, fundamental food, water and shelter rights, and emergencies. For instance, for an investment arbitration tribunal borrowing from the Iran-United States Claims Tribunal or a nation's Foreign Compensation Commission or a human rights court, or *vice versa*, the controlling (and overshadowing) common denominator might be that they both concern *force majeure*, emergency or fundamental rights. At that

---

be desirable to acknowledge these "general principles" for the sake of legitimation and disclosure of its existence.

[107] *Micula v. Romania*, ICSID Case No. ARB/05/20, Decision on Jurisdiction and Admissibility, at ¶ 101 (also citing *Victor Pey Casado and President Allende Foundation v. Republic of Chile*, ICSID Case No. ARB/98/2), Award of 8 May 2008, at ¶ 414).

point, why should an international tribunal look not beyond its prototype and to what is actually the unifying thread about the cases? The importance of limiting principles cannot be overstated if judges are to think twice about the bumps before "ski[ing]" down the "slippery slope of analogies" all the way "to the bottom."[108]

Second, within the prototypes the textual languages as well as the guiding culture often are similar. In IIA cases, for example, "investment" is the operative term of coverage whereas in human rights cases "property" is the operative term and the operative term could be as broad or as narrow as the text and the culture allow. Indeed, the presence or absence of a requirement to exhaust local remedies can be an explanation of how far the international tribunal went in resolving a case or mandating a particular remedy. If the international tribunal wanted the domestic courts to develop their *own* jurisprudence, it would not make much sense for the international tribunal to do the domestic court's (even an errant domestic court's) homework for them. Same with continuous nationality or the degree of *stare decisis* effect.

How broadly or narrowly the operative terms of art are construed can be telling. Of course contextual differences, such as a fundamental water rights overtone in one case or significant commercial assumptions in other case or the *force majeure* and emergency background in yet another case, can discourage borrowing the reasoning from a given case. But careful analysis would discourage such a comparator anyway. This is one the reasons that some eminent cases are mentioned more than once in this book; we are more interested in observing the themes and strands attending a case.

Third, both within and beyond its own prototype an international tribunal will need guidance to assess the comparators (in non-discrimination cases), the standards of review (in all or almost all cases), the acceptable governmental defences (in all cases), the proper analytical frameworks to follow (in all cases), and how best to legitimise its decisions and, associatively, itself. Often the factual scenarios will be so different that one may not help ascertain the proper outcome in another. Nonetheless, at least as often it is clear how persuasive and facilitative or necessary or sufficient a particular pressure point in a given case was to

---

[108] R. Bork, THE TEMPTING OF AMERICA 169 (Free Press, 1990). While seeking the logical end-point of a proposition is the very business of courts, mercilessly pointing out the *il*logical end-point can sometimes be just a counterproductive exercise in *reductio ad absurdum*. Not only does such an approach not convince colleagues on multi-member judicial panels as well as turn off judges on a higher court (if there be one), it goes nowhere with the public at large.

the outcome there. Then, either by direct application or *a fortiori* analysis, the comparison is conducted.

Fourth, the broader subject-matter remits of some institutions—beyond just the expropriation-related context—enhances the comparative study. Jurisprudential consistency within the tribunal takes on a new significance. If legitimacy is at stake, a judge or arbitrator has to be consistent across their jurisprudence. They must do so because they are aware that intelligent, intuitive observers will discern that the flimsy distinctions (that aren't really differences at all) between the case at hand (let us call this Case B) and the earlier case the arbiter purportedly is following (Case A) are just sophistries to yield a preferred outcome. Indulging private preferences over the voice of the law, and often the intent of the signatories (especially in the IIA context), is the easiest and quickest way for a tribunal to become illegitimate. The concern that the broader remit might make the competence of the judges and arbitrators too generalist or dilute the reasoning are unpersuasive in the main.

On the contrary, having the comparative reference point of the generalist jurist's reasoning and the wider subject-matter remit subjects the reasoning to a different and interesting scrutiny. Jurists have to submit themselves to principles rather than gerrymandering out a particular result. This is not to say that intellectually solvent minds cannot somehow manufacture a neat distinction to achieve a particular result. But it is to say that such artificial distinctions become increasingly more difficult to defend before a candid world as the record develops. One check on such judicial (mis)conduct is, again, the tribunals' own quest for legitimacy. Tribunals tend to self-combust as a direct consequence of losing this virtue.

Fifth and finally, domestic politicians actually at the root of and in charge of creating the international charters, treaties, and agreements might pay attention to the doctrinal jurisprudence highlighted in this book. They also might learn from the experiences of the tribunal working within their respective precedential structures. *Stare decisis* (even when qualified as "horizontal *stare decisis*") is a touchy term à la investment arbitration, for instance. Vertical *stare decisis* creates a system of reviewability as well as of persuasive adoption by tribunals not directly bound by the pronouncements. Horizontal *stare decisis*, on the other hand, engenders merely persuasive adoption—not so different from persuasive academic authority except that case-law ventures outside the world of theories and adds something of an extra imprimatur by deciding tangible issues concerning people's lives in a certain way.

Vertical *stare decisis* retains the benefit of creating predictability and stability in the law. These considerations, along with economy, are of course pillars of law and economics and other efficiency-oriented schools of thought. Fundamental fairness, another consideration more pronounced in some other schools of thought, is neutral in this game. It cuts both ways. On the other hand, it has been argued that dispensing away with vertical *stare decisis*, as the IIA regime did, actually promoted efficiency by guaranteeing to investors a stable, predictable framework, settled and reasonable expectations, and various procedural and substantive safeguards. Debate about the meaning of these safeguards is often contentious, thus paving the way to more and more sophisticated lines of reasoning. Comparative analysis makes a real difference here.

§ 1.3—Scope and Complexity of the International Tribunals and the Exceptionalism of this Regime

Even though international tribunals are not a globally constituted system without IIAs, human rights courts and other dispute settlement bodies, they nonetheless form an elaborate and well entrenched network, are geographically wide enough, and control significant capital flows into developing countries. It is this last point that retains the potential to cause significant political and economic meltdowns between governments and investors as well as between the developed and developing worlds.

The growth and development of public international arbitration and adjudication in the modern era is usually thought to have begun from the Jay Treaty of 1794. Inter-state arbitration picked up steam in light of the earlier-mentioned *Alabama Arbitration (Great Britain v. U.S.A.)* (1872), where Great Britain (then at the very acme of her imperial glory) actually conformed to the large damages award of U.S. $15.5 million (or approximately $304 million in today's currency) issued against it. Agreement-based bilateral arbitration appeared to have practical merit, and it stopped nations for engaging in the sort of "gunboat diplomacy" that causes diplomatic crises and even military conflicts. Even the political scientist and public intellectual Michael Doyle who rejects the prudent diplomacy explanation for the existence of a "separate peace" among liberal, democratic states while accepting the premise of this "separate peace," argues that the true explanation is mutual respect among the building blocks, citizens.[109] Interactions among citizens in the various

[109] M. W. Doyle, "Kant, Liberal Legacies, and Foreign Affairs," 12 *Philosophy and Public Affairs* 205 (1983).

states "create[s] a web of mutual advantages and commitments that bolsters sentiments of public respect."[110]

It was not until 1900 that the Permanent Court of Arbitration, the first standing arbitral body, was formed as a by-product of the First Hague Peace Conference of 1899. Indeed, the Concert of Europe's failure to stop World War I led to the establishment of the League of Nations (1919-46), the first of its kind. The League was the first general political international organisation seeking to resolve international disputes and to maintain tranquillity. The international community also created the Permanent Court of International Justice (PCIJ) (1922-46), the first standing international court. Following World War II, of course, the United Nations would replace the League and the International Court of Justice (ICJ) would replace the PCIJ.

Since 1945, there has been a proliferation of dispute settlement mechanisms and processes. Some of these systems have not been used at all and some have been used only infrequently. Systems being used frequently are the World Trade Organization (WTO), the European Court of Justice (ECJ), the European Court of Human Rights (ECtHR), the Inter-American Court of Human Rights (IACtHR), the Optional Protocol procedure under the International Covenant on Civil and Political Rights (ICCPR), the Iran-United States Claims Tribunal (IUCT), and recently the International Settlement for the Settlement of Investment Disputes (ICSID), the United Nations Commission on International Trade Law

---

[110] *Id.*, at 213; at 225-231 (Doyle basing his arguments based on Immanuel Kant's theories on three pillars, *i.e.*, first, caution (voters must bear the costs of war and the risk of losing war, or as Kant put it, "If the consent of the citizens is required in order to decide that war should be declared (and in this constitution it cannot but be the case), nothing is more natural than that they would be very cautious in commencing such a poor game, decreeing for themselves all the calamities of war," see I. Kant, "Perpetual Peace" in THE ENLIGHTENMENT, ed. Peter Gay (Simon & Schuster, 1974), pp. 790-92), respect ("[d]omestically just republics, which rest on consent, presume foreign republics to be also consensual, just, and therefore deserving of accommodation"), and finally trade ties and economic welfare (states must promote trade relations in order to promote their own economic welfare and, moreover, "the international market removes difficult decisions of production and distribution from the direct sphere of state policy. A foreign state thus does not appear directly responsible for these outcomes; states can stand aside from, and to some degree above, these contentious market rivalries and be ready to step in to resolve crises.")); at 232 ("No one of these constitutional, international or cosmopolitan sources is alone sufficient, but together (and only where together) they plausibly connect the characteristics of liberal polities and economies with sustained liberal peace.").

(UNCITRAL), and the Stockholm Chamber of Arbitration (SCC). But even on these voluminous terms, the turn of the twenty-first century evinced more than just a surge; it evinced a true sea-change.[111]

A significant change is the adoption of mandatory, non-derogable dispute settlement as a component of novel regulatory regimes such as the European Union (EU), the North American Free Trade Agreement (NAFTA), United Nations Convention on the Law of the Sea (UNCLOS) (1982), WTO (1994), and now the Council of Europe and the European Convention on Human Rights (ECHR) under Protocol 11 (in force since 1998). This book observes past, continuing and future possibilities of interplay among these institutions on expropriation-related standards.

We have to appreciate the significance of the individual investor's or property owner's at least partial incorporation into the international dispute settlement process in cases where they are directly affected or concerned. In the arena of commercial disputes, ICSID and the IUCT's Claims Settlement Declaration (CSD) allow individuals access to mixed arbitration and the New York Convention for the Enforcement of Arbitral Awards (1958) extends international systems of recognition of enforcement of private arbitration to mixed cases.

In the international human rights arena too, individual claimants have been accorded standing to challenge government action. National claims commissions and the United Nations Compensation Commission serve as alternatives to diplomatic protection and provide extra-judicial remedies. Moreover, States retain the privilege of "public interest" standing

---

[111] Charles N. Brower, Charles H. Brower, II, and Jeremy K. Sharpe, *The Coming Crisis in the Global Adjudication System*, Center for American and International Law, *available at* <www.cailaw.org/ita/workshop02_brower.pdf>, pp. 2-3 ("Over the ensuing decade (1992-2001), . . . the ICC International Court of Arbitration received an additional 4,500 arbitration cases, with 566 of these cases (involving parties from 116 states) coming in 2001 alone. New cases received in 2000 by six major arbitral institutions—the American Arbitration Association ("AAA"), the China International Economic and Trade Arbitration Commission, the Hong Kong International Arbitration Centre, the ICC International Court of Arbitration, the London Court of International Arbitration ("LCIA") and the Arbitration Institute of the Stockholm Chamber of Commerce – totaled 2,046. As these numbers have risen, the cases have become increasingly complex, too, encompassing multiple contracts and hence multiple parties and issues.") (internal footnotes omitted). Both a proliferation of arbitral rules and a proliferation of arbitral institutions have led to the docketing of these cases. Some observers, however, might see the creation of the institutions and the adoption of the rules themselves as responses to the hydraulic pressure of disputes which need to be aired.

concerning some fundamental obligations. Still, the general international dispute settlement principle is that States may resolve their disputes by any and all peaceful means—phrased as "solution by negotiation, enquiry, mediation, conciliation, arbitration, judicial settlement, resort to regional agencies or arrangements, or other peaceful means of their own choice."[112]

Several considerations are now addressed. First, consider that, for most prototypes studied in this book, the governing text of the system authorises the investor to circumvent its home State before claiming violations and compensation from the host State. Gone are the days of diplomatic protection and with them the prospect of having claims vetted by the home State. Part of the reason for this departure from diplomatic protection or diplomatic espousal is the need to engender predictability for the rule of law and part of the reason is to promote stability for claimants—both investors and other property owners.[113] In the "ancient" regime of diplomatic protection, the claimant has potential recourse *only* with regard to customary international law. Even so, "customary international law alone would not provide comprehensive protection to the investor, and a state has the sole discretion as to whether or not to bring claims on behalf of one of its nationals, and may decide not to"—undoubtedly, "[t]his reinforces the importance of the terms of an investment contract, and especially any arbitration agreement contained therein."[114]

The home State may choose *not* to entangle itself in a significantly meritorious claim of its own citizen or entity against a foreign State because the home State needs the foreign State's help on an entirely different issue. What happens now? The property owner loses out. On the other hand, the home State may choose to entangle itself in a less meritorious claim of its own citizen or entity against a foreign State because the home State does need the foreign State's help. Even if the home State does espouse the claim, "there may be interminable delays

---

[112] Art. XXIII of the U.N. Charter.

[113] Interestingly, Christopher Borgen argues that international "investors cannot rely on their own States to espouse their claims before State-to-State tribunals as such tribunals are relatively slow and, in any case, there is a likelihood that States would clog tribunal dockets with such espoused claims." C. J. Borgen, *Transnational Tribunals and the Transmission of Norms: The Hegemony of Process*, 39 GEO. WASH. INT'L L. REV. 685, 673 (2007) [C. J. Borgen, *Transnational Tribunals*] (citing C. G. Garcia, *All the Other Dirty Little Secrets: Investment Treaties, Latin America, and the Necessary Evil of Investor-State Arbitration*, 16 FLA. J. INT'L L. 301, 307 (2004).

[114] R. Moloo & A. Khachaturian, *Foreign Investment in a Post-Conflict Environment*, 10 J. WORLD INVESTMENT AND TR. 341, 348 (2009).

before, if ever, the defendant state may be induced to let the matter go to arbitration."[115] Not only does this create a disparity among claimants and claims but also among the host States, a disparity led by nothing better than politics and convenience. Of course, investors of scale can just move away whereas smaller investors and most human rights claimants do not necessarily have this luxury. And it is just as true that today's happy, *i.e.*, "safe," host State might be tomorrow's unhappy home State forced to ask its investor or private entity absorb the loss.

Second, sovereign acts and behaviour of the governments are scrutinised for a wide swath of activities under several standards of review. Even investment tribunals engage with many different kinds of government conduct beyond expropriation, and their reasoning and holdings concerning jurisdiction, attribution, fair and equitable treatment, non-discrimination, and so on apply to tribunals across the board.

In addition, it is the peculiar pressure-point(s) of an *issue or case*, and not necessarily the tribunal prototype into which it is boxed, that is more determinative of its comparative relevance to another case. The origination point counts less. This approach actually empowers arbitrators and judges with the jurisdiction to award compensation to investors in the business sphere and other property owners in the human rights and other spheres. Gus Van Harten and some others refer to this competence as a "comprehensive jurisdiction"[116] but needless to say that, as with all else in this area, it is so only insofar as the bilateral investment treaty (BIT) so allows.

Third, international disputes are resolved in a system that deploys a private adjudication model "originating in the rules and enforcement structure of international commercial arbitration, presenting major challenges to public law principles of judicial accountability, openness, and independence."[117] Giving their assent to IIA's, human rights conventions and so on, voluntarily or compelled by necessity most States have become part of the network (more ambitiously put, "system"). These States have thus infused their own domestic machineries with a strongly

---

[115] See J. L. Brierly, THE LAW OF NATIONS 277 (Clarendon Press, 1963) ("[The investor] has no remedy of his own, and the state to which he belongs may be unwilling to take up his case for reasons which have nothing to do with its merits; and even if it is willing to do so, there may be interminable delays before, if ever, the defendant state may be induced to let the matter go to arbitration . . . ").
[116] See G. Van Harten, INVESTMENT TREATY ARBITRATION AND PUBLIC LAW 6 (Oxford University Press, 2007) [G. Van Harten, ITA AND PUBLIC LAW].
[117] *Id.*

international and privately structured architecture of public law adjudication and *vice versa*.

Now we come to the complexity of this system. The public law architecture just mentioned might be overlooked just due to the multi-headed hydra that denotes this complexity. To start, the system currently incorporates 70 IIA's, 5 human rights treaties, 4 major conventions on international arbitration, and 75 sets of rules of arbitration, not to mention the domestic arbitration statutes of 165 countries. There are over 3000 IIA's currently in effect, and developing countries are party to approximately four-fifth of these treaties.[118] The rate of increase has been exceptional, as there were approximately "only" 2000 IIA's in 2007.[119] National courts have at their disposal a broad range of techniques to manage jurisdictional and choice of law conflicts among different tribunals, including mandatory rules, such as *res judicata*,[120] estoppel,[121] exclusive jurisdiction,[122] fork-in-

---

[118] Anna Joubin-Bret, Marie-Estelle Rey, Jorge Weber, 'International Investment Law and Development', in Marie-Claire Cordonier Segger, Markus Gehring and Andrew Newcombe (eds) *Sustainable Development in World Investment Law* (Kluwer 2011) (observing that in2008, developing countries were parties to 76% of BITs and 81% of all *other* IIAs).

[119] A. Parra, *The Development of the Regulations and Rules of the International Centre for Settlement of Investment Disputes*, 41 INT'L LAW. 47, 53 (2007). The first BIT was signed between Pakistan and Germany in 1959, really not all that long ago (given the approximate age of international law).

[120] When a dispute is decided between two parties, on them that decision ordinarily is binding as *res judicata.* The rule applies on the domestic as well as the international level. See Article 59, International Court of Justice (ICJ) ("The decision of the Court has no binding force except between the parties and in respect of that particular case."); *Application of the Convention on the Prevention and Punishment of the Crime of Genocide (Bosnia and Herzegovina v. Serbia and Montenegro)* (Merits), I.C.J. Reports (2007), at 43-53 (subsequent to *Application of the Convention on the Prevention and Punishment of the Crime of Genocide (Bosnia and Herzegovina v. Serbia and Montenegro)* (Preliminary Objections, Judgment) (1996), at 595). A caveat is that the *res judicata* requirements in domestic as well as international law are strict as to the identity of the parties, issue(s), and cause(s). *Res judicata* effect may sometimes be escaped using the writs of *coram nobis* (brought before a trial court) or *coram vobis* (appellate court), which attacks and attempts to rebut the necessary factual predicates of the original decision.

[121] Issue estoppel and claim preclusion is a more effective way to bar a case on identical issue (but not case) that *res judicata* ordinarily will not. See, *e.g.*, *Legal Status of Eastern Greenland*, P.C.I. J. Series A/B53, Judgment (1933), at 68-9; *Case Concerning the Temple of Preah Vihear (Cambodia v. Thailand)*, Merits, I.C.J. Reports (1962), at 6, 32; *Cave v. Mills* (1862) 7 Hurlstone & Norman, 913,

the-road clauses (choosing among several remedies),[123] and *lis alibi pendens*,[124] as well as discretionary rules, such as stays, anti-suit injunctions and *forum non conveniens*.[125]

---

927 (Lord McNair) ("… a man shall not be allowed to blow hot and cold — to affirm at one time and deny at another … Such a principle has its basis in common sense and common justice, and whether it is called 'estoppel', or by any other name, it is one which courts of law have in modern times most usefully adopted").

[122] One technique is to expressly provide in the text of the relevant international instrument that the only means of managing a dispute or class of disputes under the compact is *the* stipulated method. Some good examples are Article I of the Understanding on Rules and Procedures Governing the Settlement of Disputes (DSU), *available at* <www.wto.org/english/docs_e/legal_e/28-dsu_e.htm>; the European Court of Justice (ECJ) has asserted exclusive jurisdiction with regard to intra-European Union disputes as well as a monopoly on construing European Union law, see *Eastern Sugar B.V. (The Netherlands) v. The Czech Republic*, SCC Case No. 088/2004, Partial Award (2007), at ¶¶ 130-39; and exclusive jurisdiction typically is asserted based on a contractual forum clause in the relevant agreement, see *SGS Société Générale de Surveillance SA v. Republic of the Philippines*, Decision on Objections to Jurisdiction and Declaration, 8 ICSID Rep. 515 (2004), at ¶ 138.

[123] Investment agreements, for instance, sometimes compel a choice between international arbitration or local remedies, but not both ("fork in the road" or bifurcation clauses). However, taking the local remedies route does not somehow preclude a *new* claim later based on, among other possibilities, denial of justice by the domestic courts. This point is covered in greater detail in Chapter IV (EXHAUSTION OF LOCAL REMEDIES AND CONTINUOUS NATIONALITY).

[124] When litigation is pending before one tribunal, another forum abstains from exercising jurisdiction. This is already done in private international law in response to parallel litigation. There is some argument to be made that such rules make ample sense in the field of international law arbitration. See C. McLachlan, *LIS PENDENS* IN INTERNATIONAL LITIGATION 282-94 (Brill Publishers 2009) (employing a "substantial identity" test between or among the various cases); *Case Concerning Certain German Interests in Polish Upper Silesia* (*Germany v. Poland* (1925), P.C.I.J. Series A/B, No. 7, at 19-20; *Benvenuti and Bonfant SRL v. Government of the People's Republic of the Congo*, ICSID Case No. ARB/77/2 (1980), at ¶ 1.14.

[125] While it is true that common law tribunals in the domestic context exercise discretionary powers to manage competing litigation or competing jurisdictions through *forum non conveniens* (tribunal considers whether another tribunal might be better suited to entertain the dispute and if so gives way to that tribunal), see *Spiliada Maritime Corp. Consulex Ltd.* [1987] AC 460 (HL), there seems not to be an international law equivalent. This is not to say that the same *outcome* could not be induced by the use of inherent powers belonging to the international tribunals. See, *e.g.*, C. Brown, A COMMON LAW OF INTERNATIONAL ADJUDICATION 60-71 (Oxford University Press 2007) (not referring to *forum non conveniens*) [C.

International human rights courts have proved to be less of a formalist regarding these rules than have other international tribunals, as Chapter IV will highlight. Diplomatic or inter-governmental claims commissions tend, unsurprisingly and also surprisingly, usually tend to be the most concerned with jurisdictional rules and even norms. This is to be expected because they do not wish to compound a diplomatic spat over the original issue that they have been called upon to resolve; this is surprising because in cases where evidence-gathering is difficult or even impossible and evidentiary rules themselves are challenged often, concern with remaining within the proper remit takes a lower priority than doing justice according to the applicable law.

Now we come upon fragmentation in international law. The universal problem across these techniques is the relationship among the tribunals.[126] The International Court of Justice might be asked to review an arbitral tribunal's decision—an area where the ICJ respects the jurisdictional sphere of another tribunal and has proven itself to resist collateral attacks.[127] Another way the issue may arise is that one international tribunal may be called upon to decide if there is an obligation to submit a case to another tribunal.[128] Moreover, the consolidation of related

---

Brown, A COMMON LAW OF INTERNATIONAL ADJUDICATION]; *Simone André Diniz v. Brazil*, Case 12.001, Report No. 37/02, Inter-Am. C.H.R., Doc. 5 rev. 1 at 167 (2002) (Admissibility Petition), at ¶ 29 ("The Commission does not see any indication in the record that the complaint brought before this Commission is pending before any other international procedure, and it did not receive any information indicating the existence of such a situation; likewise, there is no indication that it reproduces any petition or communication previously examined by the [Inter-American Commission on Human Rights (IACtHR)]. Accordingly, the Commission understands that the requirement of Articles 46(1)(c) and 47(d) [of the American Convention on Human Rights] have been met.").

126 Study Group on the Fragmentation of International Law: Difficulties arising from the Diversification and Expansion of International Law, Yearbook of the International Law Commission, 2006, vol. II, Part Two; C. Brown, A COMMON LAW OF INTERNATIONAL ADJUDICATION, *supra*, at Chapter One ("The Emergence of a Common Law of International Adjudication against a Background of Proliferation").

127 *Case Concerning the Arbitral Award made by the King of Spain on 23 December 1906*, Judgment (1960), I.C.J. Reports 1960, at 192, 216.

128 *Ambatielos Case (Greece v. United Kingdom)* (Jurisdiction), Judgment (1952), I.C.J. Reports 1952, at 28; *id.*, at 44 ("It may seem at first sight that there is here a possibility of a conflict between a decision of the Court finding that there is an obligation to submit a difference to a Commission of Arbitration and an eventual decision by the Commission. There is in reality no such possibility. The Court would decide whether there is a difference between the Parties within the meaning

proceedings is not an inherent or default power but it may be authorised in the case of arbitrations. Over the past fifteen years, changes in European law, the European Court of Justice's jurisdictional assertiveness, and of course the proliferation of international tribunals and mandates has led to the evolution of these techniques.

The increased frequency of the parallel proceedings is attributed to this proliferation. Another change is that whereas international tribunals once were considered to be courts of last resort because of the exhaustion of local remedies and diplomatic protection and quintessentially interstate cases were not part of a national court's diet due to non-justiciability and state immunity, *now* things are different. The exhaustion doctrine has been weakened both by international compacts and by judicial decisions, international tribunals have begun interfacing with their national counterparts, and significant alterations to non-justiciability[129] and state immunity.[130]

National and international jurisdictions increasingly overlap and intermix. Consensus is still forming around this development, and four recent phenomena highlight this point well. First is the race to judgment: each tribunal has its own distinct mandate so that, *sans* clearly expressed deference via consent, it has a positive duty to exercise its jurisdiction.[131] Second, an ultra-principle of coordination between the national and international tribunals is important and even necessary.[132]

---

of the Declaration of 1926. Should the Court find that there is such a difference, the Commission of Arbitration would decide on the merits of the difference.").

[129] *Buttes Gas & Oil v. Hammer* (No. 3) [1982] AC 888; *Kuwait Airways Corp. v. Iraqi Airways Co.* (Nos. 4 and 5) [2002] 2 AC 883; *Re AY Bank Ltd. (in liquidation)* [2006] EWHC 830 (Ch) [2006] 2 All ER (Com) 463; *The Republic of Croatia v. The Republic of Serbia*, [2009] EWHC 1559 (Ch).

[130] *Trendtex Trading Corp. v. Bank of Nigeria* [1977] QB 529; *I Congreso del Partido* [1983] AC 244; State Immunity Act 1979 (U.K.); United Nations Convention on Jurisdictional Immunities of States and their Property, at p. 590 (2004).

[131] *Lauder v. Czech Republic*, Partial Award (2001), 9 ICSID Rep. 62; *CME Czech Republic B. V. v. Czech Republic*, Partial Award (2001), 9 ICSID Rep. 121; *id.*, Final Award on Damages and Separate Opinion (2003), 9 ICSID Rep. 264.

[132] *MOX Plant Case (Ireland v. United Kingdom)*, Order No. 3, Suspension of Proceedings on Jurisdiction and Merits, and Request for Further Provisional Measures, ICGJ 366 (PCA 2003), 126 ILR 310, 42 ILM 1187 (2003); *Commission of the European Communities v. Ireland*, Judgment, Case No. C-459/03, [2006] ECR I-4635 (2006), ECJ (Grand Chamber).

Third, there is a need to defer to party autonomy and thus for the party's chosen forum.[133] But the importance of predictability also kicks in, and requires that rules not be changed drastically in the middle of the game. Notably, "[t]he jurisdiction of a Tribunal established according to the . . . [relevant] Convention is an objective matter determined by its constitutive instruments, and the Parties cannot either increase or reduce it by agreement or acquiescence."[134] Fourth, multiple parallel litigations and the consequential "clash of mandates" are problematic.[135] The confusion, unpredictability (the old devil strikes time and time again), and costs visited upon the parties and tribunals threatens not just inter-tribunal relationships but also the sustained belief of the parties that the rule of law will provide for an efficient process.

How is this system an exceptional one? Consider the following queries: To what international minimum standard or fair and equitable treatment must a foreign investor be entitled? What are the comparators for a Venezuelan investor's stake in a Chinese nuclear plant with enormous consequences for the public health and even security, and thus the very sovereignty, of the host State? What are even the bases for deducing who the comparators are likely to be? Generally speaking, in any case what are the appropriate conditions under which an expropriation-related act is recognised as an international violation?

---

[133] *Compañía de Aguas del Aconquija S.A. & Vivendi Universal v. Argentine Republic*, ICSID Case No. ARB/97/3, Decision, 6 ICSID Rep. 330 (2002); *SGS Société Générale de Surveillance SA v. Republic of the Philippines*, Decision on Objections to Jurisdiction and Declaration, 8 ICSID Rep. 515 (2004); *Tokios Tokelės v. Ukraine*, Decision on Jurisdiction, 11 ICSID Rep. 313 (2004).

[134] *Sociedad Anónima Eduardo Vieira v. República de Chile*, ICSID Case No. ARB/04/7, Memorial of Objections, at ¶ 13 (Prof. Vaughan Lowe) (2006) ("Either the dispute is within the BIT or it is not. Express or implied assertions by the Parties cannot alter the position."); *Ceskoslovenska Obchodni Banka, A.S. v. The Slovak Republic*, ICSID Case No. ARB/97/4, Decision of the Tribunal on Objections to Jurisdiction, at ¶33, *et seq.* (1999); *Autopista Concesionada de Venezuela, CA v. Bolivarian Republic of Venezuela*, Decision of the Tribunal on Objections to Jurisdiction, at ¶ 61, *et seq.* (2001).

[135] *Mexico — Tax Measures on Soft Drinks and Other Beverages (United States v. Mexico)*, Panel Report, WT/DS308/R, adopted 2005; *Mexico — Tax Measures on Soft Drinks and Other Beverages*, Appellate Body Report, WT/DS308/AB/R, adopted 2006; *Archer Daniels Midland Co. and Tate & Lyle Ingredients Americas, Inc. v. Mexico*, ICSID Case No. ARB(AF)/04/01 (2007); *Corn Products Int'l, Inc. v. Mexico*, ICSID Case No. ARB(AF)/05/2 (2009); *Cargill, Inc. v. Mexico*, ICSID Case No. ARB(AF)/05/2 (2009).

To raise *any* of these questions in an international forum, the disputes used to be resolved by negotiation[136] and, rarely, by arbitration *between or among the States*. Once the States became involved, the allegedly wronged private actor had to rely on the States to represent their interests, following the traditional, default international law canon that the State is the individual's or other private legal entity's legal representative in the international sphere. Direct standing is the modern era's response to what some have called this "arbitrary whim or caprice of state officials"[137] or even "most flagrant spoliation of private property."[138] However, the modification, or downright rejection, of this dependency framework in favour of direct standing before an international adjudicative or arbitral tribunal is somewhat complicated.

Direct standing is not a principle that international compacts uniformly provide (though it is becoming increasingly popular as entities, including investors, begin to maintain a loose tie, at best, with their country of incorporation (or "home State")). Direct standing, therefore, is a selectively applied principle. While foreign investors benefit from this now-accepted principle in international law, less privileged human rights claimants such as migrant workers denied employment rights or torture victims denied recourse or indigenous populations suffering from environmental transgressions have no such protection to invoke. Nor does there seem to be the popular and political will to enact such changes, and

---

136 Over a long time-period and a series of iterations, it has been shown in a variety of environments that the results frequently leave no party satisfied to a functional equilibrium. See, *e.g.*, S. Dahan, "Conceptualising the EU/IMF Financial Assistance Process" in *EU Balance-of-Payments Assistance for Latvia Foundations of Success*, Occasional Papers: European Commission, November 2012, p. 184 ("According to William Zartman, the negotiation process is ruled by a paradox termed the 'Toughness Dilemma' or 'Negotiator's Dilemma', which makes it characteristically indeterminate. The dilemma claims that the tougher the negotiators' behaviour is, the more likely they are to gain a larger part of the outcome but the less likely they are to achieve any outcome (agreement) at all. The dilemma also claims that the softer the negotiators behave, the more likely they are to reach agreement but the less likely they are to reach a large part of the agreed outcome.") (internal citations omitted) [S. Dahan, "Conceptualising the EU/IMF Financial Assistance Process"].

137 M.S. McDougal et al., *Nationality and Human Rights: The Protection of the Individual in External Arenas*, 83 YALE L. J. 900, 906 (1973).

138 W.L. Penfield, *Address: Is the Forcible Collection of Contract Debts in the Interest of International Justice and Peace?*, 1 AM. SOC'Y INT'L L. PROC. 129, 131 (1907).

indeed outside of the European Union almost all States have powerfully refused to grant non-investors any such status.

Given these considerations, direct standing for investors ordinarily as seen as a commercial tool to incentivise investment, rather than a sweeping move to vindicate individual rights comprehensively and without regard to the claimant's station or means. In fact, individual rights of the *citizens* needing protection in *private* law might even be harmed by such broad investor protections. One scholar has gone so far as to call direct standing for investors "an anomalous and exceptionally potent system that protects one class of individuals by constraining the governments that continue to represent everyone else."[139]

Another scholar has suggested that "host States can find it difficult to strengthen domestic social and environmental standards, including those related to human rights, without fear of foreign investor challenge, which can take place under binding international arbitration."[140] In order to attract investment, governments often offer to "freeze" the extant regulatory framework (through vehicles known as "stabilisation clauses") for projects—some of which might last up to half a century.[141]

From the government's legal standpoint, offering to do so might, for now, be the strategically efficient course of action for it makes the government's position look measured and reasonable when faced with a "legitimate expectations" challenge. Chapters V (NON-DISCRIMINATION) and VI (OTHER SUBSTANTIVE STANDARDS) will delve further into this line of argumentation.

From the sovereign's economic standpoint, it also makes sense. Two IIA practitioners state on record that from their personal experience that "[a]s FDI-exporters woo developing countries with high economic potential, often the host governments have little capacity to critically review and negotiate such agreements. Instead, they may be signed . . . [intact and unaltered,] with the hope that such treaties will open the gates

---

[139] G. Van Harten, ITA AND PUBLIC LAW, *supra,* at 10.

[140] J. Ruggie, *Protect, Respect and Remedy: a Framework for Business and Human Rights,* Report by the Special Representative of the Secretary-General on the issue of human rights and transnational corporations and other business enterprises (A/HRC/8/5) (2008), at ¶¶ 34-5; see also O. de Schutter, INTERNATIONAL HUMAN RIGHTS LAW: CASES, MATERIALS AND COMMENTARY 164-65 (Cambridge University Press, 2010).

[141] G. Van Harten, ITA AND PUBLIC LAW, *supra,* at 9-10.

of FDI and benefits will flow automatically."[142] From capital and infrastructure to managerial knowledge to raising export competitiveness, States increase their odds of receiving these goods in exchange for part of their sovereignty.[143]

Now notice something peculiar. This book substantiates that two trends—"legitimate expectations" becomes absorbed and entrenched into all the substantive standards *or* it effectively becomes a stand-alone standard and IIA tribunals may order injunctive relief, including stays—might continue. If these trends continue, then tribunals may simply begin mandating *de facto* stabilisation clauses without having to go as far explicitly. The disadvantage attending this approach is that tribunal-welfare rather than party autonomy might become the prevailing norm.

In the coming decades, this will play out through the issue of consistency. Whereas parties and even drafters of conventions and trade agreements retain the freedom to be inconsistent, unpredictability and somewhat arbitrary, international tribunals worry constantly about their own legitimacy and are less likely to do anything that seems inconsistent. Parties typically know what their needs and earlier agreed-upon rules are. Thus tribunals might overreach their policing roles and become super-drafters.

Party autonomy is not, however, absolute. It is beyond cavil that the system sometimes is accused of "disadvantag[ing] those individuals who stand to benefit from business regulation that is now foreclosed by investment treaties or from other public initiatives, the cost of which is made too high or uncertain by the threat of investor claims."[144] Considering that

---

142 R. Moloo and J. Chao, *International Investment Law and Sustainable Development: Bridging the Divide*, p. 3 (2011) (unpublished paper on file with the author).

143 R. Moloo & A. Khachaturian, *Foreign Investment in a Post-Conflict Environment*, 10 J. WORLD INV. & TRADE 340, 340 (2009) ("Through some types of foreign investment, the foreign investor can bring capital and infrastructure, as well as technical, organizational and managerial know-how to the host state. Furthermore, FDI may supplement local growth and development by, among other things: increasing financial resources for development, improving export competitiveness, boosting employment opportunities, improving the skill base of workers, enhancing technological capacity, providing access to international markets, and playing a role in an economy's integration into the global economic community.") (internal footnotes omitted)..

144 G. Van Harten, ITA AND PUBLIC LAW, *supra,* at 10; M. Waibel et al, THE BACKLASH AGAINST INVESTMENT ARBITRATION: PERCEPTIONS AND REALITY xxxviii-xxxix (Kluwer Law International, 2010); see also, *e.g.*, M. L. Satterthwaite, *Crossing Borders, Claiming Rights: Using Human Rights Law to Empower*

human rights conventions themselves are hard to create and ratify, the loss of *the* last remaining vestige of a different kind of protection by willing governments—regulation—cannot be easy.

Direct standing is, of course, just the beginning. While it is causal to the explosion of international claims, and certainly international investment claims, direct standing is just as much a symptom of the larger *causa causans:* a heightened sense in the international legal culture that business, human rights or other transnational issues should be resolved before competent international tribunals.[145] This very vector itself is a result of the world becoming a smaller and smaller place gradually.

Chapter II penetrates the complex anatomy of these issues, and address the scope and standards of review as well as several different methodological approaches undertaken by the various institutional prisms. Here we have embarked on an "experiment" of prototypes, the value of which is a matter for the reader to judge. Chapter III then discusses the relevant attribution and causation rationales underlying the ways in which international tribunals have approached the dispute settlement of expropriation and expropriation-related standards. Chapter IV engages with the exhaustion of local remedies and continuous nationality; Chapter V with non-discrimination, with what *likeness* analysis entails, and the *necessity* test; and Chapter VI with the international minimum standard, due process, fair and equitable treatment, and full protection and security.

Women Migrant Workers, 8 YALE HUM. RTS. & DEV. L. J. 1, 2 (2005) ("[G]iven that none of the primary receiving – 'host' – countries have ratified the treaty [protecting migrant workers], and that few are likely to do so in the near future, this victory is a limited one, even for human rights advocates accustomed to celebrating small achievements.") (footnotes omitted).

[145] For IIA cases, the compacts themselves create tribunals and endow them with jurisdiction. Thus the acquiescence, at least in broad strokes, of the signatory nations themselves is not in doubt. With respect to international human rights, a telling analysis comes from a Special Rapporteur of the U.N. Commission on Human Rights. See *The Realization of Economic, Social, and Cultural Rights, Final Report on the Question of the Impunity of Perpetrators of Human Rights Violations,* prepared by Mr. El Hadji Guissé, Special Rapporteur, pursuant to Sub-Commission Resolution 1996/24, E/CN.4/Sub.2/1997/8 (1997), at ¶ 131 (human rights violations committed by States, corporations or other entities frequently "do not come within the competence of a single State and, to prevent contradictions and inadequacies in the remedies and sanctions decided upon by States individually or as a group, these violations should form the subject of special attention. The States and the international community should combine their efforts so as to contain such activities by the establishment of legal standards capable of achieving such objective.").

Chapter VII (CONCLUSION) returns us to the issue of legitimacy, notably the point that most judicial legitimacy arguments appear to have missed: Legitimacy is engendered not just by following credible actors but also by having credible actors follow you. The importance of transparency, predictability and arbitrariness will also be examined here. Each chapter will explain the future possible courses of action.

Before we address these complex strands and developments, a difficult overarching question lingers: Is this an international association of States or an international community in the truest sense? On the tribunal issue, this is truly an interactive international community—and in the few gaps and spaces where it is not, it should consider the stakes and rethink its approach. This book is devoted to making that case.

§ 1.4—Review of International Expropriation Law and Limits on Control

Governments guarantee property owners and investors certain treatment, such as the right to be free from expropriation without just compensation, the right to be free from discrimination on the basis of nationality, the right to fair and equitable treatment, or the guarantee that States will honour their contractual commitments.[146] Procedurally, the existence of a domestic law guarantee or investment treaty means that if claimants believe their substantive rights have been violated they can seek redress against the host State through the dispute resolution mechanism.

Procedural rights exist to go beyond gunboat diplomacy and politicised dispute resolution in order to provide a neutral dispute resolution forum. States, for their part, draw assurance from the fact that control mechanisms "provide States the comfort they seek . . . that an international court will not venture beyond its assigned mandate,"[147] and many States remain prepared to opt out of various agreements and conventions if in theory or in practice these mechanisms prove to be wanting.

There is an important history behind this. Developing property protection in international law (especially for foreigners) has been contentious throughout the twentieth century. In the early twentieth century, many Latin American and European jurists argued that foreigners

---

[146] See S. D. Franck, *Development and Outcomes of Investment Treaty Arbitration*, 50 HARV. INT'L L. J. 435, 442 (2009) [S. D. Franck, *Development and Outcomes of ITA*].

[147] J. Katz Cogan, *Competition and Control in International Adjudication*, 48 VA. J. INT'L L. 411, 419 (2008).

are only entitled to equality of treatment under the host country's laws, what became known as "national treatment" and is discussed in Chapter V (NON-DISCRIMINATION). The United States, though, was an early and enthusiastic proponent of an international minimum standard for the treatment of the property of foreigners and opposed the Calvo Doctrine supported primarily by Latin American countries.[148] The Latin American governments pushed back against what they saw as a malleable and seemingly endless reach of *denial of justice* and related law. The Calvo Doctrine manifested this resistance.[149]

Nonetheless, flexibility, which often is a downside of such a vague international standard such as the *denial of justice*, can also be its upside. Concepts like exhaustion of local remedies, non-discrimination, and the substantive standards (due process, fair and equitable treatment, and minimum standards of treatment) covered in this book all have their roots in (or at least were consolidated by) *denial of justice*—depending on whether it is styled as "procedural" or "substantive."[150] These concepts therefore retain a doctrinal lineage and *denial of justice* an historic status that has a net beneficial effect in holding together much of international law today. If we keep including fair and equitable treatment or due process in treaties, agreements and decisions, then *denial of justice* adds some legitimacy to them. That makes it harder for charges of malleability and illegitimacy to be levelled at the system.

The Calvo Doctrine, named after the Argentinean jurist Carlos Calvo, provides that aliens are only entitled to national treatment and, therefore, does not recognize an international minimum standard of treatment for alien property.[151] It also denies the right of foreign nationals to seek diplomatic protection from their State by requiring that the foreign national submit to the jurisdiction of domestic courts.[152] The United States insisted on the Hull Rule, named after its Secretary of State Cordell Hull,

---

[148] D. Shea, THE CALVO CLAUSE: A PROBLEM OF INTERNATIONAL AND INTER-AMERICAN LAW AND DIPLOMACY 17-19 (1955); A. V. Freeman, *Recent Aspects of the Calvo Doctrine and the Challenge to International Law*, 40 A.J.I.L. 121, 130 (1946).

[149] J. Paulsson, DENIAL OF JUSTICE IN INTERNATIONAL LAW 20 (Cambridge University Press, 2005).

[150] *Id.*, at 5 (arguing that *substantive* denial of justice should be "jettisoned"). Paulsson presents interesting arguments for ridding the system of the *substantive* category so long as denial of justice itself remains on the radar.

[151] M. Sornarajah, THE INTERNATIONAL LAW ON FOREIGN INVESTMENT 37 (Cambridge University Press, 2010).

[152] *Id.*, at 121.

who, in response to the expropriation of American-held oil interests by Mexico in the 1930's, argued that "prompt, adequate and effective compensation" was required under international law.[153]

On the domestic law plane, neo-liberal economists and activists have advocated a broader definition of expropriation (known as "takings" in the United States, Canada, Australia, and much of the common-law world). Although many of the concepts related to an expropriation claim—non-discrimination, reliance, legitimate expectation, proportionality, and due process—overlap between domestic and international law, many domestic tribunals have given greater deference to governments than have international tribunals.

Whereas United States federal courts often have acknowledged direct expropriation to be likely violations of the Fifth Amendment's Takings Clause ("nor shall private property be taken for public use, without just compensation"), they have been more reluctant to hold the same for indirect expropriations; moreover, even some direct expropriations have been approved because of conflated notions of "public use" (textual language) and "public purpose" (judicial language).[154] Canadian courts frequently use the "property subset" (the expropriation must be of "sufficient severity to remove virtually all of the rights associated with the property holder's interest" in order to constitute an unlawful expropriation)[155] and "government benefit" (government must benefit in order for the expropriation to be a violation)[156] doctrines to deny claims. Perhaps because of this (or despite this or simply on an unrelated basis), the neo-liberal activism for greater property rights in international law has increased in the later part of the twentieth century and into the twenty-first.[157]

Developments in twentieth-century international expropriation law occurred alongside, and partially prompted by, European industrialisation, international Big Business expansion, socialist revolution, decolonisation of much of the developing world and the attending imperial breakups, the establishment of new States, the changes brought about by the Soviet

---

[153] *Id.*, at 212.

[154] C. E. Cohen, *Eminent Domain after* Kelo v. City of New London*: An Argument for Banning Economic Development Takings*, 29 HARV. J. L. & PUB. POL'Y 491, 493-94 (2006).

[155] *Alberta (Minister of Public Works, Supply and Services) v. Nilsson*, [1999] 70 Alta. L.R.3d 267 (Alberta Q.B.).

[156] *A & L Investments Ltd. v. Ontario*, [1997] 36 O.R. (3d) 127 (Ont. C.A.).

[157] See B.P. Schwartz & M. Bueckert, *Regulatory Takings in Canada*, 5 WASH. U. GLOB. ST. L. REV. 477, 485 (2006).

Union's fall, and the greater role of the In the post-World War II era, the issue of treatment of foreign investment, control over natural resources and sovereignty was the subject of much controversy at the United Nations and in international law.[158] Since no country is an island in the John Dunne sense (not even ones that geographically are islands), "it has become more difficult for governments who are not parties to such investment treaties to engage in open takings without paying significant compensation."[159]

Developing countries and some Western countries exercised their sovereignty by nationalising foreign-owned industries, through land reform and economic nationalism. In 1962 the United Nations General Assembly passed Resolution 1803, declaring: "Nationalization, expropriation or requisitioning shall be based on grounds or reasons of public utility, security or the national interest which are recognized as overriding purely individual or private interests, both domestic and foreign."[160]

Significant disagreement on international expropriation law continued in the United Nations in the 1970's at the same time as developing countries wanted a basic restructuring of the international economic system. As the welfare state grew larger and there were more and more social and economic regulations, the number of expropriation claims also increased. This diplomatic tension—political as well as legal—was happening alongside, and partially because of, emerging international law decisions.

In *Norwegian Shipowners' Claims* (*Norway v. United States* (1922)),[161] the Permanent Court of Arbitration recognised that intent to expropriate on the part of the host state need not be shown in order for an expropriation claim to prevail. The holding has subsequently been cited by countless arbitral tribunals as a default assumption. In the Permanent Court of International Justice (PCIJ), a similar issue came up four years later in *Case Concerning Certain German Interests in Polish Upper Silesia* or *The*

---

[158] See generally N. Schrijver, SOVEREIGNTY OVER NATURAL RESOURCES (Cambridge: Cambridge University Press, 1997) and I. Brownlie, "Legal Status of Natural Resources In International Law (Some Aspects)," 162 Rec. des Cours 245 (1979).

[159] J. M. Marlles, *Public Purpose, Private Losses: Regulatory Expropriation and Environmental Regulation in International Investment Law*, 16 J. OF TRANSNAT'L L. & POL'Y 275, 277 (2006).

[160] G.A. Res. 1803, 17 U.N. GAOR Supp. (No. 17) at 15, U.N. Doc. A/5344 (1962).

[161] 1 U.N.R.I.A.A. 307.

Chorzów Factory Case (*Germany v. Poland* (1925)).[162] Here the PCIJ held that expropriation for reasons of public utility is not unlawful *per se*. The PCIJ also held that indirect expropriation may occur through transfers of real property itself and access to that property.

The Chorzów Factory Case is also known for putting forth two compensation principles: (*i*) "[r]estitution in kind, or, if this is not possible, payment of a sum corresponding to the value which a restitution in kind would bear"; and (*ii*) "the award, if need be, of damages for loss sustained which would not be covered by restitution in kind or payment in place of it."[163] Among today's agreements and charters, Article 13 of the Energy Charter Treaty (ECT) and Article 6 of the U.S. Model BIT use the same standards in requiring compensation for expropriation or measures tantamount to expropriation.[164]

Then, in *The Oscar Chinn Case* (1934),[165] the PCIJ held that investors and business owners have no exclusive or primary right of access to a market; in other words, a State may subsidise an industry (even to the point of making the enterprise unprofitable for some investors) without giving rise to unlawful expropriation. Soon after World War II (in 1954), the United States Foreign Claims Settlement Commission was created to dispose of certain claims related to the war. In *Case Concerning Jeno Hartman* (1958),[166] the Commission found that expropriation occurs when the government deprives the owner of access to use, enjoy or sell the property (regardless of who owns the title).

In *Case Concerning Albert Bela Root* (1958),[167] the Commission found that absent just cause and a time-limit, a total prohibition the sale or occupancy of a house constitutes expropriation. Professor G.C. Christie summed up these cases: although "a State may not purport to interfere with rights to property, it may, by its actions, render those rights so useless

---

162 P.C.I.J. Series A/B, No. 7; *id.*, at 452 (stating "there can be no doubt that the expropriation . . . is a derogation from the rules generally applied in regard to the treatment of foreigners and the principle of respect for vested rights.").
163 *Id.*, at 47.
164 See ECT, art. 13; Office of the United States Trade Representative, U.S. Model Bilateral Investment Treaty, art. 6 (Nov. 2004), <www.ustr.gov/Trade_Sectors/Investment/Model_BIT/Section_Index.html> [U.S. Model BIT 2004].
165 *Britain v. Belgium* (1934), P.C.I.J. Series A/B, No. 63.
166 No. Hung.-717 (1958), United States Foreign Claims Settlement Commission.
167 No. Hung.-1625 (1958), United States Foreign Claims Settlement Commission.

that it will be deemed to have expropriated them."[168] In short, indirect and creeping expropriations could constitute "expropriation" in the legal sense.

What about the appropriate sources of consultation? The International Law Commission (ILC)'s Special Rapporteur Sir Humphrey Waldock insisted on uniformity of agreement as to whether certain subsequent practices were to be deemed relevant to interpretation but he did not insist on total consistency of practice.[169] The International Court of Justice (ICJ) and really most international tribunals consult conventions and customary law to fill in the gaps.[170] It must be noted, though, that it is a rule of thumb that a principle of international law must be "common, consistent and concordant" in order to count as customary law and/or State practice.[171]

---

[168] G.C. Christie, *What Constitutes a Taking, supra,* at 309.

[169] ILC Ybk 1964/II, 60 ("Subsequent practice when it is consistent and embraces all the parties would appear to be decisive of the meaning to be attached to the treaty, at any rate when it indicates that the parties consider the interpretation to be binding upon them. […] [But], if the interpretation adopted by the parties diverges, as sometimes happens, from the natural and ordinary meaning of the terms, there may be a blurring of the line between the interpretation and the amendment of a treaty by subsequent practice."); Commentary, ILC Ybk 1966/II, 211 ("By omitting the word 'all' the [International Law] Commission did not intend to change the rule. It considered that the phrase 'the understanding of the parties' necessarily means 'the parties as a whole'. It omitted the word 'all' merely to avoid any possible misconception that every party must individually have engaged in the practice where it suffices that it should have accepted the practice.").

[170] Article §38(1) of the ICJ Statute prescribes the sources of law for that court as follows:

"(a) international conventions, whether general or particular, establishing rules expressly recognized by the contesting states;

"(b) international custom, as evidence of a general practice accepted as law;

"(c) the general principles of law recognized by civilized nations;

"(d) subject to the provisions of Article 59,34 judicial decisions and teachings of the most highly qualified publicists of the various nations, as subsidiary means for the determination of rules of law."

[171] *Fisheries Jurisdiction Case (United Kingdom v Iceland)* (Merits) [1974] ICJ Reports 3 at 50. See also *North Sea Continental Shelf Cases (Federal Republic of Germany v Denmark; Federal Republic of Germany v Netherlands)* [1969] ICJ Reports 4 at 44 (stating that in order to count as State practice, "[n]ot only must the acts concerned amount to a settled practice, but they must also be such, or be carried out in such a way, as to be evidence of a belief that this practice is rendered obligatory by the existence of a rule of law requiring it.").

There were certain relevant stipulations. There may not be substantial dissent.[172] Absolute uniformity is not required and apart from *jus cogens* (peremptory norms)[173] States may refuse to submit to specific rules so long as they make their position clear from the outset, thereby maintaining their "persistent objector" status.[174] Moreover, customary law and State practice applications can, albeit with some difficulty, be defeated by the doctrine of opposability. And finally, the presumption now is that *opinio juris*—the belief that a course of action took place because the rule of international law so required—occupies similar rank in international law as State practice.[175]

---

[172] See *Case Concerning Military and Paramilitary Activities in and against Nicaragua (Nicaragua v United States of America)* (Merits) [1986] ICJ Reports 98.
[173] L. for "compelling law." Article 53 of the Vienna Convention on the Law of Treaties states: "For the purposes of the present Convention, a peremptory norm of general international law is a norm accepted and recognised by the international community of States as a whole as a norm from which no derogation is permitted and which can be modified only by a subsequent norm of general international law having the same character." Some of the *jus cogens* norms are commencing and continuing aggressive warfare, war crimes, crimes against humanity, piracy, genocide, apartheid, slavery and torture.
[174] *North Sea Continental Shelf, supra*, at 229, 232 (Judge Lachs). States may do so either as a member of a regional group or on account of its status as a member of the international community. See, *e g.*, *Asylum Case (Colombia v Peru)* [1950] ICJ Rep 266 at 277-78; *Fisheries Case (United Kingdom v Norway)* (Judgment) [1951] ICJ Reports 116, at 131; C. A. Bradley & M. Gulati, *Withdrawing from International Custom*, 120 YALE L. J. 202, 204 (2010) ("According to most international law scholars, a nation may have some ability to opt out of a CIL rule by persistent objection to the rule before the time of its formation (although even that proposition is contested), but once the rule becomes established, nations that are subject to it never have the right to withdraw unilaterally from it. Rather, if a nation wants to engage in a practice contrary to an established CIL rule, it must either violate the rule or enter into a treaty that overrides the rule as between the parties to the treaty."); INT'L LAW ASS'N, COMM. ON THE FORMATION OF CUSTOMARY (GEN.) INT'L LAW, STATEMENT OF PRINCIPLES APPLICABLE TO THE FORMATION OF CUSTOMARY INTERNATIONAL LAW 27 (2000) ("There is fairly widespread agreement that, even if there is a persistent objector rule in international law, it applies only when the customary rule is in the process of emerging. It does not, therefore, benefit States which came into existence only after the rule matured, or which became involved in the activity in question only at a later stage. Still less can it be invoked by those who existed at the time and were already engaged in the activity which is the subject of the rule, but failed to object at that stage. In other words, there is no 'subsequent objector' rule.").
[175] *Case Concerning the Continental Shelf (Libyan Arab Jamahiriya v Malta)* (Judgment) [1985] ICJ Reports 13 at 29; *Advisory Opinion on the Legality of the*

Some of the more prominent and recurring sources of customary law should be surveyed. The Vienna Convention on the Law of Treaties (VCLT), a source that this book often refers to and/or consults, is another source of customary law; Articles 31 (primary)[176] and 32 (supplementary)[177] contain the general modes of treaty interpretation. The New York Convention for the Enforcement of Arbitral Awards (1958) is another.[178] The dynamic interaction among customary law, State practice and treaty provisions[179] works in five overarching ways: First, if the international

---

Threat or Use by a State of Nuclear Weapons in Armed Conflict [1996] ICJ Reports 16; RESTATEMENT (THIRD) OF THE FOREIGN RELATIONS LAW OF THE UNITED STATES § 102(2) (1987) ("Customary international law results from a general and consistent practice of states followed by them from a sense of legal obligation.").

Some scholarship maintains that "the traditional conception of [customary international law] . . . emphasizes state practice over *opinio juris*." See, *e.g.*, S. Katzenstein, *International Adjudication and Custom Breaking by Domestic Courts*, 62 DUKE L. J. 671, 672-73 (2012) (emphasis in original) (Anthea Elizabeth Roberts, *Traditional and Modern Approaches to Customary International Law: A Reconciliation*, 95 A. J. I. L. 757, 758 (2001)).

[176] "1. A treaty shall be interpreted in good faith in accordance with the ordinary meaning to be given to the terms of the treaty in their context and in the light of its object and purpose.

.....

3. There shall be taken into account, together with the context:

.....

'any relevant rules of international law applicable in the relations between the parties.'" Typically, Articles 31(1) and (2) are understood to be "internal" to the text of the international agreement whereas (3) is understood to be "external" to the same.

[177] "Recourse may be had to supplementary means of interpretation, including the preparatory work of the treaty and the circumstances of its conclusion, in order to confirm the meaning resulting from the application of Article 31, or to determine the meaning when the interpretation according to Article 31:

(a) leaves the meaning ambiguous or obscure; or

(b) leads to a result which is manifestly absurd or unreasonable."

[178] The New York Convention provides limited "defences" to avoid enforcing a tribunal award.

[179] J. M. Marlles, *Public Purpose, Private Losses, supra,* at 277 ("While customary international law recognized early on that governments engaging in expropriation had a duty to compensate foreign investors for their losses, there were few limits on how government expropriation of foreign investments might take place, or even a clear notion of what expropriation constituted. However, in the interest of attracting capital from abroad, many countries over the last two decades have begun participating in bilateral in-vestment treaties (BITs), as well as multilateral

agreement replicates a rule already existing in customary law, then that helps elucidate the rule further.[180] Second, when a customary rule is being developed, its incorporation in a treaty might crystallise the law in the shape of that rule. It is not always easy to identify when this occurs. In situations where the practice is less developed, however, the specific treaty provision might fail to crystallise the rule as part of customary law.[181]

Third, even in cases concerning new rules, the drafting of the treaty provision might serve as impetus for its *de facto* development in State practice.[182] In addition, the rule becomes customary law only when it is accepted by States. Fourth, what is known as "instant custom" has indeed been deemed by the ICJ as denoting customary law irrespective of whether

---

investment treaties such as the North American Free Trade Agreement (NAFTA) and the Energy Charter Treaty (ECT). These treaties work to attract capital to the treaty parties by limiting the potential for host government interference with foreign investments. Moreover, the proliferation of treaties like NAFTA, the ECT, and numerous BITs has also shaped the development of the customary international law of expropriation.").

[180] *Japan – Alcoholic Beverages II*, Appellate Body Report, 1 November 1996, ¶¶ 12-13; *Legal Consequences for States of the Continued Presence of South Africa in Namibia (South-West Africa) notwithstanding Security Council Resolution* 276 (1970) (Advisory Opinion) [1971] ICJ Reports 16 at 47 ("the requirement of 'concurr[ence]' by the parties requires only 'not over[t] disagree[ment]' by them"). But see *EC – Chicken Cuts*, Appellate Body Report, 27 September 2005, at ¶ 272 ("[T]he 'lack of reaction' [from signatories] should not lightly, without further inquiry into attendant circumstances of a case, be read to imply agreement with an interpretation by treaty parties that have not themselves engaged in a particular practice followed by other parties in the application of the treaty."). As a prominent, if budding, international jurist has observed of this *EC – Chicken Cuts* doctrine, "[t]he standard so created is extremely high, with agreement sufficient to generate a valid subsequent practice for the purposes of VCLT Article 31(3)(b) only held to manifest in situations where: (a) every member of the relevant regime has actively participated in the practice; or (b) every member was positively aware of the practice through notification or participation in a forum where the practice was discussed and had accepted or at least acquiesced in it. This standard has resulted in the Appellate Body rejecting as valid every purported subsequent practice brought before it." See C Miles, *Blog: Assange v Swedish Prosecution Authority: the (mis)application of European and international law by the UK Supreme Court - Part II*, Cambridge Journal of International and Comparative Law (CJICL), June 21, 2012, *available at* <www.cjicl.org.uk/index.php/cjicl-blog/entry/assange-v-swedish-prosecution-authority-the-misapplication-of-european-and-international-law-by-the-uk-supreme-court-part-ii>.

[181] *North Sea Continental Shelf*, *supra*, at 38.

[182] *Trial of the Major War Criminals before the International Military Tribunal*, Vol. 1, Judgment, 171 at 253–4.

the salient provision was supported by State practice. Finally, for consistency's sake the VCLT is believed to be applicable (though non-binding) to the interpretation of non-treaty international instruments.[183]

This last point must be expounded. Whereas the ICJ states that the VCLT "may provide guidance" and that "other factors [must] be taken into consideration," another body named the International Tribunal for the Law of the Sea (ITLOS)[184] - Seabed Disputes Chamber (commonly known as the SBDC) states simply that the VCLT "may, by analogy, provide guidance."[185] This subtle but potentially crucial difference is derived from the understanding that "Security Council resolutions," which obviously are part of the ICJ's remit once cases are submitted to that tribunal, "are issued

---

[183] *Accordance with International Law of the Unilateral Declaration of Independence in Respect of Kosovo* [2000] ICJ Reports, at ¶ 94 (the Court must recall several factors relevant in the interpretation of resolutions of the Security Council. While the rules on treaty interpretation embodied in Articles 31 and 32 of the Vienna Convention on the Law of Treaties may provide guidance, differences between Security Council resolutions and treaties mean that the interpretation of Security Council resolutions also require that other factors be taken into account. Security Council resolutions are issued by a single, collective body and are drafted through a very different process than that used for the conclusion of a treaty ... The interpretation of Security Council resolutions may require the Court to analyse statements by representatives of members of the Security Council made at the time of their adoption, other resolutions of the Security Council on the same issue, as well as the subsequent practice of relevant United Nations organs and of States affected by those given resolutions); *Responsibilities and Obligations of States Sponsoring Persons and Entities with respect to Activities in the Area* [2011] ITLOS Seabed Disputes Chamber (ITLOS SBDC), at ¶¶ 59-60 (The fact that . . . [the Regulations on Prospecting and Exploration for Polymetallic Nodules in the Area of 2000 and the Regulations on Prospecting and Exploration for Polymetallic Sulphides in the Area of 2010] are binding texts negotiated by States and adopted through a procedure similar to that used in multilateral conferences permits the Chamber to consider that the interpretation rules set out in the Vienna Convention may, by analogy, provide guidance as to their interpretation . . . The ICJ seems to have adopted a similar approach when it states in its advisory opinion on Accordance with International Law of the Unilateral Declaration of Independence in Respect of Kosovo, that the rules on interpretation of the Vienna Convention "may provide guidance" as regards the interpretation of resolutions of the United Nations Security Council (ICJ, 22 July 2010, paragraph 94).').

[184] This body, based in Hamburg, Germany, resolves disputes arising from the United Nations Convention on the Law of the Sea.

[185] *Id.*

by a single, collective body and are drafted through a very different process than that used for the conclusion of a treaty."[186]

However, the SBDC perceives treaties and secondary international instruments to be closer in character and therefore "analog[ous]."[187] In traversing a middle path, international tribunals do not wish to be seen as following the VCLT in a servile way but nor do they wish to be perceived as unconstrained by any interpretive guidelines. In the future, as State, individual and corporate activity become even more widespread and internecine, tribunals may need to determine how to construe more effectively treaties and secondary international instruments.

International Court of Justice (ICJ) cases involving expropriation claims consist of two decisions on jurisdiction and one on the merits. In the *Interhandel Case (Switzerland v. United States)* (1959),[188] the ICJ held that the exhaustion of local remedies to be customary law; before resorting to an international court, claimants must exhaust the domestic legal process—to the maximum extent possible—of the host state.

Later, in the *Case Involving Barcelona Traction, Light & Power Co., Ltd.* (*Belgium v. Spain*) (1970),[189] the ICJ held that the country of incorporation must diplomatically espouse a corporation's expropriation claim. More recently, in the *Case Concerning Elettronica Sicula S.p.A.(United States v. Italy) (ELSI)* (1989),[190] the ICJ held that in order to be an expropriation a requisition must be a "significant deprivation,"[191] not just trivial or marginal. Each of these decisions has been taken as the starting position as general principles of public international law.

The twenty-first century's starting position was consolidated by the International Law Commission (ILC). Several points are worth mentioning. First, when a State breaches an international treaty obligation, its conduct is considered a "wrongful act." Reparation is due injuries caused by such wrongful acts. Second, the basic principle that States are obligated to make "full reparation" for any injury caused by an internationally wrongful act is set out in Article 31 of the ILC's Articles of State Responsibility.[192]

---

[186] *Id.*
[187] *Id.*
[188] Judgment, I.C.J. Rep. 1959, p. 6.
[189] Judgment, I.C.J. Rep. 1970, p. 3.
[190] Judgment, I.C.J. Rep. 1989, p. 15.
[191] *Id.*, at p. 71.
[192] See J. Crawford, THE INTERNATIONAL LAW COMMISSION'S ARTICLES ON STATE RESPONSIBILITY (Cambridge University Press 2002). The ILC's Articles on State Responsibility are considered authoritative as to the principles covered there. See, *e.g.*, ILC Article 33, comment (4) (noting the direct application in part of the

ILC Article 2 provides that "an internationally wrongful act" occurs when there is State conduct that constitutes "a breach of an international obligation of the State."[193] Thus, a government's failure to provide treatment guaranteed in some legal provision is an internationally wrongful act and it gives rise to the obligation to make full reparation for any injury caused. Finally, terms of art such as "proximate causation" and "reasonable foreseeability" are often used to suggest that "but for" causation is *not* enough to give rise to state responsibility.

§ 1.5—Conclusion

The next Chapter discusses in detail the standards and parameters attending international adjudication and arbitration. Of course, most tribunals prefer to have their decisions conform to principles (really, institutionally indispensable values) such as legal coherence, harmony and symmetry of rights, justice, efficiency and party autonomy. Sometimes this is possible only on a case-by-case basis.[194] Then too, not everyone will agree upon the right resolution in a given case because it depends, in significant part, on the weights assigned to each of these factors. The appropriate, non-arbitrary line between rigidity and flexibility will usually be a difficult one to justify but no less so than siding in a binary fashion with one camp or the other, so Advantage Neither Camp.

Appealing to the adjudicator's sense of fundamental fairness, even within (or without) the structure of certain objective criteria, seems to have striking appeal. In the course of the judicial dialogue and percolation among diverse and sometimes competing international tribunals different ideas will be exchanged, examined, and re-examined, finally culminating in the optimal norm. Let us apply throughout this book this part-aspirational, part-quixotic narrative to the international law of expropriation.

One last point must be made. This book has frequently referred to decisions and scholarship from the United States. The United States is a focal point for many nations as they formulate their own investment policies and model BIT's, often by hewing closely or responding to the

---

Articles in the context of investment protection agreements). Of course, these customary and default principles may be amended or even rejected by the controlling text.

[193] ILC Y. BK., Art. II, Vol. I (2001).

[194] Perhaps an apt example comes from Justice Potter Stewart's concurring opinion in *Jacobellis v. Ohio*, 378 U.S. 184, 197 (1964) (stating forth an "I know it when I see it" test because, in Justice Stewart's view, most rigid tests in the First Amendment-obscenity field had not been as effective as might have been hoped).

model set by the United States. Moreover, the United States' complex co-sovereignty with the States within its Union and juggling those relationships with its international obligations makes for a fascinating case-study. The lessons teach international tribunals a great deal through its triumphs, losses and grey-areas (confusions and possibilities) and it can learn much from the international judicial arena as well.

CHAPTER TWO

INSTITUTIONS AS PRISMS: AN EXPERIMENT

§ 2.1—Why This Innovation is Necessary

This Chapter and, associatively, the entire monograph is an innovative experiment. In order to explore the comparativism in depth, I found it important to choose certain effective prisms. International tribunals, like the people who compose them, help us transcend our own abstractions by viewing problems and advantages through the behaviour of concrete actors. This Chapter is devoted to articulating the institutional histories, aims and capabilities of the North American Free Trade Agreement (NAFTA) (representative of IIA regimes and tribunals), the European Court of Human Rights (ECtHR) (international human rights tribunals), and the Iran-United States Claim Tribunal (IUCT) (international diplomatic dispute settlement bodies).[1]

A crucial difference between international and domestic legal orders is that "[t]he absence of an organized judicial system in international law implies that except in very limited circumstances judicial decisions are final and judges are not subject to any constraint coming from higher judicial instances."[2] But there is a significant similarity. International tribunals, like domestic tribunals, are not monoliths. The descriptive truth, whatever the normative value, is that variables such as changing doctrine,

---

[1] This approach towards institutional prototypes has the additional advantage of focusing on and zooming into a few well-selected institutions.

[2] F. Zarbiyev, *Judicial Activism in International Law—A Conceptual Framework for Analysis*, J. OF INTERNATIONAL DISPUTE SETTLEMENT (2012) 1, 14 [F. Zarbiyev, *Judicial Activism in International Law*] ("To be sure, this does not mean that judicial behaviour is unconstrained at the international level, nor does it mean that judges are not sensitive to any systemic consideration. The point is that the finality of international judicial decisions augments the space of discretion of international judges regardless of whether discretion is utilized in practice, and therefore shapes the expectations of international legal actors.").

judges and time can make significant shifts happen. However, there is some value added by institutionally-based explanations, for each tribunal has a "center of narrative gravity."[3]

Let us explore that center. It is informed not only by the institutionally governing texts and histories but, sometimes tacitly, by the "social and political considerations which gave rise to its creation" and those that sustain it.[4] While "[a]ll judges at these tribunals may not," at any given point in time, "follow the same philosophy," an institutional check mechanism is that "deviations from what is considered to be a crucial component of an organizational identity are unlikely to occur frequently."[5] Moreover, since no *one* country controls the appointments of all or majority of the judges on a tribunal, it is unlikely (although not impossible, by virtue of soft-power) that tribunal-hijacking could be accomplished. From this front, the belief goes, the integrity of the rule of law would remain secure.[6]

---

[3] D. C. Dennett, "The Self as a Center of Narrative Gravity" *in* Frank S. Kessel and others (eds), SELF AND CONSCIOUSNESS: MULTIPLE PERSPECTIVES 103 (Psychology Press, 1992).

[4] *Prosecutor v Zejnil Delalic et al.*, Case No: IT-96-21-T, Judgment of the Trial Chamber, 16 November 1998, at ¶ 170 ("The interpretation of the provisions of the Statute and Rules must, therefore, take into consideration the objects of the Statute and the social and political considerations which gave rise to its creation. The kinds of grave violations of international humanitarian law which were the motivating factors for the establishment of the Tribunal continue to occur in many other parts of the world, and continue to exhibit new forms and permutations. The international community can only come to grips with the hydra-headed elusiveness of human conduct through a reasonable as well as a purposive interpretation of the existing provisions of international customary law.").

[5] F. Zarbiyev, *Judicial Activism in International Law, supra,* at 12.

[6] Of course, it is not impossible that a bloc of countries with aligned interests might control judicial appointments. But that proposition simply is more difficult to achieve. All said and done, there remains some evidence that governments do "use their appointment power to influence the judicial behaviour of courts." See *id.*, at 18, n. 93 (citing "R. O. Keohane, Andrew Moravcsik and Anne-Marie Slaughter, 'Legalized Dispute Resolution: Interstate and Transnational' (2000) 54 International Organization 471 (mentioning the rumour that 'the German government sought to rein in the ECJ by appointing a much less activist judge in the 1980s'); R. H. Steinberg, 'Judicial Lawmaking at the WTO: Discursive, Constitutional, and Political Constraints' (2004) 98 AJIL 247, 264 (noting that, while interviewing candidates to the WTO Appellate Body's membership, the USTR focuses, among other things, on their judicial philosophy)"); see also E. Voeten, *The Politics of International Judicial Appointments*, 9 CJIL 387 (2009).

However, such deviations theoretically *could* happen. What if they do? Which deviations are to be rejected and which must be accepted?[7] Now think of the phenomenon from a time-series perspective. The same observation about tribunal deviations and identities might be made about the customary law that international tribunals help propagate. If their deviations from customary law or, for that matter, "organizational identity" occur with substantial frequency, they will either be adopted as doctrinal norms or be rejected by a backlash.[8]

It is incontrovertible that "[t]he development of international law has always been a process of applying . . . established legal principles to circumstances not previously encountered."[9] More often than not novel propositions are deduced from well-established ones. Professor Suzanne Katzenstein argues that international tribunals should allow these deviations from customary law to percolate, in the wholesome public interest of maintaining a full marketplace of ideas.[10] She further urges tribunals to decide these cases, as they do not have discretionary jurisdiction, on judicially minimalist "narrow and unambitious grounds" for procedural

---

[7] J. Patrick Kelly, *The Twilight of Customary International Law*, 40 VA. J. INT'L L. 449, 450–51 (2000) (discussing how difficult it is to determine the point(s) at which customary international law crystallises); R. Higgins, *Policy Considerations and the International Judicial Process*, 17 INT'L & COMP. L. Q. 58, 68 (1968) (quoting Gerald Fitzmaurice, "Judicial Innovation—Its Uses and Its Perils—As Exemplified in Some of the Work of the International Court of Justice During Lord McNair's Period of Office," *in* CAMBRIDGE ESSAYS IN INTERNATIONAL LAW; ESSAYS IN HONOUR OF LORD MCNAIR 24, 24 (1965)) (stating Judge Fitzmaurice's view that, "[i]n practice, courts hardly ever admit a *non-liquet*. As is well known, they adapt existing principles to meet new facts or situations.").

[8] It must be remembered that customary international law is not some sort of shibboleth, the mere recitation of which causes an immediate reaction. In fact, there is an internal tension in customary international law (as it is within many instances of *stare decisis*): "a state initiates a change in [customary international law] by deviating from the existing widespread practice and engaging in new conduct. In this sense, the evolution of [customary international law] requires its own breaking. At the time it occurs, the legal status of the break with [customary international law] is uncertain. It is unclear whether the custombreaking state is violating [customary international law] or changing it. The legality of the deviation is determined by how other states respond—whether they decide to accept the proposed break with [customary international law] or to adhere to the existing rules." See S. Katzenstein, *International Adjudication and Custom Breaking by Domestic Courts*, *supra*, at 672-73.

[9] *Oil Fields of Texas v. Iran*, 12 I.U.C.T.R. 308, 361 (1982).

[10] See S. Katzenstein, *International Adjudication and Custom Breaking by Domestic Courts*, *supra*, at at 673 *et seq*.

and substantive reasons (echoing the Cass Sunstein approach to the domestic tribunal context).[11] Some history, including international legal history, is made by the victors. Since the sovereignty-investment encouragement-status in the community of nations balance is a delicate one, this judicial minimalist approach is said to minimise the "Mandatory View" irony: the disparate exit methods for sovereigns from customary international law as opposed to treaties.[12]

The institutional similarities and differences between the three prototypical institutions, and the general system each represents, will become clearer. The functioning procedures of the tribunals are explained briefly simply because they "matte[r]."[13] International tribunals are not readily interchangeable with one another. Indeed, "[c]ourts with different procedures do not have the same kind of constituencies depending on how their procedure relates to the domestic interest groups and the extent to which access to the court and the enforcement of the decisions of the latter are 'legally insulated from the will of individual national governments.'"[14]

One procedural similarity imposes a significant effect on the development of doctrine: Timing of cases and its relationship with the development of customary international law. Experience across international law as well as expropriation specifically suggests that "newly emergent issues will often lack a treaty regime for a time."[15] At the same time, an international tribunal typically, though not always,[16] "cannot decline a case and wait for an issue to percolate—even though this is precisely what the evolutionary process of [customary international law] traditionally

[11] *Id.*, at 701, n. 136 (citing C. R. Sunstein, *Testing Minimalism: A Reply*, 104 MICH. L. REV. 123, 125 (2005)).

[12] See, *e.g.*, C. A. Bradley & M. Gulati, *Withdrawing from International Custom*, 120 YALE L. J. 202, 204 (2010) ("Unlike treaties, the rules of CIL do not arise from express negotiation, and they do not require any domestic act of ratification to become binding. Although these differences might suggest that nations should have greater flexibility to withdraw from rules of CIL than from treaties, the conventional wisdom is precisely the opposite.").

[13] F. Zarbiyev, *Judicial Activism in International Law, supra,* at 27.

[14] *Id.*, at 27 (citing R. O. Keohane, Andrew Moravcsik and Anne-Marie Slaughter, 'Legalized Dispute Resolution: Interstate and Transnational' (2000) 54 International Organization 481).

[15] C. A. Bradley & M. Gulati, *Withdrawing from International Custom, supra,* at 209.

[16] A creative tribunal might be able to postpone the grand question until a future day, and indeed this is just what Professor Katzenstein recommends. See S. Katzenstein, *International Adjudication and Custom Breaking by Domestic Courts, supra*, at 701 *et seq.*

requires."[17] This, in effect, means that "international courts will adjudicate and invalidate breaks with custom before other states have had an opportunity to respond, engaging in . . . 'preemptive' or 'early' adjudication."[18]

Moreover, one cannot help wondering if there is such a concept as an over-active body of customary international law, meaning that "longstanding [customary international law] issues (such as the immunity of heads of state and limits on the extraterritorial application of national law) are still not regulated by any comprehensive treaties"[19] and there seems not to be any incentive or impetus to develop those areas even more fully through treaty adoption. Political dialogue and conversation concerning these issues have a natural tendency to stymie and become increasingly staler if active efforts of issue development are not made. After all, the only methods of customary law alteration are presumed to be interstitial and blissfully organic.[20] There are no obvious means of reversing the consensus in the sense that no clear and definitive goals, for instance the consent of two-thirds of a particular body, are known.

Lastly, I should add that among a few other institutions the ICJ was considered but, apart from its use-of-force jurisprudence,[21] to some scholars "its case law reveals a court more attracted by a transactional

---

[17] See S. Katzenstein, *International Adjudication and Custom Breaking by Domestic Courts*, *supra*, at 673-74.

[18] *Id.*

[19] C. A. Bradley & M. Gulati, *Withdrawing from International Custom, supra,* at 209.

[20] *Id.*, at 212, n. 35-36 (citing Anthony D'Amato, *The President and International Law: A Missing Dimension*, 81 A. J. I. L. 375, 377 (1987) ("Existing customary law, then, contains the seeds of its own violation; otherwise it could never change itself."); Michael J. Glennon, *How International Rules Die*, 93 GEO. L.J. 939, 957 (2005) ("[C]ustomary international law is thought to be altered by acts that initially constitute violations of old rules; that is how it changes."); G.J.H. Van Hoof, RETHINKING THE SOURCES OF INTERNATIONAL LAW 99 (1983) ("It must be quite an extraordinary system of law which incorporates as its main, if not the only, vehicle for change the violation of its own provisions."); Michael Akehurst, *Custom as a Source of International Law*, 47 BRIT. Y.B. INT'L L. 1, 8 (1974-75) ("There is no doubt that customary rules can be changed in this way, but the process is hardly one to be recommended by anyone who wishes to strengthen the rule of law in international relations."); Jacob Katz Cogan, *Noncompliance and the International Rule of Law*, 31 YALE J. INT'L L. 189, 193 (2006) (contending that "noncompliance—particularly operational noncompliance—is a necessary component of less capable legal systems, including international law")).

[21] D. Shelton, *Form, Function, and the Powers of International Courts*, 9 CJIL 563 (2009).

justice approach specifically tailored to address the contingencies of individual cases rather than by large-scheme purposes."[22] This approach then carries over to the rest of the book. This Chapter is innovative and experimental, an experiment whose results I have been advised to retain in the final version.

§ 2.2—North American Free Trade Agreement (NAFTA) and the International Investment Agreement (IIA) Tribunals

It is generally believed that IIA's are components of a system as well as a legal culture that employs international arbitration to "entrench . . . beyond the reach of majoritarian control . . . rules for the free movement of transnational capital."[23] The North American Free Trade Agreement (NAFTA) is a prominent part of this system. It includes an especially broad provision on expropriation. The most relevant provisions are noted: Article 1139 defines "investments" to include enterprises, debt and equity securities, loans, real estate and other in-/tangible property, and capital interests. Article 1102 guarantees "to investors of another Party treatment no less favo[u]rable than that it accords, in like circumstances, to its own investors with respect to the establishment, acquisition, expansion, management, conduct, operation, and sale or other disposition of investments."

Article 1103 guarantees most favoured nation treatment to *all* signatories. Article 1105 guarantees a minimum standard of treatment: "investments of investors of another Party treatment in accordance with international law, including fair and equitable treatment and full protection and security."

Finally, Article 1110 in Chapter Eleven of the NAFTA provides that

> No party may directly or indirectly nationalize or expropriate an investment of an investor of another Party in its territory or take a measure

---

[22] F. Zarbiyev, *Judicial Activism in International Law*, *supra*, at 13 ("the ICJ seems more inclined toward the philosophy of 'settlement of individual cases'. The characterization of this court as 'the guardian of legality for the international community as a whole' is in fact a vast exaggeration . . .) (citing Separate opinion of Judge Lachs, *Questions of Interpretation and Application of the 1971 Montreal Convention arising from the Aerial Incident at Lockerbie*, ICJ Reports 1992, 3, 26)).

[23] D. Schneiderman, *Investment Rules and the New Constitutionalism*, 25 LAW & SOC. INQUIRY 757, 757 (2000).

> tantamount to nationalization or expropriation of such an investment ("expropriation"), except:
>
> (a) for a public purpose;
> (b) on a nondiscriminatory basis;
> (c) in accordance with due process of law and [National Treatment]; and
> (d) on payment of compensation… .

Moreover, Article 1131 provides that NAFTA tribunals "shall decide the issues in dispute in accordance with this Agreement and *applicable rules of international law*." To date, there have been a total of 61 notices to commence arbitration filed by corporations and investors under NAFTAs Chapter Eleven investor provisions, with a total of U.S. $28 billion claimed.[24] Of these 61 notices, 26 have been against Canada; 16 against Mexico; and 19 against the United States.

The North American Free Trade Area, comprising Canada, Mexico and the United States, was established in 1992 by the NAFTA. Like several other regional economic integration agreements, such as the European Communities (EC), the European Free Trade Association (EFTA) or Mercado Común del Sur (Mercosur), NAFTA's objective is to remove trade barriers, create a common market, and promote economic cooperation between participating States. However, unlike most similar agreements, NAFTA does not create an integrated legal system, much less a structured dispute settlement system.

NAFTA parties "reinterpret" the agreement through the NAFTA Free Trade Commission (FTC) when some prior case has revealed a contentious grey-area.[25] Whether it is good for signatory nations to do so *retrospectively*, sometimes against the reliance of investors, is a different question. That issue has not really stopped the signatories. While the EC and the EFTA have permanent international courts to settle disputes between member States, individuals and the organisation's institutions on

---

[24] J. Coe, *Taking Stock of NAFTA Chapter 11 in Its Tenth Year: An Interim Sketch of Selected Themes, Issues, and Methods,* 36 VAND. J. TRANSNAT'L L. 1381, 1385 (2003); N. Caulfield, NAFTA AND LABOR IN NORTH AMERICA 201-13 (University of Illinois Press, 2010). There might be opportunities that were not pursued by states (and thus opportunity costs) out of fear, so the amount that NAFTA has cost its signatories is probably more than the compensation and legal costs that have been imposed by IIA tribunals on States.

[25] For some reinterpretations offered and suggested, see T. Weiler, *NAFTA Investment Law in 2001: As the Legal Order Starts to Settle, the Bureaucrats Strike Back*, 36 INT'L L. 345 (2002).

implementing the agreements (and domestic laws enforcing those agreements), NAFTA dispute settlement is less institutionalised and more fragmented, relying mostly on *ad hoc* arbitration.

Under the NAFTA, there are four main dispute resolution processes, named after corresponding chapters of the agreement: Chapter Eleven (investment disputes), Fourteen (financial services), Nineteen (anti-dumping and countervailing duties), and Twenty (general dispute settlement procedure). Chapter Eleven disputes are between a private party and a party to the NAFTA whereas Chapters Fourteen, Nineteen and Twenty handle inter-state disputes. Chapter Eleven, like other recent BIT's, was a conscious step away from the diplomatic protection regime.

Chapter Eleven establishes a mechanism for the settlement of investment disputes that assures both non-discrimination and certain absolute standards among investors of the Parties to the Agreement in accordance with the principle of international reciprocity and due process before an impartial tribunal. A NAFTA "investor" is "a company organised in accordance with the law of a Contracting Party."[26]

Possible Fora for NAFTA Arbitration

A NAFTA investor who alleges that a host government has breached its investment obligations under Chapter Eleven may, at its option, might choose among several *ad hoc* arbitration options. The same options are available to most other BIT's (over 2300 BIT's now in action, as of 2010);[27] NAFTA's jurisprudence influences and is influenced by them. Two of the more prevalent arbitration options are:[28]

(1) The World Bank's International Centre for the Settlement of Investment Disputes (ICSID): Under the ICSID Convention, the Centre provides facilities for conciliation and arbitration of

[26] "Definition of Investment and Investor," Negotiating Group on the Multilateral Agreement on Investment (MAI), OECD, *available at* <www.oecd.org/daf/mai/pdf/ng/ng962e.pdf> (1996) (last accessed October 1, 2011).

[27] United Nations Conference on Trade and Development (UNCTAD), *available at* <www.unctadxi.org> (last accessed October 1, 2011); see also International Centre for Settlement of Investment Disputes (ICSID), *available at* <www.worldbank.org/icsid/about/about.htm>.

[28] Disputes have also been entertained in the Permanent Court of Arbitration (PCA). See, *e.g.*, *Vito G. Gallo v. The Government of Canada*, UNCITRAL, Award (redacted version), 2011.

investment disputes between Contracting States and nationals of other Contracting States. The jurisdiction of ICSID is set forth in Article 25(1) of the Convention. According to Article 25(1), "[t]he jurisdiction of the Centre shall extend to any legal dispute arising directly out of an investment, between a Contracting State (or any constituent subdivision or agency of a Contracting State designated to the Centre by that State) and a national of another Contracting State, which the parties to the dispute consent in writing to submit to the Centre." Importantly, the ICSID Convention under Article 42(1) consults convention and general principles of international law to fill in the gaps.[29]

ICSID is, in a fact, "an international organization with . . . [158] member states," of diverse economic and political conditions, "created to provide structure and rules for the arbitration of international investment disputes between a government and an investor of a foreign state."[30] Under ICSID Rules, an investment must satisfy three criteria, "namely (i) a contribution made by the investor, (ii) a certain duration of the project, and (iii) a participation to the risks of the transaction."[31] The unresolved question is about the role played by a potential fourth consideration that comes from the Preamble of the ICSID Convention: must an investment contribute to the economic development of the host State in order for it to be a "protected" investment?[32]

---

[29] *Amco Asia Corp. v. Indonesia*, *ad hoc* committee decision of May 16, 1986, 1 ICSID Rep. 509, 515 (1993) (Article 42(1) "authorizes an ICSID tribunal to apply rules of international law only to fill up lacunae in the applicable domestic law and to ensure precedence to international law norms where the rules of the applicable domestic law are in collision with such norms."); *Kloeckner Industrie-Anlagen GmbH v. Cameroon*, ad hoc committee decision of May 3, 1985, 2 ICSID Rep. 95, 122 (1994); *Liberian Eastern Timber Corp. v. Liberia*, award of Mar. 31, 1986, 2 ICSID Rep. 343, 358-59 (1994).

[30] K. Claussen, *Comment: The Casualty of Investor Protection in Times of Economic Crisis*, 118 YALE L. J. 1545, 1547, n. 11 (2009).

[31] Y. Banifatemi, "Unresolved Issues in Investment Arbitration," *Modern Law for Global Commerce*, p. 13, Congress to celebrate the fortieth annual session of UNCITRAL Vienna, July 2007, *available at* <www.uncitral.org/pdf/english/congress/Banifatemi.pdf> (last accessed September 1, 2011).

[32] See, *e.g.*, *Salini Costruttori S.p.A. and Italstrade S.p.A. v. Morocco*, Decision on Jurisdiction, ICSID Case No. ARB/00/4, at ¶ 52 (2001); *Joy Mining Machinery Limited v. Egypt*, Award on Jurisdiction, ICSID Case No. ARB/03/11 (2004);

Occasionally, annulment committees review an ICSID tribunal's decision even though "[t]here is no *formal* system of appellate review under the . . . Convention" and "[a]n unsuccessful party may only apply for annulment of an award on narrow, circumscribed grounds."[33] Finality is prioritised over substantive error-correction in ICSID. As will become clearer in the ensuing chapters, annulment of an ICSID award is a demanding process that focuses on process-oriented, rather than accuracy-oriented, issues. Moreover, from the monetary point of view it was decided through a 1984 amendment to Administrative and Financial Regulation 14 that "in annulment proceedings, the applicant for annulment would instead be solely responsible for making the necessary advance payments."[34] The reader can draw her own conclusions about how much the ICSID system wanted to encourage annulment proceedings or, conversely, how much it wished to generate profit through the losing party's instinctive temptation to seek annulment of the tribunal's award.[35]

The practical side is that enforcing monetary damages is more feasible and more effective, since a rights-based "primary remedy requires the defendant state to act and is not internationally enforceable as a claim for pecuniary damages."[36] Under the ICSID Convention's own terms, tellingly, "a tribunal would exceed its powers in deciding on a non-requested remedy and put the award in danger of annulment."[37] Altogether, by the end of 2011, 450 cases

---

CSOB v. The Slovak Republic, Decision on Jurisdiction, ICSID Case No. ARB/97/4 (1999).

[33] See J. T. Kurtz, *ICSID Annulment Committee Rules on the Relationship between Customary and Treaty Exceptions on Necessity in Situations of Financial Crisis*, 11 AM. SOC'Y INT'L L. International Economic Law Edition 30 (2007), *available at* < www.asil.org/insights071220.cfm#author>.

[34] A. Parra, *The Development of the Regulations and Rules of the International Centre for Settlement of Investment Disputes*, 41 INT'L LAW. 47, 59-60 (2007); see generally A. Parra, THE HISTORY OF ICSID (Oxford University Press, 2012).

[35] A current ICSID practitioner, in our private conversation, likened the later scenario to city police officers generating a "fair bit of revenue for government treasury" through parking tickets.

[36] See C. Schreuer, *Non-Pecuniary Damages in ICSID Arbitration*, 20 ARB. INT. 325 (2004).

[37] See A. van Aaken, "Remedies in International Investment Law and National State Liability," *in* INTERNATIONAL INVESTMENT LAW AND COMPARATIVE PUBLIC LAW 734 (S. Schill, ed.) (Oxford University Press 2010) (citing ICSID Convention, Art 52(1)(b)); T. Wälde and B. Sabahi, "Compensation, Damages and Valuation in

generally have been filed in various IIA tribunals. ICSID remains the venue of choice by claimants for several reasons, including the prospect of avoiding domestic judicial review (a consequence of UNCITRAL, which is explicated below).

(2) The United Nations Commission for International Trade Law (UNCITRAL) rules: The international arbitration community has no obvious preference for ICSID over UNCITRAL or *vice versa*, but several UNCITRAL advantages over ICSID are that provisional measures issued by an UNCITRAL may be binding and may also be enforced in the domestic courts; an UNCITRAL party may directly go to the domestic courts to seek a provisional measure (in ICSID, hard-to-achieve agreement between the parties is needed); confidentiality does not automatically attach in an ICSID arbitration without the agreement of the parties; and, unlike ICSID, the UNCITRAL rules explicitly provide that a tribunal "may order security for costs in order to protect the party against whom the measures are ordered should it subsequently be determined that the measures were unjustified."[38]

Proposing a New Configuration for Arbitral Panels: Having the Balance Just Right

Before I present my "3+2 Institutional Guardians" proposal for a new kind of panel configuration, it is important to understand how the system currently operates. I propose very little tinkering with the details of the presently-discharged functions. Contrasted with ICSID's finality emphasis, UNCITRAL decisions may be appealed to a domestic court. This allows for some forum-shopping and treaty-shopping and often a second bite at the apple.[39] Another difference between ICSID and UNCITRAL is that consistency is easier to maintain in ICSID cases because, unlike UNCITRAL, their awards are not subject to domestic court challenges. The ICSID tribunal in *El Paso Energy International Co. v. Argentina* (2006)[40] captured this point:

International Investment Law" *in* THE OXFORD HANDBOOK OF INTERNATIONAL INVESTMENT LAW 1049, 1059 (2008) (P. Muchlinski et al., eds).

[38] UNCITRAL Art. 26 (3) (emphasis added).

[39] M. Waibel, THE BACKLASH AGAINST INVESTMENT ARBITRATION: PERCEPTIONS AND REALITIES 92 (Kluwer Law International, 2010).

[40] ICSID Case ARB/03/15, Decision on Jurisdiction (2006), at ¶ 39.

> ICSID arbitral tribunals are established ad hoc, … and the present Tribunal knows of no provision, … establishing an obligation of *stare decisis*. It is nonetheless a reasonable assumption that international arbitral tribunals, notably those established within the ICSID system, will generally take account of the precedents established by other arbitration organs, especially those set by other international tribunals.[41]

Alternatively, both in ICSID and in UNCITRAL the investor may forego investment arbitration and go directly for the remedies available in the host country's domestic courts. An important feature of the Chapter Eleven arbitral provisions is the enforceability in domestic courts of final awards by arbitration tribunals.

One important difference between NAFTA panels and the other two institutions is that the arbitrators are chosen by the parties directly (parties agree themselves) or indirectly (parties each choose an arbitrator and they arbitrators then agree on who the third arbitrator will be).[42] Certain non-

---

[41] The point has been echoed elsewhere too. See F. Zarbiyev, *Judicial Activism in International Law, supra* at 26-27 ("*ad hoc* arbitral tribunals often pay careful attention to the systemic considerations even though what they are primarily called upon to interpret are purely bilateral treaties"); *Saipem SpA v Bangladesh*, ICSID Case No ARB/05/7, Award, 30 June 2009, at ¶ 90 ("The Tribunal considers that it is not bound by previous decisions. At the same time, it is of the opinion that it must pay due consideration to earlier decisions of international tribunals. It believes that, subject to compelling contrary grounds, it has a duty to adopt solutions established in a series of consistent cases. It also believes that, subject to the specifics of a given treaty and of the circumstances of the actual case, it has a duty to seek to contribute to the harmonious development of investment law and thereby to meet the legitimate expectations of the community of States and investors towards certainty of the rule of law"); *Bayindir Insaat Turizm Ticaret ve Sanayi A Ş v Pakistan*, ICSID Case No ARB/03/29, Award, 27 August 2009, at ¶ 145. However, there are exceptions. See *Romak SA v Uzbekistan*, PCA Case No AA280, Award, 26 November 2009, at ¶ 171 ("Ultimately, the Arbitral Tribunal has not been entrusted, by the Parties or otherwise, with a mission to ensure the coherence or development of "arbitral jurisprudence." The Arbitral Tribunal's mission is more mundane, but no less important: to resolve the present dispute between the Parties in a reasoned and persuasive manner, irrespective of the unintended consequences that this Arbitral Tribunal's analysis might have on future disputes in general").

[42] Frequently, investors choose one arbitrator and the government selects the second. The presiding arbitrator, however, is selected in a different manner. The ICSID Convention allows the parties to agree on the presiding arbitrator. Absent such agreement, the Convention provides a default rule. ICSID Convention art. 37(2)(b), Mar. 18, 1965, 17 U.S.T. 1270. In UNCITRAL arbitration, the party-appointed arbitrators choose the chair. UNCITRAL Art. 7(1).

NAFTA IIA fora for arbitration are Stockholm Chamber of Commerce (SCC), International Chamber of Commerce (ICC), the Cairo Regional Centre for International Commercial Arbitration (CRCICA), and the London Court of International Arbitration (LCIA).

There has been much discussion about bias in the IIA regime—specifically, bias "favor[ing] the production of outcomes that systematically favor particular actors, such as investors, or developed countries").[43] Here, in actuality, we are confronting a dilemma between the integrity of the IIA structural regime and party autonomy. I believe it is over-simplistic to pose the "key policy question" as "how do we ensure that regulatory outputs generally accord with the interests of IIL's principals?"[44] The revered Jan Paulsson accurately states the objective as "improv[ing]" the "[IIA] syste[m's] legitimacy by eliminating actual bias or by making public perceptions of bias less easy to hold."[45] Some distinguished jurists propose that there be a permanent panel of IIA judges[46] or that a more rigorous set of standards for arbitrator ethics[47] be formulated.

The latter seems meritorious, at least at first glance, but the former is not without substantial drawbacks: A permanent panel might needlessly meddle with party autonomy with a frequency and on a level than is currently necessary. One effective solution might be to have the Secretariat of the arbitration forum appoint two additional arbitrators (one from a developed nation, another from a developing nation) to the tribunal of (now) five arbitrators. These last two arbitrators shall have the mandate of not just being legally correct but also, perhaps most importantly, in charge of smoking out the biases from the facts or proceedings concerning the case.

---

[43] J. W. Yackee, *Controlling the IIL, supra,* at 431-32 ("whether real or perceived, has led some observers to suggest the desirability of structurally guaranteeing the independence of [IIA] decision-makers, particularly arbitrators").

[44] *Id.*

[45] *Id.* (referring to J. Paulsson, *Moral Hazard in International Dispute Resolution*, Inaugural Lecture as holder of Michael R. Klein Distinguished Scholar Chair, University of Miami School of Law (April 29, 2010), available at <www.arbitration-icca.org/media/0/12773749999020/paulsson_moral_hazard.pdf>).

[46] Charles N. Brower & Stephan W. Schill, *Is Arbitration a Threat or a Boon to the Legitimacy of International Investment Law?*, 9 CHI. J. INT'L L. 471, 475 (2009); G. Van Harten, INVESTMENT TREATY ARBITRATION AND PUBLIC LAW, *supra*, at 180-84.

[47] C. A. Rogers, *Fit and Function in Legal Ethics: Developing a Code of Conduct for International Arbitration*, 23 MICH. J. INT'L L. 341, 422 (2002).

Finally, no tribunal award may be handed down unless these two arbitrators are in agreement. While there is a risk of slowing down deliberations and thus imperiling the cause of alacrity (a primary reason for the IIA system in the first place), the list of the hold-outs and the entire line-up of arbitrators must be published if after a stipulated amount of time there is no agreement between the two Secretariat appointees. Since the Secretariat may choose not to reappoint arbitrators, this should act as a check against redundant hold-outs without needlessly compromising judicial independence. There seems to be an urgent need to engender confidence in the stakeholders through a mechanism that empowers the institutional guardians, and this precarious balancing might achieve the correct outcomes systematically. In this vein, I would also allow visible, to mean non-anonymous, third-parties with significant interest in the outcome of the arbitration to file challenges to dismiss certain arbitrators for manifest bias as to the outcome.[48] Doctrinal or philosophical bias will not suffice although bias in the furtherance of direct or indirect economic gain will.

A practical point about the expected reward and cost of bringing or keeping (as opposed to settling) a case is important because it affects the claims put forth and principles created. Because NAFTA and other investment arbitration cases usually are more expensive to pursue than human rights and dispute settlement cases, the expense factor plays a greater role for the former than for either of the latter classes. Gary Born has referred to IIA tribunals as part of the "second-generation" of international tribunals that "have been frequently and successfully used in vitally important fields, in part because they issue effective and enforceable decisions," relative to earlier institutions, such as the ICJ. [49]

The same applies to the potential for public embarrassment for both investors and governments (for public relations purposes); although investors, as claimants, *initially* are on the offensive and governments, as respondents, on the defensive, a government's decision to settle might have more to do with politics and outside pressure, *path-dependence* or monetary gain—some form of capital—that keeps certain claims from

---

[48] The reason is simple. Parties (and their counsel) know that the main players in the IIA universe are so few that a request to disqualify may well be construed as disrespect towards or lack of cooperation with the tribunal system. Such a request could turn out to be counterproductive. Moreover, in the immediate dispute(s), it might reasonably be assumed that an arbitrator who had been asked to disqualify herself or himself might tend to be impatient or less than fully receptive to the arguments of the Party which sought the recusal.

[49] G. Born, *A New Generation of International Adjudication*, 61 DUKE L.J. 775, 775-76 (2012).

developing.[50] The psychologist and behavioural economist Dan Ariely shares his insight on "arbitrary coherence," meaning that "although initial prices … are 'arbitrary', once those prices are established in our minds they will shape not only present prices but also future prices."[51] Such "initial prices" could be synonymous with the line-drawing and value-, premise- and assumption-identification in which judicial decisions are continually engaged.[52]

It must be recognised that the non-judicial character of international arbitration often makes it a preferable forum for dispute settlement (over courts) for three critical reasons. First, litigation in a foreign court might be complex, time-consuming, expensive, and potentially difficult to enforce. Second, arbitral awards ordinarily avoid a long appeals route; parties might distrust the efficiency, substantive or procedural law or integrity of a local legal system. Third, the arbitrators are agreed upon by both parties.[53]

Earlier this Chapter has discussed investor-claimants' primary interest in monetary damages. Not to be underestimated, then, is that few such litigants are out to make test cases: "[l]itigants are unlikely to make arguments that stray from existing law (as created, shaped, and revealed by prior cases), because they know that doing so would significantly

---

[50] T. Wälde, "*'Equality of Arms' in Investment Arbitration: Procedural Challenges*" *in* ARBITRATION UNDER INTERNATIONAL INVESTMENT AGREEMENTS: A GUIDE TO THE KEY ISSUES 163 (Oxford University Press, 2010) [T. Wälde, "*'Equality of Arms*'"]; *id.*, at 164 (discussing the "methods of undue interference": "corruption," "direct or indirect pressure on arbitrators," "intimidation of local and international counsel, experts and witnesses," "obstruction of legal representation" and "financial attrition by the much better funded party," among others); O. A. Hathaway, *Path Dependence in the Law: The Course and Pattern of Legal Change in a Common Law System*, 86 IOWA L. REV. 101 (2003) [O. A. Hathaway, *Path Dependence*].

[51] D. Ariely, PREDICTABLY IRRATIONAL 26 (Perennial, 2009).

[52] F. Zarbiyev, *Judicial Activism in International Law, supra,* at 28 ("Market actors are well aware of the tremendous impact that anchoring has on the price that customers are ready to pay for a given product and deploy appropriate strategies to take benefit of it. For instance, when a new product is introduced into a market of similar products at a relatively higher price, the best marketing strategy to make this price look like a 'natural' one is to differentiate that product to the point that the prices of similar products could not be used by customers as an anchor.").

[53] S. Finizio & W. Miles, THE INTERNATIONAL COMPARATIVE LEGAL GUIDE TO INTERNATIONAL ARBITRATION 41-44(Global Legal Group, 2010).

decrease their likelihood of success and perhaps even risk sanctions for putting forward an argument with an insufficient legal basis."[54]

Thus the advisory role of the officialdom and official institutions remains significant. The shadow once visibly cast by diplomatic protection has been lessened and made less *formal*—but it has not vanished completely. Diplomatic protection has just become less visible. The paradigm earlier set by investor-government interactions make a difference, and like diplomatic protection, the role of *stare decisis* too has mutated but is alive and well.

The system has developed a solution to stop self-combusting. The trend-lines show that once a number of implausible claims are rejected (sometimes in stern language) by the tribunals, the risk of filing such claims become prohibitively expensive and such cases significantly decrease.[55] To some extent, this might disincentivise the filing of an otherwise meritorious claim with a fighting chance even years after being rejected because circumstances have changed drastically. Some instances of this are inevitable.

Whereas the IUCT and the ECtHR largely have declined to take on the difficult questions presented, the NAFTA tribunals have sometimes waded into difficult waters rather unnecessarily—even when a narrower ground would have sufficed. Some scholars attribute this to lack of competence, and recommend that "one or even two members of" an IIA "tribunal . . . be recognized authorities in the increasingly specialized international economic law components of the broader field of public international law."[56]

The "integration of other disciplines, such as international human rights law and international environmental law" is an imperative in a field as quickly evolving as investment law.[57] As Chapter VI (OTHER SUBSTANTIVE STANDARDS) will highlight and as some scholars favourably attribute to the World Trade Organization (WTO) dispute settlement process, a high quality of reasoning and result, especially on esoteric issues, could come from "a broader public international law outlook of a number of [tribunal] members, who do not come from the insider community of international economic law specialists."[58]

---

[54] O. A. Hathaway, *Path Dependence*, *supra*, at 128.
[55] *Id.*, at 173.
[56] R. Howse & E. Chalamish, *The Use and Abuse of WTO Law in Investor-State Arbitration: A Reply to Jürgen Kurtz*, 20 EUR. J. INT'L L. 1087, 1109 (2009) [R. Howse & E. Chalamish, *Use and Abuse of WTO Law in ITA*].
[57] *Id.*, at 1111.
[58] *Id.*

While the NAFTA-IIA world (where public remedies have traditionally not been possible, although this is changing) and the IUCT (retrospective) can provide only monetary damages, the ECtHR may also provide injunctive relief enjoining the enforcement of expropriatory measures. Another key difference, probably a result of their separate aims and functions, is that whereas NAFTA and other IIA tribunals are constantly subject to public criticism,[59] the other two institutional prisms have largely been immune.

§ 2.3—European Court of Human Rights (ECtHR) and the International Human Rights System

Institutional and ideological change in international human rights tribunals bears some resemblance with domestic tribunals. Such change in the international fora contains five basic motifs: (*i*) "[E]xtensive as well as affirmative . . . commands" (with the "commands run[ing] not to one or two acts but to a whole course of conduct, typically to both general policy and details"); (*ii*) "Administrative . . . character" of the decrees, "essentially supersed[ing] the authority of the defendant body to manage its own business, subject to executive and legislative accountability" along with the lawful intervention of the domestic courts; (*iii*) "[S]tructural decrees are legislative in the double sense of entailing fundamental alterations of policy direction and of frequently requiring augmentation of financial resources"; (*iv*) "[C]ontinuing judicial involvement in the implementation and modification of the decree" in order to cope with the "new regime of organi[s]ational behavio[u]r" being ushered in and (*v*) Even when deeply "innovative" in "character" (not always a virtue in the

---

[59] A. DePalma, *NAFTA's Powerful Little Secret; Obscure Tribunals Settle Disputes, But Go Too Far, Critics Say*, N.Y. TIMES, Mar. 11, 2001, at B1 ("Their meetings are secret. Their members are generally unknown. The decisions they reach need not be fully disclosed. Yet the way a small group of international tribunals handles disputes between investors and foreign governments has led to national laws being revoked, justice systems questioned and environmental regulations changed."); Editorial, *The Secret Trade Courts*, N.Y. TIMES, Sept. 27, 2004, at A1 ("[T]he arbitration process itself is often one-sided, favoring well-heeled corporations over poor countries, and must be made fairer than it is today."); *Arbitration and Secrecy: Behind Closed Doors — A Hard Struggle to Shed Some Light on a Legal Grey Area*, ECONOMIST, Apr. 23, 2009, at 68; A. Beattie, *Concern Grows over Global Trade Regulation*, FIN. TIMES, Mar. 12, 2008, at 9; A. Beattie, *From a Trickle to a Flood — How Lawsuits Are Coming to Dictate the Terms of Trade*, FIN. TIMES, Mar. 20, 2007, at 13.

law), such human rights decrees have proven "resistant" to being quashed or even truncated.[60] The ECtHR typifies this composite.

Unifying the various strands and organs of international law, despite some unavoidable fragmentation, "necessarily involves the international protection of human rights."[61] This unification might confer several advantages upon the international legal order, namely "improved economy of time and resources—both human and material—as well as the promotion of higher standards of effective protection."[62] Professor Tom Ginsburg accurately states, in the domestic context, that "[n]o political institution, even a democratically legitimate one, ought to be able to suppress basic liberties."[63] He also observes that this principle "surreptitiously" carries over to the international human rights context.[64]

The principle encompasses, within the subject-matter of "basic liberties," governmental acts involving and proximately relating to expropriation. Professors Ginsburg, Dapo Akande and José Alvarez have pointed out that while the ICJ has not ruled that the United Nations Security Council acted beyond the scope of its authority (ensconced in Chapter VII of the U.N. Charter) in developing findings that it is acting to defend peace and security—the Charter contains no explicit judicial review mechanism—the ICJ "considered the issue in *dicta*" and "refused to explicitly deny that the court has the power to review the security council's actions."[65]

---

60 D. L. Horowitz, *Decreeing Organizational Change: Judicial Supervision of Public Institutions*, 32 DUKE L. J. 1265, 1266-68 (1983).

61 M. Pinto, *Fragmentation or Unification Among International Institutions: Human Rights Tribunals*, 31 INT'L L. & POL. 833, 841 (1999) [M. Pinto, *Fragmentation or Unification*]

62 *Id.*

63 T. Ginsburg, JUDICIAL REVIEW IN NEW DEMOCRACIES 2 (Cambridge University Press, 2003).

64 *Id.*, at 5.

65 *Id.*, at 6; "Questions of Interpretation and Application of the 1971 Montreal Convention Arising from the Aerial Incident at Lockerbie (Libya v. US; Libya v. UK)," 3, 114 *I.C.J.* (1992) (Provisional Measures); "Application of the Convention on the Prevention and Punishment of the Crime and Genocide (Bosnia/Herzegovina v. Yugoslavia (Serbia and Montenegro))," 3 *I.C.J.* (1996) (Request for Provisional Measures). See also D. Akande, *The International Court of Justice and the Security Council: Is There Room for Judicial Control of Decisions of the Political Organs of the United Nations?,* 46 INT'L & COMP. L. Q. 309 (1997); J. Alvarez, *Judging the Security Council,* 90 A.J.I.L. 1 (1996). I have used "acts" or "actions" somewhat frequently in the course of this undertaking. The next chapter will address the kinds of expropriatory actions and perhaps omissions too that are compensable.

The United Nations, of course, has neither a "democratic" structure nor one "wherein majority rule has ever been unconstrained" (after all, "the institutional entrenchment of particular founding nations through the veto power of the Security Council" precludes both conditions).[66] Still, it is telling (even if not significantly extraordinary) that not only international but also non-expropriation issues in public law are also confronting various versions of the judicial review question. It should also be added that it is absolutely uncontested that "[l]iberal democracies," including Convention signatories, "are particularly respectful of the rule of law"[67] and, *sans* extreme circumstances and exigencies, do not disobey judicial decisions.

Most scholars and practitioner-architects of international law seem to agree that among the pillars deserving the status of permanence are "the consent already given to the monitoring body's jurisdiction and the *pro homine* criteria for the interpretation of legal rules."[68] Unification has its drawbacks too, notable of which are "the usual reluctance of states to consent to new jurisdictions and the inherent danger of tinkering with jurisdictions that have already been accepted."[69]

Fittingly, our second prototype is the tribunal created by the European Convention on Human Rights ("Convention for the Protection of Human Rights and Fundamental Freedoms") (ECHR). The ECHR was opened for signature in 1950, came into force in 1953, and is, to an extent, a product of its Cold War history. The objective of the Convention was to protect the core human rights values of the Council of Europe,[70] and to encourage a cohesive democratic bloc of countries as reinforcement against the resurgence of fervent national socialism and totalitarian communism.[71]

---

[66] *Id.*

[67] R. O. Keohane, Andrew Moravcsik and Anne-Marie Slaughter, 'Legalized Dispute Resolution: Interstate and Transnational' (2000) 54 International Organization 478-79; see also *Hassan & Tchaouch v Bulgaria*, ECtHR, Judgment of 26 October 2000, at ¶ 87.

[68] M. Pinto, *Fragmentation or Unification, supra,* at 841.

[69] *Id.*

[70] Founded in 1949, the Council of Europe attempts to integrate Europe by stressing legal standards and protection of human rights. The ECtHR is the final supervisory tribunal over human rights issues among member states of the Council of Europe. See L. Wildhaber, *A Constitutional Future for the European Court of Human Rights*, 23 HUM. RTS L.J. 161, 162-63 (2002) [L. Wildhaber, *A Constitutional Future*].

[71] A. Moravcsik, *The Origins of International Human Rights Regimes: Democratic Delegation in Postwar Europe*, 54 INT'L ORG. 217, 221 (2000).

The ECtHR was created to enforce these goals, and has referred to the Convention as "a constitutional instrument of European public order."[72]

The ECtHR perhaps rightly perceives itself to be the premier human rights court in the world and is conscious that steps it takes will be copied elsewhere, notably in the Inter-American Court on Human Rights and the African Court on Human Rights.[73] About a decade ago, the ECtHR described its imperatives in these terms: "Although the primary purpose of the Convention system is to provide individual relief, its mission is also to determine issues on public-policy grounds in the common interest, thereby raising the general standards of protection of human rights and extending human rights jurisprudence throughout the community of Convention States."[74] Its self-perception as a "community servant court" is informed by its view that its "judgments in fact serve not only to decide those cases brought before the Court but, more generally, to elucidate, safeguard and develop the rules instituted by the Convention" and to address disputes in other international human rights regimes.[75] In its discharge of that difficult role, the ECtHR has spoken of the need to maintain a "fair balance" between the public interests and fundamental individual rights.[76]

All 47 of the Council of Europe member States are party to the ECHR (thus including approximately 800 million people), and a condition of membership is the Convention's ratification at the earliest opportunity.[77] The current members of the Council of Europe, who are the ECHR's signatories, consist of the European Union (EU), the European Economic Area (EEA), Turkey and most of the former Soviet Bloc. Article 1 of Protocol No. I to the ECHR provides:

---

[72] *Loizidou v Turkey*, ECtHR, Judgment of 23 March 1995, at ¶ 75; *Bosphorus Hava Yolları Turizm ve Ticaret Anonim Şirketi v Ireland*, ECtHR, Grand Chamber, Judgment of 30 June 2005, at ¶ 156; *Behrami and Behrami v France* and *Saramati v France, Germany and Norway*, ECtHR, Grand Chamber, Decision of 2 May 2007, at ¶ 145.

[73] J. M. Pasqualucci, THE PRACTICE AND PROCEDURE OF THE INTER-AMERICAN COURT OF HUMAN RIGHTS 139-40 (Cambridge University Press, 2003); G. H. Thune, "The Right to an Effective Remedy in Domestic Law: Article 13 of the European Convention on Human Rights," *in* D. Gomien (ed.), BROADENING THE FRONTIERS OF HUMAN RIGHTS: ESSAYS IN HONOUR OF ASBJORNE EIDE 79 (1993).

[74] *Karner v. Austria*, ECtHR, Judgment of 24 July 2003, at ¶ 26.

[75] *Ireland v. United Kingdom*, ECtHR, Judgment of 18 January 1978, Series A 25, at ¶ 154; *Guzzardi v. Italy*, ECtHR, Judgment of 6 November 1980, Series A No 39, at ¶ 86.

[76] *Beyeler v. Italy* [GC], no. 33202/96, § 107, ECHR 2000-I.

[77] L. Wildhaber, *A Constitutional Future, supra*, at 165.

> Every natural or legal person is entitled to the peaceful enjoyment of his possessions. No one shall be deprived of his possessions except in the public interest and subject to the conditions provided for by law and by the general principles of international law.
>
> The preceding provisions shall not, however, in any way impair the right of a State to enforce such laws as it deems necessary to control the use of property in accordance with the general interest or to secure the payment of taxes or other contributions or penalties.[78]

Article 6(1) provides that "in the determination of his civil rights and obligations or of any criminal charge against him, everyone is entitled to a fair and public hearing within reasonable time by an independent and impartial tribunal established by law." Article 15 allows "derogations" from the protections only in times of public emergency and just to the extent required.

The ECtHR plays different roles in each of the following scenarios: between European nations' domestic courts and the European Court of Justice (ECJ);[79] between the domestic systems and the ECtHR, and

---

[78] *Anheuser-Busch Inc. v. Portugal* [GC], no. 73049/01, ECHR 2007-I, at ¶ 62 ("the first rule, set out in the first sentence of the first paragraph, is of a general nature and enunciates the principle of the peaceful enjoyment of property; the second rule, contained in the second sentence of the first paragraph, covers deprivation of possessions and subjects it to certain conditions; the third rule, stated in the second paragraph, recognises that the Contracting States are entitled, amongst other things, to control the use of property in accordance with the general interest ... The three rules are not, however, 'distinct' in the sense of being unconnected. The second and third rules are concerned with particular instances of interference with the right to peaceful enjoyment of property and should therefore be construed in the light of the general principle enunciated in the first rule").

[79] The ECJ has learned from its past experiences with several domestic courts of last resort, namely the German Constitutional Court:

The dynamic between the then-called Court of Justice of the European Communities (ECJ) and the German Constitutional Court provides a good illustration for this pattern. In the 1970s the German Constitutional Court heavily criticized the human-rights deficit of the EC law and claimed a power of judicial review with regard to EC law as long as this situation was not remedied. The ECJ took this warning very seriously and elaborated an extremely creative human-rights jurisprudence to the point that a decade later the German Constitutional Court took note of this well-settled jurisprudence and abandoned its claim of judicial review of EC law as long as the latter meets the standards of the German Constitution in terms of the protection of fundamental rights. Now compare this episode with the analysis of the constitutionality of the Maastricht Treaty carried out by the same German Constitutional Court. In this analysis the Constitutional Court addressed a warning to the ECJ about the limits of the judicial extension of

between the ECJ (holding famously that the European Communities brought forth "a new legal order of international law")[80] and the ECtHR. A recent change is that Protocol No. 14 of the ECHR (2010) and the Treaty of Lisbon (2009) allow the European Union to accede to the Convention. At the ECtHR, complaints may be brought by individuals or other contracting signatories, and—rare for any court—the ECtHR may also issue advisory opinions (as a means of forewarning member States). Both Article 1 (right to property) and Article 35 (exhaustion requirement) of Protocol No. I make the "general principles of international law" a source of law.

The ECtHR's general docket encompasses more than property rights cases. Sometimes, there is overlap between the ECHR provisions that, for instance, involve both equality under Article 14 *and* property rights under Article 1. The Court defines "property" broadly, including not just real property, cash and cash equivalents but also social welfare, inheritance rights and employment—the means of providing freedom from desperation.[81] There is another strategic reason that the ECtHR's general docket is important for our analysis: the face-saving expectation that tribunals will not behave inconsistently based on the "politics" of a case

---

the scope of the constituent treaties due to the requirement of democratic legitimacy enshrined in the German Constitution. . . . [O]ne should not lose sight of the fact that in terms of judicial modus operandi the ECJ's human rights jurisprudence was much more audacious than the jurisprudence concerning the powers of the EC institutions: there was no textual basis for the former, whereas the latter was mainly grounded on teleological readings of the black-letter provisions of the EC treaties. See F. Zarbiyev, *Judicial Activism in International Law—A Conceptual Framework for Analysis*, J. OF INTERNATIONAL DISPUTE SETTLEMENT, (2012), 1, 6-7 [See F. Zarbiyev, *Judicial Activism in International Law*].

[80] See *van Gend & Loos v Nederlandse Administratie der Belastingen*, Case 26/62 [1963] ECR 1, 12; *Commission v Luxembourg and Belgium*, Joined Cases 90, 91/63 [1964] ECR 625, 631; *Flaminio Costa v ENEL*, Case 6/64 [1964] ECR 585, 593.

[81] L. Wildhaber, *A Constitutional Future*, *supra*, at 163; C. Sunstein, *On Marshall's Conception of Equality*, 44 STAN. L. REV. 1267, 1273 (1992) (defining freedom from desperation with regard to Justice Thurgood Marshall's jurisprudence in terms that reflect the ECtHR (with uncanny precision): "At a minimum, that role entailed *vigilance over discrimination with respect to education* [and other fundamental rights] . . .; *an attack on caste systems*; and a *willingness to look skeptically at any state action that allowed people to be subject to desperate conditions*.") (emphasis added). The ECtHR seems to embody that "[p]rocedure is the means; full, equal and exact enforcement of substantive law is the end." R. Pound, *The Etiquette of Justice*, 3 PROCEEDINGS NEB. ST. BAR ASSN. 231 (1909).

and who the perceived winners and losers of a logical argument are. Eloquently, Jon Elster calls this "the civilizing force of hypocrisy,"[82] suggesting essentially that "it is not always easy for a dissatisfied actor publicly to oppose a judicial expansion of the scope of publicly valued causes: when an actor takes public commitments to certain principles, its reputation would be seriously damaged if it did not accept what can pass for rational consequences of those principles."[83]

The Court is divided into five Sections, to which each of the judges is assigned. Judges sit in Committee of three judges, Chambers of seven judges and a Grand Chamber of 17 judges.[84] Judges are elected, from the three candidates each contracting State nominates, by majority vote in the Parliamentary Assembly of the Council of Europe. When there is an unfavourable outcome in a Section, subject to the tribunal's rules an appeal might be taken to the entire Grand Chamber.

In the mid-twentieth century, the political conditions of the members of the Council of Europe ranged from the strongly pro-capitalist to those on communism's verge. Thus the rights which were included in the Convention had to reflect a "core minimum of the values necessary to create and maintain a democratic society, while also respecting and allowing for the different [and unique] social, economic and political conditions which prevailed in the signatory states."[85] In cases of systemic abuses or bias, there is more pressure on the ECtHR to use Convention tools to carve out a protected property right. Indeed, the Court has justified its use (albeit limited) of the exhaustion of local remedies as an incentive to force governments to build up their own judicial systems.[86] In doing so, the Court has connected procedure with substance.

---

[82] J. Elster, "Strategic Uses of Arguments" *in* Kenneth Arrow and others (eds), BARRIERS TO CONFLICT RESOLUTION 251 (W. W. Norton, 1995).

[83] See F. Zarbiyev, *Judicial Activism in International Law, supra,* at 30 ("This is certainly one of the explanations of the judicial 'courage' of the ECtHR.").

[84] For the ECtHR's perspective on the Grand Chamber reforms generated by Protocol XIV, see <www.echr.coe.int/NR/rdonlyres/57211BCC-C88A-43C6-B540-AF0642E81D2C/0/CPProtocole14EN.pdf>, May 2010 (last accessed September 2, 2011).

[85] H. Mountfield, *Colloquium Article: Regulatory Expropriations in Europe: the Approach of the European Court of Human Rights*, 11 N.Y.U. ENVT'L L.J. 136, 138 (2002).

[86] S. D'Ascoli & K. M. Scherr, "The Rule of Prior Exhaustion of Local Remedies in the International Law Doctrine and its Application in the Specific Context of Human Rights Protection," European University Institute Working Paper Law No. 2007/02 (2007), p. 11.

According to the public pronouncements of some scholars,[87] the geopolitically broad jurisdiction of the ECtHR gives "private parties direct access"[88] and "creat[es] a constituency for" its decisions that are "able to pressure domestic government institutions to take heed and comply with those judgments."[89] The geopolitical diversity also indicates diverse values and legal systems but there is a common denominator of real and/or aspired culture of human rights guaranteed in the law.[90] Without this element, the supranational human rights regime may have been a failure from the very outset. Moreover, the very existence of an international human rights system denotes the belief held by its drafters and organisers that regard or lack thereof for human rights in one jurisdiction has impact on others.[91]

Chapter IV (EXHAUSTION OF LOCAL REMEDIES AND CONTINUOUS NATIONALITY) explains that State compliance with the judgments of the international human rights tribunals remains a powerful litmus test of effectiveness for the tribunals.[92] When the exhaustion requirement makes

[87] L. R. Helfer & A. Slaughter, *Toward a Theory of Effective Supranational Adjudication*, 107 YALE L.J. 273, 277 (1997) [L. R. Helfer & A. Slaughter, *Toward a Theory of Effective Supranational Adjudication*]; E. Alkema, *The European Convention as a Constitution and its Court as a Constitutional Court*, in P. Mahoney *et al.* (eds), PROTECTING HUMAN RIGHTS: THE EUROPEAN PERSPECTIVE 41 (2000).

[88] L. R. Helfer, *Redesigning the European Court of Human Rights: Embeddedness as a Deep Structural Principle of the European Human Rights Regime*, 19 E.J.I.L. 125, 132 (2008) [L. R. Helfer, *Redesigning the European Court of Human Rights*].

[89] L. R. Helfer & A. Slaughter, *Toward a Theory of Effective Supranational Adjudication, supra,* at 387 ("The ECJ deliberately wooed national courts, and the ECHR earned support from courts, administrative agencies, and some national legislators.").

[90] E. E. Fosse, "The Future of Human Rights Measurement: Towards an International Survey of Rights," Issue Paper: Carr Center for Human Rights Policy, Harvard Kennedy School of Government, August 2008 ("Although there are bound to be cultural differences in perceptions of human rights, the claims about cultural particularity are often overstated.").

[91] The thirteenth century Persian poet Sa'di Shirazi mentioned: "If one member is afflicted with pain, / Other members uneasy will remain." John Dunne's "No man is an island, entire of itself."

[92] C. Hillebrecht, "Making Courts Count: International Human Rights Tribunals and the Problems of Measuring Compliance," Issue Paper: Carr Center for Human Rights Policy, Harvard Kennedy School of Government, August 2009 ("State compliance and the subsequent strengthening of human rights protections is both the impetus for international human rights tribunals like the European Court of Human Rights (ECtHR), the Inter-American Commission on Human Rights and

little sense for a non-functioning judicial system, then it is deemed not just to be waived but actually *satisfied*. Because the Convention's signatories' participation is not to be taken for granted, the ECtHR cooperates with the domestic governments both on jurisdiction and merits. The ECtHR's approach to expropriation cases shows its self-restraint with a practical edge. As a supranational human rights tribunal, the Court seems to be open to deferring to the domestic governments, repudiating them only if the violations are egregious or clearly unreasonable or if the government has made no good-faith effort.

The all-important role of fact-finder in a given case, for instance, is generally reserved for the national courts.[93] The ECtHR states often that it cannot "assume the role" or "take the place" of national institutions.[94] This is how the ECtHR has persuaded its signatories to conform to the ECtHR's decisions. One caveat is that, since 2000, the ECtHR's "embeddedness in national legal systems" has increased significantly: "[I]n a stark reversal of past practice," the Court has "beg[u]n to specify *remedies* that national governments must provide to individuals whose rights they have violated," especially in "systemic human rights problems affecting large numbers of similarly situated individuals."[95]

International human rights tribunals generally, and the ECtHR in particular, "have the potential to generate significant . . . decrees requiring that governmental bodies reorganize themselves so that their behavior will comport with certain legal standards. Such decrees, addressed to school systems, prison and mental hospital officials, welfare administrators, and public housing authorities, insert . . . [human rights] courts in the ongoing business of public administration."[96]

---

the Inter-American Court of Human Rights (IACtHR) and their most daunting challenge.") [C. Hillebrecht, "Making Courts Count"].

[93] *Sokurenko & Strygun v. Ukraine*, App. nos. 29458/04 and 29465/04 (2006), at p. 13 (joint dissenting opinion of Judges Lorenzen and Maruste) (citing *Vidal v. Belgium,* 12351/86 (1992); *Edwards v. United Kingdom*, App. no. 4647/99 (2002), at ¶ 34) (the ECtHR usually abstains from figuring out what domestic legislation means as well "the credibility of witnesses and the relevance of evidence to the issues in the case").

[94] *Observer and Guardian v. United Kingdom*, Series A No. 216 (1991), p. 30.

[95] L. R. Helfer, *Redesigning the European Court of Human Rights: Embeddedness as a Deep Structural Principle of the European Human Rights Regime*, 19 E.J.I.L. 125, 142 (2008).

[96] D. L. Horowitz, *Decreeing Organizational Change: Judicial Supervision of Public Institutions*, 32 DUKE L. J. 1265 (1983) [D. L. Horowitz, *Decreeing Organizational Change*].

The ECtHR declares fewer than 5% of the applications filed to be admissible.[97] The Court could, if it wishes, whittle down the percentage by requiring at least a surface plausibility of the facts alleged by the claimant in her pleading; plausibility is of course more demanding as a standard than what is merely conceivable. The ECtHR does not seem to be particularly likely to disallow in its entirety pleading in the alternative (pleading of multiple inconsistent claims). This is assuming the domestic courts have failed to deliver justice in a spectacularly incompetent fashion. Disallowing pleading in the alternative might be further limited the scope of decision-worthy cases. There is a cost, of course, namely that the time, attention, and at times even scope of the highly decision-worthy cases is diminished when the ECtHR simultaneously tackles so much.

What happens in the other international human rights tribunals? In the IACtHR, for example, governments have felt themselves free to assert that "the 'automatic' processing of manifestly unfounded petitions could generate unnecessary disquiet, in addition to diverting material and human resources available in the Commission and the member states for processing petitions that should be declared inadmissible *ab initio*."[98] The Brazilian government has even gone so far as to contend that "any petition which, based on the presentation by the petitioner *or* the State, is groundless or out-of-order" should be held inadmissible (unless "based on" is not code for presumptive deference, which it appears to be).[99] The placement of the word "or" produces some bewilderment and even consternation, for it amounts to giving the State rather a *carte blanche*.

Nor is this governmental assertion readily reconcilable with the very next sentence in the Brazilian government's contention submitted in this 2002 jurisdictional decision: "[t]he so called *pro homine* principle, which governs international systems for the protection of human rights—and according to which the states bear the burden of proof—only makes sense in a context of likely and well-founded allegations. Otherwise, one runs the risk of undermining the transparency and juridical security of the system."[100] Small comfort that thought is—just as "likely and well-founded allegations" of the claimant must be agreed upon by the tribunal,

---

[97] *Id.*; Statistics: 1/1-31/8/2011, European Court of Human Rights [ECtHR Statistics], *available at* <http://www.echr.coe.int/NR/rdonlyres/7B68F865-2B15-4DFC-85E5-DEDD8C16CAC1/0/Statistics_2011.pdf> [Statistics: 1/1-31/8/2011, ECtHR].

[98] *Simone André Diniz v. Brazil*, Case 12.001, Report No. 37/02, Inter-Am. C.H.R., Doc. 5 rev. 1 at 167 (2002) (Admissibility Petition), at ¶ 18.

[99] *Id.*, at ¶ 19.

[100] *Id.*

so must the State's. The *pro homine* principle cannot somehow be *less* beneficial to the human rights claimant than it is to the State. In reality, of course, at this threshold stage of admissibility *prima facie* consideration of the facts is the established standard.[101]

In the ECtHR, this development concerning admissibility[102] was instituted to handle surging dockets (both as to applications filed each year and pending applications).[103] The ECtHR is a workhorse institution, at least as far as the volume of cases go. Limits faced by the ECtHR are, at least in part, logistical: (*i*) the Court's case-load is enormous, with 46,750 applications lodged just in 2011 and 1165 judgments, including 987 judgments finding at least one Convention violation (as of August 31, 2011);[104] (*ii*) it also has little direct enforcement capacity though (and

---

[101] *Id.*, at ¶ 31 ("The standard of appreciation of these rules is different from that required to decide on the merits of a complaint. The IAC[t]HR must make a *prima facie* evaluation to examine whether the complaint states facts indicative of an apparent or potential violation of a right guaranteed by the Convention, and not to establish the existence of a violation.").

[102] See ECtHR Statistics, *supra*. Some of the other developments: "First, the Court adopted the role of a first-instance finder of fact where states failed to investigate alleged human rights violations. Secondly, the ECtHR expanded its interpretation of Article 13 of the Convention, a provision that requires an effective domestic remedy for violations of protected rights and freedoms."

[103] European Ministerial Conference on Human Rights, Resolution I, Institutional and Functional Arrangements for the Protection of Human Rights at National and European Level (Rome, 3 - 4 Nov. 2000); Council of Europe, *Explanatory Report to Protocol No 14 to the Convention for the Protection of Human Rights and Fundamental Freedoms amending the control system of the Convention* (13 May 2004), at ¶ 14 ("Only a comprehensive set of interdependent measures tackling the problem from different angles will make it possible to overcome the Court's present overload").

[104] Statistics: 1/1-31/8/2011, ECtHR; L. Caflisch, *The Reform of the European Court of Human Rights: Protocol No. 14 and Beyond*, 6 HUM. RTS. L. REV. 403, 404 (2006) ("With its 45 judges and about 250 Registry lawyers, the Court is presently confronted with an accumulated case-load of 82,600 applications, out of which 45,550 were made in 2005, the yearly capacity of absorption of the Court now being at around 28,000 cases"); P. Leach, *Access to the European Court of Human Rights – From a Legal Entitlement to a Lottery?*, 27 HUM. RTS. L.J. 11 (2006); C. Hillebrecht, "Making Courts Count," *supra,* at 1 ("Limited enforcement capabilities and rapidly expanding caseloads hamper the tribunals' work. Empirically based composite indicators of states' compliance with the tribunals' rulings can improve the tribunals' ability to facilitate compliance and provide an incentive for member states to comply with the human rights tribunals more readily, thus strengthening human rights practices.").

perhaps *because* of which) it exercises significant compliance-measuring capacity;[105] and (*iii*) the subject-matter of its jurisdiction deters the ECtHR from reaching out to decide non-human rights questions — except when it arguably does.

The ECtHR sometimes is called upon to resolve questions touching upon politics and commerce—with Soviet Bloc countries' accession to the Convention, cases about "minorities in conflict with [a] central government" and cases about "terrorism, violence, and civil strife" have become more and more common.[106] But those cases always are doctrinally anchored to some discrete human rights provision of the Convention. Somewhat cautiously, the ECtHR walks a fine line between the two big-tent schools of the judicial power debate: the *neofunctionalists* (privileging the autonomy of a European institution) and *intergovernmentalists* (privileging many networks of member states over European umbrella organisations).[107]

In many ways, that balancing strategy is the symptomatic problem for all international human rights tribunals. The tribunal's reward would be to rebuff the image as a mere "paper tige[r]" facing a "serious deficit in enforcement capacity" and "trying to do more oversight and enforcement with relatively fewer resources." [108] But what makes the ECtHR symptomatic of international human rights tribunals generally is that, as earlier mentioned, its self-image and general image is that of the leading international human rights tribunal globally.

The ECtHR's priorities, subliminal thinking, and of course bottom-line decisions carry a stamp of credibility and legitimacy that makes them amenable to being followed in close cases by other international human rights tribunals—as well as by certain other international tribunals. The Court's insistence on parties' obedience with its provisional measures is just another area where it has borrowed from the Inter-American Court of

---

[105] C. Hillebrecht, "Making Courts Count," *supra,* at 2 (stating the – ECtHR: "Multiple datasets tracking what states have done or have yet to do; Fractures compliance records of individual cases and countries." Inter-American Commission on Human Rights Groups into three categories: "full, partial or pending compliance; Obscures details of compliance; creates incentive to do as little as possible." Inter-American Court of Human Rights: "Produces compliance reports for some, but not all, cases; Valuable information but no aggregation or accompanying data.").

[106] P. Mahoney, *Speculating on the Future of the Reformed European Court of Human Rights*, 20 HUM. RTS L.J. 1, 3 (1999).

[107] A. S. Sweet, *The Judicial Construction of Europe* 111 (Oxford University Press, 2004); P.C. Schmitter, *Three Neo-Functional Hypotheses About International Integration*, 23 INT'L ORG. 161, 163-6 (1969).

[108] C. Hillebrecht, "Making Courts Count," *supra,* at 1.

Human Rights.[109] Wise parents do not hesitate to learn from their offspring, it has been said. However, the ECtHR does have its own share of problems and confusions, as the following chapters will underscore. That angle is not just symptomatic but is simply a microcosm of the potentially graver problems facing other international human rights tribunals worldwide.

Nonetheless, international human rights has travelled the long road—from the Universal Declaration of Human Rights' "only minimally legalized," "not overly precise,[110] and weakly institutionalized" character

---

[109] *Mamatkulov and Askarov v. Turkey*, Application nos. 46827/99, 46951/99, ECHR-GC (2005), at ¶¶ 50-53 (". . . In its judgment of 17 September 1997 in *Loayza Tamayo v. Peru*, the Inter-American Court of Human Rights ruled that the State "has the obligation to make every effort to apply the recommendations of a protection organ such as the Inter-American Commission, which is, indeed, one of the principal organs of the Organisation of American States, whose function is 'to promote the observance and defence of human rights' ... 53. The Inter-American Court has stated on several occasions that compliance with provisional measures is necessary to ensure the effectiveness of its decisions on the merits . . . In two orders requiring provisional measures, the Inter-American Court of Human Rights ruled that the States Parties to the American Convention on Human Rights "must fully comply in good faith (*pacta sunt servanda*) with all of the provisions of the Convention, including those relative to the operation of the two supervisory organs of the American Convention [the Court and the Commission]; and that, in view of the Convention's fundamental objective of guaranteeing the effective protection of human rights (Articles 1 § 1, 2, 51 and 63 § 2), States Parties must refrain from taking actions that may frustrate the *restitutio in integrum* of the rights of the alleged victims") (citing *Case of Loayza-Tamayo v. Peru*, Merits, Judgment of September 17, 1997, Series C No. 33; *Case of Hilaire, Constantine and Benjamin et al. v. Trinidad and Tobago*, Merits, Reparations and Costs, Judgment of June 21, 2002, Series C No. 94); *id.*, at ¶ 113 ("In a number of recent decisions and orders, international courts and institutions have stressed the importance and purpose of interim measures and pointed out that compliance with such measures was necessary to ensure the effectiveness of their decisions on the merits. In proceedings concerning international disputes, the purpose of interim measures is to preserve the parties' rights, thus enabling the body hearing the dispute to give effect to the consequences which a finding of responsibility following adversarial process will entail."); *id.*, at ¶ 124 ("The Court observes that the ICJ, the Inter-American Court of Human Rights, the Human Rights Committee and the Committee against Torture of the United Nations, although operating under different treaty provisions to those of the Court, have confirmed in their reasoning in recent decisions that the preservation of the asserted rights of the parties in the face of the risk of irreparable damage represents an essential objective of interim measures in international law.").

[110] The UDHR makes the elementary declaration that "[a]ll humans are born free and equal in dignity and in rights," Universal Declaration of Human Rights, Dec.

in 1948 to the modern "human rights regime" which "has evolved into harder forms over time."[111] This is not an insignificant or inconsequential achievement. The ensuing chapters explore those "forms."

§ 2.4—Iran-United States Claims Tribunal (IUCT)

The IUCT was set up to assess claims of nationalisation and expropriation of United States and Iranian citizens' investments in each other's jurisdictions after the 1979 Iranian Revolution.[112] Relations were so tense that Algeria had to broker the deal, hence the term "Algiers Accords." Iran consented partially out of the need to assure the community of nations that their investments in the new Islamic Republic of Iran would be secure and partially out of the need to defreeze the $10-12 billion that was locked up in the United States (and some of its allies).[113] There is support enough in customary law for an injured State "to affirm its rights through 'counter-measures.'"[114]

One former IUCT law clerk assures me that in the early years "the big fear was that Iran could just walk out—we," to mean the IUCT as an

---

10, 1948, U.N. Doc. A/810, art. 1; Article 11's assertion that criminal defendants are "presumed innocent until proved guilty," id. art. 11, and finally Article 17's mandate that "no one shall be arbitrarily deprived of their property," id. art. 17.

[111] Kenneth W. Abbott, Robert O. Keohane, Andrew Moravcsik, Anne-Marie Slaughter, and Duncan Snidal, *The Concept of Legalization*, 54 INT'L ORG. 17, 21 (Summer 2000) (footnote added).

[112] C. N. Brower & J. D. Brueschke, THE IRAN-UNITED STATES CLAIMS TRIBUNAL 3-4 (Martinus Nijhoff Publishers, 1998) [Brower & Brueschke, THE IUCT].

[113] A. Mouri, THE INTERNATIONAL LAW OF EXPROPRIATION AS REFLECTED IN THE WORK OF THE IRAN-U.S CLAIMS TRIBUNAL 4-5, 29, 167 (Martinus Nijhoff Publishers, 1994) [A. Mouri, INTERNATIONAL LAW OF EXPROPRIATION - IUCT]; see also General Principles (A), Algiers Accords ("Within the framework of and pursuant to the provisions of the two Declarations of the Government of the Democratic and Popular Republic of Algeria, the United States will restore the financial position of Iran, in so far as possible, to that which existed prior to November 14, 1979. In this context, the United States commits itself to ensure the mobility and free transfer of all Iranian assets within its jurisdiction . . .").

[114] *Case Concerning the Air Services Agreement of March 27, 1946 Between the United States of America and France*, 18 R.I.A.A. 417, 443 (1978). These counter-measures must be proportionate to, some say, "the amount of compulsion necessary to get reparation," H. Lauterpacht, 2 OPPENHEIM'S INTERNATIONAL LAW 141 (1952), while others suggest that the counter-measure must be proportionate "to the act motivating them," see *Naulilaa Case*, 2 R.I.A.A. 1011, 1028 (Portugal v. Germany) (1928).

institution and as an experiment, "had to be extremely sensitive to politics."[115] But Iran did consent and agreed to deposit $1 billion in the IUCT's Security Account in order to meet its obligations and to satisfy the awards.[116] As one scholar puts it, not only was the Islamic Republic of Iran the originator of the arbitration proposal, "the mechanism of the Security Account serves the American favourite triple formula of 'prompt, adequate and effective' compensation. By the expedited and eased method of payment out of the Security Account, the 'promptness,' and by the hard currency of its balance, i.e., the U.S. dollar, the 'effectiveness' conditions are fulfilled."[117]

From the United States' point of view, the background was set with the series of Hickenlooper Amendments[118] to federal law requiring, not just empowering, the President to terminate foreign aid to any nation which has seized American-owned property,[119] has nullified or refused to honour contracts with Americans[120] or has "imposed or enforced discriminatory taxes or other exactions, or restrictive maintenance or operational conditions,"[121] and which has somehow fallen short of "discharg[ing] its obligation under international law . . . including speedy compensation for

---

[115] See, *e.g.*, R. Davis, "The Decision to Freeze Iranian Assets," *in* REVOLUTIONARY DAYS: THE IRAN HOSTAGE CRISIS AND THE HAGUE CLAIMS TRIBUNAL, RECORD OF A CONFERENCE HELD AT NEW YORK UNIVERSITY SCHOOL OF LAW ON THE FIFTEENTH ANNIVERSARY OF THE ALGIERS ACCORDS 10 *et seq* (A. F. Lowenfeld, eds.) (Juris Publishing, Inc., 1999); J. Amuzegar, IRAN'S ECONOMY UNDER THE ISLAMIC REPUBLIC 169 (I.B. Tauris, 1997).

[116] M. Mohebi, DEVELOPMENTS IN INTERNATIONAL LAW: THE INTERNATIONAL LAW CHARACTER OF THE IRAN-UNITED STATES CLAIMS TRIBUNAL 333 (Martinus Nijhoff Publishers, 1999).

[117] *Id.*

[118] Foreign Assistance Act of 1961, Pub. L. No. 87-195, 77 Stat. 386 (1963) (codified as amended at 22 U.S.C. § 2370(e)(1)(1994)) (First Hickenlooper Amendment); Pub. L. No.89-171, 79 Stat. 653 (1964), codified at 22 U.S.C. § 2370(e)(2) (1994) (Second Hickenlooper Amendment) (passed specifically to overrule the United States Supreme Court's decision in *Banco National de Cuba v. Sabbatino*, 376 U.S. 398 (1964), and to disabuse federal courts from using the act of state doctrine to "decline . . . to make a determination on the merits giving effect to the principles of international law in a case in which a claim of title or other right to property is asserted be any party . . . based upon . . . a confiscation or other taking.").

[119] 22 U.S.C. § 2370(e)(1)(A) (1982).

[120] *Id.* at § 2370(e)(1)(B).

[121] *Id.* at § 2370(e)(1)(C).

such property in convertible foreign exchange, equivalent to the full value thereof . . . ."[122]

With the Iranian Revolution and the takeover of the United States Embassy in Tehran, the stage was set for a take-no-prisoners approach. Nonetheless what we have to be admiring of is the cool-headed diplomacy which ensued, due in no small part to the Canadian Ambassador to Tehran at the time, for the 99 hostages to be freed and for the financial deal through the IUCT to be negotiated.

The IUCT has produced a substantial amount of jurisprudence on expropriation. So far more than 4000 cases have been filed and over 800 awards and decisions issued.[123] The Tribunal consists of nine members: three chosen by Iran, three by the United States and the remaining three chosen by the Iranian and American arbitrators.[124] The Tribunal hears claims in chambers of three members. The Tribunal is the first international arbitral tribunal since World War II to consider a significant number of expropriation claims. Tribunal decisions are based on Article V of the United States and Iranian Claims Settlement Declaration (CSD) that states in part:

> The Tribunal shall decide all cases on the basis of respect for law, applying such choice of law rules and principles of commercial and international law as the Tribunal determines to be applicable... [125]

While the cases illustrate many different types of expropriation it is unclear to what extent the jurisprudence can be used to generalize about general principles of international law and state practice, as the Tribunal's jurisdiction covers "expropriations or other measures affecting property rights" and the Tribunal applied the terms of the 1955 Treaty of Amity between Iran and the United States. The Treaty of Amity provides: "property shall not be taken except for a public purpose, nor shall it be taken without the prompt payment of just compensation." Similarly, Article II of the CSD broadly spells out relief for "expropriations or other measures affecting property rights."

---

[122] *Id.* at § 2370(e)(1).

[123] "Communiqué," Iran-U.S. Claims Tribunal (2011), *available at* <www.iusct.org/communique-english.pdf> (last visited July 5, 2011).

[124] Former legal assistants (clerks) inform the outside world that the IUCT's judges often engage in deliberation of the cases right along with their clerks in a cohesive environment. Of course, the clerks are there only for research assistance and carrying out the tasks that come up. The judges are the ones vested with the voting and decision-making authority.

[125] Claims Settlement Declaration, January 19, 1981 *in* (1981) 1 I.U.C.T.R. 9.

The Tribunal's decisions deserve close attention for several reasons: First, the sheer body of jurisprudence, and its breadth, currently filling 28 volumes of Iran-U.S. Claims Tribunal Reports cannot blithely be ignored. Second, a wide variety of expropriation cases—from expulsion of U.S. nationals to straight-forward direct or indirect expropriations to appointing managers for companies to vandalism—arose where the Tribunal applied international law. Third, leading international law practitioners and arbitrators participated as counsel and members of the Tribunal, thorough submissions of fact and law were presented to the Tribunal and the resulting decisions provide a review of international expropriation law.

Fourth, although formally the Tribunal did not *have* to apply international law principles—Article V of the CSD puts the ball in the IUCT's court—it did so. This telling move indicates the Tribunal's method of bringing legitimacy to its diplomatically-fraught decisions—both through the distinguished international law jurists who sat on the IUCT and the sources they invoked.[126]

Indeed, much of the cross-pollination happened through the overlapping judicial personnel.[127] Unlike Harold Koh's *transnational legal process theory*—interactions "whereby international legal norms seep into, are internali[s]ed, and become embedded in domestic legal and political processes" via "executive action, legislation, and judicial decisions which take account of and incorporate international norms" [128] —this book primarily is focused on the horizontal cross-pollination happening *among* international tribunals. Some scholars are complimentary about the IUCT's influence on international law.[129] IUCT arbitrator Judge George Aldrich himself noted that "the Tribunal has created a jurisprudence that

---

[126] See generally T. L. Stein, *Jurisprudence and Jurists' Prudence: The Iranian-Forum Clause Decisions of the Iran-U.S. Claims Tribunal*, 78 AM. J. INT'L L. 1 (1984); R. P. Lewis, *What Goes Around Comes Around: Can Iran Enforce Awards of the Iran-U.S. Claims Tribunal in the United States?*, 26 COLUM. J. TRANSNAT'L L. 515 (1987); D. D. Caron, *The Nature of the Iran-United States Claims Tribunal and the Evolving Structure of International Dispute Resolution*, 84 A.J.I.L. 104 (1990) [D. D. Caron, *The Nature of the Iran-United States Claims Tribunal*].

[127] C. N. Brower & J. D. Brueschke, *supra*, at 642 (stating that "able and competent lawyers and judges" sit on the Tribunal — admittedly Brower himself is an IUCT arbitrator). Judges like Brower and Hans Van Houtte also sit on investment tribunals, facilitating that cross-pollination.

[128] H. Koh, *Transnational Legal Process*, 75 NEB. L. REV. 181, 205 (1996) (emphasis added).

[129] R. P. Alford, *The American Influence on International Arbitration*, 19 OHIO ST. J. ON DISP. RESOL. 69, 86 (2003) ("[t]he significance of [IUCT] decisions as persuasive authority is second to none.").

represents a significant contribution to the development of international law, including international commercial law."[130]

Still, there are a number of problems with the IUCT's precedential value for cases beyond. First, the unique circumstances of revolutionary Iran means that the types of regulatory expropriation the Tribunal was adjudicating are different from the regulatory expropriations in stable environments (and that "the hostile nature of the relationship between the United States and Iran has so politicized the Tribunal").[131] Even though Judge Charles Brower, unlike Judge Aldrich noted earlier, of the IUCT has been rather modest about the wider influence of his Tribunal, the next few chapters will underscore evidence to the contrary (and qualify both Aldrich and Brower) both as to the past and as to future potential:

> the [IUCT] awards constitute *lex specialis* and therefore are not relevant beyond the Tribunal itself; the at times hostile nature of the relationship between the United States and Iran has so politicized the Tribunal that its decisions are suspect; the third-country Chairmen have been subjected, and have improperly yielded, to intense forms of pressure asserted by the State Party-appointed Members; and finally, the awards of the Tribunal are merely decisions in cases and therefore not worthy of being afforded any significant persuasive weight in international law.[132]

Second, as noted above, the Tribunal's subject-matter jurisdiction covers expropriation as well as other "measures affecting property rights," thus creating some initial confusion. But the IUCT has expressly grounded most of its decisions in state responsibility and has explained what the exact violation was (expropriation itself or something tangential), clarifying things substantially. Third, the backward-looking nature of the IUCT means that the IUCT's decisions do not, with any certainty, incentivise or disincentivise any government or private behaviour—not the case with the NAFTA or the ECtHR.

---

130 G. A. Aldrich, THE JURISPRUDENCE OF THE IRAN-UNITED STATES CLAIMS TRIBUNAL 43 (Clarendon Press 1996) ("the Tribunal has created a jurisprudence that represents a significant contribution to the development of international law, including international commercial law.").

131 C. N. Brower & J. D. Brueschke, THE IUCT, *supra*, at 644; D. D. Caron, *The Nature of the Iran-United States Claims Tribunal, supra* (arguing that the IUCT's decisions are not "persuasive" precedent because they involve a "special type of arbitration").

132 C. N. Brower & J. D. Brueschke, THE IUCT, *supra*, at 644.

§ 2.5—Conclusion

Completing this discussion is the case-law issue. Of course, there is no *stare decisis* or even a system of precedent in the IIA universe, but there is an effort to maintain consistency and predictability or to address similar and dissimilar outcomes in other cases. IIA tribunals nonetheless have demonstrated an increasing tendency to cross-reference each other, to adopt similar rationales, and to meticulously examine previous awards and decisions; this discourse is thus being called an "emerging jurisprudence" in investment arbitration.[133]

Each of the three institutions deals with recognised international law principles. That has never been in doubt. It is the complex ways in which they *do* the interpreting (constrained by their own textual prescriptions)—how they construe decisions and conventions—that this book is concerned with.

This book also considers the techniques through these institutions interact with each other and how they try to earn and/or preserve legitimacy. Sometimes an institution will develop an important lead first espoused by itself or by another international tribunal. Of course in international law, the International Court of Justice (ICJ)[134] and the ICSID[135] (which often govern NAFTA tribunals[136]) both expressly say that precedent is binding only in the particular case. For the IUCT, there is no provision calling for binding precedent but the IUCT usually follows its own decisions; notably, the IUCT decisions have significantly influenced investment arbitration awards.[137]

The ICJ's approach to *stare decisis* might help future international tribunals. On the issue of precedent, Judge Shahabuddeen acknowledges that the ICJ is "competent to reverse its previous holdings on the law," but maintains that the ICJ "is not expected to exercise that competence lightly and without good reason" since "mere marginal superiority of a new ruling

---

133 T. Wälde, "'*Equality of Arms*,'" *supra*, at 165.

134 Art. 59, 33 U.N.T.S. 993, ICJ Statute ("[t]he decision of the Court has no binding force except between the parties and in respect of that particular case."). A key case, mainly because of its vagueness about *stare decisis's* controlling authority in international law, is the International Court of Justice's (ICJ) *Aerial Incident of 3 July 1988* (1989), *Islamic Republic of Iran v. United States*, 1989 I.C.J. 132 (December 13) (separate concurring opinion of Judge Shahabuddeen).

135 Art. 53, ICSID Convention; see also C. Schreuer, ICSID CONVENTION: A COMMENTARY 1082 (2001).

136 Art. 1136 (1), NAFTA.

137 C. S. Gibson & C. Drahazol, *Iran-United States Claims Tribunal Precedent in Investor-State Arbitration*, 23 J. OF INT'L ARB. 521, 524 (2006); G. Kauffman-Kohler, *Arbitral Precedent: Dream, Necessity or Excuse?: Freshfields Lecture*, 23 ARB. INT'L 357, 368 (2006) [G. Kauffman-Kohler, *Arbitral Precedent*].

should not suffice."[138] Judge Shahabuddeen's separate opinion advocated a two-part test: first, to apply "twin tests of clear error and public mischief as known to the upper levels of judicial activity in many jurisdictions;" and second, a cost-benefit approach to deciding whether "the injustice created by maintaining a previous but erroneous holding must decisively outweigh the injustice created by disturbing settled expectations based on the assumption of its continuance."[139]

How about vertical *stare decisis* (relevant for the ECtHR)? A heightened standard—not just error or misapplication of law—has been promoted for vertical *stare decisis*, *viz.* a higher court reviewing a lower court. Either the relevant law must not have been applied or been applied blatantly incorrectly. The obligation is very different when horizontal and/or advisory *stare decisis* is concerned. None of the three institutions has any enforcing capacity of its own; it has to rely on domestic (national and sometimes sub-national) actors to comply.

The ECtHR's approach to *stare decisis* has, first and foremost, to do with developing an internally consistent body of law.[140] Second, following what is called "strategic legitimation," the ECtHR "ground[s] its decisions in authoritative precedent on politically sensitive cases"[141] to earn the respect of the signatories. The ECtHR also "uses more authoritative precedent when it decides cases from countries where domestic courts commonly use precedent in their judgments and" where "the persuasive value of case law citation is highest."[142] Nonetheless, "country-specific factors, such as legal culture, are irrelevant in determining the authority of precedent."[143] What predominantly matters in the ECtHR is "the legal substance of cases."[144]

Chapters V (NON-DISCRIMINATION) and VI (OTHER SUBSTANTIVE STANDARDS) will show that the NAFTA panels arguably have defined

---

[138] *Islamic Republic of Iran v. United States*, at 132; M. Shahabuddeen, PRECEDENT IN THE WORLD COURT 97-8 (Cambridge University Press, 2007).

[139] *Id.*

[140] It is not that the ECtHR has no *stare decisis* system. Its *stare decisis* system, though, is built on *arrêt de principe* and *jurisprudence constant* — "which are similar to [common law] *stare decisis* except that they do not require adherence to a legal principle that has been applied only once before." G. Kauffman-Kohler, *Arbitral Precedent, supra*, at 360.

[141] Y. Yupu & E. Voeten, *The Role of Precedent at the European Court of Human Rights: A Network Analysis of Case Citations*, p. 1, Southern Illinois University Carbondale, Conf. Proceed'gs (2010).

[142] *Id.*, at 2.

[143] *Id.*

[144] *Id.*

property and investment the most broadly and have also been the most dissonant about whether or not there is a requirement to exhaust local remedies (though consensus now seems to be that there is no such requirement). The ECtHR's *dignitarian* constitutional model has alternated between deference to domestic actors and respect for individual property rights, but those swings have generally been reasoned and not arbitrary.

The ECtHR has interpreted the exhaustion requirement somewhat loosely, property (and related) rights substantially broadly, and many considerations less importantly than advancing human rights in the Council of Europe. It must be emphasised, however, that the ECtHR has made good-faith efforts to reasonably bring related notions into the sweep of human rights. The IUCT has had the advantage of being free from setting precedent for future government or claimant conduct, and has to some extent relaxed the requirements of proving an expropriation claim. It has done so with a keen eye on its *force majeure* history.

Chapter III (ATTRIBUTION AND CAUSATION) shows how attribution and causation work in the most interesting institution, the IUCT, and why that is important for NAFTA and the ECtHR—and indeed for all emerging international legal institutions. Compliance with the various international instruments needs not only be "measured" (as Harvard University's Kennedy School of Government-based Courtney Hillebrecht has so insightfully expressed) but also realised in actuality. Tribunals yearn to "[d]emonstrate successes to stakeholders," to "[m]aximize limited resources," to "[n]avigate enforcement problems," and to "[s]hore up perceived legitimacy."[145]

States seek to "[d]emonstrate commitment to human rights," to "[e]arn positive publicity and political capital," to "be evaluated against a fair rubric, not unrealistic, hypothetical standards" via "indicators that take capacity into account . . . ."[146] Investors and property owners wish to prevail through stable, predictable, somewhat uniform investment-liberalised rules. When there is confusion and the prospect of regulatory or direct expropriations, they want a clear mandate from the international tribunal rooting out that possibility. Finally, activists and academics want to "[h]ol[d] States . . . [and private parties] accountable," to "[d]evelop best practices," to "[u]nderstand the tribunals using both quantitative and qualitative methodologies."[147] Each actor in the international expropriation law complex has an interest and incentive in realising this compliance.

Just how they do so is the subject of the next Chapter's inquiry.

---

[145] C. Hillebrecht, "Making Courts Count," *supra,* at 1.
[146] *Id.*
[147] *Id.*

CHAPTER THREE

ATTRIBUTION AND CAUSATION: "FOR WANT OF A NAIL ... THE KINGDOM WAS LOST"

§ 3.1—Introduction

This Chapter concerns institutional ethos. It is about really entering the minds of the international tribunals empowered to decide if an expropriation has taken place and, if so, what compensation is to be afforded the claimant(s). Initially, I was beset with some self-doubt about showing subliminal linkages between and among doctrines developed by the tribunals. However, in this endeavour I came to be heartened by the late Professor Ian Brownlie's thoughtful assertion that "the appearance of new, apparently defined, legal categories is of doubtful value."[1] He adds that "[t]he difficult cases cannot be made less difficult by the invention of categories"—no matter who makes them.[2] There is if not exactly a unity then at least a set of intrinsic connections among the various facets to the international law of expropriation. It is the lawyer's commission to make them applicable to the immediate case.

Until now, we have discussed the "prism" institutions and how they came about. This Chapter discusses how they reason, what their premises and assumptions are, how they decide if a respondent State is responsible ("attribution"), and what degree of nexus counts as proximate causation ("for want of a nail ... the kingdom was lost").[3] After all, as far as public

---

[1] I. Brownlie, 1 SYSTEM OF THE LAW OF NATIONS: STATE RESPONSIBILITY 197-98 (1983).

[2] *Id.* Labels, without more, are just semantics. The power of labels, and perhaps even more importantly their *predictive* power about particular outcomes, lies in the characteristics and implications they confer and, in some circumstances, the dignity they will.

[3] B. Franklin, "For want of a nail," *Poor Richard's Almanack* (1758); *Holmes v. SIPC*, 503 U.S. 258, 287 (1991) (Scalia, J., concurring) ("'for want of a nail, a

impression of (and public confidence in) judicial work is concerned, judicial *justification* for a particular outcome may well be quite different from judicial *motivations* for that decision. An elephant waits in the room. Regarding both short- and long-term results, there is a constant tug of war between investors and property owners, who typically want to make it easier to show attribution and state responsibility, and governments (as defendants), who usually do not.[4] The identities of David and of Goliath lie in the eye of the beholder. On a rare occasion, governments in support their investors against another State might sing a pro-investor protection tune, as Chapter VI (OTHER SUBSTANTIVE STANDARDS) will address. These unexpected alliances can be significant.

Overall, international human rights and diplomatic courts have relaxed these requirements, whereas IIA tribunals generally police the requirements strictly. The broad or narrow parameters in the texts are only *part* of the explanation. A more holistic explanation is that the human rights tribunals were designed to preserve and even expand human rights on the international plane rather than be procedurally particular. Likewise, instruments which govern the diplomatic tribunals essentially presuppose *force majeure*—composed of externality, unpredictability, and irresistibility[5]

---

kingdom was lost' is a commentary on fate, not the statement of a major cause of action against a blacksmith.").

[4] Special interest takes sides in this on-going conflict. For some of the literature, see Public Citizen: "NAFTA Chapter 11 Investor-to-State Cases: Bankrupting Democracy Lessons for Fast Track and the Free Trade Area of the Americas," *available at* <www.citizen.org/documents/ACF186.PDF> (2001); S. Weintraub, "The Unending Campaign against NAFTA," Issues in International Political Economy, *available at* <http://csis.org/files/publication/issues201002.pdf> (2010) ("NAFTA had two central objectives — to increase mutual trade and encourage FDI into Mexico in order to stimulate Mexican economic growth. The reasoning was that the richer Mexico becomes, the better this is for U.S. exporters. Mexico is the second largest market for U.S. exports after Canada. The U.S. export level was [U.S.] $132 billion in 2008, three times greater than it was before NAFTA. Mexico's exports to the United States in 2008 were $216 billion, five times greater than they were before NAFTA."); Lobby for Cyprus, relating to *Loizidou v. Turkey*, App. No. 40/1993/435/514 (1996), *available at* <www.lobbyforcyprus.org/media.aspx?id=37> (last accessed September 17, 2012); V. C. Igbokwe, N. Turner & O. Aginam (eds.), FOREIGN DIRECT INVESTMENT IN POST-CONFLICT COUNTRIES (Adonis & Abbey Publishers, 2010); K. R. Gray, Foreign *Direct Investment and Environmental Impacts – Is the Debate Over?*, Reciel 11(3) 2002.

[5] The event was not caused by (externality), was not and could not be foreseen by (unpredictability), and was unpreventable by (irresistibility) the party claiming the *force majeure* defence. See D. Maskow, *Hardship and Force Majeure,* 40 AM. J.

—where many lines between state responsibility and private responsibility, attribution and non-attribution, are believed to be obfuscated.[6]

This hypothesis is boosted by the fact that some public interest advocates who file briefs and make arguments in various tribunals when the *result* supports their *cause célèbre* are curiously silent or even opposed when the same reasoning brings a *contrary* result.[7] Let us make no mistake: Certain premises of this subliminal—what is perhaps even "pheromonal"[8]—reasoning derive from the social, biological, economic and experiential factors influencing the members composing the tribunals.

These elements constitute the value system to some extent undergirding the work of international law through international tribunals.[9] In this Chapter and indeed throughout this work, I have tried to avoid prolific use of circular arguments, for while their probative value extends to the original proposition it does not extend to "anything new."[10] In his characteristically tongue-in-cheek fashion, Benjamin Franklin had warned us against the wrongful deployment of circular arguments, stating that "[i]t is so wonderful to be a rational animal, that there is a reason for everything that one does."

I have it on good judicial and lawyerly authorities, and this Chapter attempts to show, that at least some dispassionate analysis of state responsibility *is* possible because we really must watch what the tribunals do in cases over time, not just what they say. Rhetoric, without corresponding

---

COMP. L. 657 (1992); S. Hedley, *Carriage by Sea: Frustration and Force majeure*, 49 CAM. L. J. 209 (1990). *Deus ex machina* events might fall within the *force majeure* category.

[6] "*Force majeure*," Digital Licensing Information, Online Library, Yale Law School, *available at* <www.library.yale.edu/~llicense/forcecls.shtml> (last accessed June 11, 2010; *Sambiaggio Case* (1903) X U.N. RIAA 500, 521.

[7] B. Choudhury, *Recapturing Public Power: Is Investment Arbitration's Engagement of the Public Interest Contributing to the Democratic Deficit*, 41 VAND. J. TRANSNAT'L L. 775 (2008); F. G. Jacobs, *Judicial Dialogue and the Cross-Fertilization of Legal Systems: The European Court of Justice*, 38 TEX. INT'L L.J. 547 (2003).

[8] The usage of this word has been justified in Chapter I (INTRODUCTION).

[9] Some institutional considerations affect the entire tribunal, albeit member-to-member by varying degrees; some pheromonal considerations influence some members and some other such considerations influence other members. Even ultra-textualism at the cost of pragmatism and purposivism is a decision of sorts, since pragmatism and purposivism are very much in the mainstream and not believed to be so wildly absurd as to be beyond comprehension — even by the respected minds who oppose these philosophies.

[10] R. Bork, THE ANTITRUST PARADOX, *supra*, at 78.

action, might be no more than lip-service that lulls the polity into a false sense of security and runs a dagger through the prospect of transparency. The writing on the wall does not yet assert that international law is nothing more than "dressed-up" (a phrase used by one of the aforementioned authorities) international politics of the moment.[11] The choices made by the tribunals—signalling behaviour is more like it—are manifested in the assumptions, premises, semiotics, subtexts and of course dispositions actually rendered by the tribunals.

Another example concerns the Treaty of Amity, concluded between the United States and Iran in 1955, decades before the Revolution. The Treaty contained a "just" compensation provision which was of some significance. While the United States claimed that the Treaty still applied before the IUCT, Iran vigorously resisted this interpretation. Iran claimed that the "United States' conduct during and after the Islamic Revolution in Iran, which resulted, according to Iran, in the Treaty of Amity, at least by implication."[12] Right at its beginning, the IUCT therefore was forced to confront a "politically sensitive and difficult situation."[13] Putting a wrong foot here might have bankrupted the Tribunal's legitimacy, in no small part because so early in the process the Tribunal might have committed a *faux pas* by committing itself to a specific doctrinal route with all its compensation ramifications.

In *Oil Fields of Texas v. Iran* (1982), the IUCT held the Treaty not directly relevant and instead focused on customary law: "it is . . . important to establish *a rule under international law* that each succession must have as a consequence that the surviving company *is under an obligation to pay appropriate compensation taking into account all the circumstances of the Case.*"[14]

Time makes many revelations. Judicial bulbs quietly planted one day eventually may blossom. Perhaps this does not happen the next week, month or year but in some cognisable shape or form it does happen. Lawyers and jurists who can then connect the dots can appreciate the

---

[11] The very rejection of diplomatic protection as a requirement has the effect of removing the politics of the moment by one degree from the work of the tribunals. This is not to say that other considerations and developments cannot re-interject politics right back into the calculus.

[12] M. Mohebi, DEVELOPMENTS IN INTERNATIONAL LAW: THE INTERNATIONAL LAW CHARACTER OF THE IRAN-UNITED STATES CLAIMS TRIBUNAL 335-36 (Martinus Nijhoff Publishers, 1999). Iran eventually did relent when in the mid-1980's it gave up the argument concerning the Treaty of Amity's inapplicability.

[13] *Id.*

[14] 12 I.U.C.T.R. 308.

pedigree, thus adding value to the doctrine through the golden thread of heritage, and also decipher what the limits of the doctrine are. The new doctrine then is spun as just an application of a greatly established, ancient and revered concept.

Nor is this attitude categorically disingenuous, for the line between the old and the novel tends often to be a debatable one. A variant of the debate between the old and the new is that between the hyper-principled and the somewhat pragmatic. Meritorious and persuasive arguments might be constructed for either position with effective gusto. This seems to be the essence of the lawyer's craft, ergo judicial tradition, as it is viewed in many international and domestic tribunals. Consider an ECtHR example. In a Bosnian case involving the applicability of equality principles along ethnic and racial lines, Judge Mijović of the ECtHR plainly observed that "[d]ifferential treatment of individuals belonging to [constitutionally forbidden category of discrimination,] '[o]thers' was an issue left to be dealt with once the situation in Bosnia and Herzegovina was less sensitive, and from that perspective the Court has accepted that it was initially justified."[15] He was not hiding the ball regarding the role of pragmatism in his tribunal's "avoidance" or "postponement" strategies. International human rights tribunals feel—and I use this word because the basis for deduction here is more psychological than logical—that they sometimes must intervene in politically sensitive cases, but there is no reason they cannot do so in a delicate, pragmatic, problem-solving manner.

During the course of my interviews with politicians and international lawyers, a shorthand term ("Bellwether Briefs") became even more relevant. It refers to what litigators already know, simply that certain defining and seminal briefs that are either doctrinally entrepreneurial or that which otherwise chart a new path. Another dimension to bellwether briefs refers to briefs or even model BIT's from leading governments, signalling a shift in strategy or policy. In fact, model BIT's are a form of relatively low-risk signalling behaviour that test the waters before taking

---

[15] *Sejdic and Finci v. Bosnia and Herzegovina*, Application nos. 27996/06 and 34836/06 (2009), at 49-50 (concurring and dissenting) ("The majority's conclusion that the relevant constitutional provisions were not intended to establish ethnic domination, as argued by the applicants, but indeed to stop a brutal conflict and to secure effective equality between the warring parties, i.e. constituent peoples, is correct, as is the majority's conclusion that the impact of these provisions is different treatment on ethnic grounds. However, was this arrangement justified, and if yes, are the relevant grounds still present and significant? The Grand Chamber preferred to leave this question half-answered, while I thought that a detailed answer to this question would have been the most important response.").

an optimally-executed dive. It should interest IIA experts that their approach has also taken root in the international human rights sphere. Over the coming years, the interaction between the two worlds on this score will be fascinating to observe.

Diction, language and tone of all judicial opinions matter. Another consideration of importance is the political behavior on the part of domestic politicians, trade and investment negotiators and diplomats that judicial opinions propel into action. I am not aware of any studies where practitioners, academics or tribunals attempting to decipher a judicial opinion's turn of phrase or even holding might fall back on something as imprecise as tone (at least in relation to the rigours of *ratio*). Doubtless, though, that this plays a role at least subconsciously. The controlling opinion or award may not have reached the significant (what might even colloquially be called "high-stakes" or "jackpot") question perhaps because the earlier case did not require that question to be redundantly reached or because the parties had not expressly raised it or some other jurisdictional reason (or even etiquette concerning the expected judicial form). Nonetheless the earlier opinion wanted to signal its intent that its proclivities ran in a particular direction and that come noon, it would take an evolving or evolved norm around which a consensus had been formed—and deliver.

So what does make the difference? Society (or at least civil society) ponders greatly over ethnicity, gender, sexual orientation and some other factors. However, these considerations cannot be the only answer because people sharing some or all of those attributes often decide very simple to very complicated cases differently.[16] Moreover, these factors are tempting because they are the most obviously phenotypical, thus risking vast over-inclusiveness and under-inclusiveness. An adjudicator who has lived a silently and secretly suffering life inside her or his mind may, despite all the visible trappings of privilege, feel a kinship or affinity with the underdog that is at least as potent as that which is felt by an adjudicator who grew up in significantly more modest and difficult circumstances. Monolith-shattering moves can sometimes be desirable.

The answer, therefore, is more complex. It lies in perceptions, or more precisely how those other more obvious "biographical" factors work in tandem with self-perceptions and society's perceptions of oneself. For

[16] See, *e.g.*, M. Minow, MAKING ALL THE DIFFERENCE 111 (Cornell University Press, 1990); *id.*, at 55 ("Perceptions and assessments of difference pick out the traits that do not fit comfortably within dominant social arrangements even when those traits could easily be made irrelevant by different social arrangements of different rules about what traits should be allowed to matter.").

instance, does the judge see herself as a victim and feel a particular empathy for the underdog or the power balance between the potent and the underdog? Alternatively, does the judge see absolute and pure self-sufficiency ("up by one's own bootstraps") instead of dependency as the way to go? How the subject chooses to weigh some perceptions vis-à-vis other perceptions perhaps makes the most decisive difference.

Professor Martha Minow's position that "there is no objective stance but only a series of perspectives—no neutrality, no escape from choice in judging"[17] should be qualified and reined in by adding that the approach taken by other tribunals, impartiality, and purpose(s) and motivation(s) of the skilled negotiator*s* (there will be many negotiators, with often-divergent interests)—there might not be any singular purpose or motivation and it is more likely than not that there might be internal contradictions, as Chapter V's exegesis of the "intentionalist approach" will cover—who drafted the instrument, including which considerations they have weighed and how, do matter. Sometimes they can be unequivocally supportive of the direction that runs counter to the judge's own deeply-held beliefs.

Wise judges, conscious of the province of their role, do not perform acts of chicanery. It is *only* when the controlling law is muddled and hopelessly confusing that the judge might look, often subconsciously, to her own life and experiences to decide the case properly. This process need never be as slanted as a psycho-biographical cross between a "Desert Island Discs"-style introspection about the judge's personal choices and a "This is Your Life"-type documentary series about personal experiences. These nefarious considerations can be, in fact and not just in theory, avoided in tribunal analysis. Indeed, self-indulgence has no role at all to play in that most solemn of obligations. It follows, then, that international tribunals should not embody the "Father of Baseball Umpires" Bill Klem's belief that something "ain't nothin'[, a ball or a strike,] till I call it."[18] Law itself dies a little if Klem's observations live on.

---

[17] *Id.*, at 56. *Cf.* G. Abi-Saab, *The Normalization of International Adjudication: Convergence and Divergencies*, 43 NYU J INT LAW & POLITICS 10 (2010) (each international judge must "relate to the legal universe in which he is supposed to act, through his own understanding of the international judicial function and what it implies for the role of the international judge as well as his understanding of the specific mandate of the tribunal.").

[18] See P. S. Karlan, *The Supreme Court, 2011 Term — Foreword: Democracy and Disdain*, 126 HARV. L. REV. 1 (2012) [P. S. Karlan, *Democracy and Disdain*] (citing *Bill Klem Quotes*, BASEBALL ALMANAC, *available at* <www.baseball-almanac.com/quotes/quoklem.shtml> (last accessed November 15, 2012)).

We should not forget, moreover, that the answer also lies in the constant exogenous-to-endogenous dialectic that adjudicators undergo. This is true for all of us. How we are perceived *by* the world feeds our perception *of* the world, and *vice versa*. Consciously or not, arbitrators respond to those dialogues. They give voices to those particular responses. This is corroborated by the fact that judges often change their own perceptions of issues over time, perhaps as a result of their own re-evaluations and re-weighing of various considerations that determine tribunal outcomes. Those instances of re-evaluations and re-weighing derive themselves from these cyclical dialogues.

It is appropriate, then, that the forward-looking feature of this book is concomitant with causation. There is no cause for shell-shock since surprises in international law do not always come totally unexpectedly. There are tea-leaves which may be read effectively in light of special institutional circumstances, tribunal priorities, and the spirit of the age. Formal doctrines leading to a prejudiced result, for instance, against a particular racial, gender or sexual orientation will be modified, tacitly in application if not explicitly in theory, in order for the tribunal to avoid what it might consider an intolerable outcome jeopardising the entire value of this international law configuration. This modification might be judicially minimalist (saying, in essence, "Let us eschew addressing the merits, if reasonably possible, or at least wait until the dust has settled a little")[19] or squarely merits-based.

Let us now shift gears to the notion of state responsibility. When the expropriation or adverse interference with property is conducted by actors whom the government was unwilling or unable to control *and* from whose conduct the government profits, state responsibility results. More importantly, the Islamic Republic of Iran profited (primarily or exclusively) from most of the expropriations and interferences with property.

On the other side, the timeliness, orderliness and stability of the IIA changes—prospective legislative acts or prospective executive orders—took *force majeure* out of the equation. No imminent harm or urgency being incessantly at stake in the IIA tribunals and the international human rights systems, relatively strict attribution and causation requirements had to be met before those tribunals. Moreover, the IIA attribution problem is rare since the identity of the regulator is not usually hidden (unlike the diplomatic courts and sometimes the ECtHR and the IACtHR); more interesting from the IIA perspective is the degree of causation sought by

[19] See S. Katzenstein, *International Adjudication and Custom Breaking by Domestic Courts*, *supra*, at 701 *et seq*. (citing C. R. Sunstein, *Testing Minimalism: A Reply*, *supra*, at 125).

tribunals. International human rights tribunals have handled relatively few attribution issues but several proximate causation questions.

Now a point about precedent in international law: While the confusion is regrettable, efficiency and equity both point to the recommendation that "[l]egal precedent in international dispute settlement is neither to be worshipped nor ignored."[20] The expropriation law community seems to be split on the precedential value of the IUCT and other diplomatic tribunals because they tend to be unique judicial bodies with only some common points of comparison with IIA and human rights tribunals—as the situation presently stands. But periods of unrest in the ECtHR, and whatever lies in the IIAs' future, keep alive the possibility that these two institutions might someday find the IUCT's manner of coping with attribution and causation useful. Most of the discussion in this Chapter uses the IUCT as a focal point through whose optic we look at the IIA and the human rights tribunals' attribution-causation analyses. Moreover, international human rights instruments (unlike how IIA instruments and the instruments governing diplomatic courts generally act) impose negative as well as positive obligations on the State.

---

[20] G. Guillame, *The Use of Precedent by International Judges and Arbitrators*, J INT. DISP. SETTLEMENT (2011) 2 (1): 5 ("In international law, the *stare decisis* rule has been excluded since 1922, but permanent jurisdictions constantly refer to their previous decisions. Nonetheless, the former are still led to reassess their jurisprudence by various methods in order to take into consideration the evolutions of the law and of international society. Regional jurisdictions are more inclined to do so than global ones. As for arbitral tribunals, they have recourse to legal precedents in a very variable manner according to the area: interstate relationships, international trade, investment or sport. Furthermore, the increase in the number of courts and arbitral institutions introduces the question whether precedents from one dispute settlement institution are relevant to others. The question arises when two courts or tribunals apply the same national law or treaty and when they apply general international law. The challenge is to navigate between two risks: that of jurisprudential incoherence and that of government by judges."). See also J. W. Yackee, *Controlling the International Investment Law Agency*, 53 HARV. INT'L L. J. 391, 426 (2012) (stating that this is not aided by the fact that "[p]recedent in early [international commercial arbitration] was weak, in large part because of the relative lack of past cases available for argumentation and citation and because of strong norms against public disclosure of reasoned awards. If awards are not published, they remain largely invisible except to the parties and the arbitrators immediately involved. Third parties will thus be unable to refer to these past arguments in order to bolster their own claims, just as arbitrators will be unable to undergird their own decisions with references to past decisions of other arbitrators.").

Causation and attribution become harder to prove when the question involves positive obligations. To prove a claim in tort law, for instance, it is "not enough that one has been prevented from obtaining performance of a contract as a result of the actor's conduct."[21] However, what about *inaction*?[22] Should *but-for* causation even be used then? Could the State have stopped such a violation?

A recognised international law principle is that "[r]esponsibility [can] be triggered where the . . . state failed to exercise due diligence and thus adequately protect the . . . [claimant],"[23] when the State hired someone who in the course of performing her duties violated primary rights. This is when the chain of attribution can be traced back to the State. But this does not mean that positive obligations are acceptable *even* when the State is not the initiator. Inverses, converses or other neat logical somersaults do not typically work when the question is riddled with various exceptions, conditions and degrees. They do not work here.

This Chapter discusses the rationales supporting each of the arguments. Due to the diplomatic tribunals' rich jurisprudence on attribution, this Chapter uses force majeure and specifically the diplomatic courts as the lens through which it considers expropriation in the rest of international dispute settlement.

§ 3.2—International Law of State Responsibility

This section lays out some basic principles of state responsibility. Those in charge of parameterising and articulating the Draft Articles of the International Law Commission (ILC) have a difficult task.[24] ILC Article 4 articulates the law of state responsibility: "any conduct of a State organ is an act of the State, that is, it is attributable to the State."[25] Article 11

---

[21] RESTATEMENT (SECOND) OF TORTS, § 766B (1979), cmt. P.

[22] A. Redfern & M. Hunter, REDFERN AND HUNTER ON INTERNATIONAL ARBITRATION 493-4 (Oxford University Press, 2009).

[23] C. Hoppe, *Passing the Buck: State Responsibility for Private Military Companies*, 19 E.J.I.L. 989, 993 (2008) [C. Hoppe, *Passing the Buck*].

[24] It has been said, and with good reason, that "no other codification project goes so deeply into the 'roots,' the theoretical and ideological foundations of international law, or has created comparable problems." See M. Spinedi and B. Simma, "Introduction," *in* Spinedi and Simma eds., UNITED NATIONS CODIFICATION OF STATE RESPONSIBILITY vii (1987).

[25] A. C. Smutny, "State Responsibility and Attribution: When is a State Responsible for the Acts of State Enterprises," 17, 28 in *International Investment Law and Arbitration: Leading Cases from the ICSID, NAFTA, Bilateral Treaties and*

observes that a State is responsible only for its own acts, thus differentiating between public and private actions: "The conduct of a person or groups of persons not acting on behalf of the State shall not be considered as an act of the State under international law."[26] When systemic human rights abuse is involved and it costs the State little to intervene, the state might violate some positive international obligation if it does not.[27]

There is also a key difference between "primary" and "secondary" rules. The primary rules "make up the bulk of the content of the Law of State Responsibility; they are the substantive obligations allegedly violated."[28] They tell us *what* the actionable claims are. The secondary rules, basically the procedural components including the IUCT's CSD requires all cases to be filed by the January 19, 1982, filing deadline, indicate how those primary rules claims are to be resolved; they serve as the bridge between the claimant and the award sought. Attribution, causation, and *force majeure* rest between-the-lines and determine how and with what level of scrutiny each rule is to be interpreted.

The IUCT's practice, in relation to the NAFTA tribunals and the ECtHR, is set forth here. That practice is a specific counterpoint to the generalised and rather abstract work of the ILC and raises two particular problems: attribution amidst revolutionary circumstances and the attribution of the acts of State-owned or State-controlled corporations. The

---

Customary International Law (T. Weiler, ed.), 2005. The Law of State Responsibility, arguably the oldest element of international law, constantly undergoes changes.

[26] Report of the ILC on the Work of its Thirty-Second session, U.N. Doc. A135/10 (1980) [hereinafter Report of the ILC (1980)], reprinted in [1980] 2 Y.B. INT'L L. COMM'N 31, U.N. Doc. AI CNA/Ser. A/1980/Add. 1 (Part 2).

[27] An often-cited case is *Neer v. Mexico,* 4 R. Int'l Arb. Awards (15 October 1926), p. 4 ("[t]he treatment of an alien, in order to constitute an international delinquency, should amount to an outrage, to bad faith, to willful neglect of duty, or to an insufficiency of governmental action so far short of international standards that every reasonable and impartial man would readily recognize its insufficiency."). The necessary benchmark for relief, therefore, is high and different from other expropriation-related standards. The point is addressed in Chapter VI.

[28] See D. D. Caron, "The Basis of Responsibility: Attribution and Other Trans-Substantive Rules" *in The Iran-United States Claims Tribunal: Its Contribution to the Law of State Responsibility* 109-110 (1998) [D. D. Caron, "The Basis of Responsibility"]; see also C. S. Gibson & C. Drahozal, *Iran-United States Claims Tribunal Precedent in Investor-State Arbitration*, 23 J. OF INT'L ARB. 521, 524 (2006) [C. Gibson & C. Drahozal, *IUCT's Influence on Investor-State Arbitration*]. These two articles provided the initial inspiration for this chapter, especially its structure.

practical difficulties in applying the ILC's draft work are pronounced here because the theoretical propositions are not conclusive about "how rules of evidence and requirements of proof are to be constructed" to these "different specific contexts."[29]

Most international tribunals apply, in the beginning, the *prima facie* test: "jurisdiction is satisfied if, prima facie, the facts alleged are capable of constituting violations of the Treaty under a prima facie determination of the meaning and scope of the Treaty provisions relied on."[30] The IUCT's jurisdiction is broader than that required by the Law of State Responsibility. It certainly is broader than the ECtHR's Article 1 remit under the ECHR and the NAFTA tribunals' Chapter Eleven remit. Article II(1) of the CSD establishes the IUCT "for the purpose of deciding claims of nationals of the United States against Iran and claims of nationals of Iran against the United States."[31]

These nationals may bring their claims under Article VII(3) against "the Government ..., any political subdivision ..., and any agency, instrumentality, or entity controlled by the Government ... or any political subdivision" of Iran or the United States as the case may be.[32] For starters, subdivisions of federal states definitely count as an attributable entity in all prototypes. This point is addressed later in this Chapter under the first rationale of attribution, *searching for agency*.

This sweeping range of potential respondents, particularly "entities controlled by the Government," reaches well beyond what "State" customarily implies. As the IUCT held in *International Technical Products v. Iran* (1985),[33] "the phrase 'Iran' as used in the [CSD] is a broader concept than 'the Government of Iran'" is understood to be in international law. The word "Government" typically refers to the political organisation that is generally in control and held accountable, whereas "Iran" transcends time and governmental authority and is a more inexact term of art.[34]

---

[29] See D. D. Caron, "The Basis of Responsibility," *supra*, at 110-111.

[30] See *Introductory Note:* Saipam S.p.A. v. The People's Republic of Bangladesh, ICSID REV.—FOREIGN INVESTMENT L. J. 95, 96 (2009).

[31] CSD, art. II (l).

[32] CSD, art. VII (3).

[33] 9 I.U.C.T.R. 206, 238, n. 35 (1985-II).

[34] The precision required here and contradistinction often implied reminds one of Humpty Dumpty, who employed words to mean "just what [he chose them] to mean — neither more nor less." See L. Carroll, ALICE IN WONDERLAND AND THROUGH THE LOOKING GLASS 198 (Messner 1982). There is also value in remembering Charles Dickens's description in *Bleak House* that it was "dirty little unfortunate" Peepy's "*large* head" which was stuck "between two iron railings." See C. Dickens, BLEAK HOUSE 25-6 (1853) (emphasis added). Details matter.

Furthermore, the sweeping language in the choice of law clause (Article V) allowed these claims of nationals to be decided *both* on the basis of private domestic law and public international law. The investment arbitration community has its own take: if it were an IIA-based claim, then of course international law would directly have to govern. What, though, if the claim is not treaty-based or premised on some other express choice of law? "[I]n the absence of any express choice of law by the parties" on a question of an IIA breach, the IIA community's consensus is that at least under ICSID Article 42(1), "the Tribunal must apply a system of concurrent law."[35] Nor does it appear that UNCITRAL, the Stockholm Chamber of Commerce or the other fora have taken or will in the near future take a different approach, given the inherent wisdom of this approach.

There are obvious advantages and limitations attending this approach. The approach has an immediately sensible and moderate appeal for lawyers and judges. Then there is also the controversy. Of course "apply[ing] a system of concurrent law" is a sensitive task fraught with potential for disputes over exactly where the specified choice of law was silent and how to interpret that silence. Should the silence be construed to mean that the general international law principles should kick in or is it, ironically enough, the command of this general principle of international law, "structurally" interpreted, that this silence means that the choice of law instrument authorises nothing more?

All this said, this prevailing default rule requiring the application of "concurrent law" means that even though "[t]he law of the Contracting State is recognized as paramount within its own territory, . . . [it] is nevertheless subject to control by international law."[36] If, on the other

---

Dickens wanted to convey the exact extent of Peepy's misery. Without pointing out the ratio of the head's size to the space between the railings, perhaps not even a writer as gifted as Dickens could have captured the child Peepy's whole peril and excruciating agony. Words can get us past our own abstractions and limitations, and they can make a difference when the law is in a state of flux and good ideas are still finding a home within that law. See, *e.g.*, T. Endicott, *Law and Language*, in THE OXFORD HANDBOOK ON JURISPRUDENCE AND PHILOSOPHY OF LAW 935-68 (J. Coleman & S. Schapiro, eds.) (Oxford University Press, 2002) (quoting Demosthenes, 350 B.C.E.: "[O]ur polity consists of words" and "[T]he power of words can damage the city.").

[35] *LETCO v. Liberia*, Award, 2 ICSID Rep. 358, 359 (allowing compensation for the revocation of a license granted a foreign investor).

[36] *Id.*, at 372 (emphasis added); see also *Benvenuti and Bonfant Srl v. The Government of the People's Republic of Congo*, 1 ICSID Rep. 330, 349 (1980) (because of no agreement between the parties about the choice of law applicable, "the Tribunal applies the law of the contracting State which is a party to the

hand, the claim involves a breach of contract and there is no agreed-upon choice of law, then "the effect and execution of [the claim] are governed *primarily* by [domestic law]."[37]

Now it is true, of course, that the tribunal in *SOABI v. Senegal* (1988)[38] did make this sweeping statement. But it must be contextualised. While the forum is international and even some of the law may be international, the *primary* source of law, with which the IIA tribunal commences its analysis, in contractual cases must be domestic law. In annulling a tribunal's award, the annulment committee in *Klöckner v. Cameroon* (1985)[39] rejected the general reference to equitable principles of public international law even as a matter of form (and therefore *a fortiori* also as a matter of substance): "[T]he arbitrators may have recourse to the 'principles of international law' only *after* having inquired into and established the content of the law of the State party to the dispute (which cannot be reduced to *one* principle, even a basic one) and *after* having applied the relevant rules of the State's law."

Another IIA tribunal, *Compañía del Desarrollo de Santa Elena SA v. Costa Rica* (2000),[40] went in the opposite direction. As far as its diction informs us, *Santa Elena's* view of all types of claims was that "[t]o the extent that there may be any inconsistency between the two bodies of law, the rules of public international law must prevail." While the legendary Christoph Schreuer and August Reinsich correctly articulate that "tribunals have"—and they add the word "unequivocally"—"sought to follow carefully the instruction to apply the host State's domestic law as well as international law,"[41] deeper inspection reveals that these tribunals are not singing in one voice about the domestic-international law balance across international dispute settlement.

---

dispute as well as the principles of international law in this matter."); *SPP v. Egypt*, 3 ICSID Rep. 189 (1992) (stating that if domestic law does not resolve the question or if international law is violated by the exclusive application of domestic law, international law governs); *Cable TV v. The Federation of St. Christopher (St. Kitts) & Nevis*, 13 ICSID Rev.-FILJ 328, 371 (1998) ("The Agreement is silent on the matter of applicable law and, in the circumstances, in accordance with Article 42(1) of the Convention the law of the Federation and applicable international law will apply.").

[37] *SOABI v. Senegal*, 2 ICSID Rep. 221 (1988).

[38] *Id.*

[39] 2 ICSID Rep. 121, 122 (emphasis in original).

[40] 15 ICSID Review-FILJ 191. *Santa Elena* is an aberration for yet another reason (the "sole effects test"), as Chapter VI explains.

[41] C. Schreuer & A. Reinisch, Legal Opinion, *CME Czech Republic BV (The Netherlands) v. Czech Republic* (Partial Award, 2001), at ¶ 37, May 2001.

The obvious suspect to which this difference of opinion may be attributed is respect for sovereign domestic laws. The lurking alternative may well be, depending on the case, the flexibility and adaptability that public international law principles typically afford tribunals which domestic law of a jurisdiction may not. Forum shopping, the *res judicata* principle, and wider latitude in claiming a procedural or substantive violation denote just some of these differences. Generally speaking, tribunals cannot really function if they avoid equitable principles of public international law.

In the IUCT context, the details run deep. The private law claim could be brought against the agent or accessory of Iran (making the IUCT a "private transnational arbitral tribunal questions of private law which might in other circumstances be justiciable before domestic courts") but *only* the Islamic Republic was open to the public law claim (making the IUCT also a "an international or interstate tribunal dealing with the rights and duties of States under public international law").[42]

Because the private actor or Iran distinction (and thus private law or public law distinction) can be difficult to navigate, the IUCT has insisted on *naming* and *identifying* the proper respondent. There have not *yet* been any cases in the ECtHR making this a determinative issue. Just two examples outside our institutions suggest that this is a real possibility: the first is the International Criminal Court's (ICC) indictment of Omar al-Bashir (the Sudanese president) in 2008 for genocide, crimes against humanity, and war crimes under the Rome Statute.[43]

The second is the precedent set by the ICJ in the *Nicaragua Case* (*Case Concerning Military and Paramilitary Activities in and against Nicaragua (Nicaragua v. United States* (1986)))[44]: state responsibility results when agents work under the direction of and for the profit of the respondent State; when the State encourages the agents; and when a State puppeteers the leaders in power in the other State. But we should not

---

[42] It is the sweeping attribution to "the Government of Iran" or "United States" that leaves many questions unanswered. For an early analysis of the IUCT, see D. Jones, *The Iran-United States Claims Tribunal: Private Rights and State Responsibility*, 24 VA. J. INT'L L. 259, 260-61 (1984) [D. Jones, *Iran-United States Claims Tribunal*].

[43] Indictment against Omar al-Bashir, by Luis Moreno-Ocampo, The Hague, July 14, 2008, *available at* <www.icc-cpi.int/NR/rdonlyres/A2BA9996-67C3-4A5F-9AD2-B20A7FD2D176/277757/ICCOTPST20080714ENG.pdf>.

[44] 1986 I.C.J. Rep.14.

forget that the ICJ was careful to separate mere encouragement from attribution.[45]

Here and now, a doctrinal aside (of sorts)—only "of sorts" because ironically enough it might actually be the most important aspect of this book—is warranted. Principled pragmatism is entirely suitable and might even be a requisite part of the judicial function when the textual instrument leaves open that possibility. But the instrument must leave that possibility open for gap-filling. The adjudicator or arbitrator's worldview is not a worthy substitute for the textual command. The tribunal is obligated to infer that had the drafters of the instrument wanted to retain no ambiguity or space for discretion they would have been explicit in saying so.

Common sense suggests that this principle is ever more so applicable in instruments whose other parts are explicitly laden with exceptions. Therefore let us put ourselves in *this* Tribunal's pragmatic shoes: its pragmatism about the situation on the ground. Pragmatism is not the same thing as adjusting the law too swiftly to the contemporary fads and trends before ascertaining if those trends will endure. Three reasons that counsel against off-the-cuff changes and knee-jerk reactions are grounded are threefold: (*i*) Administrability: This process includes shifting the entire apparatus of State and the private sector over to the new model, and sometimes is fraught with transition costs and risks); (*ii*) Intellectual tunnel vision because most principals will not be comparativists in the truest possible sense and elegant inertia might be seen to seep in; and (*iii*) "[T]he law's distrust of novelty."[46] Think of the slow-moving tortoises which signify the majesty of the law.[47]

---

[45] *Id.*, at ¶ 9.

[46] S. Breyer, "Economic Reasoning and Judicial Review" (Lecture), British Institute of International and Comparative Law (2007), pp. 6-7 [S. Breyer, "Economic Reasoning and Judicial Review"] ("[T]hree additional policy-related factors that more directly explain why economic reasoning has not played a greater role in legal decision-making . . .[:] The first has to do with the law's need and preference for administrable rules. The second concerns a certain tunnel vision, present among both economists and lawyers, that inhibits each from taking full account of the other's discipline. distrust of novelty – a fact that often requires new approaches, such as economic approaches, slowly to win acceptance in other institutions before a court will introduce them into the law. The third involves the law's distrust of novelty – a fact that often requires new approaches, such as economic approaches, slowly to win acceptance in other institutions before a court will introduce them into the law."). The same arguments could be transposed for social and scientific considerations.

[47] H. MacNeil, *Descriptions of the Friezes in the Courtroom of the Supreme Court of the United States and of the East and West Pediments of the Building Exterior*,

Amidst tremendous chaos, evidence and documentation to prove attribution is often hard to find, then there is the burden of proof problem to grapple with in order to establish attribution, and even if it were found no clear answer may be readily discernible. In such cases, public law claims against States might be brought. The IUCT has to decide if there was government "control," "[t]he two main indicators of [which] are the identity of its shareholders and the composition and behaviour of its board of directors, which must be examined together."[48]

Nor are these factors, even taken together, enough to establish "control" and then, if "control" *is* proven, there still remains the expropriation inquiry to undertake. Both inquiries are somewhat fact-specific.[49] Without a strong attribution jurisprudence, resolution might not come easily or strike neutral, dispassionate observers as legitimate. Credibility and legitimacy are absolutely essential to *and* interdependent within the calculus of an international (or, for that matter, domestic) tribunal's function.[50]

---

p. 9 (describing the United States Supreme Court sculpture as "The last figures; Left - Study and pondering of judgments; Right - A tribute to the fundamental and supreme character of this Court. Finale - The fable of the Tortoise and the Hare").

[48] *Foremost Corp. v. Iran*, 10 I.U.C.T.R. 228 (1986-I); see also *PepsiCo v. Iran*, 13 I.U.C.T.R. 3, 19 (1986-IV); *First Nat'l City Bank v. Banco Para El Comercio Exterior de Cuba*, 462 U.S. 611, 626-7 (1983) ("instrumentalities and agencies are accorded a presumption of independent status" though presumptions *are* rebuttable). For scholarly literature, see, *e.g.*, J. Chalmers, *State Responsibility for Acts of Parastatals Organized in Corporate Form*, 84 A.S.I.L. Proc. 60, 63 (1991) ("[T]he presumption against piercing the corporate veil in the public sector need not be the same . . . [W]holesale importation of the limited liability/corporate veil metaphor is not appropriate."). For an alternative perspective, see D. J. Levinson, *Making Government Pay: Markets, Politics, and the Allocation of Constitutional Costs*, 67 U. CHI. L. REV. 345, 354-57 (2000).

[49] *Saghi v. Iran*, 5 I.U.C.T.R 251, 265-6 (1984) ("[t]he jurisdictional question whether a company was controlled by the Government of Iran is distinct from the question whether the company has been expropriated.").

[50] *Baker v. Carr*, 369 U.S. 186, 267 (1962) (Frankfurter, J., dissenting) (observing that a tribunal's "authority — possessed of neither the purse nor the sword — ultimately rests on sustained public confidence in its moral sanction."); J. G. Merrills, INTERNATIONAL DISPUTE SETTLEMENT 308 (3rd ed.) (Cambridge University Press, 1998) ("The point is not that better judgments will increase the readiness of statesto use adjudication, which seems unlikely, nor even thatbetter judgments will mean that cases will have different results, though no doubt this will sometimes happen. The point is rather that *as a technique for dealing with international disputes, adjudication has properties which are uniquely valuable, but to survive requires practitioners both willing and able topreserve its integrity.*") (emphasis added).

In the IIA context, there is no better illustration than the work of the tribunal in *Compañía del Desarrollo de Santa Elena SA v. Costa Rica* (2000), discussed just a short while ago in a different context.[51] A prime step in deciding whether or not there has been an expropriation is assessing "the extent to which the measures taken have deprived the owner of the normal control of his property."[52] This loss of control must be "irretrievabl[e]"[53] and the property rights must be rendered "practically useless"[54]—plus the loss must be for a significant period of time—in order to be considered an expropriation.

In its *Santa Elena* award, the ICSID tribunal held that "[t]here is ample authority for the proposition that a property has been expropriated when the effect of the measures taken by the state has been to deprive the owner of title, possession or access to the benefit and economic use of his property."[55] Since the grand question in that case boiled down to the exact date of expropriation, the tribunal decided this point was when the Costa Rican government issued its decree. At this juncture, the "practical and economic use of the Property by the Claimant was irretrievably lost."[56]

The *Santa Elena* tribunal would turn out to be on loggerheads with the NAFTA tribunal in *S. D. Myers v. Canada* (2001)[57] and *Feldman v. Mexico* (2003),[58] which held that partial deprivation of control did not necessarily

---

[51] ICSID Case No. ARB/96/1, Final Award (2000). The curious fact is that *Santa Elena* was a rare award at the heart of which was no IIA, just customary international law. See *id.*, at ¶ 65.

[52] *Id.*, at ¶ 76.

[53] *Id.*, at ¶ 80-81.

[54] *Id.*

[55] *Id.*, at ¶ 77.

[56] *Id.*, at ¶ 80-81.

[57] *S.D. Myers, Inc. (U.S.) v. Canada*, First Partial Award, at ¶¶ 117, 123, 127, 40 I.L.M. 1408 (2001); *id.*, at ¶ 283 ("[a]n expropriation usually amounts to a lasting removal of the ability of an owner to make use of its economic rights although it may be that, in some contexts and circumstances, it would be appropriate to view a deprivation as amounting to an expropriation, even if it were partial or temporary.").

[58] ICSID Case No. ARB(AF)/99/1, Award, at ¶¶ 1, 7; ¶ 152 ("[T]he regulatory action (enforcement of long-standing provisions of Mexican law) has not deprived the Claimant of control of the investment, CEMSA, interfered directly in the internal operations of CEMSA or displaced the Claimant as the controlling shareholder. The Claimant is free to pursue other continuing lines of export trading, such as exporting alcoholic beverages, photographic supplies, or other products for which he can obtain from Mexico the invoices required under Article 4, although he is effectively precluded from exporting cigarettes. Thus, this Tribunal believes there has been no 'taking' under this standard . . . .").

qualify as an expropriation. Nor did the *Santa Elena* tribunal distinguish between *control* and *use* (frequently using the two differently nuanced terms rather interchangeably), as NAFTA awards have found it necessary to do. Finally, the *Santa Elena* tribunal cited the *Tippets, Abbett, McCarthy, Stratton v. TAMS-AFFA Consulting Engineers of Iran* (1984)[59]decision of the IUCT in asserting that a deprivation has to be more than "merely ephemeral" in order to qualify as an expropriation.[60] Customary international law demanded as much, as *Santa Elena* understood it.

One final case in point is *Azurix Corp. v. Argentina* (2006).[61] Despite possessing a concession from the Province of Buenos Aires, Azurix Corp.'s request to increase tariffs for water and sewage delivery was rejected. Understanding the whole point of creeping or gradual expropriations—further dissected in Chapter V (NON-DISCRIMINATION)—the tribunal in *Azurix Corp.* held that "cumulative steps which individually may not qualify as an expropriating measure may have the effect equivalent to an outright expropriation."[62] In this particular dispute, inadequate deprivation of control was considered fatal to the corporation's claim: "Azurix did not lose the attributes of ownership, at all times continued to control [its Argentine subsidiary] and its ownership of 90% of the shares was unaffected. No doubt the management of [Azurix's Argentine subsidiary] was affected by the Province's actions, but not sufficiently for the Tribunal to find that Azurix's investment was expropriated."[63]

Let us now shift focus to the attribution aspect of the IUCT's jurisprudence. In *Fedders Corporation v. Loristan Refrigeration* (1986),[64] for example, claimant Fedders named *only* Loristan Refrigeration Industries and General Industrial Corporation as respondents and left Iran out. However, because its claim was for expropriation (and thus a public international law claim), Fedders was required to name the government of Iran as respondent and seek an amendment of its claim to do so. Otherwise, it would have been a gladiator fighting against imaginary lions, to paraphrase (and perhaps stretch the meaning of) the august Cardozo.[65] This pernickety insistence with accurate nomenclature ("Islamic Republic of Iran" as opposed to "Loristan Refrigeration") might, to some, seem like

---

[59] 6 I.U.C.T.R. 219 (1984).

[60] *Id.* (citing *Tippets, Abbett, McCarthy, Stratton v. TAMS-AFFA*, Award No. 141-7-2, (Jun. 22, 1984) (reprinted in 6 Iran-U.S. Cl. Trib. Rep. 219, 226 (1986)).

[61] ICSID Case No. ARB/01/12, Award (Jul. 14, 2006).

[62] *Id.*, at ¶ 308.

[63] *Id.*, at ¶ 322.

[64] 13 I.U.C.T.R. 97 (1986-IV).

[65] B. Cardozo, LAW AND LITERATURE 34 (1931).

a petty issue. But it can be determinative. And there is a point: the correct defendant must be identified or innocent third-parties could be besmirched or otherwise be deemed liable. Some domestic jurisdictions, governing their own civil procedure in suits, have a notice requirement.

In *Flexi-Van Leasing v. Iran* (1986),[66] the claimant named "The Government of the Islamic Republic of Iran" as respondent in a case that really was a private domestic claim but which, because of the way that the pleading was phrased, was considered just as a public international law claim and rejected the claim. When asked to reconsider, the IUCT dismissed the request, stating that "all of the claims were directed solely against the *Government* and all were explicitly decided by the [IUCT]."[67]

In cases where the claimant was ambiguous about a public or private claim, the IUCT had to decide this question for itself. In *McLaughlin v. Iran* (1986),[68] for example, the claimant asserted breach of contract private law claims against Isiran, a completely State-owned corporation. The claimant also asserted rather an oblique, unspecified and unclear claim against the Islamic Republic, which if it had matured would have been a public international law claim. The IUCT granted the breach of contract claims but dismissed the public law claim against Iran.[69]

Along similar lines, in *SEDCO v. The National Iranian Oil Company (NIOC)* (1987),[70] the IUCT first held that the NIOC's taking SEDCO's drilling equipment was an "appropriation," and then noted the dual nature of the claim: if the "NIOC is considered to have acted in a purely private capacity, its conversion of [the drilling equipment] would be unsupported by the rights of sovereignty which may justify expropriation."[71] In both *McLaughlin* and *SEDCO*, the IUCT did not want to overstep its bounds and do the claimants' job (of specifying the respondent and thus what sort of claim applied) *for* them. Even for a *force majeure* court that consciously and deliberately has cut back on deferring to the State, there are limits.

No matter *how* the IUCT decided the case, "awards against any respondent falling within the broad Article VII(3) definition of 'Iran' were to be paid with monies drawn from the Security Account," which is "a fund established under the Algiers Accords with released assets of the Government of Iran."[72] Nonetheless the IUCT "was careful in the

---

[66] 12 I.U.C.T.R. 335 (1986).
[67] *Id.*, at 357 (emphasis added).
[68] 12 I.U.C.T.R. 146 (1986-II).
[69] *Id.*, at 156.
[70] 15 I.U.C.T.R. 23 (1987-II).
[71] *Id.*, at 34-35.
[72] D. D. Caron, "The Basis of Responsibility," *supra*, at 118.

disposition to specify *which* respondent was liable, a specification forcing the Tribunal to distinguish between a holding that the government of Iran was liable on the merits of a public international law claim" *versus* "Iran's responsibility to satisfy . . . an award in favour of a private municipal law claim against an Iranian-controlled private corporation."[73]

However, we still must grapple with the issue of "state responsibility." This "state responsibility" label, as it were, is not just semantics, and there are some important deductions to be made here. Although the IUCT has never come out and said this expressly (to the extent I am aware), I believe the arrows point to the fact that the IUCT has been trying hard to create persuasive case-law outside its own relatively narrow context.[74]

Consider three pieces of evidence. First, after all the IUCT had realized its own powers of persuasion when, in 1982, it adopted the UNCITRAL Arbitration Rules ("with certain amendments") and soon thereafter other international bodies followed suit.[75] The IUCT "has applied [the Rules] since then in hundreds of published orders, decisions and awards, has contributed greatly to their wide acceptance."[76] Third, on the compensation

---

[73] *Id.* (emphasis added). But in *Flexi-Van*, *supra,* at 352, the IUCT held that "the Government of Iran is not automatically liable for contractual obligations belonging to a company which is considered to be controlled by it within the meaning of Article VII, paragraph 3, of the [CSD]."

[74] But see C. N. Brower & J. D. Brueschke, THE IUCT, *supra*, at 644.

[75] Charles N. Brower, Charles H. Brower, II, and Jeremy K. Sharpe, *The Coming Crisis in the Global Adjudication System*, Center for American and International Law, *available at* <www.cailaw.org/ita/workshop02_brower.pdf>, pp. 2-3. Around 1985, the U.N. General Assembly developed the UNCITRAL Model Law, promoting consistency among States' arbitration laws by encouraging reform and modernization in ways that are consistent and workable with the Model Law. Important arbitral venues such as France, England, Switzerland and The Netherlands revamped their arbitration codes. *Id.*, at 4; Model Law on International Commercial Arbitration, United Nations Commission on International Trade Law, U.N. GAOR, 40th Sess., Supp. No. 17, at 81-93, U.N. Doc. A/40/17 (1985), reprinted in 24 I.L.M. 1302 [hereinafter UNCITRAL Model Law]; see also G.A. Res. 40/72, U.N. GAOR 40th Sess., Supp. No. 53, at 308, U.N. Doc. A/40/72 ("[r]ecommend[ing] that all States give due consideration to the Model Law on International Commercial Arbitration, in view of the desirability of uniformity of law of arbitral procedures and the specific needs of international arbitration practice."); see also D. Krishan, "Thinking about BITs and BIT Arbitration: The Legitimacy Crisis that Never Was" 111 *in* NEW DIRECTIONS IN INTERNATIONAL ECONOMIC LAW: IN MEMORIAM THOMAS WÄLDE (Todd Weiler & Freya Baetens, eds.) (Martinus Nijhoff Publishers, 2011).

[76] *Id.* (For their part, "[t]he UNCITRAL Arbitration Rules in turn have prompted,

front, the IUCT breathed new life into the ICJ's *Chorzow Factory Case* when it observed that decision's utility—despite the fact that the Chorzow Factory case "is nearly sixty years old, this judgment is widely regarded as the most authoritative exposé of the principles applicable in this field and is still valid to day."[77] Third, to be sure, preserving a historical record might be part of the answer but it cannot be the whole answer, or it would be a very tedious exercise indeed on the part of the IUCT.

A more persuasive answer might be the IUCT's insistence on avoiding any further diplomatic crises by justifying every trace of attribution that is determined. This would help vindicate the Tribunal's own existence. But this answer, in tandem with the historical-record justification, too falls short of being absolutely and thoroughly convincing.

The complete answer lies in legitimacy, *along with* resolution of the immediate concern and serving as a prophylactic against the creation of greater problems here and elsewhere. Even if the Tribunal's intent was not to seek legitimacy through these means,[78] surely this was an inevitable consequence. International tribunals must know that their *sui generis* status and other institutional limitations might limit its influence in the larger world of expropriation jurisprudence. By delineating what is *lex specialis* and what is *lex generalis*, the diplomatic courts have given other institutions a roadmap to follow its cases.

To follow up with the case-law and consistency analysis in Chapter II (Chapter § 2.5 - INSTITUTIONS AS PRISMS), Jutta Brunnée and Stephen Toope argue that "the compliance pull of the treaty norms" are "stronger if the relevant norms meet the requirements of interactional law—congruence with shared understandings, adherence to criteria of legality, and enmeshment of norms in a practice of legality."[79] As Chapter I (INTRODUCTION) articulated, there are reasons to think each prototype has

and in some cases strongly influenced, the development of other sets of rules.").

[77] *Amoco Inter'l Fin. Corp. v. Iran*, Partial Award, Iran-U.S. Cl. Trib., No. 310-56-3 (14 July 1987).

[78] Since the Tribunal consists of multi-member panels, it would be difficult, though not impossible, to show that there was a definitive institutional ethos attending this justification. Even explicit institutional commands contained in the founding text(s) may be deviated from, so there is no guarantee *per se*.

[79] J. Brunnée & S. Toope, LEGITIMACY AND LEGALITY IN INTERNATIONAL LAW: AN INTERACTIONAL ACCOUNT 100-01 (Cambridge University Press, 2010) [J. Brunnée & S. Toope, LEGITIMACY]; see also C. J. Borgen, *Transnational Tribunals and the Transmission of Norms: The Hegemony of Process*, 39 GEO. WASH. INT'L L. REV. 685 (2007).

its own means and opportunities of perpetuating its own unique innovations as well as international law's general norms.

Legitimacy is earned not just by following other international institutions but by engaging in a genuine conversation whereby they also follow you—in short, by being exemplary.[80] Indeed, irrespective of whether precedent is formally "binding" on any tribunal, persuasiveness is a decision's greatest security and logical impotency its greatest threat.[81] It must be remembered that the best, most effective speakers are excellent listeners because they simply must be. It is a necessary predicate. You cannot speak effectively unless you address what your listener needs resolved, and *vice versa*. Often the post-treaty interactions within the signatories and beyond "will . . . lead parties" or the corresponding tribunal(s) "to clarify or refine the terms of the treaty."[82] Indeed, such a phenomenon of gaining compliance "feed[s] back into law-making activities, by reasserting the original norm, by shifting, or even abandoning it."[83] This cycle sometimes occurs just subconsciously within the tribunal-politician-civil society-investor quadrangular complex.

Brunnée and Toope insist, first, that just because law-making or treaty interpretation is "institutionalized" does not alone make it "interactional" and, second, that *both* institutionalisation and an interactional character are necessary (one cannot be dispensed with just because the other is amply available).[84]

Mark Weidemaier ties consistency in case-law with legitimacy. He then argues that "reasoned decisions," above all other factors, serve this function. In Weidemaier's view, these elements "facilitate[e] private ordering, guiding future lawmaking efforts, and providing some assurance that the dispute resolution system meets externally imposed standards of

---

[80] R. Wolfrum & V. Röben, LEGITIMACY IN INTERNATIONAL LAW 19-24 (Springer, 2008) (presenting some reasons for the legitimacy deficit in international law and where and how to fill in the gaps).

[81] More than a quarter century ago, the great jurist Alexander Bickel felicitously stated that "the future will not be ruled; it can only possibly be persuaded." See A. Bickel, THE LEAST DANGEROUS BRANCH 98 (Yale University Press, 1986). This is not to deny or even to gloss over the reality that premises and facts that constitute the foundation of most difficult and topical legal questions do change over time. Hence, "the future" typically does not inculpate or exculpate the earlier decision based on whether those premises have held up over time. Rather, the test tends to be whether the key assumptions made were sensible, logical and faithful to the facts present at the time the decision was rendered.

[82] J. Brunnée & S. Toope, LEGITIMACY, *supra*, at 101.

[83] *Id.*

[84] *Id.*, at 101-02.

legitimacy."[85] This is a manifestation of the Brunnée-Toope interactional model's "congruence with shared understandings" criterion at work.[86] Weidemaier too suggests that legitimacy plays a particular role in party-financed dispute resolution systems since "the arbitrator must produce an award that is enforceable; the parties are hardly likely to appreciate financing a dispute resolution process that does not, in fact, resolve their dispute."[87]

The IUCT's procedural practices have blunted the impression that the IUCT is somehow a kangaroo court that is in vogue only because it is the latest exciting development. Investment arbitrators have taken up the IUCT's invitation. Human rights courts, as this Chapter has already noted, may follow suit as the jurisprudences converge. Another subtle factor is that the IUCT was in full force when the IIA tribunals were just coming to their own; given the personnel overlap (judges, arbitrators, and commentators), it could not have escaped the IUCT that it needed to avoid being plagued by the legitimacy problems that had haunted or were then haunting the IIA tribunals.[88]

---

[85] W.M.C. Weidemaier, *Toward a Theory of Precedent in Arbitration*, 51 WM. & MARY L. REV. 1895, 1917 (2010) [W.M.C. Weidemaier, *Precedent in Arbitration*]; T. E. Carbonneau, *Rendering Arbitral Awards with Reasons: the Elaboration of a Common Law of International Transactions*, 23 COLUM. J. TRANSNAT'L L. 579, 605 (1985); J. Coe, *Transparency in the Resolution of Investor-State Disputes — Adaptation, Adoption, and NAFTA Leadership*, 54 U. KAN. L. REV. 1339, 1356 (2006); A. von Staden, *Deference or No Deference, That is the Question: Legitimacy and Standards of Review in Investor-State Arbitration*, IISD, July 19, 2012, *available at* <www.iisd.org/itn/2012/07/19/deference-or-no-deference-that-is-the-question-legitimacy-and-standards-of-review-in-investor-state-arbitration/#_ftn2> ("Carefully designed and justified standards of review enable arbitral tribunals to recognize this embeddedness and the legitimacy of the interpretation and application of investment treaty provisions by respondent states in line with the pursuit of their regulatory objectives.").

[86] J. Brunnée & S. Toope, LEGITIMACY, *supra*, at 101.

[87] W.M.C. Weidemaier, *Precedent in Arbitration*, *supra*, at 1917-18.

[88] G. Bottini, *Should Arbitrators Live on Mars? Challenge of Arbitrators in Investment Arbitration*, 32 SUFFOLK TRANSNAT'L L. REV. 341, 341 (2009) ("Legitimacy of investment arbitration is becoming one of the main concerns of all the institutions and persons involved in the process."); W.W. Burke-White & A. von Staden, *Investment Protection in Extraordinary Times: The Interpretation and Application of Non-Precluded Measures Provisions in Bilateral Investment Treaties*, 48 VA. J. INT'L L. 307, 373 (2008) (asserting that international arbitration's legitimacy could be raised by a "margin of appreciation" in courts); D. D. Caron, *Investor-State Arbitration: Strategic and Tactical Perspectives on Legitimacy*, 32 SUFFOLK TRANSNAT'L L. REV. 513, 514–15 (2009) [D. D. Caron,

The Gibson-Drahozal study (published in the year 2007) uses citation analysis and more qualitative metrics to survey the IUCT's impact on 118 submissions in 16 NAFTA cases and other ICSID awards[89]: 29 IUCT decisions have been cited with some frequency and mainly for non-discrimination and other substantive reasons, *not* jurisdictional reasons. One might have grave reservations about citation analysis for its own sake as an accurate metric[90] but the Gibson-Drahozal study does justify its citations (and several *non*-citations) by constructively analysing the IUCT awards.

In fact, "the four most cited awards (*Amoco International Finance v. Iran* (1987),[91] *Phillips Petroleum v. Iran* (1989),[92] *Starrett Housing v. Iran* (1983), [93] and *Tippets, Abbett, McCarthy, Stratton v. TAMS-AFFA Consulting Engineers of Iran* (1984)[94]) all deal with issues of when expropriation occurs and the standard of compensation in the event of expropriation, issues that are central to many investor-state arbitrations."[95] Only 9 out of 43 ICSID awards, or just above twenty percent, cited the IUCT for jurisdictional purposes.[96] The holdings of these cases will become clearer in the coming chapters.

Investor-State Arbitration] (noting that procedural and substantive legitimacy are important); M. Waibel, *Opening Pandora's Box: Sovereign Bonds in International Arbitration*, 101 A.J.I.L. 711, 723 (2007) ("Legitimacy of ICSID arbitral awards depends on respecting this adjudicatory mission . . . ."); J. Kalb, *Creating an ICSID Appellate Body*, 10 UCLA J. INT'L L. & FOREIGN AFF. 179, 202 (2005) (arguing that reasoning *and* result inform a tribunal's legitimacy).

[89] C. Gibson & C. Drahozal, *IUCT's Influence on Investor-State Arbitration, supra,* at 540 (this list includes "twenty memorials on jurisdiction only and thirty-four memorials on the merits, as well as replies, rejoinders, supplemental briefs, and post-hearing submissions by the parties").

[90] First, not all citations are created equal and attributing the same weight to one citation over another is to ignore the values of varying authors, tribunals, quality of the scholarship, and the significances of the issue being at the heart of the specific citations (although it is true that the very fact that judicial opinions across the board are *authoritative* suffices to make them "important"). Second, some consider it a tragic fallacy of our epoch that there is an administrative impetus to quantify all things (worse perhaps, in these critics' eyes, that there is an effort to work almost exclusively off some *faux*-omniscient list).

[91] 15 I.U.C.T.R. 179 (1987).

[92] 15 I.U.C.T.R. 179 (1989).

[93] 4 I.U.C.T.R. 122 (1983).

[94] 6 I.U.C.T.R. 219 (1984).

[95] C. Gibson & C. Drahozal, *supra*, at 540.

[96] *Id.*, at 541.

Citing another judicial institution, however famed, is pointless unless the citer actually engages with what the other institution has contended. The parties have that first-mover-advantage in their submissions and memorials, thus setting the tone for the tribunals to react. Here too Gibson and Drahozal observe that "citation to [IUCT and other diplomatic court] precedent was much more common in submissions on the *merits* than in submissions limited to *jurisdiction*."[97] It might not be a coincidence that the most frequently cited IUCT precedent in the investment arbitration submissions matched up with those tucked inside decisions.[98] Moreover, the trend-lines show no significant drop in the IUCT's precedential value in IIA submissions or awards.[99] The IUCT classification of case types is provided below:[100]

---

[97] *Id.* (emphases added).

[98] *Id.*, at 543 (the most frequently cited Tribunal awards in the NAFTA submissions were *Phillips Petroleum and Starrett Housing,* followed by *Tippets, Amoco Inter-national Finance, Phelps Dodge,* and *Sola Tiles.*)

[99] *Id.*, at 541 ("First, the number of ICSID awards citing Tribunal precedent has increased over time, with 10 ICSID awards citing Tribunal precedent from 2002 to 2006, and only 4 from 1997 to 2001. Secondly, a large part of that increase certainly is due to the increasing number of ICSID awards, as illustrated by a comparable increase in recent years in the number of ICSID awards that do not cite Tribunal precedent. Thirdly, based on this limited data, there does not appear to have been a significant depreciation of Tribunal precedent or a substantial displacement of Tribunal precedent by citations to ICSID awards . . . .").

[100] This chart is modified and adopted from D. Caron, "The Iran-U.S. Claims Tribunal and Investment Arbitration: Understanding the Claims Settlement Declaration as a Retrospective BIT" (Chapter 10) in THE IRAN-U.S. CLAIMS TRIBUNAL AT 25 380 (C. Gibson & C. Drahozal, eds.) (2007).

Table I: IUCT Case Types

Type of Claim	*Respondent*	*Applicable Law*	*Outcome*
Claims of nationals based on public international law	The State (the Islamic Republic of Iran or the United States)	Governing rules of public international law, in conformity with Art. V	The State is named in the *dispositif* as the responsible, or not responsible, party
Claims of nationals based on domestic private law	Entities within Art. VII(3) CSD: "Government ..., any political subdivision ..., and any agency, instrumentality, or entity controlled by the Government"	Relevant rules of general or municipal private law, as found under Art. V	The Art. VII (3) respondent is named in the *dispositif* as the responsible, or not responsible, party

§ 3.3—Attribution Rationales

Three main rationales are used to justify attribution. First, the rules involve a search for a close enough relationship of the act *to* the State: "the search for agency," namely "who can be said to be in control of the actor, who provided the actor authority, or can the actor be said to be acting on behalf of the State." [101] The IUCT's jurisprudence is constantly trying to pinpoint *de jure* and *de facto* agency.

The second and third rationales have to do with actors' *de facto* exercising state power (with or without authorisation, even when no principal-agent relationship exists) and continuity of responsibility when the insurrectional movement *becomes* the new power of the state, respectively.

Then this Chapter considers the *encouragement* of control, *i.e.*, not necessarily who controlled but rather who goaded, encouraged, or tolerated (when stopping was within reasonable reach of the State) control of some third party. Finally, the Chapter investigates certain situations where the rules of attribution support the continuity of responsibility: "(1) the attribution to one government of the acts of the previous government, even if the change in government came about through revolution; and (2)

[101] See D. D. Caron, "The Basis of Responsibility," *supra*, at 128.

the attribution to the State of the acts of the government of that State made during its earlier existence as an insurrectional movement."[102]

After this, the Chapter examines the difficulty of applying "agency" to loosely-defined entities such as insurrectional movements. Then the Chapter considers the attribution to the State of the acts of an entity—everything from a quasi-public organisation to a commercial corporation —which the government owns, controls, *or* for which it appoints the manager.[103]

The attribution questions might be easier to resolve if there were some consensus as to whether damage and/or profiting by the state is a requisite for there to be state responsibility.[104] That would at least make evidence of the expropriation, if any, traceable to the actor and help preclude claims where the claimant can show no damage. NAFTA specifically and investment arbitration generally so require but the answer is far from obvious in the ECtHR and the IUCT. The NAFTA tribunal in *Merrill & Ring Forestry, L.P. v. Canada* (2010)[105] expanded:

> [T]he primary obligation is quite clearly inseparable from the existence of damage. Indeed, a finding of liability without a finding of damage would be difficult to explain in the context of investment law arbitration and would indeed be contrary to some of its fundamental tenets.

For the ECtHR, *J.A. Pye (Oxford) Ltd v. United Kingdom* (2005)[106] is illustrative as an outlier. Whereas other ECtHR decisions hint at or expressly state that the state must, in some form, be the beneficiary, *Pye* (in its original incarnation at the Fourth Section of the ECtHR) does not. The Fourth Section in *Pye* declared incompatible with Article 1 the English law of adverse possession dating back to the twelfth century.[107] Then, upon an appeal by the United Kingdom, the Grand Chamber

---

[102] *Id.*, at 129.

[103] The word "or" here is used to indicate the possibility (perhaps true in some cases) that the government has targeted some companies or entities for forced puppeteering. Sometimes this is motivated by the fact that the company is in a much-needed sector, such as banks or construction, or to inflict political reprisals against opponents or dissidents.

[104] J. Crawford, THE INTERNATIONAL LAW COMMISSION'S ARTICLES ON STATE RESPONSIBILITY 84 (2002).

[105] UNCITRAL, ICSID Administered Case (NAFTA) (2010), at ¶ 245.

[106] App. no. 44302/02, ECHR-IV (2005).

[107] W.F. Walsh, A TREATISE ON THE LAW OF REAL PROPERTY 642 (Baker, Voorhis & Co., 1915); see also M. J. Dixon, MODERN LAND LAW 428 (Taylor & Francis, 2011).

reconsidered and reversed by a 10-7 vote on the rationale that the loss of land was "the result of the operation of the generally applicable rules on limitation periods for actions for recovery of land."[108] Under these rules, "at the end of the limitation period, the paper owner's title to unregistered land was extinguished."[109] Finally the ECtHR labelled this expropriation a "control of use" as opposed to "deprivation of possessions" under Article 1 of Protocol I.[110]

Law of adverse possession takes from *A* and gives to *B*. The doctrine does not imply that the State or any of its actors profited from the taking. Moreover, *A's* reliance interests are not disturbed because adverse possession has been law for almost a millennium (and the particular statute in *Pye* had been law from before the claimant even owned the property). Proving that *B* (the beneficiary) is an "actor" or "parastatal" of the state is, of course, a different matter.

Not even these facts were enough to stop the ECtHR from finding an Article I property rights violation; nor did the Court justify this outlier. The initial effect of *Pye* in the ECtHR's Fourth Section, until it was reversed by the Grand Chamber, was to throw into legal doubt the "ancient legal device" of cognovit, and so on.[111] This phenomenon, for instance,

---

[108] *J.A. Pye (Oxford) Ltd and J.A. Pye (Oxford) Land Ltd v. the United Kingdom*, Application no. 44302/02, at ¶ 65 (Grand Chamber) (2007) (distinguishing away cases involving "legislative provision[s] which permitted the State to transfer ownership in particular circumstances" or "social polic[ies] of transfer of ownership"). See also *AGOSI v. the United Kingdom*, 24 October 1986, § 52, Series A no. 108; *Air Canada v. the United Kingdom*, 5 May 1995, § 34, Series A no. 316-A; *Gasus Dosier- und Fördertechnik GmbH v. the Netherlands*, 23 February 1995, Series A no. 306-B.

[109] *Id.*

[110] *Id.*, at ¶ 66 (stating as justification for this classification that "[t]he statutory provisions which resulted in the applicant companies' loss of beneficial ownership were thus not intended to deprive paper owners of their ownership, but rather to regulate questions of title in a system in which, historically, twelve years' adverse possession was sufficient to extinguish the former owner's right to re-enter or to recover possession, and the new title depended on the principle that unchallenged lengthy possession gave a title. The provisions of the 1925 and 1980 Acts which were applied to the applicant companies were part of the general land law, and were concerned to regulate, amongst other things, limitation periods in the context of the use and ownership of land as between individuals.").

[111] *D. H. Overmyer Co. v. Frick Co.*, 405 U.S. 174 (1972) ("The cognovit is the ancient legal device by which the debtor consents in advance to the holder's obtaining a judgment without notice or hearing, and possibly even with the appearance, on the debtor's behalf, of an attorney designated by the holder. It was

did not readily conform to the legitimacy criteria of the Brunee-Toope "interactional model," for it is presumptively inconsistent with the "adherence to criteria of legality" requirement.[112]

Let us now examine state responsibility rationales carrying significant transfers of knowledge.

Rationale One: Agency

This is about searching for agency—a connection "between the actor and the State whereby the actor may be said to have acted for or at the direction of the State."[113] Two ways of establishing such a connection: "(1) by presumption of a link in certain defined cases, or (2) by . . . establish[ing] a link by proving a principal-agency relationship." [114] Showing agency (of *de jure* or *de facto* organs) is the only way that automatic, total and unqualified state responsibility is established, as per the ICJ.[115]

Before addressing the agency question, we should note that the assumptions for IIA are somewhat different from those applicable to the international human rights and diplomatic courts. The textual differences, in part, and prudential considerations, at least in equal part, inform each institution's expropriation jurisprudence. Some of the latter considerations are: (*i*) operating successfully within the textual proviso; (*ii*) earning compliance from signatories as well as actors outside; and (*iii*) maintaining the balance between principle and flexibility by adapting, discerningly, to new circumstances and challenges. This Chapter and the next two Chapters will substantiate how the tribunals have tried to do so, have

---

known at least as far back as Blackstone's time. 3 W. Blackstone, *Commentaries* *397. In a case applying Ohio law, it was said that the purpose of the cognovit is 'to permit the note holder to obtain judgment without a trial of possible defenses which the signers of the notes might assert.' *Hadden v. Rumsey Products, Inc.*, 196 F.2d 92, 96 (CA2 1952). And long ago the cognovit method was described by the Chief Justice of New Jersey as 'the loosest way of binding a man's property that ever was devised in any civilized country.' *Alderman v. Diament*, 7 N.J.L. 197, 198 (1824). Mr. Dickens noted it with obvious disfavor. *Pickwick Papers*, c. 47. The cognovit has been the subject of comment, much of it critical.") (internal footnotes omitted).

[112] J. Brunnée & S. Toope, LEGITIMACY, *supra*, at 100-03.

[113] D. D. Caron, "The Basis of Responsibility," *supra*, at 129.

[114] *Id.*

[115] *Application of the Convention on the Prevention and Punishment of the Crime of Genocide (Bosnia and Herzegovina v. Serbia and Montenegro)*, Judgment of 26 Feb. 2007, at ¶ 392.

failed, and what they can learn from as well as teach each other and emerging international law regimes.

Certainly, the IUCT was created from catastrophe, which includes *force majeure* and revolutionary conflict. Both the international human rights system and the IIA network are capable of resolving *force majeure* disputes. But the ECtHR, as a human rights court, has shown greater sensitivity to human rights exigencies whereas the NAFTA regime, like the rest of the IIA network, is just not intended at vindicating non-corporate, individual rights concerns. I should mention, however, that § 3.5 in this Chapter explains that IIA tribunals might be called upon to decide exigency cases involving essential human needs (both positive and negative), such as food,[116] water,[117] air[118] and other environmental concerns.

IIAs typically make no such assumptions about the alleged violation, which typically is a foregone conclusion accepted by the IUCT. This author has uncovered no evidence that this was a conscious decision on the NAFTA authors' part; it might have just been the result of oversight. This strengthens the argument that there is a need for knowledge transfer on this point, thus contributing to the central thesis of this book. Only in rare cases, where the IUCT acknowledges a violation, will that Tribunal actually reject that there was the intent to violate property rights. NAFTA, by contrast, has an elaborate and complex process to glean the perpetrators' "intent."[119] Due to the precarious position of IIA's generally and their dependence on consent, the intent of the signatories is paramount.[120] This is further discussed in Chapter VI (OTHER SUBSTANTIVE STANDARDS).

---

116 Report of Jean Ziegler, Special Rapporteur on the right to food to the Commission on Human Rights, U.N. General Assembly, A/HRC/7/5 (2008).

117 See generally J. Salzman, DRINKING WATER: A HISTORY (The Overlook Press, 2012).

118 See generally J. C. Juergensmeyer, *Control of Air Pollution Through the Assertion of Private Rights*, 34 DUKE L.J. 1126 (1967); B. M. Kramer, *Transboundary Air Pollution and the Clean Air Act: An Historical Perspective*, 32 U. KAN. L. REV. 181 (1983).

119 L. Anenson, *Defining State Responsibility under NAFTA Chapter Eleven: Measures "Relating to" Foreign Investors*, 45 VA. J. INT'L L. 675, 708 (2005) [L. Anenson, *State Responsibility under NAFTA Chapter Eleven*].

120 See, *e.g.*, *Tokios Tokelés v. Ukraine,* ICSID, Decision on Jurisdiction (2004), at ¶ 39 ("We emphasize here that Contracting Parties are free to define their consent to jurisdiction in terms that are broad or narrow; they may employ a control-test or reserve the right to deny treaty protection to claimants who otherwise would have recourse under the BIT. Once that consent is defined, however, tribunals should give effect to it, unless doing so would allow the Convention to be used for

We return to the agency issue. The first test of agency is about figuring out whose acts are attributable and whose are not; the second focuses on the types of principal-agent relationships that might be attributable to the State if they work and effectuate an international wrong. There is some support in common law, as articulated and condensed by William Blackstone, for the proposition that expropriatory acts are *necessarily* "committed by the [sovereign]" with "the intervention of its officers, for whom, the law, in matters of right, entertains no respect or delicacy," therefore it makes no sense to draw these agency-based distinctions.[121] Distinctions without a difference, might be his point. Nonetheless there are varying degrees and kinds, questions of vicarious liability, and other specific issues which should be addressed.

(1) The De Jure Test: Acts are Attributable to the State because the State Itself Gives Authority to the Actor

The first step is to define "government" according to the municipal law of the State involved. The acts of certain actors are presumptively attributable to the State because the State by its own law has admitted to such a relationship. Thus acts of the various branches of the government as well as governmental ministries and agencies which carry out governmental functions are presumptively attributable to the State. It makes no difference whether the organ is legislative, executive, or judicial organs, or whether it is up in the chain of command or subordinate.[122]

---

purposes for which it clearly was not intended.").

[121] Whether Blackstone is behaving tactfully or these simply are his genuine views, he appears to rest the culpability on the shoulders of the agents and presents the sovereign as an unwitting perpetrator in the denial of property rights to its subjects and citizens. See W. Blackstone, *Commentaries on the Laws of England,* Vol. III. p. 255 ("but injuries to the rights of property can scarcely be committed by the Crown without the intervention of its officers, for whom, the law, in matters of right, entertains no respect or delicacy, but furnishes various methods of detecting the errors and misconduct of those agents by whom the King has been deceived and induced to do a temporary injustice."). As a mere pipsqueak, I am heartened that Chief Justice John Marshall interpreted Blackstone in the same way, see *Marbury v. Madison*, 5 U.S. 137, 165 (1803) (construing Blackstone to have suggested, in this context, that "personal injury from the King to a subject is presumed to be impossible . . .").

[122] See Report of the ILC to the General Assembly, U.N. Doc. Al9010/Rev. 1 (1973). Similarly, §207 of the Restatement provides that a state is responsible for the acts of

f the government of the state,

The IUCT always attributed to Iran the acts of its officials and ministries; it did not matter whether they were judicial, legislative, or executive. In this sense, the IUCT is in lock-step with NAFTA, the IACtHR and the ECtHR. In *Oil Fields of Texas v. Iran* (1986),[123] for example, the IUCT attributed the acts of the Iranian courts to the Islamic Republic. In particular, the IUCT found that "[t]he interference with the use of the three blow-out preventers as caused by the [blocking order of the] Court amounts to a taking," and thus presumably an act attributable to Iran.[124]

International human rights tribunals appear to take this doctrine rather seriously. Even in a politically-charged case such as *Loizidou v. Turkey* (1996),[125] where Turkey allegedly had raided, invaded and had taken over a Northern Cypriot woman's home, the ECtHR chose to get involved and to find an Article 1, Protocol I violation. *Either* judicial abstention from politics *or* some human rights issue was going to lose. Both could not win,[126] which is an issue familiar to international human rights tribunals dealing with collective expulsion cases.[127] Should prudential concerns stay

---

(b) the government or authorities of any political subdivision of the state, or
(c) any organ, agency, official, employee, or other agent of a government or of any political subdivision, acting within the scope of authority or under color of such authority.

123 12 I.U.C.T.R. 308 (1986-III).

124 *Id.*, at 319.

125 App. No. 40/1993/435/514.

126 At least part of the reason for the fact that in "the present state of international case law there seems to be no room for the political question doctrine" is that "[t]here is no clear separation of powers in international law." See F. Zarbiyev, *Judicial Activism in International Law—A Conceptual Framework for Analysis*, J. OF INTERNATIONAL DISPUTE SETTLEMENT (2012) 1, 14 [F. Zarbiyev, *Judicial Activism in International Law*] ("[The ICJ's] position can be roughly summarized as follows: to the extent that international law has something to say about a case, international judges can hear it whatever its political implications or sensitivity. Admittedly, international judges do have political sensitivity. As the ICJ's *Nuclear Weapon* and *Kosovo* opinions show, international judges may well be largely deferential when it comes to questions of 'high politics'. However, the point is that there is no elaborate doctrine capable of ensuring certain predictability about judicial behaviour and shaping the expectations of actors.").

127 *Hirsi Jamaa and Others v. Italy*, Application no. 27765/09, n. 50, ECHR-GC (2012) (Concurring opinion of Judge Pinto de Albuquerque) ("The due procedure provision of Article 4 of Protocol No. 4 is of much broader personal scope than the one provided for in Article 1 of Protocol No. 7, since the former includes all aliens regardless of their legal and factual status and the latter includes only aliens lawfully resident in the expelling State.") (citing *Matter of Haitians and*

a tribunal's hand from reaching these difficult issues? Where is the textual backing for such a doctrinal step? How specific does the textual backing need to be? How is a tribunal to know when it is encroaching on the political authorities and when it is just discharging its required function? The *Loizidou* decision, including its political ramifications, is not unlike a recent decision by the ACtHPR, so it is arguable that the consensus is being crystallised in this direction.[128]

In *Loizidou*, geographical barriers made little practical difference. On the attribution issue, the ECtHR found that state responsibility "could arise when it exercised effective control—lawful or not—in an area outside its national territory as a consequence of military action."[129] That the act was *ultra vires* domestic law is irrelevant to the existence of attribution.[130] Otherwise, committing clearly *ultra vires* acts might constitute a perverse

---

Dominicans of Haitian-origin in the Dominican Republic regarding Dominican Republic, order of 18/08/2000); *Konstantin Markin v. Russia*, Application no. 30078/06, n. 25, ECHR-GC (2012) ("[T]he Inter-American Court of Human Rights has affirmed the State's obligation to adopt the "the measures required for children's existence to develop under decent conditions") (citing *Case of Acevedo Buendía et al. ("Discharged and Retired Employees of the Office of the Comptroller") v. Peru*, Preliminary Objection, Merits, Reparations and Costs, Judgment of July 1, 2009, Series C No. 198; Advisory Opinion OC-17/02 of 28 August 2002, *Case of the "Five Pensioners" v. Peru*, Merits, Reparations and Costs, Judgment of February 28, 2003, Series C No. 98).

[128] See *Center for Minority Rights Development (Kenya) and Minority Rights Group International on behalf of the Endorois Welfare Council vs. Kenya*, African Court for Human and Peoples' Rights, Case No. 276/2003 (2010) (mandating the Government of Kenya to restore the Endorois sub-tribe to their ancestral lands and to compensate them for earlier dislocation and expropriation); V. Mosoti (Counsel, Environment and International Law Unit, Legal Vice Presidency, World Bank), *Endorois Welfare Council vs. Kenya*, Law, Justice and Development: World Bank (2010), *available at* <http://web.worldbank.org/WBSITE/EXTERNAL/TOPICS/EXTLAWJUSTICE/0,,contentMDK:22782014~pagePK:148956~piPK:149081~theSitePK:445634,00.html#2._> ("This decision is far-reaching for many reasons, among them, it is the first to determine who indigenous peoples in Africa are, and what their rights are. It is also the first by an international tribunal to find a violation of the right to development.").

[129] *Loizidou, supra*, at 14.

[130] Article 46 (1) of the Vienna Convention on the Law of Treaties states: "A State may not invoke the fact that its consent to be bound by a treaty has been expressed in violation of a provision of its internal law regarding competence to conclude treaties as invalidating its consent unless that violation was manifest and concerned a rule of its internal law of fundamental importance."

incentive for some culprit agency, instrumentality or other actor working for the State (and thus the State itself) to escape liability.

Loizidou held it was relevant to the attribution inquiry that the governmental organ, while engaged in some official act, violated international law. That the government *also* violated domestic law was just another on the list.[131] Otherwise States could hide behind the fact (as a "defence") that domestic legislation or directives already had banned the wrong; and vicarious liability would be precluded. The IIA tribunal in *GAMI v. Mexico* (2003)[132] concurred in this stance by citing Article 27 of the Vienna Convention on the Law of Treaties: "A party may not invoke the provisions of its own internal law as justification for its failure to perform a treaty."

The *GAMI* tribunal then referred to the *Selwyn Case* (1903),[133] involving a Great Britain-Venezuela arbitration, as rather a kind of hologram. The point was to state firmly that the IIA tribunal's jurisdiction to decide "whether there have been breaches of international law by any agency of [the] government" is distinct from a "determin[ation] whether the expropriation was legitimate under [domestic] law."[134] The two issues were separate and the position of the domestic courts on domestic law could not derecognise an international violation. The same is true for

[131] *Id.*, at 14-16.

[132] UNCITRAL, Final Award on the Merits (2004), at 17-18 (citing *The Betsy* arbitration between the U.S. and Great Britain: "the affirmance of an illegal condemnation, so far from legitimating the wrong done by the original seizure and precluding the neutral from seeking reparation for it . . ., is peculiarly that very act which consummates the wrong . . . ") (J.B. Moore, HISTORY AND DIGEST OF INTERNATIONAL ARBITRATIONS TO WHICH THE UNITED STATES HAS BEEN PARTY 3184 (1898)). The next Chapter will show that this secondary wrong by judicial failure has always been an important issue in exhaustion.

[133] 9 UNRIAA 380.

[134] UNCITRAL, Final Award on the Merits (2004), at 17-18 (citing *The Betsy* arbitration between the U.S. and Great Britain: "the affirmance of an illegal condemnation, so far from legitimating the wrong done by the original seizure and precluding the neutral from seeking reparation for it . . ., is peculiarly that very act which consummates the wrong . . . ") (J.B. Moore, HISTORY AND DIGEST OF INTERNATIONAL ARBITRATIONS TO WHICH THE UNITED STATES HAS BEEN PARTY 3184 (1898)). The next Chapter will show that this secondary wrong by judicial failure has always been an important issue in exhaustion.

States trying to "preclude an investor from seeking protection under the BIT on the ground that its own actions are illegal under its own laws."[135]

The next three chapters contain excerpts of, or cite, paeans to sovereignty, so an international violation does not necessarily mean a violation of domestic law. Nor should that matter. In Chapter § 3.5, the book addresses a relevant recent example coming from the pen of the august and erudite Judge Charles Brower, who surely belongs in the highest pantheon of the international law jurists of our age. *Selwyn* had articulated that

> [i]nternational arbitration is not affected jurisdictionally by the fact that the same question is in the courts of one of the nations. Such international tribunal has power to act reference thereto, and if judgment has been pronounced by such court, to disregard the same so far as it affects the indemnity to the individual, and has power to make an award in addition thereto in aid thereof as in the given case justice may require.
>
> Within the limits prescribed by the convention constituting the parties have created a tribunal superior to local courts.[136]

Who, then, were the attributable governmental organs? Let us start with the easiest categories. Organs whose acts were attributed to the State included, in the case of Iran, acts of the Ministry of Housing, the Ministry of Industries and Mines, and the Iranian National Industrial Organization.[137] The same is true for all government departments.

Federalism and Subsidiarity

The notion of co-sovereignty should not be misunderstood as that of *imperium in imperio* (a state within a state). On federalism, the IUCT easily decided what constituted a "political subdivision" of the State because the internal law of the State provided the necessary guidance;[138]

---

[135] *Kardassopoulos v. Georgia*, Decision on Jurisdiction, ICSID Case No. ARB/05/18 (2007), at ¶ 182 ("a host State cannot avoid jurisdiction under the BIT by invoking its own failure to comply with its domestic law").

[136] J. H. Ralston, VENEZUELAN ARBITRATIONS OF 1903 322, 327 (1904).

[137] *Cal-Maine Foods*, *supra*, at 58.

[138] See *Emanuel Too & Greater Modesto Insurance Associates v. United States*, 23 I.U.C.T.R. 378-384 (1989-III), ("[t]here is no dispute that the State of Arizona is a 'political subdivision' of the United States and therefore included in the term 'United States' as defined in Article VII, paragraph 4."); *Iowa State University of Science & Technology v. Iran*, 13 I.U.C.T.R. 271 (1986-IV); *State University of New York v. Iran*, 13 I.U.C.T.R. 277 (1986-IV).

the ECtHR[139] and NAFTA[140] respond similarly, and in the ECtHR and other human rights courts the "margin of appreciation" is justified in part because of varying conditions across jurisdictions. An important overlap with private law claims is that those jurisdictional decisions, especially where the IUCT has had to decide if a particular respondent was an Iranian "agency," can be helpful.[141]

Regarding NAFTA, there have been some *unsuccessful* domestic law claims that the trade agreement violates the rights of States and private entities protected by the United States and Canadian Constitutions.[142] That principle likely is transposable to other international compacts and certainly to those in which the United States is a signatory, a point that international lawyers engaged in cases over agreements to which the United States is a signatory might appreciate.

In a recent case now pending before the United States Supreme Court, the brief of the Yale Law School Center for Global Legal Challenges (YLSCGLC) observes, initially, that there are a series of structural, political and diplomatic[143] checks placed by the United States Constitution

---

[139] For ECtHR, see P. Mahoney, *Universality Versus Subsidiarity in the Strasbourg Case Law on Free Speech: Explaining Some Recent Judgments*, 1997 EUR. HUM. RTS. L.REV. 364 for the long list of cases, and see P. G. Carozza, *Subsidiarity as a Structural Principle of International Human Rights Law*, 97 AM. J. INT'L L. 38, 48 (2003).

[140] For NAFTA, see *Loewen Group v. United States*, ICSID Case No ARB(AF) /98/3, Final Award on the Merits (2003) (Mississippi's conduct, in the color of state law, renders the *United States* the respondent); *The Federalist* No. 51, p. 323 (C. Rossiter ed. 1961) (J. Madison).

[141] Some *de jure* agencies are recognised by IUCT cases: *Intrend Int'l v. Iran*, 3 I.U.C.T.R. 110 (1983-II) (air force); *Unidyne Corp. v. Iran*, 22 I.U.C.T.R. 138 (1993) (navy); *McCollough Inc. v. Iran*, 11 I.U.C.T.R. 3, 6 (1986-II) (the Ministry of Post, Telegraph & Telephone); and *State University of New York*, *supra* (the Ministry of Culture and Education).

[142] See, *e.g.*, *The Council of Canadians et al. v. Canada*, Reasons for Decision, Court File no. 01-CV-20841 (2005) (claiming a "breach of binding and fundamental constitutional principles including the rule of law, democracy, constitutionalism and federalism"); *Made in the USA v. United States*, 56 F. Supp. 2d 1226 (N. D. Ala. 1999), 242 F.3d 1300 (11th Cir.) (2001) (refusing to nullify NAFTA); see also J. Goldstein, LEGALIZATION AND WORLD POLITICS 156-57 (MIT Press, 2001); B. Ackerman & D. Golove, *Is NAFTA Constitutional?*, 108 HARV. L. REV. 799 (1995).

[143] One "diplomatic" implication in the YLSCGLC Brief is questionable and suspect: "It would be highly unlikely for a foreign state to enter into a treaty whose true purpose was to circumvent the limits imposed on the U.S. federal government's legislative power. Suggestions to the contrary lack any empirical

on the federal government's Treaty Power. After all, a constitutional exercise of this power requires only that the President sign the treaty and that two-thirds of the Senators present assent to it.[144] The House of Representatives[145] and the States[146] are excised from this equation completely.

---

support in centuries of treatymaking practice. See Mark Tushnet, *Federalism and International Human Rights in the New Constitutional Order*, 47 WAYNE L. REV. 841, 862 & n.99 (2001) ("Why would the negotiating partner simply do the U.S. treaty-maker a favor?")." See *Bond v. United States*, 12-158 (2012), Brief for Yale Law School Center for Global Legal Challenges, at 17 [*Bond v. United States* (2012), YLSCGLC Brief].

Let us explore the reasons. First of all, it is the "highly unlikely" cases that often tend to require judicial resolution. Second, the alleged "lack" of "empirical support in centuries of treatymaking practice" does not foreclose the possibility of this form of negotiation occurring in the future. The prospect is especially ripe because of many nations with diverse as well as complex economic and political situations entering into agreements with one another. Third, to answer Professors Tushnet, Meyer and Hathaway's (an impressive and daunting triumvirate) collective question: The "negotiating partner" might "do the U.S. treaty-maker . . . [*this*] favor" in order to (*i*) gain something else from the U.S. treaty-maker prospectively or to compensate the U.S. treaty-maker for something else; and (*ii*) use this particular instance (and the rights of States and/or citizens) as a chip. An appearance of *quid pro quo* gains traction when the President of the United States and the premier of another State engage in this sort of deal-making that has the effect of making irrelevant a treaty-ratification arm of their government.

Of course, the reader must remember that Professors Hathaway and Meyer were wearing their advocacy hats and not their academic hats when requesting the Supreme Court to deny this petition for certiorari. See *Bond v. United States* (2012), YLSCGLC Brief, at 26 ("*Counsel for Amicus Curiae*") (emphasis in original). As such, their strategy is understandable.

[144] U.S. Const., Art. II, § 2, Cl. 2.

[145] The assent of the House of Representatives is necessary for any federal legislation to be enacted and in appropriations cases the House must be the originator, as per the Constitution. Therefore, it would be ironic if in situations where a treaty might truncate *constitutional* rights the assent of the House is not deemed to be essential. See also *United States v. Lara*, 541 U.S. 193, 201 (2004) (explaining that although "[t]he treaty power does not literally authorize Congress to act legislatively, for it is an Article II power authorizing the President, not Congress, to make Treaties," "treaties made pursuant to that power can authorize Congress to deal with 'matters' with which otherwise 'Congress could not deal.") (internal citations omitted). Any valid understanding of "Congress" must include the House of Representatives.

[146] The assent of three-fourths of all States is required for a constitutional amendment to be ratified, after two-thirds of the House of Representatives and the

Mindful perhaps that a "We Know Best and the System *Should* Work Most of the Time Over the Long Haul" mentality[147] might not persuade the Supreme Court, the Oona Hathaway-Jeffrey Meyer brief finally admits that there are constitutionally-authorised "rights-protecting checks."[148] The most consequential of these checks is that the treaty at issue may not "alienate any great, essential right" of the individual or the State (which is after all a co-sovereign, along with the Government of United States).[149] What the treaty may do is address "matters of the sharpest exigency for the national well being that an act of Congress could not deal with but that a treaty followed by such an act could, and it is not lightly to be assumed that, in matters requiring national action, 'a power which must belong to and somewhere reside in every civilized government' is not to be found.'"[150]

There is support enough in the precedents of the Supreme Court to adjust the flexible doctrine to varying circumstances. I must add that, if such a case directly on the facts arises, I suspect that most savvy advocates today will take a step back from the remarkable proposition that the treaty power should be the "normative" part of the governmental powers apparatus, taking up various assignments not reasonably closely authorised by the Constitution but which "should" be had.[151] Be that as it may, the

---

Senate (Members present) already have passed the amendment. The President has no structural role in the constitutional amendment process.

[147] Certain observers might call this complete judicial abdication, not merely an exercise in judicial restraint.

[148] *Bond v. United States*, 12-158 (2012), Brief for Yale Law School Center for Global Legal Challenges, at 18 [*Bond v. United States* (2012), YLSCGLC Brief].

[149] *Id.* (citing 3 The Debates in the Several State Conventions, on the Adoption of the Federal Constitution, as Recommended by the General Convention at Philadelphia in 1787, at 514 (Jonathan Elliot ed., William S. Hein & Co., Inc. 2d ed. 1996) (1891)). The brief goes on to underpin Supreme Court precedents to its proposition: "'It would not be contended,' this Court wrote in 1890, that the treaty power "extends so far as to authorize what the constitution forbids." *De Geofroy v. Riggs*, 133 U.S. 258, 267 (1890). Treaties may not 'contravene any prohibitory words to be found in the Constitution.' *Missouri v. Holland*, 252 U.S. 416, 433 (1920). There is an important distinction between the violation of affirmative constitutional guarantees and the violation of "some invisible radiation from the general terms of the Tenth Amendment." Id. at 434. The former is firmly prohibited, while the latter does not constrain the treaty power, id. at 433-434, because "[t]o the extent that the United States can validly make treaties, the people and the States have delegated their power to the National Government and the Tenth Amendment is no barrier." *Reid v. Covert*, 354 U.S. 1, 18 (1957) (plurality opinion))."

[150] *Missouri v. Holland*, 252 U.S. 416, 433 (1920) (citation omitted).

[151] See *id.*

Supreme Court has obliquely referred to the comity principle in the law of nations as extending to "all proper subjects of negotiation between our government and the governments of other nations."[152] The YLSCGLC brief appeared to make good use of this proposition.[153] How the United States Supreme Court responds to the claim will likely unfold soon (but, sadly, not before this book goes to press).

Even Alexander Hamilton in *The Federalist Papers* recognised that in order to gain the confidence of foreign interests it was vital for the United States to speak in one voice on foreign policy questions, broadly speaking. Indeed, Hamilton had deemed this to be a crucial flaw in the erstwhile valid Articles of Confederation.[154] Although the United States Constitution ranks itself as co-equal with federal laws and treaties, it has been understood that since the Constitution is the fount of all textually authorised power, it supersedes all other instruments.[155]

"A Collectivity of Organs"

Judge Kashani's dissent in *Economy Forms Corp. v. Iran* (1984),[156] is a genuine *tour de force* but it is noteworthy for a specific doctrinal reason as well. On a question of "entit[ties] controlled by the Government of Iran" in private domestic law claims, he gave a strongly *de jure* definition of *agency*. He argued that the "Government of Iran" is "a collectivity of organs of the central government whose representative role for the political system of the Iranian nation is beyond doubt."[157] Judge Kashani further argued that "aside from the government . . . , another category of

---

[152] *De Geofroy v. Riggs*, 133 U.S. 258, 266 (1890).

[153] *Bond v. United States* (2012), YLSCGLC Brief, at 10.

[154] *The Federalist* No. 22, at 151 (Alexander Hamilton) (Clinton Rossiter ed., 1961) ("The treaties of the United States, under the present Constitution [of the Confederation], are liable to the infractions of thirteen different legislatures, and as many different courts of final jurisdiction, acting under the authority of those legislatures. The faith, the reputation, the peace of the whole Union, are thus continually at the mercy of the prejudices, the passions, and the interests of every member of which it is composed. Is it possible that foreign nations can either respect or confide in such a government? Is it possible that the people of America will longer consent to trust their honor, their happiness, their safety, on so precarious a foundation?").

[155] See, *e.g.*, *Marbury v. Madison*, 5 U.S. 137 (1803).

[156] *Economy Forms v. Iran*, 5 I.U.C.T.R. 1 (1984-I) (Kashani, J., dissenting).

[157] *Id.*, at 3.

juridical persons exists under public law which has been termed 'government agencies' pursuant to Iranian law."[158]

Other than government agencies and organs, there may be instrumentalities which, "although not *de jure* part of the government, are *de jure* empowered by the law of the host State to exercise" at least *some* elements of governmental authority.[159] The Tribunal's practice suggests that generally the acts of such entities are attributable when they exercise the power of the state.

Notice, for instance, that in *Hyatt International Corporation v. Iran* (1985),[160] the claimant alleged the expropriation by the Islamic Republic of Iran of claimant's hotel management contract rights. The *Hyatt International* expropriation, though, was conducted by the Bonyad Mostazafan ("Foundation for the Oppressed"). Iran argued in the IUCT that the Bonyad Mostazafan was a "non-government charity foundation" and thus neither a respondent nor an entity whose acts could be attributable to Iran. In an interlocutory award, the IUCT noted that so long as the group "plays an investigative or prosecutorial role in the discovery and seizure of properties eligible for confiscation," and may "call upon governmental agencies and institutions for aid in this pursuit," it is an *instrumentality*.[161]

Thus the instrumentality, unlike the agency, is not *de jure* a part of the government. Instead, it is an entity that is authorised to exercise governmental powers. The limits of the instrumentality category were obvious in *Schering Corporation v. Iran* (1984).[162] Here claimant alleged that Iran was responsible for the actions of the "Workers' Council" at Schering's Iranian subsidiary which had banned the payment of intercompany debts, and expropriated claimant's property. The Tribunal then had to inquire whether the acts of the Workers' Council were attributable to the Iranian government (the respondent named in the case).[163]

The Tribunal noted that Article 104 of the Constitution of the new Islamic Republic provided that Workers' Councils will be organized in a way that "safeguard[s] Islamic justice in the preparation of programs, and in the coordination of progress in the affairs of industrial and agricultural

158 *Id.*, at 3-4; 4-5.

159 Report of the ILC (1980), *supra*, at 31.

160 9 I.U.C.T.R 72 (1985-II).

161 *Id.*, at 88.

162 5 I.U.C.T.R. 361 (1984-I).

163 *Id.,* at 369.

production units."[164] Everybody agreed that the Councils were not *de jure* organs; there was no dispute at all on this point. The issue was whether the Workers' Councils were *de jure* authorized to exercise governmental authority. The IUCT concluded that Workers' Councils were not so authorised: they had no "duties [other] than basically representing the workers' interests vis-à-vis the management of companies and institutions and to cooperate with the management." [165]

That the group had been launched by the State did not make it a state instrumentality; otherwise countless private as well as quasi-public groups could be and perhaps would be deemed "governmental" for attribution purposes. Again the IUCT did not want to create any more diplomatic or internal tension and instead focus on rebuilding diplomatic relations, the first step was to sort out the expropriation-related questions.[166] Thus, the *de jure* test points to two basic groups of entities whose acts presumptively are considered acts of the state: entities which *de jure* are regarded as organs or agencies of the State, and entities which *de jure* are authorised to exercise governmental power.

(2) Purely Private Capacity and the De Facto Test (Acts are Attributable to the State Because the Actor, although not De Jure a Part of the State, in fact Acted on Behalf of the State)

When government actors act in a purely private capacity, that is not necessarily a principal-agent relationship. The ILC Commentary on Article 11 states the acts of persons, "who have the status of organs of the State, ... which relate to their private life and have no connection with the machinery of the State" are not attributable to the State.[167]

There is an employer *versus* sovereign distinction in international law (thus placing some public law claims into the private law domain). Similarly, then, must there also be a requirement that the perpetrators' acts were somehow connected to their official duties? Some connection has indeed been understood to be required: Every employer (and States as employers) probably has *some* actors prone to violating rights guaranteed

---

[164] *Id.*

[165] *Id.*, at 370 (footnote omitted); *Schering Co.*, *supra*, at 374 (Mosk, J., dissenting).

[166] M. Brunetti, *Iran-United States Claims Tribunal, NAFTA Chapter 11, and the Doctrine of Indirect Expropriation*, 2 CHI. J. INT'L L. 203, 205 (2001) [M. Brunetti, *IUCT-NAFTA-Indirect Expropriation*].

[167] Report of the ILC (1975), *supra*, at 70-71.

in the instrument, and it makes little sense to punish employers for the extraneous bad acts by those actors. Thus the presumption attributing to the State the acts of *de jure* government actors may be rebutted by showing that the officials' acts "relate to their private lives" and that "they do not have a [sufficiently relevant] connection with the machinery of the State."[168] This exception is part of the IUCT's jurisprudence, and is a doctrine worth adopting by our other institutions. Such a proposition carries additional weight since it comes from a *force majeure* court committed to protecting property rights.

In *Yeager v. Iran* (1987),[169] the IUCT found that Iran was responsible for the acts of an agent of Iran Air, a government-owned airline, who illegally required claimant to pay extra money for a plane ticket he had already purchased. In its reasoning, following the *de jure* test, the IUCT stated that "[a]ssuming government control over Iran Air," the conduct of an organ is attributable "even if in a particular case the organ exceeded its competence under internal law or contravened instructions concerning its activity."[170] Just because an act was *ultra vires* domestic law, or for that matter required by or consistent with domestic law, is not enough to make a violation non-attributable.[171]

The IUCT also recognised an exception to this presumption that other institutions should consider as well: a particular act will be not attributable if the organ was acting in a "purely private," rather than official, capacity "even if it has used the means placed at its disposal by the State for the exercise of its function."[172] The IUCT concluded that the agent acted in a purely private capacity because there was no indication that the Iran Air agent in *Yeager* "was acting for any other reason than personal profit, or that he had passed on the payment to Iran Air."[173]

Interesting, the IUCT seems to require that the claimant, not the respondent, establish that the act was not one of a purely private capacity. That is where the burden of proof rests. The Tribunal then noted that "[s]uch conduct by a private individual might be attributable to Iran, if

---

[168] D. D. Caron, "The Basis of Responsibility," *supra*, at 136.

[169] 17 I.U.C.T.R. 92 (1987-IV).

[170] *Id.*, at 110-11.

[171] Among other sources, see Articles 26 ("Every treaty in force is binding upon the parties to it and must be performed by them in good faith") and 27 ("A party may not invoke the provisions of its internal law as justification for its failure to perform a treaty") of the Vienna Convention on the Law of Treaties (VCLT) (1969).

[172] *Yeager, supra*, at 110-11.

[173] *Id.*

expressly or tacitly approved by Iran Air, or if Iran Air negligently failed to exercise appropriate control over its employees."[174] The IUCT's evidentiary burden on the claimant expanded the private capacity exception to the *de jure* presumption.

Now notice what this exception means (by contraposing it): had the IUCT accepted attribution because the state could not control the extraneous acts of these *de jure* or *de facto* actors: that would impose an overly demanding positive obligations requirement. It would require the State to keep tabs on the whereabouts of its actors in their entirely private capacity, *viz.* where they go, what they do in their leisure, whom they meet, etc.

Not only would this be expensive for the State, it might cause ruthless vetting of all candidates and thus invade the privacy of its actors—many of them innocent. Importantly, this determination might deter effective government work by discouraging conscientious and benign candidates from applying. Such economically inefficient remedies forced on the State will result in a dead-weight loss.[175]

The cost might be institutional legitimacy for international tribunal decisions that are theoretically helpful to some claimants but economically harmful to many innocent citizens (without giving them any future deterrence-related benefit). In some cases of principal-agent relationship, though, the IUCT *does* require positive obligations. This Chapter will address that point soon.

Now we address the creation of the IUCT and developments after the Shah's 1979 dethronement. Outside the *de jure* actor test, the principal-agent relationship must be established on a case-by-case, *de facto* basis. The revolutionary institutions that arose after the revolution in parallel to the official institutions squarely posed issues of *de facto* agency for the IUCT.

In 1979, *two* revolutions took place in Iran: the Shah was ousted in February; and the social and economic revolution in November (symbolised by the U.S. Embassy occupation). Between February and November, there was some apparent calm, "as the revolution seemed to pause to consider

---

[174] *Id.*

[175] W. M. Landes & R. Posner, *Trademark Law: An Economic Perspective*, 30 J.L. & ECON. 265, 268-70 (1987); R. Bork, THE ANTITRUST PARADOX: A POLICY AT WAR WITH ITSELF 107 (Basic Books, 1978); G. Calabresi & A. D. Melamed, *Property Rules, Liability Rules, and Inalienability: One View of the Cathedral*, 85 HARV. L. REV. 1089 (1972).

its direction since its initial objective, the downfall of the Shah, had been achieved."[176]

During this interregnum, some U.S. and other Western corporations even *returned* to Iran or reinvested money, time and other capital in Iran. On the ground, regional and ethnic groups "such as the Kurds sought greater autonomy, while the communists, moderate constitutionalists, and mullahs sought to establish their quite different political visions of Iran."[177]

This flurry of activities created two *parallel* systems of government.[178] The *de jure* government, led by Prime Minister Bazagan, consisted of the *Majlis* (legislature), the military and the courts. Around the same time, "an unofficial revolutionary system of government emerged in Iran, organizationally originating from the mosque and led by mullahs, but also populated by many socialists and communists."[179] Thus there was a time in 1979, between the toppling of the Shah and the new Islamic Republic of Iran, "when a number of groups that were not *de jure* a part of the state exercised elements of governmental authority."[180]

These actors could no longer be called "revolutionaries" because the revolution was now over. Some of them were in the government and many surviving ex-revolutionaries had profited from the revolution.[181] But so had many others (including completely private actors) and often indirectly and without knowledge.[182] Is profit enough to constitute attribution? Expropriations (and sometimes vandalism) conducted by the unofficial parallel (and sometimes paramilitary) government presented the IUCT with some difficult attribution questions.

The IUCT's cases on this point began with *Pereira v. Iran* (1984).[183] *Perreira* had to do with "actions of an element of the parallel government, the Revolutionary Guards, substantially after they were *de jure* recognized

---

[176] *Yeager, supra*, at 110-11.

[177] *Id.*, at 139.

[178] E. Abrahamian, IRAN BETWEEN TWO REVOLUTIONS 527 (Princeton University Press, 1982).

[179] *Yeager, supra*, at 139.

[180] *Id.* Judge Holtzmann's dissent in *Sea-Land v. Iran*, 6 I.U.C.T.R. 175, 201 (1984-II), observed: "[t]he contents of the subsequently adopted Constitution of the Islamic Republic of Iran demonstrate that the installation of the Islamic Republic did not result in the displacement of the revolutionary forces, but only in the ratification and institutionalization of their roles."

[181] D. Jones, *Iran-United States Claims Tribunal, supra*, at 260.

[182] A. Mouri, THE INTERNATIONAL LAW OF EXPROPRIATION AS REFLECTED IN THE WORK OF THE IRAN-U.S. CLAIMS TRIBUNAL 175 (Martinus Nijhoff Publishers, 1994).

[183] 5 I.U.C.T.R. 198 (1984-I).

by the Islamic Republic."[184] In other words, in *Pereira* the acts of the Revolutionary Guards were attributable to Iran because they were a *de jure* part of the government.

This does not resolve future cases of the same feather. In some of those cases, the IUCT failed to address whether the attribution analysis perhaps should be different during the brief period between revolution and the new *de jure* order.[185] But eventually in *Yeager,* three years after *Perreira*, the IUCT focused instead on attribution—and on disincentivising certain state behaviour.

This concern for incentives and disincentives was strange behaviour for a retrospective court. The IUCT stated that "attributability of acts to the State is not limited to acts of organs formally recognized under internal law" because "[o]therwise a State could avoid responsibility under international law merely by invoking its internal law."[186] But maybe the audience was outside the IUCT as well. This too might have been a nod to seeking legitimacy, and probably did trigger that effect (within and beyond the IUCT).

(3) Attributing to the State the Acts of Commercial Enterprises Owned, Managed or Controlled by the State

In general, the IUCT has followed the tendency of other jurists[187] to accept that the "corporate" label means that the commercial business is somewhat different from a State's normal attributes, namely governing and sovereignty. But it is not necessarily a defence against state responsibility.[188] Unlike the ECtHR, IIA's are mainly corporate in their orientation. Indeed no IIA case has come up, nor can it, where the claimant's basic shape is not corporate or commercial. The institutions also have in common certain individual rights priorities, sometimes raised

---

[184] *Id.*, at 226.

[185] *Computer Sciences v. Iran*, 10 I.U.C.T.R. 269, 303 (1986-I) (attributing to Iran expropriations by a Revolutionary Committee in April 1979); *Bechtel v. Iran*, 14 I.U.C.T.R. 149, 157 (1987-I) (attributing to Iran the appointing of a new manager for a private corporation and thus controlling the company by the Revolutionary Committee in April 1979); *Sola Tiles v. Iran*, 14 I.U.C.T.R. 223, 233 (1987-I) (attributing to Iran the impoundment order of a Revolutionary Committee in June 1979).

[186] *Id.*, at 103-4 (¶¶ 42-43).

[187] See *CME v. Czech Republic*, UNCITRAL (Partial Award) (2003), *supra*, at ¶ 74 (separate opinion of I. Brownlie), and cases cited therein.

[188] C. Hoppe, *Passing the Buck, supra*, at 991.

by the claimant and sometimes by the State. For instance, the State's "public interest" justification often contains human rights overtones.

Under recognised international law, a state may be held responsible for the acts of a state-owned company if the company has the status of an organ of the government under internal law, if it exercises elements of governmental authority, or if it is *acting on behalf of the State* (subject of discussion in this Section).[189] Consider the language of the Commentary to the ILC Draft Articles: the State behaves not just as a private commercial actor but as a commercial actor leveraging its sovereign power when it "use[s] its ownership interest to direct . . . [an entity's] acts" against the claimant's interests.[190] The acts of such State-owned corporations are not attributable "unless a sufficiently strong principal-agent relationship is shown between the State and the State-owned corporation."[191]

One place where the issue merges with international human rights law (and topically so) is the responsibility of State-contracted corporations accused of violating legal rights.[192] For its part, the United Nations Conference on Trade and Development (UNCTAD) states that IIA "protection [may be restricted] only to direct investments or investments made though a locally established enterprise, thereby emphasizing that only a contribution based on a transfer of finance and managerial control over the investment will be sufficient to warrant protection, given the greater commitment of resources and risk that this entails on the part of the investor."[193]

---

[189] I. Brownlie, "Legal Status of Natural Resources In International Law (Some Aspects)," 162 Rec. des Cours 245-7 (1979).

[190] *Plama Consortium Ltd. v. Bulgaria*, ICSID Case No. ARB/03/24 (2008) (Award), at ¶296.

[191] D. D. Caron, "The Basis of Responsibility," *supra*, at 164. Moreover, the Commentary to the ILC Draft Articles on State Responsibility state: "Since corporate entities, although owned by and in that sense subject to the control of the State, are considered to be separate, prima facie their conduct in carrying out their activities is not attributable to the State, unless they are exercising elements of governmental authority . . . ." see Commentary to Article 8 of the ILC Articles, p. 107, ¶ 6.

[192] R. Wolfrum, "State Responsibility for Private Actors: an Old Problem of Renewed Relevance," *in* M. Ragazzi (ed.), INTERNATIONAL RESPONSIBILITY TODAY: ESSAYS IN MEMORY OF OSCAR SCHACHTER 423 (Martinus Nijhoff Publishers, 2005) [R. Wolfrum, "State Responsibility for Private Actors"].

[193] *Scope and Definition*, UNCTAD Series on Issues in International Investment Agreements II, 2011, p. 10 [*Scope and Definition*, UNCTAD Series] ("In more recent years, . . . the use of a tightly defined 'closed list' of protected assets has also become the practice of some countries in their IIAs. This allows for a wide

Unlike with traditional *de jure* actors' attributable acts (noted in the first rationale), cutting back on attribution for State-controlled commercial enterprises gives the state "flexibility and advantages (*e.g.*, segmentation and limitation of potential liabilities)"[194] that it would not otherwise have. Along with rejecting punitive damages for States, some tribunals have also refused to make states pay for lost-profits.[195] A similar strain, about not discouraging a government's commercial behaviour, is also present in the certain IIA tribunals: "Fear of liability may cause governments to shy away from bold regulatory action in the interests of health."[196]

This might help explain tribunals' treading carefully. Another way to see this issue is that piling on the risk of liability may scare States away from entering arbitration, human rights or dispute settlement agreements in the future. Consent, after all, is the point of origination. On the other hand, culprits might not be forced to make the victims financially whole. Like with the private-capacity problem in the previous section, here too international law has been concerned about incentives and disincentives. Here too the tribunals must make a subjective "value judgment" as well as an efficiency one about the preferable course of action.

In *CME Czech Republic BV (The Netherlands) v. Czech Republic* (2003),[197] an IIA tribunal, Professor Brownlie's separate opinion (as arbitrator) grounded this practicality in a new principle of great proportions. *CME* is relevant because Article 5 of this Czech Republic-The Netherlands BIT shares, verbatim, the same text as NAFTA Chapter Eleven. Professor Brownlie argued that states have a responsibility to their citizens and tribunals a duty not to induce a "national economic disaster."[198] Brownlie sowed a seed: "even States responsible for wars of aggression and crimes against humanity are not subjected to economic ruin."[199]

CME was a remarkable case for two significant reasons: (*i*) the staggering award of U.S. $353 million cost the Czech Republic an amount

---

range of interests to be protected but with a clear set of defining characteristics allowing for a clearer distinction to be drawn between covered and uncovered assets and transactions.").

[194] R. Wolfrum, "State Responsibility for Private Actors," *supra,* at 165; M. Brunetti, *IUCT-NAFTA-Indirect Expropriation*, *supra*, at 205-09.

[195] *Himpurna v. PLN,* (2000) XXV Yearbook of Commercial Arbitration 13 (asserting that granting lost-profits might "impoverish the host State"). A caveat is that this award concerned an international commercial arbitration, not IIA.

[196] *S.D. Myers, Inc. v. Canada* (UNCITRAL), Final Award on Merits, at ¶ 203 (2000).

[197] UNCITRAL, Final Award, at ¶ 74 (separate opinion of I. Brownlie, Arbitrator).

[198] *Id.*

[199] *Id.*, at ¶¶ 75-79; K. Ripinsky & S. Williams, DAMAGES, *supra*, at 356.

equal to its entire health care budget; (*ii*) a little more than a week before the pro-Dutch award against the Czech Republic, on the *same* facts and a *verbatim* United States-Czech Republic BIT a differently composed IIA tribunal had dismissed the claim.[200] Indeed, the very same actions of the Czech Media Council—giving regulatory advice that led to the divestiture of a TV station—that the *CME-The Netherlands* tribunal called a "coercion" and an "intentional undermining"[201] of the investment the *CME-U.S.* tribunal deemed not to be "conduct on the part of the Media Council which would amount to an unfair and inequitable treatment."[202]

Good luck proving "coercion." The IIA tribunal in *Plama Consortium Ltd. v. Bulgaria* (2008),[203] for its part, set rather a high bar to prove "coercion": even though *Plama* did not fix the outer boundary or supply an all-purpose test, it did state that so long as claimant retained "considerable negotiating leverage" it would find coercion very difficult to prove. Although it is hornbook law that whoever pays the piper calls the tune, forcing the piper to do so is presumptively questionable. Counsel may not have entered into evidence, as incredibly difficult to prove, the subtle or direct threats or a culture of license-permit nepotism that might pervade the regime. We have all got to do a better job of allowing into evidence credible and persuasive attestations that indicate that there is a pervasive problem of corruption. This, if nothing else, would still facilitate the process of proving (by satisfying a sufficient burden) that there was an unlawfully corrupt atmosphere promoted—or wilfully tolerated—by the State.

In theory, of course, the doctrine of *ratione personae* determines whether or not an investor has met the jurisdictional hurdle to pursue an IIA claim.[204] The more teleological approach would recommend that the

---

[200] *Lauder (U.S.) v. Czech Republic,* UNCITRAL, Final Award (2001).

[201] *CME (The Netherlands) v. Czech Republic,* UNCITRAL, Final Award (2003), at ¶ 582, 593, and 611.

[202] *Lauder (U.S.) v. Czech Republic,* UNCITRAL, Final Award (2001), at ¶ 295.

[203] ICSID Case No. ARB/03/24 (2008) (Award), at ¶ 300 ("Undoubtedly, Claimant was under pressure to accept [the State-owned and -operated] Biochim Bank's position; but it was free not to accept it and refuse to make further investments on those conditions. It still had *considerable negotiating leverage* at that time, given Respondent's *strong desire* to see Nova Plama continue operations.") (emphases added to highlight the subjective nature of the standard put forth). The *Plama* tribunal then added that it found no evidence "that Respondent exercised undue pressure on Nova Plama to force it into accepting burdensome conditions." *Id.*, at ¶ 301.

[204] M. Sasson, SUBSTANTIVE LAW IN INVESTMENT TREATY ARBITRATION 51–64 (Kluwer Law International, 2010).

objective and purpose of the ICSID Convention or the salient forum or convention be the main lodestar[205] while the more formalistic approach[206] might recommend that the text and stipulations of the relevant international compact play the decisive (and perhaps the exclusive) role; in reality, a complementarity between the two approaches is needed. The "treaty shopping" possibility (a distinct one) reveals to some scholars that "ordering international investment relations on a truly bilateral basis with rights and benefits only accruing to nationals of one specific home State is an increasingly illusionary undertaking, since the nationality of corporate investors has become as fungible as capital in global markets."[207]

Continuous and shareholder nationality is explored in greater detail in the next chapter (Chapter § 4.5).

---

[205] Article 31(1) of the Vienna Convention on the Law of Treaties states: "A treaty shall be interpreted in good faith in accordance with the ordinary meaning to be given to the terms of the treaty in their context and in the light of its object and purpose." See also I. Sinclair, THE VIENNA CONVENTION ON THE LAW OF TREATIES 153 (2nd ed. 1984) ("There is no doubt that Articles 31 to 33 of the Convention constitute a general expression of the principles of customary international law relating to treaty interpretation.").

[206] R. Posner, *Legal Formalism, Legal Realism, and the Interpretation of Statutes and the Constitution*, 37 CASE WESTERN RESERVE L. REV. 181 (1987) ("[Formalism denotes that] the use of deductive logic to derive the outcome of a case from premises accepted as authoritative. Formalism enables a commentator to pronounce the outcome of the case as being correct or incorrect, in approximately the same way that the solution to a mathematical problem can be pronounced correct or incorrect.").

[207] S. W. Schill, "Investment Treaties: Instruments of Bilateralism or Elements of an Evolving Multilateral System?", Paper for the 4th Global Administrative Law Seminar (2008), at 14, *available at* <www.iilj.org/GAL/documents/Schill.pdf>; *id.*, at 13, 15 [S. W. Schill, "Investment Treaties"]. See also, for an elucidation of "complex corporate group structures," *Scope and Definition*, UNCTAD Series on Issues in International Investment Agreements II, 2011, pp. 12-13 (explaining "the use of holding or shell companies, incorporated in jurisdictions enjoying investment treaty relations with host countries, as a means of enhancing protection under IIAs, especially where the home country of the parent company has no treaty in place with a given host country. The reference to interests in companies typically does not require that the investor's interest or participation in the company be a controlling one. Indeed, minority shareholdings are generally protected under IIAs and arbitral tribunals have supported this approach") (citing R. Dolzer and C. Schreuer, PRINCIPLES OF INTERNATIONAL INVESTMENT LAW 54–55 (Oxford University Press, 2008); C. McLachlan et al., INTERNATIONAL INVESTMENT ARBITRATION: SUBSTANTIVE PRINCIPLES 187–189 (Oxford University Press, 2007)).

Professor Brownlie's "National Economic Disaster" Defence

For now, we return to Professor Brownlie's "national economic disaster" argument in *CME (The Netherlands) v. Czech Republic* (2003). It has large implications for international law beyond the world of investments. His *CME* statement was not somehow *lex specialis* and thus limited to the Czech Republic-Netherlands BIT at issue in *CME*. The sweep and context of the assertion suggest that it has grand implications for much of international law. To call this a slippery slope would amount to an excruciating understatement.[208]

Notice the heights that Professor Brownlie sets himself to achieve. (He does not quite get there due to his sad demise a mere seven years later in 2010.) In his *CME* opinion, Brownlie lays down the markers. He refers to the Japanese Peace Treaty (1951)[209]—and the Marshall Plan also comes to mind—but until now these have been voluntary measures, not necessarily ones *required* by international law. If this half-evolved butterfly develops more fully, it might one day become *jus cogens* or a peremptory norm.[210] If it does not, it will simply return to its chrysalis having made lesser marks than its original promise portended. Marks and impact, however, it will make.

That this particular trajectory might have been envisioned by Professor Brownlie should not surprise anyone. His view of extant and emerging rights has always been an expansive one. He considered "right to social security" (Article 9 of the International Covenant of Economic and Social

---

[208] This is the proverbial "little lattice window" in *Oliver Twist.* See C. Dickens, THE ADVENTURES OF OLIVER TWIST (N.Y.: Thomas Y. Crowell & Co.), p. 184 ("It was a little lattice window, about five feet and a half above the ground: at the back of the house: which belonged to a scullery, or small brewing-place, at the end of the passage. The aperture was so small, that the inmates had probably not thought it worth while to defend it more securely; but it was large enough to admit a boy of Oliver's size, nevertheless. A very brief exercise of Mr. Sikes's art, sufficed to overcome the fastening of the lattice; and it soon stood *wide open* also.") (emphasis added).

[209] *Lauder (U.S.) v. Czech Republic, supra*, at ¶79.

[210] In April 2012, I delivered a presentation on this very topic at a London boutique law firm specialising in international law, and the overwhelming consensus was that this Brownlie observation has slipped off the radar. Unsurprisingly, even more controversial was the issue whether the host State's inability to be resilient or its enduring this collapse in the first place should be accorded leniency or at least mitigation and to which extent, *i.e.*, mere mitigation as to compensation or plenary dismissal of the claims.

Rights (the ICESCR)); the "right to housing" (Article 11); and the "right to the highest attainable standard of physical and mental health" to be "second-generation rights."[211] Brownlie's notion of "third-generation rights"—"not [yet] part of existing law, but . . . 'emerging'" nonetheless—include "the right to food, the right to a decent environment, the right to development, and the right to peace."[212]

Rights they are certainly, which no one doubts. But peremptory norms are just different in kind. In international law, peremptory norms remain the ultimately trump-cards in that ordinary defences such as "persistent objections,"[213] even those claimed by States purportedly to protect their own sovereignty, fail in the face of peremptory norms such as "the prohibition of aggression, slavery and slave trade, genocide, racial discrimination and apartheid, torture, the basic rules of international humanitarian law applicable in armed conflict and the principle of self-determination."[214] And here of course the State would be seeking a peremptory norm-based defence.

---

[211] I. Brownlie, PRINCIPLES OF PUBLIC INTERNATIONAL LAW 540–41 (6th ed.) (Oxford University Press, 2003) [Brownlie, PRINCIPLES OF PUBLIC INTERNATIONAL LAW]. See also C. Tomuschat, HUMAN RIGHTS: BETWEEN IDEALISM AND REALISM 24–57 (Oxford University Press, 2003).

[212] Brownlie, PRINCIPLES OF PUBLIC INTERNATIONAL LAW, *supra*, at 541.

[213] The persistent-objection doctrine states that if a State objects to a newly emerging rule in international law from the beginning, such a rule shall not apply to the State. See *Judgment on Asylum Case Between Columbia and Peru*, ICJ Rep. (1950), pp. 266, 277 and 228; *Judgment on Fisheries Case, United Kingdom v. Norway*, ICJ Rep. (1951), p. 116. In the *Fisheries* case, the ICJ held that "in any event the ten-mile rule would appear to be inapplicable as against Norway inasmuch as she has always opposed any attempt to apply it to the Norwegian coast." *Id.* There is some dispute as to whether the persistent objection doctrine is consistent with international law, which requires as a prerequisite for customary rules in international law the consent of sovereign States.

[214] See Draft Articles on Responsibility of States for Internationally Wrongful Acts, Commentaries, Art. 40, ¶¶ 4-6, *in Report of the International Law Commission on the Work of Its Fifty-third Session*, U.N. GAOR, 56th Sess., Supp. No. 10, U.N. Doc. A/56/10 (2001). There may always be controversy about what constitutes a peremptory norm but what appears not to be particularly disputed is that "[a] feature common to [*jus cogens* norms], or to a great many of them, evidently is that they involve not only legal rules but considerations of morals and of international good order." Special Rapporteur *Third Report on Law of Treaties,* Commentary on art. 17, ¶ 76, U.N. Doc. A/CN.4/SER.A/1958/Add.l., *reprinted in* 2 Y.B. INT'L L. COMM'N 41 (1958); see also S. Knuchel, *State Immunity and the Promise of* Jus Cogens, 9 NW. U. J. INT'L HUM. Rts. 149, 154, n. 19 (2011).

Such an unprecedented step would convert what is, at best, a rationale advanced by host States to *mitigate* compensation into a full and irrebuttable *defence*.[215] Article 62 (1) (b) of the Vienna Convention on the Law of Treaties states that *unless* "the effect of the change is *radically* to transform the extent of obligations still to be performed under the treaty," "[a] fundamental change of circumstances which has occurred with regard to those existing at the time of the conclusion of a treaty, and which was not foreseen by the parties, may not be invoked as a ground for terminating or withdrawing from the treaty."[216]

Imagine that the State might be able to meet the obligations after thirty years of heavy taxation, but not necessarily any casualties or mortality; is this "radical" enough to escape liability?[217] The tiered analysis or line-drawing will require proportionality analysis by the tribunal entertaining such a dispute. An attendant fear is that it might lead to severe unpredictability or lopsided bias based on the specific tribunal's proclivities.

Professor Brownlie also cites the ICJ's *Gulf of Maine* (1984)[218] decision for its concern "for the livelihood and economic well-being of the population of the countries concerned" in deciding the remedy. But unlike Brownlie in *CME*, the *Gulf of Maine* citation (even if it is *ratio*, which is not clear) looks at population welfare as *one of many* criteria, not necessarily the determinative consideration.[219]

In the maritime delimitation context at least, the ICJ has deemed factors such as development status of the State, along with population and the extent of surrounding area, to be "strange to . . . [the] nature" of the

---

[215] Article 53 of the Vienna Convention on the Law of Treaties does provide some support to Professor Brownlie: "A treaty is void if, at the time of its conclusion, it conflicts with a peremptory norm of general international law. For the purposes of the present Convention, a peremptory norm of general international law is a norm accepted and recognized by the international community of States as a whole as a norm from which no derogation is permitted and which can be modified only by a subsequent norm of general international law having the same character."

[216] Emphasis added.

[217] Perhaps to substantiate what Article 53 means, Article 61 (1) states: "A party may invoke the impossibility of performing a treaty as a ground for terminating or withdrawing from it if the impossibility results from the permanent disappearance or destruction of an object indispensable for the execution of the treaty. If the impossibility is temporary, it may be invoked only as a ground for suspending the operation of the treaty."

[218] *Case Concerning Delimitation of the Maritime Boundary in the Gulf of Maine Area (Canada/United States of America)*, I.C.J. Rep. 1984, at ¶ 237.

[219] *Id.*

analysis.[220] *Gulf of Maine* attempted to forewarn the ICJ from disguising "catastrophic repercussions for the livelihood and economic well-being of the population of the countries concerned" as the result (inexorable or somewhat foreseeable) of "equitable criteria and the use of appropriate methods."[221]

Consider the domino effect. Doctrinally speaking, the Brownlie prescription would have the effect of expanding the *force majeure* rule to include all or most disasters or ostensible disasters—irrespective of the proximate source. The delicate causal link created between certain assertions of state responsibility and *force majeure* will not able to bear the strain. If the reviewing standard is deferential, then the State could resort, with impunity, to "national economic disaster" not so much as a genuine defence but as a convenient pretext to hide, preserve and maybe even surreptitiously enhance the real reason. It might be too intrusive and too disrespectful of sovereignty for the international tribunal to *tell* the host State what problems the State is likely to face.[222] Needless to say, the

---

[220] *Continental Shelf Case (Libyan Arab Jamahiriya/Malta),* ICJ Rep. 1985 p. 13, 40-41 ("[A]lthough there may be no legal limit to the considerations which States may take account of, this can hardly be true for a court applying equitable procedures. For a court, although there is assuredly no closed list of considerations, it is evident that only those that are pertinent to the institution of the continental shelf as it has developed within the law, and to the application of *equitable principles* to its delimitation, will qualify for inclusion. Otherwise, the legal concept of continental shelf could itself be fundamentally changed by the introduction of considerations strange to its nature.") (emphasis added); *Maritime Delimitation in the Area between Greenland and Jan Mayen (Denmark v. Norway)*, ICJ Rep. 1993, p. 38, 62 (stating that "the tendency of customary law, like the terms of Article 6, has been to postulate the median line as leading prima facie to an equitable result."); *Continental Shelf Case (Tunisia/Libyan Arab Jamahiriya),* ICJ Rep. 1982 p. 18, 77-8; *Guinea-Guinea-Bissau Maritime Delimitation* (1985) 77 ILR 635, 688-89. For Professor James Crawford's take on "equitable principles" and a term of art such as "relevant circumstances," see J. Crawford, ed., BROWNLIE'S PRINCIPLES OF PUBLIC INTERNATIONAL LAW 290 (8th ed.) (Oxford University Press, 2012) [J. Crawford, ed., BROWNLIE'S PRINCIPLES].

[221] *Gulf of Maine, supra,* at ¶ 237. Even if we argue that this probably was just *dictum*, we definitely cannot ignore that it is unclear whether the Court was more concerned with transparency or with the consideration itself.

[222] E. Haas, *Beyond the Nation State: Functionalism and International Organization* (1948); C. Eagleton, *The Task of an International Lawyer* A.J.I.L., 435 (1947); *Self-Determination in the United Nations* A.J.I.L., 88 (1953); M. Hudson, *Integrity of International Instruments*, A.J.I.L., 105 (1948); M. McDougal, *Peace and War: Factual Continuum With Multiple Legal Consequences* A.J.I.L., 63 (1955).

tribunal might need to have these answers in order to decide if the host State has been driven to this brink of economic collapse on account of its *own* culpability, the investor's culpability and/or a third-party's culpability. This possibility is explicated in the context of the "necessity" defence in Chapter V (NON-DISCRIMINATION).

Even if the tribunal were inclined to retrieve these answers one serious obstacle are the resources to conduct the fact-finding. That factor cannot be downplayed. The challenges of fact-finding in international tribunals (entity-State and inter-State disputes), including access to information held by the opposition and the difficulties attending a correct determination of facts resulting from complex, large-scale phenomena, have been well-recounted.[223] Who will pay? Will we have to create or recognize a new doctrine called fact-finders' fees and costs (like attorney's fees) and a specific allocation model? If tribunals elect not to open this Pandora's Box at all, then these questions might not arise.

Brownlie also cites use-of-force literature from other aspects of international law.[224] Connecting these other aspects of international law with the IIA universe, Brownlie might have been revolutionising how IIA and property regimes view the consequence of economic disasters. Brownlie could not have wanted to make this consequence a *necessary* element; nor would that make sense, given the manifold possibilities of violations of international law.

However there is an argument to be made for this consequence going a significant way in being *sufficient* in denying the relief sought by the investor: Nations consensually sign IIA's and other international compacts in order to attract or develop investments and other resources (foreign or domestic) but if the cost of adhering to such compacts is so high as to be catastrophic, then it makes intuitive sense from the respondent State's (and by warning, other States too) to disavow the compact. Needless to say, the friction will intensify when the IIA, property rights and other international law communities realise the high stakes.

Future IIA tribunals, parties and other stakeholders may choose to distinguish *Gulf of Maine* completely from IIA cases; as an inter-State case in the ICJ, *Gulf of Maine* dealt with a clash of boundary interests implicating a categorically higher question of sovereignty and sovereign

---

[223] See, *e.g.*, J. Crook "Fact-Finding in the Fog: Determining the Facts of Upheavals and Wars in Inter-State Disputes" *in* R. Alford and C. Rogers, eds., THE FUTURE OF INVESTMENT ARBITRATION 341 (Oxford University Press, 2009).

[224] Professor Brownlie cites: I. Brownlie, INTERNATIONAL LAW AND THE USE OF FORCE BY STATES 142-3 (1963) and P. d'Argent, LES RÉPARATIONS DE GUERRE EN DROIT INTERNATIONAL PUBLIC, Bruxelles and Paris, 2002.

dignity than most IIA cases ever could. Most IIA cases are fundamentally about recovering investments or being compensated for them. Secondly, *Gulf of Maine* concerned customary international law whereas IIA, international human rights and other cases deriving from a textual instrument would give presumptive weight to the text and might hold that protections not expressly secured in the text are not extant at all. In other words, there are some creative ways of distinguishing among textual instruments as well as between customary law and textual instruments.

Finally, perhaps the greatest point of distinction would be that *Gulf of Maine* asserted that the consequence of economic disasters *might* incentivise a particular judgment but that "there is no reason to fear any such danger in the present case on account of the Chamber's choice of delimitation line . . . ."[225] In an important sense, then, this could all be moot or hypothetical anyway. From one standpoint, this somewhat-capricious "sweepstakes" angle undermines the one important advantage that might have recommended the Brownlie approach: predictability. After all, an absolute rule could remove much of the guess-work from the otherwise complex deference analysis. However, it turns out that the Brownlie approach is in reality no more predictable than the approach(es) currently activated.

Professor Brownlie presents his idea as deference to a Nation's sovereignty. But that was not how *Gulf of Maine* necessarily saw it: the *Gulf of Maine* considerations are triggered *only* when the formal factors are in equipoise.[226] Although the tribunals have not been clear about the necessary, sufficient, and facilitating aspects of the test, the Brownlie formulation makes clear that the sovereign dignity of the State and the welfare of its people both play *some* role and to a very great extent.[227] But it is exactly the controlling but subliminal, between-the-lines reasoning that only occasionally surfaces because of candid jurists and arbitrators. [228]

[225] *Gulf of Maine, supra,* at ¶ 238.

[226] K. Ripinsky & S. Williams, DAMAGES, *supra*, at 355-9 (pointing to the "effect on a state's welfare" to justify the balance that must be struck.)

[227] R. Wright, *Causation in Tort Law*, 73 CAL. L. REV. 1735, 1739 (1985); W. Landes & R. Posner, THE ECONOMIC STRUCTURE OF TORT LAW 142 (1987); G. Calabresi, *Concerning Cause and the Law of Torts*, 43 U. CHI. L. REV. 69, 86-87, 105-08 (1975).

[228] This might be so but there remain other ethical and transparency-related issues which are hitherto unaddressed. See, *e.g.*, C. N. Brower, *Keynote Address: The Ethics of Arbitration: Perspectives from a Practicing International Arbitrator*, 5 B. J. I. L. 1 (2010); R. M. Mosk, *Attorney Ethics in International Arbitration*, 5 B. J. I. L. 32 (2010); E. P. Triantafilou, *Is a Connection to the "Public Interest" a Meaningful Prerequisite of Third Party Participation in Investment Arbitration?*, 5

These jurists and practitioners appreciate that "judgments which are inadequately reasoned, based on points not raised in argument, or which evade crucial issues are defective."[229]

Sometimes this balance can seem to be too deferential—to the point of abdicating review. Consider *Flexi-Van Leasing v. Iran* (1986) (mentioned already), where the claimant claimed that Iran expropriated its contract rights with a private (but government-controlled) Iranian company Star Line. The IUCT found that despite the Star Line contract expropriation (by Bonyad Mostazafan, an instrumentality), the company "remained a separate legal entity, and surely did not become an organ or department of the Government."[230] This ruled attribution out but provided something of a roadmap:

> The mere fact that the Government through the Foundation controls Star Line does not as such encompass an expropriation of the Claimant's rights that derive from its lease agreements with Star Line.... The Claimant does not assert that the Government has itself interfered with its contract rights, but rather that it has done so through the Foundation. To give rise to an expropriation claim this would require that . . . Star Line had acted under orders, directives, recommendations or instructions from the Foundation or the Government when it did not pay the rentals or return the leased equipment to the Claimant.[231]

Judge Holtzmann's dissent thought the claimant had indeed offered this proof: when "the Government confiscates a company, ousts the former management without regard for, or recourse to, normal corporate procedures, and then installs its own representatives . . . assuming management functions over what it considers public property,"[232] this constitutes compensable expropriation. In fact, profits actually earned through this period or the expected opportunity cost, whichever is greater, ordinarily is deemed to be the amount owed in compensation.

Second, Judge Holtzmann noted that the Tribunal held the acts of Star Line and Iran Express not attributable because there was no specific

---

B.J.I.L. 38 (2010); A. Sabater, *Towards Transparency in Arbitration (A Cautious Approach),* 5 B.J.I.L. 47 (2010); R. Teitelbaum, *A Look At The Public Interest In Investment Arbitration: Is It Unique? What Should We Do About It?*, 5 B.J.I.L. 54(2010); L. Mistelis & J. D. M. Lew, eds., PERVASIVE PROBLEMS, *supra*.

229 J. G. Merrills, INTERNATIONAL DISPUTE SETTLEMENT, *supra,* at 308. In the very next sentence, Professor Merrills suggests that these criticisms apply "to some recent [, to mean pre-1998,] international decisions." *Id.*

230 *Flexi-Van Leasing*, *supra*, at 348.

231 *Id.*, at 348-49.

232 *Id.*, at 360 (Holtzmann, J., dissenting).

evidence of State direction of the two companies. In Judge Holtzmann's view, the IUCT in *Flexi-Van* "impos[ed] an impossible evidentiary burden in holding that Flexi-Van cannot recover damages because it did not produce documents that are within the sole control of a confiscated company or the Government representatives who managed it."[233]

In the IUCT, government interference with the control of a private corporation does not inherently convert all "subsequent acts of the private corporation" into "acts of the State."[234] Still, this patchwork of attribution rules in the IUCT presents "grave proof problems for claimants who must seek evidence from either a hostile or opaque defendant government."[235] The IUCT's virtual impossibility of proof of government control is evident in the following passage from *Flexi-Van*:

> Even if ... representatives of the Foundation [for the Oppressed] were directly involved in decisions not to return containers to the Claimant, this did not constitute the kind of government interference that would amount to expropriation of Flexi-Van's contract rights. Before Star Line came under Government control, it had defaulted on rental payments and failed to return containers under the agreements in question. It was taken over by the Foundation, Star Line continued to refuse rental payments and to return containers as it had done before. The evidence described does not bear out that this was done on the instruction of the Government.[236]

Even with the onus decidedly on the State, an *ad-hoc* inquiry is almost unavoidable. The relative uncomplicated rule of NAFTA (no signatory can interfere with the "appoint[ment] to senior management positions individuals of any particular nationality")[237] provides more predictability. But the ECtHR's proportionality analysis, best described in *James v. United Kingdom* (1986)[238] is more unpredictable still than the IUCT test. The ECtHR has not had a significant body of cases directly related to government takeover of management, so the *James* formula remains its

---

[233] *Id.*, at 362.

[234] D. D. Caron, "The Basis of Responsibility," *supra,* at 168. See also R. Lillich, ed., INTERNATIONAL LAW OF STATE RESPONSIBILITY FOR INJURIES TO ALIENS 270-3 (1983); insurrections, civil wars, revolutions and armed external intervention have generated cases like *United States-Iran Hostages Case*, 19 ILM 553 (1980), or *Nicaragua v. United States*, 25 ILM 1023 (1986); C. F. Amerasinghe, STATE RESPONSIBILITY FOR INJURIES TO ALIENS 152-6 (Clarendon Press, 1967) [C. F. Amerasinghe, STATE RESPONSIBILITY].

[235] D. D. Caron, "The Basis of Responsibility," *supra,* at 168.

[236] *Flexi-Van Leasing*, *supra*, at 349.

[237] NAFTA, Art. 1107 ("Senior Management and Boards of Directors").

[238] App. No. 8793/79 (1986).

standard test. In *James*, it was established that the first prong is to decide if the aim is "legitimate" and second if there is "a reasonable relationship . . . between the means employed and the aim sought."[239] If a tribunal decides to keep a flexible test, then the prescription followed by international human rights tribunals is preferable.

Back in the IUCT- *Flexi-Van* context, the Tribunal made clear that it is highly sensitive to *separate* corporate identity with regard to financial institutions. Thus, "whe[n] a claimant alleged that it was unable to withdraw funds deposited with a private bank that had been nationalized by the Islamic Republic of Iran," the IUCT held that "the nationalization of the bank did not necessarily mean that the private monies held by the bank had been expropriated."[240]

This, in effect, distinguished between the financial institutions' ownership and their operations.[241] The argument is weak because a supermajority of the ownership in the case of financial institutions *is* the control over the mobility and flow of capital, and that flow can be directed in whichever direction as the controller chooses.[242] Like in *BP Exploration Company (Libya) Ltd. v. Libya* (1973),[243] the controller might devise ingenious ways to profit himself, his supporters or those who might perpetuate the controller's grip on power. Thus the controller remains the controller permanent. For this to happen, the controller does not even need a supermajority of the financial institutions' assets. Where it is the claimant who unlawfully procures the investment, IIA tribunals and prominent academic lawyers are developing elaborate jurisdictional and admissibility rules.[244]

---

[239] *Id.*, at ¶ 50.

[240] *Flexi-Van Leasing*, *supra.*, at 362.

[241] See, *e.g.*, *Pereira, supra*, at 226; *United Painting v. Iran*, 23 I.U.C.T.R. 351, 374-76 (1989-II); see also C. N. Brower, *The Iran-United States Claims Tribunal*, RECUEIL DES COURS 224, 291-94 (1990).

[242] This is the same reason that denying compensation but giving restitution to high-volume factory owners and high-volume financial institutions is small consolation, given their lost profits (both past and future) caused by the expropriation. Furthermore, given Iran's immediately pre-1979 emerging market status, the capital there was significant. See R. P. Buckley, THE INTERNATIONAL FINANCIAL SYSTEM: POLICY AND REGULATION 64 (Kluwer Law International, 2009).

[243] 53 ILR 297, 329 (1973).

[244] C. Miles, *Corruption, Jurisdiction and Admissibility in International Investment Claims*, 10 J. INT. DISP. SETTLEMENT 34, 42 (2012) ("Where the corruption in question relates to the procurement of the investment, and the relevant international investment agreement includes a 'legality requirement' as a condition

Some support comes from Articles 49,[245] 50[246] and 51[247] of the Vienna Convention on the Law of Treaties which deem fraud, corruption and coercion by another negotiating State to be reason enough to invalidate a State's consent and from the tort doctrine of *ex turpi causa non oritur action* (the illegality defence).[248] The assumption is that if the rules would apply to an offending State then they also would apply to the investor availing itself of a forum and rules deriving from the offense caused by that home State.

Now observe what happened in *International Technical Products Corp. v. Iran* (1985),[249] and subsequent cases. In *International Technical*, the claimant named Iran, but not Bank Tejarat (a completely State-owned bank), as respondent. This concerned a claim alleging expropriation of the claimant's property by Bank Tejarat. The claimant had to prove that Tejarat's actions are attributable to Iran.

The IUCT stated that, under these circumstances, the claimant needed to prove either (*i*) that while taking the property Bank Tejarat itself acted as a state organ ("perform[ed] governmental functions"), *or* (*ii*) that the Iranian Government or an organ was an accessory to the property transfer ("performed governmental functions.").[250]

---

of the tribunal's jurisdiction, then the matter is a question of jurisdiction. If, in the alternative, the corruption post-dates the investment, or the international investment agreement contains no 'legality requirement', then the matter is a question of admissibility.").

[245] "If a State has been induced to conclude a treaty by the fraudulent conduct of another negotiating State, the State may invoke the fraud as invalidating its consent to be bound by the treaty."

[246] "If the expression of a State's consent to be bound by a treaty has been procured through the corruption of its representative directly or indirectly by another negotiating State, the State may invoke such corruption as invalidating its consent to be bound by the treaty."

[247] "The expression of a State's consent to be bound by a treaty which has been procured by the coercion of its representative through acts or threats directed against him shall be without any legal effect."

[248] Under *National Coal Board v. England* [1954], AC 403, [1954] 1 All ER 546, in order for the *ex turpi* defence to attach and thus to immunise the defendant is the finding that the tort suffered by investor or owner is not only connected to, but also proportionate to, appellant's actions. Causal connection, sometimes proximate, between the tort and the illegal act is required. See also *The Illegality Defence in Tort: Consultation Paper 160* (2001) 71-72, 79-85, 135-136 §889, Restatement of Torts (Second) (1997).

[249] 9 I.U.C.T.R. 206 (1985).

[250] *Id.,* at 207-8; see also *American Bell International v. Iran*, 12 I.U.C.T.R. 170 (1986-III).

Unlike banks and financial institutions, regarding private corporations for which there were State-appointed managers, the IUCT was strongly pro-attribution. But there still are nuances. Sometimes the *inherent* act of the Iranian government appointing managers could be an expropriation, since the State took it and profited from it. This disfavour of free-riding, often known as a "sweat of the brow" argument, is a common pillar of civil procedure in many domestic law systems as well. Why should it be surprising that it is relevant in international law too? In *SEDCO v. NIOC* (1987),[251] discussed earlier in this chapter, the IUCT held that whenever "there is no reasonable prospect of return of control, a taking should conclusively be found to have occurred as of that date."

The IUCT in *SEDCO* found no "reasonable prospect of return" because both the text of the Iranian legislative bill appointing the managers (again, a nod to domestic legislation) and the "statements made only a month earlier"[252] by the government pointed in that direction. Similarly, in *Starrett Housing* (1983), the IUCT found the date of appointment to be the starting date of expropriation (the clock began tolling that day)—despite the fact that the government soon thereafter asked the claimant to return.

Still, was this a genuine invitation or was this invitation a Trojan Horse'esque trap? The latter is more likely. The invitation was untenable, the IUCT found, "because the conditions on which the claimant truly could return were severely prejudiced" by the claimant-averse proposed legislation in the pipeline and the lack of "compensation for any reduction in the value of its shareholding and contractual rights."[253] The claimant had every reason to fear that upon return he would be greeted with life- and property-threatening difficulties, and the uncertain political climate in Iran around then informed the IUCT's analysis.

Similar cases may well arise in the Venezuelan and Argentine contexts, given how certain Latin American states currently are engaged in vast nationalisation programmes. Not only might this spill onto IIA fora but also the IACtHR. The case also has invaluable parallels with the award in *Kuwait v. Aminoil* (1982),[254] where the Kuwaiti authorities enacted a Decree Law which terminated a lucrative petroleum concession granted to

---

[251] *SEDCO v. NIOC*, *supra*, at 278-79 (1985-II); *Starrett Housing*, *supra*, at 155 (observing that "assumption of control over property by a government does not automatically and immediately justify a conclusion that the property has been taken").

[252] *Id.*

[253] *Id.*; D. D. Caron, "The Basis of Responsibility," *supra*, at 160.

[254] 21 I.L.M. 976, at 997 (1982).

the American Independent Oil Company (Aminoil) and nationalising Aminoil's other facilities in Kuwait. The Decree Law had the effect of compelling a transfer of property rights away from the hands of foreign nationals.

However, we should not infer attribution from the very act of manager appointments by the government. Breaking this streak is *Tippets, Abbett, McCarthy, Stratton v. Iran* (1984).[255] Here the IUCT rejected an attribution claim for the August-November 1979 period because the government-selected manager and the claimant were able to work together during this time. This implies that the claimant would have been at least marginally better off in the IUCT had it failed (as unwilling or unable) to cooperate with the manager.

What is interesting is that at least one scholar would put "[i]nterference with the day-to-day operations of an investment" down as *quasi-de jure* expropriations, rather than any form of regulatory expropriations at all.[256] This scholar adds: "With-out the ability to direct the day-to-day operations of an investment, or select the personnel who operate the investment, one can hardly be said to hold even physical possession of the investment in question."[257] The obvious benefit to the claimants' bar (or at least to the claimants) is that *de jure* expropriations are significantly easier to prove because the only questions left to be resolved at that point are whether the expropriations are allowable and, if not, what the compensation must be.

Practical considerations, rather than formal factors alone, seem to have guided the IUCT in each of these cases. In that sense, the Tribunal was consistent. Generally, however, the government's appointing managers was deemed only "*an* important factor in finding a taking,"[258] and not necessarily *the* dispositive one. One consideration is clear: the IUCT has insightfully reached beyond the "corporate form" and cared about what is

---

[255] 6 I.U.C.T.R. 219, 225 (1984-II).

[256] J. M. Marlles, *Public Purpose, Private Losses: Regulatory Expropriation and Environmental Regulation in International Investment Law*, 16 J. OF TRANSNAT'L L. & POL'Y 275, 300, n. 129 (2006) ("Interference with the day-to-day operations of an investment should be imagined as a quasi-physical taking, in that management's oversight of the ordinary operations of an investment (such as a factory) is equivalent to physical possession of the investment. With-out the ability to direct the day-to-day operations of an investment, or select the personnel who operate the investment, one can hardly be said to hold even physical possession of the investment in question.").

[257] *Id.*

[258] *Id.*, at 277 (emphasis added).

happening on the ground.[259] Perhaps this choice was made for legitimacy's sake, or perhaps just to arrive at the right conclusion.

Rationale Two: Actors' De facto Exercising Governmental Authority—with or without Active Governmental Authorisation

Must a State have attributed to it the acts of entities *de facto* exercising elements of governmental authority, even if those entities are not authorized to exercise that authority and no principal-agent relationship actually exists? Customary international law states that such acts are to be attributed "unless the State can show it is not capable of controlling the actor *de facto* exercising governmental authority."[260]

Unlike in the private capacity context in the first rationale's analysis, here the IUCT recognised a positive obligation—even though in reality the difference between a private capacity exception and exercising *de facto* government authority is blurred, at best.[261] It is not always clear whether or not an *agent provocateur* is actually a government, revolution or regime agent. "[S]ince it is always difficult to establish a *de facto* rather than *de jure* principal-agent relationship," the prevailing principle is that when the State does not try to control actors "exercising elements of governmental authority," this fact "establishes a relationship."[262] This is considered enough to trigger positive obligations on the State's part.

In this *de facto* relationship (not formally one of agency), the actor acts on behalf of the state. *Yeager* addresses *de facto* principal-agent relationships and this principle to solve evidentiary problems. In *Yeager*, the IUCT referred to various customary norms and finally found "sufficient evidence . . . to establish" certain findings: (*i*) the Revolutionary Guards "after 11 February 1979 were acting in fact on behalf of the new government," or they "at least exercised elements of governmental authority

---

[259] D. D. Caron, "The Basis of Responsibility," *supra*, at 166; A. Mouri, INTERNATIONAL LAW OF EXPROPRIATION – IUCT, *supra*, at 204.

[260] ILC Draft Article 8 (1975); see also J. Mertus, *Considering Nonstate Actors in the New Millennium: Toward Expanded Participation in Norm Generation and Norm Application*, 32 N.Y.U. J. INT'L L. & POL. 537, 552–56 (2002).

[261] What is also remarkable is that this difference in who bears the burden of proof runs somewhat contrary to a recognised international law principle, best stated in UNCITRAL rule 24.1 ("Each party shall have the burden of proving the facts relied on to support its claim or defence"). *Yeager* and other cases, below, suggest that the IUCT applied this burden-shifting both to facts and to the law.

[262] D. D. Caron, "The Basis of Responsibility," *supra*, at 142-3.

in the absence of official authorities"; (*ii*) they did so "in operations of which the new Government must have had knowledge and to which it did not specifically object."[263]

Moreover, the "presumption of attribution for actors that are *de jure* part of the State is accompanied by an exception," namely "the presumption that the acts of entities *de facto* exercising governmental authority are attributable may be rebutted."[264] Here the rebuttal would have to show that the actor was, for practical purposes, *beyond* the state's control. Thus, for example, the *Yeager* Tribunal held that the "acts of the Guards were attributable to Iran" unless *Iran* "show[ed] that it did not and could not control the Revolutionary Guards [when they were functioning in their official capacity]."[265]

Rationale Three: Continuity of Responsibility

The James Bonds of the world are difficult to trace in the chain of responsibility—that is how 007's tracks are designed to remain covered. A third rationale addresses another doctrine of attribution found in the ILC's Draft Articles: "The act of an insurrectional movement which becomes the new government of a State shall be considered as an act of that State."[266] This rationale goes the furthest in attributing certain violations to the Revolutionary Guards.

The attribution of the "acts of an insurrectional movement to the State can neither be explained nor grounded on notions of agency or encouragement of control since the revolutionary movement is by definition neither an agent nor subject to the control of the State."[267] Thus the ILC acknowledged that the explanations are not necessarily or completely convincing.[268] NAFTA tribunals do not face this peculiar problem. By contrast, the ECtHR has struggled deeply, if imperceptibly, with the continuity problem.

So far the problem has not *directly* challenged the ECtHR's property jurisprudence but it *has* been faced by that Court. In a largely-overlooked case that will produce significant effects, in *Behrami & Behrami v. France*

---

[263] *Id.*, at 103-4.
[264] *Id.*, at 143.
[265] *Yeager*, *supra*, at 110, ¶ 61.
[266] Report of the ILC (1980), *supra*, at 31. Article 15 (1) and Article 15 (2) deal with the situation where an insurrectional movement results in a new State.
[267] *Id.*
[268] *Id.*, at 100 (Article 15 commentary) (followed in *Rankin v. Iran* 17 I.U.C.T.R. 135, 143 (1987-IV)).

(2007) [269] the ECtHR attributed the actions of both U.N. Interim Administration for Kosovo (UNMIK) and the NATO Kosovo Force (KFOR) exclusively to the United Nations because their actions were authorized by U.N. Security Council Resolution 1244.[270]

The ECtHR did not acknowledge the effective control of certain member states over KFOR's actions as a criterion for the attribution of responsibility for potential human rights violations. Instead, the ECtHR relied on the "overall control of the Security Council."[271] This totality-of-the-circumstances test—"effective operational control"—invites the same charges of subjectivity, potential for predilection and arbitrariness, and institutional illegitimacy. Neither the IUCT nor the ECtHR has learned from the other's shortcoming on this front (perhaps because of the vagueness in the totality-of-the-circumstances test), which is tragic since it is a problem they share.

How the IUCT has dealt with continuity of responsibility is connected to how this issue actually works. International organisations and "[foreign] governments [try] to exert some control over revolutionary movements" by asserting that if the "movement is at some point successful" it "will then be responsible for their exercise of governmental authority."[272] The IUCT endorsed this "justification of principle" in several decisions.[273] We return to *Yeager*, where CSD Paragraph Eleven was in question. Paragraph Eleven provides that

---

[269] App. no. 71412/01 (2007).

[270] The ECtHR's actions here would be consistent with its approach in *Banković v. Belgium and 16 Other Contracting States*, App. no. 52207/99 (2001), where the ECtHR recognised "extraterritorial acts as an exercise of jurisdiction only where the State, through effective control of the territory and its inhabitants, exercises public powers normally exercised by the government of that territory." *Id.*

[271] For a more in-depth analysis of *Behrami*, see P. Bodeau-Livinec, G. P. Buzzini, & S. Villalpando, *Case Report:* Agim Behrami & Bekir Behrami v. France; Ruzhdi Saramati v. France, Germany & Norway, in 102 A.J.I.L. 323 (2008). See also K. M. Larsen, *Attribution of Conduct in Peace Operations: The "Ultimate Authority and Control" Test*, 19 EUR. J. INT'L L. 509 (2008).

[272] D. D. Caron, "The Basis of Responsibility," *supra*, at 144 (citing ILC Draft Article 15: "In the case where the insurgents triumph ... [t]he resulting State apparatus is in reality the continuation of both the organizations which confronted each other.... It is therefore logical to attribute to the State the acts of organs of its preceding organization and the acts of organs of the organization that grew up during the insurrection.").

[273] *Id.*

> the United States will promptly withdraw all claims now pending against Iran ... and will thereafter bar and preclude the prosecution against Iran of any pending or future claim of the United States ... arising out of events occurring before the date of this declaration related to ... (D) injury to the United States nationals or their property as a result of popular movements in the course of the Islamic Revolution in Iran which were not an act of the Government of Iran.

This paragraph discusses claims relating to the detention of 52 Americans in the U.S. Embassy in Tehran, so the U.S. claimants argued that "paragraph 11 only bars claims by those nationals or claims related to that particular incident."[274] For its part, Iran wanted a broader (and more favourable) rule from the IUCT: "it applies to all claims related to injury caused by popular movements."[275] In the end, the Tribunal decided that no matter how CSD Paragraph Eleven is interpreted, it applied only to popular movements "which are not an act of the Government of Iran."[276] Iran might still be responsible for popular movements which are attributable to the Government under international law.[277]

There are some basic questions about applying the continuous responsibility principle. How are we to attribute acts to an insurrectional movement? Which rules apply—do insurgencies operate under the same rules of agency as nations? For starters, customary international law is murky as to "what primary rules, *i.e.*, substantive obligations, are applicable"[278]: the IUCT has decided that the "primary rules binding the insurrectional movement were the same as those binding the State of Iran at the time."[279]

Remarkably, the IUCT has, in fact, applied the *same* agency rules to the insurgency that it used for States. Not known is whether this was because of an absence of any other rules (the absence remains) or because the same rules seemed appropriate to the IUCT.

§ 3.4—Attributing Acts to an Insurrection

Article 15 of the ILC Draft only grants the possibility of attributing the acts of insurrectional movements; it does not tell us how to apply this in practice. Deciding that the acts of the insurgency are later attributable to

[274] *Id.*, at 145, n. 105.
[275] *Id.*
[276] *Yeager*, *supra*, at 99.
[277] *Id.,* at 100.
[278] D. D. Caron, "The Basis of Responsibility," *supra*, at 146.
[279] *Id.*

the new government still leaves open the issue of deciding what the insurgent acts *are*. The Tribunal tended to apply the same agency rules to the insurgency that it used for States. It also tended to seek individuated proof of such agency relationships rather than establishing presumptions.

A "legally significant connection" test—used by both ECtHR and NAFTA (as Chapters V (NON-DISCRIMINATION) and VI (OTHER SUBSTANTIVE STANDARDS) will show)—is as vague and malleable as the IUCT's test. This vagueness leads tribunals to "fea[r] that, without the imposition of jurisdictional obstacles to recovery . . ., there [will] be no stopping point short of intolerable consequences."[280] Jurisdictional bars, such as the exhaustion of local remedies, have been used especially in NAFTA cases in order to bar various claims (some of which might be meritorious); the next Chapter will address that point.

These tendencies made recovery by claimants very difficult. For example, in *Yeager* the IUCT cited customary law to argue that the "statements and acts of Ayatollah Khomeini are attributable to the new Government, as it is beyond doubt that he was the leading organ of the revolutionary movement which became the new Government."[281]

Similarly, in *Short v. Iran* (1987)[282] the IUCT held that "[t]he acts of supporters of a revolution cannot be attributed to the government following the success of the revolution just as the acts of supporters of an existing government are not attributable to the government." The *Short* Tribunal compared the insurgency to a State and suggested that the rules it would use to decide whether an act is attributable to a State are the rules it should use in deciding whether an act is attributable to an insurgency.

But then the question is: Whether the rules of attribution used to find agency in the case of States necessarily work also with an insurgency. Similarly, the key question is "whether the evidentiary rules one uses in the case of a single incident involving a unitary, stable, and relatively transparent State apparatus should differ from the case of multiple incidents arising amidst revolutionary circumstances."[283] Judge Brower's

---

[280] L. Anenson, *State Responsibility under NAFTA Chapter Eleven*, *supra*, at 725; see also NAFTA, *supra*, art. 1102; Claimant Methanex Corporation's Counter-Memorial on Jurisdiction, *Methanex Corp. v. United States*, *supra*, at 48–49 (arguing that if its national treatment claim is allowed, the U.S. defence based on "relating to" would be moot).

[281] *Yeager*, *supra*, at 101.

[282] 16 I.U.C.T.R. 76, ¶ 34 (1987-III)

[283] D. D. Caron, "The Basis of Responsibility," *supra*, at 147.

Short dissent argued that the evidentiary requirements needed to be made far less demanding.[284]

Agency in Insurrectional Movements

One might support an insurrection for many unrelated motives and this support did not necessarily imply that the supporter was the state's foot soldier (even a *de facto* one) or that the support profited the government. As a result, there were very few cases in which the IUCT held Iran responsible for injuries caused to United States citizens during revolutionary circumstances.[285] An insurgency often is "relatively unorganised and this makes it extremely difficult to determine who, in fact, acts on behalf of the insurgency."[286] Thus, proving *who*—and if agents of a revolutionary organisation, agents of *which* of the several revolutionary organisations—was difficult.

In *Short* and in *Arthur Young & Co. v. Iran* (1987),[287] the IUCT rejected the request to attribute to Iran the acts of revolutionaries which the claimants alleged caused their unlawful expulsion from Iran. In its award, the IUCT conceded that Iran was responsible for the acts of this revolutionary organisation.[288]

The IUCT emphasised that "the acts of supporters of a revolution cannot be attributed to the government following the success of the revolution just as the acts of supporters of an existing government are not attributable to the government."[289] But it had not been established "who these 'agents' were and how they were associated with the Government of Iran."[290] The Tribunal said that "attribution of acts to the State is justified only when the identity of acting persons and their association with the State is established with reasonable certainty."[291] In both cases, the IUCT's methodology was to apply the agency rules ordinarily used for states.

The standard for identifying the revolutionaries is not impossible. In *Yeager*, the IUCT found that "the claimant sufficiently identified the

[284] *Short*, *supra*, at 100 ("It is the Award's failure thus to adapt traditional concepts to *unique events* that is especially disappointing.").
[285] *Pereira, supra*, at 99; *Computer Sciences Corp. v. Iran*, *supra*, note, at 303.
[286] D. D. Caron, "The Basis of Responsibility," *supra*, at 148.
[287] 17 I.U.C.T.R. 245 (1987-IV).
[288] *Short*, *supra*, at 76.
[289] *Id.*, at 85.
[290] *Arthur Young & Co. v. Iran*, 17 I.U.C.T.R. 245, 257 (1987-IV).
[291] *Id.*, at 257.

people who expelled him from Iran as Revolutionary Guards, and that these Revolutionary Guards were, in fact, agents of the Revolutionary Government."[292] The revolutionaries and their mercenaries wore unmistakable armbands and took the claimant out to a building that the revolutionaries had captured. Again, the Tribunal applied the exact same rules it would have used for a state.

The question still lingers whether the IUCT's *search for agency* was correct amidst revolutionary circumstances. The rules of attribution when looking for a *de facto* agency relationship "between the actor and the State during a period of stability and involving two relatively open societies" make sense but in revolutionary times it has value *only* when the chance of showing any relationship or proving the act is meaningful.[293]

Sometimes it may just be plain fortuitousness (such as a distinctive smell, a previously-known location or an armband) that might decide who recovers relief on an expropriation-related claim. The burden of proof in this legal test requires purely circumstantial evidence. Faith in the rule of law to identify and rectify the problems is admirable. Blind faith against the odds is simply arrogant and audacious. Some might also accuse such acts of blind faith of being irresponsible.[294] Requiring luck, which the claimant cannot control, might be a foolhardy way to risk some important primary rights. To the extent that the necessity is outweighed by the risk in a given subset of circumstances, the reliance on chance should be kept at a station no greater than that of a necessary evil.

Let us explore the inevitable implications. On the one hand, it will signal perpetrators to cover their tracks well, thus removing the deterrent. On the other hand, good-faith (and *only* good-faith) government efforts probably should not be punished or discouraged;[295] this is at least partly

---

[292] *Yeager*, *supra*, at 100-01.

[293] D. D. Caron, "The Basis of Responsibility," *supra*, at 147; *Daley v. Iran*, 18 I.U.C.T.R. 232, 237 (1988-I). For a list of the difficulties, see *Daley*, *supra*, at 240, at ¶ 27; and *Stewart v. Iran*, 24 I.U.C.T.R. 116,119, at ¶ 12 (1990-I).

[294] Even the great Alexander Pope would not have extrapolated "chance" from the domain of "writing|" to that of international wrongfulness. See A. Pope, *Sound and Sense* (1711) ("True Ease in Writing Comes from Art, not Chance, / As those move easiest who have learn'd to dance.").

[295] In their influential book THE ECONOMIC STRUCTURE OF TORT LAW (1987), Landes and Posner suggest a zero-liability rule in good-faith cases. They stretch the argument a little bit further both to state and to private conduct. Landes and Posner then assert that in this situation private liability cannot be any greater than state liability and liability might even deter good samaritans: "imposing liability on potential rescuers will cause them to avoid activities in which they might encounter a duty to rescue — so that there might actually be less rescuing if

because no deterrence value is vindicated by punishing good-faith mistakes, except perhaps incentivising caution, meticulousness and circumspection.[296] But of course these values cannot be incentivised if the good-faith "mistake" is a product of chance or accident. Human rights courts and other dispute settlement bodies that will face this question, and in the course of their lives they all will, must come up with their own answers.

Causation in *Force Majeure* or Other Chaotic Environments

Just because the context is chaotic does not free the claimant from the obligation to prove causation and attribution. The claimant's burden might be seen by the tribunal in a more "understanding" light and thus mitigate the expectation of a certain degree of stricture but it does not remove the burden. The burden is especially mitigated, though (again) far from removed, when the chaos or disorder is caused by the State's own behaviour. The claimant retains the burden of proving that it has suffered an injury caused by the wrongful act(s) of the sovereign; a mere assertion by the Claimant of having suffered injury is insufficient.[297]

---

liability is imposed." I. Ayres, A THEORETICAL FOX MEETS EMPIRICAL HEDGEHOGS: COMPETING APPROACHES TO ACCIDENT ECONOMICS, 82 NW. U. L. REV. 837, 841 (1988) (reviewing the Landes-Posner book).

[296] H. Schäfer & C. Ott, THE ECONOMIC ANALYSIS OF CIVIL LAW 381-83 (Edward Elgar Publishing, 2004).

[297] *Mavrommatis Jerusalem Concessions* (Greece v. U.K.), 1925 P.C.I.J. (ser. A) No. 5 (Mar. 26), p.51 (requiring attribution and noting that "no loss to M. Mavrommatis has been proved."); *Batchelder Claim*, (26, July 1954), 22 International Law Reports, pp. 864-8 ("[I]t is necessary for the claimant, or the Government claiming on his behalf to submit proof that such loss occurred as a result of the war or, at least, to submit sufficient evidence of a casual connection between the war and the loss that the burden of rebuttal would be shifted to the Italian Government. In the instant case, an examination of the evidence submitted by the claimant leads to the conclusion that there is in the record neither proof that the loss was caused by the war nor evidence sufficient to oblige the Italian Government to prove the contrary."); *H.A. Spalding, Inc and Ministry of Roads and Transportation of the Islamic Republic of Iran*, Award No. 212-437-3 of 24 Feb. 1986, at ¶¶ 35, see 10 Iran-U.S. CTR, 22, at 33 ("Consequently, the Tribunal concludes that the Claimant had not carried its burden of proving its claim. To the extent the claim is based on alleged performance of services of which Respondents received the benefit Claimant has not satisfied the Tribunals either that such services were performed or, if any were rendered, requested by the Respondents so as to create a justified expectation of compensation. Insofar as the claim is based on explicit contractual rights the Tribunal notes that one contract may have been

What degree of nexus is needed to show attribution in revolutionary and insurrectional circumstances? Requiring very strict proximate causation is not practical. On the other hand, governments are not, cannot be and "should not be insurers of foreign nationals present during revolutionary circumstances."[298] Governments may find on their hands mobs that they are unable to control. Finding a middle ground is hard.

Let us do a recap of causation's influence in the development of state responsibility. Although causation was a major issue in the nineteenth and early twentieth century arbitral awards, causation has not figured very much in recent attempts to consolidate the law of state responsibility, and is underdeveloped.

It is well-known and accepted that "causation serves as a limit on the scope of State Responsibility for attributable acts" since "[e]ven if . . . an act is attributable to the defendant State it does not necessarily follow that the act was the cause in fact."[299] Nor does it mean that the act was "the legal cause of, the injury on which the claim is premised."[300] Causation is

---

concluded but that there is no evidence proving damages resulting from any breach of the contract. Therefore Claimant's claim is dismissed."); Report of Robert W. Bonynge, Mixed Claims Commission (United States and Germany) 1934, *William R. Hier Case* ("the claimant failed to discharge the burden of proof resting upon him to prove pecuniary damages suffered by him for which Germany was liable"); *id.*, *Turner C. Gillenwatter Case* ("the claimant had failed to discharge the burden resting upon him to establish the real treatment complained of"); *Levis & Levis v. Fed. Rep. of Germany*, 5 Decisions of the Arbitral Commission on Property, Rights and Interests in Germany, vol. II (Nos. 24-61), 1959, p. 206 ("While recognizing the difficulties encountered by the victims of former National-Socialist persecution in supplying proof, mere allegations submitted by a complainant cannot be accepted as prima facie evidence, at least where facts basic to the establishment of the claim are concerned. A reversal of the burden of proof could only arise if it had been sufficiently shown that the defendant held documents of evidential value which it refused to submit"); *Vaso Turajlich case*, Foreign Claims Settlement Commission of the United States, Decisions and Annotations, 1968, Decision, Y-53, p. 38 (unsupported argument of causation and attribution are especially inadequate when confronted with the weight of opposing documentary evidence tendered by the sovereign-respondent). I am particularly grateful to Professor Reisman's submission in *United States v. Canada*, LCIA Case No. 81010 (May 1, 2009) (Opinion with respect to Selected International Legal Problems in LCIA Case No. 7941), at ¶¶ 50-55, for these resources.

[298] D. D. Caron, "The Basis of Responsibility," *supra*, 102-4.

[299] *Id.*, at 153.

[300] *Id.*

also a potential, "conceptual limit to be employed in ascertaining the quantum of compensation owed to the injured state."[301]

The prevailing rule is that "[g]overnments like individuals are responsible only for the *proximate and natural consequences* of their acts."[302] Furthermore, the IUCT's position is that the strength of the chain, rather than the number of links, is what matters.[303] On the causation question, the ILC seeks "the presence of a clear and unbroken causal link between the unlawful [attributable] act and the injury for which damages are being claimed."[304]

Likewise, *Short* held that the international responsibility of a State can be engaged where the circumstances or events causing the departure of the alien, viz. expulsion, are attributable to it by proximate causation.[305] NAFTA cases, most notably *Methanex v. United States* (2005)[306] and *Glamis Gold, Ltd. v. United States* (2006),[307] have reaffirmed this "pragmatic objection" doctrine: to design the chain of causation in a way averse to "the potential for an unending sequence of financial losses"[308] and that which strikes a balance between attracting investment and maintaining sovereignty. International human rights tribunals would do well to adopt this test.

Less clear, however, is whether the rules of attribution can have the consequence of limiting state responsibility to something *less* than responsibility "for the proximate and natural consequences of a State's

---

[301] *Id.*

[302] *Dix Case*, 9 R.I.A.A. 119, 121 (U.S.-Venezuela Mixed Claims Comm'n 1903) (emphasis added).

[303] For a series of perspectives, see *Behring Int'l, Inc. v. Iran*, 8 I.U.C.T.R. 238, 271 (1985) (proximate cause as well as reasonable foreseeability is required); *Administrative Decision*, No. II, 7 R.I.A.A. 23, 29–30 (U.S.-Germ. Mixed Claims Comm'n 1923) ("[I]t matters not how many links there may be in the chain of causation … provided there is no break in the chain and the loss can be clearly, unmistakably, and definitely traced, link by link, to Germany's act."); *Hoffland Honey Co. v. Nat'l Iranian Oil Co.*, 2 I.U.C.T.R 42 (1983) (dismissing claim because the claimant was unforeseeably harmed by effects of the respondent).

[304] *Id.* at 171-2. For an mildly sardonic expression of this requirement, see W. Page Keeton et al., PROSSER AND KEATON ON THE LAW OF TORTS § 41, at 264 (5th ed. 1984) ("In a philosophical sense, the consequences of an act go forward to eternity, and the causes of an act go backward to the dawn of human events, and beyond.").

[305] R. L. Cove, *State Responsibility for Constructive Wrongful Expulsion of Foreign Nationals*, 11 FORD. INT'L L. J. 802, 803 (1987).

[306] UNCITRAL, Final Award on the Merits (2005).

[307] ICSID Case No. ARB/01/12, IIC 24 (2006).

[308] L. Anenson, *State Responsibility under NAFTA Chapter Eleven, supra*, at 704.

acts."[309] Does the rule which provides that the act of a private person is not attributable to the State mean that a State cannot be responsible for the consequences of that private act, even if that act was a foreseeable consequence of other actions of the State? Putting it a little different, is a state responsible for starting a public actor-private actor domino chain reaction that causes injury?[310]

Draft Article 27 of State Responsibility articulates that assistance to another State constitutes an unlawful act "if it is established that it is rendered for the commission of an internationally wrongful act carried out by the latter [State]."[311] Early twentieth century arbitral awards suggest that the State *can* be held responsible in such circumstances. In the *Portuguese Colonies Damages Case* (1928), [312] Portugal attributed responsibility to Germany "for damages in Portuguese Angola, even though such damages were the direct result of an uprising by the indigenous peoples of Angola."[313] Portugal claimed that the uprising was a foreseeable consequence of German military operations in Angola.[314]

Do such events make *all* collateral damages (because of expropriation and other primary rights violations) actionable and attributable to the State? Is there a ceiling (other than the logic of proximate causation) on damages? Assuming proximate causation is all that exists, then does it supply us with an adequate limiting principle? What if the military action (the initiator's actions, generally) had brought positive as well as negative consequences for the now-claimant? What if the military action had been necessary for Germany's self-preservation?

The *Portuguese Colonies Damages Case* tribunal did not answer all these questions; it simply reasoned that "it would not be equitable to leave the victim to bear damages that the perpetrator of the initial illicit act foresaw and perhaps wanted" just because "in the chain of causation there are intermediate links."[315] But no matter what, it is "necessary to exclude

---

[309] *Dix*, *supra*, at 121.

[310] Report of the ILC (1993), *supra*, at 168.

[311] Draft Articles on State Responsibility with Commentaries Thereto Adopted by the International Law Commission on First Reading (1997), Doc. 97-02583; see also I. Brownlie, SYSTEM OF THE LAW OF NATIONS: STATE RESPONSIBILITY 23 (1983).

[312] *Responsabilité de l'Allemagne a Raison des Dommages Causes dans les Colonies Portugaises du Sud de l'Afrique*, 2 R.I.A.A. 1011 (1928).

[313] D. D. Caron, "The Basis of Responsibility," *supra*, at 154.

[314] *Responsabilité de l'Allemagne a Raison des Dommages Causes dans les Colonies Portugaises du Sud de l'Afrique*, *supra*, at 1031.

[315] *Id.*; See *United States v. Comstock*, 176 L. Ed. 2d 878, 900 (2010) (Kennedy, J., concurring in judgment) ("the analysis depends not on the number of links in the

some damages so that one does not extend responsibility to damages not [ordinarily] connected to the initial act."[316] Foreseeability and intent figure in; in the absence of these factors there could not be causation.

Now imagine that a private actor intervenes between the act of the State, its organs, instrumentalities or insurrectional movements. Obviously the injury looks "distant from th[e] act because of other intervening actors."[317] In the ICJ (notably in the *Hostages Case* (1980)[318] and the *Nicaragua Case* (1986)[319]), this would probably be enough to break the chain of causation.

Not so in the IUCT, and there is not yet an obvious reason why in *force majeure* cases the ICJ and the IUCT might come up differently. Nor is the seriousness of the urgency in the cases so dramatically different. The one speculative answer is that, unlike the ICJ, the IUCT's practice and rules are exclusively grounded in *force majeure*, as are the mentalities of the judges.

In the IUCT, despite the presence of possibly independent private actors in the chain, there might be responsibility and attribution. Never has a pro-attribution view in these circumstances claimed a majority. Nor has it been ruled out decisively; the IUCT majority has just resolved the cases on other grounds. In *Grimm v. Iran* (1983),[320] the IUCT held that Iran's failure to protect the life of a U.S. national is not a measure "affecting-property-rights" (as the CSD requires) and thus outside the Tribunal's jurisdiction. An IIA tribunal, *Noble Ventures, Inc. v. Romania* (2005),[321] has suggested that such failure-to-act claims under the Full Protection and Security standard are governed by a due diligence standard rather than by strict liability. Two other cases are marginally relevant.

Grimm merits additional discussion. The *Grimm* majority did not resolve the causation question. But Judge Holtzmann's dissent argued that "international law firmly establishes that a widow has a property right in support by her husband."[322] Holtzmann would have gone further and held the present Government of Iran responsible not only for insurgent acts but more generally "for acts in furtherance of the achievement of the goals of

---

congressional-power chain but on the strength of the chain.").

[316] *Id.*

[317] D. D. Caron, "The Basis of Responsibility," *supra*, at 158.

[318] *United States v. Iran*, 1980 I.C.J. 3, 30, at ¶ 59.

[319] *Nicaragua v. United States*, 1986 I.C.J., at ¶¶ 93-122

[320] 2 I.U.C.T.R. 78 (1983-I).

[321] ICSID Case No. ARB/01/11.

[322] *Grimm*, *supra*, at 2 (Holtzmann, J., dissenting).

the Islamic Revolution."[323] Judge Khalilian's separate opinion in *Emanuel Too v. Greater Modesto Insurance Associates & the United States* (1989),[324] was open to the same view.

Neither Judge Khalilian nor Judge Holtzmann deduced that *Rankin v. Iran* (1987)[325]—decided four years after *Grimm* but two years before *Emmanuel Too*—had already laid the groundwork for sweeping, generalised liability: the revolutionaries, who later constituted the Islamic Republic, could "have reasonably been expected to initiate or prompt the types of harassment and violence that were suffered by individual U.S. nationals."[326] Combining this with Judge Holtzmann's position might create a strong enough chain to justify attribution.

While Judge Holtzmann's aims in *Grimm* are admirable, we quickly run into some practical problems. First, the claimant's victory may well be Pyrrhic and even counterproductive because, on the merits, the claimant would find it difficult to gather evidence and also show that the culprits were revolutionaries and *not* just irate private citizens (pretending that this distinction exists). Second, this might have a chilling effect on speech and protest during future revolutions in jurisdictions that accept this Holtzmann prescription.

This, ironically, would have no after-the-fact effects for IUCT—even though the rule might arise from that tribunal—but significant impact on NAFTA panels and the ECtHR. The latter two institutions, of course, regulate prospective behaviour. It is possible that the IUCT in *Short,* though clearly tempted, did not take the Holtzmann stance in *Grimm* because of the same concerns. The IUCT might have been guided by the scope to earn legitimacy on account of other international law institutions using *its* "reasoned decisions" (in Mark Weidemaier's words).[327] In any case, this approach has yielded the IUCT significant dividends, as the Gibson-Drahozal study explains.

---

[323] *Id.* at 13.

[324] 23 I.U.C.T.R. 378-384 (1989- III).

[325] 17 I.U.C.T.R. 135, 141, 147 (1987-III) (holding that there is no *de facto* difference between political conditions such as "acts of unorganized mobs and individuals" forcing someone to give up their rights and laws that de jure accomplish the same end).

[326] *Id.*

[327] W.M.C. Weidemaier, *Precedent in Arbitration, supra*, at 1917-18.

§ 3.5—Passing Obligations on to the New Government

This section engages with essential topics that underlie attribution and causation, much like attribution and causation themselves underlie primary and secondary rules and the relationship between the two.

Force Majeure, Geography, Corporate Coverage, and Definition of "Investment"

We begin with the interpretive methodology. International law generally deems policy matters to be distinct from the question whether Property X is *ultra vires* the legal definition of "investment," but ICSID tribunals have been sensitive to the possibility that "[a] direct relationship can . . . be established if those general measures are adopted in violation of specific commitments given to the investor in treaties, legislation or contracts."[328] In most of international law, the all-too-crucial definition question has been framed in the following way:

> the Tribunal must examine the current and past practice of ICSID and the practice of States as evidenced in multilateral and bilateral treaties and agreements binding on States . . . . It is for the Tribunal to determine the meaning or definition of 'investment' for this purpose as a question of law. Opinions of experts on the theory and practice of multinational corporations are not to be identified with the teachings of the most highly qualified publicists of the various nations, which as such constitute subsidiary means for the determination of rules of law. Only subject to Article 59 of the Statute of the International Court of Justice are judicial decisions to be considered as such subsidiary sources of law.
>
> . . . . .
>
> The Tribunal is of the view that *de lege ferenda* the sources of international law on the extended meaning or definition of investment will have to be found in conventional law or in customary law.[329]

---

[328] *CMS Gas Transmission Company v. The Republic of Argentina*, ICSID Case No. ARB/01/8, Decision of the Tribunal on Objections to Jurisdiction, at ¶¶ 26-27 (2003) ("[Q]uestions of general economic policy not directly related to the investment, as opposed to measures specifically addressed to the operations of the business concerned, will normally fall outside the jurisdiction of the [ICSID definition of 'investment']. A direct relationship can, however, be established if those general measures are adopted in violation of specific commitments given to the investor in treaties, legislation or contracts. What is brought under the jurisdiction of the [relevant IIA] is not the general measures in themselves but the extent to which they may violate those specific commitments").

[329] *Mihaly International Corporation v. Democratic Socialist Republic of Sri*

First, we address the geography and *force majeure* issue now or soon to be on the front burner. We have already discussed the "national of another Contracting State" language from the ICSID Convention earlier in this Chapter. Now it is important to understand what "investment" does or does not cover. Investment regimes typically do not receive a large number of direct *force majeure* cases, even though a camouflaged version might be in the offing: a water rights expropriation case called *Bayview Irrigation District v. Mexico* (2007)[330] in the NAFTA. Future IIA cases "may raise a variety of complex public and international law questions, including human rights considerations."[331]

In *Bayview Irrigation District*, the NAFTA tribunal denied jurisdiction because the water rights "investment" was conducted *in* Texas and affected *by* Mexico and not made *in* Mexico.[332] Geography mattered to the tribunal and it typically matters across the board in the IIA universe.[333] IIA's typically cover "entities established" in the host State. By this time it is hornbook law that "entity" is "[a] thing that has a real existence."[334] Claimants are deemed to be an "investor" "if it is a thing of real legal existence that was founded on a secure basis in the territory of [the host

---

Lanka, ICSID Case No. ARB/00/2, Award (2002), at ¶¶ 58-60.

330 ICSID Case No. ARB (AF)/05/1.

331 *Suez v. Argentina*, Order in response to a petition for transparency and participation as amicus curiae, ¶ 18 (2005). A case currently in gestation involves a tobacco company's challenge to tobacco packaging measures imposed by the governments, which claim that the measures promote health warnings. See *Philip Morris Brand Sàrl, Philip Morris Products S.A., and Abal Hermanos S.A. v. Uruguay,* ICSID Case No. ARB/10/7.

332 *Bayview*, *supra*, at ¶103.

333 An effective model Article 1 (4) of the Lebanon-Republic of Korea BIT (2006), stating the following: "'Territory' means the territory of the Contracting Parties, including the territorial sea as well as the maritime areas including the exclusive economic zone, its seabed and subsoil adjacent to the outer limit of the territorial sea over which the State concerned exercises, in accordance with national and international law, jurisdiction and sovereign rights." Another is Article 1, at ¶ 10, of the Energy Charter Treaty (1994): "'Area' means with respect to a state that is a Contracting Party: the territory under its sovereignty, it being understood that territory includes land, internal waters and the territorial sea; and subject to and in accordance with the international law of the sea: the sea, sea-bed and its subsoil with regard to which that Contracting Party exercises sovereign rights and jurisdiction."

334 See THE NEW SHORTER OXFORD ENGLISH DICTIONARY 830 (Thumb Index Edition 1993).The dictionary definition of "establish" ordinarily is to "[s]et up on a permanent or secure basis; bring into being, found (a…business)." *Id.*, at 852.

State] in conformity with its laws and regulations."[335] Again, we notice an international tribunal's deference to "laws and regulations" of the host State.[336] This issue will resurface soon, a few pages later, because its complexities cannot go unaddressed.

After analysing whether it was a "foreign investment" and concluding that it was "wholly confined" to Texas,[337] the IIA tribunal dismissed the claims. How the *Bayview* or other tribunals might resolve the dispute if the investment is only primarily confined to the home State or within the exclusive or primary operational reach of the host State but within the physical territory of some other State is not entirely obvious.

Another tribunal, in *Abaclat et al. v. Argentina* (2011),[338] developed the territorial-link test to answer some of these questions: securities entitlements in the form of Argentinean bonds acquired by the claimants in secondary securities markets outside Argentina were indeed investments "made in the territory of" Argentina for purposes of the definition of investment in the Argentina-Italy BIT.[339] Stating that "[w]ith regard to investments of a purely financial nature, the relevant criteria should be where and/or for the benefit of whom the funds are ultimately used, and not the place where the funds were paid out or transferred," the *Abaclat* tribunal found that "the funds generated through the bonds issuance process were ultimately made available to Argentina, and served to finance Argentina's economic development."[340]

In this respect, *Bayview* is similar to *Tokios Tokelés v. Ukraine* (2003), an IIA arbitration involving a local investor's company incorporated in a foreign jurisdiction. First, *Bayview* shows clear potential for a dispute

---

[335] See, *e.g.*, *Tokios Tokelés v. Ukraine,* ICSID, Decision on Jurisdiction (2004), at ¶ 28.

[336] *Id.*

[337] *Bayview*, *supra*, at ¶ 103.

[338] *Giovanna a Beccara and Others v. Argentine Republic*, (*Abaclat et al v. Argentina*), ICSID Case No. ARB/07/5, Decision on Jurisdiction, 4 August 2011, at ¶ 374.

[339] Article I of this BIT covers "any contribution or asset invested or reinvested by physical or juridical persons of one Contracting Party in the territory of the other."

[340] *Abaclat, supra,* Decision on Jurisdiction, at ¶ 378; Dissenting Opinion, George Abi-Saab, 28 October 2011, at ¶ 78 (stating that "the financial securities instruments that constitute the alleged investment, i.e. the security entitlements in Argentinean bonds, have been sold in international financial markets, outside Argentina, with choice of law and forum selection clauses subjecting them to laws and fora foreign to Argentina. In fact, they were intentionally situated outside Argentina and out of reach of its laws and tribunals. There is no way then to say (and no legal basis for saying) that they are legally located in Argentina.").

regarding essential elements—some might even call them positive rights, such as food, water, shelter and clothing that the domestic laws of some States (Everyone's Regulator) requires the States to *guarantee* all persons within their jurisdiction—and thus clear potential for a *force majeure* dispute.

Second, we can observe an important conflict of laws, or conflict of principles, trend: Although there arguably is an international law principle that "[a]ny activities undertaken within the State party's jurisdiction should not deprive another country of the ability to realise the right to water for persons in its jurisdiction," [341] the IIA text's geographic limitation was understood to control the scenario. If such a positive right is guaranteed in national law or constitution, then may the State escape or at least diminish liability before an IIA tribunal for harming the investor? Does it, or should it, make a difference that the class of rights at issue here is so heightened? Is there potential for a *jus cogens*-based exception to the default rule precluding States from escaping international liability on account of a domestic law *requirement* to protect fundamental rights?

Such a situation might strike some observers as distinguishable from the Brownlie prescription where the State need not have a domestic law *obligation* to do so and also from non-*jus cogens* situations. Depending on the granularity in which the guarantee is codified in internal law, the State might be able to claim under Article 46 of the Vienna Convention on the Law of Treaties an exemption.[342]

Next, we address the corporate coverage issue. Along this vein, it is important to articulate where we currently are regarding the definition of an "investment" in IIA law. The IIA tribunal in *Alps Finance and Trade v. Slovak Republic* held that the government acquisition of some "receivables" from a private firm could not be deemed a protected investment not just under the salient BIT but also under customary international law. The United Nations Conference on Trade and Development (UNCTAD) suggests that coverage may be withheld from "portfolio shares . . . . [T]he risk involved in some portfolio investments for the investor would not be as high as that involved in a direct investment, since the former investment could normally be pulled out of a host country more easily than the latter."[343]

---

[341] General Comment (No. 15), *The Right to Water (Arts. 11 and 12 of the International Covenant on Economic, Social and Cultural Rights,* UN Doc. E/C.12/2002/11*)* (2002), at ¶¶ 31, 35-6.

[342] The State should be aware that Article 23 poses something of a conflict with Article 46.

[343] *Scope and Definition*, UNCTAD Series on Issues in International Investment

Adhering to the award in *Romak v. Uzbekistan* (2009),[344] the *Alps Finance* tribunal, which was operating under the UNCITRAL rules, held that even though the BIT's definition of covered investments protected "every kind of assets," it is the *source* of the asset that controls. This seems to be largely consistent with *Renta 4 S.V.S.A. v. Russian Federation* (2009),[345] an award concerning American Depositary Receipts (ADRs), issued by certain New York banks and backed by the stock of the corporation which had been nationalised by the Russian government. ADRs were the source of the claim in *Renta*, and because the Spain-Russia BIT did not limit its coverage just to ordinary shareholders ADRs were a covered source and constituted an "'rights deriving from' an investment."[346]

Under this BIT, "investors" included natural persons ("*persona fisica*") or corporate bodies ("*persona juridica*") but did not include "collective investment funds" containing a tripartite decision-making structure.[347] The tribunal's stated basis was that coverage applied only to "corporate bodies" and individuals; moreover, it was stated in the *Renta* award on jurisdiction, that Spanish law did not consider "collective investment funds" to be recognised or recognisable "corporate bodies."[348]

Concerning the "collective investment funds" at issue here, the custodianship, ownership and management of assets were divided among different entities. Judge Charles Brower's separate opinion, believing that Spanish law's definition was inferior in relevance to the tribunal's construction of international law, stated that the tribunal's "interpretive approach violates the principle of the primacy of international law over domestic law and the principle that international treaties must be interpreted autonomously, i.e., not in accordance with the domestic legal orders of the contracting State parties involved."[349] The Brower position is entirely consistent with the earlier-explicated (in Chapter § 3.3) trend-lines running through *Selwyn-Loizidou-GAMI*, involving the three great pillars of international law analysed in this book (diplomatic dispute resolution, international human rights and IIA awards).

While many contemporary IIA's contain "trusts," "firms," and/or "associations" within the definition of "investor," not all do. Fund managers

---

Agreements II, 2011, pp. 10-11 (citing M. Sornarajah, THE INTERNATIONAL LAW ON FOREIGN INVESTMENT 227-28 (Cambridge University Press, 2004)).

[344] *Romak S.A. v. The Republic of Uzbekistan* (UNCITRAL), Award (2009).

[345] SCC, Mar. 29, 2009.

[346] *Id.*, at ¶ 143-44.

[347] *Id.*

[348] *Id.*

[349] *Id.*, at ¶ 28 (Separate opinion of Judge Charles Brower).

and trustees would be well-advised to "review . . . existing investment structures to ascertain if they can or should be modified to maximize . . . [IIA] protection (e.g., where appropriate and possible, by interposing holding companies between the fund and its foreign assets that might qualify as an "investor" under an applicable [IIA])."[350] It is becoming increasingly more common to have joint ventures, and the question then might be if the whole investor operation is severable and, if not, which textual instrument or customary law gives rise to a cause of action.[351]

What about contracts as sources of investments? When the source of an investment is a contract, then the contract itself is the relevant investment. The game does not end there, for a contract must meet some requirements: (*i*) a "certain duration of performance of the contract,"[352] (*ii*) capital contribution,[353] (*iii*) assumption of risk,[354] and (*iv*) "participation in the risks of the transaction."[355] These conjunctive criteria have been joined by another factor *necessary* for the in-flow to be deemed an "investment"

---

[350] T. G. Nelson, et al, "Possible Gaps in Bilateral Investment Treaty (BIT) Coverage for Managed Investment Funds," *supra*, at 1 ("Sovereign states can therefore be expected to cite Renta in future disputes as a basis for denying . . . [IIA] protection to unincorporated funds and similar investment vehicles organized along legal forms not recognized for protection under the relevant . . . [IIA]. The outcome of any future challenge will depend on many factors, including the specific wording of the BIT or FTA — not all of which are drafted the same way as the Spain-Russia BIT. . . . Such an exercise demands careful attention to the terms of any potentially applicable . . . [IIA], as well as to the tax and other legal consequences of any restructuring.").

[351] J. Bray, "Strengthening the Economic Dimensions of Peacebuilding" *in* PRACTICE NOTE 3: FOREIGN DIRECT INVESTMENT IN CONFLICT-AFFECTED CONTEXTS 2, International Alert, *available at* <www.international-alert.org/sites/default/files/publications/practice_note3_march2010.pdf> (2010) ("Some foreign investments take the form of entirely new ventures. Others are purchases of existing businesses, or joint ventures with local or international partner companies. Joint ventures provide a means of sharing both the financial costs and the risks of the business, as well as sharing expertise. Foreign companies often particularly value the local knowledge and business contacts provided by their in-country partners.").

[352] *Salini Costrutorri S.p.A. and Italstrade S.p.A. v. Morocco*, ICSID Case No. ARB/00/4, Decision on Jurisdiction (2001), at ¶ 52. In some academic and judicial literature, there seems to be this general insistence on sufficient length, though the ICSID Convention's most formalistic reading would not

[353] See also *Alps Finance and Trade AG v. Slovak Republic*, UNCITRAL, Award, 5 March 2011, at ¶ 231; *id.*, at ¶ 241.

[354] *Id.*

[355] *Fedax NV v. Republic of Venezuela*, ICSID Case No. ARB/96/3, Decision on Objections to Jurisdiction (1997), at ¶ 43.

within the IIA context: "contribution to the host State's economic development."[356]

This requirement, if widely accepted,[357] could cause problems down the road: *Actual* contribution to the host State's economic development depends not just on the intent and effect of the investor's behavior but also the behavior of various actors, including the host State itself, over which the investor or for that matter the government might not have very much control. Moreover, innumerable foreign portfolio investments "tak[e] the form of smaller shareholdings that are not accompanied by management control."[358] They do not satisfy the aforementioned condition of substantial contribution, of course, but nor can these foreign portfolio investments be considered non-"investments" (for ICSID or other purposes).

---

[356] *Kardassopoulos v. Georgia*, Decision on Jurisdiction, ICSID Case No. ARB/05/18 (2007), at ¶ 116. See also *Alps Finance and Trade AG v. Slovak Republic*, UNCITRAL, Award, 5 March 2011, at ¶ 231; *id.*., at ¶ 241 ("A more than abundant number of cases have contributed to elucidate the notion of investment under the ICSID Convention and, more in general, international customary law. It is now common ground that the necessary conditions or characteristics to be satisfied for attributing the quality of 'investment' to a contractual relationship include: (a) a capital contribution […], (b) a significant duration […] and (c) a sharing of operational risks […]."); *id.*, at ¶ 245 ("The constant jurisprudential trend has led the most prominent doctrine to exclude in categorical terms that a mere one-off sale transaction might qualify as an investment. The Tribunal cannot ignore the general consensus formed around the above doctrine."); R. Dolzer, "The Notion of Investment in Recent Practice," *in* LAW IN THE SERVICE OF HUMAN DIGNITY: ESSAYS IN HONOUR OF FLORENTINO FELICIANO 263 (Charnovitz, Steger and Van den Bossche, eds) (Cambridge University Press, 2005) (stating that there is a difference between the economic definition of an "ordinary transfer" of funds and the legal definition of "investment").

[357] For reasons including and ranging beyond those I have presented, *Salini* has been criticised widely.

[358] J. Bray, "Strengthening the Economic Dimensions of Peacebuilding" *in* PRACTICE NOTE 3: FOREIGN DIRECT INVESTMENT IN CONFLICT-AFFECTED CONTEXTS 3, International Alert, *available at* <www.international-alert.org/sites/default/files/publications/practice_note3_march2010.pdf> (2010) ("Portfolio investment has tended to imply less commitment to the host country in times of crisis, in part because it is much easier to sell shares than physical assets."). Less commitment to the host State does not mean no or even insubstantial commitment. It would all depend on "substantial" from whose perspective, the investor's (Certain sum of money? Certain proportion of the investor's resources? An absolute threshold?) or the State's (Certain proportion of the GDP or GNP? Certain proportion of the State's budget? An absolute threshold?).

In addition, even assuming that the prior issues somehow turn out not to be problematic, some "successful" contributions, *i.e.*, contributions that meet this test, might unfairly be *less* of a result of the investor's behavior than some "unsuccessful" contributions. In short, the shortcoming of this last criterion is the vast room for play it accords extra-investor behavior factors. In any case, another IIA tribunal has ruled that ordinary and short-term "sale and purchase contracts entered into by the Claimants are pure commercial transactions that cannot on any interpretation be considered to constitute 'investments' within the meaning of Article 25 of the ICSID Convention."[359]

Not every recent IIA tribunal has regarded the term "investment" this way. The tribunal in *White Industries v. India* (2011) (also operating under UNCITRAL rules) stated: "having regard to the definition of 'investment' in the BIT, which clearly include[s] White's rights under the Contract, and the decisions of other tribunals that rights aris[ing] from contracts may amount to investments, the Tribunal concludes that the fact that White's rights under the Contract may be *in personam* rather than *in rem* does not exclude the Contract from qualifying as an investment."[360]

There was more to the *White Industries* award. The *White Industries* tribunal also rejected the minimum requirements identified in *Alp Finance* and *Romak* (colloquially known as the *Salini* factors).[361] What happens when an investment already exists? The tribunal in *Chevron Corp. and Texaco Corp. v. Republic of Ecuador* (2012) stated that such an investment "remains protected by [the IIA] even after the enterprise in question may

---

[359] *Global Trading Resource Corp. and Globex International, Inc. v. Ukraine*, ICSID Case No. ARB/09/11, Final Award (2010), at ¶ 57; *id.*, at ¶ 56 (stating that "having viewed the contracts concluded by Global with Alan-Trade as nominee for the Ukrainian State Reserve, and having heard the parties' answers to the questions raised by it during the oral hearing, the Tribunal is compelled to the conclusion that these are each individual contracts, of limited duration, for the purchase and sale of goods, on a commercial basis and under normal CIF [cost, insurance, and freight] trading terms, and which provide for delivery, the transfer of title, and final payment, before the goods are cleared for import into the recipient territory; and that neither contracts of that kind, nor the moneys expended by the supplier in financing its part in their performance, can by any reasonable process of interpretation be construed to be 'investments' for the purposes of the ICSID Convention.").

[360] UNCITRAL, Final Award, 30 November 2011, at ¶ 7.4.7.

[361] *Id.*, at ¶¶ 7.4.8 and 7.4.9; see also *Salini v. Morocco*, Decision on Jurisdiction, ICSID Case No. ARB/00/4.

have failed ... Issues of orderly liquidation and the settlement of claims may still arise and require [international legal protection] ..." [362]

Moreover, it appears to be the UNCTAD position that "[e]xtending protection to those [intellectual property rights or IPRs] that are not protected under domestic law of a State may lead to an undue restriction of regulatory discretion in dealing with such rights in the context of the need for technology and skills transfer as part of its development policy."[363] The UNCTAD would extend this principle to all investments and accordingly recommend that "only investments made in accordance with host country law could be given protection."[364] When the factors in this calculus are in equipoise and no clear answer is evident, it appears that IIA tribunals place the burden on the State. They pay special heed to the operative provision's "material objective"[365] by refusing to give effect to "artificial trap[s] depriving investors of the very protection the BIT was intended to provide."[366]

Lastly, IIA's have taken various stances on loans, bonds, and debts: Some have excluded certain debt securities and loans;[367] some have proposed a test to determine what is an "investment" *within* this category;

---

[362] *Chevron Corp. and Texaco Corp. v. Republic of Ecuador*, PCA CASE NO. 2009-23, Third Interim Award on Jurisdiction and Admissibility, at ¶3.107 (2012) (citing *Mondev v. United States*, ICSID Case No. ARB(AF)/99/2, Final Award (2002)).

[363] *Scope and Definition*, UNCTAD Series on Issues in International Investment Agreements II, 2011, pp. 10-11 [*Scope and Definition*, UNCTAD Series 2011].

[364] *Id.* ("[I]nvestments that fail to abide by the law of the host country, as applied upon entry and establishment, will lose the protection of the IIA, as they do not qualify as protected investments due to their illegality. Depending on the exact formulation of the requirement, it could conceivably be used to deprive an investor of the treaty protection for serious violations of host country law admitted during the life of an investment, i.e. after it is made.").

[365] *Desert Line Projects LLC v. Yemen*, ICSID Case No. ARB/05/17, Award (2008), at ¶ 106.

[366] *Id.*

[367] *Scope and Definition*, UNCTAD Series 2011, *supra,* at 32 ("Canada's model BIT (2004) . . . provides an example of a definition that excludes certain debt securities and loans: Debt securities and loans with the original maturity of less than three years (Article 1(III) and (IV); Debt securities of a State enterprise and loans to a State enterprise, regardless of their original maturity (Article 1(III) and (IV); A loan to or debt security issued by a financial institution which are not treated as regulatory capital by the Party in whose territory the financial institution is located; and [t]he extension of credit in connection with a commercial transaction, such as trade financing.").

[368] and others still have "chosen to exclude sovereign debt securities from covered investments, as IIA obligations could interfere with debt restructuring or rescheduling in case of default or financial difficulties."[369] In various forms, other international law prototypes will face this question in the coming years. In Chapter I, I have articulated that treasury policy, unless discriminatory under National Treatment or Most Favoured Nation, typically carries the presumption of being *intra vires*. In fact, facially neutral policies typically need have both a discriminatory purpose and a discriminatory effect in order to be considered *ultra vires* general principles of international law. Discriminatory purpose, in particular, can be identified by policies that have no motivation other than discrimination, substantive departure(s) from normal policy, and legislative and/or administrative history. Presumptions can, however, be rebutted if the amount of debt restructuring poses an exorbitant burden on the claimants in an unexpected and unforeseeable manner or if there is serious and substantial risk of a virulent pattern of defaults developing.

Yet another alternative, exercised by the Peru-United States Free Trade Agreement, is "to limit an investor's ability to bring an investor–State claim based on a debt restructuring where holders of 75% or more of the outstanding debt have agreed to the restructuring."[370] The three-quarters fraction is, of course, adjustable to fit different circumstances. IIA's and indeed any instrument whose exclusive purpose, at least ostensibly, is to promote capital flow and encourage FDI may elect not to extend coverage to non-business assets [371] NAFTA is a prime example.[372] This common-

---

[368] Article 10.28, Peru–United States FTA (2006) ("Some forms of debt, such as bonds, debentures, and long-term notes, are more likely to have the characteristics of an investment, while other forms of debt, such as claims to payment that are immediately due and result from the sale of goods or services, are less likely to have such characteristics.").

[369] *Scope and Definition*, UNCTAD Series 2011, *supra,* at 32-33.

[370] *Id.*

[371] Article 1139, NAFTA (1992) ("interests arising from the commitment of capital or other resources in the territory of a Party to economic activity in such territory . . ."); Article 1, Belarus–Czech Republic BIT (1996) ("The term 'investment' shall mean every kind of asset invested in connection with economic activities by an investor of one Contracting Party . . . "); Article 72(a), Japan–Singapore EPA (2002) ("For the purposes of this Chapter, 'loans and other forms of debt' [...] and 'claims to money and claims to any other performance under contract' [...] refer to assets which relate to a business activity and do not refer to assets which are of personal nature, unrelated to any business activity"). See also *Phoenix Action Ltd v. Czech Republic*, ICSID Case No. ARB/06/5, Award, 15 April 2009, at ¶ 142 (smoking out and rejecting efforts to gain access to ICSID rather than to actually

sense proposition needs no textual ratification and might be construed direct by tribunals. Whether tribunals choose to do so will be a different question. Only time will tell.

International human rights tribunals have faced cases that might help the IIA analysis in certain respects.

Saga of the International Human Rights Tribunals

Before the international human rights tribunals, the attribution rule has come to mean that the Court is not competent to protect rights which do not have their basis in the Convention.[373] Across their jurisprudence, international human rights tribunals have "endeavoured to link every positive obligation to a clause of the Convention."[374] The next two chapters will reflect on how the Convention texts has been a golden thread connecting the already-tenuous positive obligations to plenary decisions of the international human rights tribunals.

Positive obligations complicate the attribution question, especially regarding *force majeure*. The question becomes—whose responsibility was it to make sure this did *not* happen? The international human rights jurisprudence in non-property areas of human rights law will make a significant difference, and has yet to (in large part), in how this State Responsibility issue is addressed in the property context.

An important trend is emerging these days. The ECtHR and the IACtHR are grounding their positive obligations (substantive or procedural) in a "combination of the standard-setting provisions of the [Conventions] and [the *specific* textual provisions] of that text."[375] Thus the obligation to "take necessary measures" to secure freedom of expression is drawn from Article 10 along with Article 1;[376] "the

---

attempt to engage in economic activities in the host State).

[372] *Id.*

[373] *Johnston v. Ireland* [1986] 9 E.H.R.R. 203, at ¶¶ 65-68; J. Akandji-Kombe, *Positive Obligations under the European Convention on Human Rights: A guide to the implementation of the European Convention on Human Rights*, HUM. RTS. HANDBOOK 7-8, 7th ed. (Council of Europe, 2007) [J. Akandji-Kombe, *Positive Obligations Handbook*].

[374] *Id.* See also P. Dumberry, *Is a New State Responsible for Obligations Arising from Internationally Wrongful Acts Committed before its Independence in the Context of Secession?*, 43 CANADIAN Y.I.L. 419, 422 (2005).

[375] *Id.*, at 7-8.

[376] *Id.*, at 8; see also *Verein Gegen Tierfabriken (Vgt) v. Switzerland*, App. no. 24699/94 (2001).

obligation to protect property from the combination of the same Article 1 and Article 14 of Protocol No. 1."[377] Property rights cannot be understood in institutional isolation, as Chapters V (NON-DISCRIMINATION) and VI (OTHER SUBSTANTIVE STANDARDS) show.

The ECtHR cases of *Assanidzé v. Georgia* (2005)[378] and *Ilaşcu v. Moldova and Russia* (2004)[379] generally bear this out. In these cases, Article I of the ECHR is seen as the bedrock of the ECHR regime, to the point of being an independent source of positive obligations. For instance, in *Assanidzé*, the Court found that Article I implicitly required the implementation of a state system such as to guarantee the Convention system over all its territory and with regard to every individual.

In *Ilaşcu*, the Court considered that in cases "where part of its territory, by reason of a separatist regime, escaped its control and authority, the state nevertheless continued to bear in respect of the population in that territory the positive obligations"[380] borne of Article 1: "it was required to take the measures necessary, on the one hand to restore its control over that territory and, on the other, to protect the persons living there."[381]

Jean-Francois Akandji-Kombe has considered describing these general obligations as "quasi-autonomous."[382] They are so only insofar as they generate solely by virtue of Article I of the Convention. But they are not absolutely so, "because their observance can be tested only on the occasion of an application alleging violation of one of the substantive rights secured by the [ECHR]."[383]

The very business of international human rights tribunals is to be context-based and, specifically, *force majeure*-sensitive. In no other circumstances has this tribunal-type been so willing to impose positive obligations and to dovetail Convention provisions to protect human rights (not to mention, become involved in deeply political issues) than in *force majeure* cases with a high degree of abuse. Perhaps this is attributable to the tribunals' appreciation of the on-the-ground and grassroots reality in *these* cases where political machinations and arm-twisting have the distinct proclivity to overtake the relatively faint voice of human rights.

---

[377] *Id.*, at 8; see also *Broniowski v. Poland*, App. no. 31443/96 (2001).
[378] App. no. 9808/02.
[379] App. no. 48787/99.
[380] See J. Akandji-Kombe, *Positive Obligations Handbook*, at 9.
[381] *Id.* The ECtHR's *Loizidou* case, already discussed, was directly about *negative* obligations, so it did not concern the joint ECHR provisions.
[382] *Id.*
[383] *Id.*

Moreover, history and the lack of effective political or legal systematic mechanisms to cure any abuses have not been encouraging. One could argue that in these cases property rights often are seen as a core guarantee for people's survival that must be attained by all or almost all possible means. Yeoman farmers to middle-class people frequently have property as the sole means to eke out a lawful living in various jurisdictions. The universality of expropriation comes to the fore.

The Iran-United States Claims Tribunal (IUCT)'s Experience with Force Majeure

The ILC's Draft Articles identify five distinct circumstances as potentially "precluding wrongfulness."[384] Amongst these the IUCT has only examined *force majeure*. Interestingly, the rules regarding *force majeure* complement those regarding attribution because the State can invoke *force majeure* only if the force is not a result of its own actions or, in other words, if the *force majeure* condition is not attributable to the State. Thus, discussion regarding *force majeure* often raises the same issues raised by the Tribunal's efforts to engage with the public aspects of a government-owned or controlled private corporation.

The Tribunal acknowledged on several occasions the international law principle that a State is not responsible for its failure to prevent wrongful acts when such acts are totally beyond its control.[385] Iran, for example, was generally not held responsible for the failure of the Shah's government to prevent injuries to aliens occurring during the general chaos resulting from the revolution. Moreover, the IUCT also seemed to apply the principle of *force majeure* to the insurrection movement by not attributing to the insurrection movement general acts of violence by unidentified revolutionaries not acting under the control of the insurgent government.

Iran could not invoke the revolution as *force majeure* precluding the wrongfulness of its acts. The reason is pretty simple: The revolution was of the new government's own (at least in significant part) making and the new government surely profited from the revolution![386] For instance, in

---

[384] See Chapter V of the ILC Draft Articles, Report of the ILC (1980), *supra*, at 33-34. The other circumstances listed in Chapter V of the ILC Draft are consent (article 29), countermeasures in respect of an internationally wrongful act (article 30), fortuitous event (article 31) and distress (article 32).

[385] See *Sea-Land, supra*, at 166.

[386] Governments and regimes often come and ago all over the world. Rarely, however, does the very regime *type* change quite so drastically. So sweeping a change did not escape the IUCT's grasp; nor did it fail to inform the IUCT's

Phillips Petroleum v. Iran (1989),[387] the Government-controlled NIOC cited *force majeure* as the reason for its failure to carry out its obligations under a joint venture with Phillips. NIOC argued that the "oil workers, who were hostile to foreign oil companies, would have prevented NIOC from resuming relations with [claimant]."[388] The Tribunal rejected this argument because the oil workers ultimately followed Khomeini's and the regime's directions, and therefore could not have been an "independent and effective force beyond the control" of the *new* Government.[389]

One critical exception, in which Iran is excused from responsibility apparently on the basis of regarding the revolution as a *force majeure* circumstance, is *Sea-Land Service v. Iran* (1984).[390] In *Sea-Land*, the claimant alleged the taking of its interest in a sea-container operation during the first half of 1979. The claimant alleged, among other things, that an Iranian labour official made "efforts ... to enforce a policy of employment of exclusively local labour."[391] Although Judges Lagergren and Kashani in the majority decided that "it appears such efforts were made," they concluded:

> [I]t is generally acknowledged that the state of administrative chaos which prevailed in Iran throughout the first few months of 1979 make it unsafe to attribute any such ostensibly governmental acts to the revolutionary Government that subsequently came to power.... Against a background of continued uncertainty and changes in control, it strikes the Tribunal as virtually impossible to use such acts as the basis of a finding of expropriation.[392]

This analysis conflates proof of an alleged act, attribution to the State, the significance of the act (if attributable to the State), and whether the revolutionary upheaval constitutes *force majeure*: If the act has happened and has been caused by an official, then it is attributable to the State and it constitutes expropriation. The benefit of separating the questions is revealed best in Judge Holtzmann's discussion of revolutionary conditions:

> The Majority absolves PSG of responsibility for its non-performance on the ground that its failures were due to 'a state of upheaval in PSG's

analyses.

[387] *Phillips Petroleum v. Iran*, 21 I.U.C.T.R. 79, 82 (1989-I).

[388] D. D. Caron, "The Basis of Responsibility," *supra*, at 174.

[389] *Id.*

[390] 6 I.U.C.T.R. 175 (1984-II).

[391] *Id.*, at 177.

[392] *Id.*, at 179.

> internal management which is consistent with the general picture of disruption which characterized Iran in months leading up to the success of the Revolution.' This observation is not only vague but also is applied with surprising carelessness. Even if the Majority were to assume that such disorganization within PSG did exist, and constituted an excuse for PSG's breaches in the 'months leading up to the success of the Revolution,' that success had occurred by February 1979.
>
> . . . No Party in this proceeding has ever contended that conditions of upheaval continued into August 1979, nor does any evidence in this or other cases before the Tribunal suggest such a widespread or lengthy breakdown of government.... Thus, unless the Majority considers that conditions of upheaval continued indefinitely, PSG must at some point be chargeable with its failure to provide the conditions for which Sea-Land had bargained.[393]

Simply put, although *force majeure* situation may preclude wrongfulness, it does so only as long as the circumstances permit it. This is something the IUCT rigorously scrutinises. In awards such as *Phillips*, Iran's defence against a public international law claim was not immunised by its invoking *force majeure*. In contrast, a State-owned company or a private entity controlled by the Government defending against a private municipal law claim could invoke the revolution as a *force majeure* circumstance relieving them of their responsibilities *under a contract*. We have already established that invoking domestic law's condemnation of an expropriation is not enough for the State to escape responsibility.

Specifically, the separate corporate existence of such entities created a presumption both that their actions were not the acts of the State and that the acts of the State—"such as support of the insurrectional act or process"—were beyond their control.

Predecessors, Successors and Obligations

It comes with the territory, and literally so. A successor government succeeds to the obligations as well and is responsible for the wrongful acts (and sometimes omissions) of predecessor regimes.[394] That the ILC Draft Articles impose international responsibility for wrongful acts on the

---

[393] *Id.*, at 199 (footnotes omitted).

[394] For instance, the RESTATEMENT (THIRD) OF THE FOREIGN RELATIONS LAW provides that the capacities, rights, and duties of a State "are not affected by a mere change in the regime or in the form of government or its ideology." RESTATEMENT (THIRD), *supra*, § 208, cmt. a.

"State"—rather than just on the *government* of the State—might mean something conceptually larger.

This difference indicates that a current government of a State "is responsible for obligations incurred by the State even if such obligations were incurred by a predecessor regime."[395] Succession of obligations showed up in IUCT and ECtHR practice. NAFTA has yet to face any such case and it is unclear what might happen, though IIA panels' tendency to cross-reference prevailing norms suggests that they will not probably stray too far from IUCT-international human rights practice.

Many claimants before the Tribunal asserted claims against the Islamic Republic of Iran based on acts or omissions allegedly made by the Shah's government. The Tribunal consistently held that acts of the previous government could be attributed to the Government of the Islamic Republic of Iran. The same is true of ECtHR cases, with the narrow but critical exception that, unlike the IUCT, the ECtHR has often faced the question of occupation by a foreign power and has decided to deny admissibility to those claims.

In *Short*, for instance, the IUCT stated that "[w]here a revolution leads to the establishment of a new government the State is held responsible for the acts of the overthrown government insofar as the latter maintained control of the situation."[396] In *Short*, the Tribunal found that "Iran" was not responsible for the failure of the Shah's government and of the secret SAVAK (*Sāzemān-e Ettelā'āt va Amniyat-e Keshvar*; National Intelligence and Security Organization) police to stop revolutionaries from expelling the claimant and others similarly situated.

The IUCT actually *assumed* that the acts of the Shah's government were attributable to the Islamic Republic of Iran, but found no responsibility because the Shah's government at the time in question had lost effective control.[397] Finding responsibility here would have been ironic, since the Shah's government and inner circle profited the least from the revolutionaries' acts. Therefore unless these acts were to be made attributable to the new regime, the claims would be caught in a no-man's-land and would become irrecoverable.

Some might believe that even the assumption of attribution (in the first prong) is erroneous because the change-over from the Shah to the Islamic Republic was a fundamental and contentious break from one regime *type* to another, wherein the successor regime's very inception and culture was defined *against* those of the predecessor regime. But that method of

[395] Report of the ILC (1975), *supra*, at 100.
[396] *Short, supra*, at 84.
[397] *Id.*, at 85.

determining attribution may well not suffice in all (or even most) situations. Unsurprisingly, "these circumstances do not fall clearly within well developed and discussed doctrines of law."[398] The details must be assessed in light of the "controlling rules," which must in turn "be derived from principles of international law applicable in analogous circumstances or from general principles of law."[399]

In *Oil Fields of Texas v. Iran* (1982), the IUCT was charged with deciding whether the National Iranian Oil Company ("NIOC") should succeed to the debts and obligations of the Oil Service Company of Iran ("OSCO").[400] While overlap of personnel might be a clue,[401] it is neither necessary nor sufficient. Superior indicators of succeeding obligations might be posed in the following interrogatory forms: (*i*) Is the agenda fundamentally the same?; (*ii*) Is control being exercised by the same authorities? (which might be termed the *font-of-power* test); (*iii*) Which authorities or actors are expected to profit?; and (*iv*) Did the predecessor regime explicitly or implicitly give an indication as to who will underwrite the debts and obligations?[402] The role of formalism is limited here and States are generally not to be allowed to escape liability due to clever acts

---

[398] *Oil Fields v. Texas*, 12 I.U.C.T.R. 308, 361 (1982).

[399] *Id.*

[400] *Id.* ("From the inception of OSCO in 1973, its relations with NIOC were . . . of a complex nature and the circumstances in this case are unique.").

[401] *Id.* ("The evidence in this case shows that performance of the tasks assigned by NIOC to OSCO was not abandoned after 1979, but was instead undertaken directly by NIOC itself, with OSCO personnel and within an organisational framework previously created in many instances by OSCO. The factual circumstances of NIOC's assumption of control over 362 OSCO's personnel and operations and its taking over of the contracts with sub-contractors and consultants resulted in NIOC's *de facto* succession to OSCO's rights and obligations with respect to these subcontractors and consultants.").

[402] *Id.* ("As to the legal consequences of this de facto succession it should be pointed out that NIOC since the creation of OSCO in 1973 through the cash call procedure provided for in Article 10 of the 1973 Service Contract invariably had provided OSCO with the funds necessary in order to meet OSCO's contractual obligations. It can be assumed that those doing business with OSCO relied on the fact that NIOC would continue to provide those funds to OSCO through the cash call procedure. From the point of view of general principles of law it would be difficult to accept that the de facto succession which took place would have as a consequence that NIOC could totally escape its previous obligation to provide the funds necessary to meet the contractual liabilities arising out of contracts entered into by OSCO for the provision of services and goods regarding operations relating to exploration, development and production of crude oil and natural gas.").

or omissions.[403] "[N]o formal corporate merger or succession in accordance with Iranian law" need have taken place in these circumstances for liability to attach.[404] Although the facts are to be channelled by these tests, there must also be a high degree of qualitative attention paid the facts themselves.

In the ECtHR sphere, Montenegro's separation from the State Union constituted secession—the creation of a new State arising from the breakup of a predecessor State—with Serbia regarded as the "continuator" State that retains the legal identity of the State Union and Montenegro the "successor" State with a new legal identity. Montenegro nonetheless was held to be responsible for violations of Convention rights, including property protection; in *Bijelic v. Montenegro and Serbia* (2009),[405] Montenegro was held accountable for its wrongful conduct committed after the June 3, 2006, dissolution of the Union. The Court did not apportion responsibility between predecessor and successor States.[406]

The early 1990's wave of European succession events has given the ECtHR occasion to delineate its succession jurisprudence relating to property. The earliest decision in which state responsibility and succession intersected was *Jasinskij v. Lithuania* (1998).[407] *Jasinskij's* ripples have powerfully affected the ECtHR. *Jasinskij* pitted applicants who had purchased (presumptively invalid) Soviet Union state bonds against the newly independent Lithuania. The case concerned the redemption of state bonds purchased before the 1991 collapse of the Soviet Union in the territory of Lithuania, and the Republic of Lithuania's and the Russian Federation's refusal to honour the debt.[408]

---

[403] *Id.* ("If a *de facto* succession of rights and obligations in a certain held has taken place without the observance of such rules under the applicable national law, it is even more important to establish a rule under international law that such succession must have as a consequence that the surviving company is under an [o]bligation to pay appropriate compensation taking into account all the circumstances of the case.").

[404] *Id.* ("Rules in national law on merger and succession normally contain provisions in order to safeguard the interests of the creditors of the company which ceases to exist.").

[405] App no. 19890/05 (2009).

[406] *Id.*, at ¶¶ 69-70; see also A. C. Buyse, *A Lifeline in Time – Non-Retroactivity and Continuing Violations at the ECHR*, 75 NORDIC J.I.L. 63, 86-7 (2006); M. J. Volkovitsch, *Righting Wrongs: Towards a New Theory of Delictual Responsibility for International Delicts*, 92 COLUM. L. REV. 2162, 2173 (1992).

[407] App no 38985/97, EComHR (1998).

[408] *Id.*, ¶1.

After attempting (and failing) to induce Lithuania to purchase the bonds through domestic courts the applicants brought their complaints before the Commission. The European Commission of Human Rights questioned "whether Lithuania has any responsibility for these debts of the former Soviet Union" and concluded that Lithuania could not "be seen as a successor of the Soviet Union in respect of these debts."[409] Factors attending this analysis must be: number and proportion of the members of the senior leadership of the successor State who are holdovers from the previous regime; proximate causal link between the core philosophies and other connections of the two regimes; and whether the successor State actively or tacitly chose to profit or will have chosen to profit from the predecessor regime's debts.

Jasinskij was a precursor to the succession issues that the ECtHR and the Commission would face after the January 1993 dissolution of Czechoslovakia and its subsequent breakdown into the Czech and Slovak Republics.[410] Among the earliest cases against the successor States to come before the Commission were *J.A. v. Republique Tceque* and *Szmora and Hlavsova v. Republique Tcheque* (1994).[411]

The European Commission in *J.A.* accepted its jurisdiction to review pre- January 1993 acts in the territory of the former Czechoslovakia, but not in *Szmora* and *Hlavsova*.[412] In most cases to reach the ECtHR the individual Slovak and Czech Republics were each held accountable for acts predating their independence without resistance from either respondent government (at least on this ground).[413] Eventually the ECtHR devised a standard formula to handle succession issues:

> The period to be taken into consideration began on 18 March 1992, when the recognition by the former Czech and Slovak Federal Republic, to

---

[409] *J.A. v. Repulique Tcheque*, App. no. 22926/93 (1994).

[410] B. E. Brockman-Hawe, *European Court of Human Rights,* Bijelic v. Montenegro and Serbia (Application No 19890/05) (2009) in CURRENT DEVELOPMENTS: INTERNATIONAL COURTS AND TRIBUNALS, 59 I.C.L.Q. 845, 859 (2010) [B. E. Brockman-Hawe, *European Court of Human Rights*]. The anatomy and material for this section of the Chapter comes from this Brockman-Hawe article.

[411] *Szmora and Hlavsova v. Republique Tcheque*, App. no. 23122/93 (1994).

[412] *Id.*, at p. 15.

[413] See, *e.g.*, *Konecny v. Czech Republic*, App nos. 47269/99; 64656/01; 65002/01 (2004), at ¶ 62; *Skodakova v. Czech Republic*, App. Nos. 71551/01 (2004), at ¶ 30; *Chovancik v. Slovakia*, App. no. 54996/00 (2003), at ¶18.

which Slovakia [or the Czech Republic] is one of the successor States, of the right of individual petition took effect.[414]

The IUCT has repeatedly held the Government of the Islamic Republic of Iran responsible for terminating contracts entered into by the Shah's erstwhile government. In *Phillips Petroleum*, the IUCT explained its decision holding Iran liable for the taking of claimant's rights under a contract with the former regime by stating that "[a] revolutionary regime may not simply excuse itself from legal obligations by changing governmental policies, nor take for the public benefit without compensation businesses operated by foreign private persons under the previous regime."[415]

The IUCT's *Phillips Petroleum* award was distinguished from an earlier decision in *Questech v. Ministry of National Defence of Iran* (1985).[416] The *Questech* Tribunal had "allowed the Ministry of National Defence to terminate a contract entered into during the time of the Shah's government."[417] Invoking "changed circumstances,"[418] the IUCT cited the top-priority importance of sensitive military contracts, especially ones involving Americans.[419] The IUCT observed that these national security details were critical to U.S. interests—though the CSD's Article II *text* makes no such exception, a point glossed over by the IUCT.

Unlike with the IUCT succession crisis, the ECtHR has faced foreign occupations. That has been enough to distinguish the ECtHR's approach and to deny admissibility in like cases. In *von Maltzan v. Germany* (2005),[420] the ECtHR's Grand Chamber considered the issue of succession to responsibility in an instance where one State incorporated another. *Von Maltzan* concerned claims of compensation for property that had been expropriated in East Germany between 1945 and 1949 (in the Soviet Occupied Zone of Germany) and after 1949 (when the area formally became the German Democratic Republic (GDR)).

---

414 *Konecny*, at ¶¶ 62-3.

415 *Phillips*, *supra*, at 111.

416 9 I.U.C.T.R. 107, 121 (1985-II)

417 *Id.*

418 *Id.*, at 122-23. Altered conditions such as "changes in the political conditions as a consequence of the Revolution," "the different attitude of the new government and the new foreign policy towards the United States," and the "drastically changed significance of highly sensitive military contracts," even if true during the time period in question in the case, were at issue in *Questech*.

419 *Id.*

420 App. nos. 71916/01, 71917/01 and 10260/02 (2005).

In *von Maltzan*, the ECtHR determined that the reunification of the GDR with the Federal Republic of Germany (FRG) in October 1990 did not, in fact, confer jurisdiction upon the Court: "[t]he FRG does not have any responsibility for acts committed at the instigation of the Soviet occupying forces or for those perpetrated by another State against its own nationals," and it did not matter that "the GDR was subsequently succeeded by the FRG, for it is 'political' obligations that are at issue in the present case."[421] What is "political," according to the *von Maltzan* Court, has to be reliably specific to the respondent State's current reality.

By and large, the ECtHR has regarded succession to responsibility for acts otherwise attributable to the Soviet Union as clear and undisputed.[422] But one dissenting jurist strongly, and somewhat persuasively, proposed to reject the succession framework. Notably, in *Lepojić v. Serbia* (2007),[423] Judge Kreca's dissent argued that the "reasoning of the Court . . . seem[s] legally dubious and self-contradicting in the light of the relevant rules of international law and common sense respectively." Why? Serbia the Republic was, in Judge Kreca's view, a "continuator," *not* a successor, to the territory of Serbia on the eastern side of the Iron Curtain.[424]

The new or "continuator" regimes within the State still have the task of deciding whether and how to attract investment. New and emerging markets do become available, from the investor's standpoint. Post-conflict governments, "whether transitional or permanent in nature," must "create profitable opportunities in strategically chosen areas." [425] The legal protections authorised to investors have value only if they are enforceable. In fact, "when there is no applicable [IIA], it is imperative that any investment agreement with the host-state contain an arbitration clause, with appropriate waivers of sovereign immunity, to allow investors to enforce their contractual rights directly against the host-state."[426] It is absolutely essential for investors not to rely on customary international law in making investment decisions, for customary law tends to be

---

[421] *Id.*, at ¶ 81.

[422] See *EVT Company v. Serbia*, App. no. 3102/05 (2007), at ¶ 32; *Vrencev v. Serbia,* App. no. 2361/05 (2008), at ¶35; *Jevremovic v. Serbia* (App. no. 3150/05) ¶ 63 (2007); *V.A.M. v. Serbia* (App. no. 39177/05) (2007) ¶76; *Lepojić v. Serbia,* App no 13909/05 (2009), at ¶24.

[423] *Lepojić, supra*, at ¶ 11 (Kreca, J., dissenting); B. E. Brockman-Hawe, *European Court of Human Rights*, *supra*, at 859.

[424] *Id.*

[425] R. Moloo & A. Khachaturian, *Foreign Investment in a Post-Conflict Environment*, 10 J. WORLD INVESTMENT AND TR. 341, 345 (2009).

[426] *Id.*, at 347.

somewhat malleable and tends also to lack the structural frame of legal protection (usually through the high card of reciprocity).

Another strategy for investors in transitional economies to cover themselves is political risk insurance. These tend to be private insurers as well as government insurers "provided by investors' home states (such as the Overseas Private Investment Corporation, an independent U.S. government agency) as well as organizations such as the Multilateral Investment Guarantee Agency (MIGA), which is part of the World Bank Group."[427] Private insurance plans usually have a shorter time period of coverage and a lower degree of expertise on offer.[428]

The last two strategies are anti-corruption and physical security. Anti-corruption protects Investor A by denying all foreign and domestic investors the loopholes to gain unfair advantages over one another. One proposed technique might be to constitutionally grant the legislature the power to block foreign financial contributions over a certain threshold to particular parties or candidates in domestic elections.[429] The last strategy,

---

427 *Id.*, at 349 ("MIGA may remove impediments to investment in developing member countries and may also coordinate with other agencies, such as the International Financial Corporation, to promote foreign investment.").

428 *Id.*

429 Constitution-drafting in various post-Arab Spring governments, African states and perhaps soon in certain Latin American States might find this to be useful. One proposed Constitution of Tunisia contains in Article XVIII a structural model:

1. Each person or entity retains the plenary right to be free from all private and public corruption. The State shall actively encourage persons and entities to petition the State and other private and public actors for a redress of grievances. Such persons and entities, their evidence, and all potential for extortion related to their disclosure must be given complete protection by the State. The State shall, at the behest of a court, constitute an independent panel to investigate any incidences of public and/or private corruption. An independent anti-corruption Ombudsman should be appointed as the first point of referral for citizens; the Ombudsman can choose to investigate cases at his or her discretion. Access should be given to the Ombudsman of information held by government which is related to a current investigation. The State may choose to regulate private corporations if it is notified by the Ombudsman and or the judiciary of corruptive practices taking place.
2. Nothing in this Constitution shall be construed to forbid governments from imposing content-neutral limitations on private campaign contributions or independent political campaign expenditures. Nor shall this Constitution prevent governments from enacting systems of public campaign financing, including those designed to restrict the influence of private wealth by offsetting campaign spending or independent expenditures with increased public funding.
3. All authorities within Tunisia shall, when compelled by a fair and reasonable request, disclose all relevant and non-confidential information to the petitioner.

physical security, forms the crux of the customary law standard Full Protection and Security (FPS). When the State fails to provide a claimant with that protection, an FPS claim is in theory available under customary law. In recent memory, positive[430] and negative[431] experiences abound. This strategy, along with the others, are worthy of serious consideration by investors.

See THE NEW CONSTITUTION OF TUNISIA: CHOICES AND DECISIONS (The Wilberforce Society: University of Cambridge, 2012) (R. Dasgupta & G. Bangham, eds.). See also Guy-Uriel Charles, *Mixing Metaphors: Voting, Dollars, and Campaign Finance Reform* (Review Essay), 2 ELECTION L. J. 271 (2003).
Among other domestic law instruments, the Eritrean Constitution, ratified in 1997, contains a sweeping anti-corruption provision, which some experts (and lay persons) have thought imprecise and saddled with the potential to be laden with judge-made exceptions. The text is provided:
Article 11 – Competent Civil Service
1. The Civil Service of Eritrea shall have efficient, effective and accountable administrative institutions dedicated to the service of the people.
2. All administrative institutions shall be free from corruption, discrimination and delay in the delivery of efficient and equitable public services.
See also D. L. Horowitz, CONSTITUTIONAL CHANGE AND DEMOCRACY IN INDONESIA (Cambridge University Press, 2013) ("What the insiders did was a thoroughgoing democratization. But the problems that remained as a result of the insiders having the inside track, namely corruption networks and a variety of other pathologies, are still there . . . It is simply a far-better than-it-might-have-been story . . . because of the way political leaders chose to proceed, opting for a course that risked public confidence in what they were doing, for the sake of avoiding even greater risks.").

[430] R. Moloo & A. Khachaturian, *Foreign Investment in a Post-Conflict Environment, supra,* at 352 ("a good example of increased security enticing foreign investment is the case of Basra, the main commercial center of Iraq. The city, which holds approximately 70% of Iraq's oil reserves and is the country's sole deepwater port, has shown a significant turnaround after an Iraqi-led military operation launched by Prime Minister Nouri al-Maliki,. . . rid the city of gunmen—primarily the Sadr-loyalist Mahdi army—and ended over two years of fighting among rival gangs.") (internal footnotes omitted).

[431] *Id.* ("One example is in the case of foreign oil companies in Nigeria, where militant groups have attacked oil facilities, affecting foreign investor operations. In the summer of 2008, militants attacked an oil facility off the Nigerian coast, forcing Royal Dutch Shell to halt production for its Bonga oilfield and blocking some 220,000 barrels of oil per day. A few hours after the Bonga attack, another militant group blew a hole in a Chevron pipeline, cutting production of another 120,000 barrels of oil per day. Several foreign investors, such as Total SA have already cited security concerns as the reason for dwindling investment on land in Nigeria.") (internal footnotes omitted).

§ 3.6—Conclusion and Continuing Debates

Because the IUCT is a retrospective body that does not create economic incentives or disincentives for the future, a *force majeure*-centric exception was allowed to slide. Such a carve-out had but a conceptual impact by "seriously eroding such succession" rules ordinarily observed in international law.[432] We are back to the non-uniformity problem and the lack of vertical *stare decisis*, from which IIA tribunals (almost) uniquely suffer. The dissonance in the GATT/WTO regime over private action's role in attribution might also be mitigated by the presence of vertical *stare decisis*, though it would of course create a different regime-type which GATT/WTO signatories may not necessarily want.[433]

All international tribunals studied in this book have been led by economic, political and, in a word, prudential concerns in defining state responsibility. This is not a pejorative. These institutions have done so by "engaging in . . . consequential analysis"[434] on their own idiosyncratic terms. As we saw in many categories of cases, the *de facto* behaviour of States leaves us with many haunting attribution questions. The future of Brownlie's "national economic disaster" test also remains to be seen. Another important issue that remains to be decided is the nature of remedies, articulated in Chapter I (INTRODUCTION).

In international law, the general rule always has been that perhaps there could be pecuniary relief (depending on the merits of the dispute) ordered by international tribunals but certainly no injunctive relief. Partly this understanding has been born of self-preservation because some international tribunals deem themselves to be safer if they do not overreach and are less effective. This is at the core of their reluctance to order injunctive relief, including contempt proceedings or judicial

---

432 B. E. Brockman-Hawe, *European Court of Human Rights*, *supra*, at 859.

433 See A. Okubo, *Environmental Labeling Programs and the GATT/WTO Regime*, 11GEO. INT'L ENVTL. L. REV. 599, 630–31 (1999) (stating a list of authorities to argue that private action "will fall outside the scope of the GATT/WTO regimes"); M. P. Vandenbergh, *Climate Change: The China Problem*, 81 S. CAL. L. REV. 905, 942–43 (2008) (explaining and substantiating the claim that the risk of WTO litigation risk rises when the government mandates certain programs). But see also S. M. Villalpando, *Attribution of Conduct to the State: How the Rules of State Responsibility May Be Applied Within the WTO Dispute Settlement System*, 5 J. INT'L ECON. L. 383, 408–09 (2002) ("[I]n some cases, the conduct of a 'private party' could be directly attributed to the State, thereby entailing the latter's responsibility under the WTO agreements.").

434 See L. Anenson, *State Responsibility under NAFTA Chapter Eleven, supra*, at 717.

penalties (*astreintes*). This seems to be the default rule unless it is the ICJ to whose jurisdiction they have expressly consented.

Several recent IIA tribunals have recently resisted this traditional understanding,[435] thus setting up a titanic debate over this question. One of these tribunals, *Micula v. Romania* (2008), also indicated its view that at a remedy need not be particularly mentioned in the textual instrument(s) in order to be available to a tribunal.[436] As Professor W. Michael Reisman recently explained in a submission, "under the customary international law of State Responsibility as codified by the International Law Commission, cessation of a wrongful act or a breach of an international obligation is the first requirement for eliminating the consequences of a wrongful act."[437]

---

[435] *Micula v. Romania*, ICSID Case No. ARB/05/20, Decision on Jurisdiction and Admissibility 2008), at ¶ 166 ("Under the ICSID Convention, a tribunal has the power to order pecuniary or nonpecuniary remedies, including restitution, i.e., re-establishing the situation which existed before a wrongful act was committed. . . . The fact that restitution is a rarely ordered remedy is not relevant at this stage of the proceedings. . . . [T]he fact that such a remedy might not be enforceable pursuant to Article 54 of the ICSID Convention should not preclude a tribunal from ordering it. Remedies and enforcement are two distinct concepts.") (citing International Law Commission, Articles on Responsibility of States for Internationally Wrongful Acts, annexed to the General Assembly Resolution 56/83, UN Doc A/RES/56/83, 12 December 2001, Article 35; *Enron Corporation and Ponderosa Assets, L.P. v. Argentine Republic* (ICSID Case No. ARB/01/3), Decision on Jurisdiction of 14 January 2004, ¶¶ 79-81); *City Oriente Ltd. v. Republic of Ecuador*, ICSID Case No. ARB/06/21, at ¶ 27 (2008) (arbitral tribunal is empowered to order contractual performance against host State), *Enron Corp. v. Argentine Republic* (Jurisdiction), ICSID Case No. ARB/01/3, 14 January 2004, ¶¶ 78-81 (affirming tribunal's power to order measures against States involving performance or enjoinment of particular actions), *Casado v. Republic of Chile* (Provisional Measures), ICSID Case No. ARB/98/2, 25 September 2001, ¶ 51 (ordering a State to suspend parallel, duplicative domestic proceedings is consistent with State sovereignty).

[436] *Micula, supra*, at ¶ 167 (stating that a remedy need not be particularly mentioned in order to be available: "the Tribunal finds no limitation to its powers to order restitution in the BIT, the instrument on which the consent of the parties is based. While Article 4 of the BIT dealing with expropriation only mentions compensation, it does not rule out restitution. Moreover, the rest of the BIT provisions do not preclude a tribunal from ordering restitution, if and when appropriate, for a violation of other substantive provisions.").

[437] *United States v. Canada*, LCIA Case No. 81010 (May 1, 2009) (Professor W. Michael Reisman, Opinion with respect to Selected International Legal Problems in LCIA Case No. 7941), at ¶¶ 44-46 (citing Article 30, ILC, p. 88). Article 30 provides:

The State responsible for the internationally wrongful act is under an obligation:

Moreover, "[t]he main focus of the requirement of cessation is to terminate a wrongful act of a continuing character or a wrongful act which, though not of a continuing character, is repeated by the responsible state."[438]

The ILC's Commentary has perceived the role of the cessation doctrine as that which must "put an end to a violation of international law and to safeguard the continuing validity and effectiveness of the underlying primary rule."[439] The whole point of cessation as a remedy goes to the international community's enduring interest in promoting and protecting the rule of law: "[t]he responsible State's obligation of cessation thus protects both the interests of the injured State or States and the interests of the international community as a whole in the preservation of, and reliance on, the rule of law."[440] Given this background, *Micula* was not that far out of step. *Micula* simply represents one strand of the remedies doctrine that has always existed; the conventional doctrine represents the alternative strand (no default injunctive power belongs to an international tribunal).

Other tribunals have followed the conventional canon that international tribunals have no default power to award non-pecuniary remedies.[441] One argument is that each significant instance of tinkering with the consent balance is crucial because the incentives to stay in must remain greater than the disincentives in order for the international adjudication or arbitration system, on whatever plane, to function. Perhaps a less cogent explanation is that international bodies such as the WTO have also refused to order performance-based or other non-pecuniary remedies: WTO panels and the Appellate Body are expressly disallowed from ordering such remedies whereas for most IIA awards the Convention or the IIA itself is silent.[442] Until and unless consensus on this issue changes, all we will have

---

(a) to cease that act, if it is continuing;
(b) to offer appropriate assurances and guarantees of non-repetition, if circumstances so require.

438 *Id.*, at ¶ 44.

439 Commentary to Article 30, Vol. II (Part II), YEARBOOK OF THE ILC, at p. 89, ¶ 4.

440 *Id.* See also Commentary to Article 30, YEARBOOK OF THE ILC, at p. 89, ¶ 5 ("cessation is often the main focus of the controversy produced by conduct in breach of an international obligation... [a]nd by contrast, reparation, important though it is in many cases, may not be the central issue in the dispute between States as to questions of responsibility.").

441 *Occidental Petroleum Corp. v. Republic of Ecuador* (Provisional Measures), ICSID Case No. ARB/06/11, 17 August 2007, ¶¶ 78-85 (refusing to consider award specific performance, noting inter alia sovereignty concerns), *LG&E Energy Corp., et al. v. Argentine Republic* (Damages), ICSID Case No. ARB/02/1, 25 July 2007, ¶¶ 86-87.

442 B. E. Allen, "The Use of Non-pecuniary Remedies in WTO Dispute Settlement:

to rely upon is that IIA's "provide arbitral forums in which to seek compensation" when the government "engag[es] in expropriation, in breach of its treaty commitments."[443]

A final point concerns joint (concurrent) responsibility. Joint responsibility has not really come up in the diplomatic courts, and is beyond the scope of this chapter. One cautionary note is that the issue could become an issue in international human rights and IIA tribunals. They have yet to do so. Importantly, the ILC in its commentary to Article 8 acknowledges the possibility, and propriety, of apportioning state responsibility when "injuries are not caused exclusively by an unlawful act but have been produced also by concomitant causes among which the wrongful act plays a decisive but not exclusive role." [444]

Finally, several international tribunals have recognized the consequential roles played by determinations without prejudice, burden of proof and parallel proceedings in international and/or domestic tribunals:

> Failing to provide evidence of admission of . . . [a particular kind of] investment, [a party's] request for initiation of a proceeding to settle an investment dispute is, to say the least, premature. However, in finding the request to be unfounded, the Tribunal does not say that it is frivolous, vexatious or malicious. Nor does the Tribunal's determination that the subject-matter of the dispute, if any, falls outside the jurisdiction of ICSID and beyond the competence of the Tribunal preclude whatever recourse the Claimant may have at its disposal to pursue its claim arising out of a commercial, financial or other types of dispute. The Tribunal's conclusions

---

Lessons for Arbitral Practitioners" *in* ASA PERFORMANCE AS A REMEDY: A MANUAL 281, 296 (stating that "a WTO panel's conformity recommendation eludes ready comparisons with arbitral remedies. On the surface, this recommendation might appear to resemble the traditional remedy of specific performance, as it calls for conduct in conformity with legal obligation. But this recommendation lacks the kind of coercive power . . . that stands behind a tribunal or domestic court's order of specific performance. Although the [WTO] system encourages compliance through the threat of compensation and retaliation, it lacks the coercive authority to compel compliance.") [B. E. Allen, "The Use of Non-pecuniary Remedies in WTO Dispute Settlement"].

[443] T. G. Nelson, et al, "Possible Gaps in Bilateral Investment Treaty (BIT) Coverage for Managed Investment Funds," *supra*, at 2 ("Maximizing [IIA] protection will not physically stop a hostile and determined government from engaging in expropriation, in breach of its treaty commitments. Nevertheless, BITs and FTAs do provide arbitral forums in which to seek compensation if such events occur. In some cases, the existence of potential BIT or FTA arbitral remedies may actually deter governmental seizures in the first place.").

[444] Report of the ILC (1993), *supra*, at 175.

> are declared to be without prejudice to any rights of action which may be available before other instances, national or international, with the consent of the Parties, if required.[445]

The next Chapter (EXHAUSTION OF LOCAL REMEDIES AND CONTINUOUS NATIONALITY) will discuss how this procedural question plays out in the three institutions and how it interacts with the non-discrimination and substantive standards. A difficulty in comparative analysis is that it is multi-linear; when discussing one institution, it often spills into discussion of the other(s). The next three chapters will address how the interactional model's "enmeshment of norms in a practice of legality"[446] criterion manifests itself in specific situations, cases and doctrines.

---

[445] *Mihaly International Corporation v. Democratic Socialist Republic of Sri Lanka*, ICSID Case No. ARB/00/2, Award (2002), at ¶ 61.

[446] J. Brunnée & S. Toope, LEGITIMACY, *supra*, at 101.

CHAPTER FOUR

EXHAUSTION OF LOCAL REMEDIES AND CONTINUOUS NATIONALITY

§ 4.1—Introduction

Before an international tribunal may reach the merits of a dispute, it must ensure that it has jurisdiction to do so. In short, "the question of jurisdiction of an international instance involving consent of a sovereign State deserves a special attention at the outset of any proceeding against a State Party to an international convention creating the jurisdiction"—sometimes "*proprio motu*, i.e., without objection being raised by the Party."[1]

The implication is that if it later appears that jurisdiction was improvidently established, it may retroactively be withdrawn. There also are suggestions that the jurisdictional and admissibility questions have become so fraught with complexity that remedies "simpler, quicker and more basic"[2] are needed to supplant this tragic ultra-"legalism" and over-"judicialisation" which allegedly have seeped into international arbitration.[3]

---

[1] *Mihaly International Corporation v. Democratic Socialist Republic of Sri Lanka*, ICSID Case No. ARB/00/2, Award (2002), at ¶ 56; see also *Empresas Lucchetti, S.A. and Lucchetti Peru, S.A. v. Republic of Peru*, ICSID Case No. ARB/03/4, Award (Feb. 7, 2005) (dismissing a request for arbitration for lack of jurisdiction *ratione temporis*).

[2] A. Redfern, *Stemming the Tide of Judicialisation of International Arbitration*, 2 WORLD ARB. & MED. REV. 21, 37 (2008).

[3] W. W. Park, *Arbitrators and Accuracy, supra,* at 29-30 ("Users of international arbitration are said to be unhappy with a costly and slow process that too often ignores in-house counsel, and has become infected with 'Americanized' pre-hearing discovery. General criticisms, both in the United States and Europe, tell of 'company-wide bans on arbitration clauses,' related to the business community's 'growing chorus of discontent' with the process. One commentator urges that arbitration must be repaired 'by whatever means necessary.' Another suggests that empirical studies showing business satisfaction with arbitration have been reached only by turning a 'blind eye to reality.' Even good friends of arbitration suggest

In other words, this vortex of a complex twister must be understood and handled better, as its uncertain ebbs and flows are so inextricably linked to the crux of international jurisdiction that they might bring the whole show down. Informed lawyers have a difficult time predicting how a specific tribunal might respond to close jurisdictional ("ritual[istic]") questions, rendering the international "legal system's" frequently a "mystery . . . [that is] baffling to everyday citizens" and is "preside[d] over" by "priests" (and understood only by elite practitioners and judges).[4]

There is some merit to each of the ideas offered by jurists and scholars: interim or advance decisions on costs; an arbitrator or adjudicator quickly rendering a decision based on the facts rather than the panoply of procedures; expedited proceedings; a single arbitrator instead of a multi-member tribunal; splitting proceedings into separate stages (jurisdiction, liability and damages); reforming the disparate availability of anti-suit injunctions depending on jurisdiction (it might be effective to standardise them without, to a substantial extent, abdicating individualised, "fit" considerations); stopping and reversing growing ethical and conflict of interest among international adjudicators; and a contract- and drafting process more attuned to the realities of international dispute resolution. These complex elements might compete against each other in certain instances. Several institutional systems, via the rules governing their respective fora, stipulate the order of priorities according to which the competing elements might be accommodated.[5]

Some jurists have taken note of a thematic problem: the perceived über-"Americani[s]ation" of international arbitration.[6] The controversy is threatening to overturn much procedure in international law that has taken a generation or longer to build. While this author is agnostic about all that

---

that it is 'generally admitted' that arbitration has become more and more expensive.") (internal footnotes and citations omitted).

[4] Bruce M. Nash, Allan Zullo, Kathryn Zullo, THE NEW LAWYER'S WIT AND WISDOM: QUOTATIONS ON THE LEGAL PROFESSION, IN BRIEF 238 (Running Press, 2001) (quote of Henry Miller).

[5] *Id.* (see sources cited therein); L. Mistelis & J. D. M. Lew, eds., PERVASIVE PROBLEMS IN INTERNATIONAL ARBITRATION (Kluwer Law International, 2006) [L. Mistelis & J. D. M. Lew, eds., PERVASIVE PROBLEMS]; See Emilio Cárdenas & David W. Rivkin, "A Growing Challenge for Ethics in International Arbitration," *in* GLOBAL REFLECTIONS ON INTERNATIONAL LAW, COMMERCE AND DISPUTE RESOLUTION 195 (ICC 2005, Gerald Aksen, Karl-Heinz Böckstiegel, Michael J. Mustill, Paolo Michele Patocchi and Anne Marie Whitesell, eds.) ("While there is widespread agreement about these fundamental principles of . . . international arbitration, problems arise because of their inconsistent application.").

[6] See, *e.g.*, W. W. Park, *Arbitrators and Accuracy, supra,* at 27.

this term means or even implies, it is safe to make two assertions: (*i*) correlation with American-style Alternative Dispute Resolution (ADR) does not necessarily imply causation or roots; and (*ii*) even assuming that (*i*) is false, the very foundation of international law signifies international *common-law* underpinnings. The judge-made character of several rules, at least insofar as they simply fill in the gaps, is bound to put a premium on efficiency- and equity-based balancing. It should not be all that surprising that international jurists might divine similar premises or assumptions across geography.

Finally, it is also the case that some international tribunals might learn from domestic ones in awarding costs against a party whose bad faith conduct caused delays or other disruptive inconveniences. As acknowledged, these ideas have varying degrees of merit. *The* overarching problem represents a disconnect between the political and the judicial officers engaged in the process. The former tend to be hyper-strategic (perhaps even artful) in negotiating the compacts and the latter hyper-intellectualised in interpreting the compacts. Some agreements and some awards prove to be happy exceptions to this norm.

Now we address, first, the exhaustion of local remedies and, second, the continuous nationality standards in international law.

The Significance of the Exhaustion Doctrine

Before discussing how the exhaustion of local remedies doctrine applies to (and sometimes interweaves) the decisions of various international tribunals, we discuss what the doctrine concerns and why it matters. Chapter I (INTRODUCTION) has discussed the Kantian "definitive article" that each legal person be entitled to hospitality by other states. Historically, this rule has never been thought unqualified and absolute; indeed, the rule is unspecific as to whether a violation of such a right *must* first be entertained in domestic court, what standards must be used, and a whole host of other remedial questions. What we do know is that the hospitality protection was thought important enough to be one of Kant's significantly stated "definitive articles" as the foundation of international law.

The exhaustion of local remedies doctrine requires that, with some exceptions, a claimant must seek redress from the domestic judicial process (and sometimes the administrative process too) before seeking redress in international court for violations allegedly caused by a domestic government.[7] The exceptions are the remedy is unavailable, ineffective or unreasonably delayed.[8] When this is met, the requirement is generally considered satisfied. One scholar has given the following example of a situation when the local remedy is pointless:

> National courts may be unavailable, given sovereign immunity, or undesirable, given problems with the enforceability of judgments or concerns related to the integrity of domestic rule-of-law institutions. Espousal requires lobbying [a claimant's] home state to act on its behalf before the International Court of Justice and will not result in an award payable to the [claimant]. Diplomacy can be untenable as it politicizes commercial disputes and can result in inaction.[9]

---

[7] L. Oppenheim, INTERNATIONAL LAW 153 (1912) ("a state must be given the opportunity to redress by its own means and within its own legal framework any wrong suffered by an alien"); ILC Draft Articles on Diplomatic Protection (2006), Art 14: courts "of the state alleged to be responsible"; C.F. Amerasinghe, STATE RESPONSIBILITY 169; see also *Finnish Vessels Case* (*Finland v. United Kingdom*), 3 R. Int'l Arb. Awards 1479, 1501 (1934) (the function of the local remedies rule is to permit the state to discharge responsibility in its own tribunals); *Interhandel Case*, 1959 ICJ Reports, p. 27 ("Before resort may be had to an international court in such a situation, it has been considered necessary that the State where the violation occurred should have an opportunity to redress it by its own means, within the framework of its own domestic legal system.").

[8] I. Brownlie, PRINCIPLES OF PUBLIC INTERNATIONAL LAW 495 (Oxford University Press, 2008) (arguing that the "best test" is that the effective remedy must be available with "reasonable probability"); A.A. Cançado Trindade, THE APPLICATION OF THE RULE OF EXHAUSTION OF LOCAL REMEDIES IN INTERNATIONAL LAW 1 (Cambridge University Press, 1983). See also, from the international human rights perspective, cases arising out of the African Commission on Human and Peoples' Rights: Communication Nos. 147/95 and 149/96, *Dawda Jawara v. The Gambia*, at ¶ 32 ("A remedy is considered available if the petitioner can pursue it without impediment, it is deemed effective if it offers a prospect of success, and it is found sufficient if it is capable of redressing the complaint."); Communication No.275/2003, *Article 19 v. Eritrea*, at ¶ 47 (implying that even though it is *lex specialis*, "the [general principles of] law on exhaustion of domestic remedies presupposes: (i) the existence of domestic procedures for dealing with the claim; (ii) the justiciability or otherwise, domestically, of the subject-matter of the compliant; (iii) the existence under the municipal legal order of provisions for redress of the type of wrong being complained of; and (iv) available effective local remedies, that is, remedies sufficient or capable of redressing the wrong complained of.").

[9] S. D. FRANCK, *The Legitimacy Crisis in Investment Treaty Arbitration: Privatizing Public International Law Through Inconsistent Decisions*, 73 FORDHAM L. REV. 1521, 1536-38 (2005).

Consensus seems to be that "objections to admissibility or jurisdiction [need not] be raised during any negotiations that occur during a period of mandatory delay before a dispute is referred to arbitration" or at any other pre-arbitration point.[10] There is a functional reason for this position: "As the dispute will, by definition, not have been referred to arbitration at that time, and the Statement of Claim will not have been issued, it would be impossible for the Respondent to know how the claim would be framed and accordingly impossible for it to know what objections to admissibility or jurisdiction it may wish to raise."[11]

Moreover, "since either Party could refer the dispute to arbitration it will not always be possible even to know which Party would be the Respondent."[12] Finally, there is growing support within international human rights, worthy perhaps of being cross-pollinated across international law, to shift the burden on to the claimant once the sovereign could prove that the "remedy" it had offered "was an effective one available in theory and in practice at the relevant time, that is to say, that it was accessible, was one which was capable of providing redress in respect of the applicant's complaints and offered reasonable prospects of success."[13]

---

[10] *Sociedad Anónima Eduardo Vieira v. República de Chile*, ICSID Case No. ARB/04/7, Memorial of Objections, at ¶ 9 (Prof. Vaughan Lowe) (2006) (stating that "there is as far as I am aware no support whatever in State practice or in the jurisprudence of international tribunals for the proposition that objections to admissibility or jurisdiction must be raised during any negotiations that occur during a period of mandatory delay before a dispute is referred to arbitration. There is no shortage of cases, in ICSID tribunals and in other tribunals such as the International Tribunal for the Law of the Sea, in which objections to jurisdiction and admissibility have been taken after the expiry of a 'cooling off' period to the reference of a dispute to arbitration; but there is no sign in those cases of any tribunal applying the concept of estoppel, the doctrine of unilateral acts of states, or any other doctrine or principle to bar objections to jurisdiction and or admissibility.").

[11] *Id.*, at ¶ 10.

[12] *Id.*

[13] *Akdivar and Others v. Turkey*, no. 21893/93, 16/09/1996, ECHR-Grand Chamber, at ¶ 68 ("once this burden of proof has been satisfied it falls to the applicant to establish that the remedy advanced by the Government was in fact exhausted or was for some reason inadequate and ineffective in the particular circumstances of the case or that there existed special circumstances absolving him or her from the requirement.") (referring to the judgment of 26 June 1987 of the Inter-American Court of Human Rights in the *Velásquez Rodríguez case*, Preliminary Objections, Series C no. 1, para. 88, and that Court's Advisory Opinion of 10 August 1990 on "Exceptions to the Exhaustion of Domestic

Some judicial literature and practitioner submissions also question the very existence of the default requirement in public international law that a government's local remedies be exhausted.[14] But the exhaustion requirement has become entrenched in customary international law, and investors and property owners start from the premise that this requirement exists in customary international law. What exactly it is that exhaustion requires, though, *can* be—and frequently is—adjusted to fit the unique circumstances of the case.

Many international tribunal perorations on this score are highly fact-intensive not just because it is good form but rather because the very justifications for the judicial outcome depend so keenly on the specific facts. To more "Fox"-type, top-down philosopher judges, this approach reeks of judicial arbitrariness that is ripe for confusion in future cases because no clear formula are outlined. This complaint is typically overstated, as some clear decisional rules can be gleaned from cases carrying relevant but complex facts.

The caveat is that international tribunals which tend to be overbroad in classing cases under sweeping banners of human rights, investments, emergencies and *force majeure*, and so on, would do well to recognise that often the pressure points of cases transcend categories and particular attention needs to be paid the *facts* of the case in order to ascertain the salient pressure points. Particularised attention will enhance, not diminish, this aspect of exhaustion analysis.

Those unique factors include the types of remedies available, the importance of the object in dispute, and the tribunal where it is being adjudicated. Two basic questions that frequently arise: Was the exhaustion requirement *waived*? Was it *satisfied*?[15] This is where international tribunals enter our analysis, for the exhaustion doctrine's in-built flexibility informs their decisions and reflects their perspectives.[16]

Remedies" (Article 46 (1), 46 (2) (a) and 46 (2) (b) of the American Convention on Human Rights), Series A no. 11, p 32, para. 41).").

[14] Despite the transition from diplomatic protection, keeping the exhaustion doctrine as a default suggests that the international law community accepts the importance of sovereignty and that it perhaps is oriented towards incentivising domestic systems to improve. See J. Crawford, THE INTERNATIONAL LAW COMMISSION'S ARTICLES ON STATE RESPONSIBILITY: INTRODUCTION, TEXT, AND COMMENTARIES 242 (Cambridge University Press, 2002).

[15] "Waiver" implies that some prior agreement, most likely the rules of the tribunal or the controlling text, freed the parties from the exhaustion requirement whereas "satisfying" the requirement means that the requirement exists and was met.

[16] T. Meron *Incidence of the Rule of Exhaustion of Local Remedies*, 34 B.Y.I.L. 83, 101 (1959) ("the rule must be applied with caution and only after all of the

The exhaustion requirement is a nod to the sovereignty of nations, and is supported by two rationales: (*i*) it "give[s] the respondent state a chance to redress the alleged wrong" (much like Clytaemnestra in *The Libation Bearers*)[17]; (*ii*) "the respondent state is entitled to its own appreciation of the questions of law and fact involved in the claims."[18] Exhaustion also encourages domestic jurisdictions to develop their judiciaries with the tacit understanding that the domestic courts' persistent failure to redress international wrongs will not be countenanced by the international orders to which the domestic jurisdictions have submitted. This is especially important for unstable democracies with uncertain (or perhaps close to non-existent) constitutional traditions.[19] Other such privileges flowing inevitably from sovereignty are consent (whose practical implications addressed in detail in the next Chapter) and, perhaps politically incorrectly now, the power to exclude certain persons or populations based on specific criteria.[20]

---

facts have been adequately considered. Not only is a rigid application of the rule to all cases . . . not supported by either the reasons for the rule of by the practice, but it also does not serve the interests of justice.").

[17] Aeschylus, *The Libation Bearers* (1930) (H. W. Smyth, trans.) (Clytaemnestra attempting "to make amends" (by pouring libations on Agamemnon's grave) for what Orestes calls "an irremediable deed," so that the system of justice and the Furies would spare her life).

[18] C. F. Amerasinghe, STATE RESPONSIBILITY, *supra,* at 409. Even the very theory of justice down from the classical times contains a notion of "mak[ing] amends." See Aeschylus, *The Libation Bearers* (1930) (H. W. Smyth, trans.) (Clytaemnestra trying "to make amends" by pouring libations on Agamemnon's grave, so that the system of justice and the Furies would spare her life, for what Orestes calls "an irremediable deed").

[19] See, *e.g.*, *Ždanoka v. Latvia* [GC], no. 58278/00, § 131, ECHR 2006-IV (stating that "it is not surprising that a newly established democratic legislature should need time for reflection in a period of political turmoil to enable it to consider what measures were required to sustain its achievements."); *id.*, at § 134 (domestic policy-makers ought to be given "sufficient latitude to assess the needs of their society in building confidence in the new democratic institutions, including the national parliament, and to answer the question whether the impugned measure is still needed...").

[20] THE LAW OF NATIONS, bk. II, ch. VII, § 94, p. 309 (B. Kapossy & R. Whatmore eds. 2008) ("The sovereign may forbid the entrance of his territory either to foreigners in general, or in particular cases, or to certain persons, or for certain particular purposes, according as he may think it advantageous to the state. There is nothing in all this, that does not flow from the rights of domain and sovereignty: every one is obliged to pay respect to the prohibition; and whoever dares violate it, incurs the penalty decreed to render it effectual."); see also I R. Phillimore,

Some scholars assert plainly that while final review belongs in the international legal order, the exhaustion rule "is a tribute to the respondent state and is not intended to control the administration of justice."[21] A default rule in international court is that the domestic court's judgment was "notoriously unfair and grossly unjust"[22]—the standard set by the *denial of justice*-Calvo Doctrine developments over the centuries.

Readers of this book might know, and will find the point discussed in a few pages, that IIA tribunals have formed a consensus that no such requirement readily exists on the IIA platform—at least facially. Some experts plainly believe that "[w]ithout a BIT, international investors can be at the mercy of local judiciaries, which can be bypassed or bought."[23] These sources also maintain that the whole point of entering into an IIA, *unless it clearly states otherwise,* is to have this exhaustion exemption, as a security, from the State. Moreover, the Charter of Economic Rights and Duties of States, adopted in 1974 by the General Assembly, stipulates: "In any case where the question of compensation gives rise to a controversy, the national jurisdiction of the State taking such measures shall be exhausted. However, upon agreement by sovereign States and other parties concerned, settlement of the dispute should be made through arbitration or international adjudication."[24] Where the presumptive burden lies, we can observe, is the issue in dispute.

Over the last few years, there have been what can best be called "backdoor" efforts to encourage investors or induce tribunals to submit to exhaustion (perhaps by showing the carrot of bolstering one's case) or its most significant effect: delay. If the carrot is attractive enough, that blame does not lie at the pro-exhaustion actors' doorsteps. But if the carrot is clouded in non-transparency and asymmetry of information and the carrot

---

COMMENTARIES UPON INTERNATIONAL LAW, pt. III, ch. X, p. 233 (1854) ("It is a received maxim of International Law that, the Government of a State may prohibit the entrance of strangers into the country"); 2 OF THE LAW OF NATURE AND NATIONS, bk. III, ch. III, § 10, p. 366 (C. Oldfather & W. Oldfather eds. 1934) (Pufendorf argues that "every [sovereign] may decide after its own custom what privilege should be granted in such a situation."). I attribute this collection of sources to Justice Antonin Scalia's recent opinion, concurring in part and dissenting in part, in *Arizona v. United States,* 2012 U.S. LEXIS 4872, *48-49 (Scalia, J.) (2012), decided by the United States Supreme Court in October Term 2011.

[21] *Id.*; see also A. A. Cançado Trindade, THE ACCESS OF INDIVIDUALS TO INTERNATIONAL JUSTICE 99-100 (Oxford University Press, 2011).

[22] C.F. Amerasinghe, STATE RESPONSIBILITY, *supra*, at 409-10.

[23] C. J. Borgen, *Transnational Tribunals, supra,* at 673.

[24] G.A. Resolution No. 3281 (XXIX) (1974), 14, ILM, p. 251.

is designed to *seem* necessary for an arbitral tribunal to be receptive to the claimant's arguments (whether or not it actually is),[25] then significant reassessment is needed. In addition, government arguments concerning the claimant's failure to "attemp[t] to amicably settle their dispute in accordance with" the appropriate IIA stipulation are becoming increasingly prevalent.[26] This is possible only when the IIA contains language encouraging or being open to such objections to jurisdiction.

A question that comes up frequently: *Does exhaustion require judicial finality in national courts or is an administrative or judicial failure in the earlier stages enough?* Finality usually comes when "the decision of the competent body or official" is "without appeal."[27] Unsurprisingly, some scholarship reaches back to denial of justice to retrieve an answer, or at least the factors that should inform the case-by-case answers to this question.[28]

Procedurally-speaking, the exhaustion of local remedies sees international courts as a highly-deferential appellate system which may hear disputes arising in domestic courts ("primary courts"). [29] The substantive angle to the exhaustion doctrine ties the doctrine with state responsibility itself: it "implie[s] that the obligation was breached by a

---

[25] An award of jurisdiction may formally be granted and the tribunal may still be less than fully receptive to claimant's merits arguments. Sometimes these factors are psychologically so deeply set that without active effort, on the arbitrator's part, to free themselves from the biases and "residual reservations" they cannot commence analysis on the merits on a completely unbiased slate.

[26] See, *e.g., Teinver S.A., Transportes de Cercanías S.A. and Autobuses Urbanos del Sur S.A. v. The Argentine Republic*, ICSID Case No. ARB/09/1 (2012), Separate Opinion of Dr. Kamal Hossain, at ¶¶ 7-8.

[27] ILC, *Responsibility of the State for Injuries Caused in its Territory to the Person or Property of Aliens: Revised Draft*, [1961] 2 Y.B. INT'L L. COMM. 46, art. 18(2), at 48, I.L.C. Doc. A/CN.4/34/Add.1. The touchstone of finality is what actually transpires in real life and this might depend on specific circumstances. What passes for finality in a stable environment might not work in a warzone. In cases where the right asserted would die if the international claim is not heard immediately, interlocutory appeals count as "final" for all practical purposes

[28] D. Wallace, "Fair and Equitable Treatment and Denial of Justice: *Loewen v. US* and *Chattin v. Mexico*" in T. Weiler (ed), INTERNATIONAL INVESTMENT LAW AND ARBITRATION: LEADING CASES FROM THE ICSID, NAFTA, BILATERAL TREATIES, AND CUSTOMARY INTERNATIONAL LAW 669, 682 (2005) (arguing that the answer is "understudied and unresolved") [D. Wallace, "Fair and Equitable Treatment"].

[29] *Id.*; M. Shaw, INTERNATIONAL LAW 731 (Cambridge University Press, 2003) [M. Shaw, INTERNATIONAL LAW].

complex act which was not complete *until* the rule had been applied and had failed to produce the correct result."[30]

The view is justified by the first exhaustion rationale above: the test is "whether every means at the disposal of the State['s]"[31] domestic system had been applied and still failed to redress the alleged wrong. Under the substantive view, then, exhaustion is more than just a checkbox for international jurisdiction: it is an attribute of a nation's sovereignty that cannot be given up without the nation's explicitly saying so.[32]

This substantive *versus* procedural view has become a bone of contention in investment tribunals, leading them to issue conflicting decisions. An illustrative case-study is the NAFTA. NAFTA's text, according to some authorities,[33] also waives the exhaustion requirement but that jurisprudence is more complex, and is discussed later in this chapter. However, in the international human rights systems, the answer is relatively consistent and is borne of pragmatism: if the human rights violation has not been or will not soon be redressed by the domestic judicial process, the exhaustion requirement is considered satisfied.

This Chapter uses exhaustion to show the self-perceptions of the two institutions: the investment tribunals give jurisdiction the same priority as they do to the merits *whereas*, for international human rights tribunals, jurisdiction is just a way to address and resolve the merits (the main point) and to induce domestic governments to build up their own judicial systems

---

[30] ILC Y.B. ("State Responsibility"), A/CN.4/SR.1468, p. 273 (Vol. I, 1977) (Summary record of the 1468th meeting) (emphasis added).

[31] *Id.*

[32] F. A. Mann, *Foreign Investment in the International Court of Justice: the* ELSI *Case*, 86 A.J.I.L. 92, 101 (1992) ("It is most welcome that a tribunal of high authority refuses to hold that waiver, estoppel or, one may add, acquiescence can be readily inferred from silence. It is submitted that it is only in very special circumstances that silence results in the loss of right").

[33] See, *e.g.*, W. S. Dodge, *Loewen v. United States: Trials and Errors Under NAFTA Chapter Eleven*, 52 DEPAUL L. REV. 563, 567 (2002) (noting that Chapter 11 waives the local remedies rule) [W. S. Dodge, *Loewen: NAFTA Chapter Eleven Trials and Errors*]; D. Wallace, "Fair and Equitable Treatment," *supra*, at 239-240; M. C. Porterfield, *International Expropriation Rules and Federalism*, 23 STAN. ENVT'L. L. J. 3, 64 (2003) (stating that Article 1121 "appears to permit an investor to institute a claim under Chapter 11 without first pursuing and exhausting domestic (both state and federal) remedies, so long as the investor waives his right to pursue domestic proceedings for damages"); C. F. Amerasinghe, STATE RESPONSIBILITY, *supra*, at 268-69 ("Whether an investment treaty . . . includes a waiver, express or implied, of the local remedies rule, where it would otherwise be applicable, is strictly a matter of interpreting the treaty.").

(perhaps an added benefit or even *the* primary one). The presence or absence of a unitary system at least partially explains this difference.

§ 4.2—Exhaustion in the IUCT

One of the justifications for choosing some standards of treatment for analysis is that our three institutions hold in common. The one exception is the *lack* of an exhaustion requirement for the IUCT. But even this no-exhaustion-required rule is telling of the IUCT's special dispute-settlement role (in a *force majeure* environment) and has important implications for state responsibility. In *Amoco International Finance Corp. v. Iran* (1987),[34] the IUCT held that its jurisdiction was determined exclusively by the terms of the CSD, and the CSD did not condition the IUCT's jurisdiction on exhausting local remedies.

The National Iran Oil Company (NIOC), a State-actor as respondent, had argued that Amoco had failed to exhaust its local remedies by not seeking compensation before Iran's Special Commission. *Lex specialis* under the CSD took precedence over *lex generalis*—the customary law status of exhaustion being well-established.[35] Nonetheless, the *Amoco* Tribunal *first* acknowledged exhaustion's default status and *then* proceeded to distinguish it away from the CSD's position on exhaustion.

Rexnord, Inc. v. Iran (1983)[36] had already held that "[t]he mere availability of a local remedy, whether judicial or otherwise, cannot preclude the Tribunal from jurisdiction." Four years later, in *Amoco* it became crystal-clear that actually it did not matter in the least whether the local remedy was effective. The local remedy simply did not have to be satisfied, thus mooting the effectiveness, availability, and unreasonably delay sub-class of questions.

---

[34] 15 I.U.C.T.R. 189, 196 (1987). See also D. Jones, *The Iran-United States Claims Tribunal, supra,* at 277 (with respect to the IUCT, "the traditional framework of State responsibility claims appears to have been modified in that the requirement of exhaustion of local remedies has been waived."); D. D. Caron, "The Basis of Responsibility," *supra*, at 114 ("[T]he structure of the Tribunal did not require a showing that local remedies [had been] exhausted.").

[35] An individual need not pursue those remedies that would be ineffective. See C.F. Amerasinghe, STATE RESPONSIBILITY, *supra*, at 240; B. Cheng, GENERAL PRINCIPLES OF LAW AS APPLIED BY INTERNATIONAL COURTS AND TRIBUNALS 179, n.65 (Cambridge University Press, 1987) (listing claims in which the domestic remedies rule has been removed).

[36] 2 I.U.C.T.R. 10 (1983).

Finally, it is important to keep the "time issue" in perspective. The last Chapter has explained that *SEDCO v. NIOC* (1987),[37] defined "appropriation" a certain way; another definition is that when "on the date of the government appointment of 'temporary' managers there is no reasonable prospect of return of control, a taking should conclusively be found to have occurred as of that date."[38] A second example comes from the already-mentioned *Tippetts, Abbett, McCarthy, Stratton v. Iran* (1984),[39] where the IUCT held that so long as the claimant and the government-appointed manager were able to work together, there was no illegal government "control" and thus no taking.

The *Tippetts* irony should not be lost on the reader. Had the original owners been unable to cooperate with the newly-foisted government-appointed manager, the expropriation claim is better off than if the owners did work well with the new manager. This, too, disincentivises owner-manager cooperation. It must be said, though, that the equation is not that easy. Sometimes the so-called "cooperation" might border on the coercive, which of course should not be glossed over, for "behind the atomistic rules there stands a whole series of socio-legal assumptions . . . ."[40]

These definitions are linked with time. Just because the IUCT does not require exhaustion in terms of invoking the local courts first does not mean that there is no minimum time requirement. By imposing *substantive* minimum-time requirements (rather than *procedural* ones) by recalibrating the definition itself, the IUCT achieves a similar end.[41] The only change is that the longer time period required shifts from a violation-to-admissibility in international court model (usually followed by NAFTA and the ECtHR) *to* expropriation process beginning-to-violation model (IUCT's style). This gives the State more time to correct itself but the expropriation process beginning-to-violation model suffers from an important disadvantage: it does not put the State on notice.

Chapter II (INSTITUTIONS AS PRISMS) has already discussed that the IUCT sees itself as deriving its legitimacy from its basic adherence to

---

[37] 15 I.U.C.T.R. 23 (1987-II).

[38] *Id.*, at 278-79 (1985-II). See also *Starrett Housing, supra*, at 155 (observing that "assumption of control over property by a government does not automatically and immediately justify a conclusion that the property has been taken").

[39] 6 I.U.C.T.R. 219, 225 (1984-II).

[40] C. Parry, *Defining Economic Coercion in International Law*, 12 TEX. INT'L L. J. 1, 2 (1977).

[41] While the claimant gets to escape the monetary costs of working the domestic courts, there probably is other capital spent on the waiting game. See C. F. Amerasinghe, STATE RESPONSIBILITY, *supra*, at 205.

international law not only as to the merits of an expropriation claim but even concerning jurisdiction. Something more is needed to stray the IUCT from this default position.

§ 4.3—Exhaustion before the NAFTA and the IIA Tribunals

Often, domestic judicial recourse precedes an ICSID or UNCITRAL claim, usually (but not *only*) because a state contract, for instance a license or a permit, is disputed. In those cases, the foreign investor first seeks local primary remedies. If the investor has *long-run* business interests in the host nation, then the investor is just as concerned with the holding as with the recovery of damages. The theory goes that only when local remedies have been used and justice was denied, the investment arbitration makes sense as a last-resort remedy. Article 26 (1) of the ICSID Convention assumes a waiver of exhaustion as the default position.[42]

Does NAFTA Article 1121[43] require exhaustion? Article 1121 "was intended, at the least, to limit multiple and potentially duplicative decisions on the same issue, and the best view of the provision is that it does indeed waive the local remedies rule, notwithstanding contrary suggestions by a few tribunals."[44]One driving force, throughout the IIA landscape, was the need to give foreign investors security, predictability and transparency, and to increase the likelihood that they will choose to invest in Country A as opposed to its competitors.[45] In human rights cases, the claimants do not always have the same geographical mobility, and thus

---

[42] Article 26(1): "Consent of the parties to arbitration under this Convention shall, unless otherwise stated, be deemed to consent to such arbitration to the exclusion of any other remedy."

[43] Art. 1121(1)(b) ("Conditions Precedent to Submission of a Claim for Submission"), the relevant part of the provision, states:

the investor . . . waive[s] their right to initiate or continue before any administrative tribunal or court under the law of any Party, or other dispute settlement procedures, any proceedings with respect to the measure of the disputing Party that is alleged to be a breach referred to in Article 1116, except for proceedings for injunctive, declaratory or other extraordinary relief, not involving the payment of damages . . . .

[44] See A. Bjorklund, "Waiver and the Exhaustion of Local Remedies Rule in NAFTA Jurisprudence," *in* NAFTA INVESTMENT LAW AND ARBITRATION: PAST ISSUES, CURRENT PRACTICE, FUTURE PROSPECTS 253, 255 (Todd Weiler ed., 2004) [A. Bjorklund, "Waiver and Exhaustion in NAFTA"].

[45] *Id.*, at 254.

their choices are also restricted. One of the earliest NAFTA decisions *requiring* exhaustion (*Loewen Group v. United States* (2003)[46]) has been defeated in the sphere of the arbitral community, and current consensus is that NAFTA, like other IIA's, does not require exhaustion.

Whereas BIT's, which have "fork in the road" (early bifurcation of domestic vis-à-vis international tribunal remedies) provisions, IIA's have been interpreted to "permit an investor to abandon local remedies in mid-stream, or even after those remedies have failed, but the investor may not subsequently return to local tribunals or courts."[47] By choosing IIA dispute resolution, claimants "forego their local remedies."[48] Tribunals have been known to construe IIA requirements upon claimants to compel them to file a formal written waiver and then significantly ensure that no other legal proceedings are commenced or continued.[49] Absent this step, the tribunal did indeed decline jurisdiction.[50]

Notably, Professor Andrea Bjorklund laments this rejection of the local remedies rule in the NAFTA regime (and generally in IIA). She instead proposes the restoration of a modified local remedies requirement "that includes a reasonable, but strict time-frame for those remedies to ensue, or provides a reasonable tolling period of the statute of limitations, while still maintaining a right for an individual to bring a claim directly should those remedies fail." [51] Bjorklund believes the existent language of the instrument allows for such a construction to be adopted and in any case add-ons are always possible.

Loewen and other NAFTA tribunals have entertained the exhaustion issue in interesting ways. Even though many of those tribunals' approach to exhaustion have now been held to be largely errant, their rationales nonetheless merit examination. So far as this author knows, no one has explicitly offered his hypothesis: Because the investment arbitration community was undecided about whether NAFTA's text requires

[46] ICSID Case No ARB(AF)/98/3, Award (2003), at ¶ 154.

[47] See A. Bjorklund, "Waiver and Exhaustion in NAFTA," *supra*, at 267 (referring to the NAFTA decision in *Waste Management v. Mexico*, Case No. ARB(AF)/98/2, at ¶ 27 (2000) (*Waste Management I*) ("To find unacceptable duplicity in the proceedings, the tribunal need have only 'proof that actions brought before domestic courts or tribunals directly affect the arbitration in that their object consists of measures also alleged in the present arbitral proceedings to be breaches of the NAFTA.'").

[48] *Id.*, at 255.

[49] *Commerce Group Corp. and San Sebastian Gold Mines, Inc. v. El Salvador*, ICSID Case No. ARB/09/17, Award, 14 March 2011, at¶ 84.

[50] *Id.*, at ¶ 116.

[51] A. Bjorklund, "Waiver and Exhaustion in NAFTA," *supra*, at 286.

exhaustion, they answered this threshold procedural question by engaging with *the merits*.

By "merits," I refer to important elements (necessary or sufficient) of the merits analysis. This is unusual since the procedural and jurisdictional issues ("gate-keeping" questions) ordinarily precede the merits. Like the texts of some other IIA's, the NAFTA instrument too emphasises effective procedures to resolve disputes but this does not totally preclude the exhaustion requirement.[52] A "final refusal to [cure the violation] (combined with effective obstruction and denial of legal remedies)"[53] might constitute expropriation. The IIA tribunal in *EnCana v. Ecuador* (2006),[54] dealing with tax issues, held that *only* when primary remedies are invoked and are unsuccessful may an international arbitration claim be brought.

On the denial of justice-exhaustion connection, the IIA tribunal in *Duke Energy v. Ecuador* (2008)[55] had to answer if the national judiciary had unduly interfered with a Chamber of Commerce arbitration and "justice was denied to the investor."[56] Because the claimant had not challenged a decision in domestic court, viz., had not exhausted the local remedies, the tribunal concluded that the claimants had failed to show that no adequate and effective remedies existed. They had to test it out for themselves; pointing to prior cases alone will not do. But of course *Duke Energy* is distinguishable since a denial of justice claim is categorically different from an expressly treaty-based claim.

Along similar lines, the *Loewen Group v. United States* (2003)[57] tribunal held:

---

[52] *Ethyl Corp. v. Canada*, UNCITRAL, Final Award on the Merits (1998), at ¶ 83; J. G. Merrills, INTERNATIONAL DISPUTE SETTLEMENT 118 (Cambridge University Press, 2005).

[53] *EnCana Corp v Ecuador*, LCIA Case No UN3481, UNCITRAL, Award (2006), at ¶ 194.

[54] *Id.*

[55] ICSID Case No ARB/04/19, Award (2008).

[56] *Id.*, at ¶ 392. Art II (7) of the U.S.-Ecuador BIT states: "Each Party shall provide effective means of asserting claims and enforcing rights with respect to investment, investment agreements, and investment authorizations."

[57] ICSID Case No ARB(AF)/98/3, Award, 26 June 2003, ¶ 154. This was not exactly correct since in *Mondev International Ltd v. United States*, ICSID Case No ARB/AF/99/2 (2002), ¶¶ 126. *et seq.* , the tribunal "assumed that an investor claiming denial of justice was not required to exhaust local remedies." W. S. Dodge, *Loewen: NAFTA Chapter Eleven Trials and Errors*, *supra*, at 162. Paulsson has criticized *Mondev* as wrong because *Mondev* misstates what the denial of justice means. See J. Paulsson, DENIAL OF JUSTICE, *supra*, at 111.

> No instance has been drawn to our attention in which an international tribunal has held a State responsible for a breach of international law constituted by a lower court decision when there was an available and effective and adequate appeal within the [host nation's] legal system.

1 BIT (2004), availabChapter Eleven claim against the United States, arguing that the Mississippi trial court violated the national treatment guaranteed by Article 1102. The claimant also argued that the verdict as well as the bond requirement violated the fair and equitable treatment provisions of Article 1105. Finally, the claimant asserted that, violating Articles 1102 and 1105, its investment was expropriated without compensation under Article 1110. In making its Article 1110 case, Loewen claimed that the treatment it received from the Mississippi courts interfered with its property rights and was "tantamount to expropriation."[58]

The *Loewen* tribunal rejected Loewen's Article 1105 claim because Loewen had failed to pursue "available and adequate" domestic remedies—mainly by not seeking a writ of certiorari in the United States Supreme Court (or by not seeking collateral review).[59] But certiorari is discretionary; the Supreme Court grants the writ for reasons of its own (most commonly, a split among the lower courts).[60] Jurisdiction is necessary but not sufficient to gain certiorari. The *Loewen* tribunal observed: "[t]here is a body of opinion [that] supports the view that the complainant is bound to exhaust any [local] remedy which is adequate and effective, so long as the remedy is not obviously futile."[61] European institutions, including the ECtHR, have "stressed that only direct means of redress are considered sufficient";[62] certiorari is not enough. This is also a decision that each institution has to make for itself, though given

[58] *Id.*, at ¶ 167.

[59] *Id.*, at ¶¶ 212, 217.

[60] Other reasons for granting certiorari are that the issue is of paramount and immediate national importance and/or that the denial of certiorari would allow an invalidation of some statute, ordinance or policy to stand without review having been had in the Supreme Court. See M. Meriwether Cordray & R. Cordray, *The Philosophy of Certiorari. Jurisprudential Considerations in Supreme Court Case Selection*, 82 WASH. U. L.Q. 389, 392–93 (2004).

[61] *Id.*, at ¶ 165 (internal quotation omitted).

[62] N. J. Udombana, *So Far So Fair: The Local Remedies Rule in the Jurisprudence of the African Commission on Human and Peoples' Rights*, 97 A.J.I.L. 1, 32 (2003) (citing *De Jong, Baljet, and Van den Brink v. The Netherlands*, 8 Eur. H.R. Rep. 20 (1986) (Commission Report); *Deweer v. Belgium*, 35 Eur. Ct. H.R. (ser. A) ¶ 26 (1980); *Pine Valley Developments Ltd. v. Ireland*, App. no. 43/1990 (1991)); see also *Sporrong v. Sweden*, 5 ECHR 35, 54 (1983).

NAFTA's emphasis on speediness and predictability, *Loewen* was difficult to justify.

Although Article 1121 requires that a claimant waive its right to bring claims regarding a measure that is the subject of a Chapter Eleven claim in domestic court, the *Loewen* tribunal held that "[Article 1121] says nothing expressly about the requirement that, in the context of a judicial violation of international law, the judicial process [should] be continued to the highest level."[63] An investment arbitration award that succinctly captures this point is *Jan de Nul v. Egypt* (2008)[64]:

> . . . the respondent State must be put in a position to redress the wrongdoings of its judiciary. In other words, it cannot be held liable unless 'the system as a whole has been tested and the initial delict remained uncorrected'. An exception to this rule may be made when there is no effective remedy or '*no reasonable prospect of success.*'

Although the *Loewen* tribunal "criticized the Mississippi proceedings in the strongest terms," it rejected the claimant's request for compensation.[65] The investor had not showed that *all* reasonable avenues of appeal, such as appeal via writ of certiorari to the United States Supreme Court, were denied it, and that this settlement with the Plaintiff was the only reasonable option available.[66] While making it clear that "the onus of proof rested with" the claimant in justifying its choice of remedies sought,[67] the *Loewen* tribunal strongly hinted that a Hobson's choice would be considered no choice at all.[68]

The tribunal in *Saipem v. Bangladesh* tribunal has been criticised for allegedly arbitrary line-drawing between judicial expropriation (stating that the local remedies rule does not apply because this is a "matter of the

---

[63] *Id.*, at ¶ 161.

[64] ICSID Case No ARB/04/13, Award (2008), at ¶ 258 (footnote omitted) (emphasis in original).

[65] *Loewen, supra*, at ¶ 154.

[66] *Id.*, at 217 ("our conclusion is that Loewen failed to pursue its domestic remedies, notably the Supreme Court option and that, in consequence, Loewen has not shown a violation of customary international law and a violation of NAFTA for which Respondent is responsible.").

[67] *Id.*, at 215.

[68] *Id.*, at 214 ("The question is whether the remedies in question were reasonably available and adequate."); *id.*, at 215 ("If, in all the circumstances, [a particular course of action such as] entry into the settlement agreement was the only course which Loewen could reasonably be expected to take, that would be enough to justify an inference or conclusion that Loewen had no reasonably available and adequate remedy.").

claim's admissibility") and denial of justice (local remedies rule does apply, for the context is "substantive").[69] The critics' contention is that by freeing claimants from the clutches of the local remedies rule in the former context but not in the latter, the *Saipem* tribunal failed to honour the exceptionalism of denial of justice.[70] It has also been argued that this *Saipem* approach, if it gains traction, will incentivise claimants (and sometimes even tribunals) to shoehorn their claims into the judicial expropriation class, especially when the respondents have a sullied reputation for having less efficient but still functional and non-corrupt domestic judicial processes. It has been suggested that at the heart of this approach lies the pernicious potential to do significant damage to the rationales attending the exhaustion doctrine itself. Candour, consistency and perceived institutional legitimacy might turn out to be the victims.

Powerful Parallels: The "Twistification" in *Marbury v. Madison*

While reflecting on *Loewen*, we should observe an interesting, uncommon parallel: *Marbury v. Madison* (1803),[71] the seminal case where the Supreme Court of the United States invalidated § 13 of the Judiciary Act of 1789,[72] a piece of legislation enacted by Congress, because the Court understood the Constitution's Exceptions Clause,[73] allowing the Supreme Court original jurisdiction only in cases "affecting Ambassadors, other public Ministers and Consuls, and those in which a State shall be a Party" and appellate jurisdiction in "all" other federal law questions, to

[69] *Saipem v. The People's Republic of Bangladesh*, ICSID Case No. ARB/05/7, Decision on Jurisdiction, at ¶ 151 (2007) (stating that generally the exhaustion doctrine does not apply to expropriation law).

[70] M. Sattorova, *Judicial Expropriation or Denial of Justice? A Note on* Saipem v. Bangladesh, 13 INT'L ARB. L. REV. 35 (2010).

[71] 5 U.S. (1 Cranch) 137 (1803).

[72] "The Supreme Court shall also have appellate jurisdiction from the circuit courts and courts of the several states, in the cases herein after provided for; and shall have power to issue writs of prohibition to the district courts [...] and writs of mandamus [...] to any courts appointed, or persons holding office, under the authority of the United States."

[73] U.S. Const., Art. III, Section 2, Clause 2 ("In all Cases affecting Ambassadors, other public Ministers and Consuls, and those in which a State shall be a Party, the supreme Court shall have original Jurisdiction. In all the other Cases before mentioned [within the judicial power of the United States], the supreme Court shall have appellate Jurisdiction, both as to Law and Fact, with such Exceptions, and under such Regulations as the Congress shall make.").

preclude the Act's authorization of original jurisdiction in a mandamus case to the Supreme Court.

Like in *Loewen*, the *Marbury* Court led by Chief Justice John Marshall first excoriated the *merits* of the government position, advanced by his chief nemesis President Thomas Jefferson, to tremendous effect,[74] then said the Supreme Court was bereft of *jurisdiction*. It was rather roundabout, especially since the jurisdictional question was a major constitutional issue.

Now Marshall stated as the reason (and, in his view, the vindicating principle) the authority of the Judiciary and specifically of the Supreme Court "to say what the law is."[75] In *Marbury*, like in *Loewen*, there really was no need for the Tribunal to reach the merits, at least as far as resolution of the immediate dispute is concerned (once it rejected the jurisdictional claim on grounds that required no further merits analysis). But John Marshall performed a quintessential and, according to Jefferson, characteristic "twistification"[76] to lose the immediate battle but win the war over the larger, looming question.[77]

---

[74] *Marbury*, *supra*, at 162 (acknowledging that the claimant did indeed have a "vested legal right": "Mr. Marbury, then, since his commission was signed by the President and sealed by the Secretary of State, was appointed, and as the law creating the office gave the officer a right to hold for five years independent of the Executive, the appointment was not revocable, but vested in the officer legal rights which are protected by the laws of his country. To withhold the commission, therefore, is an act deemed by the Court not warranted by law, but violative of a vested legal right."); *id.*, at 163 (stating that although "[t]he very essence of civil liberty certainly consists in the right of every individual to claim the protection of the laws whenever he receives an injury," that remedy created by statute cannot contradict the Constitution).

[75] 5 U.S. (1 Cranch) 137, 177 (1803). It is not so simple, though, as Professor Cass R. Sunstein points out in his piece *Beyond* Marbury*: The Executive's Power To Say What the Law Is*, 115 YALE L. J. 2580 (2006). Even though *Marbury* has for whatever reason gotten the first-mover-status in the lore of judicial review, it is not Marbury but an earlier case called *Hylton v. United States*, 3 U.S. (3 Dall.) 171, 174 (1796) ("After argument, the court (consisting of Wilson & Justices) delivered their opinions, but being equally divided, the defendant, by agreement of the parties, confessed judgment, as a foundation for the present writ of error, which (as well as the original proceeding) was brought merely *to try the constitutionality of the tax*.") (emphasis added), where the Supreme Court recognized judicial review.

[76] Letter from Thomas Jefferson to James Madison, 25 May, 1810, in Thomas Jefferson, *The Works of Thomas Jefferson*, ed. Paul Leicester Ford (G.P. Putnam's Sons, 1905), 11:141.

[77] This is the summer of 2012. Washington, D.C., where this author lives, is abuzz with post-mortem analysis of the health care decision from the Supreme Court of the United States. Some suggestions presently are floating around that Chief

Loewen was not all that different from *Marbury*. Of course, a decent argument could be made that, unlike a domestic court, an international tribunal is created to resolve every issue fairly appealed to it and indeed, for an ICSID tribunal, it might be reversible error (by annulment committee) not to address and resolve every question. That *Loewen* went for broke and eventually lost when other IIA tribunals refused to require exhaustion, at least formally, does not change the fact that *Loewen* did perform such a deft "twistification."

To its credit, and from its perspective, *Loewen* set the stage for tribunals to say that there is substantial value in exhaustion and thus in creating an indirect incentive for claimants to exhaust locally. Right out of the gate was one award which accepted, lock, stock and barrel, the *Loewen* position on exhaustion Along lines similar to the *Loewen* position on exhaustion, the NAFTA tribunal in *Feldman v. Mexico* (2002),[78] held that because all relevant judicial and administrative procedures were in theory and in reality open to the investor-claimant, she had to exhaust the local remedies.

Justice John Roberts's controlling opinion in *National Federation of Independent Business v. Sebelius*, 2012 U.S. Lexis 4876, * (2012), upholding the crux (the individual mandate, requiring most persons in the United States to purchase health insurance or pay a penalty) of President Barack's signature domestic policy achievement, the Patient Protection and Affordable Care Act of 2010 (PPACA), was just such a "twistification." While Chief Justice Roberts rejected the more expected twin justifications (of the Commerce Clause, U.S. Const. art. I, § 8, cl. 3, and the Necessary and Proper Clause, U.S. Const. art. I, § 8, cl. 18), thus jeopardizing a future course of Congressional action, he did form a majority with Justices Ginsburg, Breyer, Sotomayor and Kagan to uphold the mandate as an exercise of Congress's taxing power under the Constitution. Chief Justice Roberts, joined by Justices Breyer and Kagan, and with the combined votes of Justices Scalia, Kennedy, Thomas and Alito, also struck down as exceeding the Spending Clause, Art. I, § 8, cl. 1, the efforts of Congress seeking to withdraw, retroactively, state funds for States that refuse to accede to the Medicaid expansion authorized by the PPACA. See, *e.g.*, J. Rosen, "Welcome to the Roberts Court: How the Chief Justice Used Obamacare to Reveal His True Identity," *The New Republic*, June 29, 2012 ("Marshall achieved a similar act of judicial jujitsu in *Marbury v. Madison*, when he refused to confront president Jefferson over a question of executive privilege but laid the groundwork for expanding judicial power in the future.").

[78] ICSID Case No. ARB(AF)/99/1 (2002).

Four Approaches to Exhaustion

We return to the subject at hand. The arbitral community has answered the exhaustion question in four important ways: (*i*) by recalibrating the definition of "expropriation" *itself* (in various textual provisions); (*ii*) by distinguishing between expropriation of a contractual right and failure to comply with the contract; (*iii*) by asking how available and effective the remedies are; and (*iv*) recalibrating the "finality" of an international wrong—Do domestic courts have to be invoked at all? Does the "denial of justice through original judicial failure (or for that matter, at the stage of redress)" make a wrong ripe for investment arbitration?[79] "How many different judicial stages may be involved" before it becomes ripe?[80] This Chapter now discusses how these approaches fit into the jurisprudence of the investment arbitral awards as well as customary international law generally.

An illustrative passage comes from the NAFTA tribunal in the second round of *Waste Management v. Mexico* (2004) (*Waste Management II*)[81]:

> . . . the normal response by an investor faced with a breach of contract by its governmental counter-party (the breach not taking the form of an exercise of governmental prerogative, such as a legislative decree) is to sue in the appropriate court to remedy the breach. It is only where such access is legally or practically foreclosed that the breach could amount to a definitive denial of the right (i.e., the *effective taking* of the chose in action) and the protection of Article 1110 [NAFTA] be called into play . . . The Tribunal concludes that *it is one thing to expropriate a right under a contract and another to fail to comply with the contract.* Non-compliance by a government with contractual obligations is not the same thing as, or equivalent or tantamount to, an expropriation . . . Rather it is necessary to show an *effective repudiation of the right*, unredressed by any remedies available to the Claimant, which has the *effect of preventing its exercise entirely or to a substantial extent.*

First, the "expropriation" definition issue: NAFTA tribunals universally agree that customary international law, if Chapter Eleven had been inscrutable, would have determined if expropriation has occurred. The same is true of IIA tribunals and their corresponding instruments. But, as Chapters V (*Non-Discrimination*) and VI (*Other Substantive Standards*) illustrate, applying those principles to various cases often results in splits

[79] D. Wallace, "Fair and Equitable Treatment," *supra*, at 684.
[80] *Id.*
[81] *Waste Management Inc v. Mexico,* ICSID Case No ARB(AF)/00/3, Award (2004), at ¶¶ 174–175 (emphases added).

and dissonance.[82] Does the word "tantamount" expand upon the customary definition of expropriation under international law? The issue of what constitutes a "taking" is critical because it might lead to a finding of expropriation, and thus compensation, under Article 1110.[83]

The excerpt above in *Waste Management II* retains the phrase "effective taking." On the *merits*, of course, these differences among tribunals (especially with the lack of precedent) "may be the pivot on which the future of Chapter [Eleven] . . . may turn."[84] But such a finding might also decide the exhaustion issue since if a taking is "effective," then that might be a "definitive denial of the right" and the exhaustion requirement satisfied.

This kind of analysis requires the tribunal to engage with (*ex ante*) the merits. It is a settled proposition that a procedural "examination [on admissibility or other jurisdictional hurdles] is a summary analysis that does not imply a pre-judging or preliminary opinion on the merits."[85] What the tribunal cannot admit through the front door (procedural provisions in the ICSID Convention, UNCITRAL rules or the IIA itself), it might try to admit from the backdoor (interpret the substantive provisions in that way).[86]

---

[82] V. Been & J. Beauvis, *The Global Fifth Amendment? NAFTA's investment Protections and the Misguided Quest for an International "Regulatory Takings" Doctrine*, 78 N.Y.U. L. Rev. 30, 52-53 (2003) (citing Submission of the United States, *Metalclad Corp v. Mexico*, pp. 9-14 (1999)); D. M. Price, *NAFTA Chapter 11 – Investor-State Dispute Settlement: Frankenstein or Safety Valve?*, 26 CAN.-U.S. L.J. 1, 5 (Supp.2001); J. de Pencier, *Investment, Environment and Dispute Settlement: Arbitration Under NAFTA Chapter Eleven*, 23 HASTINGS INT'L & COMP. L. Rev. 409, 415 (2000). See also *Pope & Talbot, Inc. v. Canada*, UNCITRAL (NAFTA), Interim Award (2000); Award (2002).

[83] J. Paulsson & Z. Douglas, *Indirect Expropriations in Treaty Arbitrations*, *in* ARBITRATING FOREIGN INVESTMENT DISPUTES: PROCEDURAL AND SUBSTANTIVE LEGAL ASPECTS 148 (N. Horn & S. Kröll, eds.) (2004).

[84] D. Wallace, "Fair and Equitable Treatment," *supra*, at 255.

[85] *Simone André Diniz v. Brazil*, Case 12.001, Report No. 37/02, Inter-Am. C.H.R., Doc. 5 rev. 1 at 167 (2002) (Admissibility Petition), at ¶ 31.

[86] ICSID Case No. ARB/05/19, Decision on annulment, June 14, 2010, ¶ 47 ("The problem with the Tribunal's reasoning is that this is to do by the back door that which the Convention expressly excludes by the front door."); C. Schreuer, "Calvo's Grandchildren: The Return of Local Remedies in Investment Arbitration" 15 in THE LAW AND PRACTICE OF INTERNATIONAL COURTS AND TRIBUNALS 1: Koninklijke Brill (2005) [C. Schreuer, "Calvo's Grandchildren"] ("rationale in [some investment arbitration] cases" might "reintroduce[e] the local remedies rule through the back door").

This has a tragic ersatz quality, one which is potentially destabilising to the entire operation. If later tribunals, politicians and of course citizens cannot take the decision at its word, first the decision's and then the tribunal's legitimacy is imperiled. If "a jurisdictional issue is dependent on a factual determination," then "the tribunal must make that factual determination to the extent necessary for jurisdictional purposes."[87] But this does not at all enlighten us regarding the substantive or merits determination.[88]

Furthermore, the law undergoes some confusion when there is even the appearance of such backdoor activity. At the same time, however, what is an IIA tribunal entrusted to resolve a dispute to do, absent specific guidance? And specific guidance from the drafters of the original instrument or even add-ons typically does not come unless a problem is seen to severely disable dispute resolution. There is always the fear that creative and ingenious lawyers might claim that a specific rule in the text precludes, by contradistinction, *other* rules.

The *Waste Management II* tribunal had to decide how the contractual breach fits into the expropriation definition: it held that "mere non-performance of a contractual obligation is not to be equated with a taking of property, nor (unless accompanied by other elements) is it tantamount to expropriation."[89] The tribunal noted:

> [T]he normal response by an investor faced with a breach of contract by its governmental counterparty (the breach not taking the form of an exercise of governmental prerogative, such as legislative decree) is to sue in the appropriate court to remedy the breach. It is only where such access is legally or practically foreclosed that the breach could amount to a definitive denial of the right and Article 1110 be called into play.[90]

The *Waste Management II* tribunal might have been influenced by the *Loewen* tribunal's exhaustion reasoning. In fact, the *Waste Management II* award juxtaposed the concepts of judicial and non-judicial measures, in that the tribunal essentially held that a non-judicial act, for instance, non-delivery of services or failure to pay for services under a contract, should

[87] *Chevron Corp. and Texaco Corp. v. Republic of Ecuador*, PCA CASE NO. 2009-23, Third Interim Award on Jurisdiction and Admissibility, at ¶3.140 (citing *Micula v. Romania*, ICSID Case No. ARB/05/20, Decision on Jurisdiction and Admissibility 2008), at ¶ 24).

[88] A factual problem, without more, is not really comparable with a substantive determination, hence an *a fortiori* argument could not work either.

[89] *Waste Management II*, *supra*, at ¶ 174.

[90] *Id.*

first be routed through the judicial or administrative process. A narrow and limited exception was carved by the *Waste Management II* tribunal for "exercise[s] of governmental prerogative, such as a legislative decree"[91] that would presumably not be subject to adequate appeal.

The *Waste Management II* tribunal's holding limits Article 1110's scope and applicability in cases dealing with non-judicial acts. Unless the expropriatory measure was not subject to judicial or administrative review, under *Waste Management II* the only way that a claimant could prove an Article 1110 expropriation would be to show that (*i*) an appeal or other similar request for redress had been sought domestically; and (*ii*) that appeal had foundered due to a denial of justice under Article 1105. The *Waste Management II* tribunal's conclusion is consistent with the Restatement (Third) of the Foreign Relations Law of the United States, an important reference point for some international tribunals.[92]

Another case, *International Thunderbird Gaming Corp. v. Mexico* (2006)[93] goes to the same point about what "expropriation" is. What makes *Thunderbird* so interesting is that contractual violations were not even directly at issue there. What *was* at issue were legitimate expectations and reliance. Nonetheless, while arguing that Chapter Eleven defines "expropriation" strictly, Mexico (as respondent) submitted that Chapter Eleven expropriation does not cover government interferences with economic rights and contractual breaches.[94] The *Thunderbird* tribunal did not rule on the contract argument but Mexico's strategy hints that it was preparing to reject most claims about indirect interferences with expropriation.

The United States too has taken the same position—using slightly different arguments,[95] but Canada's position on the role of contractual

---

[91] *Id.* Even in the instance of a legislative decree, judicial remedies may be available to an aggrieved party. The answer to this question may be different in each unique circumstance, depending on the domestic legal system being considered.

[92] The Restatement, under Section 712 (official comment *h*), states that "[w]ith respect to any repudiation or breach of a contract with a foreign national, a state may be responsible for a denial of justice under international law if it denies to the alien an effective domestic forum to resolve the dispute[.]"

[93] UNCITRAL Arb. Award (2006), at ¶ 21.

[94] *Thunderbird*, Escrito Posterior a la Audencia ¶ 220.

[95] The United States and Canada focus mainly on the contractual breaches argument. See *Mondev*, U.S. Counter-Memorial p. 31 (quoting the NAFTA tribunal in *Azinian v. Mexico*, ICSID Case No. ARB (AF)/97/2 (1999), at ¶¶ 83 and 99: "What must be shown is that the court decision itself constitutes a violation of the treaty."); *Waste Management II*, Article 1128 Submission of Canada ¶ 5 ("A

breaches is incoherent. In *Merrill & Ring* (discussed in the previous chapter), [96] Canada put contractual breaches into "expropriation" under Chapter Eleven; and in *Waste Management II*, it did not. [97] On rare occasions, this might be the arbitration strategy of a client defending a variety of somewhat-contradictory interests or just a very public quest for the "right" answer. [98] One might imagine that Canada is respondent in some cases and supportive of the claimant in other cases. Unlike investors, governments must maintain this neat balance. In order to maintain their credibility, espousing narrow positions is a wise course of action for governments.

Canada would define "expropriation" with a strict test of "interference": this must implicate "the very fundamental aspects of an investment (*i.e.* its control, management of day-to-day operations, administration, distribution of dividends, appointment of officers, and ownership of property)."[99] So, absent a domestic law on the books denying remedies, a test this strict probably cannot be satisfied before the expropriation is a complete *fait accompli*. Thus the exhaustion process cannot even begin until this demanding definition of expropriation is met.

This delays, and probably is *intended* to delay (in fulfilling whatever motive), the whole resolution process. Of course, exhaustion is a function of more than just delay and time—it is also a function of undergoing an often-slow judicial process before the local machinery. Anyone who has undergone this can attest to the grueling anxiety and statistically higher-than-international risk of miscarriages of justice this poses.[100] Therefore,

---

NAFTA Tribunal does not have jurisdiction to determine contractual claims. A mere breach of a State of its contractual obligations with an investor, does not, in and of itself, constitute a breach of the minimum standard of treatment or an expropriation.").

[96] *Merrill & Ring v. Canada*, Counter-Memorial, at ¶ 745 (2010) (quoting *Pope & Talbot*, Interim Award, at ¶ 102).

[97] *Waste Management II*, Article 1128, Submission of Canada ¶ 5 ("A NAFTA Tribunal does not have jurisdiction to determine contractual claims. A mere breach of a State of its contractual obligations with an investor, does not, in and of itself, constitute a breach of the minimum standard of treatment or an expropriation.").

[98] R. Dworkin, *No Right Answer?*, 58 N.Y.U. L. REV. 1 (1978).

[99] See *Merrill & Ring*, Counter-Memorial, *supra*, at ¶ 745.

[100] See, *e.g.*, A. A. S. Zuckerman, "A Reform of Civil Procedure - Rationing Procedure Rather than Access to Justice",(1995) 22 J. OF L. & SOC'Y 155, 156 (even in the United Kingdom, "[d]elay itself has a way of generating litigation which leads to further delay. A great deal of money may be spent, long before discovery has even started, in litigating, at times all the way to the Court of Appeal

practitioners might find it valuable to contend, and tribunals judicious to accept, that only *part* of exhaustion's effect is achieved by this kind of delay.

Second and along related lines, notice how the *Waste Management II* tribunal distinguishes between "a right under a contract and another to fail to comply with the contract."[101] A contractual non-compliance ordinarily is not curable via IIA tribunals—for "[i]f Claimants merely ha[ve] a contractual claim, the [IIA] [t]ribunal would not have jurisdiction because a BIT is not intended to provide a substitute for regular contractual remedies."[102] In order to decide whether that line of demarcation lies, special characteristics (especially text and purposes) of the IIA forum and the textual instrument must be investigated. Only if the alleged contractual non-compliance *somehow* is appropriate for investment arbitration (potentially as a mixed claim), then I propose that it must first be required to travel through domestic courts.[103]

Not all contractual violations involving investments constitute expropriation, which is required for the remedies to be deemed exhausted. The exhaustion requirement "may apply" to "contract claims . . ., with the procedure and substance of" a "domestic tribunal['s]" decision "being subject to scrutiny before a NAFTA tribunal."[104] But "no similar exhaustion requirement would bar a claimant from seeking immediate Chapter [Eleven] arbitration regarding claims."[105]

The very fact that it is a contract observance claim diminishes its chances of getting relief. Making the contractual/non-contractual distinction becomes harder to defend if the tribunal is to avoid addressing "substantive" issues while purportedly deciding a "procedural" question.

---

and beyond, whether an extension of time should be granted or whether the action should be dismissed for want of prosecution.").

101 *Id.*

102 J. Beess und Chrostin, *Sovereign Debt Restructuring and Mass Claims Arbitration before the ICSID, The* Abaclat *Case*, 53 HARV. J. INT'L L. 505, 509 (2012) (referring to *Abaclat v. Argentina*, ICSID Case No. ARB/07/5, at ¶ 316).

103 I advance this proposal not just as a "nod to sovereignty" but also because domestic law treatment may help extricate the presumably complex cases into clear domestic and international law question strands. Moreover, it may well give the international tribunal, where the dispute will more likely than not end up, an impression of the quality of domestic justice that treated the case. On that latter point, even if a *separate* wrong is not claimed by the investor(s), it might shed light on the fairness with which *this* claim of international wrong was analysed.

104 B. W. Blades, *The Exhausting Question of Local Remedies: Expropriation under NAFTA Chapter 11*, 8 OR. REV. INT'L L. 31, 54 (2006).

105 *Id.*

Arguably, this phenomenon is even more controversial when the tribunal is deciding a gate-keeping type of procedural question. This kind of tribunal analysis highlights the *Waste Management II* and other tribunals' obvious glancing at the merits before resolving the exhaustion issue. While its practical need is understandable, as a general rule tribunals might find it more faithful to transparency and engendering public confidence if this is done explicitly.

Third, the *Waste Management II* excerpt above says that so long there is an "effective repudiation of the right" and there is the "effect" of denying the right totally or substantially, the local remedies have been exhausted.[106] While *Waste Management II* clearly *requires* this "effect," it does not require such a governmental *purpose* or *intent*. In this prong, the tribunal does not have to engage with the merits.

This is important for yet another reason: the *Waste Management II* tribunal suggested that if claims for mere breach of contract could be part of a NAFTA tribunal's docket, "Chapter [Eleven] would become a mechanism of equal resort for debt collections and analogous purposes in respect of all public (including municipal) contracts, which does not seem to be its purpose."[107] It might overburden Chapter Eleven as the haven for all remotely-relevant claims instead of respecting its formal Chapter breakdowns dealing with distinct subjects. This approach highlights *Waste Management II's* and IIA tribunals' general sensitivity to the instrument's general goals.

Fourth and finally, for cases involving some "original judicial failure" or a failure "at the stage of redress," when does the wrong become "final" and ripe for investment arbitration?[108] Would it be different for a human rights court or other forms of international tribunals? How much do the IIA-specific (and NAFTA-specific) consequences matter? This point is related to state responsibility, in the next Chapter, and is probably the most discretionary of the exhaustion criteria.

Unless, as *Waste Management II* put it, "access [to local remedies] is legally or practically foreclosed,"[109] those remedies *must* be accessed before an investor submits a claim for arbitration. While accessing them, "secondary wrongs" might take place.[110] This could be discrimination in jury selection to egregiously misleading or vague statute directing remedies and everything in between. Thus, an IIA violation might not be

[106] *Waste Management II* , *supra*, at ¶¶ 174–175.

[107] *Id.*, at ¶ 116.

[108] D. Wallace, "Fair and Equitable Treatment," *supra*, at 684.

[109] *Waste Management II*, *supra*, at ¶ 174.

[110] *Id.*

the "original or primary wrong" but *could* be caused by the "egregious" administrative or judicial review, thus constituting a "secondary wrong."[111]

The *Loewen* tribunal decided that "[a]n important principle of international law should not be held to have been tacitly dispensed with by international agreement, in the absence of words making clear an intention to do so."[112] However, "[s]uch an intention may be exhibited by express provisions which are at variance with the continued operation of the relevant principle of international law."[113] The tribunal also suggested that Article 1121's silence about the exhaustion requirement should be read in favour of requiring the rule for claims challenging judicial acts.[114] The *Loewen* tribunal formally limited its exhaustion holding to Chapter Eleven violations caused by *judicial* measures, but the tribunal also stated:

> The purpose of the requirement that a decision of a lower court be challenged through the judicial process before the State is responsible for a breach of international law constituted by judicial decision is to afford the State the opportunity of redressing through its legal system the inchoate breach of international law occasioned by the lower court decision. The requirement has application to breaches of Articles 1102 and 1110 as well as Article 1105.[115]

Loewen, in requiring a Chapter Eleven claimant first exhaust its domestic remedies, was concerned that a failure to require exhaustion "would encourage resort to NAFTA tribunals rather than resort to the appellate courts and review processes of the host state."[116] The tribunal noted that:

> Further, it is unlikely that the Parties to NAFTA would have wished to encourage recourse to NAFTA arbitration at the expense of domestic appeal or review when, in the general run of cases, domestic appeal or

---

[111] Paulsson, DENIAL OF JUSTICE, *supra*, at 57.

[112] *Loewen, supra*, at ¶ 160 (citing *Elettronica Sicula SpA (ELSI) United States v. Italy*, (1989) ICJ 15 at 42).

[113] *Id.*

[114] *Id.*, at ¶ 161 ("One thing is . . . reasonably clear about Article 1121 and that is that it says nothing expressly about the requirement that, in the context of a judicial violation of international law, the judicial process be continued to the highest level.").

[115] *Id.*, at ¶ 156.

[116] *Id.*

> review would offer more wide-ranging review as they are not confined to breaches of international law. [117]

Similarly, the IIA tribunal in *Generation Ukraine v. Ukraine* (2003)[118] held:

> [I]t is not enough for an investor to seize upon an act of maladministration, no matter how low the level of the relevant governmental authority; to abandon his investment without any effort at overturning the administrative fault; and thus to claim an international delict on the theory that there had been an uncompensated virtual expropriation. In such instances, an international tribunal may deem that the failure to seek redress from national authorities disqualifies the international claim, not because there is a requirement of exhaustion of local remedies but because the very reality of conduct tantamount to expropriation is doubtful in the absence of a reasonable—not necessarily exhaustive—effort by the investor to obtain correction.

This *Generation Ukraine* declaration, along with *Loewen's* exhaustion analysis, is an effort to keep alive the *substantive* denial of justice doctrine. It also fits the celebrated *Neer v. Mexico* (1926)[119] test that not only must the violation be egregious but also that domestic authorities must have failed to (or will have failed to) undo the wrong. In the previous chapter, we have discussed the realism that pervades a diplomatic dispute settlement body such as the IUCT. In *Oil Fields of Texas v. Iran* (1982),[120] the IUCT was commissioned with the task of determining if a judicial decision (in this case, that of the Islamic Court of Ahwaz) could be tantamount to a measure of expropriation. Holding that this expropriation amounted to a permanent deprivation of use, the IUCT revealed its reasoning: "In these circumstances, and taking into account the Claimant's impossibility to challenge the Court order in Iran, there was a taking of the three blowout preventers for which the Government is responsible."[121]

This understanding of finality (Criterion *iv* noted earlier) is not just an academic problem: Once a claim is admitted (assuming it is held to have been exhausted or satisfied), the degree to and depth in which it was exhausted carries over and affects its *merits* evaluation. The issue has been causing even more dissonance in recent years with *SGS v. Pakistan*

---

[117] *Id.*, at ¶ 162.
[118] ICSID Case No. ARB/00/9, Final Award on the Merits (2003).
[119] 4 R. Int'l Arb. Awards (15 October 1926), at p. 4.
[120] 12 I.U.C.T.R. 308, 318-319.
[121] *Id.*, at 319.

(2004)[122] and *SGS v. Philippines* (2004).[123] The obvious issue in both of these IIA cases—going in opposite directions—is umbrella clauses in IIA's converting contractual breaches into IIA violations. In these situations, "the investor has every incentive to have" such "freestanding contract claims arbitrated before" the IIA tribunal rather than "designating the host country's courts or tribunals" for this job.[124] For instance, the *SGS v. Philippines* tribunal stated that "the Parties' intention was to emphasize their commitment to comply with the substantive treatment obligations assumed under the BIT."[125]

What *are* those "substantive treatment obligations"? Do contracts fall within that category? Is the line to be drawn at contracts that implicate a State's internal functioning, and thus sovereignty? Most IIA tribunals have placed contract claims in the "substantive treatment obligations" category.[126] The issue becomes one of forum selection. There are important sovereignty concerns with letting contractual breaches be decided, in the first instance, by IIA tribunals. On the other hand, denying the IIA tribunals a chance to reach the contractual issue which might underpin the IIA question makes little sense.

One half-way solution (by this author) is for IIA tribunals to give the domestic courts the first crack at determining what the contract *says*. An advisory opinion or a prior interpretation by the highest domestic court should do. This decision will be reviewed by the IIA tribunals deferentially and only when it is clearly erroneous (no rational justification, with facts that barely rise above the "speculative level"[127]) will the international tribunal reverse that interpretation. In fact, the *GAMI* tribunal, discussed in the previous chapter, said not only will it give the highest domestic court's

---

[122] ICSID Case No. ARB/01/13 (2004).

[123] ICSID Case No. ARB/02/6 (2004).

[124] M. Wendlandt, *SGS v. Philippines and the Role of ICSID Tribunals in Investor-State Contract Disputes*, 43 TEX. INT'L L. J. 523, 532 (2008) [M. Wendlandt, *SGS v. Philippines*].

[125] *Id.*, at ¶ 77.

[126] See C. Schreuer, "Calvo's Grandchildren," *supra*, at 8 ("the majority of tribunals have found that jurisdiction is not restricted to claims asserting violations of the BITs' substantive provisions but includes contract claims"); see also, *e.g.*, *Salini v. Morocco*, ICSID Case No ARB/00/4 (2001), at ¶ 59-62; *Suez, Sociedad General de Aguas de Barcelona, S.A. and Vivendi Universal, S.A. v. Argentina,* ICSID Case No. ARB/03/19, Decision on Jurisdiction (2002), at ¶ 55; *SGS v. Philippines*, ICSID Case No. ARB/02/6, Decision on Jurisdiction (2004), at ¶ 130-35.

[127] The test was established in a pleading context by the United States Supreme Court. See *Bell Atlantic v. Twombly*, 540 U.S. 544, 555 (2007).

pronouncement the status of "authoritative[ly] expressed national law" but also that the domestic court's decisions deserve "respectful consideration . . . insofar as it applies norms congruent with NAFTA."[128]

The deferential mechanism by which the United States Supreme Court reviews state and local legislation for constitutionality inspires this solution.[129] That tribunal too has to negotiate between a lower sovereign court's right to say what the law is and the implications of that interpretation for the larger constitutional (or, in our case, IIA) question—bearing in mind that "[t]he power to determine the meaning of a statute carries with it the power to prescribe its extent and limitations as well as the method by which they shall be determined."[130]

The root of the confusion is the uncertainty as to whether a contractual breach *can* constitute an international wrong; and if it can, must it first travel through the domestic courts? Finally, how much domestic remedy is enough for it to count as exhaustion?[131] In *Azinian v. Mexico* (1999),[132] the NAFTA tribunal held that "NAFTA cannot possibly be read to create . . . a regime, which would have elevated a multitude of ordinary transactions[, including contractual breaches,] with public authorities into potential international disputes."

Azinian considered it "salutary" that a "dispute [might be resolved] without resorting to investor state arbitration under NAFTA," and thus the tribunal did not want to disincentivise "potential claimants under NAFTA . . . from seeking relief under domestic law from national courts."[133] The domestic courts were the workhorses whose support the IIA wanted to enlist, for the system knew it *needed* to, because it had no independent judicial means of enforcing the awards. In essence, we must appreciate the all-important pattern and attending deduction: If there be a "vertical" separation of authority, then the "oil for the rule-based gears"[134] had to be collaboration and cooperation rather than mutually destructive competition.

---

[128] *GAMI, supra*, at 18.

[129] See, *e.g.*, *Chicago v. Morales*, 527 U.S. 41, 61 (1999) (noting that "[w]e have no authority to construe the language of a state statute more narrowly than the construction given by that State's highest court," and deferring to the Illinois Supreme Court's interpretation); *Fiore v. White*, 531 U.S. 225, 226 (2001) (certifying a question to the state supreme court for its advisory opinion).

[130] *Smiley v. Kansas,* 196 U.S. 447, 455 (1905).

[131] M. Wendlandt, *SGS v. Philippines, supra*, at 534.

[132] ICSID Case No. ARB(AF)/97/2 (1999).

[133] *Id.*, at ¶ 86.

[134] *Bell v. Thompson*, 545 U.S. 794, 834 (2005).

Helnan v. Egypt, Biases and Annulment Committees

We take a hiatus, and we explore a recent award and its implications for the annulment committee system. An IIA case not yet on the public radar, *Helnan v. Egypt* (2010),[135] is important. *Helnan* said that the ICSID Convention's Contracting Parties had deemed arbitration as the "exclusive remedy" under Article 26. The annulment committee overruled the tribunal's determination that the investor had failed to exhaust local remedies.[136] The annulment committee also noted that for investment treaty claims, the agreement between the parties is defined as a calculus of "the BIT and . . . the ICSID Convention (which the agreement incorporates by reference) as well as . . . the filing of the investor's claim."[137]

This ICSID notion of annulment committees disapproving "excess[es] of power or jurisdiction" by tribunals is driven by a belief that "good fences make good neighbours."[138] As with UNCITRAL, though, the system relies on the good-faith of the arbitrators to be intellectually honest in their decisions: "Reasoned awards . . . may facilitate judicial review of the award; despite the limited statutory grounds for vacatur, a petition to vacate the award would be virtually impossible without a reasoned award."[139]

If all the arbitrators cared about was being upheld or not being annulled (by domestic courts for UNCITRAL or by annulment committee for ICSID), they might obfuscate the award's reasoning or make it so fact-intensive as to be virtually unreviewable. This might exacerbate the *legitimacy crisis* in the international judiciary, for "[t]ransparency of [international] decisionmaking processes is a fundamental prerequisite for democratic citizen participation, public discussion, and parliamentary control."[140] Brunnée and Toope's interactional model in international law,

---

[135] ICSID Case No. ARB/05/19, Decision on annulment (2010).

[136] Since the wisdom or legitimacy of an ICSID annulment committee does not directly apply to this dissertation, that point will not be addressed extensively. See C. Schreuer, *From ICSID Annulment to Appeal: Half-Way Down the Slippery Slope* in THE LAW AND PRACTICE OF INTERNATIONAL COURTS AND TRIBUNALS 211 (2011) [C. Schreuer, *From ICSID Annulment to Appeal*]. Since the standard for overruling is very high, viz. no effective application of the relevant law by the tribunal, it goes to show how unreasonable the annulment committee *thought* the tribunal had been.

[137] *Id.*, at ¶ 40.

[138] R. Frost, "Mending Wall" (poem), 1914.

[139] W.M.C. Weidemaier, *Precedent in Arbitration, supra,* at 1917.

[140] E. Petersmann, "International Trade Law and International Environmental Law: Environmental Taxes and Border Tax Adjustment in WTO Law and EC Law" *in*

explained in Chapter III (ATTRIBUTION AND CAUSATION), supports this assertion.

Both ICSID and UNCITRAL resemble the ECtHR's position on cooperation between that Court and the domestic systems. Stipulated in the ILC's Draft Rules on Arbitral Procedure,[141] the issue is about domestic judicial processes that constitute a fundamental miscarriage of justice, a high bar. Were enforcing uniformity a goal of the annulment committees, the lack of uniformity in tribunal decisions (both jurisdictional and merits) created by NAFTA's structure (and the structures of many other IIA's) would be mitigated. But that does not seem to be the case.

The *Helnan* annulment committee thought that this term of art ("excess[es] of power or jurisdiction" by tribunals) applies to "the scope of the task which the parties have charged the tribunal to perform in discharge of its mandate, and the manner in which the parties have agreed that task is to be performed."[142] An obvious example is that the tribunal was not functioning at all (unlikely).

Even the most decrepit and corrupt tribunals do function somehow, and short of total suspension of the judicial power by some layer of local authority it cannot really be said that the local courts are missing in action.[143] The other situation is rampant and the systemic pervasiveness of corruption that casts doubt on a wide variety of cases. The next section shows that this is a problem that the international human rights systems too faced and where they considered the local remedies exhausted.

Even if the ICSID tribunal *was* functioning, it still has to function effectively. Some "ineffectiveness" examples are "a failure to apply the law chosen by the parties (but not a misapplication of it)"[144] and "a failure

---

R. Revesz, P. Sands & R. Stewart, Environmental Law, the Economy and Sustainable Development: THE UNITED STATES, THE EUROPEAN UNION AND THE INTERNATIONAL COMMUNITY 135 (Cambridge University Press, 2008); see also R. Mackenzie & P. Sands, *International Courts and Tribunals and the Independence of the International Judge*, 44 HARV. INT'L L. J. 272, 282-4 (2003) [R. Mackenzie & P. Sands, *International Courts and Tribunal*].

[141] See ILC: "Commentary on the Draft Convention on Arbitral Procedure," U.N. Doc. A/CN.4/92, 108; see also *History of the Convention,* Documents Concerning the Origin and the Formulation of the Convention, Vol. II, Part 1, p. 518.

[142] *Helnan, supra,* ¶ 41.

[143] A subtle point is that local courts that are not functioning at all are probably located in a signatory country which has no intention of obeying the international tribunal anyway, which effectively makes this whole discourse moot and academic.

[144] *Helnan, supra,* at ¶ 41-2 (citing *Soufraki v. UAE*, ICSID Case No. ARB/02/7 (2007)) (Decision on Annulment)).

to decide a question entrusted to the tribunal."[145] Because it is the ICSID tribunal that hears the facts and retains the first right to resolve the problems, second-guessing of the relevant law by annulment committees ordinarily is not considered reason enough to intervene.[146]

In the context of the disqualification of arbitrators, for instance, Article 57 of the ICSID Convention stipulates the test to be whether "a manifest lack of the qualities" to be an arbitrator, namely the exercise of independent judgment, is lacked; Article 58 goes on to state that "if it is decided that the proposal is well-founded […] the arbitrator to whom the proposal relates shall be replaced." Of course, in the ordinary course of things the impartiality of an arbitrator is so delicate and fundamental an issue that there is very little margin of error.[147]

Nonetheless, the curious standard requiring "a *manifest* lack of the qualities" complicates the question. It might be thought to require something more than the mere "appearance of bias," which happens to be the requirement in many domestic jurisdictions. That view has not commanded significant support.[148] But there has been support for the argument that the proper standard is "the probability of actual bias,"[149] or in other words, the justifiable- or reasonable-doubt standard.[150]

---

[145] *Id.* (citing *Soufraki*, *supra*, ¶ 44; *Vivendi Universal, S.A. v. Argentina*, ICSID Case No. ARB/03/19, at ¶ 86).

[146] C. Schreuer, *From ICSID Annulment to Appeal*, *supra*, at 211.

[147] See, *e.g.*, *Amco v. Indonesia*, ICSID Case No. ARB/81/1, Decision on Jurisdiction (1983) ("This aim is to provide to host-states and investors an international device to settle their disputes, by reaching a decision which is final and binding, and offers the highest possible guarantees of legality, fairness and impartiality. It goes without saying that in this respect, an absolute impartiality of the sole arbitrator or, as the case may be, of all the members of an arbitral tribunal, is required…").

[148] *Compañía de Aguas del Aconquija and Vivendi Universal v. Argentine Republic*, ICSID Case No. ARB/97/3, Challenge Decision (2001), at ¶ 20 ("A question arises with respect to the term 'manifest lack of the qualities required' in Article 57 of the Convention. This might be thought to set a lower standard for disqualification than the standard laid down, for example, in Rule 3.2 of the IBA Code of Ethics, which refers to an 'appearance of bias'. The term 'manifest' might imply that there could be circumstances which, though they might appear to a reasonable observer to create an appearance of lack of independence or bias, do not do so manifestly. In such a case, the arbitrator might be heard to say that, while he might be biased, he was not manifestly biased and that he would therefore continue to sit. As will appear, in light of the object and purpose of Article 57, we do not think this would be a correct interpretation").

[149] See, *e.g.*, *Caperton v. A.T. Massey*, 129 S. Ct. 2252 (2009) (citing *Aetna Life Ins. Co. v. Lavoie*, 475 U. S. 813, 825 (1986) (one possible test of bias is whether a

It should be remembered that in a factually vague case, there really may not be much practical difference between appearance and probability standards. "Manifest" simply means that the loss of confidence must be premised on objectively reliable information; it is not an astronomically high and almost-impossible standard;[151] it does not require unanimity among tribunal members any more than it requires unanimity among the parties. This ICSID standard is "not far from the one which prescribe[d] the international customary law."[152] The standard for manifest satisfaction

---

certain factor would "offer a possible temptation to the average … judge to … lead him not to hold the balance nice, clear and true") (internal citations and quotation marks omitted)).

[150] *Compañía de Aguas del Aconquija and Vivendi Universal v. Argentine Republic*, ICSID Case No. ARB/97/3, Challenge Decision (2001), at ¶ 25 ("But in cases where (as here) the facts are established and no further inference of impropriety is sought to be derived from them, the question seems to us to be whether a real risk of lack of impartiality based upon those facts (and not on any mere speculation or inference) could reasonably be apprehended by either party. If (and only if) the answer is yes can it be said that the arbitrator may not be relied on to exercise independent judgment.'"); *SGS v. Pakistan*, ICSID Case No. ARB/01/13 (2004), at p. 345 ("The party challenging an arbitrator must establish facts, of a kind or nature as reasonably to give rise to the inference that the person challenged clearly may not be relied upon to exercise independent judgment in the particular case in which the challenge is made.").

[151] *Suez, Sociedad General de Aguas de Barcelona S.A. and Interagua Servicios Integrales de Agua S.A. v. Argentine Republic*, ICSID Case No. ARB/03/17, Challenge Decision of 22 October 2007, at ¶ 30 ("Independence and impartiality are states of mind. Neither the Respondent, the two members of this tribunal, or any another body is capable of probing the inner workings of any arbitrator's mind to determine with perfect accuracy whether that person is independent or impartial. Such state of mind can only be inferred [either] from conduct by the arbitrator in question, or persons connected to [him/her]. It is for that reason that Article 57 requires a showing by a challenging party of any fact indicating a manifest lack of impartiality or independence.").

[152] *Siemens A.G. v. Argentine Republic*, ICSID Case No. ARB/02/8, at 57, Award (2007); *Electricidad Argentina S.A. and EDF International S.A. v. Argentine Republic*, ICSID Case No. ARB/03/22 (2008), Annulment Commitee Decision, at ¶¶ 65-68 ("Pursuant to Convention Article 57, a lack of reliability to exercise independent judgment must be 'manifest'. We understand Respondent to propose that a lack of reliability to exercise independent judgment becomes 'manifest' when it can be 'easily understood or recognized by the mind'. Professor Schreuer indicates that the proposed test for what is 'manifest' relates not to the seriousness of the allegation, but to the ease with which it may be perceived. Something is 'manifest' if it can be 'discerned with little effort and without deeper analysis.'") (citing C. Schreuer, *A Commentary to the ICSID Convention*, *supra*); *Urbaser S.A.*

of a burden of proof is certainly no *more* rigorous than the standard required of an Annulment Committee to intercede and set aside an award.

This said, let us explore what the *Helnan* annulment committee has accomplished. Addressing the *Helnan* tribunal's reliance on *Generation Ukraine*, the annulment committee noted that the *Generation Ukraine* award concerned a low-level governmental decision. The investor's failure to seek local redress in that case was enough to disqualify the claim. This was not because of the exhaustion requirement but rather because the low-level decision was not grave enough to amount to a breach of international law to begin with. *Generation Ukraine*, therefore, was no defence.[153]

From an annulment committee's perspective, however, *Generation Ukraine* is just case-law—though it is very eminent and strikingly relevant case-law. That cannot be what the exception-laden "a failure to apply the law chosen by the parties (but not a misapplication of it)"[154] criterion, on *Helnan's* own terms, could reasonably cover. Not on a neutral reading, at least.

We must confront reality. *Helnan,* on the other hand, was about a *ministerial* decision, "for which a State may be held responsible in international law, and in respect of which no substantive requirement that an investor seek local redress should have been imposed." [155] The annulment committee concluded that because the "clear intention of the [ICSID Convention's Contracting Parties was] not to require the pursuit of local remedies as a precondition to arbitration, such a requirement were to be read back in as part of the substantive cause of action."[156]

The *Helnan* annulment committee went so far as to state clearly that "[w]here a State has agreed with a foreign investor that arbitration of disputes arising under a contract between them shall be the exclusive remedy, the exhaustion of local remedies is inferentially excluded" by

---

and Consorcio de Aguas Bilbao Bizkaia, Bilbao Biskaia Ur Partzuergoa v. Argentine Republic, ICSID Case No. ARB/07/26, Challenge Decision of 12 August (2010), at ¶ 43 ("The requirements of independence and impartiality serve the purpose of protecting the parties against arbitrators being influenced by factors other than those related to the merits of the case. In order to be effective this protection does not require that actual bias demonstrate a lack of independence or impartiality. An appearance of such bias from a reasonable and informed third person's point of view is sufficient to justify doubts about an arbitrator's independence or impartiality.").

153 *Helnan*, *supra*, ¶ at 41-4.

154 *Id.*, at ¶ 41-2 (citing *Soufraki v. UAE*, ICSID Case No. ARB/02/7 (2007)) (Decision on Annulment)).

155 *Id.*, at ¶ 45.

156 *Id.*, at ¶ 47.

contradistinction.[157] *Helnan's* implications have not yet been appreciated fully by the investment arbitration or broader international law communities.

Moreover, this remarkable statement by the *Helnan* annulment committee calls into question the default status of exhaustion in international law. If exhaustion can be done away with inferentially and by implication, then this is a new frontier. Such a step should be taken thoughtfully and cautiously. We can be confident enough to predict that sooner or later the investment arbitration community will have to grapple with *Helnan's* exhaustion problem.

The common thread of the now-errant tribunals: a substantive claim for expropriation or a violation of the fair and equitable treatment standard for denial of justice can only be admitted when the investor has sought local (administrative or judicial) redress and this was manifestly denied. This denial may take different forms, be it a refusal to access to court to "defend legal rights, a refusal to decide, unconscionable delay, manifest discrimination, corruption, or subservience to executive pressure, and it must amount to a breach of international law."[158] Presently, of course, no exhaustion is required.

Expropriation or a related violation may then be claimed and damages awarded. Thus, if there is a denial of justice, no further claim for primary remedies before national courts is necessary. The investor may then seek monetary relief before international tribunals. Asking the investor to pursue ineffective remedies would be inefficient. Still, the hurdle for a denial of justice claim needs to be set high if primary remedies are not to be lost too easily in investment arbitration.

One final note: Due to structural differences, the closest ECtHR counterpart for the NAFTA-IIA (ICSID) annulment committees is the ECtHR Grand Chamber reviewing an individual Chamber. This is where it becomes a little more complicated. An important difference between the internal reviewing mechanisms of ICSID and the ECtHR is that the ECtHR Grand Chamber is far more deferential to its individual Chamber

---

[157] *Id.*, at ¶ 45 n. 43 (also citing C. Schreuer, THE ICSID CONVENTION: A COMMENTARY ON THE CONVENTION ON THE SETTLEMENT OF INVESTMENT DISPUTES BETWEEN STATES AND NATIONALS OF OTHER STATES 938 (Cambridge University Press, 2009)); G. K. Foster, *Striking a Balance Between Investor Protections and National Sovereignty: The Relevance of Local Remedies in Investment Treaty Arbitration*, 49 COLUM. J. TRANSNAT'L L. 201, 211 (2011).

[158] J. Paulsson, DENIAL OF JUSTICE, *supra,* at 204.

about factual findings than the ICSID annulment committees are to tribunals.[159]

As the next section will explain, the ECtHR Grand Chamber is not nearly as deferential to the local courts. One arguable reason is that, on systematic human rights abuse cases where the ECtHR's scrutiny is at its peak,[160] it does not necessarily trust the domestic courts to call themselves ineffective or dysfunctional (which the human rights courts were created to help domestic courts overcome).[161] Property rights cases in the human rights courts can be, and sometimes have been, repackaged as human rights abuse cases—especially if they become a pattern.

§ 4.4—Exhaustion before the ECtHR and the International Human Rights Tribunals

Like the other two types, the IACtHR, the ECtHR, and the ACtHR too have adapted the exhaustion requirement to their contexts but unlike the IUCT the human rights courts have not dispensed with the requirement completely. The application has to be brought within six months of the final rejection in domestic courts. Notwithstanding that IUCT does not require exhaustion, its stance on state responsibility is, in most other ways, at least as relaxed as the ECtHR (as Chapter III: ATTRIBUTION AND CAUSATION underscores).[162]

In the international human rights systems, exhaustion is generally seen as a *facilitator* for, not an *impediment* to, human rights. The investment arbitration and human rights perspectives on exhaustion were coming from very different worlds. The international human rights tribunals seems to want to do more than protect human rights; the only way it can be effective is to promote a human rights *culture* in the Convention system and let the domestic systems fill in the gaps (but only the gaps). Because the Council of Europe, which is served by the ECtHR, is a diverse place

---

[159] S. C. Grover, PROSECUTING INTERNATIONAL CRIMES AND HUMAN RIGHTS ABUSES COMMITTED AGAINST CHILDREN: LEADING INTERNATIONAL COURT CASES 50 (Springer, 2009).

[160] H. Lauterpacht, "The Proposed European Court of Human Rights," in TRANSACTIONS 35 (1950); J.W.F. Sundberg, *Human Rights In Sweden: The Breakthrough of an Idea*, 47 OHIO ST. L.J. 951 (1985).

[161] *Id.*; C. Schreuer, *From ICSID Annulment to Appeal*, *supra*, at 211-12.

[162] See, *e.g.*, R. Lalive, *The First World Bank Arbitration (*Holiday Inns v. Morocco*) — Some Legal Problems*, 51 B.Y.I.L. 123, 159 (1980) ("the general unity of an investment operation" requires that "international proceedings in principle have primacy over purely internal proceedings.").

with common as well as civil law, religious differences, and other features, a "clash of civilizations" could otherwise result.

When the ECHR was enacted in 1953, domestic courts were not developed in many Council of Europe countries and this ECHR shadow was designed to quicken the pace domestically. The ECtHR has tried to do this in three sequential ways: "strengthening domestic institutions, backstopping them, and compelling them to act."[163] This shift in focus of "from independent regulation above the national state to direct engagement with domestic institutions" was thought necessary.[164] This is a classic case of "dialectical review"—"a recurring engagement among international tribunals and national courts that could ultimately yield a system of harmonized legal norms."[165]

When the local judicial process has broken down, the need for the exhaustion requirement is, simultaneously, at its peak (by working through the problems, the signatory State will learn) and its very bottom (no effective remedy to exhaust). It might be incredibly tempting for the international tribunal to intervene and supposedly rectify the structural problem by waving its magic wand. But experience teaches that tribunals should best Odysseus by resisting this seductive siren-song.[166] Not only might States not learn anything for the *future*, they might also not have experimented enough with various modalities and techniques to discharge *this* immediate judicial mandate effectively. Sometimes, however, such judicial mandates on complex structural issues become unavoidable; in such cases, maximum possible flexibility to the governmental decision-makers should be given. In any case, this contradiction has not really been addressed here or elsewhere though this author's inclination is to require most investor-claimants to invoke but not necessarily exhaust fully such remedies and to exempt human rights claimants altogether.

One of the criticisms attending the IIA waiver of the local remedies rule is that "[a]s arbitrations multiply," this high volume will be hard to

---

[163] A. Slaughter & W. Burke-White, *The Future of International Law is Domestic (or, The European Way of Law)*, 47 HARV. J. INT'L L. 327, 328 (2006) [A. Slaughter & W. Burke-White, *Future of International Law*].
[164] *Id.*
[165] See A. Bjorklund, *Reconciling State Sovereignty and Investor Protection in Denial of Justice Claims*, 45 VA. J. INT'L L. 809, 867 (2005) [A. Bjorklund, *Reconciling State Sovereignty and Investor Protection*].
[166] Homer, THE ODYSSEY 98 (Plain Label Books, reprinted 2009) ("If any one unwarily draws in too close and hears the singing of the Sirens, his wife and children will never welcome him home again, for they sit in a green field and warble him to death with the sweetness of their song.").

control and thus the role of a buffer or insulator served by the local remedies rule would have been useful.[167] But given the many cases in which the international human rights tribunals consider the exhaustion requirement satisfied only because there was no effective remedy to exhaust in domestic courts and still manages to produce a high volume of written judgments, [168] makes this fear untenable. Perhaps the detailed and time-consuming function of an IIA tribunal would have to be modified or the lengthy awards truncated, but the overall project is not yet a lost cause. This knowledge transfer on a logistical as well as jurisdictional question is significant.

We now observe several IIA-international human rights court differences. First, foreign investors' security, codified in an IIA, partly lies in not having to exhaust local remedies[169] but ECtHR claimants, who are often nationals of the government they are suing, theoretically *must* exhaust domestic remedies. Second, unlike IIA regimes, the ECtHR actually analyses the issue in detail though it usually decides close questions of whether the local remedies are generally unavailable, ineffective or delayed in favour of the claimant; the burden of proof typically rests on the State. [170] This is remarkable because the same principles of international law apply to and are cited by the ECtHR as are cited by the NAFTA tribunals; this is *un*remarkable because, as Chapter II suggests, the ECtHR's "core mandate" is "protecting civil and political liberties enshrined in the Convention," and procedure is the means.[171]

Formal remedies are inadequate in the ECtHR; what matters is "the general legal and political context in which [the remedies] operate as well as *the personal circumstances of the applicant*." [172] Not only are the

[167] A. Bjorklund, "Waiver and Exhaustion in NAFTA," *supra,* at 286.

[168] A. Slaughter & W. Burke-White, *Future of International Law, supra,* at 328-29.

[169] See, *e.g.*, J. Kurtz, "National Treatment, Foreign Investment and Regulatory Autonomy: The Search for Protectionism or Something More?," in P. Kahn and T. Wälde (eds), NEW ASPECTS OF INTERNATIONAL INVESTMENT LAW 311 (2007) (arguing that the IIA regime "prioritizes party autonomy, speed, and finality over the process of legal reasoning and justification").

[170] See, *e.g.*, M. Pinto, *Fragmentation or Unification, supra,* at 833.

[171] See L. R. Helfer, *Redesigning the European Court of Human Rights*, *supra*, at 128.

[172] See *Van Oosterwijck v. Belgium*, App. no. 7654/76 (1980), at ¶¶ 36-40 (emphasis added); see also *Akdivar v. Turkey*, App. no. 99/1995/605/693 (1996), at ¶¶ 68-69; *Khashiyev and Akayeva v. Russia*, App. no. 57942/00; 57945/00 (2005), at ¶¶ 116-117; *Isayeva v. Russia*, App. no. 57950/00 (2005), at ¶¶ 152-3. Poverty alone does not absolve the applicant from *trying* to use domestic proceedings (i.e.,

applicants' (investors') personal statuses immaterial in the NAFTA-IIA universe, but the author has unearthed no NAFTA literature (academic or judicial) on this score. This, again, is *un*remarkable because IIA's presuppose investors' financial candlepower.[173] One scholar, Lee Caplan —a lonely voice not so much in dissent as he is just close to solitary in addressing the question *at all* — argues, first, that small and medium-sized commercial enterprises are key for the prosperity of a dynamic worldwide economy in the long run and that the global IIA network needs to morph itself into becoming more accessible to smaller and perhaps nascent enterprises. [174] Caplan proposes as possible solutions political risk insurance, strategic alliances, and streamlining the IIA decision-making.[175]

Now notice a new, potentially trend-setting case in the ECtHR. In *Yukos Oil Co. v. Russia* (2011),[176] very recently the ECtHR's Grand Chamber found a property rights violation on purely procedural grounds; the State imposed disproportionately high fines and prematurely seized assets without thoughtful deliberation or a fair chance for the firm to justify itself in domestic proceedings.[177] The State had not given Yukos enough time to review the pertinent material, some of which was provided just days before the first trial.[178] After all, while the State, in its exercise of sovereignty, "may strike hard blows," it may not strike "foul ones."[179] In cases involving expropriation and criminal forfeiture, it should be an axiom in international law that although the State may be (and even must be) "diligent, strict, and vigorous in . . . enforcement [it] can also afford to be just."[180]

Cyprus v. Turkey, App. no. 25781/94 (2001), at ¶ 352 (peculiar situation of Turkish-Cypriot Gypsies)).

[173] See, *e.g.*, E. De Brabandere, "Non-State Actors in International Investment Law" *in* PARTICIPANTS IN THE INTERNATIONAL LEGAL SYSTEM: MULTIPLE PERSPECTIVES ON NON-STATE ACTORS IN INTERNATIONAL LAW 345 (J. D'Aspremont, ed.) (Taylor & Francis, 2011).

[174] L. Caplan, "A Proposed Set of Arbitration Rules for Weaker Players in Investor-State Arbitration" 240 *in* YEARBOOK ON INTERNATIONAL INVESTMENT LAW & POLICY (Oxford University Press, 2010); see also L. Caplan, "The Challenges Confronting Small Investors" *in* R. P. Alford and Catherine A. Rogers, eds., THE FUTURE OF INVESTMENT ARBITRATION, *supra,* at 459.

[175] *Id.*, at 242.

[176] App. no. 14902/04 (2011).

[177] *Id.*, at 15.

[178] *Id.*

[179] *Berger v. United States*, 295 U.S. 78, 88 (1935).

[180] R. H. Jackson, *The Federal Prosecutor*, 24 J. AMER. JUDICATURE SOC'Y 18, 18-19 (1940).

In the fullness of time, *Yukos* may be seen as a textbook case of the ECtHR saying that, whether you are an affluent corporation or a poor yeoman farmer, the total or near-complete absence of an effective remedy not only means that the claimant has exhausted whatever remedy the State had to offer but also that this is a violation *in itself*. In the IIA world, this would probably be characterised as a fair and equitable treatment or due process violation, and in the IUCT an "interference" violation. As things now stand, the ECtHR is the only international human rights court saying so, but it carries weight.[181]

Observe a trend in the coming years. If the ECtHR follows through with *Yukos's* logical implications, this will repudiate the thirty-year-old rule of *Ireland v. United Kingdom* (1978),[182] an interstate case which had rejected the substantive component to exhaustion. This might have the adverse effect of tribunals consciously or subconsciously *raising* the bar to prove exhaustion a bit higher in order to prevent the double-bonus windfall. Other human rights tribunals may follow suit. Because not a significant period of time has passed since *Yukos*, it is premature to tell what will happen. The developments will be exciting to watch.

Yukos most likely is also the only case in the three institutions where there have been concerns about how the exact identity of a party (the Russian Federation, in this case) has actually affected the decision.[183] In no other case in any of the three institutions has this been a serious issue.[184]

---

[181] N. J. Udombana, *So Far So Fair: The Local Remedies Rule in the Jurisprudence of the African Commission on Human and Peoples' Rights*, 97 A.J.I.L. 1, 4 (2003) ("[The local remedies rule's] function is procedural [in human rights courts] — is a question of admissibility and not of substance."). *Yukos* came eight years after Udombana's article, so his working assumption was that the ECtHR retains no substantive component to exhaustion.

[182] 25 ECHR (ser. A) ¶ 159.

[183] M. Lopas, *The Human Rights Brief*, Center for Human Rights and Humanitarian Law, *available at* <http://hrbrief.org/2011/10/ecthr-decision-for-russian-oil-company-emphasizes-focus-on-procedural-human-rights-violations/> (2011) (last accessed October 15, 2011) ("Antoine Buyse, senior researcher at the Netherlands Institute of Human Rights in Utrecht, explained that because the ECtHR is concerned about Russia implementing its rulings, 'the court prefers to stay on firm ground and finds violations which can be clearly argued.' . . . By dismissing the issue of political prejudice in the Yukos trial, the court averts a decision that would be much less palatable to Russia, which is the defendant state in nearly a quarter of new cases brought in 2009.").

[184] S. D. Franck, *Development and Outcomes of ITA, supra*, at 442-45 (using outcome-analysis to test hypotheses about IIA tribunal preferences between

This ties in with the legitimacy rationale guiding the institutions, and is addressed again at the end of this Chapter.

A third difference: The ECtHR has consistently held that it is not necessary for the Convention right to be explicitly raised in domestic proceedings. As long as the issue was raised *implicitly* or in *substance* or was a contractual violation, the exhaustion rule is satisfied under *Castells v. Spain* (1985).[185]

The last section has explained how this ECtHR approach contrasts with NAFTA cases—*Waste Management II, Azinian, Mondev Int'l Ltd. v. United States* (2002), [186] and *Thunderbird* connect this with state responsibility and take a more nuanced approach to what is an international law claim vis-à-vis a domestic law claim. In fact, as the last section has already noted, *all* three NAFTA signatories agree that "NAFTA does not cover breach of contract claims, absent some 'additional element'"[187] (such as denial of justice or peremptory norm).

There are caveats to the knowledge transfer. Another key NAFTA-ECtHR difference is that, unlike for many IIA tribunals including the *Loewen*-NAFTA tribunal,[188] before coming to the ECtHR one need not exhaust discretionary remedies such as seeking certiorari in a domestic court of last resort. *Loewen's* point was that a claimant might not have the right to a discretionary remedy but she definitely has the right to *seek* such a remedy, thus the claimant first had to do so. For IIA's, "procedural

---

developed and developing countries, and finding no such bias in NAFTA); G. Van Harten, *Fairness and independence in Investment Arbitration: A Critique of Susan Franck's "Development and Outcomes of Investment Treaty Arbitration,"* SSRN.com, *available at* <http://papers.ssrn.com/sol3/papers.cfm?abstract_id=1740031> (2010) (last accessed October 4, 2011) (impeaching Franck's study for lack of data and thus reliability and claiming there is no evidence either way); W. M. C. Weidemaier, *Disputing Boilerplate*, 82 TEMP L. REV. 1, 18–19 (2009) (tracing the possibility of bias in investment arbitration).

[185] App. no. 11798/85 (1992), at ¶ 32; see also *Sadik v. Greece*, App. no. 18877/91 (1996), at ¶ 33; *Fressoz and Roire v. France*, App. no. 29183/95 (1999), at ¶ 38; *Azinas v. Cyprus*, App. no. 56679/00 (2004), at ¶¶ 40-1.

[186] ICSID Case No ARB/AF/99/2.

[187] J. Pauwelyn, et al., "Standards Under the North American Free Trade Agreement," Graduate Institute, Geneva, working paper 2011, *available at* <www.graduateinstitute.ch/webdav/site/ctei/shared/CTEI/Law%20Clinic/Memoranda%202011/Standerds_NAFTA.pdf> (last visited September 24, 2011), pp. 81-87.

[188] *Loewen*, *supra*, at ¶ 210 (seeking certiorari in the U.S. Supreme Court is a required path).

protection" usually is distinct from "substantive investment protection."[189] When the case is a challenge to laws already on the books and the violation is "final" for many cases—rather than an isolated, as-applied challenge—there need not be exhaustion.

In *Cyprus v. Turkey* (2001),[190] the ECtHR held that the local remedies had to be exhausted in the Turkish Republic of Northern Cyprus (TRNC), despite the fact that Cyprus was challenging the very existence of the TRNC courts. The logical gap in the ECtHR's analysis is that it did not address whether the TRNC courts had been established unlawfully and thus had been operating in violation of a peremptory norm. This decision was not readily consistent with the ECtHR's twenty-year old decision in *Van Oosterwijck v. Belgium* (1980).[191]

In *Van Oosterwijck*, the ECtHR had held that there is no obligation to exhaust domestic remedies where there are "special circumstances which absolve the applicant."[192] Articles 40 and 41 of the ILC Draft Articles suggest that there is an important difference between an ordinary international law breach and a *jus cogens* breach. There is a strong case to be made that *jus cogens* in the *Cyprus v. Turkey* scenario is just such a "special circumstance," if there ever was one. Still, one way to reconcile *Cyprus* with the rest of the ECtHR's exhaustion jurisprudence: the alleged problem with the TRNC courts did not involve an error in process, just an error in forum. Altogether, an ECtHR composite attuned to the personal concerns and problems of the applicant emerges.

It remains to be seen if the ECtHR will take the United Nations Committee against Torture's leap and admit claims where the claimant's noncompliance with domestic procedures "could presumably not—or at least not solely—be attributed to the complainant or victim."[193] With *Ruiz-Mateos v. Spain* (1993),[194] the ECtHR has set itself up to do just this. And in *Akdivar* three years later the ECtHR deemed the remedies exhausted because of special circumstances, viz. reprisals and civil strife. *Akdivar* has strong IUCT and *force majeure* overtones. Despite the fact that the *Akdivar* Court did not cite IUCT decisions, the latter may have been

---

[189] *Maffezini v. Spain*, ICSID Case No ARB/97/7, Decision on Jurisdiction (2000), at ¶ 54.

[190] App. no. 25781/94, at ¶¶ 82-102.

[191] App. no. 7654/76.

[192] *Id.*, at ¶ 42.

[193] Comm. No. 6/1990, *Parot v. Spain*, ¶¶ 4.1–5.2, UN Doc. CAT/C/14/D/6/1990 (1995); C. Ingelse, THE U.N. COMMITTEE AGAINST TORTURE 187 (2001).

[194] App. no. 12952/87 (1993).

influential. At the very least, this increases the likelihood that there is a place for IUCT decisions in international human rights.

Moreover, nations eager to join the Council were expected to improve their human rights commitments politically and judicially. This reasoning is not so different from the *Azinian*-NAFTA tribunal's (mentioned in the previous section): resolutions in domestic court "might have the salutary effect of resolving the dispute without resorting to investor state arbitration under NAFTA."[195] In NAFTA too, the aim is to work with the domestic courts, not to disable their participation in these cases. We return to this point with the *Selmouni* case (discussed shortly).

ECHR Article 35's text itself states that the exhaustion requirement is based on recognised international law principles. The obligation to exhaust domestic remedies forms part of customary international law, under the International Court of Justice's decisions.[196] Other international human rights treaties containing an exhaustion requirement: the International Covenant on Civil and Political Rights[197] (including its Optional Protocol),[198] the American Convention on Human Rights,[199] the African Charter on Human and Peoples' Rights.[200] As the ECtHR observed in *De Wilde, Ooms & Versyp v. Belgium* (1971),[201] in the interests of quick resolution or other reasons, the State may *waive* the requirement of exhaustion.

The question now is whether a particular remedy is domestic or international. If the remedy is *domestic*, under normal circumstances it has to be exhausted before an application is filed with the Court. If, on the other hand, it is *international*, the application may be rejected under ECHR Article 35.[202] It is for the ECtHR to determine whether a remedy is

[195] *Azinian*, *supra*, at ¶ 86.

[196] *The Interhandel Case (Switzerland v. United States)*, judgment of 21 March 1959; the ILC Third Report on Diplomatic Protection (A/CN.4/523) at ¶ 83, discusses "hardship cases" where because of an accidental relationship with the respondent State it would be "impractical and unfair" to require exhaustion. *Interhandel* notes that "a general principle of law that would make the local remedies rule inapplicable in such cases is that of *ex injuria jus non oritur*." *Id.*, at ¶ 87.

[197] Article 41(1)(c).

[198] Articles 2 and 5(2)(b).

[199] Article 46.

[200] Articles 50 and 56(5).

[201] Series A no. 12, ¶ 55 (1971).

[202] The relevant part reads: "The Court shall not deal with any application submitted under Article 34 that…is substantially the same as a matter that …has

domestic or international in character: considerations include the formal character of the remedy, the controlling text in domestic and international law, the function of the remedy, and how crucial it is in a legal system.[203]

An analog is the IIA problem of distinguishing between contractual violations (squarely *domestic*) and breaches of IIA (usually *international* violations). The remedy question under the ECtHR is different from the analytical question of violations because remedies are what ultimately matter. As Chapter II (INSTITUTIONS AS PRISMS: THE ECtHR) has explained, the ECtHR has begun ordering its own remedies once domestic remedies have failed.

This development (or the euphemistic term "embeddedness"[204]) has not been challenged by the signatories—although ECHR Article 13 obligates the signatories, not the ECtHR, to provide an effective national remedy. ECtHR petitioners generally have to observe the domestic law procedures, failing which their application is likely to fall foul of the exhaustion rule.[205] If more than one remedy is available, the applicant is required to exhaust only one of them.[206]

Why have the signatories expressed little hesitation about this change? It could be because those cases are rare and egregious human rights violations, such as large-scale torture, civil strife, and risk of reprisal.[207] It could also be because remedies in those cases are ordered by the ECtHR *only after* a deferential review of the domestic court's decision and

---

already been submitted to another procedure of international investigation or settlement and contains no relevant new information."

[203] *Jeličić v. Bosnia-Herzegovina*, App. no. 41183/02 (2005), at 26.

[204] For a more extensive analysis of subsidiarity and "embeddedness" for the ECtHR and international human rights courts generally, see *id.*, at 128; Y. Arai-Takahashi, THE MARGIN OF APPRECIATION DOCTRINE AND THE PRINCIPLE OF PROPORTIONALITY IN THE JURISPRUDENCE OF THE ECHR 236 (2002); R. Keohane, *Compliance with International Commitments: Politics Within a Framework of Law*, 86 AM. SOC'Y INT'L L. (Proc. & Ann. Meeting) 176, 176 (1992) (stating that "institutional enmeshment," *i.e.*, "embeddedness," takes place "when domestic decision[-]making with respect to an international commitment is affected by the institutional arrangements established in the course of making or maintaining the commitment.").

[205] *Ben Salah, Adraqui and Dhaime v. Spain*, App. no. 45023/98 (2000); *Merger and Cros v. France*, App. no. 68864/01 (2004); *MPP Golub v. Ukraine*, App. no. 6778/05 (2005); *Cardot v. France*, App. no. 11069/84 (1991); *Michalak v. Poland*, App. no. 24549/03 (2005); *Charzynski v. Poland*, App. no. 15212/03 (2005).

[206] *Barbosa v. Portugal*, App. no. 65681/01 (2004); *Jelicic v. Bosnia and Herzegovina*, App. no. 41183/02 (2005).

[207] *Akdivar, supra,* at ¶ 16.

because the ECtHR was created precisely to handle "systemic human rights problems" in an organised way.[208] This is telling about the role and prestige of the Court today. This is not to downplay the criticism the Court is currently receiving from within and beyond the Euro-skeptic communities but that criticism is not yet strong enough to overturn the Court's regime.

A class of cases that NAFTA and the IIA's do not directly have to deal with is *interstate* cases, a textbook example of diplomatic protection. The exhaustion requirement applies to these cases, where the petitioning government alleges ECHR violations against individuals by *another signatory*.[209]

The NAFTA-IIA universe, as part of the direct-standing model, cannot really deal with this type of State-State interaction. Even in straightforward most-favoured-nation (MFN) cases where the respondent nation's treaty with a *third* nation is concerned, the fragmentation problem arises. The current state of things in this NAFTA-IIA universe is rather jumbled: *Only* when "the treaty [does not] provid[e] for a particular system of arbitration" and "the parties have [not] agreed to a highly institutionalized system, such as NAFTA,"[210] can the other treaty even be considered.

These stipulations atending the IIA universe self-perpetuate some of this jurisdictional confusion. The ECtHR's clear hierarchy makes clear who has the last word on the ECHR. One scholar notes that the ECtHR "is a court of precedents"[211]—conventional wisdom about the ECtHR as a

---

[208] *Id.*

[209] *Ireland v. the United Kingdom*, Series A no. 25, ¶ 159 (1978) (involving the "Five Techniques" of interrogation: wall-standing, hooding, subjection to noise, deprivation of sleep, and deprivation of food and drink)). But "the rule does not apply where the applicant State complains of a practice as such, with the aim of preventing its continuation or recurrence." *Denmark v. Turkey*, App. no. 34382/97 (2000), at ¶ 34 (citing *Ireland*).

[210] *Azinian*, *supra*, at ¶ 63.

[211] See M. Balcerzak, "The importance of effective remedies" *in* APPLYING AND SUPERVISING THE ECHR: THE IMPROVEMENT OF DOMESTIC REMEDIES WITH PARTICULAR EMPHASIS ON CASES OF UNREASONABLE LENGTH OF PROCEEDINGS 25, *available at* <http://www.echr.coe.int/NR/rdonlyres/82597AB6-124F-48D5-8BBB-792899EB0C6A/0/AmeliorationsRecours_EN.pdf> (last accessed October 4, 2011); see also G. Ress, *The Effect of Decisions and Judgments of the European Court of Human Rights in the Domestic Legal Order*, 40 TEX. INT'L L.J. 359, 376 (2005) (former ECtHR judge arguing that "[w]ithin the domestic legal order, the [ECHR] is only one element in the mosaic of different constitutional provisions and its interpretation in that context may differ considerably from an interpretation based on the Convention alone.").

civil law court notwithstanding. The difficult question of reconciliation with prior cases lives on.

The ECtHR rationale for the exhaustion rule is to afford the national authorities, mainly the courts, the opportunity to prevent or correct the alleged ECHR violations. The exhaustion requirement assumes that the domestic legal order will provide an effective remedy for violations of Convention rights. Prime among these authorities are *Selmouni v. France* (1999),[212] *Kudła v. Poland* (1996),[213] and *Andrášik v. Slovakia* (2002).[214] *Selmouni* put front and center a chief reason for the existence of the exhaustion requirement in the ECtHR:

> [T]he purpose of Article 35 is to afford the Contracting States the opportunity of preventing or putting right the violations alleged against them before those allegations are submitted to the Convention institutions. . . . States are [owed] an opportunity to put matters right through their own legal system. . . . [T]he machinery of protection established by the Convention is subsidiary to the national systems safeguarding human rights.[215]

Then *Selmouni* adds the caveat that

> the only remedies which Article 35 of the Convention requires to be exhausted are those that relate to the breaches alleged and at the same time are available and sufficient. The existence of such remedies must be sufficiently certain not only in theory but also in practice, failing which they will lack the requisite accessibility and effectiveness; it falls to the respondent State to establish that these various conditions are satisfied.[216]

The ECtHR's exhaustion rule is not inexorable: the Court applies the rule flexibly and without excessive formalism, given the ultimate goal of protecting human rights.[217] Surprisingly, this has not brought up charges of illegitimacy. *Selmouni* summarized that

> the complaint intended to be made subsequently to the Court must first have been made – at least in substance – to the appropriate domestic body,

---

[212] App. no. 25803/94 (1999).
[213] App. no. 30210/96 (1996), at ¶ 152.
[214] App. nos. 57984/00 (2002).
[215] *Selmouni*, *supra*, at ¶ 74.
[216] *Id.*, at ¶ 75.
[217] *Ringeisen v. Austria*, Series A no. 13 (1971), at ¶ 89; *Lehtinen v. Finland* (dec.), App. no. 39076/97 (1999).

and in compliance with the formal requirements and time-limits laid down in domestic law.[218]

The right to an effective remedy is a secondary right, and is there to support the primary human rights guaranteed in the text. There cannot be an Article 13-exhaustion right violation *without* there being a primary right violation of some sort. This should not be understood to mean that an Article 13 application can only come *after* some primary rights violation. If a violation has indeed been established in domestic law, then an applicant must surely have been given an effective domestic remedy (even if it had not been readily accessible).

In *Klass v. Federal Republic of Germany* (1978),[219] the ECtHR confirmed this view. The *Klass* line of reasoning adopted by the Court was reaffirmed two years later by the European Commission of Human Rights[220] in *Silver v. United Kingdom* (1980).[221] In *Silver,* the ECtHR held that a victim asserting an ECHR violation—with an arguable claim—should have a domestic process.[222] All that the ECtHR has given by way of an analytical structure to this "arguability test" is an easy-to-satisfy three prong test: (*i*) it should address an ECHR right or freedom; (*ii*) it should have some support in the facts proffered; and (*iii*) it must trigger a *prima facie* violation.[223]

Now comes a landmark decision in the ECtHR's exhaustion jurisprudence concerning Article 13. After years of delays in getting some

---

[218] See, *e.g.*, "The importance of effective remedies" *in* APPLYING AND SUPERVISING THE ECHR: THE IMPROVEMENT OF DOMESTIC REMEDIES WITH PARTICULAR EMPHASIS ON CASES OF UNREASONABLE LENGTH OF PROCEEDINGS 22, Directorate General of Human Rights: Council of Europe (2006) (statement of Michal Balcerzak).

[219] Series A, No. 28, 2 EHRR 214 (1978).

[220] The European Commission of Human Rights (1954-1998) was an intermediary between the complaining party and the ECtHR. Complainants could not circumvent the Commission. If the Commission found a case to be well-founded and meritorious, the Commission would then initiate proceedings on behalf of the complainant in the ECtHR. In 1998, the Council of Europe reformed the "Convention machinery" and adopted Protocol XI to abolish the Commission and allowed complainants to petition the ECtHR directly. See Prot. No. XI, ECHR, E.T.S. 155, *entered into force* 1 November 1998.

[221] App. Nos 5947/72, 6205/73, 7052/75, 7061/75, 7107/75, 7113/75 and 7136/75 (1980).

[222] *Id.*, at ¶ 113.

[223] *Boyle and Rice v. United Kingdom*, App. no. 19/1986/117/165-166 (1988).

member States to respond, in *Kudła v. Poland* (2000)[224] the Grand Chamber of the ECtHR basically said: "Enough!" The Court decided that Article 6 (1) failed to absorb Article 13's guarantees in cases where the right to trial within a reasonable time was at stake. Thus the Article 13 complaint about ineffective remedy was deemed to be a distinct claim.

As hinted above, the increasing frequency of violations of the reasonable time requirement under ECHR Article 6 (1) may have been a prime factor. The *Kudła* Court discussed "the important danger" that exists for the rule of law "within the national legal orders of the State Parties when excessive delays in the administration of justice occur in respect of which litigants have no domestic remedy."[225] In that very case, for example, Poland had waited almost four years to introduce a separate remedy to tackle such delays. The theme that resurfaces is that, to the ECtHR, exhaustion is not for its own sake. In that Court's cost-benefit analysis, when exhaustion stopped paying dividends to protect human rights in the signatories, the Court sensed its very role was to be institutionally interventionist in such a case.

Still, this was not an unrestrained Court and there were limits. Again the Court rejected arguments for a unified pan-European definition of effective remedies, including a time-bar.[226] If the Court had wanted to do this, it had had enough cover, but that would have been a needless jab in the face of members' sovereignty for the ECtHR to determine the procedural details for them.[227] It is a step to be taken only when members' obstinacy cannot be handled. It is also a classic example of the "Delegator's Dilemma."[228] Pointing this out is a high-risk strategy for the ECtHR and the Council of Europe because then the value of the Convention system also comes up for debate.

---

[224] App. no. 30210/96. See also CAN EXCESSIVE LENGTH OF PROCEEDINGS BE REMEDIED? 251, European Commission for Democracy through Law, Council of Europe (2007).

[225] *Id.*, at ¶ 148.

[226] M. Scherer & G. Born, *Bridging Cultural Gaps in International Arbitration: Introduction to The European and Middle Eastern Arbitration Review*, Global Arbitration Review Special Report, p. 5-7 (2008) [M. Scherer & G. Born, *Bridging Cultural Gaps*].

[227] See, e.g., *Handyside v. United Kingdom*, App. No. 5493/72 (1976), at ¶ 23 ("It is not possible to find in the domestic law of the various Contracting States a uniform European conception of morals. ... [This] leaves to the Contracting States a *margin of appreciation.*") (emphasis added).

[228] J. D. Donahue, J. Zeckhauser & S. Breyer, COLLABORATIVE GOVERNANCE: PRIVATE ROLES FOR PUBLIC GOALS IN TURBULENT TIMES 248 (Princeton University Press, 2011).

The ECtHR has yet to reach this far. In *Sürmeli v. Germany* (2006),[229] the ECtHR observed, mainly as *dictum*, that perhaps "the best solution" is "a remedy designed to expedite the proceedings in order to prevent them from becoming excessively lengthy" in the *first place*. After all, protracting litigation in the style of the Dickensian case of *Jarndyce v. Jarndyce* is not desirable.[230] It remains unclear if this was a policy suggestion or if the Court was preparing to execute this in a future case. Maybe both, if the policy suggestion were to go unheeded.

§ 4.5—Continuous and Shareholder Nationality: Advantages and Limitations

The law "needs to be able to point to someone or something possessing those rights and duties: '[t]here must exist something that 'has' the duty or the right.'"[231] Continuous nationality factors into the "genuine link" requirement of the ICJ.[232] The general principle in international law is that States have the freedom to decide the question of nationality in their own law, and most IIAs grant this protection to investors bearing the nationality of one of the contracting parties. Aron Broches has argued that "the parties should be given the widest possible latitude to agree on the meaning of 'nationality' and any stipulation of nationality made in connection with a conciliation or arbitration clause which is based on a reasonable criterion."[233]

In the IIA context, Christoph Schreuer has backed this point, arguing that "[a]ny reasonable determination of the nationality of juridical persons contained in national legislation or in a treaty should be accepted by an ICSID commission or tribunal" since "[d]efinitions of corporate nationality in national legislation or in treaties providing for ICSID's jurisdiction will be controlling for the determination of whether the nationality requirements of [ICSID] Article 25(2)(b) have been met."[234] In the seminal *Barcelona Traction* case, the ICJ recognised that "the process of lifting the

[229] App. No. 75529/01, at ¶ 100.

[230] See 2 C. Dickens, BLEAK HOUSE 85 (1853).

[231] J. Klabbers, *The Concept of Legal Personality*, 11 JUS GENTIUM 35, 39 (2005) (citing H. Kelsen, GENERAL THEORY OF LAW AND STATE 93 (Russell & Russell, 1945, Wedberg trans.)).

[232] *Nottebohm Case*, I.C.J. Reports 1955, pp. 4, 20 *et seq.*

[233] A. Broches, "The Convention on the Settlement of Investment Disputes between States and Nationals of Other States," 136 RECUEIL DES COURS 331, 361 (1972-II) [A. Broches, "ICSID"].

[234] C. H. Schreuer, ICSID CONVENTION: A COMMENTARY, *supra*, at 286.

veil, being an exceptional one admitted by municipal law in respect of an institution of its own making, is equally admissible to play a similar role in international law."[235]

We must be careful regarding *Barcelona Traction*, though, because it, like all ICJ cases,[236] was an inter-State case. Its holding "that incorporation is the only criterion for nationality in cases of diplomatic protection," is not necessarily applicable "with respect to agreements between the parties to treat companies of the host State as a national of the other Party under the second clause of Article 25(2)(b)" of ICSID.[237] Secondly, *Barcelona Traction* concerns customary international law which has debatable relevance for specifically codified international investment or other law.[238] Finally, even as things already stand the prevailing theory in international law does not encourage determining corporate nationality's default position *exclusively* by the nationality of the controlling shareholders.[239]

---

[235] 1970 ICJ Rep. 3, at ¶ 58.

[236] Statute of the International Court of Justice art. 34(1), June 26, 1946, 59 Stat. 1055, 8 U.N.T.S. 993 ("Only state[s] may be parties in cases before the [International] Court [of Justice]."); see also J. Collier & V. Lowe, THE SETTLEMENT OF DISPUTES IN INTERNATIONAL LAW 132–69 (1999) (explaining the scope of the ICJ's jurisdiction).

[237] *Tokios Tokelės v. Ukraine*, ICSID Case No. ARB/02/18, Decision on Jurisdiction, at ¶ 54, n. 44 (citing A. Broches, "ICSID," *supra*, at 360-01 and *Barcelona Traction, supra*, at ¶ 56 ("[t]he wealth of practice already accumulated on the subject in municipal law indicates that the veil is lifted, for instance, to prevent the misuse of the privileges of legal personality, as in certain cases of fraud or malfeasance, to protect third persons such as a creditor or purchaser, or to prevent the evasion of legal requirements or of obligations.")). Even though *Barcelona Traction* here uses the phrase "for example" (thus precluding most *ejusdem generis* connotations), it is still curious that all the examples concern some form of fraud or misrepresentation. See also *Nottebohm Case (Liechtenstein v. Guatemala)*, ICJ, Judgement, 18 November 1953; Judgement, 6 April 1955 (ICJ Reports, 1955, pp. 4-65); *Barcelona Traction, Light and Power Company, Limited (Belgium v. Spain)*, ICJ 1970, Judgement, 24 July 1964; Judgement, 5 February 1970 (ICJ Reports, 1970, pp. 3-357).

[238] See, e.g., *CMS Gas Transmission Co. v. Arg. Republic*, ICSID Case No. ARB/01/8, Decision on Application for Annulment, ¶ 69 (Sept. 25, 2007); *Total S.A. v. Arg. Republic*, ICSID Case No. ARB/04/1, Decision on Objections to Jurisdiction, ¶ 78 (Aug. 25, 2006)

[239] See, *e.g.*, A.C. Sinclair, *The Substance of Nationality Requirements in Investment Treaty Arbitration*, 20 ICSID-REV.-FOR. INV. L. J. 357, 368-378 (2005); R. Dolzer & M. Stevens, BILATERAL INVESTMENT TREATIES 34 *et seq.* (Martinus Nijhoff Publishers 1995).

Rather, the test advocated by that school of thought is holistic, with an emphasis on the formalistic criteria of incorporation and/or integration.

"Holistic" does not necessarily have to mean "malleable" though. Nowadays corporate restructuring is routinely allowed to give precedence to the place of incorporation or the corporate *siège social,*[240] *i.e.*, "the place where the legal entity's judicial and economic integration is situated."[241] Traditionally, "the test of incorporation or seat rather than control when determining the nationality of a juridical person" has been the norm, at least before ICSID tribunals and many other IIA tribunals widely.[242] The established rule in this area has been largely unmodified over the past decade or so.[243]

In practice, shareholder nationality is not a controlling part of the default IIA analysis, which is perhaps not so negative from a doctrinal point of view. This is because "[t]ribunals have come to no consensus concerning how large a stake a minority investor must have before qualifying for protection or if there should be any minimum."[244] At the same time, it is important to state unequivocally that not a single IIA

---

[240] S. W. Schill, "Investment Treaties, *supra*, at 14.

[241] H. Xanthaki, *The Establishment of Foreign Companies in France*, 17 THE COMPANY LAWYER (1996), at 28.

[242] C. H. Schreuer, ICSID CONVENTION: A COMMENTARY, *supra*, at 279-80 (citing *Kaiser Bauxite Company v. Jamaica*, Decision on Jurisdiction, Case No. ARB/74/3 (1975), 1 ICSID Reports 296, 303 (1993); *SOABI v. Senegal*, Decision on Jurisdiction, Case No. ARB/82/1 (1984), 2 ICSID Reports 175, 180-81; *id.*, at 281 ("[t]he overwhelming weight of the authority…points towards the traditional criteria of incorporation or seat for the determination of corporate nationality under Art. 25(2)(b)."); *Amco Asia Corp. v. Republic of Indonesia*, Decision on Jurisdiction, Case No. ARB/81/1 (1983), 1 ICSID Reports 389, 396 (stating that nationality under the ICSID Convention is ". . . a classical one, based on the law under which the juridical person has been incorporated, the place of incorporation and the place of the social seat. An exception is brought to this concept in respect of juridical persons having the nationality, thus defined, of the Contracting state party to the dispute, where said juridical persons are under foreign control. But no exception to the classical concept is provided for when it comes to the nationality of the foreign controller, even supposing — which is not at all clearly stated in the Convention — that the fact that the controller is the national of one or another foreign State is to be taken into account . . ..")); see also *Autopista Concesionada de Venezuela, C.A. v. Bolivarian Republic of Venezuela*, Decision on Jurisdiction, Case No. ARB/00/5 (2001), at ¶ 108.

[243] *Id.*

[244] J. D'Agostino, *Rescuing International Investment Arbitration: Introducing Derivative Actions, Class Actions, and Compulsory Joinder*, 98 VA. L. REV. 177, 188 (2012) [J. D'Agostino, *Rescuing International Investment Arbitration*].

tribunal has "dissented from the position that both controlling and minority shareholders' direct and indirect claims and investments are covered by both ICSID and every [IIA] under which these questions have arisen."[245]

Since each of these awards arose under IIA instruments, and not domestic law or contract, it must follow that foreign shareholders are entities distinct from "the local company in which they invested and have their own, independent sources of legal rights and remedies."[246] The corresponding IIA serves as a source of rights and enforcement remedies. These rights and remedies enable each international investor to seek its own claim before a properly constituted IIA tribunal, divorced from the efforts (extant or non-extant) of the local commercial enterprise, or of other investors,[247] to prevail although it is virtually certain that any

---

[245] *Id.*, at 187 (citing *CMS Gas Transmission Co. v. Arg. Republic*, ICSID Case No. ARB/01/8, Decision on Application for Annulment, ¶ 69 (Sept. 25, 2007); *Compañía de Aguas del Aconquija, S.A. v. Arg. Republic*, ICSID Case No. ARB/97/3, Award, ¶ 1.1.7 (Aug. 20, 2007); *Total S.A. v. Arg. Republic*, ICSID Case No. ARB/04/1, Decision on Objections to Jurisdiction, ¶¶ 78–81 (Aug. 25, 2006); *Suez, Sociedad General de Aguas de Barcelona S.A. v. Arg. Republic*, ICSID Case No. ARB/03/17, Decision on Jurisdiction, ¶ 49 (May 16, 2006); *Gas Natural SDG, S.A. v. Arg. Republic*, ICSID Case No. ARB/03/10, Decision on Preliminary Questions on Jurisdiction, ¶ 35 (June 17, 2005); *Camuzzi Int'l S.A. v. Arg. Republic*, ICSID Case No. ARB/03/2, Decision on Objections to Jurisdiction, ¶ 47 (May 11, 2005); *Sempra Energy Int'l v. Arg. Republic*, ICSID Case No. ARB/02/16, Decision on Objections to Jurisdiction, ¶ 41 (May 11, 2005); *Siemens A.G. v. Arg. Republic*, ICSID Case No. ARB/02/8, Decision on Jurisdiction, ¶¶ 137–142 (Aug. 3, 2004); *Azurix Corp. v. Arg. Republic*, ICSID Case No. ARB/01/12, Decision on Jurisdiction, ¶¶ 72–76 (Dec. 8, 2003); *CMS Gas Transmission Co. v. Arg. Republic*, ICSID Case No. ARB/01/8, Decision on Objections to Jurisdiction, ¶¶ 40–65 (July 17, 2003); *CME Czech Republic BV v. Czech Republic*, Case No. 403/VERMERK/2001/CME UNCITRAL Arbitration Rules, Partial Award and Separate Opinion, ¶ 418 (Sept. 13, 2001), 9 ICSID Reports 113 (2006); *Lauder v. Czech Republic*, In the Matter of an UNCITRAL Arbitration, Final Award, ¶ 177 (Sept. 3, 2001), 9 ICSID Reports 62 (2006); *Goetz v. Republic of Burundi*, ICSID Case No. ARB/95/3, Award Recognizing Settlement, ¶ 89 (Feb. 10, 1999); *Lanco Int'l, Inc. v. Arg. Republic*, ICSID Case No. ARB/97/6, Preliminary Decision: Jurisdiction, ¶ 10 (Dec. 8, 1998)).

[246] *Id.*, at 190.

[247] W. Peter, ARBITRATION AND RENEGOTIATION OF INTERNATIONAL INVESTMENT AGREEMENTS 352 (2d ed. 1995) ("[T]he distinction between the investor's rights as shareholder and the foreign enterprise's rights of control over its property can be somewhat blurred."); G. Bottini, *Indirect Claims Under the ICSID Convention*, 29 U. PA. J. INT'L L. 563, 568 (2008) ("Often the problem arises when the party to the

pecuniary relief accorded the company will raise the value of investor shares.[248]

As far as simple coverage goes, new IIA's and regional pacts seem to cover minority shareholders more expressly than older IIAs did.[249] In this respect, a possible line of attack by government counsel might be via contradistinction: if a newer IIA contains express language, then the older IIA suffering from the want thereof does not cover minority shareholders or at least shareholders with shares *de minimis*. C. F. Amerasinghe has gone on to state that despite the variance in IIA texts, some of the very first IIA's could be construed to cover minority shareholders.[250] Some commentators assert that ICSID-based "[p]rotection for indirect investments seems less intuitive [than coverage of minority shareholders is], but is entrenched."[251] The diction of Article 25(2) of the ICSID Convention[252] is such that "a company can be domestically incorporated but still covered by the convention if under foreign control."[253]

---

contract that constitutes the main investment is a local company — albeit with foreign shareholders — so that the nationality criterion will not be met since any dispute that arises will be between the host state and one of its nationals.").

[248] *Id.*

[249] See, *e.g.*, 2004 U.S. Model Bilateral Investment Treaty, *available at* <www.state.gov/documents/organization/117601.pdf> (last visited June 27, 2012); 2007 Model FIPA (Canadian Model Foreign Investment Promotion and Protection Agreement), cited in C. Yannaca-Small, OECD, INTERNATIONAL INVESTMENT LAW: UNDERSTANDING CONCEPTS AND TRACKING INNOVATIONS, A COMPANION VOLUME TO INTERNATIONAL INVESTMENT PERSPECTIVES 51 (2008); see also N. Rubins, The Notion of 'Investment' in International Investment Arbitration, in Arbitrating Foreign Investment Disputes 283, 296 (Norbert Horn & Stefan Kroll eds., 2004); United Nations Conference on Trade and Development, Scope and Definition, IIA Monitor, UNCTAD/WEB/DIAE/IA/2009/8 (2011), p. 13, available at <http://unctad.org/en/Docs/diaeia20102_en.pdf> (last accessed June 27, 2012); , the Energy Charter Treaty, art. 1(6), Dec. 17, 1994, 34 I.L.M. 381, 383 (1994); North American Free Trade Agreement, art. 1139, Dec. 17, 1992, 32 I.L.M. 605, 647–48 (1993). See also C. McLachlan et al., INTERNATIONAL INVESTMENT ARBITRATION: SUBSTANTIVE PRINCIPLES 187-189 (Oxford University Press, 2007).

[250] C.F. Amerasinghe, The Jurisdiction of the International Centre for the Settlement of Investment Disputes, 19 INDIAN J. INT'L L. 166, 177–81 (1979).

[251] J. D'Agostino, *Rescuing International Investment Arbitration, supra,* at 188.

[252] A "protected investor" is

"(a) any natural person who had the nationality of a Contracting State other than the State party to the dispute . . . but does not include any person who . . . also had the nationality of the Contracting State party to the dispute; and

"(b) any juridical person which had the nationality of a Contracting State other than the State party to the dispute . . . and any juridical person which had the

Shareholder nationality comes into play only when shareholder nationality (or whatever criterion) has expressly been agreed upon by the parties as the decisive criterion, "unless it proves unreasonable."[254] This "unreasonableness"—not a precise word or concept by any means—is nonetheless not a completely meaningless benchmark. Rather the presumption is *so* decidedly against *post-hoc* recognition that a high burden, *i.e.*, a textual clash between the Convention itself and this construction of the IIA, will be required in order to evade the natural reading of the shareholder nationality requirement.

IIA's now being constructed are inserting "denial of benefits" clauses "to restrict the benefit of the agreement only to investors who possess that nationality of a contracting party."[255] The objective is simple: "[A] host State may deny benefits of the treaty to 'letterbox' companies constituted in the territory of the other party by persons from a third country or from the host State itself."[256] More interesting still is the prospect of IIA tribunals giving "denial of benefits" clauses customary, default status in international law. If this scenario takes root, it would not be a "clause" in an international compact any more. Rather, an *anti*-clause might be needed to dispel the automatic effect of the rule.

---

nationality of the Contracting State party to the dispute . . . and which, because of foreign control, the parties have agreed should be treated as a national of another Contracting State for the purposes of this Convention."

[253] J. D'Agostino, *Rescuing International Investment Arbitration, supra,* at 189.

[254] *Autopista Concesionada de Venezuela, C.A. v. Bolivarian Republic of Venezuela*, Decision on Jurisdiction, Case No. ARB/00/5 (2001), at ¶¶ 119-20 ("[E]xercising the discretion granted by [ICSID], *the parties have specifically identified majority shareholding as the criterion to be applied. They have not chosen to subordinate their consent to ICSID arbitration to other criteria.* As a result, the Tribunal must respect the parties' autonomy and may not discard the criterion of direct shareholding, *unless it proves unreasonable*.").

[255] *Scope and Definition*, UNCTAD Series, *supra,* at 18.

[256] *Id.* ("In policy terms, the issue of establishing the nationality of an investor presents the question of the extent to which the parties to an agreement wish to link the legal coverage of the agreement with the economic ties between the parties and the covered investment. One country may be seeking to establish a generally favourable investment climate and may be prepared to extend treaty coverage to investments that have minimal economic ties with the other party, while another country may wish to extend treaty coverage only to investments with strong economic ties to the treaty partners.").

The IIA tribunal in *Aguas del Tunari v. Bolivia* (2005)[257] recognised jurisdiction concerning an investor whose home country had not had a BIT with the respondent and which interposed an entity who did have such a BIT. The issue had been easier concerning dual nationals, who the tribunal in *Champion Trading v. Egypt* (2003)[258] held could bring their claims via any *one* of their nationalities.

When faced with the claimant-party requesting arbitration different from the party which had consented to arbitration (caused by transfer of shares to the parent company), the *Banro American Resources Inc. v. Congo* (2000)[259] tribunal could identify no dispute about the nationality question and thus had had no significant "veil piercing" controversy to resolve. Rather, the tribunal denied jurisdiction to stop the parent company from seeking and enjoying diplomatic protection while its subsidiary (the claimant) pursued ICSID arbitration, which, if allowed, would violate the text, objective and in-built assumptions underlying Article 27 of ICSID.[260]

Lastly and just a year after *Champion Trading*, in *Tokios Tokelés v. Ukraine* (2004),[261] the tribunal allowed a claim brought under a BIT with the home State. Some might argue that the "genuine link" test was made virtually redundant here.[262] There is an argument to be made that

---

[257] Decision on Respondent's Objections to Jurisdiction, at ¶¶ 67 *et seq.*; see also *Saluka Investments BV v. The Czech Republic*, UNCITRAL, Partial Award (2006), at ¶¶ 222-242; *ADC Affiliate Limited and ADC & ADMC Management Limited v. Hungary*, Award (2006), at ¶¶ 335-362.

[258] Decision on Jurisdiction, at ¶¶ 3.4.1 ff.

[259] ICSID Case No. ARB/98/7, at ¶10 ("This was the case, in particular, in two situations: when the request was made by a member company of a group of companies while the pertinent instrument expressed the consent of another company of this group; and when, following the transfer of shares, the request came from the transferee company while the consent had been given by the company making the transfer.").

[260] *Id.*, at ¶¶ 13, 24. Article 27 states that "[n]o Contracting State shall give diplomatic protection, or bring an international claim, in respect of a dispute which one of its nationals and another Contracting State shall have consented to submit or shall have submitted to arbitration under this Convention, unless such other Contracting State shall have failed to abide by and comply with the award rendered in such dispute."

[261] ICSID Case No. ARB/02/18, Decision on Jurisdiction, at ¶¶ 21 *et seq.*

[262] *Id.*, at ¶¶ 21, 38, and 80; G. Van Harten, ITA AND PUBLIC LAW, *supra,* at 115 (observing that "the tribunal . . . allowed a claim against the Ukraine by a Lithuanian company that was 99 per cent owned by Ukrainains, who were thus able to leverage their ownership of a foreign firm into a claim against their own state, in effect opening the system to claims by domestic investors who shift capital to a foreign platform and then re-invest it in the home country.").

corporations and investors, especially those of scale, can opt for *any* IIA regime they prefer—the BIT regime being replaced, effectively, by an interesting, unending kind of multilateral regime.[263] The relevant solution, then, would be for negotiating States to insist on textual clauses classifying investors by sector (although this is still debatable on the facts[264]), annual income, nationality(/ies) of controlling shareholders, venue of incorporation, and so on. Or the IIA can expressly create a "genuine link" test with factors that necessarily, sufficiently, and/or significantly meet that standard.

Consider the difference this made in the *CME* arbitrations. In these arbitrations, the investors were not just invoking different nationalities *consecutively* but also *simultaneously*. The *CME-U.S.* tribunal stated that it was led in its direction (opposite to the *CME-The Netherlands* tribunal's) by the investor's "vague"[265] allegations and the fact that "Claimant or the entities he controls did not commence any administrative or other proceedings before the appropriate courts of the Czech Republic in the course of which the issue of the overall attitude of the Media Council in this affair."[266] This statement has curious consequences for the exhaustion of local remedies, discussed in the next chapter.

---

[263] *Id.*, at ¶¶ 22-23; at ¶ 23 ("The context in which the ICSID Convention and the . . . [relevant] BIT reference and define corporate nationality allows the Tribunal to disregard the Claimant's state of incorporation and determine its corporate nationality based on the nationality of its controlling shareholders, *i.e.*, to pierce the corporate veil; [t]he Tribunal should pierce the corporate veil of the Claimant in this case because allowing an enterprise that is established in [the home State] but owned and controlled predominantly by [members of the host State] to pursue ICSID arbitration against [the host State] is contrary to the object and purpose of the ICSID Convention and the . . . [relevant] BIT, namely, to provide a forum for the settlement of *international* disputes; and [t]he jurisprudence of ICSID arbitration supports the use of a "control-test" rather than state of incorporation to define the nationality of juridical entities and it also supports piercing the corporate veil in certain circumstances that apply in the present case.") (emphasis in original). But see dissenting opinion of Prosper Weil, at ¶ 14 ("To decide the jurisdictional issue the Decision should, therefore, have checked first whether the Tribunal has jurisdiction under Article 25 of the Convention — interpreted . . . in light of its object and purpose — and then, in a second stage, whether it has jurisdiction also under the bilateral investment treaty.").

[264] For multi-sector investors, for instance, is it the primary sector in which they generate a profit or are active that counts? Could they not adjust their strategy in order to go "sector-shopping" and thus to silo themselves into more favourable stipulations? Would this not bring about charges of illegitimacy?

[265] *Lauder (U.S.) v. Czech Republic,* UNCITRAL, Final Award (2001), at ¶ 261.

[266] *Id.*, at ¶ 287.

From a State's standpoint, it might be useful to prevent treaty-shopping (what might colloquially be called *multi-dipping*), meaning that once an investor invokes *one* of its nationalities, it must remain pegged to that nationality and not be free to switch later. This rule might be adopted by the relevant convention, the IIA or other international compact, or as a candid incentive-driven principle by the tribunals themselves. Such a rule is not, however, full-proof because some multi-national investors are likely to find some "lucrative" (to mean, convenient for the purposes of that arbitration) nationality; nonetheless, this rule does have the benefit of forcing investors to *choose* a nationality, remain consistent and remain predictable. It has the added benefit of putting their respective host States on notice. Moreover, in situations where a "large corporation" is split "into numerous subsidiaries" but which "overrides the liability barriers between [the subsidiaries] by having the subsidiaries and the parent company cross-guarantee each other's major debts,"[267] the corporation has every incentive to "multi-dip" and none not to. The rule minimizes the chance that through brilliant pincer-movements the corporation will be able to game the system.

Behaviour-predictive principles built into the international compact or the tribunal decision can help bring or sustain legitimacy. Legitimacy is jeopardised, if not completely lost, when the investors can freely game the system, no less and no more than when States can. Unfortunately because we do not live in a world where spiritual fulfilment (or "job satisfaction," if you will) is always deemed to be enough by all actors in the discharging of their designated functions. Therefore, principled, behaviourally-framed (to mean encouraging as well as prophylactic), and achievable rules are sometimes necessary.

§ 4.6—Conclusion

Completing this Section is the burden of proof problem—where the ECtHR differs from the NAFTA. Unlike in NAFTA, in the ECtHR whenever the government says that the local remedies have not been exhausted, it (not the applicant) bears the burden of proving that the applicant has not used a remedy that was both effective and available at the relevant time.

The second issue is the ECtHR's perception of exhaustion as means to an end, in contrast with the NAFTA-IIA approach to exhaustion as strictly jurisdictional. That end, human rights protection, leads the ECtHR to

---

[267] See R. Squire, *Strategic Liability in the Corporate Group*, 78 U. CHI. L. REV. 605, 605 (2011).

loosen the exhaustion requirements and require exhaustion only to the extent that it promotes human rights, and not for its own sake. In that endeavour, the ECtHR is helped by its unitary system and *stare decisis* effect throughout the Convention system. These advantages are not available to NAFTA.

Nonetheless, some half-way measures might be of assistance. Some "partial equivalents" that might help NAFTA are waiting periods, "local-court-first" requirements (invoke but not necessarily exhaust, and a recent case highlighted the eighteen-month requirement),[268] and "fork-in-road" (choose between domestic or international tribunal routes at some advanced stage and not rescind the choice later) provisions.[269] While the ECtHR's (and the IACtHR's and the ACtHR's) decentralisation makes it harder to have a fixed time limit (this proposal having been considered and rejected for sovereignty reasons), NAFTA does not face this problem (because it can be reinterpreted or have add-ons, see Chapter II). Where there is a right, ordinarily there should be an implied remedy unless the tribunal at that given time is jurisdictionally bereft of the power to command a fitting remedy. NAFTA tribunals have the textual authority to form some consensus about whether to tighten up the time-limit.

A point about legitimacy is appropriate. As methodology goes, this Chapter has already explained that other than the very recent ECtHR's *Yukos Oil Co.* case against Russia[270] there is no evidence for specific party-based bias (private litigant or State) in any of our institutions. This indicates that the tribunals generally take a long-arc view.

This appearance of impartiality adds doctrinal coherence to the mix, not to mention public confidence that the disagreements are in good-faith and not likely to change based on who the parties are. Cases not generally applicable and for just one moment in time are hard to defend. Our institutions have shown that large-scale conflicts and emergencies do not necessarily bring up cases *so* factually peculiar that doctrines established there have no application outside the context. This is not to say that the tribunals, especially the ECtHR and the IUCT, do not favour one *side* over the other but most outcomes have not been thought dependent on who the *exact* litigant was.

---

[268] *Teinver S.A., Transportes de Cercanías S.A. and Autobuses Urbanos del Sur S.A. v. The Argentine Republic*, ICSID Case No. ARB/09/1 (2012), Separate Opinion of Dr. Kamal Hossain, at ¶¶ 7-8.

[269] For a more extensive discussion, see C. Schreuer, "Calvo's Grandchildren," *supra,* at 15-16.

[270] *Yukos Oil Co. v. Russia*, App. no. 14902/04 (2011) (making Russia, a frequent respondent, obey the decision was a special motive force for the ECtHR).

Let us focus now on shareholder and corporate nationality. It is beyond cavil that "more attention needs to be paid in the drafting of definitions of 'investor' to actual foreign control and to the possibility of treaty shopping that a formal reading of place of incorporation test creates."[271] Negotiators would be well-advised to "supplemen[t] the country-of-organization test" by using "the company-seat test and/or requirement of real or substantial economic activities in the home State, and/or a denial-or-benefits clause (discretionary or automatic)."[272]

This assumes a certain state of IIA protection. If, however, "a government is willing to grant IIA protection to investments regardless of whether they flow from the other Contracting Party, from a third State or even from its own territory (channelled through the territory of the other Contracting Party), the country-of-organization test" should be adequate.[273] Most of all, a conversation among the various negotiators and tribunals must exist for each arm of the process to appreciate the others' needs.

So far we have seen that in causation, attribution and exhaustion, the three institutions take into account their own aims, competence and legitimacy. They may also brainstorm about ways to influence other international tribunals. We have also seen how the institutions might engage with the merits to decide procedural issues. The next two chapters will address the merits case-law attending the three institutions.

---

[271] *Scope and Definition*, UNCTAD Series, *supra*, at 99.
[272] *Id.*
[273] *Id.*

CHAPTER FIVE

NON-DISCRIMINATION: NATIONAL TREATMENT, MOST FAVOURED NATION AND DOMESTIC DISCRIMINATION

§ 5.1—Introduction

Underpinnings of Non-Discrimination: Sovereignty's Implications

Consent in one form or another is at the heart and crux of many international law disputes. Due to the realities of contemporary non-discrimination analysis conducted by international tribunals, this Chapter is about the consent of States to be judged by international tribunals. Simply put, when tribunals are assessing if a State has violated its most-favoured-nation obligation to a claimant (arising from the signatory status of the claimant's home State), it seems necessary to inquire whether the State has made an identical commitment to signatories of *other* international agreements. Yet around this relatively simple notion all manner of difficult debates have developed, as this Chapter gradually will unveil. Consent is not a mere grotto in the larger compound of international dispute settlement. In many ways, consent *is* international dispute settlement or at least the very coin of this realm.

International tribunals appear to try to strike a balance between the objective, dispassionate judicial function and the appropriate restrictions on this function. Make no mistake: At least in formal terms, the tribunal is empowered to resolve Question X from Countries A and B *only* because A and B have given their consent and submitted themselves to the tribunal's jurisdiction. A and/or B might have had various pressures—trade and investments, political, prestige in the world, and militaristic even—that induce them to enter and stay within such compacts.

There might be incentives and disincentives. There will be internal and external inconsistencies to reconcile. But whatever there is, there must be consent given by the State in order for the international legal order to decide a dispute where that State is a party. In the parlance of game theorists, equilibrium lies at the point where the risks for each party at their minimum and the rewards are at their maximum. The checks and balances between the parties are sufficiently checkmated to deliver a conflict.

Consider what happened in 1949. In the *Corfu Channel Case* (1949),[1] the ICJ held that, without the State *party(/ies)'s* consent, international tribunals cannot enter a private-public or State-State dispute.[2] A nation's right to consent (or the right to withhold consent), which flows as a necessary consequence of sovereignty, is not an easy concept to apply in difficult cases. Practitioners and academics have advanced several theories, to varying degrees of satisfaction. This Chapter recounts recent developments in order to place consent's future on the map.

Sovereignty, therefore, occupies a tricky place both as to jurisdiction and as to the substance of the determination. Its historical pedigree is strong even though the contours of its reach are not always clearly demarcated.[3] But even proponents of Parliamentary sovereignty which was exalted at common law cannot deny that the sovereign no longer can do, if it ever could (which it seems like it could indeed), "every thing that

---

[1] *Corfu Channel* (*United Kingdom of Great Britain and Northern Ireland v. Albania*) (Merits) [1949] ICJ Rep 4.

[2] M. Waibel, *Corfu Channel Case*: Continued Relevance for Contemporary International Law, Max Planck Encyclopedia of Public International Law (Heidelberg and Oxford University Press, 2011); R. Bishop, J. Crawford & W. M. Reisman, FOREIGN INVESTMENT DISPUTES: CASES, MATERIALS AND COMMENTARY 317-23 (Kluwer Law International, 2005).

[3] W. M. Reisman, *Sovereignty and Human Rights in Contemporary International Law*, 84 A.J.I.L. 866, 868-69 (1990) [W. M. Reisman, *Sovereignty and Human Rights*] ("Political legitimacy . . . was to derive from popular support; governmental authority was based on the consent of the people in the territory in which a government purported to exercise power. At first only for those states in the vanguard of modern politics, later for more and more states, the sovereignty of the sovereign became the sovereignty of the people: popular sovereignty. It took the formal international legal system time to register these profound changes. Another century beset by imperialism, colonialism and fascism was to pass, but by the end of the Second World War, popular sovereignty was firmly rooted as one of the fundamental postulates of political legitimacy. Article 1 of the [United Nations] Charter established as one of the purposes of the United Nations, to develop friendly relations between states, not on any terms, but 'based on respect for the principles of equal rights and self-determination of peoples.'") (internal footnotes omitted).

is not naturally impossible."[4] Over-reaching or an exercise in excess by the international tribunal might breed distrust of the judicial function and, gradually, even make the State's own political process complacent and deprive the political process of developing its strengths and mitigating its weaknesses after identifying them through various successes and disappointments.

Let us candidly ask of ourselves several questions. Why will the State bother to engage with the difficult business of persuading fellow citizens and the officialdom if courts—international or domestic—keep achieving all the ends? Where then is the incentive or, for that matter, the opportunity? There obviously is another side to the coin. On the other hand, refusing to exercise jurisdiction, however ingeniously motivated by the goal of avoiding, exclusively or even partially, a difficult case, might undermine public confidence in the very existence of the tribunals. A few pages later, I offer my own mechanism.

Not everyone sees the issue in dispassionate terms. There is something to be said of a developed/developing country ideological fault-line,[5] at least a correlative one. The pressing nature of this issue is made even more imminent by the fact that many developing nations are attempting to build up their regulatory structures while striking the optimal balance to attract

---

[4] William Blackstone, 1 COMMENTARIES ON THE LAWS OF ENGLAND 156 (University of Chicago Press, 1979) ("The power and jurisdiction of parliament is so transcendent and absolute, that it cannot be confined, either for causes or persons, within any bounds. . . . It hath sovereign and uncontrolable authority in making, confirming, enlarging, restraining, abrogating, repealing, reviving, and expounding of laws, concerning matters of all possible denominations, ecclesiastical, or temporal, civil, military, maritime, or criminal . . . . In short, it can do every thing that is not naturally impossible."). Nor should it be thought that even in England this view of Parliamentary sovereignty was universal. In fact, the truth was far from it. See, *e.g.*, G. S. Wood, *Federalism from the Bottom Up*, 78 U. CHI. L. REV. 705, 709 (2011) ("Although many mainstream Englishmen by the mid-eighteenth century accepted this doctrine of sovereignty, some, such as William Pitt and Lord Camden, did not, and the idea remained contested among many Anglo-Americans. . . . There were . . . alternatives to the English unitary vision of sovereignty present in mid-eighteenthcentury Anglo-American culture.").

[5] Neither the developing world nor the developed world is a monolith. The nations cross the fault-line sometimes and even within their "worlds" there are tremendous wealth disparities. Especially interesting in our time is the abundant Chinese FDI and other resources (including managerial and technological expertise) entering certain parts of Africa. See, *e.g.*, M. Davies, "How China is Influencing Africa's Development," Background Paper for the Perspectives on Global Development 2010 (Shifting Wealth), OECD (2010). The precise ramifications will become clearer in time.

foreign investment.[6] According to Muthucumaraswamy Sornarajah, developed countries "may . . . backtrac[k] on" investor and owner protection rules and "creat[e], as developing countries did in the past, significant sovereignty-based defences to liability and redra[w] the boundaries of investment protection."[7]

Luke Peterson and R. Doak Bishop, as interpreted by Joseph D'Agostino and (far less impressively) yours truly, believe that IIA's play a significant "role in the growth of international investment, especially in developing countries."[8] The Peterson-Bishop view is also that the "disintegrat[ion]" of "crucial parts of the [IIA] system" might "restrict international capital flows, improvements in the livelihoods of residents of developing nations, returns on investment in developed countries, and global economic growth itself."[9] Whether as the lesser of several evils—after all, FDI has been shown to exert greater efficiency in local economic growth than domestic investment—or because some less developed nations believe they can avoid some of the costs, some developing nations keep entering into IIA's.[10]

At the same time, however, it would be naïve to pretend that such disparity between the sovereign and the claimant is invariably a one-way street. Developed countries do not enjoy losing before IIA tribunals either.

---

[6] ASEAN Secretariat: "ASEAN Comprehensive Investment Agreement Fact Sheet" (2009), stating that FDI inflows into ASEAN in 2007 grew by 23% from the year before to US$63.3 billion.

[7] M. Sornarajah, THE INTERNATIONAL LAW ON FOREIGN INVESTMENT 4 (Cambridge University Press, 2010); see also S. Rose-Ackerman, "Do BITs Benefit Developing Countries?," & A. Joubin-Brett, "Bi-Lateral Investment Treaties 1995-2006: Trends in Investment Rule-Making" *in* R. P. Alford and Catherine A. Rogers, eds., THE FUTURE OF INVESTMENT ARBITRATION (Oxford University Press, 2008) (failing to come up with a single IIA conclusively demonstrating that IIA's attract foreign investment but reserving the question for another day's resolution based on greater empirical trends and qualitative evidence) [R. P. Alford and C. A. Rogers, eds., THE FUTURE OF INVESTMENT ARBITRATION].

[8] J. D'Agostino, *Rescuing International Investment Arbitration: Introducing Derivative Actions, Class Actions, and Compulsory Joinder*, 98 VA. L. REV. 177 (2012) (citing L. Peterson, "Out of Order," *in* THE BACKLASH AGAINST INVESTMENT ARBITRATION 483, 484-85, M. Waibel et al. eds. (Kluwer Law International, 2010); R. Doak Bishop, J. Crawford et al., "Foreign Investment Disputes," *in* FOREIGN INVESTMENT DISPUTES 1, 7–8 (Kluwer Law International, 2005)).

[9] *Id.*

[10] A. T. Guzman, *Why LDCs Sign Treaties That Hurt Them: Explaining the Popularity of Bilateral Investment Treaties*, 38 VA. J. INT'L L. 639, 653 (1998).

With greater tax incentives awarded to corporations, the governments of developed countries sometimes have to compensate foreign investors but do not always see a comparable sum of money flowing back into their coffers. A significant and timely case in point is the Sakhalin-2 "roadshow" in the Russian Federation.[11]

Consider how the 2004 Canadian Model BIT[12] and the 2004 United States Model BIT[13] highly value a sovereign's right to regulate in the promotion of certain sustainable development goals. The International Institute for Sustainable Development (IISD), which supports FDI that is friendly to sustainable development, produced a balanced Model BIT draft for Sustainable Development.[14]

The issue is a sensitive one, and it follows that the attending political spat that had led to organised dispute resolution may return with vengeance if it is not handled tactfully by the tribunals. Particularly since "international tribunals can be very creative and capable of extending considerably the scope and reach of their jurisdiction and the rules they are

---

[11] See T. Parfitt, Kremlin Attack Dog Vows to Take on Shell in the Battle of Sakhalin, THE GUARDIAN (London), Guardian Financial Pages, Oct. 4, 2006, at 25; see also *Shell's Sakhalin Rout Shines Light on Others*, PETROLEUM INTELLIGENCE WKLY, Jan. 1, 2007; S. L. Myers, *Russia Strong-arms Energy-hungry West; Moscow Can Afford to Ignore its Critics*, INT'L HERALD TRIB., Dec. 28, 2006, at 5; J. M. Marlles, *Public Purpose, Private Losses: Regulatory Expropriation and Environmental Regulation in International Investment Law*, 16 J. OF TRANSNAT'L L. & POL'Y 275, 276 (2006) [J. M. Marlles, *Public Purpose, Private Losses*] ("Due to . . . supposed violations [concerning the environment and allegedly perpetrated by Western energy companies], the Russian Ministry of Natural Resources used its regulatory power to revoke the foreign investors' environmental operating license, freezing the construction process and throwing completion of the project into doubt. However, following two and-a-half months of deadlock, in late December 2006, the foreign investors acquiesced to handing over a majority stake in the project to a government-controlled energy company and agreed to revise the contract between them-selves and the Russian government to the enormous benefit of the government. Shortly thereafter, Russian President Vladimir Putin announced that Sakhalin-2's environmental issues were 'considered resolved,' and construction was able to continue.") (internal footnotes omitted).

[12] Canadian Model BIT (2004), *available at* <http://ita.law.uvic.ca/documents/Canadian2004-FIPA-model-en.pdf>.

[13] U.S. Model BIT, *available at* <www.state.gov/documents/organization/117601.pdf> (2004).

[14] International Institute for Sustainable Development, "IISD Model International Agreement for Sustainable Development," *available at* <www.iisd.org/pdf/2005/investment_model_int_ agreement.pdf> (2005).

entrusted to interpret,"[15] international tribunals have the duty to be circumspect and modest in addressing cases that lack an obvious outcome. Until a consensus has been formed in one direction or another, tribunals would be well-advised to remain highly fact-intensive as to the analysis while exploring the doctrinal considerations on all sides.

Balancing investor rights, sovereignty with pragmatism has many potential drawbacks and advantages not just for States and powerful investors but also for ordinary persons. Structural adjustments, far from being abstract, retain the potential to have extraordinary impact on people's lives by upsetting the trade and investment, political and militaristic balance of power. The stakes are high, and the last section of this Chapter offers this author's objective reflections and suggestions.

Judicial restraint is a helpful starting point for international tribunals. In two important respects, they might take instruction from domestic courts' approaches to this canon.[16] There are two main and universally

---

[15] F. Zarbiyev, *Judicial Activism in International Law—A Conceptual Framework for Analysis*, J. OF INTERNATIONAL DISPUTE SETTLEMENT, (2012), 1, 2 ("It is striking, for instance, that the concept of erga omnes obligations, which has brought about crucial changes in the understanding and conceptualization of modern international law, owes its emergence to a mere obiter dictum contained in a judgment of the International Court of Justice.") (citing in n. 5: *Barcelona Traction*, ICJ Reports 1970, 32)) [F. Zarbiyev, *Judicial Activism in International Law*].

[16] *Id.*, at 2 (stating that there is an advantage in observing "similar experiences in the context of domestic laws"); at 8-11 (stipulating nine considerations to evaluate judicial activism: "[t]he Conception of Judicial Function;" "[t]he Degree of Determinacy in the System;" "[t]he Existence of a Hierarchically Structured Judicial System;" "Prudential Doctrines about the Relationship between the Judicial and Political Branches;" "[t]he Mechanisms of Political Control;" "[t]he Legitimating Function of Legal Academics"; "[t]he Nature of the Proceedings; Discursive Constraints;" and "Social Legitimacy Considerations"). Various articulations of judicial activism abound. Keenan D. Kmiec stipulates that the "core meanings" of judicial restraint are "(1) invalidation of arguably constitutional actions of other branches, (2) failure to adhere to precedent, (3) judicial "legislation", (4) departures from accepted interpretive methodology, (5) result-oriented judging." See K. D. Kmiec, *The Origin and Current Meanings of Judicial Activism,* 92 CAL. L. REV. 1441, 1444 (2004). Sterling Harwood, for his part, understands judicial activism to encompass one or more of these judicial behaviours: "(1) refusing to take an attitude of judicial deference ... for legislative or executive power or judgment; (2) relaxing requirements for justiciability ...; (3) breaking precedent ...; and (4) loosely or controversially construing constitutions, statutes or precedents." See S. Harwood, JUDICIAL ACTIVISM: A RESTRAINED DEFENSE 2 (Austin & Winfield, 1996); see also F. Zarbiyev, *Judicial Activism in*

agreed-upon tenets of judicial restraint: (*i*) not to "'anticipate a question of . . . law in advance of the necessity of deciding it'"[17]; and (*ii*) not to "formulate a rule of . . . law broader than is required by the precise facts to which it is to be applied."[18] Respect for the roles of the other constitutive actors is central to the concept of judicial restraint for an international tribunal. When "the price" is "the limitation of other actors' discretion" and truncation of their traditional roles,[19] judicial modesty is critical. Although Robert Howse has explained well his reasons that judicial activism is any "tendency to impose on states legal limits or constraints

---

International Law, supra, at 4 ("In the formal type of judicial activism, 'the judge deals with legal issues ... other than those which could suffice to constitute the logical structure leading up to his ruling'11 in order to contribute to what the judge conceives to be the development of law. Substantive judicial activism refers to an activism at a different level. 'Being unsatisfied with existing law, or with what he sees as lacunae in the existing law', a judge engaged in a substantive judicial activism 'will be ready', writes Thirlway, 'to indulge in something close to open law-creation in order to base his decision.'") (citing H. Thirlway, 'Judicial Activism and the International Court of Justice' *in* N Ando (ed), LIBER AMICORUM JUDGE SHIGERU ODA 75 (2002).).

[17] *Ashwander v. TVA*, 297 U.S. 288, 346 (1936) (Brandeis, J., concurring) (quoting *Liverpool, New York and Philadelphia S. S. Co. v. Commissioners of Emigration*, 113 U.S. 33, 39 (1885)). Both tenets were confirmed by Sir Hersch Lauterpacht in THE DEVELOPMENT OF INTERNATIONAL LAW BY THE INTERNATIONAL COURT 89-105 (Cambridge University Press, 1982). Some observers argue that the United States Supreme Court is not, *in practice*, actually all that restrained in charged statutory or even constitutional cases but that is a different question altogether. Here we are talking about doing what the domestic courts preach, not necessarily what they do. See also D. Luban, *Justice Holmes and the Metaphysics of Judicial Restraint*, 44 DUKE L. J. 449 (1994).

[18] *Ashwander*, *supra*, at 347. There is the wise judicial culture in international law of deciding the case on the least controversial and just sufficient basis, if at all legally and practically possible. See, *e.g.*, *Application of the Convention of 1902 Governing the Guardianship of Infants*, ICJ Reports 1958, 55, 62 ("The Court has to adjudicate upon the subject of the dispute .... It retains its freedom to select the ground upon which it will base its judgment, and is under no obligation to examine all the considerations advanced by the Parties if other considerations appear to it to be sufficient for its purpose"); *United States-Measure Affecting Imports of Woven Wool Shirts and Blouses from India*, WT/DS33/AB/R, Report of the Appellate Body of 25 April 1997, 19 ("A panel need only address those claims which must be addressed in order to resolve the matter in issue in the dispute"); *Arrest Warrant,* ICJ Reports, 2002, 3; *Accordance with International Law of the Unilateral Declaration of Independence in Respect of Kosovo*, ICJ, Advisory Opinion of 22 July 2010.

[19] F. Zarbiyev, *Judicial Activism in International Law, supra,* at 2.

not justified by the strict rule of international law,"[20] it seems that a more effective approach is also a more complex one.

There is doctrinal evidence that sovereignty-based argumentation has lost some of its erstwhile lustre in international legal conversations. In this respect, two patterns of evidence should be considered. First, conventional notions of international law hold the view that sovereign "states' freedom of action was the [presumptive] rule," and here "international obligations were naturally seen as exceptions."[21] Therefore, exceptions to this settled rule, meaning "provisions which limited state freedoms" had "to be interpreted in a restrictive manner."[22] All this seems to have changed. Armed with earlier and recent case-law, scholars have noted that this "interpretive philosophy" appears to have become obsolete.[23]

Second, there has been definitive and significant "marginali[s]ation of parties' intentions in the process of interpretation."[24] This is far more than just a theoretical prism, and for the following reason: Even though the international compact interpretation process strives "to establish the

---

[20] R. Howse, "The Most Dangerous Branch? WTO Appellate Body Jurisprudence on the Nature and Limits of the Judicial Power" *in* Thomas Cottier and Petros C Mavroidis (eds), THE ROLE OF THE JUDGE IN INTERNATIONAL TRADE REGULATION 35 (University of Michigan Press, 2003) [R. Howse, "The Most Dangerous Branch?"].

[21] F. Zarbiyev, *Judicial Activism in International Law, supra,* at 15-16.

[22] *Id.*

[23] *Compare Free Zones of Upper Savoy and the District of Gex (France / Switzerland)*, 1932 PCIJ (ser A/B) No 46, 96, 166 (maintaining that "the sovereignty of [a state] is to be respected in so far as it is not limited by her international obligations, and ... that no restriction exceeding those ensuing from these [obligations] can be imposed on [the state] without her consent"); *The S.S. 'Wimbledon' (United Kingdom, France, Italy & Japan v Germany)* 1923 P.C.I.J. (ser A) No 1, 15, 24 (articulating that "all restrictions or limitations upon the exercise of sovereignty ... must be construed as restrictively as possible and confined within [their] narrowest limits") *with* F. Zarbiyev, *Judicial Activism in International Law, supra,* at 15-16 (citing *Siemens v. Argentina* (Decision on Jurisdiction, 3 August 2004) ICSID Case No ARB/02/8, at ¶ 81; *Iron Rhine Arbitration* (PCA Award, 24 May 2005), at ¶ 53; *Aguas del Tunari S.A. v. Republic of Bolivia* (Decision on Respondent's Objections to Jurisdiction, 21 October 2005) ICSID Case No ARB/02/3, at ¶ 91; *Dispute regarding Navigational and Related Rights*, ICJ Reports, 2009, 237, at ¶ 48; *Application of the Interim Accord*, ICJ, Judgment of 5 December 2011, at ¶ 70.).

[24] F. Zarbiyev, *Judicial Activism in International Law, supra,* at 16.

common intention of the parties to the treaty,"[25] in modern international law the text has taken primacy.[26] To some, the intentionalist approach[27]

---

[25] *EC - Customs Classification of Certain Computer Equipment*, Appellate Body Report, WT/DS62/AB/R, WT/DS67/AB/R, WT/DS68/AB/R) (5 June 1998), at ¶ 93.

[26] Report of the International Law Commission to the General Assembly on the work of its 18th session, ILC Yearbook (Vol II 1966) 220 ("[T]he text must be presumed to be the authentic expression of the intentions of the parties; and that, in consequence, the starting point and purpose of interpretation is to elucidate the meaning of the text, not to investigate *ab initio* the intentions of the parties.").

Among other international tribunals, the WTO Appellate Body seems to have given this approach its seal of approval over a long line of cases. The Appellate Body does insist that *only* when text is inconclusive, the "intent and purpose" must be investigated and considered. See, *e.g.*, *U.S.-Shrimp*, WT/DS58/AB/R (1998), at ¶ 114 (stating that there must be "an examination of the ordinary meaning of the words of a treaty, read in their context, and in the light of the object and purpose of the treaty involved. A treaty interpreter must begin with, and focus upon, the text of the particular provision to be interpreted. It is in the words constituting that provision, read in their context, that the object and purpose of the states parties to the treaty must first be sought. Where the meaning imparted by the text itself is equivocal or inconclusive, or where confirmation of the correctness of the reading of the text itself is desired, light from the object and purpose of the treaty as a whole may usefully be sought."); *United States – Gasoline*, adopted 20 May 1996, WT/DS2/AB/R, p. 17; *Japan – Taxes on Alcoholic Beverages*, adopted 1 November 1996, WT/DS8/AB/R, WT/DS10/AB/R, WT/DS11/AB/R, pp. 10-12; *India – Patent Protection for Pharmaceutical and Agricultural Chemical Products*, adopted 16 January 1998, WT/DS50/AB/R, at ¶¶ 45-46; *Argentina - Measures Affecting Imports of Footwear, Textiles, Apparel and Other Items*, adopted 13 February 1998, WT/DS56/AB/R, at ¶ 47; and *European Communities - Customs Classification of Certain Computer Equipment*, adopted 22 June 1998, WT/DS62/AB/R, WT/DS67/AB/R, WT/DS68/AB/R, at ¶ 85.

[27] See, *e.g.*, *First Award under the Convention between Costa Rica and Nicaragua of 8 April 1896 for the Demarcation of the Boundary between the two Republics*, 28 Report of International Arbitral Awards, 215, 216 ("[W]e are to interpret and give effect to the treaty of April 15, 1858, in the way in which it was mutually understood at the time by its makers … . It is the meaning of the men who framed the treaty which we are to seek, rather than some possible meaning which can be forced upon isolated words of sentences."); *Iran v United States*, Case No A/18, 5 I.U.C.T.R. 251, 260 ("[T]he Vienna Convention does not require any demonstration of a 'converging will' or of a conscious acceptance by each Party of all implications of the terms to which it has agreed. It is the 'terms of the treaty in their context and in the light of its object and purpose' with which the Tribunal is to be concerned not the subjective understanding or intent of either of the Parties.").

may well be legal fiction because it arguably "does not make much difference in terms of the constraining power of . . . [international judges]."[28] Moreover, government intent is "complex and multifaceted" with political choices are "shaped by different politicians and officials with differing philosophies and perspectives."[29] Nonetheless, the intentionalist approach does "assum[e] that what one is after is the determination of the intention of the parties provides an important constraint on one's interpretive discretion whether that intention is empirically ascertainable or not."[30] No one disputes that textual interpretation by adjudicators and arbitrators lends itself to more "room for discretion" via judicial activism than does the intentionalist approach.[31]

The more sceptical among us might believe that this divergence in interpretive approaches is a *consequence*, rather than the *cause*, of differences in how we perceive sovereignty in international law. They might believe the chosen method of interpretation is merely pretextual in order to justify our specific viewpoints concerning the outcomes. This school of thought need look no further than the WTO Appellate Body's pro-"activist" (or at least pro-discretionary) reasoning in *United States—Shrimp* (1998)[32] for confirmation of their instincts. In that case, the Appellate Body understood that the codified term "exhaustible natural resources" in GATT Article XX (g) must be "read by a treaty interpreter in light of *contemporary concerns of the community of nations* about the protection and conservation of the environment."[33] Indisputably and inevitably, "the Appellate Body enhanced its own interpretive power" through such analysis.[34]

Have you ever read anything more trusting of judicial discretion as judicious discretion—one practitioner I know calls this assertion by the Appellate Body the "Tribunals Know Best" approach? Fearing perhaps that a great number of developed nations would take advantage of this imbalance or fearing the new regime of unpredictability (or both), several developing nations objected strongly: Pakistan (calling this reasoning "a recipe for adding to and diminishing the rights and obligations of

---

[28] F. Zarbiyev, *Judicial Activism in International Law, supra,* at 17.
[29] *S. D. Myers, supra*, at ¶ 161.
[30] F. Zarbiyev, *Judicial Activism in International Law, supra,* at 17.
[31] *Id.*
[32] WT/DS58/AB/R (1998), at ¶ 33.
[33] *Id.*, at ¶ 129 (emphasis added).
[34] F. Zarbiyev, *Judicial Activism in International Law, supra,* at 29.

Members"); [35] India (stating, basically, that the Appellate Body had usurped the role of the Members: "This notion expounded by the Appellate Body based on its evolutionary approach to interpretation was dangerous and not agreed by Members. Reference to 'contemporary concerns' to justify a changed interpretation of the words 'exhaustible natural resources' had amounted to either an amendment or an authoritative interpretation of the existing agreement which could only be done by Members");[36] and Mexico (arguing that "the Appellate Body had overstepped its authority in a manner that was damaging to the dispute settlement system").[37]

Nonetheless, pointing to this precedent, the Appellate Body reaffirmed this reasoning in a 2009 sequel case, stating that "We consider such reading of the terms in China's GATS Schedule to be consistent with the approach taken in *United States—Shrimp*."[38] Lastly, as an aside, some experts have argued that "Appellate Body's environment-friendly report in . . . [this] case has something to do with its desire to enhance its social legitimacy by showing that the WTO is not just about trade and money."[39]

Cause or consequence, everyone agrees that the interpretive approaches are at the very least indicative of a given international lawyer's take on sovereignty. In any case, if intent *is* important then (*i*) reckless conduct on the part of the sovereign must also be covered. The same is true of (*ii*) deliberate governmental efforts to target the extra-sensitive aspects and weaknesses of claimants (the "Achilles Heel" strategy), especially necessary to ascertain when particular claimants have been targeted. This point is expounded upon later in the Chapter ("class of one" theory). Finally, there must be (*iii*) substantial certainty or at least high

---

[35] Minutes of Meeting Held in the Centre William Rappard on 6 November 1998, WT/DSB/M/50, 5.

[36] S. Harwood, JUDICIAL ACTIVISM: A RESTRAINED DEFENSE 2 (Austin & Winfield, 1996).

[37] R. Howse, "The Most Dangerous Branch?," *supra*, at 35.

[38] See *China-Measures Affecting Trading Rights and Distribution Services for Certain Publications and Audiovisual Entertainment Products*, WT/DS363/AB/R, Appellate Body Report of 21 December 2009, at ¶ 396. While there is some merit to Fuad Zarbiyev's excellent analysis that "an illustration of the operation of discursive constraints" because "after all, the Appellate Body merely followed a precedent," (and could defend itself this way) there are those who do not believe the Appellate Body would have resolved the dispute in this direction were it not actually legally moved to this conclusion, irrespective of what precedent suggests. See F. Zarbiyev, *Judicial Activism in International Law, supra,* at 29.

[39] F. Zarbiyev, *Judicial Activism in International Law, supra,* at 30.

probability attributable to the State's intent that its action or proximately causal *inaction* will cause the harm alleged by the claimants.

Shaping Doctrine through Judicial Modesty: A Proposed Framework for International Judges

As promised earlier in the Chapter, I propose a test of general applicability. Apart from text and purpose of the various instruments, the following considerations should guide the work of international tribunals: the Objectively Superior Outcome in the Long Term, if there be one; Public Confidence in International Law; Whether the Facts Arose and Proceedings Continued in Good Faith; Incentives and Disincentives for Each Actor (and how each might act as a check or be outweighed by the others); and, perhaps most importantly, How the Decision Might Cause a Jolt to the Specific International Law Regime and to International Law generally. Giving careful and punctilious attention to *each* of these factors is necessary but not sufficient.

The need for judicial intervention is at its height when the claim is legally meritorious even under a strict interpretation. But the need for judicial intervention is also extant when the claim is legally meritorious under a broad interpretation of the salient instrument(s) and there is no (or almost no) clamouring constituency empowered with the ear of the politicians who could help redress their grievances. It bears repeating that discretionary jurisdiction,[40] if there be one, ought to be exercised even in the latter class of cases. The inverse side of this phenomenon is that States too need "collective support" before accomplishing a watershed, or really any significant, change in international law.[41] Some experts have pointed, as evidence, to the fact that "there are very few precedents of overturned

---

[40] The Court of Justice of the European Union, the ECtHR or the Appellate Body of the WTO are the bodies with compulsory jurisdiction.

[41] F. Zarbiyev, *Judicial Activism in International Law, supra*, at 17 ("Consider . . . the possibility of overturning a judicial decision with which a state is not satisfied. Since no state can unilaterally change international law, be it custom or treaty law, the threat of overturning cannot exercise a powerful constraint on judicial action, for the unsatisfied state needs collective support. Such support is difficult to obtain given that the actors, which are not directly targeted by the decision, would be unlikely to consider themselves to be affected. The very logic of political action dictates this outcome.") (internal footnote omitted).

international judicial decisions"[42]—the so-called "nuclear option" in international law.[43]

The structure and reach of a judicial opinion must provide clarity and predictability because, quite simply, that is partly why the tribunal and the regime were created in the first place. Waiting for a future case is not always an option in an often-politically or economically fraught system that lacks binding *stare decisis*, which generally characterises international law. Usually, the judicial restraint argument is stronger and international tribunals' actions more suspect when the government is told *what* (substantively or procedurally) it must or must not do (*Other Substantive Standards*—the next chapter) than when the government is told *whom* it must engage or treat equally (this Chapter).

It has also been the subliminal experience of several respected jurists that tribunal awards recognising discrimination tend to engender less public clamour than awards premised on more ambiguous or subjective criteria. People feel less robbed of their sovereignty and their right to regulate. Not to mention the prevailing view that "when it comes to questions of whether there has been unjustified discrimination under national treatment or most-favored nation clauses, there is generally much less reason for deference because the assessment of such discrimination is typically more amenable to 'objective' analysis and less subject to justifiable disagreements based on different preferences, values, or expertise."[44] A third consequential difference between non-discrimination and other substantive standards is that in non-discrimination claims the burden typically is on the State whereas with respect to claims concerning other substantive standards it is the challenger-claimant who must demonstrate that deviation from the law occurred and worked an injury upon the claimant.

In one important respect, an international tribunal perceives judicial restraint slightly differently from a domestic tribunal since a traditional canon of judicial restraint (aforementioned Tenet *ii*) inevitably conflicts

---

[42] *Id.* (citing in n. 85: "The reversal of the holding of the PCIJ's *Lotus* decision by the 1952 Brussels Collision Convention and the 1958 Geneva High Seas Convention is the most frequently mentioned example.").

[43] *Id.* (stating that "nuclear option" means that the change is "indisputably 'effective', but extremely difficult to implement.")

[44] A. von Staden, *Deference or No Deference, That is the Question: Legitimacy and Standards of Review in Investor-State Arbitration*, IISD, July 19, 2012, *available at* <www.iisd.org/itn/2012/07/19/deference-or-no-deference-that-is-the-question-legitimacy-and-standards-of-review-in-investor-state-arbitration/#_ftn2>.

with the speedy-dispute-resolution-now! *zeitgeist* of international cases, especially IIA and diplomatic crises cases. That traditional canon was thus stated simply by John Roberts, the incumbent Chief Justice of the United States: "[i]f it is not necessary to decide more to dispose of a case, in my view it is necessary not to decide more."[45]

Generalities are allowed some exceptions, but only as long as those exceptions do not swallow the rule. If that occurs, it is time for new generalities. When investors or owners come to international tribunals, in IIA and diplomatic crises and sometimes even in human rights cases, they come assured with the promise of speedy-resolution-now. This author's position is that *(i)* if the case would have ended up in the same posture after a few rounds when bounced back to a different court; *(ii)* if the looming, grand question would have been unavoidable; *(iii)* if the parties (or at least one party) wants such a resolution, and *(iv)* if the benefits to be accrued by a small amount of fact-finding are grossly outweighed by the costs of postponing this decision,[46] the large question(s)—before domestic

[45] C. Sunstein, Op-Ed., *The Minimalist*, L.A. TIMES, May 25, 2006, at B11 (quoting the address given by Chief Justice Roberts at the Georgetown University Law Center graduation ceremony in 2006). The nub of this statement is judicial restraint and deference to the policy makers, who on the federal level are coequal to the Supreme Court. Even though The Chief Justice voted to invalidate campaign finance restrictions under the First Amendment's free speech guarantee in *Citizens United v. Federal Election Commission*, 130 S. Ct. 876, 919 (2010), and used a variation of the same phrase in his concurring opinion ("[W]hile it is true that '[i]f it is not necessary to decide more, it is necessary not to decide more,' . . . sometimes it *is* necessary to decide more.") (emphasis in original) when he was reaching a broader question without which the outcome still would have been the same, he also deferred to Congress in upholding President Obama's signature health-care bill, the Patient Protection and Affordable Care Act (PPACA), in *National Federation of Independent Business v. Sebelius*, 2012 U.S. Lexis 4876, * (2012), on the constitutionally-protected taxing power of Congress rather than the more well-known Commerce Clause power (discussed in Chapter IV). The Chief Justice might distinguish the two situations somewhat by saying, as he did, that "[t]here is a" world of "difference between judicial restraint and judicial abdication," *Citizens United*, *supra,* at 919 (2010). Still, a more difficult question lingers: Where does the tipping point between "judicial restraint" and "judicial abdication" lie? Perhaps the answer is whether, in the aggregate, there is a vulnerable population to whose valid claims the policymakers just would not "'give ear.'" See *United States v. Virginia*, 518 U.S. 515, 531 (1996) (citing *Goesaert v. Cleary*, 335 U.S. 464, 467 (1948)).

[46] For example, trial judges facing imminent prospect of evidence or witness tampering know this well.

and certainly before international tribunals—ought to be decided without further delay.

Why is this especially relevant to international tribunals? Far from being just an intellectual exercise, this resolution might help avert wars, economic meltdowns, diplomatic crises, trade and investment misunderstandings due to real or perceived non-transparency, and other manifestations of tension. Whereas domestic courts can take their own time and several rounds to resolve all the issues incrementally, since litigants frankly might have nowhere else to go,[47] international tribunals are expected by the signatories which have created them to deliver comprehensive and clear resolution.

In fact, Chapter IV (EXHAUSTION OF LOCAL REMEDIES AND CONTINUOUS NATIONALITY) has already stated that, on the IIA platform, a tribunal's error is fatal (to mean, vulnerable for annulment) by annulment committees to commit "a failure to apply the law chosen by the parties (but not a misapplication of it)"[48] or to commit "a failure to decide a question entrusted to the tribunal."[49] From composition of the IIA tribunal to reversibility, it is the parties who are the very epicentre of the process. Parties have certain limitations, of course, namely that they must hew consistently with the Convention governing the forum and the specific IIA governing their behaviour but even those issues take into account (in significant part) the policy considerations and practical difficulties confronting the parties. This systemic arrangement contemplates that the umpires will be deployed simply to "call balls and strikes"—and almost no one comes to the ballgame to see them.[50]

Non-discrimination has a long history and has become a pillar of modern international law. The two most common dimensions to non-discrimination are *national treatment (NT)* and *most favoured nation treatment (MFN)*. NT and MFN mainly pertain to international trade and

---

[47] This is assuming that litigation is the only reality and that settlement, mediation and arbitration options are not available.

[48] *Id.*, at ¶ 41-2 (citing *Soufraki v. UAE*, ICSID Case No. ARB/02/7 (2007)) (Decision on Annulment)).

[49] *Id.* (citing *Soufraki*, *supra*, at ¶ 44; *Vivendi Universal, S.A. v. Argentina*, ICSID Case No. ARB/03/19, at ¶ 86).

[50] "Chief Justice Roberts 2006 Commencement Address," Georgetown University Law Center, available at <http://apps.law.georgetown.edu/webcasts/eventDetail.cfm?eventID=144> (May 21, 2006). This, again, is not to suggest that the case-law does not carry over to other cases or even other tribunals. We have learned that it does. It simply is to suggest that dispute resolution takes primacy among tribunal objectives.

investment law. But the often-overlooked dimension to non-discrimination is *domestic discrimination*, where the State discriminates amongst its own nationals, citizens, and people who live there. If there is any principle at the heart of international law principles forbidding domestic discrimination, it is that measures imposing and/or substantially perpetuating "second-class citizenship" presumptively violate international law.[51] We might call this the *anti-subordination principle*, the existence and even thriving of which need to preclude—indeed, it will enhance—a healthy notion of diversity in international law.

Under NT, the contracting parties may not treat domestic participants more favourably than foreign participants[52] though it may treat them worse.[53] Notably in the NAFTA case of *Bayview v. Mexico* (2007) (already mentioned),[54] the tribunal concluded that "because the claimants' position would implicitly afford foreign investment greater protection than is typically granted domestic investment, the records surrounding the

[51] See, *e.g.*, *Sejdic and Finci v. Bosnia and Herzegovina*, Application nos. 27996/06 and 34836/06 (2009), at ¶ 57; *East African Asians v. the United Kingdom*, nos. 4403/70 et al., Commission's report of 14 December 1973, § 208, Decisions and Reports 78; *Cyprus v. Turkey* [GC], no. 25781/94, § 310, ECHR 2001-IV..

[52] NT is the requirement that nationals or residents of another country no less favourably than domestic nationals in like situations. NT requires equivalent, not necessarily identical, treatment. See National Treatment for Foreign-Controlled Enterprises, OECD, *available at* <www.oecd.org/dataoecd/32/21/1954854.pdf> (last accessed October 4, 2011); U.N. General Assembly Resolution 3281 Art. 2(2) (1974) (recognising NT and MFN protections for foreign investors).

[53] This does not sit well in some circles. For a representative list, see J. E. Stiglitz, *Regulating Multinational Corporations: Towards Principles of Cross-Border Legal Frameworks in a Globalized World Balancing Rights with Responsibilities*, 23 A.J.I.L. 451, 468 (2008); V. Lowe, Oxford Univ., *Fair and Equitable Treatment in International Law*, Remarks at the Annual Meeting of the American Society of International Law (Mar. 30, 2006), *in* 100 Proc. Ann. Meeting (AM. SOC'Y INT'L L.) 73, 74 (2006).

[54] ICSID Case No. ARB (AF)/05/1, at ¶ 95; see also C. Lévesque, "*Bayview Irrigation District v. Mexico:* The Case," in SUSTAINABLE DEVELOPMENT IN WORLD TRADE LAW 412 *et seq.* (Kluwer Law International, 2011) (M. Segger & M. Gehring et al., eds.) [M. Segger & M. Gehring, SUSTAINABLE DEVELOPMENT IN WORLD TRADE LAW].

drafting of Chapter [Eleven] would have to demonstrate the intent to provide such broad applicability."[55]

The *Bayview* default status, then, is at-par foreigner-domestic treatment, not disparity. Most other IIA decisions are largely silent on this exact question. And under MFN, the contracting parties may not differentiate between foreign participants from different States.[56] The international law position was summarised the U.S.-Mexican Claims Commission in the *Hopkins Case* (1926),[57] where the commission rejected the Mexican government's argument that the new government had lawfully nullified the previous government's obligations:

> it not infrequently happens that under the rules of international law applied to controversies of an international aspect a nation is required to accord to aliens broader and more liberal treatment than it accords to its own citizens under its municipal laws. … There is no ground to object that this amounts to a discrimination by a nation against its own citizens in favor of aliens. It is not a question of discrimination, but a question of difference in their respective rights and remedies. The citizens of a nation may enjoy many rights which are withheld from aliens, and, conversely, under international law aliens may enjoy rights and remedies which the nation does not accord to its own citizens.

To this end, the NAFTA tribunals in *GAMI* and in *S.D. Myers v. Canada* (2000)[58] have cited *Hopkins* approvingly.

NT and MFN working in tandem are still not full-proof, however. A State may strategically immunise itself with a "decoy" or "shill" strategy ("a disguised restriction on international [investment]")[59]: By *not* expropriating some less valuable investments (or at least investments it desires less), even in the same sector, from the home nation of the highly-

---

[55] N. Shapiro, *Comment: International Arbitration – ICSID Jurisdiction Under NAFTA – Bayview Irrigation District v. United Mexican States*, ICSID Case No. ARB(AF)/05/1, Award 19 June 2007, 32 SUFFOLK TRANSNAT'L L. Rev. 1, 5 (2008).

[56] MFN is "treatment accorded by the granting State to the beneficiary State, or to persons or things in a determined relationship with that State, not less favourable than treatment extended by the granting State or to a third State or to persons or things in the same relationship with that third State." Article 5 of the Draft Articles on most-favoured-nation clauses (ILC Draft), in ILC YEARBOOK: VOL. II, p. 21 (1978).

[57] 4 UNRIAA 41, 47.

[58] 8 ICSID Rep., at ¶ 260.

[59] Article XX of the GATT 1994.

valued investment it *is* targeting for expropriation.[60] Thus covering itself with misdirection and strategic immunity the State may evade liability even after causing the most invidious discrimination, at little gross expense and no net expense.

We should face reality here. It will be next to impossible for claimants to reveal and *prove* the mischief and chicanery at work here. Another potential obstacle lying between a smooth NT/MFN doctrine and a workable system, as the last subsection of this Chapter will show, is that MFN's actionability is in peril. Here too consent is omnipresent and influential.

Jan Paulsson argues that "the very fact of being foreign creates an inequality."[61] Paulsson's logic, if stretched, might endorse in some circumstances advantages upon the foreigner (not available to the national) that compensate for this inherent disadvantage being an outsider, burdened by those vestiges.[62] Paulsson and his school of thought justify this argument using the incentivising-development rationale. Foreign investors "seek to reduce the risk of investment abroad through investment protection."[63] This phenomenon, the argument goes, ends up "lower[ing] the cost of capital for capital-importing countries and accelerates their

---

[60] The screenplay of the popular television show THE WEST WING (ep: *The Benign Prerogative*, Season V, episode XII) seems to have understood this point and felicitously called the victims of such strategic thinking "packing peanuts." Those who end up on the losing side of this most formalist of equations tend generally to be unwitting victims of some socioeconomic and/or legal accident, rather than any grand-design. They also tend to be those whose cases are grouped together based on some over-inclusive or under-inclusive (and perhaps both) trait(s) instead of sensible individualised consideration.

[61] J. Paulsson, DENIAL OF JUSTICE IN INTERNATIONAL LAW 149 (Cambridge University Press, 2005) (arguing that because "host states can unilaterally change any protection offered under their domestic laws," there is an inherent "risk . . . in the asymmetrical relationship between a private investor and a sovereign state.") [J. Paulsson, DENIAL OF JUSTICE].

[62] Despite the fact that this premise has a noble lineage, it is also true that today's investors typically are not penurious outsiders lacking clout in the domestic system. In fact, it is often true that *foreign* investors have greater clout (that they owe to their affluence) than do less privileged domestic claimants. If we are to draw categories using broad brush strokes, then international human rights claimants but not IIA claimants might be exempt from the "influence-less outsider" status and its associated procedural and substantive implications.

[63] N. DiMascio & J. Pauwelyn, *Nondiscrimination in Trade and Investment Treaties: Worlds Apart or Two Sides of the Same Coin?*, 102 A.J.I.L. 48, 55 (2008) [N. DiMascio & J. Pauwelyn, *Nondiscrimination in Trade and Investment Treaties*]

economic development through investment promotion."[64] On the whole, this might be true. But sectoral and country-specific road-mapping does not reveal this to be the unequivocal and unqualified truth, and efforts made by certain developed countries reflect this reality.[65]

Non-discrimination's international human rights relevance is different from its IIA relevance where NT and MFN apply. Article 14 of the ECHR forbids its contracting parties from discriminating on several bases, namely "sex, race, colour, language, religion, political or other opinion, national or social origin, association with a national minority, property, birth or *other* status."[66] But Article 14 does not *explicitly* forbid discrimination on the basis of nationality.

Here the relevant *tertium comparationis* (shared attribute(s) or "likeness") comes into play, and will prove relevant for each of the

---

[64] See *id.*; A. T. Guzman, *Why LDCs Sign Treaties That Hurt Them: Explaining the Popularity of Bilateral Investment Treaties*, 38 VA. J. INT'L L. 639, 669-74 (1998) (discussing how the incentives are different for several categories of developing countries); J. W. Salacuse & N. P. Sullivan, *Do BITs Really Work? An Evaluation of Bilateral Investment Treaties and Their Grand Bargain*, 46 HARV. INT'L L.J. 67, 74 (2005). Turning the developed-developing country balance on its head, in recent times the argument could be made that when large multinationals invest in small developing countries, the asymmetry may sometimes work the other way. If so, the party needing protection is not so much the foreign investor, but rather the host country. See S. D. Franck, *Development and Outcomes of ITA*, *supra*, at 442.

[65] See, *e.g.*, Canadian Model BIT (2004), Annex B.13(1)(c) ("Except in rare circumstances, such as when a measure or series of measures are so severe in the light of their purpose that they cannot be reasonably viewed as having been adopted and applied in good faith, non-discriminatory measures of a Party that are designed and applied to protect legitimate public welfare objectives, such as health, safety and the environment, do not constitute indirect expropriation.") ("rare circumstances" might include specific violations of the agreement to which the State had submitted); see, for even more expansive language, International Institute for Sustainable Development, "IISD Model International Agreement for Sustainable Development," *available at* <www.iisd.org/pdf/2005/investment_model_int_ agreement.pdf> (2005) ("Consistent with the right of states to regulate and the customary international law principles on police powers, bona fide, non-discriminatory regulatory measures taken by a Party that are designed and applied to protect or enhance legitimate public welfare objectives, such as public health, safety and the environment, do not constitute an indirect expropriation under this Article.").

[66] Art. 14, ECHR (emphasis added). Under the EU, though, discrimination is forbidden only on the basis of sex, racial or ethnic origin, age, disability, religion or belief and sexual orientation.

institutions. Dissimilar treatment is discrimination only when the subjects so treated are otherwise similarly situated. "Discrimination implies unreasonable distinction," and expropriations that "*invidiously* single out property of persons" are presumptively unreasonable.[67] Likeness analysis also helps detect *de facto* discrimination and the earlier-mentioned "decoy" discrimination.

An important example came in *Petrov v. Bulgaria* (2008),[68] where the ECtHR decided that "[w]hile the Contracting States may be allowed a margin of appreciation to treat differently married and unmarried couples in . . . taxation, social security and social policy," there is no apparent reason to deny unmarried couples the right of contact when one of them is in police custody while giving it to married couples. *Petrov's* rationale, rejecting the positive law-made rationale, was that context and function of the rights matter; whether or not two individuals are "like" depends not just on their innate status but also on the specific rights they seek.[69] The IUCT and the NAFTA regime could draw instruction from *Petrov's* analysis.

Some of the relevant categories in a multi-factor likeness analysis that could assist the NAFTA, the ECtHR and the IUCT are market-competitive relationship; end-uses (functionality); demand and supply substitutability; and how they satisfy the regulatory purpose (including the environmental impact).[70] The other factors have to do with WTO/GATT *products* that do not readily apply to us. Even though from a pragmatic standpoint the non-discrimination jurisprudence of our three institutions is the most predictable aspect, there remains some doctrinal dissonance. Confusions

---

[67] THIRD RESTATEMENT 200, American Law Institute (1987) (emphasis added).

[68] App. no. 15197/02 (2008).

[69] The Court has extended this "other" equality to individuals on the basis of fatherhood (*Weller v. Hungary*, App. no. 44399/05 (2009)), membership in organisations (*Danilenkov v. Russia*, App. No. 67336/01 (2009); *Grande Oriente d'Italia di Palazzo Giustiniani v. Italy*, App. no. 26740/02 (2007)), military rank (*Engel v. The Netherlands*, App. nos. 5100/71, 5101/71, 5102/71, 5354/72 and 5370/72 (1976)), parenthood of a child born to unmarried parents (*Sommerfeld v. Germany*, App. no. 31871/96 (2003); *Sahin v. Germany*, App. no. 30943/96 (2003)), and place of residence (*Carson v. United Kingdom*, App. no. 42184/05 (2010)).

[70] GATT Panel Report, *Treatment by Germany of Imports of Sardines (Germany – Sardines)*, G/26 (1952), BISD 1S/53, ¶ 13; GATT Panel Report, *Canada/Japan – Tariff on Imports of Spruce, Pine, Fir (SPF) Dimension Lumber (Japan – SPF Dimension Lumber)*, L/6470 (1989), BISD 36S/167, ¶ 5.13 ff; GATT Working Party Report, *The Australian Subsidy on Ammonium Sulphate (EEC – Animal Feed Proteins)*, GATT/CP 4/39 (1950), BISD II/188, ¶ 4.2.

discourage investors and property owners from bringing claims or take them off track from bringing potentially *winnable* claims.

Some questions come up: Is disparate effect enough? Need there be a discriminatory intent or purpose? How do the non-discrimination standards in our different institutions interplay? This Chapter will analyse the patterns and explain how the non-discrimination principles interact in these institutions. The chart below (Y = Yes; N = No) encapsulates the non-discrimination standards.

	IUCT	***International Human Rights Instruments***	***IIA's***
NT	*Y*	*Y*	*Y*
MFN	*Y*	*Y*	*Y*
Domestic Discrimination	*N*	*Y*	*N*

§ 5.2—Non-Discrimination before the IUCT

Differential treatment of various persons, or classes of investors, is not automatically forbidden under the IUCT. Like non-discrimination in international human rights law,[71] such differentiation is "unreasonable" only if it lacks some "objective justification," not grounded in the forbidden classifications or somehow showing that the two comparators are not similarly situated.

In *American International Group v. Iran* (1983),[72] and again in *Amoco International Finance Corporation v. Iran* (1987),[73] the IUCT recognised a non-discrimination principle at work in the customary international law of expropriation, even though the CSD's text says nothing specific about it. The Tribunal went so far as to find protected NT and MFN rights.

Exactly *what* standard this non-discrimination principle requires is a closer question,[74] and here the *Amoco* parties totally disagreed with each

[71] M. Pellonpaa, EXPULSION IN INTERNATIONAL LAW 113 (1984).

[72] 4 I.U. C.T.R. 96, 105.

[73] 15 I.U.C.T.R. 189, 196 ("Discrimination is widely held as prohibited in the customary international law of expropriation"); see *id.*, at ¶¶ 139-40 for a rich explanation about the parties' positions.

[74] P. H. Sand, *Lessons Learned in Global Environmental Governance*, 18 B.C. ENVTL. AFF. L. REV. 213, 224 (1991) [P. H. Sand, *Lessons Learned*]; N. Schrijver,

other. The *Amoco* claimant argued that the Iranian government's expropriation of Khemco Company was discriminatory because, though all comparable and similarly situated U.S. interests in Iran *were* expropriated, "in another of [Iran's] joint ventures, the Japanese share of a consortium, the Iran-Japan Petrochemical Company [,named "UPC,"] was not expropriated."[75]

Iran countered, claiming that its Single Article Act (passed in the immediate aftermath of the Revolution) applied to the whole oil industry. Iran also claimed that honouring the terms of the UPC contract and had to do with specific economic, not political or diplomatic, circumstances: unlike the Khemco plant, "the operation of the UPC joint venture was not closely linked with other contracts relating to the exploitation of oil fields" and "that UPC was not yet an operational concern at the relevant time . . . ."[76]

Recognising the non-discrimination principle,[77] the IUCT found "it difficult, in the absence of any other evidence, to . . . conclu[de] that the expropriation of a concern was discriminatory only from the fact that another concern in the same economic branch was not expropriated."[78] There is always the chance that non-expropriation of the UPC was a "twistification" by Iran to cover itself with misdirection. Had the IUCT wanted, it could have put the burden squarely on Iran to prove that this was non-discriminatory towards the Khemco plant.[79] But this does not seem to have been the case. The IUCT's explanation of its likeness analysis should not, though, give chills to the anti-expropriation camp:

> Reasons specific to the non-expropriated enterprise, or to the expropriated one, or to both, may justify such a difference of treatment. Furthermore, as observed by the arbitral tribunal in *Kuwait v. American Independent Oil Company (AMINOIL)*, 21 ILM 1019 (1982) . . . a coherent policy of nationalization can . . . be operated gradually in successive stages. In the present Case, the peculiarities discussed by the Parties can explain why

---

SOVEREIGNTY OVER NATURAL RESOURCES: BALANCING RIGHTS AND DUTIES 349 (Cambridge University Press, 2008) [N. Schrijver, SOVEREIGNTY OVER NATURAL RESOURCES].

75 *Amoco*, *supra*, at 195.

76 *Id.,* at 196-97.

77 *Id.*, at 197.

78 *Id.*

79 Of course there remains the tacit possibility that the Tribunal did not defer to the State quite as greatly as many commentators have presumed and even then to the Tribunal the claimant's non-discrimination argument seemed to be at a loss.

> UPC was not treated in the same manner as Khemco. The Tribunal declines to find that Khemco's expropriation was discriminatory.[80]

To be sure, the IUCT kept itself open to *stronger* evidence adduced by the claimant—yes, here the burden was higher than just showing that there was differential treatment. Whether this evidence is hard to come by when state actors have basically been told how to escape liability, as Chapter III (ATTRIBUTION AND CAUSATION) shows, is a different question altogether. Moreover, notice how the IUCT endorsed the principle of showing non-discrimination through gradual or "creeping expropriations" ("coherent policy of nationalization can . . . be operated gradually in successive stages") and thus endorsed the possibility of showing "creeping expropriations" themselves.[81] The *Azurix* tribunal stated in 2003 that "[w]hen considering multiple measures," a finding of expropriation "will depend on the duration of their cumulative effect."[82]

While I have always been inclined to define "creeping expropriations" this way, some scholarship and even jurisprudence deem "creeping expropriations" as interchangeable with "regulatory expropriations" and "regulatory takings." The latter operative term of arts, of course, are defined as "any scenario in which a capital-importing state uses its regulatory powers to deprive foreign investors of their property or the effective enjoyment thereof."[83]

A non-discrimination claim in international tribunals can also be demonstrated by proving that there is no legitimate regulatory purpose

---

[80] *Id.*

[81] *Id.*; see also *Azurix Corp. v. Argentina*, ICSID Case No. ARB/01/12, Award (Jul. 14, 2006) ("cumulative steps which individually may not qualify as an expropriating measure may have the effect equivalent to an outright expropriation.").

[82] *Id.*, at ¶ 313. Even though the *Azurix* tribunal stated that "[t]here is no specific time set under international law for measures constituting creeping expropriation to produce that effect," the tribunal nonetheless was on the same page as previous arbitral awards that a single policy (not "creeping" or gradual measures) would not be expropriatory if it only led the property to be "out of the control of the investor for a year." Id. (citing *Wena Hotels Ltd. v. Egypt*, ICSID Case No. ARB/98/4, Committee Decision on Application for Annulment, 41 I.L.M. 933 (2002)).

[83] J. M. Marlles, *Public Purpose, Private Losses, supra,* at 276 (citing RESTATEMENT (THIRD) OF FOREIGN RELATIONS LAW OF THE UNITED STATES § 712 rep. note 7 (1987); Elyse M. Freeman, *Note, Regulatory Expropriation Under NAFTA Chapter 11: Some Lessons From the European Court of Human Rights*, 42 COLUM. J. TRANSNAT'L L. 177, 181 (2003); Rainer Geiger, *Regulatory Expropriations in International Law: Lessons from the Multilateral Agreement on Investment*, 11 N.Y.U. ENVTL. L.J. 94, 96 (2002)).

benefiting (or likely to benefit)—not just essential or necessary to—the public welfare. But do not expect the State to simply roll over and do not expect the tribunals to forget that claimants "bear a significant burden to produce evidence of the state's wrongful purpose . . . ."[84] Claimants might elect to undertake several strategies to defeat the deference which is accorded the State:

*(i) Direct-Evidence-of-*Scienter *Strategy:* "Any direct evidence of improper purpose, such as international communications of government officials indicating protectionism" or other violations.[85] But this kind of obvious proof "will often be unavailable and tribunals . . . [might] be willing to consider whether other forms of evidence are sufficient."[86] Hence, we explore alternatives.

(ii) Symptomatic-Effects Strategy: "[A] wrongful purpose should have certain symptomatic effects (*e.g.*, benefits to domestic investors at the expense of foreign investors)."[87]

(iii) Typical-Practices Strategy: "Whether the enactment of the measure is consistent with the state's typical practice is also significant as an anomalous measure may indicate that the state was motivated by other purposes."[88] Moreover, "tribunals may also examine the substantive merits of a measure as evidence that the measure was highly disproportional, irrational, or not scientifically justified may suggest that it was used as a pretext for an improper objective."[89]

Even with the governmental deference typically involving empirical information factored into the equation (showing, most likely, that benefits accruing for the public consumption now or in the future are to be considered attributable to the challenged measure), the measure or policy would fail the first prong of the non-discrimination analysis.

---

[84] R. Moloo & J. Jacinto, *Environmental and Health Regulation*, *supra*, at 55.
[85] *Id.*, at 55 (citing *S.D. Myers, Inc. v. Government of Canada*, NAFTA/ UNCITRAL, Partial Award, at ¶¶ 161-195 (Nov. 13, 2000)). The *S. D. Myers* tribunal had to evaluate the documentary evidence contained in the record suggesting Canada's protectionist intent.
[86] *Id.*, at 55-56.
[87] *Id.*
[88] *Id.*
[89] *Id.*

It is also true that the regulatory purpose inquiry is a discrete element within the non-discrimination obligation.[90] Where economic injury results from a *bona fide* non-discriminatory regulation within the police powers of the State, compensation is not required. A governmental measure will be discriminatory if it results "in an actual injury to the alien …with the intention to harm the aggrieved alien" to favour national or some other nation's companies.[91]

The IUCT has consistently required a legitimate public purpose.[92] A series of decisions underscore this point. For instance, the IUCT's *American International Group,* with which this Section opened, concerned Iran's expropriation of an insurance company through its new Law of Nationalization of Insurance Companies and Credit Enterprises (LoNICCE). There the IUCT stated that

> it cannot be held that the nationalization of Iran America was by itself unlawful, either under customary international law or under the Treaty of Amity . . . as there is not sufficient evidence before the Tribunal to show that the nationalization was not carried out for a public purpose as part of a larger reform program, or was discriminatory.

In *INA v. Iran* (1985),[93] again through the LoNICCE, Iran had nationalised the 20% equity interest owned by U.S. claimant. There the IUCT's broadened its grip on this form of non-discrimination by throwing in all kinds of expropriation along with the most obvious nationalisation. According to the IUCT:

> [E]xpropriations for a public purpose and subject to *conditions provided for by law*—notably that category which can be characterised as 'nationalisations'—are not *per se* unlawful. A lawful nationalisation will, however, impose on the government concerned the obligation to pay compensation.[94]

---

[90] According to the Third Restatement, "[o]ne test suggested for determining whether regulation and taxation program are intended to achieve expropriation is whether they are applied only to alien enterprises." See RESTATEMENT OF THE LAW THIRD, THE FOREIGN RELATIONS OF THE UNITED STATES, American Law Institute 712 (1987).

[91] See R. Dolzer & M. Stevens, BILATERAL INVESTMENT TREATIES 97-8, *supra*.

[92] M. Shaw, INTERNATIONAL LAW, *supra*, at 745. But see Brownlie, *supra,* at 545 (expressing reservations about such a requirement).

[93] 8 I.U.C.T.R. 373 (1985).

[94] *Id.*, at 391 (emphasis added). Rosalyn Higgins has argued that the issue is really one of who has to bear the cost of taking care of the public interest. Must it be

The IUCT imposes modest public-purpose requirements on the expropriating State. This was confirmed by the *Amoco* partial award:

> [a] precise definition of the 'public purpose' for which an expropriation may be lawfully decided has neither been agreed upon in international law nor even suggested. It is clear that, as a result of the modern acceptance of the right to nationalize, this term is broadly interpreted, and that States, in practice, are granted extensive discretion.[95]

The IUCT in *Amoco* did not say that this discretion knows no bounds. Thus "[a]n expropriation, *the only purpose* of which would have been to avoid contractual obligations of the State or of an entity controlled by it, could not . . . be considered as lawful under international law."[96] *Amoco* also deemed it to be "generally accepted [in international law the principle] that a State has no right to expropriate a foreign concern only for financial purposes."[97]

The margin of appreciation, though, becomes relevant at a critical point. For instance, expropriation for the sole or primary aim of obtaining the revenues for "the exploitation of national resources [for] the development of the country,"[98] would not necessarily be illegitimate. In *Amoco*, the IUCT looked to a combination of public purpose and reliance (along the lines of NAFTA's "reasonable investment-backed expectations"[99]) to decide if the public purpose requirement had been satisfied:

> it could not be doubted that the Single Article Act was adopted for a clear public purpose, namely to complete the nationalization of the oil industry in Iran initiated by the 1951 Nationalization of the Iranian Oil Industry Act, with a view to implementing one of the main economic and political objectives of the new Islamic Government.[100]

Nationalisation or expropriation legislation enacted for the public purpose, and for which the company had had 26 years of warning, is enough to satisfy the regulatory purpose requirement. Although it *can* be

---

society as a whole, represented by the state, or the owner of the particular property? See R. Higgins, *The Taking of Property by the State: Recent Developments in International Law*, 176 RECUEIL DES COURS 276, 277 (1982).

95 *Amoco*, *supra*, at 103.

96 *Id.*, at 104 (emphasis added).

97 *Id.*

98 *Id.*

99 *Azurix Corp. v. Argentina*, ICSID Case No. ARB/01/12, Award (2006), at ¶ 301.

100 *Amoco*, *supra*, at 105.

rebutted, it is *prima facie* evidence of such a purpose. Hearkening back to *INA's* "conditions provided for by law" language, we can see that this reliance factor, however tacitly, was already at work two years before *Amoco*. Reliance, a consideration discussed in more detail in the next Chapter (OTHER SUBSTANTIVE STANDARDS), acts as a check against abrupt expropriations or interferences with legitimate expectations.

Nonetheless the presumption is that absent these abrupt zigzags by the State, the tribunals must defer to government policies of what its needs are, its statistical forecasts, and the like since sovereignty so requires and, well, voters are the ones who have to fix the deeper directional problems, not international tribunals, or they might compromise their own legitimacy in a manner almost impossible to repair. This underrated argument requires further analysis.

"Dictator Paradox"

International law presumes that the State understands its own needs best and is politically accountable (to voters) and to future international agreements (to the community of nations). Since liberal principles presume that "morally autonomous citizens hold rights to liberty" and to consent, "the states that democratically represent them have the right to exercise political independence."[101] This political independence is not just from foreign intervention but also undemocratic and "soul-less despotism" of domestic dictators.[102]

Absolute power allows the dictator to realize their basest ambitions truly and fully.[103] It precludes the remote possibility that they could ever

---

[101] M. W. Doyle, "Kant, Liberal Legacies, and Foreign Affairs," *supra*, at 213.

[102] I. Kant, "Perpetual Peace" (1795) in THE PHILOSOPHY OF KANT 454, ed. Carl J. Friedrich (New York: Modem Library, I949).

[103] R. A. Caro, THE YEARS OF LYNDON JOHNSON xiv (2012) ("But although the cliché says that power always corrupts, what is seldom said, but what is equally true, is that power always reveals. When a man is climbing, trying to persuade others to give him power, concealment is necessary: to hide traits that might make others reluctant to give him power, to hide also what he wants to do with that power; if men recognized the traits or realized the aims, they might refuse to give him what he wants. But as a man obtains more power, camouflage is less necessary. The curtain begins to rise. The revealing begins."). Justly elected and removable Presidents who are dependent on other Branches to enact their agendas in a functioning Republic are assuredly the very antithesis of dictators. My point simply is that if Presidents can thus be "revealed," then so can dictators — far more easily because dictators fear neither future elections nor the judgment upon

be ejected from office.[104] How the deferential standard might work for states like Saddam Hussein's Ba'athist Iraq or Libya's Gaddafi regime that do not have such internal political accountability has never been answered satisfactorily.[105] But before we get carried away it must be mentioned that "democracy" is a label placed on certain kinds of governments that fall beyond a certain line on the continuum. It should not escape our notice, of course, that what constitutes a "democratic" regime lies often in the eye of the beholder. That said, there exists a school of thought entitled "democratic perfectionists" believes that "there [might] exist electoral deficiencies that call into question the democratic character of mature democracies."[106]

This "Dictator Paradox" suggests that if voter accountability inherent in the political process is one rationale behind deference to the sovereign respondent, then dictatorial regimes should not benefit from *this* rationale—to the international human rights claimant's needless detriment.[107] After all, as W. Michael Reisman points out,[108] consent of the

---

their legacies (because they most likely believe they will be able to rig those just as well as they may have rigged the elections).

[104] If dictators believed they could (or even should) be ejected easily, they probably would not be dictators in the first place.

[105] See N. DiMascio & J. Pauwelyn, *Nondiscrimination in Trade and Investment Treaties, supra,* at 57 (arguing that "if investment treaties are meant to prohibit acts that countries are unlikely to want to undertake anyway, there is reason to interpret investment disciplines with a high degree of deference to the regulating country.").

[106] See Guy-Uriel Charles, *Can Mature Democracies Be Perfected?*, 9 ELECTION L. J. 157, 157 (2010).

[107] What I call the *expansive subaltern thesis* simply means that covers parties disadvantaged by their lack of socioeconomic candlepower and those accidentally caught in formalism's web. What often happens is that even benign decision-makers, including governments and civil society actors, yield to group-think and draw group- and identity-based boundaries — in essence, "box" entities — that are over-inclusive and/or under-inclusive. Some people sometimes win in this game unfairly and some people sometimes lose but the people's respect for the rule of law always loses. That respect for the rule of law, if it is to survive at all, must consistently remain enshrined in the public firmament.

[108] See W. M. Reisman, *Sovereignty and Human Rights, supra,* at 867-68. Reisman states that "[i]n international law, the sovereign had finally been dethroned." *Id.*, at 868. Dethronement or not, I believe that the role of the sovereign has simply morphed and shifted over to the people, giving birth and shine to the international law norm of popular sovereignty.

governed is a nonnegotiable pillar of customary international law.[109] The contemporary incarnation of sovereignty is *popular* sovereignty, as opposed to the "sovereign's sovereignty."[110] The reader can anticipate the dictator-sovereign's counterargument, brought up in Chapter I, that they are entitled to reap the rewards of the "Hobbesian security reparation" theory. However, that theory presumes that this "reparation" is in return for protecting and preserving the lives and property of those within the sovereign's borders. Since dictators typically do no such thing, the theory does not apply.

The sovereign might still gain deference but it should not be imputed to this rationale; this is not just a cosmetic point of semantics. Respect due

---

[109] See, *e.g.*, *id.*, at 867 ("In the Universal Declaration of Human Rights, a document then describing itself as 'a common standard of achievement' but now accepted as declaratory of customary international law, Article 21(3) provided that '[t]he will of the people shall be the basis of the authority of government; this will shall be expressed in periodic and genuine elections which shall be by universal and equal suffrage and shall be held by secret vote or by equivalent free voting procedures.' Of course, there had been regional pacts based upon similar notions, much as there had been holy alliances based on their antithesis. The significance of this statement in the Universal Declaration was that it was now expressed in a fundamental *international* constitutive legal document.") (emphasis in original and internal footnotes omitted).

[110] This Reisman phrase basically refers to an absolute ruler's or dictator's "sovereignty" to do as she or he pleases. *Id.*, at 869 ("International law still protects sovereignty, but — not surprisingly it is the people's sovereignty rather than the sovereign's sovereignty."). See *id.*, at 869 ("Under the old concept, even scrutiny of international human rights without the permission of the sovereign could arguably constitute a violation of sovereignty by its 'invasion' of the sovereign's *domaine réservé*. The United Nations Charter replicates the 'domestic jurisdiction-international concern' dichotomy, but . . . [unsupportable is] the contention that internal human rights are 'essentially within the domestic jurisdiction of any state' and hence insulated from international law."). In the early twentieth-century, say 1923, when *Tinoco* ((*Great Britain v. Costa Rica*), 1 R. Int'l Arb. Awards 369 (1923), *reprinted in* 18 AJIL 147 (1924)) was decided, the twin tests were "*de facto* control" and national sovereignty, meaning that a seizer of power was entitled to sovereignty in international law so long as she or he held on to this power. During these "L'état, c'est moi" days, the State was the ruler and the ruler the supreme embodiment of the State. But the "constitutive policy of international human rights" has caused a powerful and enduring paradigm shift. See W. M. Reisman, *Sovereignty and Human Rights, supra,* at 870 (citing M. S. McDougal, H. D. Lasswell & W. M. Reisman, "The World Constitutive Process of Authoritative Decision," *in* M. S. McDougal and W. M. Reisman, INTERNATIONAL LAW ESSAYS 197 (1981)).

democracies and self-determination rights worldwide requires this important step by international courts, a step that has been ratified by international covenants (most notably in human rights).[111] Other potential reasons in *favour* of deference are too many to list. Suffice it to mention that stability of agreements, predictability, and legitimate expectations[112] are just some of the reasons. Though imprecise, a rough approximation was phrased by the Central American Treaty of Peace (also known as the Treaty of Washington) in 1908: "The Governments of the High Contracting Parties shall not recognize any other Government which may come into power in any of the[s] . . . Republics as a consequence of a *coup d'état*, or of a revolution against the recognized Government, so long as the freely elected representatives of the people thereof have not constitutionally reorganized the country."[113]

---

[111] See, *e.g.*, United Nations Declaration on the Elimination of All Forms of Racial Discrimination, GA Res. 1904 (XVIII) (Nov. 20, 1963); International Convention on the Elimination of All Forms of Racial Discrimination, opened for signature Mar. 7, 1966, 660 UNTS 195; Declaration on the Elimination of All Forms of Intolerance and of Discrimination Based on Religion or Belief, GA Res. 36/55 (Nov. 25, 1981); Convention concerning Forced or Compulsory Labour, June 28, 1930, 39 UNTS 55; International Convention on the Suppression and Punishment of the Crime of Apartheid, GA Res. 3068 (XXVIII) (Nov. 30, 1973); Convention against Discrimination in Education, Dec. 14, 1960, 429 UNTS 32; Convention concerning Equal Remuneration for Men and Women Workers for Work of Equal Value, June 29, 1951, 165 UNTS 303; Convention on the Elimination of All Forms of Discrimination against Women, GA Res. 34/180 (Dec. 18, 1979); Declaration on the Protection of All Persons from Being Subjected to Torture and Other Cruel, Inhuman or Degrading Treatment or Punishment, GA Res. 3452 (XXX) (Dec. 9, 1975); Convention against Torture and Other Cruel, Inhuman or Degrading Treatment or Punishment, GA Res. 39/46 (Dec. 10, 1984); Code of Conduct for Law Enforcement Officials, GA Res. 34/169 (Dec. 17, 1979); and Declaration of Basic Principles of Justice for Victims of Crime and Abuse of Power, GA Res. 40/34 (Nov. 29, 1985); and several conventions on social welfare and the familial and cultural rights. See also Resolutions Adopted by the General Assembly During its 20th Session, 20 UN GAOR Supp. (No. 14) at 53-65, UN Doc. A/6014 (1965) (several resolutions concerning non-selfgoverning territories).

[112] The "legitimate expectation" rationale works both for investors and owners challenging a government action as it does for signatory States attempting to hold each other to their ostensible and consented-to commitments.

[113] The more precise phrasing "as a *necessary* consequence of a *coup d'etat*, or of a revolution against the recognized Government" would have entailed deeply fact-intensive but-for causation, which might be difficult for international bodies to assess. The Treaty of Washington's language privileges administrability and the even appearance of illegitimacy *over* absolute precision. There is something to be

After all, unless the change in the type of regime has been drastic, sudden and unforeseeable, the signatories knew not just the present state but also the possibilities to which they were they were consenting to when they did so. Agreements assume risks, and sometimes risks go wrong. Risks, therefore, are excusable or may be implicitly waived only with enumerated and/or severe exceptions.

Chapter III (ATTRIBUTION AND CAUSATION) has explained that the Vienna Convention on the Law of Treaties allows exceptions based primarily in fraud, error and corruption. Moreover, Article 46 ("A State may not invoke the fact that its consent to be bound by a treaty has been expressed in violation of a provision of its internal law regarding competence to conclude treaties as invalidating its consent unless that violation was manifest and concerned a rule of its internal law of fundamental importance") of the same makes it quite difficult for a signatory to avoid compliance based on a conflict-with-domestic-law argument.

This is easier said than done, of course. What if the nation's highest court recognises, over spirited dissents and by a close vote, years after the signing of the treaty and centuries after the adoption of the Constitution, its supreme law, a constitutional interpretation that is inconsistent with the treaty? Is that constitutional principle necessarily "manifest" or "of fundamental importance"? What factors are to guide such an inquiry? Need the Nation's highest tribunal have been unanimous? How are we to determine, objectively and uniformly, how strong the arguments on either side need be? Would this not inject a new level of subjectively-fraught discretion and render the international tribunal into something of a super-Supreme Court of a Nation? Surely, "manifest" is not necessarily equivalent to a consensus since, in a split panel, both the judges in the majority and the minority may with good reason claim that application of the law in question is "manifest." Trying to situate international law into the domestic law framework, we will encounter such questions galore.

---

said for the fact that, unlike the sciences and the other social sciences, the law moves slowly since people expect it to have stability and predictability. Before taking a plunge into the unknown, the law needs to explore its options very carefully under a variety of scenarios for a long time. Most importantly perhaps, the law's quirk is to balance the equities and sometimes take the overprotective and over-inclusive step *only if* the risk and danger in not doing so are substantially large, imminent and greater than the adverse consequences of taking the over-inclusive step. See, *e.g.*, S. Breyer, "Economic Reasoning and Judicial Review," *supra*, at 6-7.

International law literature generally points to political accountability as a requisite foundation[114] but what might happen in its absence is not entirely clear. In their relatively recent path-marking work *Complementary Constraints*, Jide O. Nzelibe and Matthew C. Stephenson assume "voter welfare" to be *the* end-goal of any regime, and advance various reasons that particular democratic mechanisms—in this case, unilateral authority, mandatory separation of powers regime, and voluntary separation of powers regime—might be effective.[115] The mechanisms clearly are secondary in this equation. But if "voter-welfare" becomes "voter-irrelevance," then the original assumptions must be reassessed.

Behavioural Incentives: Entering into and Honouring Agreements

States do not want to discourage other States from doing future IIA business with them or companies from contracting with them. *This* we know. But how much and what sacrifices the States are prepared to make, is the relevant inquiry. Not so different at all from what Professor Haskell referred to as "'thin' conception of human sociability—whereby human

[114] V. Perju, *Provocation: Law's Republics*, 125 HARV. L. REV. F. 204, 204 (2012) (stating as two of the three "premises" of this particular argument that "[f]irst, the relevance for any polity of the exercises in self-government of other political communities, as encoded in their constitutional laws and cultures, is not self evident and must therefore be justified. Second, that justification must place domestic and foreign law within a unitary framework . . . ."). Subsequently, the question naturally arises: Which "self" are we discussing here, *i.e.*, who gets to make this determination? Typically, the presumption in international law is that the voters — enabled and qualified to do so by universal suffrage — get to make this determination. See Preamble, VCLT ("Having in mind the principles of international law embodied in the Charter of the United Nations, such as the principles of the equal rights and self-determination of peoples, of the sovereign equality and independence of all States, of non-interference in the domestic affairs of States, of the prohibition of the threat or use of force and of universal respect for, and observance of, human rights and fundamental freedoms for all, . . .").

[115] J. O. Nzelibe and M. C. Stephenson, *Complementary Constraints: Separation of Powers, Rational Voting, and Constitutional Design*, 123 HARV. L. REV. 617, 645-6 (2010) ("When voters are able to observe not only the policy outcome, but also the decisions that led to the adoption of the final policy, the structure of the separation of powers affects the number of degrees of freedom voters have to influence government decisions. Imperfectly informed voters can adopt more refined strategies when they can condition their voting strategies on a larger number of observed paths to a policy outcome.").

nature wars between the desire for rational order amongst each other and conflicting self-interests"?[116] The State's regulatory purpose determination is overridden only in rare and exceptional instances—"exceptional" not just in degree but also sometimes in kind.[117]

Two such exceptions, earlier hinted at, are extreme politicisation and bias in the process (as opposed to public purpose in a socioeconomic sense) or when it is intended to be to the benefit of the government decision-makers. For instance, in *BP v. Libya* (1973),[118] Judge Lagergren (as the sole arbitrator) held that the expropriation of the claimant's concession rights "violate[d] public international law as it was made for purely extraneous political reasons and was arbitrary and discriminatory in character." Here a dictator's private benefit was at issue and openly admitted by Libya (as respondent) in so many words.

Is a discriminatory *effect* enough for proving a violation? The CSD text says little, and the IUCT is conflicted on the *intent* versus *effect* issue. Still, language in the *American International Corporation, INA,* and *Amoco* trifecta of the IUCT's non-discrimination jurisprudence suggests that a well-documented evidentiary pattern (effect), joined with other factors, could be evidence of discriminatory intent. While it is tempting to believe that the very creation of the IUCT and specifically the Preamble of the Algiers Accords ("acceptable resolution of the crisis") admits of this "effect," there are two logical drawbacks: (*i*) Preambles typically do not have overwhelming legal force on such fundamental matters; and (*ii*) the "acceptable resolution of the crisis" language might, at best, admit of a general problem but it most likely does not transfer that assumption over to *each* claim. Textually, the most that could be said of the IUCT's governing instruments is that the "acceptable resolution of the crisis" wording facilitates but does not automatically trigger the sufficiency of this effect.

On the discriminatory effect issue, there usually is no textual help in the IIA's (including NAFTA). However, one NAFTA tribunal has filled in the gap and held that discriminatory effect and persuasive evidence that the "inten[tion]" was "primarily" discriminatory in that same direction suffices. [119] Many international human rights instruments use what linguists would call "active verbs." The ECHR, for instance, affirmatively

---

[116] J. D. Haskell, *Hugo Grotius in the Contemporary Memory of International Law, supra,* at 275.

[117] R. Dolzer & M. Stevens, "Bilateral Investment Treaties," *supra*, at 98; N. Schrijver, SOVEREIGNTY OVER NATURAL RESOURCES 345.

[118] 53 ILR 297, 329 (1973).

[119] *S.D. Myers v. Canada*, Award, at ¶ 194.

gives Contracting Parties the authority to "enforce such laws as [they] dee[m] necessary to control the use of property" and guaranteeing private property rights "subject to the conditions provided for by law." The ACHR, in Article 21, similarly allows the signatories "[to] subordinate such use and enjoyment to the interest of society" and Article 14 of the ACHPR "only" permits "encroach[ment] upon in the interest of public need or in the general interest of the community and in accordance with the provisions of appropriate laws."[120]

Along these lines, instructive is Article III:1 GATT, which states that measures "should not be applied to imported or domestic products so as to afford protection to domestic production."[121] The WTO Appellate Body has stressed that the words "so as to afford protection" are about protectionist *effect* in NT and MFN cases, not about protectionist *intent*.[122] The Appellate Body and its panels quietly have taken the IUCT approach that strong, consistent patterns of evidence may show intent.[123] The next section will show that the ECtHR and the IUCT are on the same page jurisprudentially regarding this issue. The WTO-property or -investment protection transferable knowledge has some value. Legal and policy issues, such as market access, scientific uncertainty, and services, and

---

[120] The use of the word "only" seems somewhat ironic because the exception could potentially swallow the rule.

[121] WTO Appellate Body Report, *Japan – Taxes on Alcoholic Beverages (Japan – Alcoholic Beverages II)*, WT/DS8/AB/R, WT/DS10/AB/R, WT/DS11/AB/R (1996), at 25 f.

[122] *Id.*, at 29 ("It is irrelevant that protectionism was not an intended objective if the particular tax measure in question is nevertheless, to echo Article III:1, 'applied to imported or domestic products so as to afford protection to domestic production.'"); see also *Chile – Taxes on Alcoholic Beverages (Chile – Alcoholic Beverages)*, WT/DS87/AB/R, WT/DS110/AB/R (2000), ¶ 61f, 71; *Korea – Taxes on Alcoholic Beverages (Korea – Alcoholic Beverages)*, WT/DS75/AB/R, WT/DS84/AB/R (1999), ¶ 149.

[123] WTO Panel Report, *Mexico – Tax Measures on Soft Drinks and Other Beverages (Mexico – Taxes on Soft Drinks)*, WT/DS308/R (2006), ¶ 8.91 ("the declared intention of legislators and regulators of the Member adopting the measure should not be totally disregarded"); WTO Panel Report, *Indonesia – Autos*, WT/DS55/1(1998), ¶ 14.115 ("the nature of the discrimination, which is to promote a national industry by giving it advantages vis-à-vis imported products, is clearly designed so as to afford protection to domestic production"); WTO Appellate Body Report, *Canada – Certain Measures Concerning Periodicals (Canada – Periodicals)*, T/DS31/AB/R (1997), at 30 ff (addressing Canada's submissions about the protectionist intent of the measures).

institutional issues, such as compliance, enforcement and dispute settlement, apply in both situations.[124]

One last scenario has not come up in the IUCT but it should be noted anyway because it has IIA implications for the future. A defence available to respondents in NT *or* MFN cases is that the measure does not give an additional edge to domestic participants or participants from some other nation because any even remotely competing domestic products from some other nation are totally absent. If a complainant challenges a measure which causes *de facto* (but not *de jure*) discrimination, then the analysis will focus on the measure's effect in a *specific* situation. The analysis will vary based on whether it is a perfect competition or oligopoly or monopoly system. And lastly, "the absence of a credible non-protectionist purpose could also be considered as circumstantial evidence of a protectionist purpose."[125]

Although some scholars have urged the IUCT and other tribunals to clear the air about where the "regulatory purpose" analysis is concerned, they also acknowledge that this is just an academic aspiration[126] "From a practical standpoint," it makes no difference whatsoever "whether the regulatory purpose is considered under the comparator clause, the 'less favourable treatment' element or as a distinct and separate element."[127] Still, the author agrees that this "transparency" (or at least non-opacity) "would enhance legal security and facilitate the parties to a dispute to build their legal arguments"[123] on sounder footing. I also agree that likeness analysis cannot realistically avoid taking regulatory purpose into account.

That guidance should have come from the parties themselves rather than devised much later by the IUCT.[129] Altogether, charges of illegitimacy and judges-overstepping-bounds aside, the IUCT has succeeded in given

---

[124] See M. Segger & M. Gehring, SUSTAINABLE DEVELOPMENT IN WORLD TRADE LAW, *supra,* at 39-68.

[125] See N. Diebold, *Non-Discrimination and the Pillars of International Economic Law – Comparative Analysis and Building Coherency*, SOC'Y OF INT'L ECON. L., Working Paper No. 2010/24 (2010), p. 23 ("While the complainant seeks to show protectionism, the respondent [State] may submit evidence demonstrating that the measure was adopted with the objective to protect a public interest, such as health, morals, order, environment, natural resources, etc.").

[126] See *id*., and other scholars cited therein.

[127] *Id*., at 14.

[128] *Id.*

[129] *Id.* (stating that "due to the lack of a textual basis, adjudicating bodies mostly rely on the comparator clause or to a lesser extent on the element of 'less favourable treatment.'").

clarity to difficult non-discrimination questions. More than anything else, the IUCT was asked in 1981 to clean up a political and diplomatic mess, which in large part it has.

§ 5.3—Non-Discrimination before the ECtHR and the International Human Rights Tribunals

The ECtHR has a *general* docket on Article 14 discrimination cases that must be reconciled with cases concerning property non-discrimination. Thus some of the analysis in this section comes from the ECtHR's discrimination jurisprudence *generally*. The most important of these premises is the "likeness" analysis concerning comparators, a point concerning which there seems to be agreement among our three institutions: "[D]iscrimination means treating differently, without an objective and reasonable justification, persons in similar situations."[130] Moreover, "[n]o 'objective and reasonable justification' means that the distinction in issue does not pursue a 'legitimate aim' or that there is not a reasonable relationship of proportionality between the means employed and the aim sought to be realised."[131] We have thus covered legitimate aim and proportionality in one broad stroke. These issues deserve to be explicated.

Moreover, the ECtHR does face questions about nationality discrimination by governments. For instance, in *Gaygusuz v. Austria* (1996),[132] the Court decided that denying someone emergency assistance solely because of their nationality violated Articles 1 and 14. But the Court faces questions which have at their core *all* kinds of discrimination; it is the Court's province to decide which bases to permit. This is the only domestic discrimination court among our institutions.

This Chapter has already noted that Article 14 of the ECHR has a "such as" phrasing. The words "such as" should not imply boundless judicial discretion. But just *how* to apply *ejusdem generis* is of course up to the ECtHR.[133] Also notice the word "other" in Article 14, intended as a catch-all term to cover invidious status-based discrimination. [134]

---

[130] *Sejdic and Finci v. Bosnia and Herzegovina*, Application nos. 27996/06 and 34836/06 (2009), at ¶ 42.

[131] *Id.* (citing *Andrejeva v. Latvia* [GC], no. 55707/00 (2009), § 81).

[132] App. no. 17371/90.

[133] *Ejusdem generis* would cover only the matters belonging to the same subject matter or the same category of subject as to which the clause relates.

[134] *Sejdic and Finci v. Bosnia and Herzegovina*, Application nos. 27996/06 and 34836/06 (2009), at ¶ 39 ("Article 14 complements the other substantive

Furthermore, it should be noted that the term "other's" almost-inescapable elasticity also takes into account the different socioeconomic conditions in different signatories: what might be a stigma in one country might be innocuous in another, thus weakening the case for a *de facto* discrimination violation. Unlike NAFTA which, according to Articles 1102 and 1103, requires signatory governments to treat Investor A in Sector 1 of Foreign Country Z the way it would treat (or better)[135] its own nationals as well as Sector 1 investors of any other foreign countries, the ECtHR and the IUCT are not specific about *who* the comparators are—thus making the study even more interesting. On this score, most other IIA's tend to take the NAFTA line.

The prohibition on discrimination in Article 14 is one of the fundamental rights. However, this provision is not self-executing; it is dependent on the rights and privileges that the State gives. For example, the applicant claiming that she was discriminated against with regard to her private property rights will most likely rely on Article 14 along with Article 1. The claimant will not have to establish that there was another violation in order to prove that there was discrimination, although she

---

provisions of the Convention and the Protocols thereto. It has no independent existence since it has effect solely in relation to 'the enjoyment of the rights and freedoms' safeguarded by those provisions. Although the application of Article 14 does not presuppose a breach of those provisions – and to this extent it is autonomous –, there can be no room for its application unless the facts at issue fall "within the ambit" of one or more of the latter.") (citing *Abdulaziz, Cabales and Balkandali v. the United Kingdom*, 28 May 1985, § 71, Series A no. 94; *Petrovic v. Austria*, 27 March 1998, § 22, Reports 1998-II; and *Şahin v. Germany* [GC], no. 30943/96, § 85, ECHR 2003-VIII).).

[135] Some politicians in the NAFTA free trade area have tried to tamp down on this "better" angle. For example, the Kerry Amendment in the United States wanted to say that a trade agreement "shall ensure that foreign investors are not granted greater legal rights than citizens of the United States possess under the United States Constitution … [and] ensure that standards for minimum treatment … shall grant no greater legal rights than United States citizens possess under the due process clause of the United States Constitution." Proposed Kerry Amendment to H.R. 3009, S.A. 3430, 107th Cong., 148 CONG. REC. S4504 (2002); enacted into federal law as 19 U.S.C. § 3802(b)(3) (2004). What instead was passed said that one of the main objectives in IIA negotiations is "reduc[ing] or eliminat[ing] artificial or trade-distorting barriers to foreign investment, while ensuring that foreign investors in the United States are not accorded greater substantive rights with respect to investment protections than United States investors in the United States…." Trade Act of 2002, Pub. L. No. 107-210, § 2102(b)(3), 116 Stat. 933, 995 (2002). See also A. Bjorklund, *Reconciling State Sovereignty and Investor Protection, supra,* at 890.

might have to prove that she either already owned a property or her ownership or possession was thwarted by the law. The equality provision "applies also to those additional rights falling within the general scope of any Convention article, for which the State has voluntarily decided to provide."[136]

The burden then falls on the State to establish that the differential treatment was in accordance with the law, pursued a legitimate aim and that the means employed were proportionate to that aim. When it is an expropriation issue that is being disputed, the "margin of appreciation"[137] given to the State is wider than when gender, nationality and social status are employed to classify. A related "rationale behind the doctrine is that because of their proximity to complex factual matters and the life of their societies, national authorities are 'in a better position than the international judge to give an opinion' on the necessity of human rights restrictions."[138] In fact, the High Level Conference on the Future of the European Court of Human Rights has issued several declarations insisting on the margin.[139]

---

[136] *Sejdic, supra*, at ¶ 39 (citing *Case "relating to certain aspects of the laws on the use of languages in education in Belgium" v. Belgium* (Merits), 23 July 1968, § 9, Series A no. 6; *Stec and Others v. the United Kingdom* (dec.) [GC], nos. 65731/01 and 65900/01, § 40, ECHR 2005-X; and *E.B. v. France* [GC], no. 43546/02, § 48, ECHR 2008).

[137] See generally H. C. Yourow, THE MARGIN OF APPRECIATION DOCTRINE IN THE DYNAMICS OF THE EUROPEAN HUMAN RIGHTS JURISPRUDENCE (Springer, 1996). Human rights bodies in Costa Rica and Finland have adopted the ECtHR approach. See I/A Court HR, Proposed Amendments of the Naturalization Provisions of the Constitution of Costa Rica, Advisory Opinion OC-4/84 of 19 January 1984, Series A No 4, at ¶ 62; Human Rights Committee, *Hertzberg et al. v Finland*, Communication No 61/1979, UN Doc CCPR/C/OP/1, at ¶ 10.3.

[138] F. Zarbiyev, *Judicial Activism in International Law, supra,* at 15 (citing *Ireland v United Kingdom* ECtHR, Judgment of 18 January 1978, Series A 25, at ¶ 207; *Handyside v United Kingdom*, ECtHR, Judgment of 7 December 1976, Series A 24, at ¶ 48; *Müller et al. v Switzerland*, ECtHR, Judgment of 24 May 1988, Series A 133, at ¶ 35.)

[139] Izmir Declaration adopted by the High Level Conference on the Future of the European Court of Human Rights organised within the framework of the Turkish Chairmanship of the Committee of Ministers of the Council of Europe, 26–27 April 2011 (stating that the Declaration "[i]nvites the Court, when examining cases related to asylum and immigration, to assess and take full account of the effectiveness of domestic procedures and, where these procedures are seen to operate fairly and with respect for human rights, to avoid intervening except in the most exceptional circumstances."); Brighton Declaration adopted by the High Level Conference on the Future of the European Court of Human Rights organized at the initiative of the United Kingdom Chairmanship of the Committee of

Three deductions about the generalisations and applications attending "margin of appreciation" in international law must be addressed. First, the "margin of appreciation" doctrine is not "conceptually generalizable" across subject-matter areas or even jurisdictions.[140] The example one scholar gives is that while it would "be hard to convince international judges that national authorities are in a better position to judge the legality of the use of nuclear weapons,"[141] on fact-specific issues concerning health, safety, and "morals"[142] (the traditional police powers) the "margin of appreciation" must kick in. But the margin "left to national authorities is," in theory if not always in fact, "subject to substantial limits."[143] One might not necessarily agree with Fuad Zarbiyev but he, to his credit, calls it as he sees it: "In these circumstances one could hardly believe that such a flexible standard could exercise any meaningful constraint on the discretion of international judges."[144]

Second, while classes and categories of cases do give us a shorthand description, some scholars and judges believe that broad classes do not usually supersede in importance the specific facts of a case.[145] Professor Brownlie's admonition to this effect, with which Chapter III commences, rings true. This is certainly true in terms of removing the presumptive burden. If the presumptive burden of proof lies on the State and the facts favor the claimant, an overbroad classification in the law most likely will not cause the State to prevail in a given dispute.

Ministers of the Council of Europe, 19–20 April 2012 (requesting the ECtHR to accord "due regard to the State's margin of appreciation" and petitioning the Council of Europe's Committee of Ministers to propose an amendment to add the principles of subsidiarity and margin of appreciation in the Convention's Preamble).

140 F. Zarbiyev, *Judicial Activism in International Law, supra,* at 15.

141 *Id.*

142 Of course, international human rights jurisprudence limits what aspects and permutations of "morals" the State may regulate, for the term "morals" is a strikingly broad, value-laden term often carrying serious doctrinal and practical implications.

143 F. Zarbiyev, *Judicial Activism in International Law, supra,* at 15.

144 *Id.*

145 See generally I. Berlin, THE HEDGEHOG AND THE FOX (Weidenfeld & Nicolson, 1953). While the categorical versus non-categorical approach often makes a difference as to the sweep or posture, it is rare that it makes a difference as to the very outcome of a case. Such a rare case, in the immigration context, was just heard by the United States Supreme Court in *Moncrieffe v. Holder*, 132 S.Ct. 1857, No. 11-702 (2012).

Third, and on a point related to the first deduction, "margin of appreciation" probably applies *most* directly to legal questions where the human rights dimension is unsettled and where no clear consensus has been formed. It might be gallant to suggest (or to wishfully infer) that the ECtHR is leading the charge for the vindication of rights. But the factual reality is that the ECtHR "has been reluctant to be too intrusive about questions of society that divide European or particular national societies in an important way."[146] Consider that in the suits concerning same-sex marriage,[147] euthanasia,[148] divorce rights[149] or display of crucifixions in state school classrooms,[150] the ECtHR has refused to recognise Convention violations.[151] The common denominator across this category is that findings of Convention violations, at the times that the cases arrived at the Court, might have torn the Council of Europe apart or at least discredited it. Nothing close to a consensus exists yet on any of these questions. As social policy and thinking evolve on these questions, the ECtHR may well return to the issues and reverse itself. Thus proceeds the "margin of appreciation" saga. After all, the variables attending the judicial calculus are a "constantly shifting phenomen[a]" and perhaps there is even some merit to the claim that "no international court could afford the luxury of [complete] logical consistency in this regard."[152]

---

[146] F. Zarbiyev, *Judicial Activism in International Law, supra,* at 31.

[147] *Schalk & Kopf v. Austria*, Application no. 30141/04, ECtHR, Judgment of 24 June 2010.

[148] *Pretty v. United Kingdom*, Application no. 2346/02, ECtHR, Judgment of 29 April 2002.

[149] *Johnston and others v. Ireland*, Application No. 9697/82, ECtHR, Judgment of 18 December 1986.

[150] *Lautsi v. Italy*, Application no. 30814/06, ECtHR, Grand Chamber, Judgment of 18 March 2011.

[151] The ECtHR did refuse to sanction the death penalty, which has roundly been rejected by the Council of Europe signatories. See *Öcalan v. Turkey*, App. No. 46221/99, at ¶ 196 (2005) ("It may be questioned whether it is necessary to await ratification of Protocol No 6 by the three remaining States before concluding that the death penalty exception in Article 2 has been significantly modified. Against such a consistent background, it can be said that capital punishment in peacetime has come to be regarded as an unacceptable, if not inhuman, form of punishment which is no longer permissible under Article 2."). The *Öcalan* decision is laden with an evolutionary understanding of the Convention. See, *e.g.*, E. Bodansky, Ocalan v. Turkey *(Mirja Trilsch and Alexandra Ruth): ECHR decision on trial by Turkey of Kurdish separatist leader*, 100 A.J.I.L. 180 (2006).

[152] F. Zarbiyev, *Judicial Activism in International Law, supra,* at 31-32. A comparison of the ECtHR's tones in two contexts might be revelatory. Compare the defensive tone in *Golder v United Kingdom*, ECtHR, Judgment of 21 February

A caveat concerning the judicially-crafted “margin” doctrine with varying implications for different situations is warranted. This should not be taken as a great “gotcha!” moment by certain common lawyers. Yes, the respective international tribunal may well have conducted itself *anyway* in the “judge-made law” tradition of common law.[153] But here it is not absolutely clear as some might believe since the texts of the salient human rights instruments already authorise, through various “derogation” clauses, such a demarcation between the categories of rights sought to be vindicated.

We have studied the ECtHR text on property. In similar language, Article 14 of the African Charter on Human and Peoples’ Rights (ACHPR)[154] states: “The right to property shall be guaranteed. It may only be encroached upon in the interest of public need or in the general interest of the community and in accordance with the provisions of appropriate laws.” Contrast this with the unequivocal rejection of many kinds of status-based discrimination, for Article 2 of the African Charter states: “Every individual shall be entitled to the enjoyment of the rights and freedoms recognized and guaranteed in the present Charter without distinction of any kind such as race, ethnic group, color, sex, language, religion, political or any other opinion, national and social origin, fortune, birth or other status.”

Moreover, Article 21 (1) of the Inter-American Convention states: “Everyone has the right to the use and enjoyment of his property. The law may subordinate such use and enjoyment to the interest of society.”[155]

1975, Series A, No 18, at ¶ 36 (“This is not an extensive interpretation forcing new obligations on the Contracting States: it is based on the very terms of the first sentence of Article 6 para. 1”) with the resonance and self-confidence in *Société Colas Est and others v France*, Judgment of 16 April, 2002, at ¶ 41 (“Building on its dynamic interpretation of the Convention, the Court considers that the time has come to hold that in certain circumstances the rights guaranteed by Article 8 of the Convention may be construed as including the right to respect for a company's registered office, branches or other business premises”). This contrast and juxtaposition was brought to my attention via Fuad Zarbiyev’s prize-winning article, at 31-32, n. 189.

[153] O. W. Holmes & G E. White, THE COMMON LAW xxvii (Harvard University Press, 2009) (articulating “external” (including “prejudices,” “intuitions,” and “motives of public policy”) and “internal” factors).

[154] Adopted June 27, 1981, OAU Doc. CAB/LEG/67/3 rev. 5, 21 I.L.M. 58 (1982), *entered into force* Oct. 21, 1986.

[155] The rest of this Article states: “2. No one shall be deprived of his property except upon payment of just compensation, for reasons of public utility or social

Contrast *this* with the Inter-American Convention's utter prohibition on status-based discrimination: Article 1 (1) states that "The States Parties to this Convention undertake to respect the rights and freedoms recognized herein and to ensure to all persons subject to their jurisdiction the free and full exercise of those rights and freedoms, without any discrimination for reasons of race, color, sex, language, religion, political or other opinion, national or social origin, economic status, birth, or any other social condition." The reason for the difference in protecting property rights vis-à-vis status rights might be the mobility of property ownership in contrast with the immobility of race, sex, ethnicity, and national origin;[156] it might be the historical branding that attends some rights; or it might be something else.

Be that as it may, the key elements informing the tribunal analysis are the *treatment* to which the investor or owner was subject (interfering with her ownership or possession) and showing "likeness": this treatment was unreasonably different from those offered to others in comparable situations. The ECtHR has itself held that "Article 14 safeguards individuals, placed in similar situations, from any discrimination in the enjoyment of the rights and freedoms set forth in those other provisions."[157]

Using this prescription, the ECtHR sometimes turns down Article 1 expropriation claims while granting Article 14 discrimination claims.[158] Discrimination here is broader than in NT and MFN cases; presumably, the comparators and the bases for comparison can be everyone and anyone—domestic or international. The national identity of the comparator is irrelevant in the ECtHR, unlike in IIA-related NT and MFN cases. The international human rights systems' general prescription appears to be epitomised by an observation made by the Constitutional Court of South Africa: "It is only if there is a willingness to protect the

---

interest, and in the cases and according to the forms established by law. 3. Usury and any other form of exploitation of man by man shall be prohibited by law."

[156] *Sejdic and Finci v. Bosnia and Herzegovina*, Application nos. 27996/06 and 34836/06 (2009), at ¶ 43 ("Ethnicity and race are related concepts. Whereas the notion of race is rooted in the idea of biological classification of human beings into subspecies on the basis of morphological features such as skin colour or facial characteristics, ethnicity has its origin in the idea of societal groups marked in particular by common nationality, religious faith, shared language, or cultural and traditional origins and backgrounds. Discrimination on account of a person's ethnic origin is a form of racial discrimination . . .").

[157] *Inze v. Austria*, App. no. 8695/79, at p. 14 (1987).

[158] *Inze*, *supra* (legislation preferred legitimate children over illegitimate children in property inheritance); *Marckx v. Belgium*, App. no. 6833/74 (1979) (same).

worst and the weakest amongst us, that all of us can be secure that our own rights will be protected."[159]

Legislation on spatial planning, taxes and environmental protection may interfere with property rights.[160] These provisions normally make a distinction between different social and economic groups, occasionally on the ground of property. In *Pine Valley Developments Ltd. v. Ireland* (1991),[161] the applicants bought land and sought a planning permit to build warehouses and offices. Despite a 1982 law dictating that the permit should be granted, it was denied to this claimant (but granted to others) and the property's economic value diminished substantially.

The claimant alleged discrimination in comparison with other landowners. The Government had advanced no justification whatsoever for the differential treatment between claimant and those who had been granted permission—there being little doubt that claimant and these comparators were in the same category. We see how in *Pine Valley* the reliance (reasonable and legitimate expectations) factor, through the 1982 Act, is relevant. If the State had created a sure reliance, then its retrospectively repeal strengthens the argument that a violation happened. Although NAFTA has not yet faced any serious *force majeure* cases (it still might), which might adjust the "reasonableness" of the expectations, other IIA tribunals seem to have attempted to strike a fine balance.[162]

---

[159] *S v Makwanyane and Another* (CCT3/94) [1995] ZACC 3, at ¶ 88 (Chaskalson P); *id.*, at ¶ 156 (Ackermann J.) ("We have moved from a past characterised by much which was arbitrary and unequal in the operation of the law to a present and a future in a constitutional state where state action must be such that it is capable of being analysed and justified rationally. The idea of the constitutional state presupposes a system whose operation can be rationally tested against or in terms of the law. Arbitrariness, by its very nature, is dissonant with these core concepts of our new constitutional order. Neither arbitrary action nor laws or rules which are inherently arbitrary or must lead to arbitrary application can, in any real sense, be tested against the precepts or principles of the Constitution.").

[160] *Doran v. Ireland*, App. no. 50389/99 (2003); *Andrášik v. Slovakia*, App. nos. 57984/00, 60226/00, 60237/00, 60242/00, 60679/00, 60680/00 and 68563/01 (2002); *Di Sante v. Italy*, App. no 56079/00 (2004); *Giummarra v. France*, App. no. 61166/00 (2001); *Paulino Tomás v. Portugal*, App. no. 58698/00 (2003); *Johtti Sapmelaccat Ry v. Finland*, App. no. 42969/98 (2005).

[161] App. no. 43/1990.

[162] See *Enron Corporation and Ponderosa Assets, L.P. v. Argentina*, ICSID Case No. ARB/01/3 (2007), at ¶ 231-32 (referring to the Argentinean economic crisis and arguing that "just as it is not reasonable for the licensees to bear the entire burden of such changed reality neither would it be reasonable for them to believe that nothing happened in Argentina since the [investor's] License was approved").

Nonetheless, *Pine Valley* was also the case where the ECtHR held that environmental protection is "clearly a legitimate aim in accordance with the general interest" for Article 1.[163] This was inevitable because, as the next Chapter will show, the contagious, dispersing nature of environmental effects means *first* that government may intervene to protect public health and *then* skews the balance in favour of the central government.[164]

Another *Pine Valley* lesson is about the shifting burden of proof. In environmental cases (or cases with a possible environmental dimension), in the beginning the burden of proof is on the claimant; when the claimant *prima facie* meets that burden, the burden shifts to the respondent expropriator.[165] The respondent then loses if it cannot furnish a single justification for the discrimination.

Another discrimination case (on property grounds) is *Chassagnou v. France* (1999),[166] and undoubtedly is more challenging than *Pine Valley*. In *Chassagnou*, the French Republic had enacted a law requiring the owners of estates smaller than 20 hectares to transfer their hunting rights to hunting associations. The claimants, falling into this classification, argued that this was unlawful discrimination.

The ECtHR had ample discretion to construe the "likeness" factors. Were two small estates alike because they were estates or were they alike because they were small estates? Conversely, the same goes for large estates or mid-sized estates, and so on. The ECtHR held that the *effect* of the French legislation was that only small landowners were victimised in breach of Article 14 taken in conjunction with Article 1 of Protocol No. I.

We make four observations in total. The first three are: (*i*) Like the IUCT's model (indicating basically that evidence can show violation), the *Chassagnou* Court held that effect was enough even if the evidence proffered was not empirically dug up over years and a large number of cases; (*ii*) The ECtHR had a clear choice in how it applied the likeness test, whichever way it went the result would have been justifiable, and it

---

[163] *Pine Valley, supra*, at 32.

[164] See *Trail Smelter Arbitral Tribunal,* 33 A.J.I.L. 182, 331 (1939) ("no State has the right to use or *permit the use* of its territory in such a manner as to cause injury by fumes in or to the territory of another or the properties or persons therein, when the case is of serious consequence and the injury is established by clear and convincing evidence."); K. Harrison, PASSING THE BUCK: FEDERALISM AND CANADIAN ENVIRONMENTAL POLICY 44 (University of British Columbia Press, 1996).

[165] M. Goldhaber, A PEOPLE'S HISTORY OF THE EUROPEAN COURT OF HUMAN RIGHTS 80, 126 (Rutgers University Press, 2009).

[166] App. nos. 25088/94, 28331/95 and 28443/95.

may deliberately have chosen a pro-weaker party interpretation;[167] (*iii*) the Court's "in conjunction with" language. The twin relationship between Article 14 and Article 1[168] was summarized by the *Chassagnou* Court itself:

> Where a substantive article of the Convention has been invoked both on its own and together with Article 14 and a separate breach has been found of the substantive Article, it is not generally necessary for the Court to consider the case under Article 14 also, though the position is otherwise if a clear inequality of treatment in the enjoyment of the right in question is a fundamental aspect of the case.[169]

The *fourth* observation involves the usefulness of the legislation and its relationship to the regulatory purpose. The preamble to this Chapter has already observed that *de jure* differentiations which cause detriment to foreigners strengthen the case for unlawful discrimination. The same is true when there is "the possibility of alternative means achieving the same end."[170] Like the IUCT's regulatory purpose doctrine in non-discrimination, in the ECtHR too the respondent properly is given a chance to justify the measure by proving its (*i*) legitimate regulatory aim; and (*ii*) a strong nexus between the measure and the now-recognised legitimate objective ("reasonable relationship of proportionality between the means employed and the aim sought to be realised").[171] This is a point of knowledge-transfer from which most, if not all, international tribunals will benefit.

---

[167] Compare with *Krimstock v. Kelly*, 306 F.3d 40, 53-4 (2nd Cir. 2001) (opinion by Sotomayor, J.) (considering "*special* due process concerns" — "the only means to earn a livelihood," "temporal gap" between the seizure of the property and the proceeding, "the inability of innocent owners to challenge promptly," and the "inadequacy of other remedies" to decide that a quick hearing was needed) (emphasis added).

[168] R. H. Jackson, *The Task of Maintaining Our Liberties: The Role of the Judiciary*, 39 A.B.A.J. 961, 963 (1953) ("My equal right to drive an automobile may be only a claim to use of property, but it concerns my personal freedom as well.").

[169] *Chassagnou*, *supra,* at 21.

[170] *Sejdic and Finci v. Bosnia and Herzegovina*, Application nos. 27996/06 and 34836/06 (2009), at ¶ 48 (citing *Glor v. Switzerland*, Application no. 13444/04 (2009), at ¶ 94).

[171] *Van Raalte v. the Netherlands*, App. no. 20060/92, 186 (1997); *Darby v. Sweden*, Series A no. 187, p. 12 (1990). See *Trail Smelter Arbitral Tribunal,* 33 AM. J. INT'L L. 182 (1939), reprinted in R.M. Bratspies & R.A. Miller (Eds.) TRANSBOUNDARY HARM IN INTERNATIONAL LAW: LESSONS FROM THE TRAIL

As an important note, international human rights tribunals have yet to create a powerful "nexus" doctrine taking into account sovereignty or other non-regulatory purpose-related socioeconomic factors. In such cases, these tribunals should consider the WTO Appellate Body's analysis in *United States—Shrimp* (1998).[172] This case recognised a strong enough relationship (once it saw the "legitimacy" of the important public interest, in Philippe Sands' words)[173] between the import ban on shrimp that are caught without a turtle excluder device or TED (the objection) and protecting United States interests. In 1987, the United States enacted this regulation pursuant to the Endangered Species Act of 1973.[174]

The logic was that without this protection, foreign shrimp might migrate into United States waters and even harm sea turtles (irrespective of whether they are indigenous to the United States). The very reputation, existence and market value of those foreign States' properties were at stake. As were the United States' own environmental interests as well as its moral authority to influence, through soft power, the environmental practices of reluctant States.

Furthermore, the WTO Appellate Body in *United States-Shrimp* turned on its head a phrase employed by the panel—"a particular situation where a Member has taken unilateral measures which, by their nature, could put

---

SMELTER ARBITRATION 314 (Cambridge University Press, 2006) (known as *Trail Smelter I*).

[172] WT/DS58/AB/R (1998), at ¶ 33.

[173] P. Sands, "Environmental Protection in the Twenty-First Century: Sustainable Development in International Law" *in* R. Revesz, P. Sands & R. Stewart, ENVIRONMENTAL LAW, THE ECONOMY AND SUSTAINABLE DEVELOPMENT: THE UNITED STATES, THE EUROPEAN UNION AND THE INTERNATIONAL COMMUNITY 392 (Cambridge University Press, 2008) [P. Sands, "Environmental Protection in the Twenty-First Century"].

[174] *U.S.-Shrimp*, WT/DS58/AB/R (1998), at ¶ 3 ("Section 609(a) empowers the United States Secretary of State, upon consulting with the Secretary of Commerce, to 'initiate negotiations as soon as possible for the development of bilateral or multilateral agreements with other nations for the protection and conservation of … sea turtles' and to 'initiate negotiations as soon as possible with all foreign governments which are engaged in, or which have persons or companies engaged in, commercial fishing operations which, as determined by the Secretary of Commerce, may affect adversely such species of sea turtles, for the purpose of entering into bilateral and multilateral treaties with such countries to protect such species of sea turtles; … .' Section 609(b)(1) imposed, not later than 1 May 1991, an import ban on shrimp harvested with commercial fishing technology which may adversely affect sea turtles. Section 609(b)(2) provides that the import ban on shrimp will not apply to harvesting nations that are certified.").

the multilateral trading system at risk"[175]—to illustrate the high risk of environmental and political harm caused by a well-publicized episode of even *one* tainted shrimp entering the United States. Previously, floating proposals to resolve such problems have included "domestic solutions," including legislation, policy and litigation as well as "[i]nternational [l]awmaking [t]hrough [d]omestic [l]itigation."[176] Other than pre-emptive measures, not much can be done by way of recovery after the injury takes place.[177] As far as *post*-injury remedies are concerned, even the loosest interpretations of causation (specifically, culprit-identification) often do not suffice.

Under *Corfu Channel*, State A could insist on obligating other States to not knowingly injure A under the doctrine of *sic utere tuo ut alienum non laedas*. Despite the obvious differences between the international human rights tribunals and the GATT/WTO system (most obvious being the different investment-trade regime goals), international human rights tribunals might find some of the factors underlying the *United States—Shrimp* analysis helpful.[178] So might international investment tribunals, despite the well-articulated concerns that international investment law and international trade law are fundamentally different.[179]

---

[175] *Id.*, at ¶ 115 (citing Panel Report, at ¶ 7.60).

[176] S. Hsu & J. Parrish, *Litigating Canada-U.S. Transboundary Harm: International Environmental Lawmaking and the Threat of Extraterritorial Reciprocity*, 48 VA. J.I.L. 1, 2, 32 *et seq.* (2007) [S. Hsu & J. Parrish, *Litigating Canada-U.S. Transboundary Harm*].

[177] *Id.*, at 39-40 (2007) ("Historically, if a plaintiff was able to navigate the various jurisdictional barriers to suit, proving that the defendant caused the transboundary harm was another challenge. The common law was not receptive to recovery when several possible defendants existed, let alone thousands. Where a discrete and identifiable source of pollution from a single defendant imposed measurable harm, an action in nuisance would lie to abate the environmental harm, or, in a modern case, provide for a damages remedy. But modern pollution problems involving less discernible pollutants from multiple sources—such as the SO_2, VOC_s, NO_x, and $PM_{2.5}$ that literally millions of polluters emit—are ill-fitted for traditional tort remedies.") (internal footnotes omitted). For a detailed discussion of extraterritorial jurisdiction under international law, see U.N. Int'l Law Comm'n, Report of the International Law Commission, 58th Session, Annex E – Extraterritorial Jurisdiction 516, U.N. Doc. A/61/10 (2006). There is no apparent reason that this principle concerning air pollutants would not transfer over to sea turtles and water pollution.

[178] P. Sands, "Environmental Protection in the Twenty-First Century," *supra*, at 388-91.

[179] But see K. Claussen, *Comment: The Casualty of Investor Protection in Times of Economic Crisis*, *supra*, at 1546 (stating that "while the language of . . . [certain

After all, the chief purpose of IIA's is to "stimulat[ing] the flow of private capital and the economic development of the Parties," whereas the primary purpose of the GATT is to promote "reciprocal and mutually advantageous arrangements directed to the substantial reduction of tariffs and other barriers to trade and to the elimination of discriminatory treatment in international commerce."[180] Undoubtedly, in an IIA case it is the VCLT that supersedes in importance any WTO/GATT reliance. Several additional factors separate international trade law from international investment law. First, the former is more concerned with classes of traders and merchants while the latter is concerned with the individual investor, thus explaining the reason that in the former it is still very much a diplomatic protection regime where one State sues another. Second, "the WTO is designed to address obligations between and among many states, to keep the playing field even in their trade policies toward one another" while "the international investment legal regime protects the relationship between a state and a private investor."[181] In fact, attempting to "[a]ppl[y] the WTO necessity doctrine by way of analogizing to WTO case law ignores this distinction in these two relationships."[182]

Third, "one purpose of international investment law is to induce investment by assuring investors that sunk-cost projects will be subject to special protection but trade law is not at all concerned with compensating the investor."[183] Fourth, "regarding remedies, no damages are paid in trade

---

IIA's] may be similar to language in trade texts, investment law and trade law have evolved separately from one another since that language was first used. Therefore, neither body of law is germane in interpreting the other. [Moreover], the two bodies of law cannot be compared because they are distinct practice areas, each with its own purposes. Textual parallels they may share are not appropriate tools for interpretation."); *id.* (observing that "[r]ather than applying principles from international investment law, . . . [some] tribunal[s]," such as the tribunal in *Continental Casualty Co. v. Argentine Republic*, ICSID (W. Bank) Case No. ARB/03/9 (Sept. 5, 2008), have been known to "appl[y] principles of international trade law in interpreting the treaty to reach its conclusion.").

180 K. Claussen, *Comment: The Casualty of Investor Protection in Times of Economic Crisis*, *supra*, at 1550-51. Kathleen Claussen draws our attention to the the WTO Appellate Body's decision in Appellate Body Report, *European Communities—Measures Affecting Asbestos and Asbestos-Containing Products*, WT/DS135/AB/R (Apr. 5, 2001). This case defined "necessity" with respect to the consequences that measures adopted by one sovereign would have on the flow of goods. *Id.*, at ¶ 172.

181 *Id.*

182 *Id.*

183 *Id.*

law. When found to be in breach of the GATT by the WTO's Dispute Settlement Body, a state incurs restrictions on trade." [184] However, "[i]nvestments . . . are governed by bilateral treaties requiring that compensation be paid to a private investor."[185] This last point constitutes a tangible difference, for such "alternate remedies may incentivize states to act differently and consider that which is 'necessary' in trade interactions to be altogether distinct from that which is 'necessary' in the context of investment relationships."[186] The comparative guidance is certainly not mandatory for either area of law but it simply is a constructive source of helpful premises even if the assumptions (and thus potentially the deductions) might be different.[187]

It could be articulately argued that when a State's own conduct even in part induces or produces its repositioning on the very brink of economic or security collapse, the expropriation conducted by the State is compensable for the IIA-centric purpose of protecting investor rights has gone dishonoured.[188] The justification would basically be a variation on the *ex turpi causa non oritur actio* doctrine, indicating that the defendant cannot preclude claimant's arguments for relief by asserting its own past errors as a defence (modifying the subject from the claimant to the respondent-sovereign).

Considering that even in a GATT/WTO case (and thus obviously inter-State) such as *United States – Shrimp* where two (or more) sovereign interests brushed up against each other, the right to self-defence and the right against suffering a "knowing" injury were recognised as supreme. Consequently, the *a fortiori* argument could be advanced that surely when only one of the parties is a State in such a situation and efforts to find perfect tailoring have either failed or are bound to be futile, the Sovereign

---

[184] *Id.*

[185] *Id.*

[186] *Id.*

[187] *Id.*; *Continental Casualty Co., supra*, at ¶ 192 ("Since the text of Art. XI derives from the parallel model clause of the U.S. FCN treaties and these treaties in turn reflect the formulation of Art. XX of GATT 1947, the Tribunal finds it more appropriate to refer to the GATT and WTO case law which has extensively dealt with the concept and requirements of necessity in the context of economic measures derogating to the obligations contained in GATT, rather than to refer to the requirement of necessity under customary international law.").

[188] *Id.*, at 1550-51. *Continental Casualty Co., supra,* is the anomaly among the cases in point. In the requests for arbitration filed against Argentina, due to its enactment of the Emergency Law devaluing the peso with tremendous alacrity, only in *Continental Casualty* did the sovereign prevail essentially because of its "necessity" defence.

has significant leeway in pursuing policies that are over-inclusive and/or under-inclusive.[189]

Returning to *Chassagnou*, it should be mentioned that Judge Caflisch's separate concurring opinion there first recognised the two-prong "aims and effects" nexus test and subsequently pointed out France's self-contradictory position. Simply put, Judge Caflisch's punctiliously detailed opinion pointed out the weakness of the French Republic's rationale:

> The Government have not shown that the discrimination imposed is even useful for the purpose of achieving the aim pursued. On the contrary. The French parliament requires small landowners to make considerable sacrifices, which they can avoid only with great difficulty. On the other hand, it leaves it up to large landowners to preserve game stocks on their own land without restricting their property rights in any way (Article L. 222-14 of the Countryside Code); the duties it imposes on them are both undemanding and vague, a fact which, moreover, casts doubt on the effectiveness of the Law as a whole. What is more, it is hard to see how and why landholdings larger than 20 hectares in area could be effectively managed by their owners whereas the opposite is true of smaller areas. It is therefore difficult to argue that there is a reasonable relationship of proportionality in a situation where considerable sacrifices are imposed on some landowners but not on others, especially when the discriminatory system thus established is not, in the final analysis, as effective as desired.[190]

Judge Caflisch's rather scintillating closing act also had a policy suggestion under the guise of (and along with) conforming to the Convention:

---

[189] C. D. Cunningham, "Affirmative Action: Comparative Policies and Controversies,"*in* INTERNATIONAL ENCYCLOPEDIA OF THE SOCIAL AND BEHAVIORAL SCIENCES 212 (Neil J. Smelser & Paul B. Baltes eds., Elsevier, 2002) ("In contrast to India, affirmative action programs in the US have not used consistent criteria for defining group boundaries or for selecting eligible groups. For example, one US federal court struck down a law school admission program at the University of Texas, in part because only blacks and Mexican Americans were eligible for affirmative action consideration; Hispanic Americans, Asian Americans and Native Americans were excluded (Hopwood v. State of Texas, [78 F.3d 932 (5th Cir. 1996)]). Many people who oppose affirmative action programs in the United States because they use racial categories such as black, African American, or Latino claim that equally effective and more equitable programs can be developed using only class categories, such as low-income . . . .").

[190] *Chassagnou*, *supra*, at 24.

> The [French] system would perhaps work better if it were applicable to all owners, large and small, and if its geographical scope were more extensive. In the absence of a reasonable relationship of proportionality between the aim pursued and the discriminatory mechanism instituted by the Loi Verdeille, one should conclude, as the Court has done, that there has been a violation of Article 1 of Protocol No. 1 taken together with Article 14 of the Convention.[191]

In finding a violation, Judge Caflisch, like the Grand Chamber itself (though Judge Caflisch's explanation above is arguably more complete), did much more than require a "legitimate aim" and proportionality. Judge Caflisch reached deep into the facts of the case and text of the French legislation to dissect, and ultimately reject, the nub of the French government's argument (colloquially speaking, "spin"). This new judicial pronouncement undoubtedly was more stringent than a "reasonable relationship" (or "rational basis") test.

Tacitly, the Grand Chamber established "heightened scrutiny"[192] for discrimination against the disadvantaged party when the alleged discriminatory bases concern certain groupings. To international human rights tribunals, protected groups include migrants, vilified racial and religious minorities, and other actors lacking clout and/or retaining vestiges of stigma[193] — in short, "those who are disadvantaged in the

---

[191] *Id.* The good judge is a distinguished jurist, and he is not known for playing games or chicanery. Nonetheless, this "work better" language resembles extra-constitutional policy concern, for the wisdom of laws typically are not the province of judges — only the lawfulness is.

[192] This is a well-known test in the United States, and a measure must have an exceedingly persuasive justification and be narrowly tailored to meet this end in order to pass scrutiny. See *United States v. Virginia*, 518 U.S. 515 (1996), and cases cited therein.

[193] See, *e.g.*, Joint Statement by UN Experts, the IACHR [Inter-American Commission on Human Rights] Rapporteur on the Rights of Migrants and the ACHPR [African Commission on Human and Peoples' Rights] Special Rapporteur on Refugees, Asylum Seekers, Internally Displaced Persons and Migrants (press release), African Commission on Human and Peoples' Rights, December 19, 2012, available at <www.achpr.org/press/2012/12/d139/> ("Respect for the right to liberty and security of person implies that liberty is the rule and detention, the exception. States have the obligation to establish a presumption in favor of liberty in domestic law. The automatic, mandatory or punitive use of migrant detention not only violates migrants' right to liberty, but also affects *others of their human rights.*") (emphasis added); *Minersville School Dist. v. Gobitis*, 310 U.S. 586, 606 (1940) (Stone, J., dissenting) (intolerable will be "the surrender of the [legal] protection of the liberty of small minorities to the popular will. We have previously

struggle for existence."[194] These are bases upon which individuals might claim that customary international law entitles them to the special solicitude of the courts.[195] Individuals or groups craving this judicial recognition need to strike the right balance of having just enough political power of being a cognisable group but not having so much political power that tribunals decide to expend their capital elsewhere. This Zero-Sum Game also highlights the competition *among* disadvantaged groups to earn this political power or alternatively judicial solicitude. International human rights tribunals have not taken this step for litigants of a non-disadvantaged status.[196]

The ECtHR has thus been the most pioneering in saying explicitly that there needs to be a weighing of the public interest and the governmental measure, though the next Chapter will show that the IIA tribunals too have adopted this approach. Perhaps tribunals do not want to value the merit of

---

pointed to the importance of a searching judicial inquiry into the legislative judgment in situations where prejudice against discrete and insular minorities may tend to curtail the operation of those political processes ordinarily to be relied on to protect minorities.") (*Gobitis* was overruled and Justice Stone's dissent resurrected in *West Virginia State Board of Education v. Barnette*, 319 U.S. 624 (1943)).

[194] R. H. Jackson, *The Federal Prosecutor, supra,* at 19.

[195] This invites a paradox because, quite simply, a group must be quite possessed of political power to have its case litigated, an expensive and draining process, before international tribunals will deem that group to be "powerless." The Catch-22 is that if a group has no political power then it also might not have a significant and distinct identity — it should surprise no one to learn of this correlation — and on the other hand if it has a great deal of political power and simply wants ratification of its group status, then the courts might refuse them this special solicitude. The legislature, the courts will say, are there to receive these groups with open arms.

[196] Even in the corporate *Yukos* case, where the property rights claim won, this was very much on procedural grounds. See *Yukos Oil Co. v. Russian Federation*, App. no. 14902/04 (2012), at ¶ 657 ("On the whole, given the [exceedingly rapid] pace of the enforcement proceedings, the obligation to pay the full enforcement fee and the authorities' failure to take proper account of the consequences of their actions, the Court finds that the domestic authorities failed to strike a fair balance between the legitimate aims sought and the measures employed.");¶ 652 ("[N]either the seizure order of 14 July 2004, which set in motion the process of auctioning OAO Yuganskneftegaz . . . , nor any of the subsequent decisions, including the judicial decisions in the context of the company's complaints against the actions of the bailiffs . . . , mentioned or discussed in any detail possible alternative methods of enforcement and the consequences that they might have on the future of the company.").

a public-interest determination made by the government,[197] though they are already weighing the public interest with the right asserted. A minor public interest (not difficult to divine, even if it is manufactured or fabricated *after* the expropriation) may well weigh heavier on the scales of efficiency, cost, reliance and fairness than a property right to a disadvantaged party—a category towards which, we have noted, the international human rights tribunals tend to show solicitude.[198]

More candid judicial and academic scholarship is needed in this area (including in our institutions), least of all because the public might attribute to the tribunals an inclination to decide cases on bases not openly articulated or acknowledged. That would add unnecessary confusion and scuttle public confidence in the tribunals. In the next section (NAFTA and IIA), we will look into the standard of scrutiny that property-expropriating and investment-restrictive measures have to satisfy in non-discrimination challenges.

§ 5.4—Non-Discrimination Before the NAFTA and the IIA Tribunals

Non-discrimination prohibits measures which differentiate *de jure* on the basis of nationality[199] and also measures which differentiate *de facto*—but only on the basis of the nationality of claimants (unlike the ECtHR's broader scope). Non-discrimination in international investment law has a

---

[197] N. Diebold, *Non-Discrimination and the Pillars, supra*, at 21 ("the adjudicating bodies need to have the authority to evaluate the objective value or importance of the allegedly protected public interest. This may be a difficult task as it entails to second guess the national values of sovereign contracting parties with different institutional, political or religious traditions."); M. Scherer & G. Born, *Bridging Cultural Gaps*, *supra*, at 7.

[198] *Id.*, at 23 ("the protection of a minor public interest may reinforce the conclusion that a measure is not discriminatory in cases where the measure differentiates *de facto* between remotely competing market entities and has a low qualitative and quantitative effect on foreign entities. Conversely, a universally very important public interest, such as human life and health, may be used to justify measures which differentiate on a formal basis or between strongly competing market entities to the detriment of predominantly foreign entities.").

[199] If one reads Articles 1102 (NT) and 1103 (MFN) in a vacuum, one could argue that these provisions do not say what the basis for the discrimination is, so long as investors of protected nationalities *are* discriminated against. But this hyper-textual interpretation has not prevailed — the necessary assumption is that text, distinct from context, matters a great deal — and does not even appear to be a possibility in the near future, so we will work with the prevailing interpretation.

distinct meaning not shared by human rights: though in both systems, claimants circumvent their home States (and exercise direct standing), before an investment tribunal the claimant's status is still very much bound up in its nationality.[200]

Exceptions and the "Necessity" Test

The difficulty will not me offend.
For I perceive the way to life lies here.
Come, pluck up, heart; let's neither faint nor fear.
Better, though difficult, the right way to go,
Than wrong, though easy, where the end is woe.

— John Bunyan, *The Pilgrim's Progress*

Before we address the non-discrimination test that NAFTA uses, let us understand *what* the IIA purportedly leaves intact and *why* it is not so simple. These exceptions (and their connection to the "necessity" test, explained soon) are inextricably connected with non-discrimination and substantive standards claims brought under the relevant IIA. In conducting what is inevitably a sensitivity analysis, it must be remembered (and contextualised) that "[t]he ultimate goal of the harmonization of . . . measures is to prevent the use of such measures for arbitrary or unjustifiable discrimination between Members or as a disguised restriction on international trade . . . [or investment], without preventing Members from adopting or enforcing measures which are both 'necessary to protect' human life or health and 'based on scientific principles', and without requiring them to change their appropriate level of protection."[201]

NAFTA, for one, stipulates that its provisions should not prevent a signatory from "providing a service or performing a function" in the following categories: environmental measures,[202] "law enforcement, correctional services, income security or insurance, social security or

---

[200] G. De Búrca, "Unpacking the Concept of Discrimination in EC and International Trade Law," *in* C. Barnard & J. Scott (eds), THE LAW OF THE SINGLE EUROPEAN MARKET: UNPACKING THE PREMISES 181 (2002); see also N. Diebold, *Non-Discrimination and the Pillars, supra*, at 24 (arguing that one reason for fragmentation in applying the non-discrimination principle, in cases where "the factual and economic settings" are thoroughly different, is "pure arbitrariness.").

[201] *EC-Hormones*, WT/DS26/AB/R, WT/DS48/AB/R, at ¶ 177 (1998).

[202] Art. 1114, NAFTA.

insurance, social welfare, public education, public training, health, and child care."[203] This sounds generous but there is a caveat.

First, it is an almost uniformly accepted principle of international law (and perhaps of judicial construction anywhere) that exceptions cannot swallow the rule. Furthermore, "the prevention of 'abuse of the exceptions'" is a fundamental goal of construction.[204] Second, just because a State may *provide* a service does not mean it can do so discriminatorily or in violation of due process, fair and equitable treatment or minimum standards, IIA awards have maintained (as this Section and the next Chapter will show). Thus the service guarantees in Articles 1101 and 1114 belabour what is already implied, perhaps to make doubly, or perhaps exponentially, certain that tribunals do not overreach into these protected carve-out fields. The WTO Appellate Body, for its part, has focused on context, object and purpose in making these evaluations.[205] It has stated that "[t]he general design of a measure, as distinguished from its application, is . . . to be examined in the course of determining whether that measure falls within one or another of the paragraphs [containing the exemptions]."[206]

Many IIA's contain a "necessary to" clause, and thus IIA tribunals have to answer the "necessity" question. Especially regarding NAFTA's environmental exception, the necessity test looms large. Language such as "necessary to secure compliance with laws and regulations . . . [otherwise consistent] with [Chapter Eleven]," "necessary to protect human, animal or plant life or health" and "[to] conserv[e] . . . living or non-living exhaustible natural resources,"[207] raises more questions than it answers: Is this expropriation "necessary to" the government's achieving some legitimate regulatory purpose? Achieving *what* degree of success in the regulatory aim is "necessary"? How broadly should each of these exceptions (or *chapeaux*) be construed? Which interpretive philosophies should govern?

In some quarters, the operative term "necessary" is contextualized by the caveat that a Condition A might be necessary for the success of a Condition B without A being necessary for the very existence of B. Others counter by suggesting that because this caveat would fundamentally change the relationship between A and B, it is over-broad to fit the label "necessary." According to this school, "essential" states an absolute *sine*

---

[203] Art. 1101, NAFTA.

[204] See, *e.g.*, *United States-Gasoline*, WT/DS2/AB/R, p. 22.

[205] *U.S.-Shrimp*, WT/DS58/AB/R (1998), at ¶ 116.

[206] *Id.*, at ¶ 115.

[207] Art. 1106 (6), NAFTA.

qua non whereas the looser term "necessary" requires only that the measure be narrowly tailored to the aim or purpose, provided the latter is legitimate.

The most commonly used (and highly sophisticated) necessity test comes from GATT/WTO, not the IIA universe. Although trade and investment policies focus on different goals—"*liberalization* of trade flows, in the case of trade, and *protection* and *promotion* of foreign investment, in the case of investment"[208]—some aspects of the necessity test carry over.[209]

Another consideration that carries over is the danger in "selective incentives" and "add-ons" (reinterpretations), as "they [may] skew an otherwise symmetrical system of reciprocal rights and obligations."[210] Instead, one scholar suggests that the "credibility of multilateral agreements" might be better-served if drafters and tribunals "start . . . with an asymmetrical regime that does not even pretend to treat states equally, and instead differentiates treaty obligations according to each party's special circumstances."[211] Try as some jurists might, they cannot refute that there is indeed some, though by no means overwhelming, support for this "special and differentiated treatment" proposition.[212] This might be regarded, at least potentially, as the IUCT and ECtHR approach.

---

[208] N. DiMascio & J. Pauwelyn, *Nondiscrimination in Trade and Investment Treaties*, *supra*, at 54 (stating that "the trade regime is about overall welfare, efficiency, liberalization, state-to-state exchanges of market access, and trade opportunities — not individual rights.") (emphases preserved); T. Waelde & A. Kolo, *Environmental Regulation, Investment Protection and 'Regulatory Taking' in International Law*, 50 INT. & COMP L.Q. 811 , 836 n. 112 (2001) ("A foreign investor, [unlike a foreign trader], is heavily exposed for the long-term to significant political and now regulatory risk, both in developing and developed countries.").

[209] D. T. Blackmore, *Eradicating the Long Standing Existence of a No-Precedent Rule in International*
Trade Law — Looking Toward Stare Decisis *in WTO Dispute Settlement*, 29 N.C. J. INT'L L. & COM. REG. 487, 512–14 (2004) (stating the usefulness of WTO decisions) (emphasis in original); J. Bacchus, *Groping Toward Grotius*, 44 HARV. INT'L L.J. 533, 540 (2003) ("As we said in the very first ruling of the WTO Appellate Body, WTO rules cannot be viewed in 'clinical isolation' from the broader corpus of international law.").

[210] P. H. Sand, *Lessons Learned, supra,* at 224.

[211] *Id.*

[212] The ACIA, which states the socioeconomic development of a country to be the primary objective of IIA (this assumption cannot be ignored), 'recognis[es] the different levels of development within ASEAN, especially the least developed Member States which require some flexibility including special and differential

It does not take a soothsayer to make a common-sense inference: Over the next few decades the consent function might adjust this chessboard. This attitude is, however, in serious tension with the IIA no-special-treatment attitude, so how its future plays out in IIA's will be interesting to observe. Today's detractors might become tomorrow's defenders if it appears that, in a landscape where developing countries have lost the incentive to maintain their presence, "special and differentiated treatment" is the necessary evil which keeps them there.

Amending the treaty text has not proven to be an effective remedy, in the long- or short-terms. First, "amending treaties is often costly and time-consuming, especially where the treaty, like the Energy Charter Treaty, is broadly multilateral."[213] Moreover, "attempt[s] to 'fix' [the IIA's] regulatory takings problem is indicative of the inherent difficulties that states have in clarifying contested [IIA] concepts via better treaty text."[214] The reason

---

treatment.' See Article 17, ASEAN Comprehensive Investment Agreement (1998), available at <www.asean.org/documents/FINAL-SIGNED-ACIA.pdf>, at paragraph 2. The ACIA also contains a Special and Differential Treatment clause offering "technical assistance and commitments to newer ASEAN Member States in accordance with their individual stage of development." See R. Moloo and J. Chao, *International Investment Law and Sustainable Development: Bridging the Divide*, pp. 15-16 (2011) (unpublished paper on file with the author) ("While the ACIA does not make clear the meaning of 'Special and Differentiated Treatment', we may glean the basis of this concept from its use in the international trade arena, where developing countries have demanded a global recognition that binding multilateral agreements amongst states of such diverse economic statuses, which demand the same amount of liberalization along the same timetables, could be counterproductive to their development."). It seems important to highlight this general commitment by ACIA to catering to its Member States's varying stages of development: "It is recognized that particular pressures on the balance of payments of a Member State in the process of economic development may necessitate the use of restrictions to ensure, inter alia, the maintenance of a level of financial reserves adequate for the implementation of its program of economic development." See Article 16 (Measures to Safeguard the Balance of Payments), ASEAN Comprehensive Investment Agreement (1998).

213 J. W. Yackee, *Controlling the International Investment Law Agency*, 53 HARV. INT'L L. J. 391, 416-425-26 (2012).

214 *Id.*; see also Marc R. Poirier, *The NAFTA Chapter 11 Expropriation Debate Through the Eyes of a Property Theorist,* 33 ENVT'L L. 851, 904 (2003) ("we do have an international legal standard for regulatory takings. We just do not know what it means. The problem cannot be escaped by giving up on current international law and setting out to draft a clearer treaty provision. 'Attempts to restate regulatory takings doctrine in clearer form — whether of the distillation or

simply is that superior treaty texts, as much as they foreclose some problems, they open up others—largely because imaginative counsel deliver contradistinction-based argumentation, arguing primarily that Situation A (in the treaty text) used a particularly emphatic linchpin phrase to warrant an unfavourable result, whereas Situation B (their case) does not.

Back to the GATT/WTO "aims and effects" test: It balances several factors, namely (*i*) the relative importance of the public interest; (*ii*) how the measure promotes the regulatory purpose and the public interest; (*iii*) the effect of the measure on the aims of the institution itself; and (*iv*) if less drastic and equally or more effective alternatives are available.[215] From an FDI or trade attraction standpoint, some emerging IIA's (especially starting in the 1990's), including the NAFTA, maintain predictability by "covering all sectors" (in the pre-establishment phase, unless indicated otherwise in the annex) as well as "providing clarity as to which non-conforming restrictions are maintained or can be introduced."[216] Moreover, "unilateral liberalization after the entry into force of the treaty is automatically bound at these lower levels of restrictiveness, meaning that going back to previously maintained restrictions is not possible."[217]

The NAFTA tribunal in *Pope & Talbot v. Canada* (2000)[218] accepted Canada's position and decided that "circumstances" had to be construed

---

"start over" variety — sooner or later almost always rely on terms or procedures that reinsert vagueness into the formulation.'").

[215] WTO Appellate Body Reports, *Korea – Measures Affecting Imports of Fresh, Chilled and Frozen Beef*, WT/DS161/AB/R, WT/DS169/AB/R (2001), at ¶ 164; *United States – Measures Affecting the Cross-Border Supply of Gambling and Betting Services*, WT/DS285/AB/R (2005), at ¶ 306; *Dominican Republic – Measures Affecting the Importation and Internal Sale of Cigarettes*, WT/DS302/AB/R (2005), at ¶ 70.

[216] A. Berger, et al., "Do Trade and Investment Agreements Lead to More FDI? Accounting for Key Provisions Inside the Black Box," Working Paper, WTO (2010),
available at <www.wto.org/english/res_e/reser_e/ersd201013_e.pdf>, at p. 6; *id.*, at 18 (while "liberal admission rules promote bilateral FDI," IIA's "offering nothing specific to foreign investors, in terms of liberal admission or effective dispute settlement, leave bilateral FDI unaffected or even induce a substitution of source").

[217] *Id.*

[218] *Pope & Talbot v. Canada*, NAFTA/UNCITRAL, Canada's First Phase Counter-Memorial (2000), at ¶¶ 185-97.

broadly[219]—a stance that governments are bound to like. *Pope & Talbot* also recognised that States can come up with "some rational justification" for the differentiation without trying too hard, so the scrutiny needs to smoke out the biases.[220] On the other hand, "justifications" too elaborate may also be invented and inauthentic.

This test does not tell us which factors are necessary, which are sufficient, and their relative weights.[221] Flawed or not, it is making a reappearance in recent IIA cases.[222] Elaborating on the WTO relevancy in the IIA context, some academic criticism attends "not [an IIA tribunal's] misreading of GATT/WTO law but its failure to consider the division of labour between Fair and Equitable Treatment and National Treatment obligations, as developed by recent investment law jurisprudence, in ensuring that *generally* investors are not worse-treated than domestic actors."[223] Assuming, though, that both FET and NT claims are put forth, the tribunal's analysis might be confusing but it will not necessarily be wrong.

The second and perhaps more meritorious criticism is that understanding and applying the competition factor[224]—competition with investors from other nations and with those from the home State—is a WTO-NAFTA/IIA-international human rights tribunal transferable tool. Another transferrable tool is the goods/services distinction that allows WTO panels and appellate bodies some flexibility not usually assumed by IIA tribunals. A similar distinction between expropriation of real or other property and investments vis-à-vis market share or access might deliver greater clarity.[225] Since the IIA's themselves often do not contain this distinction, tribunals have not candidly acknowledged its implications.

Nicolas Diebold defends the test, in the trade *as well as* IIA contexts, as freeing "the arbitral tribunals" from applying "a specific threshold, such as 'necessary' or 'related to.'"[226] Diebold also appreciates that the test

---

219 The tribunal rejected the claimant's argument that the test was met if claimant produced like products or services as the comparators. *Pope & Talbot v. Canada*, NAFTA/UNCITRAL, Investor's First Phase Memorial (2000), at ¶¶ 63-72.

220 *Pope & Talbot v. Canada, supra*, at ¶¶ 80-81.

221 The confusion was highlighted clearly in a case, *Occidental Exploration and Prod. Co. v. Ecuador*, UNICTRAL, Final Award (2004), at ¶¶ 176-78.

222 N. DiMascio & J. Pauwelyn, *Nondiscrimination in Trade and Investment Treaties, supra*, at 65.

223 R. Howse & E. Chalamish, *Use and Abuse of WTO Law in ITA, supra,* at 1102.

224 *Id.*, at 1115.

225 E. Chalamish, *The Future of BITs, supra,* at 219.

226 N. Diebold, *Non-Discrimination and the Pillars, supra,* at 23.

"would add the extent to which the measure contributes to the protection of the policy objective as an additional factor to the overall analysis."[227] Although Diebold's second point is superb, the first one largely misses this author's argument. Bringing in the factor-based approach invites a greater problem: it would add tremendous arbitrariness (especially in non-precedential systems like IIA's) while doing away with rigidness. Some experts might deem Diebold's Pincer movement-like approach to be penny-wise and pound-foolish in its flexibility and uniformity trade-off strategy. The effort to find an effective medium should go on.

Certain factors "necessary" to the finding of a violation are injury visited upon the claimant or close threat of an injury; intent *or* pattern of effect in situations where the State has the duty to appreciate that only marginal cost on its part is required to rectify the violation; and of course actual disparate effect or the proximate threat thereof. Other than the complex obvious factors it is difficult to justify any one factor as "sufficient." It should be said though that if disparate impact *and* disparate effect are demonstrated along with likeness, that generally comes within striking distance of being quite sufficient, provided the State fails to make an overpowering showing of a compelling governmental interest—goals not just approximately necessary in some situations but absolutely essential for the success of the State's sovereign mission.

Perhaps in some contexts tribunals will find positive discrimination or the inclusion of certain historically and presently disadvantaged groups or the evening out of opportunities to be such compelling interests. It is deemed to be legally acceptable to protect, for a time, such groups without over- or under-generalization whom the "infernal laws" and conditions "of . . . [disadvantage] have prevented . . . from acquiring an education, understanding the . . . laws of contract, or of managing the ordinary business of life."[228] However, when the preferences become stereotypical and over-generalised, thus irrational—in short, no longer "fitted for purpose" and left to continue solely or largely to cater to special interests (or to ingratiate the authorities with the special interests)—the very identity of the injured party is understood to alter. It is important to remember that while the comparator or likeness analysis is class-based, the

---

[227] *Id.*

[228] THE AMERICAN ANNUAL CYCLOPÆDIA AND REGISTER OF IMPORTANT EVENTS 142 (D. Appleton, 1867) (Speech by Rep. Thaddeus Stevens, of Pennsylvania, on the floor of the House of Representatives, December 18, 1865).

injured claimant's claim is always staked in their capacity as an *individual* or as representing *individuals*.[229]

Faithful to the largely co-extensive stipulations of both most IIA's (including NAFTA Chapter Eleven) and the GATT text was the Appellate Body's *United States—Malt Beverages* decision: interpreting the clause that regulatory measures "should not be applied . . . so as to afford protection to domestic production," the Appellate Body held that "legitimacy of . . . regulations should be determined primarily on the basis of their purpose and their market effects, *i.e.*, whether they have a *bona fide* regulatory purpose and whether their effect on conditions of competition is to create a protective advantage in favor of domestic products."[230] This analysis across our institutions could be informed by protectionist *versus* non-protectionist purpose or effect, social welfare policy, and even revenue-collection.

Consider a simple example. A government wants to expropriate a private entity's 5000-acre plot of land for an essential plant to pump out pollutants in the water (public purpose met). When government could conduct this project in 20 years and could instead take just 1000 acres and perform the project in 30 years, is the former "necessary"? If we choose the 1000 acres/30 years option, what marginal costs would be incurred (on top of the 5000 acres/20 years option)? This requires case-by-case inquiries, and that what goes into that inquiry needs structure and methodology.[231]

---

[229] Questions of affirmative action or preferential policies— class- or group-based anti-subordination principle cases — may well arise before international tribunals, as they have before domestic tribunals. In such situations, the complex principles of individualism, anti-subordination, inclusiveness, past *versus* present discrimination, and socioeconomic disadvantage come into play. See, *e.g.*, C. D. Cunningham, "Affirmative Action: Comparative Policies and Controversies," *supra,* at 211 ("These Israeli [preferential] programs [benefiting the Sephardim] do not aim to combat current discrimination or to compensate for past discrimination. There is no history of Ashkenazi dominance and exploitation of the Sephardim comparable to the treatment of African-Americans in the US or the lower castes in India. Rather the programs have been justified in terms similar to the current constitutional discourse in India, recognizing that the combination of initial socioeconomic disadvantage with the continuing influence of informal networks would perpetuate a society divided along the Sephardi-Ashkenazi line, thus requiring affirmative action to counteract these social forces.").

[230] GATT B.I.S.D. (39th Supp.) at 208 (1993), at ¶ 5.

[231] Some scholars think of "necessity" as a stand-alone standard while others consider it part of non-discrimination. There already is good scholarship available

One advantage the GATT/WTO necessity test has going for it is point (*iii*): the effect of the measure on the aims of the institution itself. Earlier in this Chapter we have already discussed the IUCT's and the ECtHR's focus on either promoting settlement without needless hassle or promoting human rights. Notably, in Judge Caflisch's *Chassagnou* opinion (in the ECtHR) we saw a vivid demonstration of an international tribunal scrutinising to see if the measure met *the government's own* purported public purpose as well as the tribunal's. This internal coherency test sometimes is, and some would have it always be considered, built into the *rationality* criterion. [232] Despite an intrinsic appeal of the internal coherency test, it suffers from a fundamental flaw: the tribunal's task is to ascertain whether the asserted justification is consistent with *a* legitimate public purpose, not necessarily the one that is offered by the government. This makes the task harder but also more faithful to logic and reason, not to mention to the institutional interests of international law.

Some international and domestic tribunals have used the *rationality* criterion (typically the bare-minimum requirement for a measure to satisfy) to expand the law without openly saying so. If the tribunal sees that the timing or the facts are just not ideal for a bold pronouncement, it has the option of formally leaving the doctrinal framework intact but fleshing out the contents in a way that plants seeds for future movements or gives other actors within and beyond the system the relevant clues to make those changes. Later, when the time *is* right the overseeing tribunal formally can put its imprimatur. Yet another advantage of the GATT/WTO test is that it tells us what to consider in answering what

---

but it is mainly in the WTO/GATT area, which might one day be transposed to the IIA and human rights context. See N. Diebold, *Non-Discrimination and the Pillars, supra*, at 23; M. Cossy, "Some Thoughts on the Concept of 'Likeness' in the GATS," *in* M. Panizzon et al (eds), GATS AND THE REGULATION OF INTERNATIONAL TRADE IN SERVICES 327 (2008); M. Krajewski and M. Engelke, "Commentary to Article XVII," *in* R. Wolfrum et al (eds), WTO - TRADE IN SERVICES: MAX PLANCK COMMENTARIES ON WORLD TRADE LAW 396-412 (2008); A. Mattoo & A. Subramanian, *Regulatory Autonomy and Multilateral Disciplines: The Dilemma and a Possible Resolution*, 1 J.I.E.L. 303, 315 (1998).

[232] Perhaps the sociologist Erving Goffman was right in stating that "an individual who implicitly or explicitly signifies that he has certain social characteristics ought in fact to be what he claims he is." See E. Goffman, THE PRESENTATION OF SELF IN EVERYDAY LIFE 13 (Anchor, 1959). By analogy, rationales behind government measures might need to satisfy the same internal coherency requirement.

degree of success is "necessary."[233] The suggestions laid down here by the GATT/WTO Appellate Body might be unrealistic, sovereignty-encroaching and even vague but they certainly are *less* vague than the alternatives.

Consider what the Appellate Body has done. It has interpreted rather restrictively the "necessary to protect human, animal or plant life or health" test of Article XX(b) or the "relating to the exhaustion of natural resources" test of Article XX(g).[234] These policies can be upheld only if no "less GATT-consistent" means can be found.[235] The *Korea—Beef Case* (2001)[236] held that these measures have to be "indispensable or of absolute necessity or inevitable to secure compliance certainly fulfil the *requirements*" of another GATT provision, Article XX(d). Not surprisingly (given past language), the burden of proof "falls not on the claimant but on the government seeking to justify the measure."[237] A dissenting school of thought believes that a generous helping of deference to the government is in-built (or should be) into the "necessity" test as a means of balancing out the erosion of public interests.[238]

Over time, though, the Appellate Body has loosened up the "necessity" test. In the *EC—Asbestos Case*,[239] it read "necessity" to mean *less* trade-restrictive, not *least* trade-restrictive. Narrow tailoring is required; the *least*-drastic-means test is not. Here the Appellate Body shifted the burden

---

[233] The analysis was set forth by the author in *Competing Constitutional Ideals in the United States'* Force Majeure-*Federalism Cases: Calling the Shots in Disaster Management*, 13 E. J. L. R. 140-41 (2011).

[234] R. Moloo & J. Jacinto, *Environmental and Health Regulation*, *supra*, at 56 (stating that "relating to"-like provisions "d[o] not extend to whether the measure is necessary or the most rational, proportional, or efficient response").

[235] See D. C. Esty, GREENING THE GATT: TRADE, ENVIRONMENT, AND THE FUTURE 48, Volume 1994, Part 2 (Peterson Institute, 1994) (observing first that the test could "forc[e] attention to the means chosen to pursue environmental goals." Esty later says that GATT/WTO has dropped this balancing act, thus "eviscerating Article XX"); P. F. J. Macrory, A. E. Appleton & M. G. Plummer, THE WORLD TRADE ORGANIZATION: LEGAL, ECONOMIC AND POLITICAL ANALYSIS 844-5 (Springer 2005).

[236] Report of the Appellate Body, *Korea — Beef*, WT/DS135/AB/R (2001), ¶ 161 (emphasis added) ("At one end of this continuum lies 'necessary' understood as 'indispensable'; at the other end, is 'necessary' taken to mean as 'making a contribution to.'"). Does including certain exceptions exclude others? Not necessarily, when the word "including" is there to keep options open.

[237] R. Dasgupta, *Competing Constitutional Ideals*, *supra*, at 140.

[238] J. D. Mortenson, *The Meaning of "Investment": ICSID's* Travaux *and the Domain of International Investment Law*, 51 HARV. INT'L. L.J. 257, 312-13 (2010).

[239] Report of the Appellate Body, *European Communities — Measures Affecting Asbestos and Asbestos-Containing Products*, WT/DS135/AB/R (2001).

from the State to the claimant (as the second prong of the test goes). This is consistent with the GATT panel decision in *Tuna/Dolphin I and II* that "necessary" just means "predictable" and "unavoidable,"[240] "the latter in the sense that all reasonably available international co-operative arrangements must have been exhausted."[241] The Appellate Body requires that in most scenarios a "proportionality-based, *ad-hoc*, case-by-case analysis balancing many factors" be used.[242] Still, this is no cure-all for the unpredictability.

One clear pattern is that the availability of less restrictive measures can be shown, as in the *Reformulated Gasoline Case* (1996),[243] by "applying statutory baselines to domestic as well as [all] foreign refiners or permitting foreign refiners to use individual baselines"—choices "reasonably available to the [respondent] to achieve its goal."[244] Once the claimant has shown that the respondent's actions were not "necessary," the burden shifts or should shift.[245] As it occurred in the ECtHR's *Pine Valley* case, if the respondent cannot even furnish an "administrative complexity" justification using "standard means of documentary evidence and third party verification," its probability of losing the dispute increase greatly.[246]

Of course, just the State's mere mention of a problem as too "administrative[ly] comple[x]" will not salvage its policy forever.[247] It might buy the State some time though. If years pass and no attributable progress occurs and there has been no attempt to deliver progress either, then deep judicial scepticism towards the policy may rightly seep in. And deference might be at an end. Similarly, if the problem directly involves or touches upon sensitive issues at the crux of the instrument's protection, the standard of review is strict.

Under this standard, only a most overpowering or compelling governmental interest is required, along with narrow tailoring (neither

---

[240] GATT Doc. DS21/R, 30 ILM 1594 (1991); 33 ILM 839 (1994).

[241] P. Sands, PRINCIPLES OF INTERNATIONAL ENVIRONMENTAL LAW 960 (Cambridge University Press, 2003) [P. Sands, INTERNATIONAL ENVIRONMENTAL LAW].

[242] R. Dasgupta, *Competing Constitutional Ideals*, *supra*, at 141.

[243] *U.S. — Standards for Reformulated and Conventional Gasoline*, Panel Report (1996), WT/DS2/R; *Appellate Body Report* (1996), WT/DS2/AB/R, 35 ILM 603 (1996).

[244] P. Sands, INTERNATIONAL ENVIRONMENTAL LAW, *supra*, at 962.

[245] *Id.*

[246] *Id.*

[247] *Id.*

over-inclusive nor under-inclusive) to achieve this end.[248] Deference is not a permanent cure-all. It is limited temporally, on the facts of the case and the standard of review.

It is not at all easy to contend "that a [S]tate's determinations under a treaty's non-precluded measure provision as to what measures are necessary to protect its essential security interests or public order should not receive at least some deference; still, a number of tribunals, though not all, have held otherwise, in part because of a dubious mixing of treaty and customary law."[249] In 2004, the United States rewrote the salient clause in its most recent model BITs to explicitly confer the self-judging power of necessity upon the IIA tribunal.[250] The next Chapter addresses the deference point extensively.

How the IIA Non-Discrimination Analysis Operates

Let us now address what informs the non-discrimination analysis. As with the IUCT and the ECtHR, the sequence goes this way: (*i*) identify the comparators that are in "like circumstances" with the investor; and then (*ii*) determine whether the investor received *less* favorable treatment than the comparators.[251]

Most NAFTA tribunals openly admit that the measure's practical *effect* is the main factor in deciding if the claimant received less favorable treatment. Still, showing patterns of evidence pointing to protectionist

---

[248] See, *e.g.*, *Sejdic, supra*, at ¶ 44 ("Article 14 does not prohibit Contracting Parties from treating groups differently in order to correct 'factual inequalities' between them. Indeed, in certain circumstances a failure to attempt to correct inequality through different treatment may, without an objective and reasonable justification, give rise to a breach of that Article.") (citing *Case "relating to certain aspects of the laws on the use of languages in education in Belgium"*, *supra*, § 10; *Thlimmenos v. Greece* [GC], no. 34369/97, § 44, ECHR 2000-IV; and *D.H. and Others v. the Czech Republic* [GC], no. 57325/00, § 175, ECHR 2007).

[249] A. von Staden, *Deference or No Deference, supra.*

[250] See, *e.g.*, 2012 United States Model Bilateral Investment Treaty [US Model BIT], Art. 6 (1) lit. a; 2004 US Model BIT, Art. 18.

[251] R. Moloo & J. Jacinto, *Environmental and Health Regulation: Assessing Liability Under Investment Treaties*, 29 BERK'Y J. INT'L L. 1, 57 (2011) [R. Moloo & J. Jacinto, *Environmental and Health Regulation*]; *Pope & Talbot v. Canada*, NAFTA/UNCITRAL, Award on the Merits of Phase 2 (2001), at ¶¶ 73-104.

intent can go a long way; the *S.D. Myers v. Canada* (2000)[252] tribunal made clear, however, that this evidence of intent is not *required* to win a discrimination claim. Similarly, *International Thunderbird Gaming Corp. v. Mexico* (2006)[253] stated that the claimant need not "show *separately* that the less favourable treatment was motivated because of nationality."

IIA tribunals might start by adopting the IUCT's intent *versus* effects analytics. That will require some judicial analysis (especially difficult when there is no precedent) in the NAFTA-IIA world. Their first step is to decide if, in investment cases, tribunals are even concerned about the expropriating sovereign's intent;[254] and secondly how to adjust the evidence requirement to the IIA's own context. But should these changes be made through the amendment process or even by returning to the drawing board to create a new IIA? Do the inherently-tenuous international tribunals have the competence to fill in all the gaps?

In the NT/MFN non-discrimination analysis, the first issue is whether the expropriatory measure has a legitimate regulatory purpose. NAFTA cases have asked this question within and beyond the environmental and public health context. Rahim Moloo and Justin Jacinto remind us that in the NAFTA case *GAMI Investments Inc. v. Mexico* (2005),[255] the *only* claimed regulatory purpose was the survival and solvency of the local sugar industry.[256]

If the State successfully, viz. using a legitimate basis, differentiates between the claimant and the comparators, then they are not similarly situated or in "like circumstances."[257] *Methanex v. United States* (2004)[258] is a perfect case-study for this proposition. There the U.S. regulation (a

---

[252] NAFTA/UNCITRAL, Partial Award, at ¶ 252-54 (2000); A. Newcombe & L. Paradell, LAW AND PRACTICE OF INVESTMENT TREATIES: STANDARDS OF TREATMENT 232-319 (2009).

[253] UNCITRAL (NAFTA), at ¶ 177.

[254] As Chapter VI (OTHER SUBSTANTIVE STANDARDS) will show, though most IIA tribunals see some role for "intent," some would totally cut off any intent-violation connection. See *Siemens AG v. Argentina*, ICSID Case No. ARB/02/08, Award (2007), at ¶ 299.

[255] *GAMI v. Mexico*, Award, 44 ILM 545 (2005), at ¶¶ 114-15.

[256] R. Moloo & J. Jacinto, *Environmental and Health Regulation: Assessing Liability Under Investment Treaties*, 29 BERK'Y J. INT'L L. 1, 54 (2011) [R. Moloo & J. Jacinto, *Environmental and Health Regulation*].

[257] See, *e.g.*, *Pope & Talbot v. Canada*, *supra,* at ¶ 79; see also R. Dolzer & C. Schreuer, PRINCIPLES OF INTERNATIONAL INVESTMENT LAW, *supra*, at 181-83 (providing cases arguing how "like circumstances" might involve legitimate differences).

[258] UNCITRAL, Final Award on the Merits (2005).

California Executive Order) arguably affected the claimant Methanex but not the comparators: Methanex's investment was situated "in an environmentally sensitive area or utilized an environmentally harmful production process."[259] The United States' rejoinder (accepted by the tribunal) is logically strong:

> [R]egulations limiting business activities in certain environmentally sensitive areas or imposing additional limitations on emissions where air pollution is more severe will not *ipso facto* violate national treatment even though some of these regulations may be applied to some operations and not to other, competing operations. In those cases, direct competitors may be deemed not to be in like circumstances for the purpose of the measure at issue because of their operations' differing locations.[260]

Some scholars argue that this is really a test of whether the State could show that its differential treatment was justified and, importantly, that its public interest was necessary enough to encroach on investor rights.[261] The trouble with this argument is the NAFTA's wording,[262] and indeed most IIA's do not openly give the tribunals this remit. Chapter Eleven's sweep covers all bases with regard to investment-related activities and gives tribunals no authority to excuse a public interest-based encroachment *once* investment rights of a foreigner are acknowledged.

Methanex addressed this interpretive point head-on and presumed that "the text [manifests] the drafters' intentions."[263] Had the drafters wanted to thus authorise the tribunals on an important issue, they would have said so. Nonetheless the NAFTA-IIA tribunals persist. This NAFTA tendency strongly resembles the ECtHR's tacit refusal to weigh the merit of a State's public-interest determination, though both NAFTA tribunals and the ECtHR do so circuitously. Who bears the burden of proving a legitimate regulatory purpose in NAFTA remains unclear,[264] unlike the

---

[259] R. Moloo & J. Jacinto, *Environmental and Health Regulation, supra*, at 55.

[260] *Methanex v. United States, supra*, U.S. Rejoinder on the Merits, (23 Apr. 2004) ¶ 159.

[261] See, *e.g.*, M. N. Kinnear, A. Bjorklund, J. F.G. Hannaford, INVESTMENT DISPUTES UNDER NAFTA: AN ANNOTATED GUIDE TO NAFTA CHAPTER ELEVEN 1102 (2009).

[262] Art. 1102(1), NAFTA ("Each Party shall accord to investors of another Party treatment no less favorable than that it accords, in like circumstances, to its own investors with respect to the establishment, acquisition, expansion, management, conduct, operation, and sale or other disposition of investments.").

[263] *Methanex, supra*, at ¶ 142.

[264] See, *e.g.*, *Pope & Talbot v. Canada, supra* , at ¶¶ 78-82 (burden on the State); *United Parcel Service of America, Inc. v. Canada*, NAFTA/UNCITRAL, Award

IUCT's and the ECtHR's relatively clear approaches. The investor certainly bears the burden of proving it is similarly situated (in "like circumstances" with) the comparators.

This is not to oversell the NAFTA tribunals' intrusiveness in *how* it weighs a State's proffered legitimate purpose. Unlike the ECtHR in *Chassagnou*, NAFTA typically does this weighing with deference.[265] For example, in *Pope & Talbot* the tribunal just looked at "whether there is a reasonable nexus between the measure and a rational, non-discriminatory government policy,"[266] not whether the action was actually necessary. The ECtHR, if the reader recalls from the last section, waded far deeper into the usefulness of the French law.

Several other NAFTA awards must be pointed out. In *Feldman v. Mexico* (2002),[267] the tribunal looked at whether there was "*any* rational justification in the record" for the less favorable treatment. This approach is hard to square with *S. D. Myers'* fear of easily-producible (or manufacturable) "rational justification"[268] but is just how *Glamis Gold, Inc. v. United States* (2009) tribunal required a "*prima facie* showing of legitimacy under the [fair and equitable treatment (FET) and due process] standard[s]."[269] Moloo and Jacinto insightfully argue that "such . . . deference may be too substantial in the context of applying the NT/MFN standards" since NT and MFN—unlike the FET "baseline" standard—"typically provide full protection against nationality-based discrimination."[270]

In short, a broad "like circumstances" test (such as the one that the State preferred in the *Pope & Talbot* award) protects States from being held liable for some discriminatory *effect*. But that high deference is not necessarily proper for discriminatory *intent* cases. This *S.D. Myers* versus *Feldman- Glamis Gold* tension on the non-discrimination standard needs to be resolved.

---

on the Merits (2007) ¶¶ 83-86 (burden on the investor); M. Kinnear et al., *supra*, at 1102-26 (arguing that shifting the burden makes it too easy for the investor); N. DiMascio & J. Pauwelyn, *Nondiscrimination in Trade and Investment Treaties*, *supra,* at 86 (arguing that the investor should bear the *full* burden of demonstrating nationality-based discrimination).

[265] R. Moloo & J. Jacinto, *Environmental and Health Regulation, supra*, at 54-6, has helpfully compiled this list.

[266] *Pope & Talbot v. Canada*, *supra*, at ¶ 81.

[267] *Feldman v. Mexico*, ICSID Case No. ARB(AF)/99/1, Award (2002) ¶ 182 (emphasis added).

[268] *Pope & Talbot v. Canada*, *supra*, at ¶¶ 80-81.

[269] NAFTA/UNCITRAL, Award (8 June 2009) ¶ 356.

[270] R. Moloo & J. Jacinto, *Environmental and Health Regulation, supra*, at 55-6.

While legislative or executive acts of direct or regulatory expropriation are understandably deemed compensable under various standards, there is a logical limit. Acts of treasury policy such as adjustment of interest rates, federal funds rates, discount rates, and money supply are better limited to non-discrimination. There remains the fear that recognising a generalised breach concerning matters of treasury policy, *outside* the obvious, limited and sequestered-off province of non-discrimination, might in the long-run prove to be an unprecedented encroachment of the prerogatives of a sovereign. It might be the straw that broke the camel's back (jeopardised the functioning of the IIA). In short, this is an excellent, effective and even necessary place to demonstrate that meaningful deference may be accorded the sovereign even in the IIA sphere.

Most-Favoured-Nation Clauses: A Turbocharged Supernova

If a country makes two MFN promises to two different countries, then it cannot treat them both better than it treats the other; it must give them equal treatment—that is, unless the MFN clause of IIA-*One* is not even enforceable in some *other* IIA arbitration. Why enter into an MFN guarantee if the other signatory has already promised MFN treatment to another party and the other MFN clause is not enforceable in arbitration (unless there are sectoral, time or other distinctions)? Whether the treatment is equal can be resolved within the established framework (despite its flaws), and has been addressed earlier in this Chapter.

Consider the following IIA awards which have interpreted the MFN clause to guarantee the best level of treatment. *Archer Daniels Midland Company and Tate & Lyle Ingredients Americas, Inc. v. Mexico* (2007)[271]: "Claimants and their investment are entitled to the best level of treatment available to any other domestic investor or investment operating in like circumstances." *Loewen Group v. United States* (2000)[272]: MFN requires "a comparison between the standard of treatment accorded to a claimant and the most favourable standard of treatment accorded to a person in like situation to that claimant." Lastly, *Methanex v. United States* (2005)[273]: "the investor or investment of another party is entitled to the most favourable treatment accorded to some members of the domestic class."

Therefore, the implications are important when an IIA claimant cannot rely on the MFN-based dispute settlement provisions of the respondent's

[271] ICSID Case No. ARB (AF)/04/5, at ¶ 205.

[272] ICSID Case No ARB(AF)/98/3, at ¶ 140.

[273] *Methanex, supra*, at ¶ 21.

IIA with *another* State. This challenges the very actionability and effectiveness ("teeth," if you will) of MFN, though the supporters of this view point out that important international law principles and cases are in their favour[274] even if most current case-law is not.[275]

We look to the differences, if any, between national and international orders for an answer. Here, the consent of States and sovereignty play a prominent role, for "international law has force [only] when enough countries honour it."[276] Consent is not, by definition, coercive, and it is an essential attribute of sovereignty. Sovereignty, though, should not be conflated with party autonomy because sovereignty comes first, remains the default principle throughout arbitration or litigation before an international adjudicator, and permits the parties only to fill in certain gaps.[277] States' incentives or disincentives explain their varying degrees of compliance with international law—based on rational choice theory.[278]

---

[274] Z. Douglas, *The MFN Clause in Investment Treaty Arbitration: Treaty Interpretation off The Rails*,
J. INT'L DISP.SETTL'T, 2010, p. 5 ("[t]he decision in *Maffezini, infra,* was the first time that a party has been permitted to rely upon an MFN clause to modify the jurisdictional mandate of an international tribunal. Across the hundreds of years of activity of international courts and tribunals leading up to *Maffezini*, there had only been judicial pronouncements against such a device, including the International Court of Justice's judgment in the *Anglo-Iranian Oil Company Case* and the British-Venezuelan Mixed Claims Commission's decision in *Aroa Mines*.").

[275] See, *e.g.*, *Suez, Sociedad General de Aguas de Barcelona, S.A. and Vivendi Universal, S.A. v. Argentina*, ICSID Case No. ARB/03/19, Decision on Liability (2010); *Suez, Sociedad General de Aguas de Barcelona S.A., and InterAguas Servicios Integrales del Agua S.A. v. Argentina*, ICSID Case No. ARB/03/17, Decision on Liability (2010), and cases cited therein.

[276] M. J. Glennon, THE FOG OF LAW, *supra,* at 27.

[277] *Waste Management Inc v. Mexico*, ICSID Case No. No. ARB(AF)/98/2, Award (2000) (*Waste Management I*) (2000), at ¶¶ 4-7, 14-31, 16 ("The essential constituent elements which constitute the institution of arbitration are the existence of a conflict of interests, and an agreement expressing the will of the parties or a legal mandate, on which the constitution of an Arbitral Tribunal is founded. This assertion serves to confirm the importance of the autonomy of the will of the parties, which is evinced by their consent to submit any given dispute to arbitration proceedings. Hence, it is upon that very consent to arbitration given by the parties that the entire effectiveness of this institution depends."); *Waste Management Inc v. Mexico*, ICSID Case No. ARB(AF)/00/3, Award (2000) (*Waste Management I*), Mexico's Preliminary Objection concerning the Previous Proceedings, Decision of the Tribunal (2002), ¶¶ 2-3, 19-50.

[278] M. J. Glennon, THE FOG OF LAW, *supra,* at 27.

Professor Brownlie even argued that consent is such a determinative fulcrum that "even the *erga omnes* character of the principle of self-determination," as understood in the ICJ's *East Timor Case* (1995),[279] "will not help it to overcome the limitations of jurisdiction on the basis of consent."[280] After all, the jurisdiction of international tribunals exists "only because and *in so far as* the parties have so desired."[281] State A's safeguard against State B is that neither State may ordinarily be taken before an international tribunal for a particular claim without its consent. Put simply, the level of granularity a tribunal uses determines if a specific violation alleged is a "claim" in itself. Consent also makes a difference as to the reviewability of certain third-party MFN claims before international tribunals.

Consider the award of the IIA tribunal in *Maffezini v. Spain* (2000).[282] The *Maffezini* tribunal observed "that today dispute settlement arrangements are inextricably related to the protection of foreign investors."[283] *Maffezini* deduced from this axiom that an international tribunal could take up a primary-rule violation so long as *some* related international obligation connects the respondent to the tribunal at issue. This is an easy threshold to satisfy in most cases.

---

[279] *East Timor (Portugal v. Australia)*, 1995 I.C.J., 90.

[280] I. Brownlie, THE RULE OF LAW IN INTERNATIONAL AFFAIRS: INTERNATIONAL LAW AT THE FIFTIETH ANNIVERSARY OF THE UNITED NATIONS 42 (Martinus Nijhoff Publishers, 1998); compare *Status of Eastern Carelia Case*, [1923] PCIJ, Ser. B, No. 5, P. 7 ("no State can, without its consent, be compelled to submit its disputes with other States either to mediation or to arbitration, or to any other kind of pacific settlement" even where the opinion is "advisory" only formally but actually binding) with *Interpretation of Peace Treaties Case*, [1950] ICJ 65, p. 29 ("no State, whether a Member of the United Nations or not, can prevent the giving of an Advisory Opinion which the United Nations considers to be desirable in order to obtain enlightenment as to the course of action it should take.").

[281] Declaration of Judge *ad hoc* Verhoeven, *Armed Activities on the Territory of the Congo*, ICJ Reports 2001, 684; see also *Status of Eastern Carelia*, PCIJ (series B, No 5) 27 (stating that "no State can, without its consent, be compelled to submit its disputes with other States either to mediation or to arbitration, or to any other kind of pacific settlement."); *Rights of Minorities in Upper Silesia*, PCIJ (ser A, No 15) 1928, 22; *Corfu Channel, ICJ Reports 1948*, 27; *Anglo-Iranian Oil Co, ICJ Reports* 1952, 103; *Monetary Gold, ICJ Reports* 1954, 32; *Continental Shelf, ICJ Reports 1984*, 22; *Land Island and Maritime Frontier Dispute, ICJ Reports* 1990, 133; *East Timor, ICJ Reports* 1995, 101.

[282] ICSID Case No. ARB/97/7, at ¶ 54 (Decision on Jurisdiction) (2000).

[283] *Id.*

Jan Paulsson is among the most active proponents of the *Maffezini* view: "the principle that national investment laws may create compulsory arbitration without privity is beyond cavil."[284] To Paulsson, these welcome developments augur "a new world of arbitration where the claimant need not have a contractual relationship with the defendant,"[285] thus ruling out this relationship requirement altogether.

Paulsson's argument runs into a textual problem from the New York Convention (mentioned in Chapter I): Article II (1) requires an "agreement in writing" regarding submitting a case to international arbitration.[286] Article 25(1) of the ICSID Convention, moreover, states that the ICSID Tribunal only has jurisdiction in disputes between a contracting state and the national of another contracting state, where the parties have "consented in writing" to submit to ICSID. There remains much uncertainty about how specific this consent must be or what forms it can take.

The tribunal in *Siemens AG v. Argentina* (2004)[287] did not find these textual problems insurmountable. *Siemens AG* further found that IIA's have "as a distinctive feature special dispute settlement mechanisms not normally open to investors. Access to these mechanisms is *part of the protection* offered under the Treaty. It is *part of the treatment* of foreign investors and investments ... ."[288] Simply put, for MFN third-party purposes it could not make the least possible difference if the right was procedural or substantive.[289] The right existed.

---

[284] J. Paulsson, "Arbitration Without Privity" *in* T. Walde, (ed.), THE ENERGY CHARTER TREATY 325 (Kluwer Law International, 1996); see also J. Paulsson, "Dispute Resolution" in R. Pritchard, (ed.) ECONOMIC DEVELOPMENT, FOREIGN INVESTMENT AND THE LAW (Kluwer Law International, 1996).

[285] *Id.*, at 325.

[286] Furthermore, Article II (2) defines an "agreement in writing" as an "arbitral clause in a contract or an arbitration agreement, signed by the parties or contained in an exchange of letters or telegrams."

[287] ICSID Case No. ARB/02/8, at ¶ 102 (Decision on Jurisdiction) (2004) (emphasis added).

[288] *Id.*, at ¶ 102-03.

[289] Rationales backing this up state that access to arbitration is either a jurisdictional protection "inextricably related" (*Maffezini, supra,* at ¶ 54) to substantive treatment, a natural "part of the treatment of foreign investors and investments," (*Siemens AG, supra,* at ¶ 102) "an integral part of the investment protection regime," (*Suez, supra*, at ¶ 57) or inherently (and this goes the furthest) "a substantive protection" (*Gas Natural SDG, S.A. v. Argentina,* ICSID Case No. ARB/03/10, Decision of the Tribunal on Preliminary Questions on Jurisdiction (2005), at ¶ 31).

The *Maffezini* tribunal further stated "that a distinction has to be made between the legitimate extension of rights and benefits by means of the operation of the clause, on the one hand, and disruptive treaty-shopping that would play havoc with the policy objectives of underlying specific treaty provisions, on the other hand."[290] Juggling between and negotiating the two sets of consequences, the *Plama* tribunal articulated "one, single exception" to the general *Maffezini* principle: "an MFN provision in a basic treaty does not incorporate by reference dispute settlement provisions in whole or in part set forth in another treaty, unless the MFN provision in the basic treaty leaves no doubt that the Contracting Parties intended to incorporate them."[291] Several post-*Plama* tribunals have backed up that award,[292] including on the basis that Article 31 of the Vienna Convention on the Law of Treaties would be violated by a contrary interpretation.[293] Other views state that putting so high a burden runs

---

[290] *Maffezini, supra*, at ¶ 63.

[291] *Plama Consortium Limited v. Bulgaria*, ICSID Case No. ARB/03/24, Decision on Jurisdiction (2005), at ¶ 223; *id.*, at ¶ 198 (". . . [A]n agreement of the parties to arbitrate . . . should be clear and unambiguous."); *id.*, at ¶ 200 ("[The] reference [in the MFN clause] must be such that the parties' intention to import the arbitration provision of the other agreement is clear and unambiguous"); *id.*, at ¶ 204 ("the intention to incorporate dispute settlement provisions must be clearly and unambiguously expressed."); *id.*, at ¶ 218 ("an arbitration clause must be clear and unambiguous and the reference to an arbitration clause must be such as to make the clause part of the contract (treaty).").

[292] See, *e.g.*, *Telenor Mobile Communications A.S. v. Hungary*, ICSID Case No. ARB/04/15, at ¶ 90, Award (2006) (stating that "[t]his Tribunal wholeheartedly endorses the analysis and statement of principle furnished by the *Plama* tribunal."); *Vladimir Berschader and Moïse Berschander v. The Russian Federation*, SCC Case No. 080/2004, at ¶ 90, Award (2006) (articulating that "the present Tribunal will apply the principle that an MFN provision in a BIT will only incorporate by reference an arbitration clause from another BIT where the terms of the original BIT clearly and unambiguously so provide or where it can otherwise be clearly inferred that this was the intention of the contracting parties."); *Wintershall Aktiengesellschaft v. Argentine Republic*, ICSID Case No. ARB/04/14, at ¶ 167, Award (2008) (stating that "ordinarily and without more, the prospect of an investor selecting at will from an assorted variety of options provided in other treaties negotiated with other parties under different circumstances, dislodges the dispute resolution provision in the basic treaty itself – unless of course the MFN Clause in the basic treaty clearly and unambiguously indicates that it should be so interpreted: which is not so in the present case.").

[293] See, *e.g.*, *Telenor Mobile, supra*, at ¶ 91 ("Article 31 of the 1969 Vienna Convention on Treaties requires a treaty to be interpreted 'in good faith in accordance with the ordinary meaning to be given to the terms of the treaty in their

contrary to the notion that the treaty, including its consent clause, must be interpreted fairly, neither restrictively nor liberally—nor with undue solicitude for the principle of *effet utile*.[294]

---

context and in the light of its object and purposes.' In the absence of language or context to suggest the contrary, the ordinary meaning of 'investments shall be accorded treatment no less favourable than that accorded to investments made by investors of any third State' is that the investor's substantive rights in respect of the investments are to be treated no less favourably than under a BIT between the host State and a third State, and there is no warrant for construing the above phrase as importing procedural fights as well. It is one thing to stipulate that the investor is to have the benefit of MFN investment treatment but quite another to use an MFN clause in a BIT to bypass a limitation in the very same BIT when the parties have not chosen language in the MFN clause showing an intention to do this, as has been done in some BITs.").

[294] *Oil Platforms (Islamic Republic of Iran v. United States of America),* Preliminary Objections, Judgment of December 12, 1996, Separate Opinion of Judge Higgins, p. 857, at ¶ 35 ("It is clear from the jurisprudence of the Permanent Court and of the International Court that there is no rule that requires a restrictive interpretation of compromissory clauses. But equally, there is no evidence that the various exercises of jurisdiction by the two Courts really indicate a jurisdictional presumption in favour of the plaintiff. (I make no reference in these observations as to the jurisdictional standards applicable for establishing a competence sufficient for the ordering of provisional measures.) The Court has no judicial policy of being either liberal or strict in deciding the scope of compromissory clauses: they are judicial decisions like any other."); *Amco Asia Corporation v. Republic of Indonesia* (Jurisdiction), (1983) 1 ICSID Reports 389 at p. 394 (". . . like any other conventions, a convention to arbitrate is not to be construed restrictively, nor, as a matter of fact, broadly or liberally. It is to be construed in a way which leads to find out and to respect the common will of the parties: such a method of interpretation is but the application of the fundamental principle *pacta sunt servanda*, a principle common, indeed, to all systems of internal law and to international law. Moreover – and this is again a general principle of law–any convention, including conventions to arbitrate, should be construed in good faith, that is to say by taking into account the consequences of their commitments the parties may be considered as having reasonably and legitimately envisaged."); *SPP v. Egypt*, Decision on Jurisdiction, 14 April 1988, 3 ICSID Reports 143 ("Thus, jurisdictional instruments are to be interpreted neither restrictively nor expansively, but rather objectively and in good faith, and jurisdiction will be found to exist if—but only if—the force of the arguments militating in favor of it is preponderant."); *Mondev Int'l Ltd. v. United States*, ICSID Case No. ARB(AF)/99/2 (2002), at ¶ 43 ("In the Tribunal's view, there is no principle either of extensive or restrictive interpretation of jurisdictional provisions in treaties. In the end the question is what the relevant provisions mean, interpreted in accordance with the applicable rules of interpretation of treaties."); *Fisheries Jurisdiction Case* (Spain v. Canada), ICJ

Many IIA awards have relied on *Maffezini* and will be jeopardised if *Maffezini* is repudiated. There is no guarantee that IIA signatories will issue a reinterpretation—or that the signatories in other IIA's would. Moreover, investor and State expectations have already been built up. Alleged IIA violations, or at least claims arising from alleged facts connected to IIA transgressions, happening *between* the time that *Maffezini* is repudiated and some remedy is found will face confusion. Although *Maffezini* has been controversial because of the widely applicable and explosive implications it wrought, both doctrinally and financially, it does not seem to have been roundly rejected in the IIA community.[295] Surely, part of the reason is that there is no consensus or ostensible recognition of the fact that *Maffezini* has been functionally unworkable, a partly appropriate test for rejecting the award.

Not everyone sees things the *Maffezini*-MFN way, of course.[296] Rejecting *Maffezini's* ostensible "harmoni[s]ation and enlargement of the scope of such [MFN] arrangements" justification,[297] the *Plama* tribunal stated that the likely "effect" when "an investor has the option to pick and choose provisions from the various BITs" is "chaotic," "actually counterproductive to harmoni[s]ation" and thus "cannot be the presumed intent of Contracting Parties."[298] This last logic jump requires the

---

Reports 1998 pp. 432, 451-2, at ¶¶ 37-38), 452-456, at ¶¶ 44-56; *Case concerning the Aerial Incident of 10 August 1999 (Pakistan v. India)*, 39 ILM 1116 (2000) at p. 1130, at ¶ 42; *Ethyl Corporation v. Canada* (Jurisdiction), decision of 24 June 1998, (1999) 38 ILM 708 at p. 723, at ¶ 55. See also "Consent to Arbitration," in DISPUTE SETTLEMENT 32, United Nations Conference on Trade and Development, *available at* <http://unctad.org/en/docs/edmmisc232add2_en.pdf>.

[295] See, *e.g.*, F. O. Vicuña, *Reports of [Maffezini's] Demise Have Been Greatly Exaggerated*, Journal of International Dispute Settlement, Vol. 3, No. 3 (2012), pp. 479–481.

[296] Decisions not entirely consistent with the *Maffezini*-MFN position are *Salini Costruttori S.p.A. and Italstrade S.p.A. v. Jordan*, ICSID Case No. ARB/02/13, Decision on Jurisdiction (2004) and *Plama Consortium Limited v. Bulgaria*, ICSID Case No. ARB/03/24, Decision on Jurisdiction (2005). Among other governments, the United States believes *Maffezini* has been wrongly decided.

[297] *Maffezini, supra*, at ¶ 62.

[298] *Plama*, *supra*, at ¶ 219. To be fair, the *Maffezini* tribunal was acutely aware of the risks attending this approach — "[T]here are some important limits that ought to be kept in mind. As a matter of principle, the beneficiary of the clause should not be able to override public policy considerations that the [C]ontracting [P]arties might have envisaged as fundamental conditions for their acceptance of the agreement in question, particularly if the beneficiary is a private investor, as will often be the case. The scope of the clause might thus be narrower than it appears at first sight." *Maffezini, supra,* at ¶ 62. Moreover, the *Maffezini* tribunal supplied

assumption that rules "actually counterproductive to harmoni[s]ation" categorically "cannot be the presumed intent of Contracting Parties." This probably is mostly true but we cannot be certain that *sometimes* certain IIA configurations are constructed in a manner that leaves intact a sufficiently wide grey-area.[299]

There is also a more fundamental, First Principles-type argument concerning *Maffezini*. Opposed to what she sees as *Maffezini's* expansion of international jurisdiction where she argues it does not belong, in her recent separate opinion in *Impregilo S.p.A. v. Argentina* (2011) [300] Arbitrator Brigitte Stern argued that "the jurisdictional treatment is *never* inherent in the substantive treatment on the international level." She conceded that in domestic systems, usually when there is a primary right there is also a remedy to have it enforced; if the administrative means fail, then there is always judicial review.[301]

Stern's argument is not without a pedigree. In fact, Stern went back to the First Principles of rights (primary rules) and remedies (secondary rules) in national vis-à-vis international law systems:

> On the national level, when there exists a substantive right, there is always automatically a means to protect such a right through the jurisdictional system. In other words, on the national level, jurisdictional treatment is inherent in substantive treatment. In contrast, on the international level, most rights cannot be enforced through a jurisdictional process, it is only when, exceptionally, the State has given its consent—consent to other

---

four significant examples: (i) exhaustion of local remedies requirement; (ii) fork in the road provision; (iii) "if the agreement provides for a particular arbitration forum, such as ICSID, for example, this option cannot be changed by invoking the clause, in order to refer the dispute to a different system of arbitration"; and (iv) "if the parties have agreed to a highly institutionalized system of arbitration that incorporates precise rules of procedure." *Id.*, at ¶ 63.

[299] In conversations with the author, several negotiators have acknowledged this reality. If the IIA must "sell" before the public and the legislature, as one negotiator from a sub-Saharan African state admitted, then it must be "fuzzy enough" to "make us and the other Party feel like we, they, are winning." He further goes on to classify this strategy as a "P.R. exercise, pure and simple — there is little that is noble in this IIA-drafting approach." The author remains agnostic as to the alleged "nobility" (or "ignobleness") of the project.

[300] ICSID Case No. ARB/07/17, at ¶ 45 (Final Award) (2011) (Professor Brigitte Stern, Arbitrator) (concurring and dissenting opinion) (asserting that there is a "profound difference between the national legal orders and the international legal order").

[301] M. Elliot, "The Modified *Ultra Vires* Principle" *in* THE CONSTITUTIONAL FOUNDATIONS OF JUDICIAL REVIEW 106 (Hart Publishing, 2001).

> States for accepting the jurisdiction of the ICJ or consent to foreign investors for accepting international arbitration—that such a 'jurisdictional treatment' complements the substantive treatment granted by the international rules.[302]

This, again, is about consent. International tribunals depend on the explicit consent of the States to have some aspect of their MFN commitments (*outside* the currently-disputed IIA) considered. The ICSID tribunal in *Telenor Mobile Communications A.S. v. Hungary* (2006)[303] put the burden on the claimant in these situations:

> In the absence of language or context to suggest the contrary, the ordinary meaning of 'investments shall be accorded treatment no less favourable than that accorded to investments made by investors of any third State' is that the investor's *substantive rights* in respect of the investments are to be treated no less favourably than under a BIT between the host State and a third State, and there is no warrant for construing the above phrase as importing *procedural rights* as well.

A significant problem with this argument is that it presupposes (as it must, to reach its destination) that (*i*) the primary-secondary rules difference exists (this author agrees); and (*ii*) the difference is an important enough default rule or norm in international law that for third-party investors to trigger a *Maffezini*-type MFN clause they must show "specifically negotiated" text and relevant drafting history.[304] This latter point is less obvious.

But Stern's argument is not just about consent. It just as importantly concerns the delicate balance between inducing a signatory to stay within the fold and keeping the international arbitration and adjudication system potent enough to fulfil its mandate through predictability, legitimacy, efficiency and equity. On the point of requiring a "specifically negotiated" text and drafting history, let us face the facts here. Often this is too high and too randomly applicable a burden. Circumstantial evidence controls the determination whether such a deviation from the default status was thought through. This evidence might include speeches of negotiators

---

[302] *Id.*; see also *Council of Canadians, CUPW and the Charter Committee on Poverty Issues v. the Attorney General of Canada*, Ontario Sup. Ct. of Justice, Case Number No. 01-CV-208141 (2003), at ¶ 35 (affidavit of M. Sornarajah).

[303] ICSID Case No. ARB/04/15, Award (2006), at ¶ 92.

[304] Y. Banifatemi, "The Emerging Jurisprudence on the Most-Favoured-Nation Treatment in Investment Arbitration," in A. Björklund, Ian Laird & Sergey Ripinsky (eds)., INVESTMENT TREATY LAW: CURRENT ISSUES III 269 (BIICL, 2009) [Y. Banifatemi, "The Emerging Jurisprudence on the MFN Treatment"].

(extremely rarely available),[305] surreptitiously included ("tucked-inside") text and government interpretations in which other the signatories concurred (restatements and add-ins).[306]

The reinterpretations and insertions may come from governments hedging their bets, not putting a potentially deal-breaking provision on the negotiating table, and instead hoping to influence future tribunal awards based on these reinterpretations. Another problem with add-on government *interpretations* is that, whether or not the process is transparent, it does not engage the civil society (including corporations, NGO's, small businesses, etc.) in the same in-depth way that the original compact does. Nor do add-ons typically require ratification by the Legislature (that some signatory nations might require the Executive to attain for international compacts).

Sometimes this will be the result of no deliberate process but just luck. Yas Banifatemi argues that Brigitte Stern's *Impregilo* standard,

> in a somewhat absurd manner, impl[ies] that dispute resolution provisions are more specifically negotiated than other treaty provisions. It is, however, presumed that, when entering into a treaty, the State parties intend to write what they write. There is no difference in nature, in terms of drafting, between the fair and equitable standard, the prohibition of expropriations without compensation, the prohibition of discriminatory or arbitrary conduct, or dispute resolution provisions.[307]

The anti-*Maffezini* counterrevolutionaries have shown no intention of backing down[308] and hint that they might even outnumber (not in the

---

[305] The minutes of these conclaves are not typically well-known or at least well-known with any credibility or certitude because, as one senior government official from one East Asian nation's treasury ministry told me, "[t]hese negotiations can't function in a fish-bowl. A lot that is discussed and is kept or stricken would incense a lot of special interest groups. We walk in and shut the door behind. If some constituency later blames us, we transfer responsibility to the other guys. We are both right, we are both wrong, we are certainly all constrained by politics." It reflected eye-opening candour on this Treasury official's part.

[306] See S. D. Franck, *Development and Outcomes of ITA*, *supra*, at 438, 440, 448, 485-488; L. E. Peterson, *UK Bilateral Investment Treaty Program and Sustainable Development: Implications of Bilateral Negotiations on Investment Regulation at a Time When Multilateral Talks Are Faltering*, BRIEFING PAPER (The Royal Inst. of Int'l Affairs, Sustainable Development Programme, London), 2 (2004), *available at* <www.iisd.org/pdf/2004/trade_bits.pdf>.

[307] Y. Banifatemi, "The Emerging Jurisprudence on the MFN Treatment," *supra*, at 269.

[308] *Id.*, at 5 (urging that it is not a "legally convincing argument to rely on former cases as if they were binding precedents").

number of cases but in the number of arbitrators)[309] the *Maffezini* position. Given this landscape, what will happen to MFN in IIA arbitrations depends largely on how the IIA community resolves this issue. IIA's will face a significant confusion and unpredictability if this particular doctrine is overturned.

This MFN position is the only counter-prevailing or minority position that this dissertation red-flags so prominently. The dissertation does so because it has strong potential to make waves in the future. This dissenting position has been overlooked by most scholarship and, more alarmingly, by the drafters of newer agreements.[310] The only point of agreement between the various camps is that from the political brokers of these agreements there has been near-complete radio silence. The issue just does not seem to percolate up to the public sphere from Parliaments, Congresses, and executive agencies in charge of crafting these agreements.[311] The commentators have almost exclusively been from the scholarly and IIA communities, not consistent with the interactional model recommendations of Brunnée and Toope.[312]

Had politicians and negotiators listened to the tribunals, and the tribunals received valid signalling that they could be heard, idea-sharing might have had a shot; it might have led to more sophisticated IIA instruments—with sectoral-, geographical-, and even timing-based MFN clauses. A blackout regarding this dimension takes a direct hit on the

---

[309] *Id.*, at ¶ 5 (arguing that "if one looks at the number of arbitrators that are in favour of applying the MFN clause to dispute settlement rather than at the number of awards, that the picture looks almost balanced, because of the repeated involvement of some of the arbitrators.")

[310] See M. Malik, *Recent Developments in International Investment Agreements: Negotiations and Dispute*, IV Annual Forum for Developing Country Investment Negotiators Background Papers New Delhi, October 27-29, 2010, *available at* <www.iisd.org/pdf/2011/dci_2010_recent_developments_iias.pdf> (last accessed October 2, 2011), and sources cited therein (no evidence that the drafters have picked up on these nuances); J. Kurtz, *A General Investment Agreement in the WTO? Lessons from Chapter 11 of NAFTA and the OECD Multilateral Agreement on Investment*, Jean Monnet Working Paper 6/02, N.Y.U. Law School (2002), *available at* <http://centers.law.nyu.edu/jeanmonnet/papers/02/020601.pdf> (offering solutions that are developed and developing country-centric rather than more focused and granular such as sector-based and/or competition-based).

[311] Part of the reason, certainly, is that the public has not shown itself to be overwhelmingly concerned about the issues yet. Absent that appetite, which can only be built by education and awareness campaigns, it is difficult to see policy-makers investing the energy and resources into seeking public input over the issue.

[312] J. Brunnée & S. Toope, LEGITIMACY, *supra*, at 88-102.

legitimacy component down the line. In the interest of candour, it should be pointed out that while domestic politicians can opt-out through various mechanisms, domestic *courts* are duty-bound to enforce and execute an award, no less so because the "restrictive theory" concerning sovereign immunity is the guiding norm and principle in various jurisdictions.[313]

§ 5.5—Conclusion and Potential Developments

On non-discrimination, the three institutions have much to teach each other procedurally and substantively. But the wealth of judicial and scholarly literature in the GATT/WTO and other international regimes should also be considered.

One final point of knowledge transfer pertains to non-discrimination. Two potentially winning arguments in both the ECtHR (corporate and commercial cases) and more naturally in the IIA universe are addressed. First, the reader might consider adjusting the "public interest" rationale. From a host State's perspective, the advantage offered by investors is that they make "valuable contributions to society worthy of protection, including capital investments, creating employment opportunities and transferring technology."[314]

What might happen if investors and property owners build on this argument using fact- and data-based cost-benefit analysis to show that their contribution to the public interest is greater than or equal to non-expropriated investors whose investments are otherwise attractive candidates for expropriation? This legal strategy could challenge the allegedly expropriating State by checkmating it in the electoral sphere.

Moreover, even if nothing happens in the *tribunals*, the public could be incentivised to pay attention to the unfolding of this saga. If the State forgoes this investment, it will be harder for the State to justify that decision to its constituents. Of course, as we have discussed, if it is a State

---

[313] J. W. Yackee, *Controlling the International Investment Law Agency*, 53 HARV. INT'L L. J. 391, 416-416, n. 118 (2012) ("the New York Convention and the ICSID Convention strictly limit the grounds upon which a domestic court might refuse to recognize an [IIA] award, and the spread of the so-called 'restrictive theory of sovereign immunity' means that in many jurisdictions a state on the losing end of an award will have difficulty relying on sovereign immunity principles to avoid enforcement or execution.") (citing G. Born, *A New Generation of International Adjudication*, 61 DUKE L.J. 775, 826–31 (2012)).

[314] R. Moloo & J. Jacinto, *Environmental and Health Regulation*, *supra*, at 36 (citing R. Moloo & A. Khachaturian, *Foreign Investment in a Post-Conflict Environment*, 10 J. WORLD INV. & TRADE 340 (2009)).

where a traditional understanding of "voter-welfare" is absent from the equation, such as a dictator state, it is an entirely different conversation altogether. In that conversation, the rationale for deference is severely weakened.

Second, is it discrimination when the State targets one particular investor or owner? This is an interesting argument that has not really come up in any of our institutions (at least not voluminously or prominently enough to occupy precious law library space). But even if you give the State all the deference in the world, it still might come across to an international tribunal as "irrational," because it is arbitrary, for the State to target a specific investor just out of bare animus for that investor. Absent a narrowly-tailored measure to meet a legitimate aim and where superior (to mean, more specific) alternatives existed and no emergency or "necessity" could be divined, the expropriation-related conduct is presumably a violation. It is therefore compensable.

The United States Supreme Court recently faced and rejected a "class of one" discrimination claim (in the public employment context) but the seed for this jurisprudence was planted both in the majority opinion and the dissent.[315] In fact, the Court's majority did not actively dispute the "class of one" theory as an acceptable premise.[316] Whether such a claim is brought under non-discrimination or the substantive standards, it might be meritorious. As the next Chapter will show, international tribunals have used a variety of verbal formulae to disapprove "class of one"

---

[315] *Engquist v. Oregon Dep't of Agriculture*, 553 U.S. 591 (2008) (accepting that "class of one" discrimination claims *may* be constitutionally cognisable but disapproving them in the context of government jobs); *id.*, at 610 ("Unless state action that intentionally singles out an individual, or a class of individuals, for adverse treatment is supported by some rational justification, it violates" the equal protection guarantee of the Constitution) (Stevens, J., dissenting, and citing *Village of Willowbrook v. Olech*, 528 U S. 562 (2000)). See also R. C. Farrell, *The Equal Protection Class of One Claim:* Olech, Engquist, *and the Supreme Court's Misadventure*, 61 S.C. L. REV. 107 (2009).

[316] It might be that the *Engquist* majority opinion did not wish to question the intrinsic value of the "class of one" theory for two reasons: the controlling precedent indicated otherwise and the overruling of the precedent would have eroded precious judicial capital unnecessarily since the immediate case about public employment discrimination would have been decided the same anyway. Some lower courts have refused to extend *Engquist* beyond its public-employment context. See, e.g., *Analytical Diagnostic Labs Inc. v. Kusel*, 2d Cir., No. 08-6297-cv, 10/4/10 (case involving medical laboratory's claim that the New York Department of Health subjected it to an especially intense and microscopic degree of regulatory scrutiny).

discrimination under substantive standards but not directly under the non-discrimination provisions. It will be interesting to observe the implications and relevance of the aforementioned State's "Achilles Heel" strategy in this context.

For the reasons we have discussed earlier in this Chapter (with respect to the IIA-international trade law differences and their relevance to the "necessity" defence), the "class of one" theory is absolutely suitable to IIA cases, not to mention to the international human rights scenario. After all, unlike the WTO/GATT regime whose focus is on sustaining the transnational flow of goods, "the international investment legal regime protects the relationship between a state and *a* private investor."[317] The private investor has demonstrable agency in IIA.

One guess is that the tribunals have not wanted to open up the Pandora's Box of non-discrimination because, historically, they have seen that the Pandora's Box of Fair and Equitable Treatment (FET) and other substantive standards have been enough to reckon with. The same works *vice versa*. All in all, these prospects for the future are much more than just legal strategies; addressing this argument will enrich the decisions.

Finally, despite the judicial focus of this Chapter and the fact that asking signatories to "negotiate either an exhaustive or an enumerative list of [protected] public interests"[318] is unlikely to be helpful, what *is* needed is a citizenry-legislative-tribunal dialogue on how to move forward.[319] Supposing, even tacitly, that citizens are some abstract units useful solely for the purpose of electing politicians who then deputise experts to negotiate the treaty misses a key part of the equation.[320] Whatever be the future of or even wisdom in Professor Brownlie's "national economic disaster" argument (in Chapter III), the smallest and yet the most consequential boson are the citizens. Their *de facto* marginalisation from the elevated conversation makes the international system needlessly vulnerable to becoming irrelevant and quickly so. Irrespective of whether it is a domestic or an international tribunal, and perhaps even more so if the latter, "disdain" for the democratic and political processes spells

---

[317] K. Claussen, *Comment: The Casualty of Investor Protection in Times of Economic Crisis*, *supra*, at 1550-51 (emphasis added).

[318] N. Diebold, *Non-Discrimination and the Pillars, supra*, at 23.

[319] R. Mackenzie & P. Sands, *International Courts and Tribunal, supra,* at 283-85.

[320] P. Sands, "Litigating Environmental Disputes" *in* T. Mensah, T. Ndiaye & R. Wolfrum, LAW OF THE SEA, ENVIRONMENTAL LAW, AND SETTLEMENT OF DISPUTES 323 (Martinus Nijhoff Publishers, 2007) (connecting own interpretation of "sustainable development" with the "competing societal demands") [P. Sands, "Litigating Environmental Disputes"].

catastrophe for the tribunal system and by association for the rule of law that the tribunals are discharged to vindicate.[321]

Let us face facts. The negotiation process is delicate and extremely difficult to achieve, often more so than a tribunal award or even a series of tribunal awards in a particular direction. Negotiation requires interpersonal orientation, strategic dilemma, and methodological direction. With respect to the latter component, "[d]efining the formula is cooperative by nature, whereas the detail phase is competitive." Formula-defining "encompasses the overarching framework which sets the items to be covered or the sense of justice governing the [formula]" — "[i]t must not only identify a shared perception, reference structure, and idea of justice, but also be comprehensive and relevant to the needs of all parties" — while detail-stipulation "comprises distributive details, ideally implementing the general terms which the formula establishes."[322]

The template might not be easy to follow. But we also cannot shun the conversational process which inevitably implicates negotiations and re-negotiations. In this vein, it is critical to remember that "[n]egotiation which begins by establishing a clear formula will tend to produce a more positive-sum or integrative result, whereas negotiation in the reverse order will tend to be more zero-sum or distributive."[323] Integrative outcomes tend to be sounder and more enduring outcomes.

---

[321] See, *e.g.*, P. S. Karlan, *Democracy and Disdain, supra,* at 2 ("Sometimes the Justices seem barely able to hide their disdain for the other branches of government."); *id.*, at 13 (arguing that the question transcends invalidation of democratically adopted or authorised measures — "Indeed, several of the most striking examples of judicial disdain involve cases in which Justices voted to sustain the law being challenged, or in which the Court was called upon to mediate a conflict between different levels of government. Rather, the problem is that the Court's decisions convey a broad message about the democratic process itself that may undermine public confidence in the democratic process going forward. The Court's dismissive treatment of politics raises the question whether, and for how long, the people will maintain their confidence in a Court that has lost its confidence in them and their leaders."). But see R. E. Barnett, *The Disdain Campaign*, 126 HARV. L. REV. FOR. 1, 1 (2012) (criticising Karlan's insistence on judicial "attitudes" towards democracy as opposed to the substance of their determinations — claiming that Professor Karlan "faults [some jurists] not so much for the doctrines they purport to follow, or outcomes they reach, but for the attitude they allegedly manifest toward Congress and the people."). This too is a cautionary tale.

[322] S. Dahan, "Conceptualising the EU/IMF Financial Assistance Process," *supra*, at 185.

[323] *Id.*

The *Maffezini*-MFN controversy is a cautionary tale for all of us. Enhancing the role of *amicus curiae* might assist in generating the big-picture consistency and give interested parties the impression that they are being consulted.[324] Ironically, there has been more transnational judicial dialogue and greater efforts have been undertaken to induce this dialogue than there have been intra-system dialogue among the various negotiation, legislative and judicial organs.[325] Transnational dialogue and cooperation (judicial or otherwise) is laudatory, and indeed most diplomatic and economic crisis-resolution has this dialogue as its inception. But more must be done and a greater number of angles explored.[326] The scholarly community and eventually the citizenry will need to get involved and legitimacy will be secured only when the tribunals show an interest in listening to them.

As Chapter III explains legitimacy, a key player is a decision's reasoning; it can trigger a dialectical chain reaction with the other participants in society. Otherwise, the system itself might be undermined because international tribunals, by their very nature, are tenuous. The consent question morphs its precise form and continues to live on.

---

[324] J. A. VanDuzer, *Enhancing the Procedural Legitimacy of Investor-State Arbitration Through Transparency and Amicus Curiae Participation*, 52 McGILL L.J. 681, 706–08 (2007).

[325] M. A. Waters, *Mediating Norms and Identity: The Role of Transnational Judicial Dialogue in Creating and Enforcing International Law*, 93 GEO. L.J. 487 (2005).

[326] See, e.g., Anne-Marie Slaughter, A NEW WORLD ORDER 108–27 (2004); Robert O. Keohane & J. S. Nye, *Transgovernmental Relations and International Organizations*, 27 WORLD POL. 39, 41 (1974) (tracing the development of transgovernmental networks as a driver behind the creation and evolution of international policy); Kal Raustiala, *The Architecture of International Cooperation: Transgovernmental Networks and the Future of International Law*, 43 VA. J. INT'L L. 1 (2002).

CHAPTER SIX

OTHER SUBSTANTIVE STANDARDS: EXPROPRIATION, FAIR AND EQUITABLE TREATMENT, MINIMUM STANDARD OF TREATMENT, AND COMPENSATION

§ 6.1—Introduction

Let us commence with the basics. Even though there is thought to be a distinction between direct expropriations and regulatory measures to that effect,[1] the gravity of the latter may in some circumstances be tantamount to the gravity of the former.[2]

Tension between Sustainable Development and Property Rights: Spent Force or a New Dawn?

On the outset, one critical issue of terminology: The term "substantive standards" was really divined by process of elimination. The goal was to show that these standards were not variable like non-discrimination but absolute. "Absolute," though, conveyed a certain permanence and rigidity not readily consistent with these evolving, context-based standards. Thus, "substantive" seemed apt. These substantive standards include expropriation itself as well as fluid standards related to expropriation.

---

[1] *S. D. Myers v. Canada*, UNCITRAL, Final Award on the Merits (Nov. 13, 2000), at ¶ 282 ("Expropriations tend to involve the deprivation of ownership rights; regulations a lesser interference. The distinction between expropriation and regulation screens out most potential cases of complaints concerning economic intervention by a state and reduces the risk that governments will be subject to claims as they go about their business of managing public affairs.").

[2] *Id.*, at ¶ 283 ("An expropriation usually amounts to a lasting removal of the ability of an owner to make use of its economic rights although it may be that, in some contexts and circumstances, it would be appropriate to view a deprivation as amounting to an expropriation, even if it were partial or temporary.").

Regarding these standards, "[t]he tension is obvious. Too much policy space reduces the value of international obligations. Too stringent obligations overly constrain the national policy space. Finding a development-oriented balance is the challenge."[3] Chapter I (INTRODUCTION) has already discussed that the emerging consensus in the IIA sphere appears to be investment protection comes first, *then* and if at all come sustainable development objectives. In fact, "alarmed by the interpretations of relatively flexible standards of treatment of foreign investors adopted in investment awards, a number of states have decided to detail the specific content of those standards in model bilateral investment treaties and treaties in order to prevent their extensive interpretation by arbitral tribunals."[4] Therefore, the formal standards and the rigour with which the claims are evaluated take on a new scale of significance.

This tendency towards "public law challenge[s]"[5] instead of maintaining a system of "private-law-based commercial arbitration"[6] has been a source of some consternation in various international law circles. In particular, many proponents of a corporatist and capital-intensive international law system appear to object. Among this group are some

---

[3] Anna Joubin-Bret, Marie-Estelle Rey, Jorge Weber, 'International Investment Law and Development', in Marie-Claire Cordonier Segger, Markus Gehring and Andrew Newcombe (eds), SUSTAINABLE DEVELOPMENT IN WORLD INVESTMENT LAW (Kluwer, 2011). See also A. Mills, *Antinomies of Public and Private at the Foundation of International Investment Law and Arbitration*, 14 J. INT'L ECON. L. 469, 488 (2011) (the issue concerns a "balance between the public regulatory needs of states, and the private interests of investors.").

[4] F. Zarbiyev, *Judicial Activism in International Law, supra,* at 20 (citing 2004 US Model BIT, art 5; Canada's Model Foreign Investment Promotion and Protection Agreement, art 5; The United States-Dominican Republic-Central America Free Trade Agreement (CAFTA), art 10.5).

[5] S. W. Schill, *Enhancing International Investment Law's Legitimacy: Conceptual and Methodological Foundations of a New Public Law Approach*, 52 VA. J. INT'L L. 57, 67 (2011).

[6] A. von Staden, *Deference or No Deference, That is the Question: Legitimacy and Standards of Review in Investor-State Arbitration*, IISD, July 19, 2012, *available at* <www.iisd.org/itn/2012/07/19/deference-or-no-deference-that-is-the-question-legitimacy-and-standards-of-review-in-investor-state-arbitration/#_ftn2> [A. von Staden, *Deference or No Deference*] ("the intensity with which a tribunal scrutinizes the conduct of the investment's host state that is alleged to have breached one or more obligations under applicable investment treaty provisions, with a stricter standard of review tending to benefit the investor and a more lenient or permissive standard advantaging the respondent state.").

respected academics as well.[7] There is another factor concerning the hydraulic pressure on adjudicators faced with these disputes. Undoubtedly, "[t]here is a particular pressure for international judges and arbitrators to turn to public law 'standards of review' in health and environmental disputes, because they raise sensitive issues of domestic regulatory autonomy."[8]

Now please take note of the repercussions. Henceforth, the stakes are also higher for the international human rights-IIA interplay. The reason is that international human rights undoubtedly concerns "public law challenge[s]" and is seen to have an adverse influence on what some multinational corporations and investors see as the purely private law and commercial[9] arbitration-centric IIA space. What is somewhat ironic is that

---

[7] See, *e.g.*, J. Klabbers, AN INTRODUCTION TO INTERNATIONAL INSTITUTIONAL LAW 340 (Cambridge University Press, 2002) (stating that "for us internationalists, the state was, until recently, the root of all evil, so it follows that anything that attempts to reach beyond the state is laudable and praiseworthy, regardless of its precise contents … . State sovereignty needs to be overcome if life will ever get better.").

[8] C. E. Foster, *Adjudication, Arbitration and the Turn to Public Law 'Standards of Review': Putting the Precautionary Principle in the Crucible*, J INT. DISP. SETTLEMENT (2012) 3 (3): 525 [C. E. Foster, *Precautionary Principle in the Crucible*].

[9] C. Brower & J. Sharpe, *The Creeping Codification of Transnational Commercial Law: An Arbitrator's Perspective*, 45 VA. J. INT'L L. 199 (2004) ("Two notable features of contemporary life are the worldwide retreat of state authority and the privatization of functions (including dispute resolution) previously performed only by governments. These related developments have spurred the unprecedented growth of international arbitration. Increased demand for the private resolution of international commercial and investment disputes testifies (1) to the desire of parties everywhere to avoid subjecting their rights and obligations to adjudication in national courts under national law, and (2) to the great extent to which so many states have facilitated this 'privatized justice' through adoption of international treaties such as the New York Convention, modern arbitration statutes, and progressive, pro-arbitration jurisprudence.").
The authors of this article also state that the Principles of International Commercial Contracts, published in 1994 by the International Institute for the Unification of Private Law (UNIDROIT) and which now govern many arbitrations, are (*i*) only "international legal principles applicable to international commercial contracts made by a distinguished group of international experts coming from all prevailing legal systems of the world, without the intervention of states or governments, both circumstances redounding to the high quality and neutrality of the product and its ability to reflect the present stage of consensus on international legal rules and principles governing international contractual obligations in the world, primarily

the pro-sovereignty actors see the system as having been oriented towards private commercial arbitration all along and they see their own efforts towards greater public law incorporation as an uphill struggle. Everyone wants to be regarded as a folk-hero but who the innocent Odette is and who the wily Odile is depends almost entirely on the judgment of the beholder.[10]

It could be argued that the balance has shifted away from private commercial arbitration towards public international law-style adjudication in *form* and the opposite way in *substance*. Some have called for an administrative and constitutional law standard, in accordance with this paradigm realignment.[11] Over the last decade or so, the use of IIA's for investment arbitration has increased manifold.

Since this trend is likely to continue and only accelerate, the tension with sustainable development-centric aims will become even more "pronounced."[12] Preambles of IIA instruments are where the objectives and purposes,[13] along with the contexts,[14] are set forth. But "the concept of

---

on the basis of their fairness and appropriateness for international commercial transactions falling within their purview ...." (citing Partial Award in ICC Case No. 7110, June 1995, excerpted in ICC Int'l Ct. Arb. Bull., Fall 1999, at 39, 49); and (*ii*) testify as to what the law should be (normative), as opposed to American Law Institute Restatements which speak to the state of the existing law (descriptive).

[10] See P. I. Tchaikovsky, SWAN LAKE (1877) (the entire play concerns Odette as the protagonist); Act III, *id.* (Odile enters).

[11] R. Moloo and J. Chao, *International Investment Law and Sustainable Development: Bridging the Divide*, p. 2 (2011) (unpublished paper on file with the author) [R. Moloo and J. Chao, *Bridging the Divide*] (citing Stephan W. Schill, *Enhancing International Investment Law's Legitimacy: Conceptual and Methodological Foundations of a New Public Law Approach*, 52 VA. J. INT'L L. 57 (2011); William W. Burke-White and Andreas von Staden, *Private Litigation in a Public Law Sphere: The Standard of Review in Investor-State Arbitrations*, 35 YALE J. INT'L L. 283 (2010)).

[12] *Id.*, at 4.

[13] Preambles are where the purpose and objectives are set forth, and often preambles are the first places where tribunals look in order to determine the contents. See, *e.g.*, *Case concerning the Arbitral Award of 31 July 1989 (Guinea-Bissau v. Senegal)*, Dissenting Opinion of Judge Weeramantry [1991] ICJ Reports 53, 67 ("An obvious internal source of reference is the preamble of the treaty. The preamble is a principle and natural source from which indications can be gathered of a treaty's objects and purposes even though the preamble does not contain substantive provisions"); E Suy, "Le Préamble" *in* E. Yakpo and T. Boumedra (eds), LIBER AMICORUM JUDGE MOHAMMED BEDJAOUI 253-69 (Kluwer 1999).

[14] See Vienna Convention on the Law of Treaties (1969) 1155 U.N.T.S. 331, Article 31(2) ("context for the purpose of the interpretation of a treaty shall

sustainable development" "commonly" has not been "include[d]"[15] in IIA preambles. Several scholars contend that this phenomenon provides "a real opportunity to encourage the use of sustainable development norms in adjudicating investment disputes involving developing countries, and to reconcile some of the tensions between investment and sustainable development."[16]

Before the Chapter delves into sustainable development's expanding role in international law, it is appropriate to note that some scholarship urges the IIA community (a consideration which does not, of course, directly apply to international human rights systems or other areas within international law) to strike a note of caution against an over-aggressive use of the police powers. At the bottom of the slippery slope lies the reality that "the protection against expropriation without compensation would become altogether meaningless if states were able to escape the compensation obligation by disguising all expropriations as regulations."[17] What might be lost is the special legitimacy of IIA as a tool of FDI encouragement and orderly resolution of country-country disputes by giving relatively quick and meaningful judicial access to investors and avoiding international confrontation between or among nations.[18]

---

comprise, in addition to the text, including its preamble . . .'); Draft Articles on the Law of Treaties with Commentaries, (1966) 2 Y.B. Int'l L. Comm. 1, 221 ("Paragraph 2 seeks to define what is comprised in the 'context' for the purposes of the interpretation of the treaty That the preamble forms part of a treaty for purposes of interpretation is too well settled to require comment . . .").

[15] Marie-Claire Cordonier Segger and Andrew Newbcombe, "An Integrated Agenda for Sustainable Development in International Investment Law" in Marie-Claire Cordonier Segger, Markus Gehring and Andrew Newcombe (eds) SUSTAINABLE DEVELOPMENT IN WORLD INVESTMENT LAW (Kluwer, 2011) 107, 108.

[16] R. Moloo and J. Chao. *Bridging the Divide, supra,* at 4.

[17] *Id.*, at 10-11 (citing R. Moloo & J. Jacinto, *Environmental and Health Regulation*, *supra*, at 19).

[18] *Id.*, at 11 ("[A] more balanced approach is beginning to take shape, namely, that the expropriation standard revolves around whether the regulation under dispute is legitimate. In order to determine legitimacy, a tribunal must look at: 1) the degree of interference with investment, 2) the investor's legitimate expectations in relation to the use and enjoyment of the investment, and 3) the character of the regulatory measure, including purpose: the regulation must be *bona fide*.") (citing R. Moloo & J. Jacinto, *Environmental and Health Regulation*, *supra*, at 24; *Continental Casualty Company v. Argentine Republic*, ICSID Case No. ARB/03/9, Award, at ¶ 276 (2008); *Glamis Gold, Ltd. v. United States*, NAFTA/UNCITRAL, Award, at ¶ 356 (2009); *Tecnicas Medioambientales Tecmed S.A. v. United Mexican States*, ICSID Case No. ARB(AF)/00/2, Award, at ¶ 121 (2003)).

Sustainable development principles are *now* present in the Kyoto Protocol,[19] the Energy Charter Treaty (ECT),[20] the United Nations Framework Convention on Climate Change (UNFCCC),[21] the United Nations Convention on Biological Diversity,[22] the WHO Framework Convention on Tobacco Control,[23] and the United Nations Convention to Combat Desertification,[24] among other conventions. Sustainable development has never truly and completely taken off in the IIA sphere though it has greater immediate potential in international human rights. Part of the reason for this tardy development in IIA is that the legal status of sustainable development is unclear and less than settled. It was not until 1987 that a functional definition of "sustainable development" was crafted.

At that point in time, the United Nations World Commission on Environment and Development commissioned what became known as the Brundtland Report; the Report's task was to specify sustainable development's significance and parameters. The Report defined sustainable development as "development that meets the needs of the present without compromising the ability of future generations to meet their own needs."[25] The Brundtland Report also observed that a "mere increase in flows of capital to developing countries will not necessarily contribute to development."[26]

Let us explore this theme further. In 1992, half a decade after the publication of the Brundtland Report, the Rio Declaration and its associated roadmap of implementation, Agenda 21, became the "seminal documents" of sustainable development[27]—they are "popularly held to be

---

[19] Kyoto Protocol to the UN Framework Convention on Climate Change (1997), *available at* <www.unfccc.de/fccc/docs/cop3/protocol.html>.

[20]See Energy Charter Treaty (1995), *available at* <www.encharter.org/fileadmin/user_upload/document/EN.pdf>, Article 26(6).

[21] United Nations Framework Convention on Climate Change (1997), *available at* <http://unfccc.int/resource/docs/convkp/conveng.pdf>.

[22] United Nations Convention on Biological Diversity (1992), *available at* <www.cbd.int/>.

[23] World Health Organization Framework Convention on Tobacco Control (2003), *available at* <www.who.int/fctc/text_download/en/index.html>.

[24] United Nations Convention to Combat Desertification (1994), *available at* <www.unccd.int>.

[25] G. H. Brundtland, Our Common Future: The Report of the World Commission on Environment and Development 43 (Oxford University Press, 1987).

[26] *Id.*

[27] Rio Declaration on Environment and Development, 13 June 1992, adopted by the UNCED at Rio de Janeiro (1992) U.N. Doc A/CONF. 151/26 (Vol. 1),

significant for any meaningful elaboration of the concept because they establish objectives, set targets and standards."[28] Remarkably, these documents helped expand the notion of sustainable development beyond its erstwhile ken of environmental sustainability; it now included "social and economic sustainability, especially in developing country contexts" as well.[29]

The 1992 Rio Declaration on Environment and Development recognises that *human development* is no less fundamental to the notion of sustainable development.[30] It is fitting to note that the Vice President of the ICJ, Judge Weeramanstry has done the same, under the "The Concept of Sustainable Development" broad rubric.[31] In 1994, long before sustainable development reached public consciousness, Article 19 of the Energy Charter Treaty incorporated the term: "In pursuit of *sustainable development* and taking account of its obligations under international agreements concerning the environment to which it is a party, each country shall strive to minimize in an economically efficient manner harmful Environmental Impacts... ."[32] Then in 1997, the Programme of Further Action to Implement Agenda 21, came in the form of a United Nations General Assembly Resolution. It stressed that "economic development, social development, and environmental protection are three

---

reprinted in I.L.M. 874, 1992 [Rio Declaration]; see also R. Moloo and J. Chao, *Bridging the Divide, supra,* at 5-7.

[28] P. Schwartz, *Sustainable Development in International Law,* 5 Non-State Actors and International Law 127, 130 (2005) (stating that these documents "provide no composite formal definition of the concept of sustainable development.") [P. Schwartz, *Sustainable Development in International Law*].

[29] R. Moloo and J. Chao, *Bridging the Divide, supra,* at 5.

[30] Rio Declaration, *supra*, Principle 1 (emphasis added).

[31] *Case Concerning the Gabčíkovo-Nagymaros Project (Hungary/Slovakia)*, Judgment of 25 September 1997, ICJ Reports 1997, ¶ 2 ("Had the possibility of environmental harm been the only consideration to be taken into account in this regard, the contentions of Hungary could well have proved conclusive. Yet there are other factors to be taken into account - not the least important of which is the developmental aspect, for the Gabčíkovo scheme is important to Slovakia from the point of view of development. The Court must hold the balance even between the environmental considerations and the developmental considerations raised by the respective Parties. The principle that enables the Court to do so is the principle of sustainable development.").

[32] Article 19, Energy Charter Treaty, 2080 U.N.T.S. 95 (1994) (emphasis added).

interdependent and mutually reinforcing pillars of sustainable development."[33]

A sequel to the Rio Declaration- Programme of Further Action to Implement Agenda 21 chapter was assembled in 2002. In that year, the World Summit on Sustainable Development (WSSD) drafted the 2002 Johannesburg Declaration, stating "a political commitment to sustainable development from world leaders."[34] The Declaration was accompanied by the Johannesburg Plan of Implementation, addressing issues such as poverty reduction and "eradication, consumption and production, the natural resource base, health, small island developing states, regional initiatives, means of implementation, and the institutional framework."[35] The Johannesburg Plan of Implementation reaffirmed certain basic principles of international law concerning sustainable development.[36] According to this Plan, governmental authorities commit themselves to "enhance the benefits developing countries can draw from foreign direct investment."[37]

In the wake of the Johannesburg Plan, the International Law Association published the New Delhi Principles on Sustainable Development, thereby stipulating the principles concerning sustainable development. The enumeration, however succinct, is not exhaustive and contains seven principles:

> 1) The duty of states to ensure sustainable use of natural resources; 2) The principle of equity and the eradication of poverty; 3) The principle of common but differentiated responsibilities; 4) The principle of the precautionary approach to human health, natural resources and ecosystems; 5) The principle of public participation and access to information and justice; 6) The principle of good governance; and 7) The principle of

---

[33] Programme to Further Agenda 21 (1997) UN Doc. A/RES/S-19/2; see also R. Moloo and J. Chao, *Bridging the Divide, supra,* at 6.

[34] World Summit on Sustainable Development, 'Johannesburg Declaration on Sustainable Development' (2002) UN Doc. A/199CONF.20; see also R. Moloo and J. Chao, *Bridging the Divide, supra,* at 6.

[35] R. Moloo and J. Chao, *Bridging the Divide, supra,* at 6.

[36] Marie-Claire Cordonier Segger and Andrew Newbcombe, "An Integrated Agenda for Sustainable Development in International Investment Law" in Marie-Claire Cordonier Segger, Markus Gehring and Andrew Newcombe (eds) SUSTAINABLE DEVELOPMENT IN WORLD INVESTMENT LAW (Kluwer 2011) 107, 108 [M. Cordiner Segger and A. Newcombe, "An Integrated Agenda for Sustainable Development"].

[37] M. Cordonier Segger and A. Newcombe, "An Integrated Agenda for Sustainable Development," *supra*, at 108-109.

integration and interrelationship, in particular in relation to human rights and social, economic and environmental objectives.[38]

Moloo and Chao are undoubtedly correct in praising "[t]he relative simplicity and accessibility of these principles" and attributing "the current [successful] discourse on sustainable development" to those considerations,[39] sooner or later the political "discourse" will need to become framed legal standards. Greater precision will be required of the sustainable development norms.

There is another aspect of sustainable development "not included in the New Delhi Declaration, but potentially quite relevant in international investment disputes."[40] It is "a real bee in the bonnet" to investors and corporations, as one elderly jurist who is a committed IIA practitioner, described to me bluntly. This aspect is corporate responsibility. The WSSD, for its part, underscored "corporate responsibility and accountability" as an important method of attaining the status of sustainable development.[41] It is not alone in pursuing this aim.

Other organizations which have laboured to encourage and elevate the cause of corporate responsibility include the Organization for Economic Cooperation and Development (OECD) through its Guidelines for Multinational Enterprises. These Guidelines constitute a "comprehensive set of principles for responsible business practices in human rights, transparency, and the environment, amongst others."[42] How the tension between sustainable development and investor interests plays out will be interesting and consequential to observe. Sustainable development is already considered "a part of modern international law by reason not only

---

[38] R. Moloo and J. Chao, *Bridging the Divide*, *supra*, at 6; see also New Delhi Declaration Of Principles Of International Law Relating to Sustainable Development, International Law Association (ILA) Resolution 3/2002 in ILA, Report of the Seventieth Conference, New Delhi (ILA 2002); see also Marie-Claire Cordonier Segger, "Significant developments in sustainable development law and governance: A proposal," 28 Natural Resources Forum 61 (2004).

[39] R. Moloo and J. Chao, *Bridging the Divide, supra,* at 6.

[40] *Id.*

[41] Plan of Implementation of the World Summit on Sustainable Development (2002) UN Doc. A/CONF.199/20, 49.

[42] R. Moloo and J. Chao, *Bridging the Divide, supra,* at 7; see also OECD Guidelines for Multinational Enterprises (2008); P. Feeney, "The Relevance of the OECD Guidelines for Multinational Enterprises the Mining Sector and the Promotion of Sustainable Development," OECD Global Forum on International Investment, Paris, France (2002).

of its inescapable logical necessity, but also by reason of its wide and general acceptance by the global community."[43]

The future role and legal status of sustainable development will be a matter of pushing the needle subtly and perhaps subliminally. Whatever the state of official recognition in the meantime and "[e]ven if sustainable development is viewed as an objective rather than a principle of international law," sustainable development's "invocation by States may still engage a certain interstitial normativity helping to push or pull other principles into play, and encouraging States to use certain legal or institutional mechanisms to secure progress toward sustainable development as a policy objective."[44] This "interstitial normativity" triggers within States and within international tribunal thinking processes that might fairly be characterised as "adjudicatory, administrative and deliberative."[45]

If and when the sustainable development *defence* becomes a peremptory norm in international law, as it certainly is on the inevitable track of becoming, it might have broad consequences.[46] The parallels with Professor Brownlie's "national economic disaster" defence, analysed earlier in Chapter § 3.3, are significant. While sustainable development might have reached the status of being some legal norm, it is not yet a

---

[43] *Case Concerning the Gabčíkovo-Nagymaros Project (Hungary/Slovakia)*, Judgment of 25 September 1997, ICJ Reports 1997, para 95.

[44] M. Cordiner Segger and A. Newcombe, "An Integrated Agenda for Sustainable Development," *supra*, at 109-110.

[45] P. Schwartz, *Sustainable Development in International Law, supra,* at 141 ("The legal status of sustainable development is that it is used whenever its elements are to be clarified, interpreted, modified or distinguished in the context in which they may be employed… the legal character of sustainable development as an aspect of that law goes beyond legislative and judicial processes (that may confer obligations relevant for pursuing sustainability) to include adjudicatory, administrative and deliberative processes.").

[46] Article 15.1 of the Budapest Treaty between the Czechoslovak Socialist Republic and the People's Republic of Hungary (September 16, 1977), governing the dispute, states that "the Contracting Parties shall ensure, by the means specified in the joint contractual plan, that the quality of the water in the Danube is not impaired as a result of the construction and operation of the System of Locks." Hence, there was express textual warrant in the Treaty to affirm the virtues and application of the sustainable development norm within the Treaty's context. That the ICJ chose to make grand, widely-applicable and extra-treaty pronouncements highlights the overarching importance of sustainable development to the ICJ. The ball is up in mid-air and appears to be oriented towards peremptory-norm land. The crowds are watching almost in slow-motion, and if pushed by the bookies at this time they might bet that sustainable development will end up as a peremptory norm.

peremptory norm by any means.[47] Simultaneously, however, it is accurate to suggest that while "principles and norms of international law may be in a constant state of creation and flux, at some point such norms," including sustainable development, do "reach a tipping point where they become accepted and applied in all appropriate forums."[48]

How do experts in the IIA domain, not to mention foreign investors, react to these developments concerning (and expanding the role of) sustainable development in theory and in practice? Defensively and without undiluted jubilation. The aforementioned veteran jurist said, "we never wanted this pollution. If it keeps going in this direction, international law is just going to become a spent force."[49] There is more to the investor community's concerns, which stem from fear of illegitimacy derived from arbitrary or insufficiently clear standards of review. The converse to the argument is that "properly designed standards of review can enhance the legitimacy of . . . [international dispute settlement] (including genuinely democratic legitimacy), especially when it comes to public-law-type disputes, and may thus be able to mitigate some elements of the frequently asserted 'legitimacy crisis' of, and 'backlash' against, investment arbitration," among other international law areas.[50]

---

[47] Part of the reason is that sustainable development has not been at the forefront of the discussion long enough, but a more directly attributable cause is that advocates of sustainable development have not yet adequately demonstrated its connection to the very survival and success of international law — in the proximate way that peremptory norm has proven itself to be.

[48] R. Moloo and J. Chao, *Bridging the Divide, supra,* at 8.

[49] Even pro-sustainable development activists must acknowledge that he has a point, and that point is grounded in consent theory: Sustainable development, due simply to its seductive power and potential for virtually unending judicial discretion, has a life of its own. If not clearly cabined, it might lead to outcomes that the signatories never envisioned or approved when entering into the compact(s).

[50] A. von Staden, *Deference or No Deference, supra* ("[G]overnance arrangements . . . [in international law] ultimately needs to be empirically seen as legitimate by both sides to the disputes to assure its institutional survival and maintain compliance, not only from an abstract normative vantage point."); see also W. Burke-White & A. von Staden, *Private Litigation in a Public Law Sphere: The Standard of Review in Investor-State Arbitrations*, 35 YALE J. INT'L L. 283 (2010) [W. Burke-White & A. von Staden, *Private Litigation in a Public Law Sphere*]; A. von Staden, *The Democratic Legitimacy of Judicial Review Beyond the State: Normative Subsidiarity and Judicial Standards of Review*, Jean Monnet Working Paper 10/11 (2011).

Now let us address the substantive standards related to expropriation, in addition to Expropriation itself: *Fair and Equitable Treatment (FET)* and *Minimum Standard of Treatment (MST)* (also sometimes known as the *International Minimum Standard (IMS)*).[51] Due process in the conduct of an expropriation often is encompassed within FET and is addressed that way in this Chapter. This is the currently prevailing IIA nomenclature but both the diplomatic and the international human rights tribunals use criteria similar to FET-MST. Each concept evolves and is usually applied using a generally subjective test—with some guideposts.[52] In the NAFTA arbitration of *ADF Group Inc. v. United States* (2003),[53] Canada's submission encapsulates this evolutionary argument:

> Canada's position has never been that the customary international law regarding the treatment of aliens was 'frozen in amber at the time of the *Neer*[54] decision'. Obviously, what is shocking or egregious in the year 2002 may differ from that which was considered shocking or egregious in 1926. Canada's position has always been that customary international law can evolve over time, but that the threshold for finding violation of the minimum standard of treatment is still high.[55]

As with other tests (in previous chapters), applying these considerations and knowing their relative weights is not easy.[56] Because it is easy to get lost in this forest, we use the FET-MST terms as breadcrumbs. The terms FET and MST are not strictly coextensive but they do have some tests and

---

[51] There is some support for the fact that FET too is borne of IMS.

[52] ICSID Case No ARB(AF)/00/1, Award (2003), at ¶ 179, referring to the Transcript of the Oral Hearing, Vol. II, 16 April 2002, pp. 492-493. Also Post Hearing Transmission of the United States (2002), p. 20 (U.S. Submission: these provisions not "frozen in time").

[53] *Id.*, Second Submission of Canada Pursuant to NAFTA Article 1128 (2002) ¶33.

[54] *USA (L.F. Neer) v. Mexico* (1926), 4 R.I.A.A. 60 (Gen. Cl. Comm'n 1926).

[55] Candidly, the ICSID tribunal in *Mihaly International Corporation v. Democratic Socialist Republic of Sri Lanka*, ICSID Case No. ARB/00/2 (2002), at ¶ 33 stated that "the definition of 'investment' was left to be worked out in the subsequent practice of States, thereby preserving its integrity and flexibility and allowing for future progressive development of international law on the topic of investment." Thus that tribunal, *inter alios*, put the focus on State practice, tribunal behavior and forward-looking evolution of phraseology rather than a fixed historic meaning.

[56] Ioana Tudor too grapples with the vagueness and leaves it for a "bright mind" to "propos[e] suitable concepts for this area of the law." I. Tudor, THE FAIR AND EQUITABLE TREATMENT STANDARD IN THE INTERNATIONAL LAW OF FOREIGN INVESTMENT 226 (Oxford University Press, 2008) [I. Tudor, *FET*].

standards in common.[57] Definitions-wise, these terms are self-explanatory. Decisions and awards have given content and meaning to the standards.[58] Typically, "acts that would give rise to a breach of the minimum standard of treatment prescribed by the [applicable IIA] and customary international law as those that, weighed against the given factual context, amount to a gross denial of justice or manifest arbitrariness falling below acceptable international standards."[59]

Unlike FET, IMS/MST has a long doctrinal pedigree; nonetheless, many of the international violations long identified under other labels often hinted at procedural components now overlapping with FET.[60] Under NAFTA, for instance, FET in the text of the NAFTA now is co-

---

[57] R. Dolzer & C. Schreuer, PRINCIPLES OF INTERNATIONAL INVESTMENT LAW 92-96 (2008) [R. Dolzer & C. Schreuer, IIL PRINCIPLES]; see also "Fair and Equitable Treatment Standard in International Investment Law," OECD Working Papers on International Investment, *available at* <www.oecd.org/dataoecd/22/53/33776498.pdf> (2004).

[58] At least one IIA case has held that the FET is not the same as MST and might require the satisfaction of a greater burden of proof and/or more stringent standards from the State. See *Enron Corporation and Ponderosa Assets, L.P. v. Argentina*, ICSID Case No. ARB/01/3 (2007), at ¶ 258 (holding that "the [FET] standard, at least in the context of the Treaty applicable to this case, can also require a treatment additional to, or beyond that of" MST or international minimum standard); *Sempra Energy International v. Argentina,* ICSID Case No. ARB/02/16 (2007) ("On many occasions," FET might be "more specific, less generic and spelled out in a contemporary fashion so that its application is more appropriate to the case under consideration.").

[59] *International Thunderbird Gaming Corp. v. Mexico,* UNCITRAL Arb. Award (2006), at ¶ 194; see also *Alex Genin et al. v. Estonia*, Award, ICSID Case No. ARB/99/2 (2001); *S.D. Myers, Inc. v. Canada*, First Partial Award, UNCITRAL (NAFTA) (2000); *Mondev International Ltd. v. United States*, ICSID Case No. ARB(AF)/99/2 (2002); *ADF Group Inc. v. United States*, Award, ICSID Case No. ARB(AF)/00/1 (2003; *Azinian v. Mexico*, Arbitral Award, ICSID Case No. ARB(AF)/97/2 (1999) *Loewen Group v. United States*, Award, ICSID Case No. ARB(AF)/98/3 (2003); *Case concerning Elettronica Sicula SpA (ELSI) (United States v. Italy),* 20 July 1989, 1989 I.C.J. 15.

[60] I. Tudor, *FET*, *supra*, at 227-79; S. Schill, "Fair and Equitable Treatment, the Rule of Law, and Comparative Public Law" *in* S. Schill, INTERNATIONAL INVESTMENT LAW AND COMPARATIVE PUBLIC LAW 152 (Oxford University Press, 2010). Tribunals often postpone the official acknowledgement of a novel doctrine until the time is right. Until that time arrives, the doctrine is presented as a necessary component of established law.

extensive with MST in customary international law.[61] Satisfying the FET standard traditionally meant that claimants must prove "egregious and shocking conduct,"[62] "subjective bad faith"[63] or "willful neglect"[64] exercised by the host state.[65] Certainly, part of the reason is that FET has a dangerously malleable quality which could upset the IIA field by upsetting the consent equation.[66] This no one will doubt.

Similarly, with regard to the MST, the NAFTA tribunal in *S. D. Myers v. Canada* (2000) held that IIA tribunals (or domestic tribunals interpreting the relevant IIA) "d[o] not have an open-ended mandate to second-guess government decision-making."[67] That recognition is attended the candid admission that governments, which are forced to make "controversial" decisions, "may appear to have made mistakes, to have misjudged the facts, proceeded on the basis of a misguided economic or sociological theory, placed too much emphasis on some social values over others and adopted solutions that are ultimately ineffective or counterproductive."[68] There might not be a remedy under the international or domestic systems, some scholars and jurists might argue. Assuming, however, that there *is*, "[t]he ordinary remedy . . . for errors in modern

---

[61] F. Zarbiyev, *Judicial Activism in International Law, supra,* at 19 (In July 2001, "[e]xtensive interpretations of the fair and equitable treatment standard of NAFTA, prompted the NAFTA Free Trade Commission, which is composed of the representatives of the three contracting parties, to issue an interpretive note pointing out that the fair and equitable treatment standard within NAFTA amounted to the same standard as the minimum treatment standard of customary international law.") (citing *Pope & Talbot v. Canada*, Final Award, 10 April 2001, at ¶ 111–17; T. Ginsburg, *Bounded Discretion in International Judicial Lawmaking*, 45 VA. J. INT'L L. 631, 662–63 (2005)).

[62] *Neer v. Mexico*, 4 Review of International Arbitration Awards (15 Oct. 1926) 4.

[63] *Alex Genin, Eastern Credit Limited, Inc v. Republic of Estonia*, ICSID Case No. ARB/99/2, Award (25 June 2001), at ¶¶ 367, 371; see also *Eudoro Armando Olguin v. Republic of Paraguay*, ICSID Case No. ARB/98/5, Award (26 July 2001).

[64] *Alex Genin v. Estonia*, *supra*.

[65] See also E. De Brabandere, *'Good Faith', 'Abuse of Process' and the Initiation of Investment Treaty Claims*, J INT. DISP. SETTLEMENT (2012) 3(3): 609.

[66] See, *e.g.*, S. Montt, STATE LIABILITY IN INVESTMENT TREATY ARBITRATION: GLOBAL CONSTITUTIONALISM AND ADMINISTRATIVE LAW IN THE BIT GENERATION 370 (Hart, 2009) (noting the "real danger that an unrestrained international investment law jurisprudence [concerning FET] could crystallize conservative rules that overprotect the *status quo*.").

[67] *S.D. Myers v. Canada*, NAFTA/UNCITRAL, First Partial Award (2000), at ¶ 261.

[68] *Id.*

governments is through internal political and legal processes, including elections."[69]

This has been the general rule. But rules tend to have exceptions. In expanding FET/MST, several IIA tribunals have used the FET standard to encompass considerations such as the legitimate expectations of the investor (the "stabilisation clauses" contained in several modern IIA's mentioned in Chapter I could be an over-compensatory response to this phenomenon),[70] stability and predictability of the legal framework, and, finally, transparency and processual fairness.[71] Put simply, the FET standard "is intended to protect the investor against arbitrary, discriminatory or unreasonable conduct."[72] Some pro-sovereignty jurists maintain that effective term of art though "legitimate expectations" and other substantive tests are, there simply is no cognisable expropriation without an actual forfeiture of property by the State. Certainly, a procedural violation *relating to* or *in the course of* challenging the alleged expropriation would be a discrete and separate violation[73] but the alleged expropriation itself would not be legally cognisable before an international tribunal. One could imagine that a jurist holding this view would tell the

---

[69] *Id.* In *S. D. Myers*, the tribunal's finding of protectionist intent led to a finding of an NT breach (Article 1102), which in turn led to its finding an MST breach (Article 1105). In 2001, the Parties subsequently issued a Note of Reinterpretation through the NAFTA Free Trade Commission, stating that a "breach of other provisions of NAFTA or of separate international agreements do not establish that there has been a breach of Article 1105(1)." See NAFTA Free Trade Commission, Notes of Interpretation of Certain Chapter 11 Provisions (July 31, 2001).

[70] *Biwater Gauff Ltd v. United Republic of Tanzania*, ICSID Case No. ARB/05/22, Award, at ¶ 602; see also *Saluka Investments BV (The Netherlands) v. the Czech Republic*, UNCITRAL, Partial Award (17 Mar 2006) ¶ 165.

[71] *Tecmed v. Mexico*, ICSID Case No. ARB(AF)/00/2, Award (2003), at ¶ 154.

[72] R. Moloo and J. Chao, *Bridging the Divide, supra,* at 11; see also R. Moloo and J. Jacinto, *Environmental and Health Regulation, supra*, at 38.

[73] With respect to such claims, one can imagine sovereign responses to requests for arbitration or human rights applications to this effect: Had supremely frivolous expropriation claims not been filed, the associated violation would not have taken place. The implication of this "but-for" causation argument might then be that either the facts dictated a dismissal of all or most of the claims against the sovereign or, conversely and as a second-best alternative, that if the other violations are recognised by the tribunal, then at least the original super-frivolity of the expropriation claim be deemed a mitigating consideration decreasing the compensation that is ordered.

claimants' counsel: "*Taking* what?"[74] The mere dashing of hopes or *oblique* intimations will not do.

Let us summarise and order these propositions. According to IIA tribunals, then, the FET inquiry includes, but may expand beyond, the following questions: (*i*) whether the State has provided a stable and predictable legal framework; (*ii*) whether the State made specific representations to the investor; (*iii*) whether due process has been denied to the investor; (*iv*) whether there is a lack of transparency in the legal procedure or in the actions taken by the State; (*v*) whether the host State has harassed, coerced, abused power or conducted other acts in bad faith with material harm falling on the investor; and (*vi*) whether any of the actions of the State can be deemed arbitrary, discriminatory or inconsistent.[75]

As for point (*vi*), it is not doctrinally at all certain that tribunals can or should, though it is now tacitly accepted that they do so, squeeze discrimination into the FET standard when there already exists a strong and reticulated non-discrimination standard. It is, however, basically settled that as form goes "access to international arbitration [is] a necessary part of FET."[76] However, in customary international law, the precise form is largely in the discretion of the State.[77]

The justification for this rule is not unlike the justification for the exhaustion rule, articulated in Chapter IV (EXHAUSTION OF LOCAL REMEDIES AND CONTINUOUS NATIONALITY): both to recognise the domestic system's sovereign flexibility but also to encourage domestic jurisdictions to build up their judicial systems. It would take "specific evidence" to rebut the presumption that "host State adjudication of treaty rights was necessarily inferior to international arbitration."[78] Even

---

[74] "Taking" implies that the alleged victim had something of concrete or realizable value which the alleged perpetrator appropriated.

[75] *Lemire v. Ukraine,* ICSID Case No. ARB(AF)/98/1, at ¶ 284, Decision on Liability (2010).

[76] *Rights of Nationals of the United States of America in Morocco (France v. United States of America),* Judgment of 27 Aug. 1952, I. C. J. Rep. 1952, p. 192, at ¶ 105.

[77] *Renta 4 S.V.S.A. v. Russian Federation,* SCC (Mar. 29, 2009), at ¶ 23 (Separate opinion of Judge Charles Brower) ("a State that does not provide to a foreign investor dispute settlement procedures at all necessarily will deny that investor fair and equitable treatment when a dispute arises. The means by which the State in questio[n] offers dispute settlement, in order to avoid a denial of justice, is largely in its discretion. It can do so by setting up a domestic court system, but it may equally provide dispute settlement by consenting to arbitration.").

[78] C. McLachlan, L. Shore & M. Weiniger, INTERNATIONAL INVESTMENT ARBITRATION: SUBSTANTIVE PRINCIPLES, p. 257. This is not to say that IIA tribunals believe that

committed deferentialists such as Andreas von Staden believe that a case-by-case approach, governed by established and stable but also flexible analytical tests, is the proper and preferred course of action.[79] Proponents of this approach must acknowledge that in many jurisdictions, particularly in some developing countries, there is a definitive absence of "consistent and transparent regulatory processes founded on principles of due process in any context."[80] From this follows the fear that "the international investment regime is imposing stringent standards for investors that developing countries cannot provide for its own citizens."[81]

Any good argument in modern international law must do its utmost to justify its main and subsidiary conclusions through a deft use of pedigree and tradition. *This* particular deferentialist argumentation links deference with legitimacy of the international tribunal, instrumentalising the various standards of *review* (different from standards of claims, such as FET, IMS, etc.).[82] This argumentation starts with the premise that "[s]tandards of review are almost entirely[83] judicially created instruments that allow the reviewing court or tribunal to adjust the scope, depth, and intensity with which it will review the acts of another (usually governmental) actor" or functionary whose conduct is attributable to the government, "based on considerations of normative appropriateness, technical expertise, politico-cultural proximity, or a mix thereof."[84] "[T]he recognition" to be deduced from this premise is that there exist "several sites of political and legal decision-making, each of which can lay a claim to legitimate authority in interpreting and applying the relevant legal norm at issue."[85]

---

this "specific evidence" is all that elusive. See, *e.g.*, *Renta, supra,* at ¶ 100 ("History is replete with examples of investment disputes which have overwhelmed the capacity of national institutions — in countries of all stages of development — for dispassionate judgment.").

[79] A. von Staden, *Deference or No Deference, supra.*

[80] R. Moloo and J. Chac, *Bridging the Divide, supra,* at 12.

[81] *Id.*

[82] Various *standards of review*, such as good faith or clear error, are built into each *claim*.

[83] A. von Staden, *Deference or No Deference, supra.* (citing n. 9, stating "The prominent exception in international law is Article 17.6 of the WTO Anti-Dumping Agreement whose explicit standards of review are, however, partly phrased in an ultimately self-defeating manner; see Steven P. Croley & John H. Jackson, *WTO Dispute Procedures, Standard of Review, and Deference to National Governments*, 90 AM. J. INT'L L. 193, 200-201 (1996).").

[84] *Id.*

[85] *Id.*

The deferentialists then argue that this recognition must "be justified precisely because it defines the relationship between different sites of legitimate political and legal decision-making from the vantage point of the reviewing court."[86] Finally comes the joint legitimacy-standards of review conclusion: "By defining reasonably deferential standards of review that grant respondent states enough freedom of choice in pursuing public interest policies that they deem necessary, . . . tribunals can recognize and protect states' legitimate regulatory interests without abdicating their judicial supervisory function, nor the protection of investor interests."[87] The European Court of Justice, the ECtHR and the IACtHR tend to have an in-built and judicially-acknowledged jurisprudence of some deference or "margin of appreciation."[88]

The caveat, of course, is that legitimacy is a protective criterion only to the extent the textual proviso, where applicable, covers the expropriatory and/or related act(s). Although it is somewhat true, as the deferentialists posit, that "the parameters of a given standard of review and the assessment of whether state action meets the specific and/or general threshold requirements under a given provision (e.g., no abuse of right, no arbitrary discrimination etc.) remain subject to judicial control,"[89] theoretically (and construed neutrally) "judicial control" is not the same as judicial *law-making*.

Assuming these premises, the only way this deferentialist chain of reasoning justifies the legitimacy-deference link is if abundance of caution and a specific version of the proper role of international tribunals bridges the logical gap. I do not contend that this would be invalid; I simply suggest that if we are to avow such extra-textual considerations we should consider doing so explicitly. It should also be recognised that the supposed purism of some deferentialists has certain in-built limits. They might realistically believe that the deference (also known as the "margin of appreciation doctrine) "provides for different degrees of deference depending on the specific rights and legal provisions at issue" and that "standards of review need to emerge endogenously out of the interpretation of concrete legal texts, not be imposed from the outside."[90]

---

[86] *Id.*
[87] *Id.*
[88] *Id.*
[89] *Id.*
[90] *Id.* (citing W. Burke-White & A. von Staden, *Private Litigation in a Public Law Sphere, supra* & S. Marks, *The European Convention on Human Rights and Its 'Democratic Society'*, 66 BRIT. Y.B. INT'L L. 209, 219 (1995)).

Wading the Ambiguities and Designing a Functional Framework

Let us now examine the contents of the various claims. In recent years, one scholar, Richard Bilder, has most eloquently attempted to infuse the IMS with, or recognise within the standard (depending how one chooses to read his work), certain ingredients. He has argued that "[w]hile . . . the precise content of the international minimum standard in relation to judicial proceedings—what constitutes a 'denial of justice' in such cases—is uncertain, . . . its general contours . . . are reasonably clear."[91]

What makes this assertion even more remarkable is that Professor Bilder was arguing that the IMS "overlaps and reinforces" non-discrimination "to some extent," and he was doing so in his official opinion to the *Loewen* tribunal.[92] The dual considerations recognised by Professor Bilder are as follows:

> On the one hand, the concept has been said to broadly embrace a discriminatory, arbitrary or capricious refusal by courts or other appropriate tribunals to entertain proceedings for the redress of injury suffered by an alien, undue delay in judicial proceedings affecting aliens, serious inadequacies in the administration of justice, or an obvious and deliberate misapplication of the law in a case involving an alien. . . . On the other hand, it appears accepted that mere error by a national court does not in itself constitute a denial of justice, absent discriminatory intent.[93]

It is true that Bilder acted as a fact-skeptic in disputing whether the *Loewen* trial in Mississippi was a violation as described by the pro-claimant submission of Sir Professor Robert Jennings, QC (as Bilder described Jennings's complaints, "'a remarkable travesty of the most

---

[91] *Loewen Group, supra*, at ¶ 16 (Submission of Prof. Richard Bilder on international law governing state responsibility for treatment of foreign investors) (2001). Compare with A.V. Freeman, THE INTERNATIONAL RESPONSIBILITY OF STATES FOR DENIAL OF JUSTICE 291-93 (1938) ("Obviously, no *a priori* or general answer to this question can be attempted ....") [A.V. Freeman, DENIAL OF JUSTICE].

[92] *Id.*

[93] *Id.* (also citing Harvard Draft Convention on Responsibility of States, art. 9, reprinted in 23 AM. J. INT'L L. SUPP. 133 ("A state is responsible if an injury to an alien results from a denial of justice. Denial of justice exists where there is a denial, unwarranted delay or obstruction of access to the courts, gross deficiency in the administration of judicial or remedial process, failure to provide those guarantees generally considered indispensable to the proper administration of justice, or a manifestly unjust judgment. An error of a national court which does not produce manifest injustice is not a denial of justice.")).

elementary notions of justice', in which a jury drawn from a "small, remote and not at all well-off African-American community'—'manipulated', 'befuddled', 'mesmerized' and 'seduced' by the 'unsavory performance' of plaintiff's counsel who, unrestrained by the trial court judge, engaged in a 'gross abuse of the system' and 'ruthless and blatant' stirring-up of the jury's 'latent' racial and nationalistic prejudice—predictably awarded 'absurdly and outrageously inflated damages' against Loewen.").[94]

Professor Bilder argued that "this misperceives, and indeed caricatures, the trial proceedings."[95] He did not, however, act as a law-skeptic, which is exactly what he would have had he challenged Prof. Jennings's claim (both implicit, in certain parts of his submission, and explicit, in other parts) that such a characterisation does indeed constitute an IMS or denial of justice violation.

Another line of attack for Professor Bilder might have been, and it may yet be taken up by other practitioners, that the background of Professor Jennings and the background of the authorities he cites both are entirely non-American. While it is *international* minimum standard that is being expounded, there exists at least a colourable claim that the IMS requires only that the alleged treatment be in the mainstream of the specific jurisdiction's conduct, not that there is an airtight, immovable particular standard applicable internationally.

The latter is a test that tribunals might be reluctant to accept because it would be almost impossible to define, so the former might be more palatable just by default. That jurisdiction-specific test, Bilder might have argued and experts as well as counsel in future cases can still argue, is an integral part of the IMS. This is not to say that there is *no* internationally-germane standard, based on the *Neer* award, whatsoever but only to say that its threshold is lower.[96]

Jennings almost anticipated an argument like the one I just articulated. This, in turn, Sir Robert attempted to counter: "The second phase [of the Loewen trial in Mississippi state court] allowed counsel to mesmerise the jury into changing their own already grossly exaggerated sum of $160 million punitive damages into 5400 million. In terms of denial of justice

[94] *Loewen Group, supra*, at ¶ 24 (Submission of Prof. Richard Bilder on international law governing state responsibility for treatment of foreign investors) (2001).

[95] *Id.*

[96] The award in *Merrill & Ring Forestry L.P. v. Canada*, Award, at ¶¶ 200-213, acknowledged that some awards and theorists have expanded the scope of MST beyond *Neer's* original contemplation.

these astonishing figures speak for themselves. These verdicts were brought about by carefully calculated, and wholly improper means. The gross denial of justice was the intended result."[97] Prof. Jennings then tried to show the incompatibility with "the letter and spirit of" "NAFTA's policy of encouraging investment" the "unexplained immense punitive damages for a breach of contract involving relatively small sums of money."[98]

Now please look closely at Professor Sir Jennings' language here. Not only was Jennings invoking the text and the purpose of the textual instrument but he was also invoking a logical disconnect that reveals, in his view, the conflict with IMS. Simply put, "unexplained immense punitive damages for a breach of contract involving relatively small sums of money" is not the normal cost of doing business in Mississippi or elsewhere in the United States.[99] Aberration from the usual norm, absent extraordinary and proportionate justifications, tends to be a powerful clue that something is rotten in the State of Mississippi.

This is the reason, in Jennings's view, that "[t]he sums awarded were so bizarrely disproportionate as almost to defy belief."[100] This is also the reason that a "legitimate expectations" argument also existed for the claimant. This is why, still, an appeal to the United States Supreme Court (as Chapter IV has explored, albeit in the exhaustion context) might have had serious merit under Supreme Court precedents concerning the Fifth and Fourteenth Amendments' guarantees of due process.[101]

IMS/MST's broadest sweep actually covers more than just the foreign investor's property and investment rights. Interestingly, it includes Full

---

[97] *Loewen Group, supra*, at ¶ 21 (Submission of Sir Robert Jennings, Q.C., on the general state of the claim).
[98] *Id.*, at ¶ 22.
[99] *Id.*
[100] *Id.*, at ¶ 21.
[101] U.S. Const. Amdts. V and XIV. The controlling Supreme Court precedent at the time of *Loewen* was (and remains) *BMW of North America v. Gore*, 517 U.S. 559, 562 (1996) ("The Due Process Clause of the Fourteenth Amendment prohibits a State from imposing a 'grossly excessive' punishment on a tortfeasor."); *id.*, at 575 ("Perhaps the most important *indicium* of the reasonableness of a punitive damages award is the degree of reprehensibility of the defendant's conduct."); *id.*, at 580 ("perhaps [the] most commonly cited *indicium* of an unreasonable or excessive punitive damages award is its ratio to the actual harm inflicted on the plaintiff. . . . The principle that exemplary damages must bear a 'reasonable relationship' to compensatory damages has a long pedigree."); *id.*, at 583 ("Comparing the punitive damages award and the civil or criminal penalties that could be imposed for comparable misconduct provides a third *indicium* of excessiveness.").

Protection and Security (FPS) protections of property protection, safety and personhood as well. This tendency was clear in *Biwater Gauff Ltd. v. Tanzania* (2008),[102] where the IIA tribunal applied investor protection rights with regard to the *persons* of the investor's employees and referred extensively to IUCT cases[103] in so doing: "the deportation of [the Claimant's] senior management, the seizure of [the Claimant's] assets and the immediate installation of [a company friendly to the Respondent]" were "abusive and unreasonable" under the U.K.-Tanzania BIT.[104] International agreements and domestic constitutions which put these terms—FET and IMS/MST—in the judicial arsenal have allowed tribunals to remedy violations not spelled out in the text. Indeed, an excessively exhaustive list may counterproductively block *other* winnable claims.

International tribunals are also different because there is a presumption of affirmative obligations owed the foreign investor by the State. In fact, the Full Protection and Security (FPS) provision contained in numerous IIA's so encapsulates. Recent occurrences in Kazakhstan, the Russian Federation, and Nigeria render the issue starkly topical.[105] The scepticism usually attending any non-negative obligations claims (or sub-claims) does not significantly affect international investment cases; whether or not it is a principle in international human rights law, however, seems not to be a settled issue.

---

[102] ICSID CASE NO. ARB/05/22.

[103] Referring to the management and control cases: *SEDCO v. NIOC* (1985); *Tippetts v. Iran* (1986); *Starrett Housing v. Iran* (1987); *ITT Industries v. Iran*, 2 IUCTR 348 (1983); *Phelps Dodge v. Iran* (1985).

[104] *Id.*, at ¶ 709.

[105] F. Ferrari & R. Rolfini, *Investing in a Dangerous World: A New Political Risk Index*, Working Paper No. 06, SACE Group, p. 3 ("The recent dispute between ENI, an Italian oil firm, and the Kazakh government over the exploitation of the oil field of Kashagan is the latest in a long list of cases where foreign investments have been threatened by government decisions or political violence acts. In April 2006, the Venezuelan government took control of the Jusepin and Dacion oil fields operated by French firm Total and Italian ENI, after they refused to change their operations into joint ventures with the state oil firm PDVSA. Under a protocol signed on December 21, 2006 the Russian government forced the entry in the Sakhalin Energy project of the state oil company Gazprom as the major shareholder, with the stakes of the other three shareholders (Shell, Mitsui and Mitsubishi) being diluted. In Nigeria, oil pipeline breaks due to vandalism and sabotage have almost doubled, from 497 to 895, between 1999 and 2004 and product loss due to pipeline ruptures has grown steadily from 179,000 to 396,000 metric tons over the same period – a figure roughly equal to four super tankers.") (internal quotation marks omitted).

The IIA tribunal in *El Paso v. Argentina* (2011) observed that the FPS standard "is no more than the traditional obligation to protect aliens under international customary law and that it is a residual obligation provided for those cases in which the acts challenged may not in themselves be attributed to the Government, but to a third party."[106] The care and vigilance that States must take to protect foreign investments and investors essentially is "a duty of prevention and a duty of repression."[107]

If, however, the alleged measures are directly attributable to the State and not to a third party, then the FPS scrutiny angle vanishes. While this language is broad, an earlier award in *AWG v. Argentina* (2010) and *Suez and Vivendi v. Argentina* (2010),[108] had limited the scope of the FPS standard ever so substantively: "Argentina is obliged to exercise due diligence to protect investors and investments primarily from physical injury, and that in any case Argentina's obligations under the relevant provisions do not extend to encompass the maintenance of a stable legal and commercial environment"—unless, of course, the IIA promised the "maintenance of a stable legal and commercial environment." The consolidated award in *AWG* and *Suez and Vivendi* considered the specific treaty language (though a neutral reading does not reveal that this would be *lex specialis*), the historic maturation of international law principles, and recent awards to reach this conclusion.[109]

Limits of the International Minimum Standard and the Lure of Investment In-Flow

States are most sensitive to being told their process is somehow inadequate or patently wrong or that their aims are illegitimate. As the previous Chapter has explained, non-discrimination somehow manages to strike most governments, investors and civil society actors as a more "objective" claim. Rightly or wrong, non-discrimination gives the impression of a neutral exercise of the judicial function. It is therefore no surprise that the "substantive standards" jurisprudence of international tribunals is the most controversial part of their work. In the eyes of some

---

[106] *El Paso v. Argentina*, ICSID Case No. ARB/03/15, Award, 31 October 2011, at ¶ 522.

[107] *Id.*

[108] Decision on Liability, 30 July 2010, at ¶ 179 (consolidated cases).

[109] *Azurix v. Argentina*, ICSID Case No. ARB/01/12 (Argentina-United States BIT), Award, 14 July 2006; *CME Czech Republic B.V. v. Czech Republic*, UNCITRAL (Czech Republic-The Netherlands BIT), Partial Award, 13 September 2001.

critics, this is where the tribunals are most likely to use malleable doctrines to bring about the "irrelevancy-impotency of the nation state, the resulting field of play for economic imperialism, and resulting opportunities to engage in regulatory arbitrage,[110] leading to problems such as environmental degradation and 'plantation production… .'"[111]

This is also the reason that IMS or denial of justice has "generally not been regarded as embracing those more 'garden-variety' and relatively inconsequential procedural or substantive errors that are endemic in every legal system."[112] International tribunals have employed, in this sense, rather a prudential approach in granting relief only to those claims that are truly "egregious."[113] Two international awards, from 1927[114] and 1932[115]

---

[110] Regulatory arbitrage could refer to any system or act restructuring the firm whereby the assets or debts are allocated to particular uses by internal or external forces. Examples include preferential tax rates, insurance policies, and the outsourcing of non-revenue-generating operations such as a firm's information technology infrastructure and internal accounting and audits. Another example is shareholder nationality often defined by country of incorporation. Chapter § 3.3 addresses this issue.

[111] D. M. Branson, *The Very Uncertain Prospect of "Global" Convergence in Corporate Governance*, 34 CORNELL INT'L L.J. 321, 352 (2001); see also C. N. Brower, *Investor-State Disputes under NAFTA: A Tale of Fear and Equilibrium*, 29 PEPP. L. REV. 43, 44 (2001) ("Canadian and U.S. writers have denounced the purportedly 'aggressive' use of investor-state arbitration as an 'offensive' weapon that has 'chilled' the exercise of regulatory authority and caused an 'alarming' loss of sovereignty. Based on the wide variety of pending claims, writers warn that Chapter [Eleven] provides foreign corporations with a reliable 'tool for attacking any legislation or regulation that they do not find beneficial to their investments.'").

[112] *Loewen Group, supra*, at ¶ 18 (Submission of Prof. Richard Bilder on international law governing state responsibility for treatment of foreign investors) (2001).

[113] Among others, two of the greatest names in twentieth-century international law (Louis Henkin and A. V. Freeman) seem to accept this axiom. See, *e.g.*, L. Henkin, et al., INTERNATIONAL LAW 715, n.3. (3rd ed. 1993) ("It is well-settled that a mere error in a decision or relatively minor procedural irregularities do not constitute unlawful denials of procedural justice. The injustice must be egregious. The decision must be 'so obviously wrong that it cannot have been made in good faith and with reasonable care' or 'a serious miscarriage of justice' must otherwise be clear'..."); A.V. Freeman, DENIAL OF JUSTICE, *supra*, at 291-93 ("Ample protection against arbitrary violations of the local law will normally be afforded within the State itself by the conventional means of appeal to a superior court. Ruling improperly on evidence, erroneously charging a jury, exceeding the decorous limits of judicial restraint with prejudicial effects for one of the parties (such as openly insulting the claimant's attorney before the jury), emotionally addressing the jurymen with the aim of kindling their hostility, and the like will usually find

respectively, drive home the point rather concisely. "[O]therwise, almost every legal case involving an alien might, in practice as well as theory, be subject to diplomatic complaint and international oversight."[116]

The IIA's sometimes are left unchallenged, in stark political terms, by the host governments themselves. Tellingly, in urging Liberian environmental and human rights activists not to press cases against the Malaysian corporation Sime Darby, President Ellen Johnson said: "If you do so all the foreign investors coming to Liberia will close their businesses and leave, then Liberia will go back to the old days."[117]

Chapter I has addressed that formally the reciprocity principle (each signatory nation possesses the same rights for their outward investors or property owners) among nations is the bedrock for the consent justification. It is just as true that

---

rectification in the wisdom of the reviewing bench. Where this does not happen, there is still left the question of whether these various deviations from regular judicial activity are sufficiently flagrant to embroil the State. For it is generally agreed that mere 'minor irregularities' in the course of the procedure will not justify interposition. As the General Claims Commission put it in the *McCurdy* case, 'the existence of some irregularities in the proceedings against an offender does not necessarily constitute a sufficient ground in itself to justify a declaration of denial of justice.' This is simply another way of stating that those violations of the local adjective law which do not have the effect of vitiating guarantees exacted by the international duty of judicial protection must be disregarded. But when does an irregularity become sufficiently gross so as to be considered as a denial of justice?").

[114] *Putnam Case*, U.S.-Mexico General Claims Commission, 4 R.I.A.A. 151, 153 (award of Apr. 15, 1927) ("Only a clear and notorious injustice, visible, to put it thus, at a mere glance, could furnish ground for an international arbitral tribunal of the character of the present, to put aside the national decision presented before it and to scrutinize its grounds of fact and law.").

[115] *Salem Arbitration* (*U.S. v. Egypt*), 2 R.I. A. A. 1161 (award of June 8, 1932) (addresses "claims only [of] exorbitant cases of judicial injustice," including "obvious discrimination of foreigners against nationals [and] palpable and malicious iniquity of judgment ... .").

[116] *Loewen Group, supra*, at ¶ 18 (Submission of Prof. Richard Bilder on international law governing state responsibility for treatment of foreign investors) (2001).

[117] "A Nobel Laureate's Problem at Home," op-ed, *New York Times*, January 20, 2012, *available at* <www.nytimes.com/2012/01/21/opinion/in-liberia-a-nobel-laureates-problem.html?_r=1> (last accessed January 21, 2012); A. Bjorklund, *Foreword, Symposium: Romancing the Foreign Investor, BIT by BIT*, 12 U.C. DAVIS J. INT'L L. & POL'Y 1, 5-7 (2005).

> many BITs are signed between countries of vastly different socio-economic statuses, with one country being the primary capital exporter and the other being the primary importer. The result is that developing countries sign agreements strongly favoring the inward investments, without any guarantees as to spill-over benefits that the investments may have to its socio-economic development. Specifically, such investments could harm sustainable development by making the government liable when it takes legitimate action to maintain environmental, social, and economic well-being.[118]

Fact or myth or just fear-mongering (which some have claimed it is), this terror of being forced to return "to the old days" has had some traction.[119] Out of 2,349 changes in national FDI laws between 1991 and 2005, a staggering 92% were in favor of creating a more hospitable environment for foreign investors.[120] Whereas manufacturing sectors have proven themselves to be open to FDI, "[n]atural resources are less so, but [multi-national corporations] have access through various non-equity forms. Even the services sector—which, traditionally, has contained many activities that are off-limits for foreign investors—has increasingly been opened, although (compared especially with manufacturing) many restrictions still apply."[121]

A significant note about the second-prong of the international-wrong analysis: Is the measure narrowly tailored to the government's objective? We know of the proposition that ceding sovereignty in international courts is not the *only* way to encourage investment. Other recognised strategies are: "the creation of sufficient number of Special Economic Zones of quality," "the proactive role of the state governments in aiding the FDI process in conjunction with the Central government and the private sector," the creation of "desirable infrastructure facilities, relaxation of small-scale industry regulations, lower commodity and utility prices, lower indirect taxes, lower import duties on raw materials, fiscal and other fillips

---

[118] R. Moloo and J. Chao, *International Investment Law and Sustainable Development: Bridging the Divide*, p. 2 (2011) (unpublished paper on file with the author).

[119] See, *e.g.*, M. Reisman, "Foreign Investment, Economic Development and National Sovereignty," Keynote Address, Seoul, South Korea, April 13, 2007.

[120] UNCTAD, World Investment Report 2006: FDI from Developing and Transition Economies, Geneva, 2006, p. 23.

[121] K. P. Sauvant, "Regulatory risk and the Growth of FDI" *in* WORLD INVESTMENT PROSPECTS TO 2011: FOREIGN DIRECT INVESTMENT AND THE CHALLENGE OF POLITICAL RISK 67-68 (Economist Intelligence Unit in co-operation with the Columbia Program on International Investment (CPII), 2007).

to encourage some specific types of investment, incentives for new business promotion, harmonization of government policies and reduction of red-tapism."[122]

The point is important because it might weaken the consent-based *de facto* coercion arguments advanced by some sovereign defendants. Dissatisfied by a sovereign's expropriation or nationalisation justifications, an international tribunal might suggest that the governmental behaviour was excessive because, if it is the case, the sovereign had not attempted (or adequately attempted) the less drastic alternatives.

Absent that effort, the sovereign bears a seriously high burden of proving that its behaviour was not drastic and needlessly pre-emptive. Of course, if it will be an obvious blind alley or is too risky or time-sensitive to attempt less drastic or draconian measures, that might be excusable. Thus, it follows that *in effect and tacitly* IIA tribunals might be able to mandate scaled-down remedies. This strategy might avoid even the mildest hint of judicial arrogance that the earlier-analysed *Micula v. Romania* (2008) framework fails to conceal.

We must also face the political reality out there. A *sturm und drang* angle: Some political leaders often are judged significantly based on the sum of money that is the FDI in-flow on their watch. This seems to be a more prominent criterion to judge the leadership in less developed countries than for those in developed economies but the latter too are not immune.[123] Unless and until that metric changes, this recurring problem will probably continue.[124] Statistically and so far empirically, several of the claims suggesting that have been shown to be hyperbolic.[125]

---

[122] N. Bajpai & N. Dasgupta, "Multinational Companies and Foreign Direct Investment in India and China," *supra,* at 2.

[123] See, *e.g.*, J. W. Salacuse & N. P. Sullivan, *Do BITs Really Work?: An Evaluation of Bilateral Investment Treaties and Their Grand Bargain*, 46 HARV. INT'L L. J. 67 (2005).

[124] See K. P. Gallagher & E. Shrestha, *Investment Treaty Arbitration and Developing Countries: A Re-Appraisal*, GLOBAL DEVELOPMENT AND ENVIRONMENT INSTITUTE WORKING PAPER, May 2011, *available at* <www.ase.tufts.edu/gdae/Pubs/wp/11-01TreatyArbitrationReappraisal.pdf>, at p. 2 ("A key argument is that these treaties elevate the rights of foreign firms over host governments, and allow those firms to directly file claims against those governments. Many claims have been targeted toward policies for the public welfare, so the story goes, and thus hinder the ability of developing countries especially to develop the proper institutions to raise their standards of living. Moreover, the costs of awards that need to be paid to claimants and the cost to carry out a case are seen as enormous by developing country standards. Taken as a whole then, these concerns make developing nations very cautious about any

This Chapter discusses the protection against non-compensable expropriation, addressing the intents *versus* effects test, the reasonable expectations factor (reliance), and the proportionality test.[126] The Chapter also addresses how the tribunals evaluate the legitimacy of a governmental measure resulting in an expropriation, and whether such an expropriatory measure triggers compensation. The issue rapidly becomes one of trying to draw a principled and non-arbitrary line of demarcation.

Past chapters (especially Chapter III: ATTRIBUTION AND CAUSATION) have laid the groundwork for this one. This Chapter will connect the dots with Chapters III, IV (EXHAUSTION OF LOCAL REMEDIES AND CONTINUOUS NATIONALITY), and V (NON-DISCRIMINATION). Particularly with reference to legitimacy and the "interactional law" model, this Chapter highlights the transferability of knowledge among the prototypical institutions in this dissertation. The Brunnée-Toope interactional model's "enmeshment of norms in a practice of legality"[127] also takes on a special significance in this Chapter simply because the application of the rules is

---

measure that could be perceived as in violation of a treaty. A growing number of actors argue that such fears can be laid to rest. Defenders claim that the system does not unfairly subject developing countries to arbitral panels. When these arguments are made, they often rely on the relatively recent empirical work by legal scholar Susan Franck. Franck's work suggests that developing countries are not subject to more claims under the system, and that investors do not win the majority of cases. When foreign investors do win, the awards paid are not necessarily large amounts.") (citing S. D. Franck, *Development and Outcomes of Investment Treaty Arbitration*, 50 HARV. INT'L L. J. 435 (2009); S. D. Franck, *Empirically Evaluating Claims About Investment Treaty Arbitration*, 86 N.C. L. REV. 1 (2007)) [K. P. Gallagher & E. Shrestha, *Investment Treaty Arbitration and LDC's*].

[125] *Id.*, at 3 ("Franck's study found that the bulk of the cases (around 90%) did indeed originate from high income countries of which 32 cases were from the U.S. Among the respondent governments, 70% were non-OECD (or developing) countries. However, only few came from low-income countries and high proportion of arbitration (45%) were subjected against upper middle income developing countries. In terms of arbitration outcomes, the ultimate winners did not appear to be significantly different for investors and respondent countries. Investors on average won less than half of the cases and even when they won, they did not win big. U.S. seemed to follow the similar trend and lose more.")

[126] The anatomy and substance of this Chapter are inspired by the Moloo and Jacinto article *Environmental and Health Regulation*, *supra,* the Bjorkland article *Reconciling State Sovereignty and Investor Protection, supra,* and the Moloo and Chao article *Bridging the Divide*. This author's analysis of this chapter commenced with these pieces.

[127] J. Brunnée & S. Toope, LEGITIMACY, *supra*, at 101.

less obvious and thus more susceptible of being challenged by parties (or their allies) who do not like particular results and scholars who do not like certain analyses (or results).

§ 6.2—Substantive Standards before the NAFTA and the IIA Tribunals

Standards have become more specific since the *Chattin v. Mexico* (1927)[128] test of manifest injustice, conscience-shocking government behaviour or "astonishing lack of [government] seriousness." All of these standards invite the judge's subjectivity, but without these prerequisites, an international claim could not succeed. *Chattin* also set the standard for deference, justified by

> concerns about sovereignty. First, because nations are permitted to organize their judicial systems as they see fit within very broad boundaries, the establishment of more precise standards risks favoring some legal systems over others. Thus, any standard must be fluid enough to encompass legal systems constructed from different legal, cultural, and political traditions. Second, publicists, national decision makers, and tribunal members have asserted that minimalist review maximizes deference to national sovereignty.[129]

---

[128] IV RIAA 282; *id.*, at 292 (like the *Neer* case, approving the possibility of positive obligations and holding that "th[is] Commission would render a bad service to the Government of Mexico if it failed to place the stamp of its disapproval and even indignation on a criminal procedure so far below international standards of civilization as the present one."). Notice how the *Chattin* arbitral commission, like the ECtHR in exhaustion cases, is justifying its decision by saying how the government will learn nothing if the commission does not decide the case a particular way; the difference is that here the commission is ruling *against* the State.

[129] A. Bjorklund, *Reconciling State Sovereignty and Investor Protection, supra,* at 867. *James v. U.K.,* 8 EHRR (1986) 123, at 1142–143 ('[T]he Court cannot substitute its own assessment for that of the national authorities'); *Karatas v Turkey* [1999] IV ECtHR 81, at 120 (Joint Partly Dissenting Opinion of Judges Wildhaber, Pastor Ridruejo, Costa and Baka)('In the assessment of whether restrictive measures are necessary in a democratic society, due deference will be accorded to the State's margin of appreciation; the democratic legitimacy of measures taken by democratically elected governments commands a degree of judicial self-restraint'); *Hormones* (AB), *supra*, at ¶ 117 ('the applicable standard is neither *de novo* review as such, nor "total deference", but rather the "objective assessment of the facts"'); *Argentina – Safeguard Measure on Imports of*

International lawyers have learned from *Chattin* and have refined the test in later cases, especially NAFTA's *Mondev, Loewen Group,* and *Waste Management II* awards. In 2002, the *Mondev* tribunal suggested "shock or surprise" (along with limits of its role) as the formula of choice. [130] *Mondev* was followed by the NAFTA arbitral panel of *Chemtura Corporation v. Canada* (2010),[131] stating that the test is whether the State's determination and process "as a whole" shows bad faith; in other words, one defect can theoretically be compensated by a different plus-factor conferred upon the claimant by the State apparatus.[132] The deference test is being applied inconsistently across the IIA sphere.

A great number of specificities and stipulations have been added to these earlier tests. On (rare) occasions, there might even have been necessary and sufficient criteria — a far greater number of the former than of the latter — that bring more of a framework to these tests. Not all cases would be resolved if such a framework were to be implemented but *some* might. For the most part, these tests are like multilayered boxes, and at their very core are some unavoidable discretion and subjectivity. Indeed, even the necessary and sufficient criteria might be debatable. Undoubtedly, the power to determine and then privilege certain values that an international tribunal might choose to arrogate to itself is not always explicit. But typically the more tacitly (clandestinely, if you will) this is done, there is all the more cause to be suspicious of its potency and influence in the decision-making process.

That discretion element can be minimized but cannot be wholly written out of an effective, workable test. Indeed, too "objective" or streamlined a test might prove not to be faithful to the overall purpose behind the analysis. After all, the majestic generalities went into the text of the instrument for a reason, and if the reason was indeed so cynical as the fact that this is all the signatories could agree upon (and were inclined to ward

---

Footwear (Footwear), WTO Doc. WT/DS121/AB/R (2000), at ¶ 121; *EC – Measures Affecting Asbestos and Asbestos-Containing Products*, WTO Doc WT/135 (2001).

[130] ICSID Case No ARB/AF/99/2, at ¶ 127. See also *Loewen Group, supra*, at ¶ 17 (Submission of Prof. Richard Bilder on international law governing state responsibility for treatment of foreign investors) (2001) ("commentators and tribunals have said that, in order to constitute a 'denial of justice,' the conduct in issue must be - the adjectives used to describe the strictness of the standard vary – 'gross,' 'outrageous,' 'egregious,' 'flagrant,' 'clearly unjust,' a 'palpable injustice,' 'manifestly unfair,' or 'manifestly iniquitous.'").

[131] UNCITRAL, Final Award on the Merits, at ¶ 134-35.

[132] *Id.*, at ¶ 144.

off conflict until another day),[133] then that pragmatism has to be a driving force in international dispute settlement.

Furthermore, most so-called "objective" tests are skewed and driven towards particular results (therefore, people) as opposed to some other results (again, consequently, people). To achieve a balanced result, perhaps the optimal approach for the adjudicator to undertake is to flexibly and sensibly apply certain "objective" criteria after checking their own biases and preconceived notions.[134]

A note of caution is warranted. "Pragmatism" is not the same thing as "convenience," however. Rather, that pragmatism includes the requirement to do as the law requires in a given case and the presumed understanding should be that the signatories understand that sometimes the tribunal awards might make them irate beyond belief. The insurance the signatories do get is that in the short and long runs diplomatic disaster is most likely avoided and there is greater stability and predictability from the investors' perspective *even if* there is no broad evidence that investment is actually attracted across sectors and host States due to IIA's.[135] In the next sub-section, we test this hypothesis and generate some deductions.

Statistics: The Tangible and Intangible Influencers on FDI In-Flow

During the course of my interviews with Fortune 500 executives, particularly those in charge of making investment decisions, that they use

---

[133] Whereas in most domestic law systems both legislatures and tribunals behave this way, it appears that in international law regimes this postponing of the grand, often dogmatic, question primarily is conducted by the signatories (who, in a manner of speaking, are the equivalents of legislatures) and less so by international tribunals. IIA tribunals and diplomatic settlement bodies have as their primary mandate dispute resolution such that international peace, harmony and comity remain intact and there is room for economic and political growth within the community of nations.

[134] Diversity of approaches has much to commend it. This "many paths to Rome" principle stands for the justification that there is not necessarily any *exclusive* one way which delivers the right result, legalistically or purposively.

[135] See, *e.g.*, S. D. Franck, *The ICSID Effect? Considering Potential Variations in Arbitration Awards*, 51 VA. J. INT'L L. 977 (2011); S. D. Franck, *Rationalizing Costs in Investment Treaty Arbitration*, 88 WASH. U. L. REV. 769 (2011); D. Smith, Note, *Shifting Sands: Cost-and-Fee Allocation in International Investment Arbitration*, 51 VA. J. INT'L L. 751 (2011); S. D. Franck, *Empirically Evaluating Claims About Investment Treaty Arbitration*, 86 N.C. L. REV. 1 (2007).

certain determinants (noted below) which international investment lawyers might not necessary think of. We have the following determinants to consider: Gross Domestic Product (GDP), GDP growth, Number of arbitrations filed, Number of arbitrations won by the state, Number of arbitrations lost by the state, Total Human Development Index designated by the United Nations (HDI), the Education index,[136] and the Income index.[137]

Trying to ascertain the FDI in-flow, we consider 84 countries, represented in a panel-data format.[138] The time period being covered is 2005-2010. Two important considerations to remember are that, first, the study had to respond to limited data availability by finding the most consistently available band of recent data that supplies predictions; second, that "a lack of adequate sample composition and size to conduct rigorous empirical work from which an analyst could draw . . . [truly] *bold* lessons."[139] Nonetheless, the statistics do provide indication of the importance of several determinants and their directions to the computation of FDI in-flow.

---

[136] L. Story, *As Companies Seek Tax Deals, supra* ("quoting Hallmark C.E.O., Donald J. Hall Jr. as stating: 'If you're looking at the competitiveness of a region, the most important thing a region can do is to focus on education. And this use of incentives is really transferring money from education to businesses.'").

[137] See United Nations Conference on Trade and Development (UNCTAD) (2012).

[138] The countries are Albania, Algeria, Argentina, Armenia, Australia, Azerbaijan, Bangladesh, Belize, Bolivia, Bosnia and Herzegovina, Bulgaria, Burundi, Cambodia, Canada, Chile, Democratic Republic of the Congo, Costa Rica, Czech Republic, Dominican Republic, Egypt, El Salvador, Estonia, Ethiopia, Gabon, Georgia, Germany, Greece, Grenada, Guatemala, Guyana, Hungary, India, Indonesia, Islamic Republic of Iran, Kazakhstan, Kyrgyzstan, Latvia, Lebanon, Lithuania, Malaysia, Mexico, Moldova, Morocco, Nicaragua, Pakistan, Panama, Paraguay, Peru, Philippines, Romania, Russia, Senegal, Serbia, Slovakia, Slovenia, South Africa, Sri Lanka, Tajikistan, Tanzania, Thailand, Trinidad and Tobago, Tunisia, Turkey, Turkmenistan, United Arab Emirates, United Kingdom, United States, Uruguay, Uzbekistan, Venezuela, Vietnam, Yemen and Zimbabwe.

[139] K. Gallagher & E. Shrestha, *Investment Treaty Arbitration and Developing Countries: A Re-Appraisal*, Global Development and Environment Institute, Tufts University (Working Paper), p. 1.

Table II: Index Scores Assigned to Host States

Host States	Human Development Index (HDI) Average (During 2005-10) Scale of 0-1	Education Index (EI) Average (During 2005-10) Scale of 0-1	Income Index (II) Average (During 2005-10) Scale of 0-1
Albania	0.729666667	0.717666667	0.608666667
Algeria	0.682166667	0.628833333	0.612333333
Argentina	0.781	0.793333333	0.688333333
Armenia	0.708666667	0.749666667	0.561
Australia	0.922833333	0.978833333	0.829166667
Azerbaijan	0.699	0.671	0.593666667
Bahrain	0.802333333	0.738833333	0.811166667
Bangladesh	0.480166667	0.401333333	0.3655
Belize	0.593333333	0.6565	0.582833333
Bolivia	0.651833333	0.732166667	0.526833333
Bosnia &	0.7255	0.7165	0.612333333
Herzegovina	0.759833333	0.788666667	0.668333333
Bulgaria	0.293166667	0.313333333	0.176666667
Burundi	0.507333333	0.500166667	0.398833333
Cambodia	0.900333333	0.911166667	0.8385
Canada	0.790666667	0.781	0.683333333
Chile	0.659	0.603	0.571333333
China	0.271	0.340166667	0.135
DRC	0.734	0.650333333	0.654833333
Costa Rica	0.789666667	0.768833333	0.725333333
Croatia	0.8605	0.928166667	0.764333333
Czech Republic	0.673166667	0.6065	0.606333333
Dominican	0.707166667	0.669833333	0.607833333
Republic	0.628333333	0.539833333	0.556166667
Ecuador	0.6645	0.621666667	0.582166667
Egypt	0.829333333	0.9165	0.734166667
El Salvador	0.339333333	0.228166667	0.2935
Estonia	0.657666667	0.646333333	0.678333333
Ethiopia	0.899833333	0.9285	0.831833333
Gabon	0.510833333	0.5405	0.367833333
Germany	0.746	0.779	0.615666667
Ghana	0.563333333	0.421666667	0.534166667
Grenada	0.618833333	0.6495	0.476833333
Guatemala	0.809333333	0.8585	0.729666667
Guyana	0.523833333	0.436166667	0.473

Hungary	0.593333333	0.557	0.495333333
India	0.693	0.6145	0.6595
Indonesia	0.6865	0.692166667	0.5595
Iran	0.727333333	0.8275	0.642833333
Jordan	0.605166667	0.714333333	0.419
Kazakhstan	0.796666667	0.861833333	0.7105
Kyrgyzstan	0.7235	0.687833333	0.671333333
Latvia	0.801166667	0.875333333	0.721333333
Lebanon	0.716666667	0.681	0.632
Lithuania	0.747666667	0.719	0.689333333
Macedonia	0.755666667	0.701166667	0.6945
Malaysia	0.638666667	0.714166667	0.478166667
Mexico	0.632166667	0.702833333	0.483166667
Moldova	0.566666667	0.433166667	0.520666667
(Republic of)	0.460666667	0.388833333	0.364833333
Mongolia	0.577666667	0.510833333	0.452
Morocco	0.442833333	0.442	0.412333333
Myanmar	0.699166667	0.5355	0.764
Nicaragua	0.492166667	0.372833333	0.454166667
Nigeria	0.753333333	0.736833333	0.662166667
Oman	0.646666667	0.622	0.533333333
Pakistan	0.7065	0.6935	0.605833333
Panama	0.631333333	0.674833333	0.493666667
Paraguay	0.801333333	0.815666667	0.719833333
Peru	0.798833333	0.720166667	0.765666667
Philippines	0.767833333	0.809666667	0.667166667
Poland	0.741	0.7785	0.6985
Portugal	0.757	0.6715	0.7715
Romania	0.445666667	0.367833333	0.400166667
Russian	0.755333333	0.778	0.650666667
Federation	0.824	0.869666667	0.744
Saudi Arabia	0.867833333	0.898333333	0.789666667
Senegal	0.606166667	0.697	0.644166667
Serbia	0.867666667	0.851833333	0.8025
Slovakia	0.674	0.674166667	0.529666667
Slovenia	0.591166667	0.701833333	0.402166667
South Africa	0.442	0.440333333	0.3505
Spain	0.668666667	0.582	0.6075
Sri Lanka	0.7475	0.696666667	0.771166667
Tajikistan	0.6835	0.622166667	0.603
Tanzania	0.686166667	0.569833333	0.679166667
Thailand	0.668333333	0.739	0.573833333
Trinidad and	0.7215	0.850833333	0.586166667
Tobago	0.828833333	0.7085	0.911333333
Tunisia	0.857666667	0.806666667	0.833333333
Turkey	0.905333333	0.934666667	0.868333333

Turkmenistan	0.764833333	0.7495	0.6715
Ukraine	0.6225	0.711833333	0.452
United Arab	0.719	0.653666667	0.672
Emirates	0.576333333	0.490333333	0.455
United Kingdom	0.441166667	0.286333333	0.433833333
United States	0.349333333	0.556	0.1825

Table III: Aggregate FDI In-Flow of Host States

Host States	**Aggregate FDI In-Flow (2005-2010) in USD ($)**
Albania	4282705116
Algeria	12158000000
Argentina	38073519167
Armenia	3674369949
Australia	136993000000
Azerbaijan	-2601734000
Bahrain	7926492614
Bangladesh	4803260428
Belize	751069160.8
Bolivia	1965811293
Bosnia & Herzegovina	4900309904
Bulgaria	40282164629
Burundi	6079235.722
Cambodia	3868568504
Canada	307778000000
Chile	69934417531
China	875785000000
DRC	*N/A*
Costa Rica	9116598161
Croatia	19989557791
Czech Republic	43290204617
Dominican Republic	10535900000
Ecuador	2450893446
Egypt	49588300000
El Salvador	774670000
Estonia	12644591377
Ethiopia	1650638044
Gabon	1191700155
Germany	264800000000
Ghana	8830331145
Grenada	621499047.4
Guatemala	4080400000
Guyana	977139000
Hungary	1375840000000
India	156586000000
Indonesia	48145342242
Iran	14700164190
Jordan	15105408276
Kazakhstan	57700832887
Kyrgyzstan	1436463281
Latvia	6513200000
Lebanon	22090546708

Lithuania	7646624383
Macedonia	2211753792
Malaysia	36562821671
Mexico	138748000000
Moldova (Republic of)	2044630000
Mongolia	3824329531
Morocco	12469633657
Myanmar	4106334263
Nicaragua	2477900000
Nigeria	38671929861
Oman	12069440832
Pakistan	21858000000
Panama	11056800000
Paraguay	1290400000
Peru	31364100509
Philippines	12496000000
Poland	90940000000
Portugal	28048647631
Romania	49470590000
Russian Federation	252450000000
Saudi Arabia	152231000000
Senegal	1528241848
Serbia	16722954305
Slovakia	13693861460
Slovenia	4383308912
South Africa	28298207016
Spain	251189000000
Sri Lanka	2989512000
Tajikistan	1160468500
Tanzania	3168105165
Thailand	51908401152
Trinidad and Tobago	6711700000
Tunisia	11160008924
Turkey	89216000000
Turkmenistan	9232100000
Ukraine	45527000000
United Arab Emirates	59567043839
United Kingdom	752994000000
United States	1281860000000
Uruguay	8368403850
Uzbekistan	3314900000
Venezuela	3751000000
Viet Nam	36233000000
Yemen	3475767683
Zimbabwe	473700000

Table IV: Awards Given in Favour of or Against Particular States

Host States	Number of IIA's Filed Against State	Number of IIA's *Won* By State	Number of IIA's *Lost* By State
Albania	2	2	0
Algeria	3	2	0
Argentina	55	3	9
Armenia	1	0	0
Australia	1	0	0
Azerbaijan	3	1	0
Bahrain	0	0	0
Bangladesh	2	0	1
Belize	1	0	0
Bolivia	9	0	0
Bosnia &	1	0	0
Herzegovina	1	1	0
Bulgaria	2	0	1
Burundi	1	0	0
Cambodia	19	3	2
Canada	3	1	2
Chile	*N/A*	*N/A*	*N/A*
China	4	2	1
DRC	4	0	1
Costa Rica	1	0	0
Croatia	15	6	4
Czech Republic	2	0	0
Dominican	12	2	1
Republic	10	2	3
Ecuador	3	1	0
Egypt	3	1	1
El Salvador	1	1	0
Estonia	1	0	0
Ethiopia	2	0	0
Gabon	2	0	0
Germany	1	1	0
Ghana	3	0	0
Grenada	1	0	0
Guatemala	6	0	2
Guyana	10	0	1
Hungary	1	0	0
India	1	0	0
Indonesia	5	1	0
Iran	10	1	2
Jordan	3	0	1

Kazakhstan	2	0	2
Kyrgyzstan	3	0	1
Latvia	3	1	0
Lebanon	2	0	0
Lithuania	2	2	0
Macedonia	18	6	4
Malaysia	4	1	2
Mexico	4	0	0
Moldova	2	1	0
(Republic of)	1	1	0
Mongolia	1	0	0
Morocco	1	0	0
Myanmar	9	2	0
Nicaragua	3	1	0
Nigeria	1	0	0
Oman	2	1	0
Pakistan	4	1	0
Panama	2	1	0
Paraguay	11	1	2
Peru	1	0	0
Philippines	9	2	0
Poland	9	1	1
Portugal	1	0	0
Romania	1	0	0
Russian	1	0	0
Federation	9	3	2
Saudi Arabia	2	0	0
Senegal	1	0	0
Serbia	1	0	1
Slovakia	3	1	1
Slovenia	1	1	0
South Africa	2	1	0
Spain	1	0	1
Sri Lanka	1	1	0
Tajikistan	1	0	0
Tanzania	8	2	1
Thailand	3	0	0
Trinidad and	14	5	2
Tobago	2	1	0
Tunisia	2	0	1
Turkey	15	6	0
Turkmenistan	1	0	0
Ukraine	2	1	0
United Arab	14	0	0
Emirates	1	0	0
United Kingdom	2	1	0

United States	3	0	1

Table V: Average GDP Growth and GDP of the Host States

Host States	GDP (Aggregate in USD) During 2005-2010	% of Annual GDP Growth (Average) During 2005-2010
Albania	65159160441	5.15
Algeria	826401000000	3.033333
Argentina	1660500000000	7.177991266
Armenia	50172380602	5.943215663
Australia	5420740000000	2.857014651
Azerbaijan	213327000000	18.50816667
Bahrain	111955000000	6.123333333
Bangladesh	459865000000	6.168931369
Belize	7718230694	2.568835049
Bolivia	87785743829	4.569174486
Bosnia & Herzegovina	90902433491	3.558
Bulgaria	252338000000	3.403435181
Burundi	9136674362	3.89548935
Cambodia	54202666529	7.829182923
Canada	8253730000000	1.529336422
Chile	1019330000000	3.913020834
China	23907500000000	11.23333333
DRC	62017641790	5.965114066
Costa Rica	164260000000	4.832798689
Croatia	348211000000	1.543659383
Czech Republic	1078200000000	3.441792728
Dominican Republic	255441000000	7.478242411
Ecuador	288359000000	3.953017673
Egypt	898344000000	5.898740335
El Salvador	119269000000	1.803415502
Estonia	114629000000	1.796334094
Ethiopia	135314000000	10.60631252
Gabon	68458489594	2.879762246
Germany	19174100000000	1.216706919
Ghana	142421000000	6.531495536
Grenada	4553816844	1.855531192
Guatemala	209766000000	3.610177589
Guyana	10231115599	3.309858719
Hungary	768454000000	0.554995734
India	7291510000000	8.338707922
Indonesia	2840510000000	5.729413408

Iran	1370160000000	4.488425964
Jordan	116973000000	6.571307751
Kazakhstan	639776000000	6.85
Kyrgyzstan	23720960279	3.566723034
Latvia	148297000000	1.711617502
Lebanon	173366000000	5.645658121
Lithuania	215560000000	2.500465226
Macedonia	48991337685	3.556149027
Malaysia	1134780000000	4.671096008
Mexico	5849860000000	2.014171111
Moldova (Republic of)	28104952481	4.038209046
Mongolia	26561600206	6.675807883
Morocco	470982000000	4.577906975
Myanmar	*N/A*	*N/A*
Nicaragua	34941853005	2.974702404
Nigeria	997560000000	6.478962477
Oman	274892000000	5.699
Pakistan	882851000000	4.810590017
Panama	126254000000	8.24022421
Paraguay	78483734526	5.16440428
Peru	686551000000	7.155785699
Philippines	916162000000	4.928439413
Poland	2500960000000	4.547019392
Portugal	1338590000000	0.512184901
Romania	913648000000	3.32433181
Russian Federation	7424650000000	4.130087546
Saudi Arabia	2360890000000	3.282624388
Senegal	68422837478	3.823404566
Serbia	219760000000	2.609
Slovakia	486665000000	5.082725671
Slovenia	272540000000	2.28133601
South Africa	1714650000000	3.566576996
Spain	8240920000000	1.369580124
Sri Lanka	217375000000	6.368636331
Tajikistan	24643285482	8.030296939
Tanzania	110297000000	6.95953319
Thailand	1485410000000	3.784479669
Trinidad and Tobago	124988000000	3.857459768
Tunisia	238234000000	4.421982966
Turkey	3737070000000	4.158933709
Turkmenistan	88968870221	11.03333333
Ukraine	770253000000	1.583333461
United Arab Emirates	1543700000000	3.51531965
United Kingdom	14597200000000	0.795835119
United States	82370600000000	1.129519194
Uruguay	160628000000	6.098156908

Uzbekistan	153717000000	8.233333333
Venezuela	15981800000000	4.921733656
Viet Nam	479548000000	7.257452035
Yemen	140582000000	4.552781331
Zimbabwe	34218974292	-2.583475713

The statistical methodology is justified on five significant grounds: First, the implications of "signaling" behaviour indicate that the arbitration claimant's specific home state is irrelevant as all the parties are affected. Second, one group of reasons motivating investors to invest in a host state is inextricable from another group of reasons. Third, while the multiplication or proliferation of tribunals means that there is now a tendency for decisions to be less binding or, more likely, completely non-binding, the reputational risks matter so significantly (often a strong motivator that leads respondent states to settle), at least in the short run, that the award still remains consequential.

Fourth, firm investors significantly consider the political risk indices because of the stamp of credibility and legitimacy they confer. This is relevant in terms of advancing or supporting a particular venture to the shareholders.[140] Investors and States also "informally" consider treaties in the negotiation process.[141] FDI is not understood to be inherently sufficient

140 I am not without my own doubts concerning how dependent potential investors are, in actuality, on the United Nations' designated indices. However, I have become increasingly inclined to believe that these indices are used for credibility purposes by a project-supportive actor within the corporate structure to persuade others to agree to bring investment to the host state in question. See also, for the credibility of these ratings, M. L. Satterthwaite, "Measuring Human Rights: U.N. Indicators in Critical Perspective," in GOVERNANCE BY INDICATORS: GLOBAL POWER THROUGH QUANTIFICATION AND RANKINGS (Davis et al, eds.) (2011); M. L. Satterthwaite, *The Trust in Indicators: Measuring Human Rights*, 27 BERKELEY J. INT'L L. 253 (2009); M. Green, *What We Talk About When We Talk About Indicators: Current Approaches to Human Rights Measurement*, 23 HUM. RTS Q'LY 1062, 1065 (2001).

141 See, *e.g.*, K. Gallagher & E. Shrestha, *Investment Treaty Arbitration and Developing Countries: A Re-Appraisal*, Global Development and Environment Institute, Tufts University (Working Paper), p. 5 ("As Luke Eric Peterson, publisher of the Investment Law Reporter said in an interview . . . : 'There is no obvious way to measure how often investment treaties are used in informal contexts by foreign investors in the context of negotiation or lobbying. However, in my experience as a journalist tracking this area, I would not be the least bit surprised if there were dozens upon dozens of such informal treaty-uses for every claim that actually gets arbitrated. Virtually every lawyer I know professes to use these treaties in negotiations on behalf of their clients with governments. As a

to rid a conflict-prone or other disaster-prone area of its problems,[142] and indeed the investors themselves seek some sort of official and impartial assurance that the investment will be a worthwhile one, in the short- and long-runs.[143] In what the scholar John Bray has called the "virtuous cycle," the hope and expectation are that "peacebuilding initiatives in the political arena create an environment conducive to well-designed investments, which themselves serve to reinforce the wider social foundations of peace" and prosperity.[144]

It should not surprise anyone to know that politicians and even presidential campaigns listen closely to investor concerns about such FDI activity, especially in emerging markets. Three reasons exist for this solicitude to investors: (*i*) Some investors are constituents; (*ii*) In any case, constituent welfare could be enhanced; and (*iii*) Geopolitical reasons might counsel competing effectively with a rival nation over the rewards attending an emerging market. The Mitt Romney presidential campaign's (2012) Working Group on U.S. Investment in Africa, for instance, contains action plans as well as legislative and tax and investment treaty proposals to incentivise certain African States to relinquish or at least diminish reliance on Chinese FDI, in the long-term strategic interest of the

---

reporter it's frustrating to know that the primary use of these treaties is in such non-arbitration contexts, but to lack fuller details of such uses - including the legal, policy and financial impacts.'").

142 J. Bray, "Strengthening the Economic Dimensions of Peacebuilding" *in* PRACTICE NOTE 3: FOREIGN DIRECT INVESTMENT IN CONFLICT-AFFECTED CONTEXTS 2, International Alert, *available at* <www.international-alert.org/sites/default/files/publications/practice_note3_march2010.pdf> (2010) (last accessed November 1, 2012) ("FDI from a variety of different commercial sectors can be an important ingredient in recovery. However, it is clear that FDI can never be the panacea. Foreign companies are themselves influenced by wider political and economic developments, and will scarcely invest at all if the host government fails to provide a conducive environment, or if the country is still considered to be unsafe. Furthermore, the impact of individual investments will depend on the extent to which they are managed in a conflict-sensitive manner.") [J. Bray, "Strengthening the Economic Dimensions"].

143 *Id.* ("During violent conflict, a variety of market systems continue to operate . . . . However, few investors – whether domestic or foreign – are prepared to commit significant sums to new wealth-creating commercial initiatives whilst fighting continues. Equally, they may be slow to make substantial new commitments for several years after wars come to an end because of enduring instability and insecurity.").

144 *Id.*

United States.[145] More likely than not, the Barack Obama Administration has similar research conducted—historically, the victorious party's or even non-victorious Administration documents are released later.

Fifth and finally, since 2000, there has been a high level of political, militaristic and economic instability globally, which has been made transparent and well-known by the e-culture. This instability and thus the political risk are likely to continue rising.[146] Not only are powerful investors more likely to know about these regional advantages and shortcomings but they are unlikely to be able to mislead their shareholders (at least the publicly traded companies) or their board of directors (all companies). The restructuring of the corporate anatomy has reverted some power, by the virtue of transparency, back to the interests actually *owning*, not just operating and/or controlling, the firm. This has generated a clearer structure guiding FDI in-flow.

Other considerations which slightly limit the scope of the study have, by no means, proved detrimental to the integrity of this analysis.[147]

---

[145] Mitt Romney Campaign 2012, *Working Group on U.S. Investment in Africa: Compendium of Action Plans and Briefing Memoranda*, Advisory Committee on Africa (January 1, 2013) (on file with the author).

[146] F. Ferrari & R. Rolfini, *Investing in a Dangerous World: A New Political Risk Index*, Working Paper No. 06, SACE Group, p. 5 ("Political risks associated to FDI are likely to continue to rise in the near future. The tensions reflect three basic facts: (i) the startling gaps in income between rich and poor countries, which provides political incentives for a backlash against foreign investment within poor host countries; (ii) the growing scramble for natural resources reflecting the rising resource demand from China and other emerging economies; and (iii) the increasing attention to environmental threats at the global scale, which put many natural-resource-based FDI projects under increased scrutiny and expose them to much greater controversy.").

[147] Five factors must be addressed. First, in marking a victory or loss, I have used a stringent test of unequivocal or almost unequivocal certainty. Doubtless, as to the figures some experts may disagree with me. Second, the reputation effect of an award is strong and carries over year to year. Combining these figures with the *aggregate* FDI in-flow and GDP and the *average* indices (HDI, Education and Income) and GDP growth — the factors that are the least analysed but potentially among the most relevant, if not determinative — has proved to be effective. Third, I have not typically counted non-public awards on the theory that if the result is unknown, the outcome may cause neither party any harm. Fourth, it is true that not every victory or loss is created equal. Nonetheless, from a perceptions-standpoint the exact size of the award or the claim staked does not mean very much to the potential investor pool, for it is the character of the alleged breach by the State that portends future behaviour. Fifth and finally, for ease of calculation some of the figures have been rounded.

A recapitulation is in order. A domestic violation does not become "final" (and thus ripe) as an international claim until the "whole legal system" of the domestic government has been given every reasonable "opportunity to correct" the original error.[148] *Loewen,* though repudiated by the arbitral community on the exhaustion point, nonetheless is important for its stance: "[t]he local remedies rule, which requires a party complaining of a breach of international law by a State to exhaust the local remedies in that State before the party can raise the complaint at the level of international law[,] is procedural in character."[149]

Waste Management II states that if there is an "effective repudiation of the right" and there is the "effect" of denying the right completely or substantially, domestic remedies have been exhausted.[150] *Waste Management II* requires this "effect" but does not necessarily require the claimant to show intent on the government's part.

Chapter III (ATTRIBUTION AND CAUSATION) has already introduced the intent *versus* effects question in the IIA universe. There is no easy answer; the answer significantly depends on the strength of the evidence. Yves Fortier and Stephen Drymer have noted that "th[is] determination of . . . when non-compensable regulation [becomes] compensable indirect expropriation" requires "a balancing of several considerations."[151] Tribunals

---

[148] B. K. Gathright, *A Step in the Wrong Direction: The* Loewen *Finality Requirement and the Local Remedies Rule in NAFTA Chapter Eleven*, 54 EMORY L. J. 1093, 1121 (2005) (observing that *Loewen's* exhaustion issue resembled the ICJ's *Ambatielos Claim* (*Greece v. United Kingdom*), 23 I.L.R. 306 (1956)). *Ambatielos* requires that before bringing an international claim a claimant "should have exhausted the possibilities of appealing to a higher court against any adverse decision of a lower one." *Id.*, at 335.

[149] *Loewen, supra*, at ¶ 149.

[150] *Waste Management II*, *supra*, at ¶¶ 174–175.

[151] Y. Fortier & S. L. Drymer, *Indirect Expropriation in the Law of International Investment: I Know It When I See It, or Caveat Investor*, 19 ICSID REV. 293, 326 (2004); *id.*, at 305 ("in order to be considered an expropriation, the effect of a regulatory measure on property rights – that is, the required level of interference with such rights – has been variously described as: (1) *unreasonable*; (2) an interference that renders rights so *useless that they must be deemed to have been expropriated*; (3) an interference that deprives the investor of *fundamental rights of ownership*; (4) an interference that makes rights *practically useless*; (5) an interference *sufficiently restrictive* to warrant a conclusion that the property has been 'taken'; (6) an interference that deprives, in whole or in significant part, the *use or reasonably-to-be-expected economic benefit* of the property; (7) an interference that *radically deprives* the economical use and enjoyment of an investment, as if the rights related thereto had ceased to exist; (8) an interference that makes *any form of exploitation of the property disappear* (*i.e.*, it destroys or

these days reject "extreme versions of the 'sole effect' or 'purpose [only]' doctrines"; instead, they "consider both the character and the practical impact of governmental measures."[152] As international law theory would have it, "rights . . . [including and] other than property rights may be "expropriated" and . . . international law makes it appropriate for tribunals to examine the purpose and effect of governmental measures."[153]

Notably, Steven Ratner has added a "third factor" to the intent-effect calculus:

> the context of the governmental measure, including its purpose and the proportionality between the harm to the investor and the benefit to the public. Although some have suggested that international law relies only on the first two criteria—together composing the so-called sole effect doctrine—the better view from a review of decisions is that this third factor is relevant.[154]

Intent to expropriate, along with actual expropriation, makes it more likely that a substantive violation will be found.[155] But the evidentiary standard to prove intent is more complex. A case in point is the NAFTA case of *Methanex v. United States* (2005):[156] California banned the gasoline additive MTBE's (Methyl tert-butyl ether) production or sale, and the claimant-investor sued. On both expropriation and FET-due process, the *Methanex* tribunal indicated that the establishment of intent pursuant to Article 1101(1) could be met by identifying "either a single or predominant purpose underlying a particular measure."[157] That reasoning

---

neutralizes the economic value of the use, enjoyment or disposition of the assets or rights affected); and (9) an interference such that the property can no longer be put to *reasonable use*.") (emphasis in original).

[152] *Id.* The term "sole effect" comes from R. Dolzer & C. Schreuer, IIL PRINCIPLES, *supra,* at 92.

[153] UNCITRAL, Final Award on the Merits, at ¶ 134-35.

[154] S. R. Ratner, *Regulatory Takings in Institutional Context: Beyond the Fear of Fragmented International Law*, 102 A.J.I.L. 475, 482-83 (2008) [S. R. Ratner, *International Regulatory Takings*].

[155] *CMS Gas Transportation Company v. Argentina*, ICSID Case No. ARB/01/8 (2005), at ¶ 280 ("such intention and bad faith can aggravate the situation but are not an essential element of the standard.").

[156] *Methanex Corp. v. United States*, 44 I.L.M. 1345 (UNCITRAL 2005) (Final Award).

[157] *Id.*, First Partial Award, *supra*, at ¶ 158.

has been followed in several other IIA awards, thereby showing its sphere of influence.[158]

The frequency with which *Methanex* has been cited shows its persuasive power and high rate of situational occurrence. This is noteworthy given the *Methanex* doctrine's relative youth (6 years). Pre-*Methanex* NAFTA cases had, in effect, applied this same "single or predominant purpose" test but that *Methanex* actually spelled out the test has raised its importance. This same test has been used by ECtHR in a series of Article I expropriation cases with varying degrees of scrutiny (*see* the next section).[159]

Now notice what the award in *Methanex* accomplished. The *Methanex* tribunal pointed out that the claimant's case would be difficult to prove—the "specific intent to harm suppliers of goods and services to such MTBE producers" could only be established through a series of inferences from alleged facts.[160] Then the tribunal noted: "[D]ecrees and regulations may be the product of compromises and the balancing of competing interests by a variety of political actors."[161] The limit to vicarious or *respondeat superior* liability is that "[w]here a single governmental actor is motivated by an improper purpose, it does not necessarily follow that the motive can be attributed to the entire government."[162] The multiple-motive cases or cases where "intent varied amongst state officials" are particularly difficult.[163] In such cases, existent literature highlights methods which

---

[158] The main NAFTA cases on this score are *Cargill v. Mexico*, ICSID Case No. ARB(AF)/05/2 (2009); *Chemtura Corp. v. Canada*, UNCITRAL, Final Award on the Merits (2010); *Merrill & Ring Forestry, L.P. v. Canada, supra* (2010). Other recent IIA cases relevant to the point are *Malicorp Limited v. Egypt*, ICSID Case No. ARB/08/18 (2011); *Nations Energy Inc., et al. v. Panama*, ICSID Case No. ARB/06/19 (2010); *Alpha Projektholding GmbH v. Ukraine*, ICSID Case No. ARB/07/16 (2010); *Ioan Micula, Viorel Micula, S.C. European Food S.A, S.C. Starmill S.R.L. and S.C. Multipack S.R.L. v. Romania*, ICSID Case No. ARB/05/20(2008); *National Grid plc v. Argentina*, UNCITRAL (2008); *Metalpar S.A. and Buen Aire S.A. v. Argentina*, ICSID Case No. ARB/03/5 (2006).

[159] *Andrejeva v. Latvia*, App. no. 55707/00 (2009); *Skodakova v. Czech Republic*, App. no. 71551/01 (2004); *Chovancik v. Slovakia,* App no 54996/00 (2003); *Scollo v. Italy*, App. no. 19133/91 (1995); *Papamichalopoulos v. Greece*, App. no. App. no. 14556/89 (1993).

[160] *Methanex Corp.*, at ¶ 153.

[161] *Id.*, at ¶ 158; see also G. Myers, *The Differing Treatment of Efficiency and Competition in Antitrust and Tortious Interference Law*, 77 MINN. L. REV. 1097, 1142 (1993).

[162] *Id.*, at ¶ 158.

[163] R. Moloo & J. Jacinto, *Environmental and Health Regulation*, *supra*, at 56.

might be used to distinguish between wrongful and bona fide regulations, focusing on the intent-motive angle.[164]

In addition, the tribunal concluded that "it is unclear whether intent must focus on the contract or the foreign investor, or whether this distinction will make any difference."[165] In *Methanex*, the tribunal "disregarded the investor's claim that harm to its economic interests from the ban on MTBE was foreseeable and sufficient to establish jurisdiction."[166] The *Methanex* facts were so unique that *Methanex* can be read as broadly or as narrowly as one chooses to read it. Indeed this distinguishing away, and not repudiating, an unhelpful prior case seems to be commonplace across international dispute settlement—even in IIA where precedent is not formally a factor.

Domestic tribunals do the same with great frequency, of course, in order not to truncate the interest of comity and reciprocity. To what extent a tribunal will adhere to a prior case requires, of course, a "sober appraisal of the disadvantages of the innovation as well as those of the questioned case, a weighing of practical effects of one against the other."[167] Each tribunal will have to decide this for itself. It might choose to maintain some internal consistency (or at least the ability to distinguish a case with a straight face) about whatever it decides, perhaps for the sake of its own legitimacy. If it does not, not only will its own legitimacy be question but so will the legitimacy of much of its prototype.

The often-ignored lesson of *Methanex* (almost alone among IIA cases) is the breadth of deference the tribunal gave the government's scientific evidence. As Chapter I (INTRODUCTION) has noted, this dominant issue is related to the competence of the judges and their evaluative capabilities; and as Chapter III (ATTRIBUTION AND CAUSATION) has discussed, it raises

---

[164] *Id.* ("There is a crucial, but not yet fully explored, distinction between an *S.D. Myers* type situation where the tribunal is able to conclude that the state's primary motive was wrongful, and a *Methanex* type situation where multiple motives are accepted as a normal part of the regulatory process. One approach would be to determine whether a legitimate motive existed that could have reasonably led to the enactment of the measure in the absence of the other motives. That approach would cover a situation where a state took action for a wrongful purpose and justified its action on some minor or tangentially related environmental or health risk. However, it would not treat as wrongful a situation where a bona fide regulation was enacted in circumstances where other incentives, such as the opportunity of domestic producers to profit, were present, which is not an uncommon attribute of environmental and health regulation.").

[165] L. Anenson, *Responsibility under NAFTA Chapter Eleven, supra*, at 710.

[166] *Id.*, at 710-11.

[167] J. Jackson, *Decisional Law and* Stare Decisis, 30 A. B. A. J. 334 (1944).

evidence-gathering difficulties and perhaps necessitates objective third-parties, such as *amici curiae*, experts and special masters, to play an important role. The tribunal found that the public health reasons given in support of the MTBE ban were supported by an "objectively confirmed . . . scientific study."[168] But it remains unclear who confirmed, after knowledgeable but dispassionate study, the *validity* of the scientific information because the tribunal just seemed to accept it rather at face value:

> [T]he Tribunal accepts the [University of California (UC)] Report as reflecting a serious, objective and scientific approach to a complex problem in California. Whilst it is possible for other scientists and researchers to disagree in good faith with certain of its methodologies, analyses and conclusions, the fact of such disagreement, even if correct, does not warrant this Tribunal in treating the UC Report as part of a political sham by California. In particular, the UC Report was subjected at the time to public hearings, testimony and peer-review; and its emergence as a serious scientific work from such an open and informed debate is the best evidence that it was not the product of a political sham . . . .[169]

Then, the *Methanex* tribunal quietly placed the burden on the claimant to show that the evidence was "scientifically incorrect."[170] The tribunal saw its commission in this sphere only to ensure that the scientific or economic evidence is "objective."[171] "Objective" refers to more than neutrality and impartiality in this context. It means that the evidence conform to the following features: "good faith, coherence, . . . proportionality and reasonableness."[172] I interpret the famously nebulous

---

[168] *Id.*, at ¶ 14.

[169] *Id.*, at ¶¶ 101-02.

[170] *Id.*, at ¶ 101 (stating that "in all material respects, the Tribunal is not persuaded that the UC Report was scientifically incorrect: the Tribunal was much impressed by the scientific expert witnesses presented by the USA and tested under cross-examination by Methanex; and the Tribunal accepts without reservation these experts' conclusions.").

[171] R. Moloo and J. Chao, *Bridging the Divide, supra,* at 11 ("One way to assess the legitimacy of a health or environmental regulation is whether there is a scientific basis for the regulation, though the tribunal does not concern itself on whether the science is correct, just that the science is objective.").

[172] L. Boisson de Chazournes, *Introduction: Courts and Tribunals and the Treatment of Scientific Issues*, JOURNAL OF INTERNATIONAL DISPUTE SETTLEMENT, Vol. 3, No. 3 (2012), p. 479 [L. Boisson de Chazournes, *Scientific Issues*]; see also M. Moïse Mbengue, *Scientific Fact-finding by International Courts and Tribunals*, J Int. Disp. Settlement (2012) 3(3): 509 (explaining that "appears that traditional

term "reasonableness" simply to parameterise off extreme or illogical positions. This is not to be a complete formalist. For instance, there is nothing questionable *per se* about timetable harmonization and avoiding duplication of scientific information. Lacking textual guidance on this front, there appears to be no customary law principle categorically forbidding "access to a common pool of information."[173]

The GATT/WTO Appellate Body, on the other hand, has sometimes sought to independently evaluate the correctness of the evidence. In 2001, it "rul[ed] that it is sufficient for a member to rely, in good faith, on scientific sources which, at the time, may represent a divergent, but qualified and respected, opinion."[174] The question is easier if this opinion is monolithic. Undoubtedly, the question becomes a difficult one once the qualified and respected scientific opinion is divergent although great deference to the sovereign is given if a "risk" which is "life-threatening" is identified and "is perceived to constitute a clear and imminent threat to public health and safety."[175] Some scholars have recommended that, in the

---

fact-finding processes are being challenged by the ever-growing number of international scientific disputes."). The scientific evidence is not worth very much if it is not internally consistent. No amount of deference can salvage the evidence unless its proponents are prepared to furnish at least a persuasive explanation for gaps of internal logic. The one conceivable exception are admittedly secret or national security-based evidence, regarding which some sort of *in camera* explanation with gag orders for counsel could be arranged.

[173] *EC-Hormones*, WT/DS26/AB/R, WT/DS48/AB/R, at ¶ 153 (1998) ("In disputes where the evaluation of scientific data and opinions plays a significant role, the panel that is established later can benefit from the information gathered in the context of the proceedings of the panel established earlier. Having access to a common pool of information enables the panel and the parties to save time by avoiding duplication of the compilation and analysis of information already presented in the other proceeding.").

[174] P. Sands, INTERNATIONAL ENVIRONMENTAL LAW, *supra*, at 976; *European Communities — Asbestos*, WT/DS135/AB/R (2001).

[175] *EC-Hormones*, WT/DS26/AB/R, WT/DS48/AB/R, at ¶ 194 (1998) ("In some cases, the very existence of divergent views presented by qualified scientists who have investigated the particular issue at hand may indicate a state of scientific uncertainty. Sometimes the divergence may indicate a roughly equal balance of scientific opinion, which may itself be a form of scientific uncertainty. In most cases, responsible and representative governments tend to base their legislative and administrative measures on 'mainstream' scientific opinion. In other cases, equally responsible and representative governments may act in good faith on the basis of what, at a given time, may be a divergent opinion coming from qualified and respected sources. By itself, this does not necessarily signal the absence of a reasonable relationship between the . . . [governmental] measure and the . . .

IIA sphere, "[t]he standard of review should be limited to examining the reasonableness of the method used to assess the facts, and not the facts in themselves."[176] Parties should remember the hedging words in this prescription—"in good faith," "at the time," and "qualified and respected."[177]

A fringe view without valid scientific (or other) basis will most likely not be accepted. Such disputes concern not just scientific and technological findings but also financial factors, such as controversies surrounding how much a 51% stake in an investment is worth, for compensation purposes. This is not a pure hypothetical. In fact, these are some of the facts attending the Spanish oil firm Repsol's December 2012 request for ICSID arbitration against Argentina. How that case unfolds will be interesting to observe.

Moreover, the Appellate Body was actually anchoring this principle to the well-established principle of legitimate expectation engendered by the State in the investors and owners. The interesting question that has hitherto not been resolved explicitly is whether a nascent scientific theory that is *initially* without much support in the scientific community (definitely "divergent," but not a "qualified and respected . . . opinion") when the State chooses to rely on it, if only for convenience's sake, but which later is proven correct independently, is an adequate defence.

However, if the legitimate expectation principle and "good faith" are the lodestars upon which the axiom is founded, then truth may not be an adequate defence. Tribunals could easily say that this is like lottery because science requires established proof and that unproven views, however deeply held, are not yet "theory." This may require the Appellate

[problem identified], especially where the risk involved is life-threatening in character and is perceived to constitute a clear and imminent threat to public health and safety."). See also S. W. Schill, *Deference in Investment Treaty Arbitration: Re-conceptualizing the Standard of Review*, J Int. Disp. Settlement (2012) 3(3): 577 (explaining that deference to the sovereign justifies and perhaps even requires that, in the IIA orbit, "the standard of review" must be "conceptualize[d] . . . within a separation of powers-framework that fuses domestic and international legal considerations in allocating power between states and arbitral tribunals.").

[176] L. Boisson de Chazournes, *Scientific Issues, supra,* at 479 (explaining that Yuka Fukunaga "argues that, in light of the fact that there are 'different truths', and considering the relevant case law (especially the *EC-Hormones* suspension case), it is not for a panel to be deciding about science).") (referring to *EC-Hormones, supra,* at ¶ 194 and to Y. Fukunaga, *Standard of Review and 'Scientific Truths' in the WTO Dispute Settlement System and Investment Arbitration*, J INT. DISP. SETTLEMENT (2012) 3(3): 559).

[177] P. Sands, INTERNATIONAL ENVIRONMENTAL LAW, *supra*, at 976.

Body's test to be ossified, and perhaps made stricter, by substituting in "theory" for the looser word "opinion."

Deciding expropriation and FET questions, the IIA tribunal in *Chemtura Corporation v. Canada* (2010)[178] noted that "its task" is "not to second-guess the correctness of the science-based decision-making of highly specialized national regulatory agencies." That role belongs to policy-makers and specialists, not those entrusted with the limited judicial function. This was right before the *Chemtura* tribunal observed, by itself (and perhaps as *obiter*), that the contested chemical "lindane has raised increasingly serious concerns both in other countries and at the international level since the 1970s."[179] The specific treaty language might make a substantial difference: under general FET principles, "[a] measure that is substantively flawed (*e.g.*, disproportionate or based on unsound science) is unlikely to be considered a breach of the FET standard if it is otherwise legitimate,"[180] though if the relevant treaty proscribes "unreasonable" conduct by the sovereign then "a *bona fide* and procedurally legitimate measure, could, in theory, be so disproportional and unjustified as to constitute a breach."[181]

Rahim Moloo and Justin Jacinto, in their groundbreaking article *Environmental and Health Regulation*, argue that "[w]hile tribunals are understandably hesitant to second-guess policy choices, it is appropriate to examine whether the measure actually followed from whatever analysis is cited *as its basis*."[182] They then proceed to state that "[i]f a state undertook a study which found that no regulation was necessary, and still acted, that action is more likely to be found arbitrary."[183] The Moloo-Jacinto contention has its obvious value but it should also be pointed out, as I have elsewhere in this book, that whatever the purported "basis" *presented by the sovereign* may be, there are not utterly invalid arguments for affirming measures that have an otherwise meritorious "basis" (*whether or not it was presented by the sovereign*). This latter approach might raise controversial and difficult questions relating to predictability and arbitrariness as well as judicial expertise[184] but it possesses intellectual honesty in ample measure.

---

[178] UNCITRAL, Final Award on the Merits, at ¶ 134-35.
[179] *Id.*, at ¶¶ 135-37.
[180] R. Moloo & J. Jacinto, *Environmental and Health Regulation*, *supra*, at 56.
[181] *Id.*
[182] *Id.*, at 54.
[183] *Id.*
[184] If some international judges and arbitrators have significant difficulty in assessing the value of scientific or other specialised evidence that is presented to them, I have difficulty imagining how they will cope with the task of

Let us put all this in the larger context of the development of intellectual history. In 1790, Edmund Burke said lamented that the "age of chivalry is dead, that of sophist[s], economists and calculators has succeeded, and the glory of Europe is extinguished forever."[185] *Sic transit gloria mundi!*, Burke believed. If the age of "sophist[s], economists and calculators has . . . [indeed] succeeded,"[186] then the flexible level of judicial deference to the scientific and economic information offered by the New Age phenomena must be carefully handled in particular cases. We must accept and to some extent embrace reality. There might be advantages to be derived from modern sources of information. The deference to government-proffered scientific opinion, one could suggest, was adequately established in *Chemtura* and *Methanex*.

The presumptive belief goes that, more so than judges (some of whom might be unelected), elected politicians and negotiators, possessed of expert resources and evidence, are in a better position to make these decisions.[187] They are also more likely to be held accountable to change the rules without being bound by a rule or systemic expectation of precedent (as judges are).[188] Politicians are largely free to change their minds, for they operate in an innovative gladiatorial arena where fresh

---

independently finding evidence that has escaped the parties and the experts (appointed by the parties). Perhaps this is where the tribunal-appointed experts raise the likelihood of such evidence coming to the fore, even though often the parties prefer to avoid the intervention of the tribunal-appointed experts.

[185] E. Burke, REFLECTIONS ON THE REVOLUTION IN FRANCE 84-85 (Macmillan, 1890, original in 1790).

[186] *Id.*

[187] Certainly, international judges, especially IIA arbitrators, are chosen on a case-by-case basis. There is the possibility that their professional security is on some level dependent on the direction of their decisions. But the same is true of so many elected domestic judges in the United States. The same also goes for far more numerous judges in common or civil law jurisdictions whose elevation to the higher tribunal is at least subtly dependent on the ideological direction of their decisions, along with their overall competence as jurists.

[188] S. Breyer, "Economic Reasoning and Judicial Review," *supra,* at 10 ("[T]he need for, and value of, bright-line rules in the law . . . explains some of the difficulty of judges' use of economic reasoning. Economic reasoning does not automatically welcome the use of bright-line rules. Economics often concerns gradations with consequences that flow from a little more or a little less. But the law . . . often seeks clear administrable distinctions of kind, not degree. . . . Bright-line rules sometimes reduce the transactions costs of judging, as such rules are easier and simpler to administer. Additionally, bright-line rules can have the benefit of providing greater clarity to the public at large, thereby reducing compliance costs and even, perhaps, litigation costs, as well.").

ideas are the stock in trade in exchange for votes and credibility. Consent of the governed and opinion polls are the prevailing indicators of legitimacy for politicians.

The judicial function, on the other hand, inherently contains a framework of promoting predictability, stability and precedent. The law simply moves slower than socioeconomic developments, and catches up only when those developments seem stable and moving definitively and progressively in the new direction. Otherwise the institutional costs of retrenchment are just disproportionately high in terms of the judicial capital they erode. Yet another difference between international judges and domestic politicians dovetails with the analysis above: "[P]oliticians do not have the same 'time horizons' as courts."[189] The fact remains that "[w]hile courts are concerned about long-standing principles, politicians feel obliged to react only when their short-term interests are at stake."[190]

One structure is not necessarily better or worse than the other but both must cooperate in order for the entire system to work effectively for the parties. If it fails to add productive value for any stakeholder, the regime's days are limited.

Amici Curiae, Special Masters, and Mass Claims

We need to start thinking whether non-scientist or non-economist arbitrators may assess this evidence themselves or appoint an impartial special master to act as an independent middleman between the parties and the tribunal. Of course, respected scientific opinion does the job to some extent. However, it is more foolhardy than valiant to suggest that respected scientific opinion, even when inscrutable or unfathomable to the lay judge, is always enough. As things currently stand, a panel of scientifically literate (to a complex level) international arbitrators and judges is difficult, perhaps impossible, to assemble in order to resolve every dispute.

Second problem occurs when scientific opinion runs in competing directions: IIA tribunals and other international fora might take instruction

---

[189] F. Zarbiyev, *Judicial Activism in International Law, supra,* at 17 (citing Karen J Alter, *Who Are the 'Masters of the Treaty'?*: European Governments and the European Court of Justice' (1998) 52 Intl Org 121, 123); id., at 130-31 (observing that "[t]he short-term focus of politicians explains why they often fail to act decisively when doctrine that is counter to their long-term interest is first established.").

[190] *Id.*

from the ICJ's "specialized approach."[191] Nor is it *ipso facto* a particularly good argument to suggest that concerns of sovereignty militate against the intrusion of special masters, since the States do not categorically or with any great frequency object to special masters and the ICJ assigns special masters in the most sensitive cases.

Liberalising the *amicus* and joint expert (selection and submission) processes to some extent might add value to the landscape.[192] *Amici* already play a significant role in the human rights network, and there are meritorious arguments potentially supporting at least a vigorously executed pilot experiment in the investment and property spheres.[193] It should be noted that several IIA legal advisors heading these government departments have mentioned to me their view that joint experts agreed upon by the parties tends to "work out far better" than *tribunal* appointments of the experts, confidentiality advisors, and special masters. As evidence, many of them pointed to the "superb" performance of Professor John R. Crook as confidentiality advisor in the recent *Softwood Lumber Dispute*.[194]

---

[191] P. Sands, "Litigating Environmental Disputes," *supra*, at 315 (referring to *Case Concerning Gabčíkovo-Nagymaros (Hungary v. Slovakia)*, 1997 ICJ Reports 7 *et seq*. 27-29).

[192] See, *e.g.*, D. B. Hollis, *Private Actors in Public International Law: Amicus Curiae and the Case for the Retention of State Sovereignty*, 25 B.C. INT'L & COMP. L. Rev. 235, 235–36 (2002).

[193] See, *e.g.*, R. Moloo, *The Quest for Legitimacy in the United Nations: A Role for NGOs?*, 16 UCLA J. OF INT'L L. & FOREIGN AFF., pp. 27-28 (2011) ("NGOs can contribute valuable information relevant to the decision-making process. NGOs are already key sources of information for the UN. For example, they are the main source of information to the UN human rights system. Without information from NGOs, the UN human rights system would have 'ground to halt' a long time ago. The information and expertise of NGOs have made valuable contributions to the UN, particularly in areas relevant to the work of the GA, including punishment for genocide, elaboration of the international protection of human rights, defence of the natural environment, banning of landmines, and addressing the AIDS crisis. The reason why NGOs are often able to contribute valuable information to the UN is that NGOs often have access to information that is unavailable to other actors on the international stage."). No one seriously believes that NGO's, by that fact alone, are entitled to more credibility or legitimacy than elected governments. But governments might be seen to have ulterior motives (as might NGO's), and the whole array of viewpoints and data might help, not hinder, the decision-making process. Credibility, both real and perceived, of the system itself is at stake.

[194] *United States v. Canada*, LCIA, Case No. 111790, at ¶¶ 49-50 (2012). See also J. R. Crook, *Preliminary Settlement of Softwood Lumber Dispute*, 100 A.J.I.L. 702,

The proposition that IIA tribunals[195] as well as the WTO Appellate Body[196] have the authority to accept *amicus curiae* briefs and expert submissions seems to be the emerging consensus. In the domestic judicial arena concerning international law questions and with impact befalling the international judicial systems, this has been done to great and stirring effect.[197] So far the execution has been prominent in the environmental and public harm context but there is no reason that the phenomenon cannot become widespread. Furthermore, this is an excellent method of encouraging the network of domestic and international judicial dialogue facilitated by private industry and social-political action NGO's. The approach could engender public confidence by impressing upon the lay public that the international tribunals are committed to transparency. Finally, there is a principle of transnational reciprocity at work here which

---

702 (2006); J. R. Crook, *United States and Canada Agree on Measures To Address Devils Lake Flooding and Ecological Protection*, 99 A.J.I.L. 909 (2005).

[195] *UPS v. Canada*, Decision on Intervention as *Amicus Curiae*, at ¶¶ 35-43 (2001) (reading its UNCIRAL Article 15(1) power to include the power "to investigate and determine the matter subject to arbitration in a just, efficient and expeditious manner"); *Methanex v. United States*, Decision on Intervention as *Amicus Curiae*, at ¶ 27 (2001) ("broadest procedural flexibility within fundamental safeguards").

[196] See., *e.g.*, *United States – Shrimp/Turtle*, *supra*, at ¶ 103-07. The Appellate Body took small steps at first via cases, before adopting, under "article 16(1) of its Working Procedures, an additional procedure setting out guidelines for applications to submit *amicus* briefs." See R. Mackenzie & P. Sands, *International Courts, supra, at* 284; see generally G. Z. Marceau & J. Hawkins, *Experts in WTO Dispute Settlement*, J INT. DISP. SETTLEMENT (2012) 3(3): 493.

[197] See, *e.g.*, S. Hsu & J. Parrish, *Litigating Canada-U.S. Transboundary Harm, supra,* at 39 ("Member firms of the Edison Electric Institute—electricity generation companies that have coal-fired power plants that emit the pollutants that flow north and foul Ontario's air—saw themselves as standing in Teck's shoes. The National Mining Association and the U.S. Chamber of Commerce also filed amicus briefs in the Ninth Circuit. Both groups were concerned with the possibility of Canadians extraterritorially applying their own law, and argued against the U.S. court setting a precedent by permitting the case to go forward."); *id.*, at n. 206 ("Brief of *Amicus Curiae* Chamber of Commerce of the United States of America in Support of Defendant-Appellant Supporting Reversal, *Pakootas v. Teck Cominco Metals*, 452 F.3d 1066 (9th Cir. 2005); Brief for *Amici Curiae* the National Mining Ass'n & the National Ass'n of Manufacturers Supporting Appellant & Reversal, *Pakootas v. Teck Cominco Metals*, 452 F.3d 1066 (9th Cir. 2005).").

makes the actions of the "first mover" tribunals virtually determinative of what will happen in the future.[198]

The ECtHR and the IACtHR are known for accepting as well as encouraging *amicus* briefs[199] and the ICJ is known for *not* doing so.[200] Although there is value in the argument that keeping the *amicus* process limited helps maintain some balance because developing country "NGOs may . . . be less well financed than their [developed] country counterparts and therefore less able to participate effectively,"[201] the system needs to trust the arbitrators' ability to sift through relevant and credible information. The tribunals may also make it clear that the information is submitted under oath and that penalty for perjury or willful equivocation is so high, within reasonable bounds, that the expected reward falls short of the expected risk that the fraudulent-information-submitting *amicus* will take on.

The costs imposed on some *amici*, especially the less financially provident ones, and of course on the parties paying for the special masters can be reduced if we allow for mass claims[202] and counterclaims. The benefits of consolidation are obvious. There is a marginal saving of time, money and various transition costs no matter which type of international class arbitration[203] is followed. Moreover, "the frequency of international

---

[198] *Id.*, at 38, n. 201 (stating that "what is good for the goose is good for the gander. If U.S. law permits such suits, then Canadian legislatures and courts may well be inclined to find that Canadian law permits the same kinds of suits.").

[199] D. Shelton, *The Participation of Nongovernmental Organizations in International Judicial Proceedings*, 88 AM. J. INT'L L. 611, 629-30 (1994).

[200] *Id.*, at 620-24.

[201] S. Charnovitz, *Two Centuries of Participation: NGOs and International Governance*, 18 MICH. J. INT'L L. 183, 275 (1997).

[202] S. I. Strong, *The Sounds of Silence: Are U.S. Arbitrators Creating Internationally Enforceable Awards When Ordering Class Arbitration In Cases of Contractual Silence or Ambiguity?*, 30 MICH. J. INT'L L. 1017, 1018, n. 2 (2009) ("Class arbitration involves 'an arbitrator [or arbitral tribunal] selected and paid by the parties, rather than an elected or appointed judge, [who] presides over a class action' and thus 'decides whether to certify a class, determines the form and manner of notice to class members, resolves all issues of law and fact, and enters an award that may bind many hundreds or thousands of class members.' W. Mark C. Weidemaier, *Arbitration and the Individuation Critique*, 49 ARIZ. L. REV. 69, 70 (2007). Many international arbitrations consist of a panel of three arbitrators. However, for ease of discussion, this Article refers to the arbitrator in the singular.") [S. I. Strong, *The Sounds of Silence*].

[203] *Id.*, at 1022 ("There are three different types of international class arbitrations: (1) a class arbitration that includes at least one defendant from a country other than the seat of the arbitration, which means that enforcement of an award will have

class arbitration will only increase as the global economy continues to expand and diversify, and as claimants who may not reside in the same country as the defendant seek to assert group or representative claims that are barred from judicial consideration by arbitration agreements."[204]

Given the evolution of the global economy, this might be a losing battle. Areas as diverse as insurance, finance, manufacturing, consumer, maritime, employment, and electronic commerce law will be affected by arbitrations. International defendants are not likely to appreciate mass claims, and their challenges "will arise at the international enforcement stage"[205]—and will likely be some variation on the theme of inadequate warrant in the governing textual proviso.[206] Sovereigns who lose at this

---

international implications; (2) a class arbitration that involves defendants that may be based in the arbitral forum but that also hold significant foreign assets that could be the subject of an international enforcement action; and (3) a class arbitration that includes claimants from outside the arbitral seat.").

[204] *Id.*, at 1018 (citing Samuel P. Baumgartner, *Class Actions and Group Litigation in Switzerland*, 27 Nw. J. Int'l L. Bus. 301, 301 (2007); see also Carole J. Buckner, *Toward a Pure Arbitral Paradigm of Classwide Arbitration: Arbitral Power and Federal Preemption*, 82 Denv. U. L. Rev. 301, 301 (2004) (describing areas where class arbitration might be on the rise); Christopher R. Drahozal, *New Experiences of International Arbitration in the United States*, 54 Am. J. Comp. L. 233, 250–55 (2006) (describing areas where international arbitration is likely to increase) [hereinafter Drahozal, New Experiences]; Edward F. Sherman, *Group Litigation Under Foreign Legal Systems: Variations and Alternatives to American Class Actions*, 52 DePaul L. Rev. 401, 407 (2002) (describing areas where class arbitration might be on the rise); Anne Marie Whitesell & Eduardo Silva-Romero, *Multiparty and Multicontract Arbitration: Recent ICC Experience*, in ICC International Court of Arbitration Bulletin, Complex Arbitrations—Special Supplement 2003, at 7, 7 (2003) (describing increase in multi-party proceedings).).

[205] *Id.*, at 1020 ("The battle will be fought particularly fiercely in cases where the arbitration agreement is silent or ambiguous about the possibility of class treatment, with losing defendants arguing that the decision to proceed as a class was presumptively improper in the absence of the parties' explicit agreement to that particular type of procedure.").

[206] Scholars have predicted that Article V(1)(d) of the United Nations' 1958 Convention on the Recognition and Enforcement of Foreign Arbitral Awards (New York Convention) ("Recognition and enforcement of the award may be refused, at the request of the party against whom it is invoked, only if that party furnishes to the competent authority where the recognition and enforcement is sought, proof that: . . . (d) The composition of the arbitral authority or the arbitral procedure was not in accordance with the agreement of the parties, or, failing such agreement, was not in accordance with the law of the country where the arbitration took place") will be the source of this challenge.

stage will likely contend that mass claims are "presumptively improper in the absence of the parties' explicit agreement to that particular type of procedure."[207]

Let us therefore appreciate what the instruments do stipulate. The IIA tribunal in *Abaclat et al. v. Argentina* (2011)[208] held that ICSID, at least, placed no bar *per se* to mass claims:

> (i) The silence of the ICSID framework regarding collective proceedings is to be interpreted as a 'gap' and not as a 'qualified silence'; (ii) The Tribunal has, in principle, the power under Article 44 ICSID Convention[209] to fill this gap to the extent permitted under Article 44 ICSID Convention and Rule 19 of the ICSID Arbitration Rules;[210] and (iii) The procedure necessary to deal with the collective aspect of the present proceedings concern the method of the Tribunal's examination, as well as the manner of representation of claimants. However, it does not affect the object of such examination.

Of course we have discussed Argentina and its nationalization before. Now the crisis manifests itself through the mass claims and "class action" dimension. In the context of sovereign debt restructuring and other issues where the aggrieved parties might be numerous—there were 60,000 here—the logistical and substantive character of IIA could go undergo a significant shift.[211] Provided that a salient common denominator exists and

---

[207] S. I. Strong, *The Sounds of Silence, supra,* at 1020 (citing, *inter alia,* A. Redfern and M. Hunter, LAW AND PRACTICE OF INTERNATIONAL COMMERCIAL ARBITRATION, ¶¶ 5-03 to 5–10, 6-01 (4th ed. 2004) (articulating the timeless problem of "pathological clauses")).

[208] ICSID Case No. ARB/07/5, Decision on Jurisdiction, 4 August 2011, at ¶ 551 (footnotes added for easy reading and clarification purposes).

[209] Art. 44, ICSID Conv. ("Any arbitration proceeding shall be conducted in accordance with the provisions of this Section and, except as the parties otherwise agree, in accordance with the Arbitration Rules in effect on the date on which the parties consented to arbitration. If any question of procedure arises which is not covered by this Section or the Arbitration Rules or any rules agreed by the parties, the Tribunal shall decide the question.").

[210] Rule 19, ICSID Arbitration Rules ("The Tribunal shall make the orders required for the conduct of the proceeding.").

[211] J. Beess und Chrostin, *Sovereign Debt Restructuring and Mass Claims Arbitration before the ICSID, The* Abaclat *Case*, 53 HARV. J. INT'L L. 505, 505 (2012) [J. Beess und Chrostin, *Mass Claims*] ("*Abaclat* is the first arbitral decision to hold that 60,000 Claimants may join in one mass claims arbitration under the institutional rules of the ICSID. If the *Abaclat* decision is followed in the future, it will likely have significant impact on sovereign debt restructuring, the drafting of

equates with a valid IIA claim, tribunal may adopt measures to consolidate the cases. Failure to do so might delay or even deny justice in *other* arbitrations.

The IIA tribunal in *Spyridon Roussalis v. Romania* held that, provided the parties have consented, the ICSID Convention allowed an IIA tribunal to determine counterclaims arising directly out of the subject-matter of the dispute. A 2-1 tribunal nonetheless refused to exercise jurisdiction to hear these counterclaims brought by Romania alleging that claimant Spyridon Roussalia had failed to make the U.S. $1.4 million payment on his relevant investment (premise of the claim).[212] The tribunal construed the consent clause of the BIT ("disputes … concerning an obligation of the latter") to limit jurisdiction to claims about the host State's obligations. In an award issued just months before the *Spyridon Roussalis* award, an UNCITRAL tribunal had pronounced that a counterclaim must have at least a "close connection" with the main claim from which it allegedly arose.[213]

Assessing the Experts (and their Opinions)

In the GATT/WTO system, members need not "automatically . . . follow what, at any given time, constituted majority scientific opinion."[214] Of course, the GATT/WTO (like some international human rights disputes) deals with inter-state cases and thus, where consent is established, sovereignty collides with sovereignty. This is especially true where transboundary, contagious harm incidentally, unknowingly or deliberately caused by one country (supported by some rational need) harms the sovereign interests and public welfare of another country.[215]

Deference, then, is not as effective a talisman (for the State) in WTO/GATT cases as it is in IIA cases. This is an important effect, or at least side-effect, of direct standing. When two parties are in dispute with

---

arbitration clauses, and the scope of ICSID jurisdiction over mass claims arbitrations.").

[212] ICSID Case No. ARB/06/1, Award, 7 December 2011, at ¶ 869.

[213] *Paushok et al v. Mongolia*, UNCITRAL, Award on Jurisdiction and Liability, 28 April 2011, at ¶ 693.

[214] *EC — Asbestos*, at ¶ 32 (rejecting Canada's "preponderant" scientific opinion suggestion).

[215] The quintessential case in point is *U.S. – Shrimp* (1998), where the United States's turtle excluder device requirement was at issue. The case is discussed in the previous chapter. For a detailed explanation, see P. Sands, PRINCIPLES OF INTERNATIONAL ENVIRONMENTAL LAW 841-42 (Cambridge University Press, 2003).

each other, it is instinctive for the tribunal to attempt to give each party no more and no less latitude than the other. Accordingly, the deference that the State receives before an investment tribunal must be less than the deference it receives before a WTO panel or appellate body where *each* party is, at least theoretically, a State (and where they neutralize each other's sovereign interests). Moreover, the WTO Appellate Body's position implies that it is possible (at least theoretically) for a tribunal to weigh the scientific evidence without being overly intrusive.

Methanex's approach to scientific correctness is important for the "intent" analysis because the result often depends on how strictly the tribunals inspect the evidence and if they allow States to invoke *post-hoc* justifications. *Post-hoc* justifications cannot be equated with "intent"—try as some might to define the term of art loosely—because intent presupposes being led to the expropriatory means *by* the legitimate public interest ("premeditation" of sorts). Andrew Newcombe expresses this as a three-part test:

> the requirement for: (i) a scientific-based risk assessment; (ii) a rational connection between an identified risk and the measure taken; and (iii) an assessment of the regulatory options available to a state to address the risk, are important factors in determining the legitimacy of the police powers measures and whether non-compensation can be justified given the risk in question.[216]

Along these lines, one NAFTA case that has really puzzled the IIA community is *Ethyl Corp. v. Canada* (1998).[217] The claimant-manufacturer of the gasoline additive MMT (methylcyclopentadienyl manganese tricarbonyl) sued Canada, arguing that Canada expropriated its assets by banning MMT importation; this was a case about market share and market access. Canada, of course, had to show public health and environmental reasons.

Like the revelation in an O Henry novel, Canada then surprised many observers. In its Statement of Defence, Canada stated that "[i]n 1994 the Department of National Health and Welfare had reviewed the available literature and assessed the direct health risk associated with exposure to airborne respirable manganese" and had found that "*current levels* of airborne respirable manganese to which the population in large urban

---

[216] A. Newcombe, *The Boundaries of Regulatory Expropriation in International Law*, 20 ICSID REV., FILJ 1, 36 (2005).
[217] UNCITRAL, Final Award on the Merits (1998).

centers are exposed are below the benchmark air level at which no adverse health risks *are expected*."[218]

Furthermore, Canada maintained that "[t]he public health and environmental impacts of long-term, lower dose exposure to airborne respirable manganese and unburned MMT are unknown."[219] This author does not wish to read ulterior motives into this repositioning but simply observes that Canada, in a telling non-move, did not point to the *precautionary principle* to justify the ban. Under this principle, coupled with the *aggregation principle*, Canada might have argued that it is the aggregate effect of the MMT in the future (not the one-actor model, but the havoc that *all* similarly-situated actors in the MMT business could wreak) that Canada was trying to nip at the bud.[220]

It is customary international law that "responsible, representative governments commonly act from perspectives of prudence and precaution where risks of irreversible, e.g. life-terminating, damage to human health are concerned."[221] Although various instruments do contain an express authorization of the precautionary principle,[222] it appears to be customary law that they generally need not. On the other hand, instruments dispelling the possibility of the precautionary principle being used as a full or partial defence must do so.

A legal system cannot function if it makes bald assumptions that all actors might wish to do something utterly impractical. At the same time,

---

[218] *Ethyl Corp. v. Canada*, Statement of Defence, at ¶ 60 (emphasis in original). This government study was the only scientific evidence that the parties mentioned.

[219] *Id.*, at ¶ 30.

[220] Fittingly perhaps, the precautionary principle is a settled aspect of international environmental law; the question is to what extent that should apply automatically to mixed questions of international environmental *and investment* law. See United Nations Conference on Environment and Development, Rio, 1992 (the "Rio Declaration") ("Where there are threats of serious or irreversible environmental damage, lack of full scientific certainty should not be used as a reason for postponing measures to prevent environmental degradation."); *Danube Dam — Gabčíkovo/Nagymaros Case* (*Hungary v. Slovakia*), 37 ILM 162, 204, 212 (1998); *AP Pollution Control Board v. Nayudu*, Supreme Court of India SOL Case No. 53 (1999) (unreported) ("it is necessary that the party attempting to preserve the *status quo* by maintaining a less-polluted state should not carry the burden or proof and the party who wants to alter it, must bear this burden"); M. J. Dixon, Case Note: *Gabčíkovo/Nagymaros Case*, 57 CAM. L. J. 1, 4 (1998).

[221] *EC-Hormones*, WT/DS26/AB/R, WT/DS48/AB/R, at ¶ 124 (1998).

[222] Article 19(1), Energy Charter Treaty, Dec. 17, 1994, 2080 U.N.T.S. 95 ("In its policies and actions each Contracting Party shall strive to take precautionary measures to prevent or minimize environmental degradation.").

however, it *must*, perhaps in an abundance of caution, actively assume that these actors might wish to act "rationally" and look out for their self-interest. This principle—prophylactic rather than *post*-injury curative—takes the long view, and was functioning here. It has some in-built deference to the State but is not widely seen as problematic or illegitimate.

Among international cases, we have rarely seen States invoking the precautionary principle (at least not expressly). One possible reason is while Canada as a *sovereign* might find the argument to its advantage, Canadian investors (at least some of whom are also citizens and constituents) might not. Taking this position now might have straitjacketed Canada in future disputes. Canada might not be able to act as a supportive amicus in those disputes.

Another reason might be that the principle is a last resort, not the first line of defence. States might prefer not to reach the precautionary principle as a defence possibly because, years later, if the fears are held to have been unfounded and not supported by empirical or other data, there is no guarantee that the tribunals will not retroactively nullify restrictions once upheld in a prior arbitration. The absence of *stare decisis* in the IIA network will not help the argument for retaining the established approach. Even in the same ICSID arbitration, perhaps the probability of this error being labeled a "misapplication" of law and thus annulled would rise dramatically if precautionary principle were the basis. Morever, because *Ethyl* was being heard under the UNCITRAL Rules, the domestic courts might be able to vacate the award.

Before we move on to other issues, it is fitting to mention one last point about Canada's strategy in the case. Now, Canada had available a third way, which was a low-risk argument that the precautionary argument was more of an "approach" than a "principle of general or customary international law."[223] This distinction mirrors the strategic argument that the United States had at least once advanced before the WTO Appellate

[223] *EC-Hormones, supra*, at ¶ 123 ("The status of the precautionary principle in international law continues to be the subject of debate among academics, law practitioners, regulators and judges. The precautionary principle is regarded by some as having crystallized into a general principle of customary international environmental law. Whether it has been widely accepted by Members as a principle of general or customary international law appears less than clear ... [The] status of the precautionary principle in international law and that the precautionary principle, at least outside the field of international environmental law, still awaits authoritative formulation.").

Body).[224] But perhaps Canada wanted nothing at all to do with the precautionary argument. It might also be the case that Canada was concerned about the doctrinal or at least strategic dilution of the precautionary argument that might leverage away Canada's credibility in the future.[225] After all, although the precautionary argument is a powerful weapon in the State's arsenal and retains the potential to "help keep States on the pathway towards the realization of common ends through international law,"[226] it is not an automatic and absolute defence. At the very least, "sufficient scientific evidence" is required to satisfy that standard.[227]

My hypothesis is strengthened by the insistence of several developed countries' IIA legal advisors that their Foreign Ministries' commitments to transparency are demonstrated by presenting on-line much of the arbitration-centric information.[228] This advisor also emphasised the inter-

---

[224] *EC-Hormones*, WT/DS26/AB/R, WT/DS48/AB/R, at ¶ 43 (1998) ("In the view of the United States, the claim of the European Communities that there is a generally-accepted principle of international law which may be referred to as the 'precautionary principle' is erroneous as a matter of international law. The United States does not consider that the 'precautionary principle' represents a principle of customary international law; rather, it may be characterized as an 'approach' – the content of which may vary from context to context.").

[225] *Id.*, at ¶ 43 ("The European Communities does not explain how 'the precautionary principle' affects the requirements in the SPS Agreement that a measure be 'based on' scientific principles and a risk assessment, and not maintained without sufficient scientific evidence. The EC's invocation of a 'precautionary principle' cannot create a risk assessment where there is none, nor can a 'principle' create 'sufficient scientific evidence' where there is none.").

[226] C. E. Foster, *Precautionary Principle in the Crucible, supra* ("Greater reliance on public international law considerations such as the precautionary principle will help to reinforce international law as a vehicle for controlling and influencing the State in relation to shared international problems, and help keep States on the pathway towards the realization of common ends through international law.").

[227] *Id.*, at ¶ 43; *id.*, at ¶ 125 ("the precautionary principle does not, by itself, and without a clear textual directive to that effect, relieve a panel from the duty of applying the normal (i.e. customary international law) principles of treaty interpretation in reading the provisions of the SPS Agreement.").

[228] Along with the government of this IIA legal advisor, other governments too insist on symmetric transparency *among* nations. The United States, for instance, has expressed particular concern on the following issues: domestic technology requirement ("The Administration crafted a new discipline to prevent Parties from imposing domestic technology requirements, i.e., requiring the purchase, use, or according of a preference to domestically developed technology in order to provide an advantage to a Party's own investors, investments, or technology");

agency working group ("I-WoG," in office parlance, I am told) within the Executive in order to come up with consistent positions. This function requires not only liaising with Commerce, Treasury, the Attorney General's Office (known as "Law and Justice" in some jurisdictions), and various other regulatory actors but also the interests of the subsidiaries. If Canada has been following the same pattern, its decision to forego the precautionary principle claim might be applauded as presbyopic (taking the long view on legal strategy) rather than suspected of being a temperamental fit.

Had Canada invoked the precautionary argument, perhaps it would have been hard to justify why Canada had not adopted a total ban on MMT rather than just an importation ban. The NT discrimination issue was stark because the MMT importation ban indicated that somehow homegrown MMT was fine but U.S. or Mexican MMT was not. Absent an exceedingly persuasive justification that involves the very integrity and functionability of the international law regime, a logical necessity or a different compelling and urgent societal interest, the sovereign must be held to its word. The case has overwhelming GATT/WTO implications and, had Canada actually *defended* its ban, the GATT/WTO likeness cases[229] could have imparted some lessons to the *Ethyl* tribunal. Such cases may yet come up.

---

participation in standard-setting ("U.S. investors may be at a competitive disadvantage when product standards in foreign markets are developed in an opaque, unpredictable, or discriminatory fashion, especially where governments use standards or technical regulations to favor domestic firms and technologies. The 2012 model BIT includes new language requiring Parties to allow investors of the other Party to participate in the development of standards and technical regulations on non-discriminatory terms. This provision also recommends that non-governmental standards bodies observe this requirement"); and delegated government authority ("Delegated government authority. The Administration developed a new footnote to clarify the standard for whether a Party has delegated governmental authority to an SOE or any other person or entity, in order to help ensure that the actions of SOEs and other entities acting under delegated governmental authority are fully covered by the BIT's obligations"). See Model Bilateral Investment Treaty: Fact Sheet, Office of the Spokesperson, U.S. Department of State, April 20, 2012, *available at* <www.state.gov/r/pa/prs/ps/2012/04/188199.htm>.

[229] See, *e.g.*, *EC — Scallops*, Request for Consultations by Canada, "European Communities – Trade Description of Scallops," WT/DS/7/1 (1995) (case settled) (while *all* species of French scallops were labelled the desirable "Coques St Jacques," *all* species of Canadian scallops from Canadian seas were labelled the less desirable "Petoncles.").

Chapter V (NON-DISCRIMINATION) has already discussed how other NAFTA cases such as *S.D. Myers v. Canada* (2000)[230] and *International Thunderbird Gaming Corp. v. Mexico* (2006)[231] establish that evidence of intent can be found in *patterns* of government behavior. Patterns of upsetting investors' reasonable expectations or failing to provide a stable and predictable system are not always enough but they go a long way in establishing expropriation.[232] In line with the previous chapter, "class of one" discrimination would be an FET violation even if it is not unpredictable or disproportionate; it simply would be arbitrary.

In fact, Jan Paulsson and Zachary Douglas argue that "one possible basis for distinguishing between compensable and uncompensable takings in a regulatory context [is] the frustration of the investor's legitimate expectations built on a reasonable reliance upon representations and undertakings by the Host State."[233] Of course, an expropriation is presumptively *ultra vires* both customary international law and the FET's legitimate expectations prong if it imposes a retroactive liability.

The IIA tribunal's award in *Occidental v. Ecuador* (2004)[234] concerned claimants who were compelled by *ex post facto* changes in the Ecuadorean tax code to reimburse VAT payments that claimants had already received. *Occidental* has been construed in some circles to preclude retroactive liability *per se* even when it is enacted through sovereignty exercises as fundamental as tax code alternations.[235] But what *Occidental* actually held was that, as per the facts in that arbitration, "[t]he tax law was changed

---

[230] NAFTA/UNCITRAL, Partial Award ¶ 252-54 (2000); A. Newcombe & L. Paradell, LAW AND PRACTICE OF INVESTMENT TREATIES: STANDARDS OF TREATMENT 232-319 (2009).

[231] UNCITRAL (NAFTA), at ¶ 177.

[232] *Impregilo S.p.A. v. Argentina*, ICSID Case No. ARB/07/17 (2011) (C. Brower, Arbitrator, concurring and dissenting) (agreeing with some of the findings of FET violation but would have found several other violations due to a "pattern directed at damaging [the claimant]" — pointing to "consistent and uncooperative behavior" by the government, *id.*, at ¶ 6).

[233] J. Paulsson & Z. Douglas, "Indirect Expropriations in Treaty Arbitrations," *in* ARBITRATING FOREIGN INVESTMENT DISPUTES: PROCEDURAL AND SUBSTANTIVE LEGAL ASPECTS 158 (N. Horn & S. Kröll, eds.) (2004).

[234] *Occidental Exploration and Production Company v. The Republic of Ecuador*, UNCITRAL/LCIA Case No. UN3467, Final Award (2004).

[235] I do not read *Occidental* in that way, and I am honored to be in Professor Schill's august company. See, *e.g.* S. Schill, INTERNATIONAL INVESTMENT LAW AND COMPARATIVE PUBLIC LAW 584 (Oxford University Press, 2010) (stating that "it was not the retroactive effect itself that was held to be a violation of investor rights, but rather the way in which the change took place.").

without providing any clarity about its meaning and extent and the practice and regulations were also inconsistent with such changes."[236]

Moreover, if this retroactive liability is "severe," is imposed "on a limited class of parties that could not have anticipated the liability, and if the extent of that liability is substantially disproportionate to the parties' experience,"[237] it adds to a non-discrimination argument in addition to an FET violation.[238] The IIA tribunal in *Tecnicas Medioambientales Tecmed S.A. v. Mexico* (2003) (*TECMED*)[239] was unmoved by the expropriation's "benefi[t] to society as a whole—such as environmental protection." *TECMED* is probably the claimants' best friend in this area, as it contains language that is more categorical than that is found in *Occidental*:

> The foreign investor expects the host State to act in a consistent manner, free from ambiguity and totally transparently in its relations with the foreign investor, so that it may know beforehand any and all rules and regulations that will govern its investments, as well as the goals of the relevant policies and administrative practices or directives, to be able to plan its investment and comply with such regulations. Any and all State actions conforming to such criteria should relate not only to the *guidelines, directives or requirements issued*, or the resolutions approved thereunder, but also to the goals underlying such regulations.[240]

On an expropriation claim, the *TECMED* tribunal found an expropriation "particularly" because "the negative economic impact of such actions on the financial position of the investor is sufficient to neutralize in full the value, or economic or commercial use of its investment without receiving any compensation whatsoever."[241]

Substantial diminution in the investment or property value seemed to be sufficient for the finding of a substantive violation in *TECMED*. This tribunal also held that "it is generally understood that [indirect expropriations] materialize through actions or conduct, which do not

---

[236] *Occidental, supra,* at ¶ 181.

[237] *Eastern Enterprises v. Apfel*, 524 U.S. 498, 528-29 (1998). Limited retroactive liability for a narrow time period, *only* in a manner absolutely required by the circumstances, might pass the legitimate expectations test.

[238] Risking that I am belabouring the obvious and the already-stated, it still bears mentioning that FET is arguably broad enough to encompass non-discrimination and a claim for FET might be more likely to succeed if it fails, or at least is suspect with regard to, the non-discrimination test as well.

[239] ICSID Case No. ARB(AF)/00/2, Award (2003), at ¶ 121.

[240] *Id.*, at ¶ 154 (emphasis added to draw attention to the specified class of instruments creating "expectations").

[241] *Id.*, at ¶ 121.

explicitly express the purpose of depriving one of rights or assets, but actually have that effect."[242] Some IIA tribunals would go further and overtly cut off the umbilical cord between intent and violation.[243] Practitioners are advised not to presume that this drastic development will bear fruit. Indeed, a "totality of the circumstances"-oriented judge might want to consider intent.

The IIA tribunal in *Azurix v. Argentina* (2006)[244] made three observations: (*i*) "there is a common thread in the recent awards under NAFTA . . . which does not require bad faith or malicious intention of the recipient State as a necessary element in the failure to treat investment fairly and equitably" but that patterns of evidence nonetheless can show the government's intent;[245] (*ii*) "the conduct of the State has to be below international standards but" these international standards evolve;[246] and (*iii*) "the frustration of expectations that the investor [must] legitimately [be] taken into account when it made the investment" since "[t]he standards of conduct agreed by the parties to a BIT presuppose a favorable disposition towards foreign investment, in fact, a pro-active behavior of the State to encourage and protect it."[247] Each observation is a valid aspect of knowledge transfer for international tribunals.

Another recent IIA tribunal, *Alpha Projektholding GmbH v. Ukraine* (2010),[248] elaborated on this last point in broad brush strokes: the State has

---

[242] *Id.*, at ¶ 114.

[243] *Siemens AG v. Argentina*, ICSID Case No. ARB/02/08, Award (2007), at ¶ 299 (holding that "the [FET and other] standard[s] [are] . . . unrelated to whether the Respondent has had any deliberate intention or bad faith in adopting the measures in question…."); *Genin v. Estonia,* ICSID Case No. ARB/99/2, Final Award on the Merits (2001), at ¶ 1024 ("in order to amount to a violation of the BIT, any procedural irregularity that may have been present would have to amount to bad faith, a willful disregard of due process of law or an extreme insufficiency of action.") (held by the *Azurix* tribunal, *infra,* to *require* intent to prove expropriation).

[244] ICSID Case No. ARB/01/12, Award (2006), at ¶ 372.

[245] *Id.*

[246] *Id.*

[247] *Id.*

[248] ICSID Case No. ARB/07/16, Award (2010), at ¶ 420. Other tribunals have expressed the same view. See *LG&E Energy Corp. v. Argentina*, ICSID Case No. ARB/02/01, Decision on Liability (2006), at ¶ 131 (holding that "the [FET, MST, IMS, and due process] standard[s] consis[t] of the host State's consistent and transparent behavior, free of ambiguity that involves the obligation to grant and maintain a stable and predictable legal framework necessary to fulfill the justified expectations of the foreign investor"); *PSEG Global Inc. v. Turkey*, ICSID Case

an obligation not "to upset an investor's legitimate expectations and [an] obligation to avoid arbitrary government action, regardless of whether there is any discriminatory element involved." This covers the obligation not to "arbitrarily chang[e] the rules of the game in a manner that undermines the legitimate expectations of, or the representations made to, an investor."[249] One possible negative consequence of this legitimate expectations factor is that it might discourage States from creating reliances as more trouble than they are worth.

The *Lemire v. Ukraine* (2010)[250] tribunal also appreciated the point of balancing between legitimate investor expectations and the public interest. However, it is important to observe that *Lemire* defers to the government as to what "public interest" includes or does not include—"balanc[ing] against the legitimate right of [the host State] to pass legislation and adopt measures for the protection of what as a sovereign it perceives to be its public interest."[251] The *Lemire* tribunal further articulated that the "wider context" here is "the economic development for both signatory countries."[252] Would the absence of this factor have made a difference? Time will tell. *AWG Group Ltd. v. Argentina* (2010),[253] decided just a few months after *Lemire*, noticeably left out the deferential wording: "in interpreting the meaning of fair and equitable treatment to be accorded to investors, the Tribunal must balance the legitimate and reasonable

---

No. 02/5, Award (2007) ¶ 250 (holding that "the [FET] obligation was seriously breached by what has been described … as the 'roller-coaster' effect of the continuing legislative changes") (citations omitted)' *Siemens AG*, *supra*, at ¶ 299 ("the current standard includes the frustration of expectations that the investor may have legitimately taken into account when it made the investment"); *Enron, supra*, at ¶232 (holding that the "stable framework for the investment" was a key element of the FET standard).

249 *Id.*, at ¶ 420.

250 ICSID Case No. ARB(AF)/98/1, at ¶ 284, Decision on Liability (2010).

251 *Id.*, at ¶ 273; see also A. von Staden, *Deference or No Deference, supra* ("it is quite clear in the context of provisions laying down the requirements for permissible expropriations that the identification of the relevant 'public purpose' for which such an expropriation may be undertaken deserves deference, in that it is not for the tribunal to replace the state's assessment of what public purposes should be pursued with its own. As long as the stated purpose is not clearly a mere pretense, tribunals generally accept it, as they do increasingly the good faith exercise of a state's police powers as non-expropriatory more generally.") (internal footnotes omitted).

252 *Id.*

253 UNCITRAL, Decision on Liability (2010), at ¶ 336.

expectations of the Claimants with Argentina's right to regulate the provision of a vital public service."[254]

The *Lemire* tribunal also observed that "[e]conomic development is an objective which must benefit all, primarily national citizens and national companies, and secondarily foreign investors. Thus, [the tribunal maintained,] the object and purpose of the Treaty . . . [was] not to protect foreign investments *per se*, but . . . [to] aid to the development of the domestic economy."[255] This pronouncement dovetails with Professor Brownlie's earlier-observed stance that "national economic disaster" is a *quasi*-absolute defence as to claims addressing expropriation and/or compensation. This analysis also has the effect of challenging (or at least ranking down) the primary IIA aim of stimulating foreign investment and the accompanying capital flow.

The presumably more popular view is that the initial baseline of the investor's or property owner's legitimate expectations may not be calibrated downwards unless it is exceedingly persuasively supported by a genuinely *compelling* justification such as saving (or trying to save) the national economy from collapse (as happened in the Argentine financial crisis cases or other emergency situations). But the *Lemire* tribunal goes deeper. By deferring to the respondent State's own idea of "public interest," *Lemire* even surpasses the Brownlie formulation.

First, it is acceptable for the international tribunal to defer, unless clearly prejudicial, to the sovereign's proffered set of facts about its conditions; it skates close to the tipping point for the tribunal to defer to the sovereign's notion of what constitutes "public interest." Not only could this result in doctrinal unpredictability, it could also confer upon sovereign respondents an automatic and significant Get-Out-of-Jail-Free card to escape liability.

Second, it does not address the proper allocation of the burdens: Such a measure, it might be argued, enables the State to "forc[e] some people alone to bear public burdens which, in all fairness and justice, should be borne by the public as a whole."[256] Moreover, Chapter III has discussed that Judge Brower's observation in *Renta* "the principle that international treaties must be interpreted autonomously, i.e., not in accordance with the domestic legal orders of the contracting State parties involved."[257] Should this autonomous construction also not be accorded by international tribunals to what "public interest" is, in light of the sovereign's

[254] *Lemire, supra*, at ¶ 273.
[255] *Id.*
[256] *Armstrong v. United States*, 364 U. S. 40, 49 (1960).
[257] *Renta*, *supra*, at ¶ 28 (Separate opinion of Judge Charles Brower).

condition?[258] In short, then, whether or not this *Lemire* rule takes off in the future will make a significant doctrinal and practical difference. This *Lemire* principle, of course, involves issues which can be traced back to 1923 (and even before, in some manifestation).[259]

Such issues concern the clash on the issue of interpretation,[260] and some suggestions are even made that sovereignty inspires analytical as well as emotional considerations on all sides.[261] A middle-ground is available: Although "states do . . . remain *legitimately* concerned with ensuring that the rules of the [international investment law] game accord with state understandings of what the rules should be"[262] and this concern

---

[258] There is likely to be at least an overlap of understanding between the international tribunal's view, taking into account the unique conditions concerning the sovereign's jurisdiction, and the sovereign's view. But to render the tribunal's view entirely dependent on the nation's own notion of "public interest" would be rather a new Rubicon in international law. *Lemire*, should it prove to have staying power on this score, may well rework some fundamental propositions of international law.

[259] See, *e.g., The S.S. 'Wimbledon' (United Kingdom, France, Italy & Japan v Germany)*, 1923 PCIJ (ser A) Nos 1, 15, 24; *Lake Lanoux case*, 12 Report of International Arbitral Awards 281, 310; *Air Service Agreement of 27 March 1946,* 18 Report of International Arbitral Awards 417, 483.

[260] The concerns of sovereignty, which give States the power of auto-interpretation, are said to "cal[l] into question the very viability of international law." See F. Zarbiyev, *Judicial Activism in International Law, supra,* at 22. Auto-interpretation, of course, "allows states to determine *uti singuli* the content of their international rights and obligations." *Id.* (emphasis in original). At the same time, however, "the interpretations of rights and obligations by states themselves are likely to be self-serving and can endanger the very existence of an objective legal order." *Id.*

[261] Some experts believe that international lawyers like Judge Brower are understandably "favourable to third-party interpretations of international law" for two reasons: (*i*) "what is at stake is nothing less than the very existence of their discipline" ; and (*ii*) "the darkest horrors of the twentieth century were committed in the name of sovereignty." See F. Zarbiyev, *Judicial Activism in International Law, supra,* at 22. I would not attribute much weight to Factor (*i*), for it exudes a certain *ad hominem* radiation, though it must be said that (*ii*) has an intuitive appeal which withstands penetrating scrutiny.

[262] J. W. Yackee, *Controlling the International Investment Law Agency*, 53 HARV. INT'L L. J. 391, 416-417 (2012) (stating that "unlike domestic agencies, the [international investment law] agency is largely decoupled from the legitimating influence and control of domestic politics, and for that reason the agency's lawmaking functions are structurally [much more] problematic than the lawmaking functions of their domestic administrative counterparts.") (internal quotation marks omitted).

should be given great regard, the right of final interpretation should lie in the international tribunal. There already are cases and doctrines which could serve as intellectual anchors.[263]

Another angle of practitioner manoeuvring is to recalibrate what a "legitimate" expectation is. If tribunals across international dispute settlement rally around a consensus that because emergency and *force majeure* situations as well as practical exigencies such as economic collapses often happen irresistibly and unforeseeably, the only appropriate rule is a simple, comprehensive one—perhaps that without an explicit promise (described by *Lemire* itself as "specific representations to the investor"[264]) by the sovereign State, no such "expectation," let alone a "legitimate" one, exists.

The legal risk borne of difficult circumstances is akin to business and commercial risk that companies often undertake. An alternative available to the tribunals is a holding that the initial baseline presumably (but with the potential to be rebutted) constituted a "legitimate expectation" in most non-urgent and/or unforeseeable situations. In these situations, "existence of . . . expectations created by host country laws, coupled with the act of investing their capital in reliance on them, and a subsequent, sudden change in those laws that led to a determination that the host country had not treated the investors fair and equitably" would be insufficient.[265]

Now we come upon *when* an expropriation is compensable: conventional wisdom is that "certain *bona fide* regulation that is non-discriminatory and within the state's police powers does not require compensation, no matter what the effect." [266] In *Feldman v. Mexico* (2002),[267] the NAFTA tribunal

---

[263] The award in *Funnekotter and others v. Zimbabwe*, ICSID CASE NO. ARB/05/6, Final Award (2009), at ¶ 103, states:

The Tribunal observes that, Zimbabwe domestic law may in this respect provide the Tribunal useful information on the situation which prevailed in Zimbabwe from 2002 to 2005. However, the Tribunal also notes that during that period there had been no state of emergency declared in that country. In any event, it is on the basis of the applicable rules of International Law that, in conformity with Article 9(3) of the BIT, the Tribunal must decide whether or not there was at the time a state of necessity which could have made lawful deprivation of property without compensation. In other words, ultimately international law, not the domestic law of Zimbabwe, must determine the effect any state of emergency would have on the dispute before the Tribunal.

[264] *Lemire*, *supra,* at ¶84.

[265] *AWG, supra*, at ¶ 226.

[266] R. Moloo & J. Jacinto, *Environmental and Health Regulation*, *supra*, at 72.

[267] *Feldman v. Mexico*, ICSID Case No. ARB(AF)/99/1, Award (2002), at ¶ 103.

accepted this approach. *Feldman* then balanced the FET-MST claims with the aim of *not* discouraging government-run commercial enterprises:

> [G]overnments must be free to act in the broader public interest through protection of the environment, new or modified tax regimes, the granting or withdrawal of government subsidies, reductions or increases in tariff levels, imposition of zoning restrictions and the like. Reasonable governmental regulation of this type cannot be achieved if any business that is adversely affected may seek compensation, and it is safe to say that customary international law recognizes this . . . .

We have seen this justification in Chapter III already, and it is appropriate for the other two institutions as well. The fear was that "governmental regulation in important areas such as health and environment would be undesirably hindered if governments were constantly worried about having to pay compensation to any foreign investor adversely affected."[268]

Intent is not the only test of expropriation but these decisions suggest that "when the measure in question is a *bona fide* regulation of general application, within the legitimate exercise of the state's police powers, a tribunal will be less likely to award compensation."[269] Both the effect and the attributes of an expropriation factor into whether compensation is owed for an expropriation.

Cases following this approach include the IIA tribunal decision in *Saluka v. Czech Republic* (2006),[270] in which the claimant argued that because the Czech government put the bank IPB (in which the claimant had invested) into forced administration, this was an unlawful expropriation. The Czech Republic countered that this was the only way to maintain a stable banking system; the turbulent banking system was the

---

[268] R. Moloo & J. Jacinto, *Environmental and Health Regulation*, *supra*, at 72; M. Reisman & R. D. Sloane, *Indirect Expropriation and its Valuation in the BIT Generation*, 74 BRIT. Y.B. INT'L L. 115, 129 (2003) ("[G]overnments must be free to act in the broader public interest through protection of the environment, new or modified tax regimes, the granting or withdrawal of government subsidies, reductions or increases in tariff levels, imposing zoning restrictions and the like. Reasonable governmental regulation of this type cannot be achieved if any business that is adversely affected may seek compensation, and it is safe to say that customary international law recognizes this.").

[269] *Id.*, at 72-3.

[270] *Saluka Investments BV (The Netherlands) v. the Czech Republic*, UNCITRAL, Partial Award (2006) ¶ 165.

result of IPB's shareholders not correcting several deep flaws previously identified by the government.[271]

The *Saluka* tribunal first observed that "[i]t is now established in international law that States are not liable to pay compensation to a foreign investor when, in the normal exercise of their regulatory powers, they adopt in a non-discriminatory manner *bona fide* regulations that are aimed at the general welfare."[272] This meant that "a State does not commit an expropriation and is thus not liable to pay compensation to a dispossessed alien investor when it adopts general regulations" within its police powers.[273] Do not allow the tone to gloss over the fact that there is plenty of in-built flexibility here: "*bona fide*," "normal exercise of their regulatory powers," "aimed at the general welfare," and of course "non-discriminatory manner."

Now consider a potentially explosive situation now in the banking sector pipelines. When the new Basel III regulations, which have been implemented by the Federal Reserve Bank of the United States and such national banks in many nations, come into effect in 2013 it may invite some challenges with respect to reserve-to-capital ratio requirements.[274] Basel III governs banks and most other financial institutions. If such an institution must hold a certain proportion of capital against default risk, despite the fact that the real risk of default is actually lower, the financial institution might engage in regulatory arbitrage. Under such circumstances, it might in fact be profitable for the financial institution to securitise the loan, for this would excise the low risk loan from its institutional portfolio. Alternatively, if the real risk is greater than the

---

[271] *Id.*, at ¶ 270.
[272] *Id.*, at ¶ 255.
[273] *Id.*, at ¶ 262.
[274] Federal Reserve Bank, Press Release, June 7, 2012 (articulating that the proposed rule-making contained in *Regulatory Capital Rules: Regulatory Capital, Implementation of Basel III, Minimum Regulatory Capital Ratios, Capital Adequacy, and Transition Provisions* as "increas[ing] the quantity and quality of capital required by proposing a new minimum common equity tier 1 ratio of 4.5 percent of risk-weighted assets and a common equity tier 1 capital conservation buffer of 2.5 percent of risk-weighted assets, and raising the minimum tier 1 capital ratio from 4 percent to 6 percent of risk-weighted assets; revise the definition of capital to improve the ability of regulatory capital instruments to absorb losses; establish limitations on capital distributions and certain discretionary bonus payments if additional specified amounts, or 'buffers,' of common equity tier 1 capital are not met; and introduce a supplementary leverage ratio for internationally active banking organizations."), *available at* <www.federalreserve.gov/newsevents/press/bcreg/20120607a.htm>.

regulatory risk then it might turn out to be profitable to make that loan and hold on to it, assuming the loan's appropriate pricing.

On a reserve-to-capital ratio requirement claim, *Saluka* would not necessarily foreclose an investor victory before an international tribunal. This naturally would not be a "direct transfer of funds mandated by the Government,"[275] but a direct transfer of funds from one bank activity to another *forbidden* by the Government. Firm choice is a common denominator in both scenarios; however, the difference is the harm caused by one course of action as opposed to another. The relatively empirical nature of the latter inquiry is warranted by *Saluka*. Noting that it is sometimes difficult to decide which expropriations are "general" and which are not, the *Saluka* tribunal employed a more balanced test:

> [i]t . . . inevitably falls to the *adjudicator* to determine whether particular conduct by a state 'crosses the line' that separates valid regulatory activity from expropriation. Faced with the question of when, how and at what point an otherwise valid regulation becomes, in fact and effect, an unlawful expropriation, international tribunals must consider the circumstances in which the question arises. The context within which an impugned measure is adopted and applied is critical to the determination of its validity.[276]

The fact-intensive decisions lay with the judge or arbitrator. A deference, if accorded at all, was to the judge, not to the claimant or the State. For support, the *Saluka* tribunal reached back to the IUCT's decision in *Emmanuel Too v. Greater Modesto Insurance Associates* (1989).[277] *Too* was appropriate to reference because of its openness to Totality-of-the-Circumstances and to what constitutes a Hobson's choice. In addition, *Too* was an appropriate yardstick for *Saluka* because both cases concerned a middle point between a revolutionary, unruly atmosphere and a stable, predictable one.[278] In *Too*, the IUCT had stood for the proposition that

---

[275] *Eastern Enterprises v. Apfel*, 524 U.S. 498, 521 (1998) (plurality opinion). Of course, the transfer principle could manifest itself in numerous situations, from affecting multinational farmers to service sectors. Under *Saluka*, the degree of interference and the character of interference would matter dispositively. This point has been addressed through other examples and variants in Chapter III.

[276] *Saluka, supra,* at ¶ 264 (emphasis in original).

[277] 23 I.U.C.T.R. 378, 387 (1989).

[278] *Too* concerned Iranian assets in the United States; although the general atmosphere was stable in the United States, the hostility greeting the claimant was disturbing. The claimant in *Saluka* was dealing with the Czech authorities who were *neither* downright arbitrary and hostile *nor* totally predictable.

> [a] State is not responsible for loss of property or for other economic disadvantage resulting from *bona fide* general taxation or any other action that is commonly accepted as within the police power of States, provided it is not discriminatory and is not designed to cause the alien to abandon the property to the State or to sell it at a distress price.

This is one of the few cases where distress sale is openly recognised as a substantial diminution in value and is therefore compensable. The *Saluka* tribunal decided that because the blame for the non-rectification of IPB's problems lies substantially with shareholders, this measure "[wa]s . . . a lawful and permissible regulatory action by the Czech Republic aimed at the general welfare of the State." [279] The tribunal added that this expropriation "does not fall within the ambit of any of the exceptions to the permissibility of regulatory action . . . recognised by customary international law."[280]

Now consider the inverse scenario, where the test is also one of culpability. If we choose to view this problem through the prism of the "necessity" test, the questions are: Was it the State's own unforeseeable fault, over a period of time or suddenly, that it had to impose the challenged measure?[281] At which the tipping point did it become necessary for the State to enact the dubious regulation? A doctrinally "purist" approach might warrant a tribunal to adopt an extreme approach in either direction, for that might be easier to justify than the more moderate approach of drawing a line somewhere else.

After all, tribunals, unlike policy-makers, are expected to be principled and causally sound in all their pronouncements. Nonetheless, a more moderate line, despite its difficulties in justification, is probably the sounder and more responsible approach. Politics is the art of the possible, and, in this crucial sense, international tribunals are commissioned to resolve disputes with decisions that can function, are accepted, are perceived as legitimate, and are likely to be enduring.

The last Chapter has already discussed creeping expropriations (expropriations in gradual stages) in the diplomatic tribunal context. Like the IUCT in *Amoco International Finance Corporation v. Iran* (1987),[282] the IIA tribunals too have refused to block compensation for the entire creeping expropriations category. This is a position that the human rights

---

[279] *Saluka,* at ¶ 275.

[280] *Id.*.

[281] I have mentioned already that it is not quite *force majeure* or even *deus ex machina* if the State is directly and foreseeably at fault.

[282] 15 I.U.C.T.R. 189, 196.

field might investigate further and even consider adopting. Charles Brower, as arbitrator in the IIA case *Impregilo S.p.A. v. Argentina* (2011),[283] connected "intent" with creeping expropriation. Judge Brower thereby raised the bar:

> although the government's underlying intentions are not a necessary legal element of an indirect or creeping expropriation claim, such a claim can be bolstered by evidence of a broader policy decision that assigns common purpose to the individual measures leading to the investor's property deprivation.

Showing intent is more important here than in other expropriation cases. The NAFTA tribunal in *Pope & Talbot v. Canada* (2000)[284] faced an investor claim about expropriation with both FET-due process's and MST's strong overtones that the way in which Canada implemented the U.S.-Canada Softwood Lumber Agreement unlawfully interfered with the claimant's business. The tribunal held first that "[r]egulations can . . . be exercised in a way that would constitute creeping expropriation."[285] Then the tribunal explained that "much creeping expropriation could be conducted by regulation, and a blanket exception for regulatory measures would create a gaping loophole in international protections against expropriation."[286] If States could execute expropriations through smaller, more incremental measures, they might escape liability altogether.[287]

In *Azurix v. Argentina* (2006),[288] the tribunal impliedly took to task an earlier tribunal,. *Lauder v. Czech Republic* (2001).[289] *Lauder* had stated that host States "are not liable for economic injury that is the consequence of *bona fide* regulation within the accepted police powers of the State."[290] The same principle was observed by the IUCT in 1985.[291] The NAFTA award in *S.D. Myers v. Canada* (2000) was not willing to "rule out th[e]

---

[283] ICSID Case No. ARB/07/17, at ¶ 22 (Final Award) (June 21, 2011) (Judge Charles Brower, Arbitrator) (concurring and dissenting opinion).
[284] *Pope & Talbot Inc. v. Canada*, NAFTA/UNCITRAL, Interim Award (26 June 2000), at ¶ 99.
[285] *Id.*, at ¶¶ 99-100.
[286] *Id.*
[287] *Id.*; see also *TECMED, supra*, at ¶ 114-16.
[288] *Azurix Corp. v. Argentina*, ICSID Case No. ARB/01/12, Award (2006).
[289] UNCITRAL, Final Award (3 Sep. 2001), at ¶ 198.
[290] *Id.* ¶ 310.
[291] *SEDCO, Inc. v. National Iranian Oil Company*, Interlocutory Award No. ITL 55-129-3 (28 Oct. 1985), reprinted in 9 Iran-U.S. Claims Tribunal Rep. 248, 273-74.

possibility" that "[r]egulatory conduct by public authorities" may in some cases be "legitimate."[292]

Methanex v. United States and *Saluka v. Czech Republic* have held an expropriation does not occur when a state adopts general regulations that are "commonly accepted as within the police power of States."[293] The same view was endorsed by the recent award in *Chemtura Corporation v. Canada* (2010).[294] A unanimous tribunal in *Chemtura* determined that Canada had not breached its IIA (in particular NAFTA) obligations when it had adopted non-discriminatory measures concerning the agricultural insecticide lindane. The *Chemtura* tribunal understood the Canadian government to have been

> motivated by increasing awareness of the dangers presented by lindane for human health and the environment. A measure adopted under such circumstances is a valid exercise of the State's police powers and, as a result, does not constitute an expropriation.[295]

The *Azurix* tribunal supported the dual approach of taking both purpose and effects into account: "[t]he public purpose criterion as an additional criterion to the effect of the measures under consideration needs to be complemented."[296] The current default position—perhaps more than just the "emerging consensus"[297]—in international law is the *joint* consideration of intent and effects. It should explicitly be engaged with by our institutions.

In examining claims about expropriation, FET-due process or MST, a superior test is one of foreseeability in intent: Intention should be attributed *only* if the perpetrator inferred or had a duty to infer that a diminution in value would occur and, despite available means, did not try to stop or minimise this diminution. As noted earlier, weighing the different aspects of a measure's "character, including its purpose . . . can be a difficult task, and . . . will require a fact-specific analysis."[298] In this,

---

[292] UNCITRAL, Partial Award (13 Nov. 2000), at ¶¶ 266, 281 ("The general body of precedent usually does not treat regulatory action as amounting to expropriation.").

[293] See *Methanex v. United States of America*, NAFTA/UNCITRAL, Award (9 Aug. 2005); *Saluka Investments BV (The Netherlands) v. the Czech Republic*, UNCITRAL, Partial Award, at ¶ 165 (17 March 2006).

[294] UNCITRAL, Final Award on the Merits, at ¶ 134-35.

[295] *Chemtura Corp. v Canada*, UNCITRAL, Final Award (2 Aug. 2010), at ¶ 266.

[296] *Azurix*, *supra*, at ¶ 311.

[297] R. Moloo & J. Jacinto, *Environmental and Health Regulation*, *supra*, at 75.

[298] *Id.*, at 75-6.

international tribunals (notably in *Azurix*[299]) may draw help from *TECMED* (mentioned already).

The *TECMED* tribunal acknowledged that just because an expropriatory measure does not discriminate and has a legitimate public interest does not mean that it is uncompensable.[300] One view is that FET-MST-due process is so indefinite that non-discrimination should be the only (or perhaps, main) test. Even if non-discrimination worked in a picture-perfect way (which the last Chapter shows is not the case), this would still be a bad idea. Conceptually at least, some treatment can be *below* MST and still be regarded as formalistically non-discriminatory.

What might also harm the expropriating State's argument is the disproportionality between the public interest and the means used to achieve that interest. Chapter V has already explained the pitfalls of the "necessity" test, which will not be belaboured here. The *TECMED* tribunal elaborated on the proportionality test:

> [W]hether such actions or measures are proportional to the public interest presumably protected thereby and to the protection legally granted to investments, taking into account that the significance of such impact has a key role upon deciding the proportionality. . . . There must be a reasonable relationship between the charge or weight imposed to the foreign investor and the aim sought to be realized by any expropriatory measure.[301]

Proportionality analysis presupposes balancing and it presupposes weights assigned to the several variables.[302] It also presupposes candour

---

[299] *Azurix*, *supra*, at ¶¶ 311-12, 316-17.

[300] *Id.*, at ¶ 121.

[301] *TECMED v. Mexico*, *supra*, at ¶ 122 (emphasis added); Y. Fortier & S. Drymer, *Indirect Expropriation in the Law of International Investment, supra*, at 326-27.

[302] J. Crawford, ed., BROWNLIE'S PRINCIPLES, *supra*, at 291 (stating that "[p]roportionality . . .is . . . a test of the equitableness of a result arrived at by other means" and then pointing out that the "*ex post facto* verification" of proportionality is either a strict*ly*, though not necessarily rigid, mathematical analysis or one that, in the delimitation context, considers "particular geographical features" and is therefore more qualitative); *North Sea Continental Shelf Cases (Federal Republic of Germany v Denmark; Federal Republic of Germany v Netherlands)* [1969] ICJ Reports 4 at 52 ("A final factor to be taken account of is the element of a reasonable degree of proportionality which a delimitation effected according to equitable principles ought to bring about between the extent of the continental shelf appertaining to the States concerned and the lengths of their respective coastlines,-these being measured according to their general direction in order to establish the necessary balance between States with straight, and those with markedly concave or convex coasts, or to reduce very irregular coastlines to their

on the part of the decision-makers, when they are expected to use objective or at times somewhat subjective metrics to conduct the analyses.[303] Especially in parallel reasoning or reasoning-by-analogy cases, it remains particularly paramount that these adjustments, whether they be direct or *a fortiori*, are spelled out for the sake of tribunal legitimacy. Most recently, the NAFTA tribunal in *Glamis Gold v. United States* (2008),[304] followed *TECMED* and *Azurix* in applying the proportionality test:

> whether measures of a State constitute a non-compensable regulation or a compensable expropriation by examining, *inter alia*, (1) the extent to which the measures interfered with reasonable and investment-backed expectations of a stable regulatory framework, and (2) the purpose and character of the governmental actions taken.

By adding the proportionality test to NAFTA's jurisprudence, *TECMED* added some clarity to the somewhat-muddled body of FET-MST law. This step "ma[de] explicit what has . . . stood in the background of regulatory takings decisions that reject the sole effect doctrine and consider the purpose and context of the government's actions."[305] Proportionality, reliance, and non-discrimination are the IIA universe's defining legacy to international expropriation law. The international human rights arena carries on this discussion.

---

truer proportions."); The Bangladesh/Myanmar Case, ITLOS Case No 16, §§ 477-99 (articulated as the "disproportionality test").

303 L. Greenhouse, "The Legacy of Lewis F. Powell, Jr.," *N. Y. Times*, Dec. 4, 2002 ("'Self-consciousness and candor are the ideals' in a judge, Prof. Laurence H. Tribe of Harvard Law School said in an interview. 'Judges are most dangerous when they think they've escaped the past and become victims of their own myth.'").

304 *Glamis Gold, Ltd. v. United States*, NAFTA/UNCITRAL, Award (2009) ¶ 356; see also *Continental Casualty Company v. Argentina*, ICSID Case No. ARB/03/9, Award (2008) ¶ 276.

305 S. R. Ratner, *International Regulatory Takings*, *supra*, at 527-8.

§ 6.3—Substantive Standards before the ECtHR and the International Human Rights Tribunals

There is a distinct pro-individual orientation of most modern human rights courts, including the ECtHR. For example, the Inter-American Court of Human Rights once stated that "[i]n concluding these human rights treaties, the States can be deemed to submit themselves to a legal order within which they, for the common good, assume various obligations, not in relation to other States, but towards all individuals within their jurisdiction."[306] Although there is not much IIA literature or jurisprudence on such retroactive imposition of obligation on States, the presumption in international human rights is that such obligations are non-retroactive. At least one international human rights tribunal has conclusively held that "the principle of non-retroactivity in the law of treaties" is a general canon of international law.[307]

But the pro-individual orientation is not so absolute and categorical as to be free of the balancing act necessary to maintain general welfare and public interest. Otherwise the States might never have entered into the compact and might be substantially incentivised to leave. In a regime dominated perhaps just by party autonomy and investor rights concerns, there might not be a role for *amici curiae* submissions that are not pro-investor. Moreover, environmental cases demonstrate that the State, as the only actor seriously encumbered with this specific concern, might be construed to have not just a right but an *obligation* to regulate in the interests of the progeny, lest they be left bereft of resources or saddled with debt.

Similarly, the African Charter on Human and Peoples' Rights was created to "meet the needs of Africa" so that "through the institution of a State, the rights of all [are] recognised, respected without discrimination, and where public authorities submit themselves to the law in all their

[306] See *Effect of Reservations on the Entry into Force of the American Convention on Human Rights*, Advisory Opinion OC–2/82, 2 Inter-Am. Ct. H.R. (ser. A) (1982), at ¶ 29.

[307] *Blečić v. Croatia*, Application no. 59532/00, 8 March 2006, ECHR-GC, at ¶ 81 (observing that "while it is true that from the ratification date onwards all of the State's acts and omissions must conform to the [European Convention on Human Rights], the Convention imposes no specific obligation on the Contracting States to provide redress for wrongs or damage caused prior to that date . . . Any other approach would undermine both the principle of non-retroactivity in the law of treaties and the fundamental distinction between violation and reparation that underlines the law of State responsibility.").

endeavours."[308] Article 12 (5) takes great pains to protect against what took place *en masse* against South Asian merchants and Caucasian farmers in many parts of the continent[309]: "The mass expulsion of non-nationals shall be prohibited. Mass expulsion shall be that which is aimed at national, racial, ethnic or religious groups." In its own way this too is an investment-welcoming provision, although this particular dimension has largely been overlooked. Article 5 (6) of the Inter-American Convention stipulates: "Punishments consisting of deprivation of liberty shall have as an essential aim the reform and social readaptation of the prisoners"; Article 6 (1) states: "No one shall be subject to slavery or to involuntary servitude, which are prohibited in all their forms, as are the slave trade and traffic in women"; and Article 6 (2) guarantees: "No one shall be required to perform forced or compulsory labor. This provision shall not be interpreted to mean that, in those countries in which the penalty established for certain crimes is deprivation of liberty at forced labor, the carrying out of such a sentence imposed by a competent court is prohibited." The examples are too numerous to recount, and they illustrate the special role of the protections in the culture of the signatories and the inter-signatory relationships. The hard truth inherent in any comparativist's life is that you never truly know if the transplant from one system into another is legitimate or not; even if democratic legitimacy is the lodestar, in a super-majority of cases the answer could be justified cogently either way.

It is because of the international human rights tribunals's "public good" (sometimes phrased as "public interest") orientation that IIA tribunals (corporatist in nature) have rarely looked to them for guidance. In *Mondev International Ltd. v. United States* (2002),[310] the NAFTA tribunal considered the ECtHR's cases[311] concerning sovereign immunity and the

---

[308] See AFR. COMM'N, NON-COMPLIANCE OF STATES PARTIES TO ADOPTED RECOMMENDATIONS OF THE AFRICAN COMMISSION: A LEGAL APPROACH, 24th Ord. Sess., OAU DOC/OS/50b (XXIV), ¶ 6 (1998).

[309] C. Clarke et al., SOUTH ASIANS OVERSEAS: MIGRATION AND ETHNICITY 151 et seq. (Cambridge University Press, 2010); J. I. Herbst, STATE POLITICS IN ZIMBABWE 37 (University of California Press, 1990).

[310] Case No. ARB(AF)/99/2 (Final Award), at ¶ 144.

[311] Those cases include *Fogarty v. United Kingdom*, Application No. 37112/97, (2002) 34 EHRR 12, ¶¶ 24-25 (citing *Fayed v. United Kingdom*, Series A no. 294-B (1994), at ¶ 65); *Tinnelly &Sons Ltd. v. United Kingdom*, 27 EHRR 249 (1999); *Osman v. United Kingdom*, 29 EHRR 245 (2000); *TP & KM v. United Kingdom,* 34 EHRR 2 (2002); *Al-Adsani v. United Kingdom*, App. no. 35763/97 (2002), at ¶ 47; *McElhinney v. Ireland*, App. no. 31253/96 (2002), at ¶ 24.

denial of access to court. After some analysis, *Mondev* distinguished not just the cases but also the *tribunals*:

> These [ECtHR] decisions concern the 'right to a court', an aspect of the human rights conferred on all persons by the major human rights conventions and interpreted by the [ECtHR] in an evolutionary way. They emanate from a different region, and are not concerned, as Article 1105(1) of NAFTA is concerned, specifically with investment protection.

Things went a little better a year later in *TECMED*. In its first reference to the ECtHR, the *TECMED* tribunal cited the ECtHR's *Matos e Silva, Lda. v. Portugal* (1996)[312] decision for the proposition that "measures adopted by a State, whether regulatory or not, are an indirect *de facto* expropriation if they are irreversible and permanent and if the assets or rights subject to such measure . . . have been neutralized or destroyed."

The *TECMED* tribunal's second ECtHR reference bought into the latter's proportionality-based "aims and effects" test. Here *TECMED* cited *James v. United Kingdom* (1986),[313] which held that

> [n]ot only must a measure depriving a person of his property pursue, on the facts as well as in principle, a legitimate aim 'in the public interest,' but there must also be a *reasonable relationship of proportionality between the means employed and the aim sought to be realised* . . . . The requisite balance will not be found if the person concerned has had to bear 'an individual and excessive burden' . . . . The Court considers that a measure must be both appropriate for achieving its aim and not disproportionate thereto.
>
> . . . .non-nationals are more vulnerable to domestic legislation: unlike nationals, they will generally have played no part in the election or designation of its authors nor have been consulted on its adoption. Secondly, although a taking of property must always be effected in the public interest, different considerations may apply to nationals and non-nationals and there may well be legitimate reason for requiring nationals to bear a greater burden in the public interest than non-nationals.

---

[312] App. no. 15777/89, at ¶18.

[313] App. no. 8793/79 (1986), ¶ 50, 63 (emphasis added) (citing *Mellacher v. Austria*, App. no. 10522/83, 11011/84, 11070/84 (1989), at ¶ 24; *Pressos Compañía Naviera v. Belgium*, App. no. 17849/91 (1995) , at ¶ 19). See also H. Mountfield, *Regulatory Expropriations in Europe: The Approach of the European Court of Human Rights*, 11 N.Y.U. ENVT'L L.J. 136 (2002); H. R. Fabri, *The Approach Taken by the European Court of Human Rights to the Assessment of Compensation for "Regulatory Expropriations" of the Property of Foreign Investors*, 11 N.Y.U. ENVT'L L.J. 148 (2002).

Regarding ECtHR-IIA cross-pollination, in a recent arbitration (*Roussalis v. Romania* (2011)[314]), the claimant extraordinarily argued that the expropriation was "in breach of the BIT—and of the European Convention on Human Rights and of its Additional Protocol—Romania failed to create a safe environment for the investor and the investment …." The claimant and the IIA tribunal relied upon, not just added as confirmatory evidence once the case was won anyway, the relevant ECHR provisions and ECtHR cases (including *Handyside v. United Kingdom* (1976)[315]).

Roussalis's implications, though, should not be read too widely. After all, it did not say that an IIA obligation would excuse a human rights obligation. Presumably it is the State's first-order obligation not to ratify contradictory international compacts or, tacitly, international compacts that conflict with domestic laws. In fact, the Inter-American Court of Human Rights was unmoved by a similar IIA-invoking argument:

> according to [Paraguay], [a Germany-Paraguay BIT] allows for capital investments made by a contracting party to be condemned or nationalized for a "public purpose or interest", which could justify land restitution to indigenous people. Moreover, the Court considers that the enforcement of bilateral commercial treaties negates vindication of non-compliance with state obligations under the [Inter-American Convention on Human Rights]; on the contrary, their enforcement should always be compatible with the [Inter-American Convention on Human Rights], which is a multilateral treaty on human rights that stands in a class of its own and that generates rights for individual human beings and does not depend entirely on reciprocity among States.[316]

A similar situation is occurring with regard to the WTO-IIA sphere parallel proceedings, and it undoubtedly "has prompted considerable debate over the extent to which findings in a WTO dispute are relevant to (or dispositive of) claims brought in an investor-state arbitration arising out of the same government measure, and *vice versa*."[317] The step needs to

---

314 ICSID Case No. ARB/06/1.

315 24 Eur. Ct. H.R. (ser A) at 29.

316 *Sawhoyamaxa Indigenous Community v. Paraguay*, Series C, No. 146 (Inter-American Court of Human Rights), at ¶ 140 (citing to *The Effect of Reservations on the Entry into Force of the American Convention on Human Rights (Arts. 74 and 75). Advisory Opinion OC-2/82 of September 24, 1982. Series A No. 2*, ¶ 29).

317 B. E. Allen, "The Use of Non-Pecuniary Remedies in WTO Dispute Settlement," *supra*, at 282; *id.*, at 281-82 ("As further evidence of the apparent convergence between the worlds of international arbitration and WTO dispute settlement, a single government measure has in two instances given rise to parallel proceedings

be taken carefully such that the cross-pollination that is currently extant between the WTO universe and IIA jurisprudence is not upset.[318]

Returning to *TECMED*, we already have seen this test in Chapter V (NON-DISCRIMINATION). Without citing the ECtHR, IIA tribunals have nonetheless gone the *James* way with the "aims and effects" test. In *Firemen's Fund Insurance Co. v. Mexico* (2006),[319] a NAFTA Chapter Fourteen case involving financial services, the ICSID tribunal said:

> To distinguish between a compensable expropriation and a non-compensable regulation by a host State, the following factors (usually in combination) may be taken into account: whether the measure is within the recognized police powers of the host State; the (public) purpose and effect of the measure; whether the measure is discriminatory; the proportionality between the means employed and the aim sought to be realized; and the bona fide nature of the measure.

Along similar lines, the tribunal in *LG&E Energy v. Argentina* (2006),[320] established that "[i]n order to establish whether State measures constitute expropriation . . . the Tribunal must balance two competing interests: the degree of the measure's interference with the right of ownership and the power of the State to adopt its policies." How about the *degree* of interference? The *LG&E Energy* tribunal explained that "the

---

before the WTO and arbitral tribunals. The softwood lumber dispute between the United States and Canada, which arose out of the US imposition of countervailing and antidumping duties, yielded a politically-charged WTO case. At the same time, Canadian investors initiated arbitral proceedings against the United States based on the same measures, seeking recovery under Chapter 11 of the North American Free Trade Agreement (NAFTA). Likewise, a Mexican tax on sweeteners gave rise to both a successful WTO challenge by the United States and NAFTA claims by US investors.").

[318] Cases in which IIA awards have cited the WTO decisions are *ADM/Tate & Lyle v. United Mexican States*, ICSID Case No. ARB(AF)/04/05, ¶¶ 73-74, 85-99, 141, 189, 212-13 (26 September 2007); *Occidental Exploration & Production Co. v. Ecuador*, LCIA Case No. UN3467, ¶¶ 153-55 (1 July 2004); *Feldman v. Mexico*, ICSID Case No. ARB(AF)/99/1, ¶ 177 (16 December 2002); *Pope & Talbot v. Canada*, Award on the Merits of Phase 2, ¶¶ 45-72 (10 April 2001); *S.D. Myers v. Canada*, Partial Award, ¶¶ 221, 244-46, 291-98 (13 November 2000). The WTO Appellate Body has cited an ICSID award (*Saipem S.p.A. v. The People's Republic of Bangladesh*) in support of its findings. Appellate Body Report, *US – Stainless Steel*, WT/DS344/AB/R, n. 313, adopted 20 May 2008.

[319] ICSID Case No. ARB(AF)/02/1, at ¶ 176(j); see also *Corn Products International, Inc. v. Mexico*, ICSID Case No. ARB(AF)/04/01, Decision on Responsibility (2008), at ¶ 87(j).

[320] ICSID Case No. ARB/02/1, Decision on Liability (2006), at ¶ 189.

measure's economic impact—its interference with the investor's reasonable expectations—and the measure's duration"[321] determine if there has been an expropriation. It is a test that the other institutions should consider adopting, albeit with pragmatic modifications. This should not be misunderstood, for the tribunal was not suggesting that the impact is *sufficient* to establish a violation—it was saying that the impact is a *necessary* factor. As with the GATT/WTO "necessity" test referred to in the last chapter, *LG&E Energy* did not prescribe relative weights for the factors.

Like *Matos e Silva* and *TECMED* (from the ECtHR and the ICSID tribunal, respectively), the *LG&E Energy* tribunal held the economic impact of the expropriation must be "substantial"[322] and permanent.[323] The *LG&E Energy* tribunal then added the important caveat that where an "investment's successful development depends on the realization of certain activities at specific moments that may not endure variations,"[324] the permanence requirement does not apply. This is an extremely important point that neither NAFTA nor the ECtHR nor the IUCT has explicitly picked up on. Applying the test will be hard—for instance, how is a State necessarily responsible for knowing when *not* to expropriate? Is this where the investor's or owner's right to a hearing has to be honored? But the issue cannot go unaddressed any longer.

The *LG&E Energy* tribunal again applied the proportionality test to the question of whether and when a State may adopt certain measures:

> With respect to the power of the State to adopt its policies, it can generally be said that the State has the right to adopt measures having a social or general welfare purpose. In such a case, the measure must be accepted without any imposition of liability, except in cases where the State's action is obviously disproportionate to the need being addressed.[325]

This developing consensus on the proportionality test first articulated by the NAFTA *TECMED* tribunal and by the ECtHR's *James* decision was followed by the *Continental Casualty v. Argentina* (2008)[326] tribunal. It is yet another point of knowledge transfer. The *Continental Casualty* tribunal differentiated between compensable expropriation and legitimate governmental regulation:

---

[321] *Id.*, at ¶ 190.
[322] *Id.*, at ¶ 191.
[323] *Id.*, at ¶ 193.
[324] *Id.*
[325] *Id.,* at ¶ 195 (emphasis added) (citing to *TECMED v. Mexico*, *supra*, ¶ 202).
[326] ICSID Case No. ARB/03/9, Final Award on the Merits (2008).

> there are limitations to the use of property in the public interest that fall within typical government regulations of property entailing mostly inevitable limitations imposed in order to ensure the rights of others or of the general public (being ultimately beneficial also to the property affected). These restrictions do not impede the basic, typical use of a given asset and do not impose an unreasonable burden on the owner as compared with other similarly situated property owners. These restrictions are not therefore considered a form of expropriation and do not require indemnification, *provided however that they do not affect property in an intolerable, discriminatory or disproportionate manner.*[327]

This line of cases makes clear that "a legitimate social or general welfare purpose to a government regulation of general application"[328] is not enough to immunise an expropriation. No matter what, "its proportionality must be assessed before a decision not to award compensation for [an expropriation] is made."[329] NAFTA and IIA tribunals are adapting this test for themselves.

These rare IIA-ECtHR cross-pollination exceptions point towards some idea-sharing. But some scholars consider the rarity a "regrettable failure," on the part of IIA tribunals, "to use all available resources and to commence a dialogue among the bodies that make important decisions about the standards for a functioning judicial system."[330] The problem probably "cuts both ways" since the ECtHR too has not referred to IIA awards with any frequency. The number of citations is negligible. Contrasted with the prolific IUCT-IIA cross-citation, the IIA-ECtHR cross-citation rate is low. But one processual concern where there should be minimum space for disagreement is the transparency expected of public officials, including in the evidentiary documentation context analysed in the previous section. There is an impressive weight of material in the international human rights system which might moor that development in other areas of international law.[331]

---

[327] *Id.*, at ¶ 276 (emphasis added).

[328] R. Moloo & J. Jacinto, *Environmental and Health Regulation*, *supra*, at 72.

[329] *Id.*

[330] A. Bjorklund, *Reconciling State Sovereignty and Investor Protection, supra,* at 861.

[331] *Stoll v. Switzerland*, Application no. 69698/01/ (2007), ECHR-GC, at ¶ 111 ("Similarly, the Inter-American Commission on Human Rights has taken the view that the disclosure of State-held information should play a very important role in a democratic society because it enables civil society to control the actions of the government to which it has entrusted the protection of its interests."); *Case of Claude-Reyes et al. v. Chile*, Merits, Reparations and Costs, Judgment of September 19, 2006, Series C No. 151, at ¶¶ 84-86 ("... In several resolutions, the

Now let us apply these prescriptions to what the ECtHR has actually *done* in expropriation cases, both on processual and on substantive grounds. In *Ruiz-Mateos v. Spain* (1993),[332] the ECtHR recognised a three-prong test to decide if the duration of (and delay in) domestic court proceedings violated Article 6(1). The *Ruiz-Mateos* test was to evaluate: (*i*) how complex the case is; (*ii*) if the applicants made reasonable effort to exhaust; and (*iii*) if the State provided effective remedies.[333] Thus the remedial question was absorbed into the analysis assessing whether there had been a violation at all. This presumably implies that remedies commensurate with the burden that the measure places on the claimant might make the violation a non-issue or at least *de minimis*.

In commercial cases, whether they are being disputed before a human rights tribunal or an IIA tribunal or some other international forum, the delay—even when the complainant is forced to exhaust domestic remedies—might strengthen the case for a procedural or substantive violation. This includes not just compensation standard[334] but also the exhaustion itself. Delays may, of course, cost commercial complainants their comparative advantage in relation to their protected comparators. Sometimes that is the precise intention of the State.

As Chapter IV (EXHAUSTION OF LOCAL REMEDIES AND CONTINUOUS NATIONALITY) has already noted, the test can also be used to determine if a claim has been exhausted in the domestic courts. The formlessness,

---

OAS General Assembly has considered that access to public information is an essential requisite for the exercise of democracy, greater transparency and responsible public administration and that, in a representative and participative democratic system, the citizenry exercises its constitutional rights through a broad freedom of expression and free access to information. In this regard, the State's actions should be governed by the principles of disclosure and transparency in public administration that enable all persons subject to its jurisdiction to exercise the democratic control of those actions, and so that they can question, investigate and consider whether public functions are being performed adequately . . . .").

[332] App. No. 12952/87.

[333] *Id.*, at 517-19. The ECtHR found a violation based on the 7 year 9 month-delay in the case.

[334] See, *e.g.*, *S. D. Myers v. Canada*, UNCITRAL, Final Award on the Merits (Nov. 13, 2000), at ¶ 284 ("[The claimant's] venture into the Canadian market was postponed for approximately eighteen months. Mr. Dana Myers testified that this delay had the effect of eliminating SDMI's competitive advantage. This may have significance in assessing the compensation to be awarded in relation to Canada's violations of Articles 1102 and 1105, but it does not support the proposition *on the facts of this case* that the measure should be characterized as an expropriation within the terms of Article 1110.") (footnotes omitted and emphasis added).

vagueness and malleability of the test indicate that it suffers from the same flaw as the *LG&E Energy* tribunal's "economic impact" test and the GATT/WTO "necessity" test.

The ECtHR has also addressed the right to a remedy in the domestic courts for improper government behaviour. In *Sporrong & Lönnroth v. Sweden* (1983),[335] the government had deprived claimants of the use of their own property for a period of 23 years and 8 years, respectively. The claimants argued that the expropriation *de jure* stripped them of their possessions and excessively restricted their property use *sans* compensation.[336] As an aside, this would have been as ideal a case as any other for the ECtHR to address the *LG&E Energy* tribunal's reinterpretation of the "permanence" test: to decide if the expropriation is compensable when the investment value is at certain peaks.

The ECtHR framed the *Sporrong* test as "whether a fair balance had been struck between the demands of the general interest of the community and the requirements of the protection of the individual's fundamental rights."[337] The prolonged expropriation and construction ban "upset this balance and imposed an excessive burden on the applicants which could only be rendered legitimate had Swedish law permitted the applicants to seek a reduction of the time limits for expropriation or to claim compensation."[338] It was not enough that there remained the possibility of *discretionary* review by the Swedish Supreme Administrative Court.[339] Generally speaking, on expropriatory matters such as housing and where a manifestly oppressive government tyrant is not present, "the Court" seems to "respect the legislature's judgment as to what is in the general interest unless that judgment is manifestly without reasonable foundation."[340]

---

[335] 5 E.H.H.R. 26, ¶ 54 (1983).

[336] *Id.*, at 35–36, 48.

[337] *Id.*, at 52-54.

[338] A. Bjorklund, *Reconciling State Sovereignty and Investor Protection, supra,* at 861-2; *id.*, at 54; M. Reisman & R. D. Sloane, *Indirect Expropriation and its Valuation in the BIT Generation*, 74 BRIT. Y.B. INT'L L. 115, 129 (2003) ("[In indirect expropriation cases] the impact of each governmental measure must be analyzed, not in isolation, but cumulatively, because, as the European Court of Human Rights wrote in this context, 'the consequences of [the state's] interference [are] undoubtedly rendered more serious by the[ir] combined use'.") (citing *Sporrong*, at ¶ 60)).

[339] *Id.*, at 57-8.

[340] *J.A. Pye (Oxford) Ltd and J.A. Pye (Oxford) Land Ltd v. the United Kingdom*, Application no. 44302/02, at ¶ 75 (Grand Chamber) (2007) (citing *Immobiliare Saffi v. Italy* [GC], no. 22774/93, § 49, ECHR 1999-V).

In *Osman v. United Kingdom* (2003),[341] a murder victim's family and injury victim himself claimed that the police had been legally negligent by *failing* "to apprehend, interview, search, or charge P, despite having extensive knowledge of his suspicious activities."[342] This is a quintessential *positive obligations* case with support in international human rights law.[343] The United Kingdom Court of Appeal dismissed the action because, in its view, there can be no negligence action against the police in investigation-related *positive obligations*. The Court of Appeal grounded its rationale in public policy.[344] The ECtHR's perception was different:

> the applicants must be taken to have had a right, derived from the law of negligence, to seek an adjudication on the admissibility and merits of an arguable claim that they were in a relationship of proximity to the police, that the harm caused was foreseeable and that in the circumstances it was fair, just and reasonable not to apply the exclusionary rule.[345]

This was no windfall, however, and the access to courts in this situation is not absolute. The Court pointed out that a government may limit the right of access to the courts but must meet still satisfy the balancing "aims and effect" test.[346] The ECtHR thus applied the test *outside* the substantive expropriation setting and took it into the processual territory. Since the no-negligence action rule in *Osman* disproportionately limited the claimant's access to a court, the ECtHR found an Article 6(1)

---

[341] 29 E.C.H.R. 245 (2000).

[342] A. Bjorklund, supra, at 864; *Osman*, *supra*, at 263.

[343] *Case of the Moiwana Community v. Suriname*, Preliminary Objections, Merits, Reparations and Costs, Judgment of June 15, 2005, Series C No. 124, at ¶ 39 (".. [a]ccording to this principle of non-retroactivity, in the case of a continuing or permanent violation, which begins before the acceptance of the Court's jurisdiction and persists even after that acceptance, the Tribunal is competent to examine the actions and omissions occurring subsequent to the recognition of jurisdiction, as well as their respective effects."); *Silih v. Slovenia*, Application nos. 71463/01, 9/04/09 (2009), ECHR-GC, at ¶¶ 159-60 (the procedural obligation to carry out an effective investigation under Article 2 has evolved into a separate and autonomous duty. . . . This approach finds support also in the jurisprudence of the United Nations Human Rights Committee and, in particular, of the Inter-American Court of Human Rights, which, though under different provisions, accepted jurisdiction *ratione temporis* over the procedural complaints relating to deaths which had taken place outside their temporal jurisdiction).

[344] *Osman*, *supra*, at 263–64 (referring to *Hill v. Chief Constable of West Yorkshire*, [1989] A.C. 53).

[345] *Id.*, at 313.

[346] *Id.*, at 315-17.

violation.[347] In property cases, the same principle would apply in conjunction with Article 1. As Chapter III (ATTRIBUTION AND CAUSATION) noted, *Osman* is Exhibit A for the ECtHR's openness to *positive obligations* as a state responsibility principle. The bar is high but not impossible.

From international human rights tribunals' description in this book and cited literature, the reader might think that these institutions' daily fare includes substantive expropriations. Not so at all. These courts have actually reviewed far fewer cases involving "the actual decision of a national court," viz. substantive expropriations, than processual ones. In *Brumarescu v. Romania* (1999),[348] the Court invalidated a Romanian court's expropriation decision on substantive grounds. In so doing, the Court tacitly held that judicial failure strengthens the case for the wrongfulness of the expropriation, whether or not the judicial failure is a substantive violation in itself.[349]

Brumarescu is important for another reason. *Brumarescu* was about the during-and-after phases of the Iron Curtain, and it implied that the obligations do pass on to the new government (as Chapter III analysed). The claimants sued in 1993, 43 years after the expropriation of a parcel of land and after a change in the governing regime.[350] The first court held this to be an expropriation and ordered the property returned but the Procurator-General of Romania had that judgment stayed under power conferred upon him by the Code of Civil Procedure.[351] Eventually, the Romanian Supreme Court of Justice vacated the lower court's decision; the property came back to the State.[352] The ECtHR held that this violated "the principle of legal certainty."[353] Reliance and reasonable owner expectations are back in the equation.

On the substantive grounds, the ECtHR held the expropriation unlawful because the public interest aim (the first prong of the "aims and effects" test) had not been proven by the State.[354] This, we have established, is the State's burden. The ECtHR was careful to state that neither the Romanian Supreme Court of Justice nor the government had

---

347 *Id.*, at 317.
348 33 E.C.H.R. 862 (1999).
349 *Id.*, at 864.
350 *Id.*, at 865.
351 *Id.*, at 865-6.
352 *Id.*, at 866.
353 *Id.*, at 864.
354 *Id.*, at 865.

shown this;[355] this tied the substantive violation with the "judicial failure" processual violation.

Now the case was over and the State had lost. But ECtHR went further and reaffirmed the second prong: proportionality. There has to be a balance between the public interest and "the protection of the individual's fundamental rights."[356] *Brumarescu* recognised that the balance does not exist "where the person concerned bears an individual and excessive burden."[357] The ECtHR then found that the dearth of public interest in the expropriation and the zero-compensation reality "for four years (between the re-appropriation of the property and the ECtHR claim) [w]as evidence of . . . disproportionality."[358]

These three cases—*Sporrong*, *Osman, Brumarescu*—are symptomatic in demonstrating that the ECtHR's substantive standards apply to at least the *positive obligations*, "judicial failure," continuing obligations, reliance, and proportionality test contexts. The analyses can be especially helpful for balancing sovereignty with human rights in an umbrella system. International human rights systems exist because their signatories recognise that human rights, with all its complex elements, in *one* signatory jurisdiction influence what happens in the others.

§ 6.4—Substantive Standards before the IUCT

The IUCT's jurisprudence should be situated in relation to the other institutions' jurisprudence. First, Chapter III (ATTRIBUTION AND CAUSATION) already has explained how reasonable expectations and reliance factor into the IUCT's expropriation analysis. It is not repeated. Second, recall from this Chapter's earlier analysis how the *Methanex* tribunal took the UC Report's scientific evidence at its word. The *TECMED* tribunal,[359] though, examined the evidence strictly (and maybe this is why *Methanex's* low, dim-wattage scrutiny has not caught on):

> [I]t [wa]s irrefutable that there were factors other than compliance or non-compliance by [claimant] with the Permit's conditions or the Mexican environmental protection laws and that such factors had a decisive effect in the decision to deny the Permit's renewal. These factors included 'political

---

[355] *Id.*, at 866.
[356] *Id.*, at 865-6.
[357] *Id.*, at 866.
[358] *Id.*, at 866.
[359] *Methanex Corp. v. United States*, 44 I.L.M. 1345 (UNCITRAL 2005) (Final Award).

circumstances.' The political circumstances referred to by the tribunal 'include[d] mounting community pressure to relocate the landfill.'[360]

Political circumstances matter, and in this respect the *TECMED*-NAFTA tribunal was on the same page as the IUCT. The political circumstances at issue in *TECMED* "include[d] mounting community pressure to relocate the landfill."[361] The *TECMED* tribunal deemed this community pressure to be a legitimate aim and then rejected the means as disproportionately excessive to the *actual* community pressure on the ground.[362]

Tellingly, the *TECMED* tribunal did not seem to distinguish itself from *Methanex's* less demanding scrutiny. Because the *TECMED* tribunal rejected as insufficient the evidence of community pressure proffered by the government, it is unclear if the tribunal would have, or future tribunals will, examine for themselves—in other words, scrutinize strictly as well as *independently*—this evidence. If so, where will they obtain the resources to conduct the fact-intensive assessment? This remains to be developed in future cases and other tribunals.

However, there is a greater inherent problem: Advocates might use as a limiting principle the argument that political pressure (whatever the extent) is less legitimate or compelling than scientific evidence. After all, most political pressure comes from *within* the community which constitutes the State. When a similar case arose in the United States Supreme Court in 2005 (*Kelo v. New London*[363]), neither the majority (which determined that "public purpose" was, by and large, tantamount to the Fifth Amendment's "public use" exception)[364] nor the dissent used the "community pressure" rationale to strengthen the State's case.

Justice O'Connor's *Kelo* dissent understood the lack of State evidence showing blight or "social harm" caused by the expropriated property to mean that a "community pressure" (to take these "well-maintained" homes to give to Wal-Mart or any private entities) would be illegitimate.[365] The dissent did not consider it a rational enough justification that such private enterprises might raise more money in profits or tax revenue—or that this

---

[360] *Id.*

[361] *Id.*

[362] *Id.*, at ¶ 128.

[363] 545 U.S. 469.

[364] Nonetheless, Justice O'Connor's *Kelo* dissent, in particular, cited *Hawaii Housing Authority v. Midkiff*, 467 U.S. 229, 245 (1984) ("A purely private taking could not withstand the scrutiny of the public use requirement; it would serve no legitimate purpose of government and would thus be void.").

[365] 545 U.S. 469, 500-01.

whole expropriatory operation might be a product of community pressure. The *Kelo* majority did not contradict this argument.

Government as the expropriating sovereign cannot point to community pressure as the culprit. If avoiding voter discontent is, without more, a legitimate public aim, then almost all aims are readily legitimate; and if they are not readily legitimate, then they can always wear the disguise of voter discontentment to pass the test (much like Professor Brownlie's "national economic disaster" defence in Chapter III). The "It's-Not-Necessarily-Us-But-It's-Our-Constituents" argument made by some politicians assumes, incorrectly, that the body politic is distinct from the voters' elected representatives or their investment negotiators. There is also the fear that approving the community-pressure rationale would, in effect, approve a certain kind of political pusillanimity as a sufficient justification and prevent politicians from living with the consequences of their difficult choices.

Moreover, when the standard is deferential it is quintessentially intrusive for an international tribunal to tell a State what *its* internal community pressure dictates or does not dictate. How can an international tribunal retain or exercise hubris enough to disregard the State's sovereign interests on a pivotal "process issue" so flagrantly? Would it not set a pernicious precedent that could engulf and eventually destroy the tribunal? Destroy the tricky concession-and-gains balance in international law? On the other hand, a State would (most likely) prefer to suffer an international tribunal's organised and dignified "intrusion" and perhaps be vindicated on the substance of the claim than to suffer a setback concerning the bottom-line of the decision. Efforts might be made to create a mechanism whereby respondent sovereigns may waive any such contempt of intrusiveness claim even though there will not be any implicit or explicit penalty for failing to do so.

Moreover, this entire controversy might be mooted or at least blunted if the parties and the tribunal are persuaded that science and technology make the inspection non-intrusive.[366] This point of knowledge transfer

---

[366] W. M. Reisman, *Sovereignty and Human Rights in Contemporary International Law*, 84 A.J.I.L. 866, 868-69 (1990) (articulating that "the concept of popular sovereignty was not [intended] to remain mere pious aspiration. The international lawmaking system proceeded to prescribe criteria for appraising the conformity of internal governance with international standard of democracy. Thanks to a happy historical conjunction, modern communications technology has made it possible to verify that conformity rapidly and economically and to broadcast it widely. . . . In functional terms, this process constitutes a new type of inclusive international recognition. Decisions to withhold recognition where the will of the people has

should be addressed by tribunals across international dispute settlement. In addition, there is the genuine and substantial risk that States might begin to use this cheeky argument as a firewall, as an inexhaustible gift that keeps giving.

Like NAFTA and the ECtHR, the IUCT recognises it as "an accepted principle of international law that a State is not liable for economic injury which is a consequence of a *bona fide* 'regulation' within the accepted police power of states."[367] In *Starrett Housing Corp. v. Iran* (1983),[368] the IUCT held that indirect expropriation is deemed to have happened when

> a State . . . interfere[s] with property rights to such an extent that these rights are rendered so useless that they must be deemed to have been expropriated, even though the State does not purport to have expropriated them and the legal title to the property remains with the original owner.

In the IUCT, a measure's effect is important but it is unclear *how* important. As Chapter III (ATTRIBUTION AND CAUSATION) pointed out, the IUCT's concern is with what actually happens, not necessarily what formally happens. But the following discussion highlights why the IUCT (and institutions following the Tribunal) should not be too hasty in rejecting the "intent" component.

SEDCO v. NIOC (1987)[369] and *Tippetts, Abbett, McCarthy, Stratton v. TAMS-AFFA Consulting Engineers of Iran* (1984),[370] established that "an act of expropriation does not require a formal decree of nationalization." In *Tippetts,* particularly, the IUCT held that "deprivation or taking of property may occur under international law through interference by a state in the use of that property or with the enjoyment of its benefits, even where legal title to the property is not affected."[371]

This *effect crystallization* is a school of thought which argues that "the form of measures of control or interference is less important than the

---

been demonstrably ignored or suppressed have increasingly led to the next stage, the institution of international programs designed to permit or facilitate the realization of the popular will.").

[367] *SEDCO, Inc. v. NIOC*, Interlocutory Award, 9 I.U.C.T.R. 248, 273-74.

[368] *Starrett Housing Corp. v. Iran*, 4 I.U.C.T.R. 122, 154 (1983); *Occidental Petroleum and Production Co. v. Ecuador*, LCIA Case No. UN 3467, Award (2004), at ¶ 85 ("expropriation need not involve the transfer of title to a given property, which was the distinctive feature of traditional expropriation under international law. It may of course affect the economic value of an investment.").

[369] 15 I.U.C.T.R. 23 (1987).

[370] 6 I.U.C.T.R. 219 (1984).

[371] *Id.*, at 220.

reality of their impact."[372] But effect does not necessarily overtake the combined forces of intent and character, and in any case the measure's intent and character play into this "reality." The IUCT has been consistent on this point. In *Tippetts*,[373] the Tribunal said that although the government's intent matters, it is "less important than the effects of the measures on the owner . . . .". In *Phelps Dodge Corp. v. Iran* (1986),[374] the IUCT reaffirmed:

> The Tribunal fully understands the reasons why the Respondent felt compelled to protect its interests through this transfer of management, and the Tribunal understands the financial, economic and social concerns that inspired the law pursuant to which it acted, but those reasons and concerns cannot relieve the Respondent of the obligation to compensate Phelps Dodge for its loss.

This test, skewed towards "effect," has just one NAFTA ally (*Metalclad v. Mexico* (2000))[375] and another in an ICSID case named *Compañía del Desarrollo de Santa Elena SA v. Costa Rica* (2000).[376] First, the *Metalclad* tribunal had to decide if an ecological decree converting investor's lands into a landfill site was an expropriation. The tribunal held that Mexico had indeed "expropriated Metalclad's investment without providing compensation,"[377] because "[the] Decree had the effect of barring forever the operation of the landfill."[378] Addressing the measure's impact, the *Metalclad* tribunal stated that

---

372 G.C. Christie, *What Constitutes A Taking Of Property Under International Law?*, 38 BRIT. Y.B. INT'L L. 307, 338 (1962).
373 *Tippetts, supra,* at 225-26.
374 10 I.U.C.T.R. 121, 130.
375 *Metalclad Corp. v. Mexico*, ICSID Case No. ARB(AF)/97/1, Final Award (2000).
376 ICSID Case No. ARB/96/1, Final Award (2000). The curious fact is that *Santa Elena* was a rare award at the heart of which was no IIA, just customary international law. See *id.*, at ¶ 65. There are those who suggest that "developing countries could be better off in a regime governed by customary international law with no BITs compared with a global BITs regime." See J. Tobin & S. Rose-Ackerman, *When BITs Have Some Bite, supra,* at p. 12, n. 13 (characterising Andrew Guzman's earlier work, see A. T. Guzman, *Why LDCs Sign Treaties That Hurt Them: Explaining the Popularity of Bilateral Investment Treaties*, 38 VA. J. INT'L L. 639 (1998), to state this position).
377 *Metalclad, supra*, at ¶ 112.
378 *Id.*, at ¶ 109.

> expropriation under NAFTA includes not only open, deliberate and acknowledged takings of property, such as outright seizure or formal or obligatory transfer of title in favour of the host State, but also covert or incidental interference with the use of property which has the effect of depriving the owner, in whole or in significant part, of the use or reasonably-to-be-expected economic benefit of property even if not necessarily to the obvious benefit of the host State.[379]

The *Metalclad* tribunal further stated that "consider[ing] the motivation or intent" was irrelevant since "the Ecological Decree would, in and of itself, constitute an act tantamount to expropriation."[380] The *Starrett-Tippetts* line of IUCT cases has made the CSD's "interference with property rights" language synonymous with the "tantamount to expropriation" language of NAFTA Chapter Eleven. Both *Metalclad's* and *Starrett-Tippetts's* "sole effects" tendency was not entirely disapprovingly cited by Judge Charles Brower in *Impregilo*.[381]

Second, the tribunal in *Santa Elena* tribunal also suggested in so many words that just the effect of the measure matters in the expropriation analysis.[382] In this respect, *Santa Elena* resembled the no-intent-please test of *TECMED*. Contrast this with the WTO/GATT idea of "not . . . limit[ing] the use of measures which are genuinely intended to achieve environmental objectives."[383] The *Santa Elena* tribunal held rather sweepingly that the intent behind the expropriation counted for little:

> While an expropriation or taking for environmental reasons may be classified as a taking for a public purpose, and thus may be legitimate, the fact that the Property was taken for this reason does not affect either the nature or the measure of the compensation to be paid for the taking. That is, the purpose of protecting the environment for which the Property was taken does not alter the legal character of the taking for which adequate compensation must be paid. The international source of the obligation to protect the environment makes no difference.
>
> Expropriatory environmental measures—no matter how laudable and beneficial to society as a whole—are, in this respect, similar to any other expropriatory measures that a state may take in order to implement its policies: where property is expropriated, even for environmental purposes,

---

[379] *Id.*, at ¶ 103.
[380] *Id.*, at ¶ 111.
[381] *Impregilo S.p.A.*, *supra*, at ¶ 51.
[382] *Santa Elena, supra,* at ¶ 54.
[383] P. Sands, INTERNATIONAL ENVIRONMENTAL LAW, *supra*, at 976-77.

whether domestic or international, the state's obligation to pay compensation remains.[384]

Now, what are some ways for the State engage in what it might view as damage-control? After *Santa Elena* was decided, the President of the *Santa Elena* tribunal publicly acknowledged the "purpose test" and supported a balancing approach.[385] Moreover, the facts of *Santa Elena* have to do with *direct* expropriation. But, whatever the facts, the language of the excerpt applies to *all* expropriations. Thus, if *Santa Elena* carries the day—even uses that are "laudable and beneficial to society as a whole" make no difference—that will be the end of all expropriation.[386] Nor does *Santa Elena* limit itself to cases where there has been a substantial diminution in value. All expropriations are fair game. Because this is the end of the road for the IUCT's "effects" jurisprudence, it should be thought through carefully by all international tribunals. This is the final point of knowledge transfer in this Chapter.

§ 6.5—Conclusion and Compensation

The intents *versus* effects test, the reasonable expectations factor (reliance), and the proportionality analysis are modern international law fixtures as substantive standards are concerned. As things now stand, a State may still conduct environmental and health regulation without being blocked by tribunals. But the "sole effects" test or overemphasis on reliance or a skewed proportionality analysis could shift the balance.

Some of the assessments might challenge a tribunal's institutional competence, whether it is the NAFTA-*Methanex* tribunal's understanding of scientific evidence (a limitation of knowledge) or the ECtHR's intervention in the politically-intense Northern Cypriot expulsion case

---

[384] *Id.*, at ¶¶ 71-72.

[385] Y. Fortier & S. Drymer, *Indirect Expropriation in the Law of International Investment, supra*, at 326; R. Moloo & J. Jacinto, *Environmental and Health Regulation*, *supra,* at 114, n. 69.

[386] This is not necessarily a fringe or half-baked view. Professor Rosalyn Higgins eloquently has argued that "interferences which significantly deprive the owner of the use of his property amount to a taking of that property. This will be so even if he remains in physical possession of that property." See R. Higgins, *The Taking of Property by the State: Recent Developments in International Law*, 176 RECUEIL DES COURS 259, 324 (1982). She did concede, though, that unlike with environmental aims, "interferences with property for economic and financial regulatory purposes are tolerated to a significant degree." *Id.*

Loizidou v. Turkey (1996), as Chapter III (ATTRIBUTION AND CAUSATION) has already explained (a limitation of enforceability). Having the balance just right is critical, and for this to happen the international institutions must remain open to idea-sharing with actors outside their own setting. It should also be remembered that international tribunals, especially ones commissioned to protect human rights across national boundaries, have a duty to be consistent. Doctrinally absolute rejections of property rights claims, even on narrow time, space, and condition-based questions, might come back to haunt them later when cases concerning other human rights issues arrive and no principled reason to distinguish the two scenarios readily exists. I regard this as the "Be Careful What You Seek" note of caution for international tribunals and their advocates.

This book would be incomplete were we not to discuss the issue of compensation.[387] While there is some doubt and disputation as to the role of IIA's in furthering FDI and short- or long-term local economic growth, the same cannot be said for the developing country-developed country disparities in the opportunity cost of losing a claim. It is definitely the case that "[t]he opportunity costs of losing a claim are much higher for developing rather than developed nations," especially a United States investor is the party.[388]

Moreover, the opportunity cost consideration is exacerbated for developing countries by the economic reality "[r]elative to government budgets and in per capita terms developing countries pay significantly

---

[387] Certain model BIT's tend to guarantee that the compensation be paid without delay, that it conform to the fair market value just before the expropriation was undertaken, that "not reflect any change in value occurring because the intended expropriation had become known earlier," and finally that it be "be fully realizable and freely transferable." See Article 6(2), Model U.S. BIT (2012).

[388] K. Gallagher & E. Shrestha, *Investment Treaty Arbitration and Developing Countries: A Re-Appraisal*, Global Development and Environment Institute, Tufts University (Working Paper), p. 9 (stating that authors take the United States as an example and that "[o]f the total U.S. wins, the average award amount has been around $47 million ($50 million excluding Canada). The average award Canada is liable to pay to the U.S. for losing arbitration is $3.9 million which is the lowest amount. Other countries face much higher penalty ranging from $9 million (Kazakhstan, Turkey and Congo Democratic Republic) to $107 million (Argentina). For the cases where U.S. has won, the average amount claimed is much higher and is around S234 million ($251 million excluding Canada). Thus compared to Canada (which can be used as a proxy for developed country), the developing countries seem to be subjected to higher amount both in terms of claims and awards."). The paper also contains per-capita figures for wins and losses.

more in damages than developed nations do."[389] These considerations, it should be remembered both by United States negotiators and treaty draftspersons and by actors elsewhere, provide a confirmatory piece of evidence that perpetuates the legitimacy crisis. My reason for making this observation is not to be even remotely put blame or responsibility any particular doorstep. It simply is to caution the various Secretariats, governments, and investors that the arbitration network functions because enough nations sustain it. That trust, once broken, could be difficult to regain.

To the critics of the current system, this pattern indicates a subliminal (almost subconscious) bias towards Americanisation of the procedural or substantive standards. In our interview, one central African developing country's lawmaker believed he was speaking for the whole subaltern of developing nations in stating that "the whole IIA regime is rigged against us. Maybe some of the East Asian countries can win by raising their export competitiveness but not us." Some other actors have the sobering view that the system is not perfect but it is better than the alternatives:

> Many forms of international dispute resolution have been tried, and will be tried in this world of sin and woe. No one pretends that international arbitration is perfect or all-wise. Indeed, it has been said that international arbitration is the worst form of international dispute resolution except all those other forms that have been tried from time to time. [390]

As far as compensation, restitution, and legal costs are concerned, there is a staggering amount of impressive literature addressing the issue.[391] Most of the fundamental conclusions are definitive though their details and degrees are not always so. Three significant points must be discussed. First, interest may be added within the award of economic damages.[392]

---

[389] *Id.*

[390] C. N. Brower, C. H. Brower, II, and J. K. Sharpe, *The Coming Crisis in the Global Adjudication System*, Center for American and International Law, *available at* <www.cailaw.org/ita/workshop02_brower.pdf>, p. 38.

[391] For a comprehensive list of cases explaining legal and proceeding-related costs issued by IIA tribunals, see B. Sabahi, COMPENSATION AND RESTITUTION IN INVESTOR-STATE ARBITRATION: PRINCIPLES AND PRACTICE 216 *et seq.* (Oxford University Press, 2011).

[392] G. Arangio-Ruiz (Special Rapporteur), *Second Report on State Responsibility*, United Nations document A/CN.4/425, at 57-59 (9 June 1989); *S.S. Wimbledon Case*, 1923 P.C.I.J. (ser. A) No. 1, at 15, 33; *Chorzow Factory Case*, 1928 P.C.I.J. (ser. A) No. 17 (13 Sept.), at 47; *Illinois Central Railroad Co. v. United Mexican States*, 4 R.I.A.A. 134, 137 (6 December 1926). As a more recent example, the United Nations Compensation Commission award concerning claims arising from

Second, tribunals have rejected the occasionally-presented government argument that compound interest is simply "punitive."[393] The presumption is that "[i]t is not the purpose of compound interest to attribute blame to, or to punish, anybody for the delay in the payment made to the expropriated owner; it is a mechanism to ensure that compensation awarded to the Claimant is appropriate in the circumstances."[394] Compound interests help to make the wronged claimant whole again by providing them with the compensation for the use during the time their property was not at their disposal.

In a recent arbitration involving not-unlike-IUCT-type chaos in the country, the tribunal stated that "if Zimbabwe had in due time paid to the Claimants the indemnity due . . . them, they would have been able to invest that sum in the currency of their choice."[395] To borrow the phrase from Judge Brower and Jeremy Sharpe, the chief legal advisor for investment arbitration at the U.S. Department of State, we might call this

---

the Iraqi invasion of Kuwait in the early 1990's is relevant. See *Awards of Interest*, Decision taken by the Governing Council of the United Nations Compensation Commission at its 31st Meeting, held on 18 December 1992, United Nations document S/AC.26/1992/16 (1993) ("interest will be awarded from the date the loss occurred until the date of payment, at a rate sufficient to compensate successful claimants for the loss of use of the principal amount of the award").

393 *Funnekotter and others v. Zimbabwe*, ICSID Case No. ARB/05/6 (2009), Respondent's Counter-Memorial, 6 July 2007, p. 29.

394 *Compañia del Desarrollo de Santa Elena S.A. v. Costa Rica*, ICSID Case No. ARB/96/1, Award of 17
February 2000, at ¶ 104. Some scholars have argued that a landmark award, *Kuwait v. Aminoil*, 21 I.L.M. 976, at 997 (1982), which was one of the first to award compound interest, should not count as persuasive authority in favour of awarding compound interest because of their view that the *Aminoil* award "only included compound interest in order to obfuscate the fact that the tribunal wanted to compensate Amoinoil without classifying the taking as an unlawful expropriation." See S. Ripinsky & K. Williams, DAMAGES IN INTERNATIONAL LAW 385, n. 111 (BIICL, 2008) (citing C. N. Brower & J. Sharpe, *Awards of Compound Interest in International Arbitration: The* Aminoil *Non-Precedent,* (2006) 3 (2) *Transnational Dispute Management,* at 159 [C. N. Brower & J. Sharpe, *Awards of Compound Interest*]). Whatever else this portion of the *Aminoil* award is, it surely counsels in favour of judicial transparency — Caesar's wife must be "beyond reproach," 1 *Thessalonians* 5:22 (King James) — to the maximum extent of candour that is possible.

395 *Funnekotter and others v. Zimbabwe*, ICSID CASE NO. ARB/05/6, Final Award (2009), at ¶ 144.

the "temporary withholding of . . . money" default rule of customary law and *lex mercatoria*.[396]

Ironically, if the investor "at all relevant times had inventory sufficient to meet all its sales requirements, *notwithstanding [a] shutdown*," that harms any damages claim about lost profits.[397] This approach, developed about a decade ago, tries to remedy the logical flaw in the cooperation with the government-appointed manager example highlighted in Chapter III (particularly the fear that this might actually create a perverse incentive on the part of the investor *not* to produce). But by inviting the tribunal to assess whether the available inventory was "sufficient o meet all its sales requirements"[398]—or whatever the standard for recovering lost profits might turn out to be—the tribunals will embroil themselves in the fact-specific analysis realm.

There is much support for the rule, and its core perimeter does not seem to be shrinking though its rationales are always in flux. The *Santa Elena* tribunal too has affirmed that the award should, at least partially, give the investor what she would have earned had she been able to invest her capital at "prevailing rates of interest"[399]—the differential suggested honouring the opportunity cost. However, this did not occur in the Zimbabwe situation: "[C]ompensation was not paid promptly at the time of dispossession, and the Claimants were therefore not able to make any investment outside of Zimbabwe."[400]

At this point, the *Funnekotter and others v. Zimbabwe* tribunal composed of highly respected jurists saw it fitting ("must" is the verb of command they employed) to "use a rate of interest taking into account the situation in that country."[401] This should not quite so surprising or stunning. Nor is it particularly unmoored from the rest of compensation

---

[396] C. N. Brower & J. Sharpe, *Awards of Compound Interest, supra,* at 152. Even the IUCT has noted that "it is customary for arbitral tribunals to award interest as part of an award for damages," even when there is "the absence of any express reference to interest in the compromis." See *Islamic Republic of Iran v. United States of America*, Dec. No. 65-A19-FT (30 September 1987), 16 Iran-United States C.T.R. 285, 289-90. See also *McCollouqh & Company, Inc. v. The Ministry of Post, Telegraph and Telephone et al.*, Award No. 225-89-3 (22 April 1986), 11 Iran-United States C.T.R. 3, 34.

[397] *Pope & Talbot Inc. v. The Government of Canada*, UNCITRAL, Award in Respect of Damages, May 31, 2002, at ¶¶ 84-86 (emphasis added).

[398] *Id.*

[399] S. Ripinsky & K. Williams, DAMAGES IN INTERNATIONAL LAW 385-86 (BIICL, 2008) (citing *Santa Elena, supra*, at ¶ 105).

[400] *Funnekotter and others, supra*, at ¶ 144.

[401] *Id.*

jurisprudence which has always recognised a "moral damages" component.[402] This was just an application of that well-established principle, one with a respected pedigree. Perhaps an effective prism is that such a cost shift or transfer is just synonymous with or tantamount to "moral damages." A public acknowledgement of this connection might place on firmer footing the *Funnekotter* approach of taking context into account to assess costs and damages.

Even when an independent firm of auditors certifies a net asset value of the expropriated property, and no one contests their assessment(s),[403] complications may arise.[404] If the *Chorzow Factory Case* test is applied and the damages amount must "wip[e] out all the consequences of the illegal acts," the length of the time period will be required for interest compounding purposes.[405] In addition, when the net asset value is lower than the "genuine value," compensation generally is higher than the net asset value.

Finally, for compensation purposes, significant debate about the difference(s), if any, between "lawful" and "unlawful" expropriation lingers, and shows no signs of attaining quiescence.[406] If we choose to

---

[402] See, *e.g.*, *Determination of Ceilings for Compensation for Mental Pain and Anguish*, Decision taken by the Governing Council of the United Nations Compensation Commission during its Fourth Session, at the 22nd meeting, held on 24 January 1992, United Nations document S/AC.26/1992/8 ("Decision 8"); Chile-United States Commission at ¶¶ 23, 31 (issuing an award of damages to the estates and family members of various decedents); YEARBOOK OF THE INTERNATIONAL LAW COMMISSION 1993, vol. II (Part II), p. 71, at ¶ 9 ("international tribunals have always granted pecuniary compensation, whenever they deemed it necessary, for moral injury to private parties").

[403] For an in-depth analysis of valuation methods applied to a case, see *CME Czech Republic BV (The Netherlands) v. Czech Republic* (2003), UNCITRAL, Final Award, at ¶ 490 *et seq.*

[404] Astute readers of expropriation awards and decisions surely have noticed that the compensation sections of the awards tend not to be as lengthy or as meticulously reasoned as the rest of the award. This pattern might be a result of the tribunal defensiveness that its deductions about particular figures and interest rates could be seen in some quarters as arbitrary or random.

[405] *Case Concerning the Factory at Chorzów (Claim for Indemnity) (Germany v. Poland)*, 1928 P.C.I.J. (ser. A) No. 17 (13 Sept.).

[406] *ADC Affiliate Ltd and ADC & ADMC Mgmt Ltd v. Hungary* (ICSID Case No. ARB/03/16), Award (2006), at ¶ 481; W. Michael Reisman and Robert D. Sloone, *Indirect expropriation and its valuation in the BIT Convention*, 2004 BRITISH Y.B. INT'L L., p. 133; Audley Sheppard, *The distinction between Lawful and Unlawful Expropriation, in the Investment Arbitratory and the Energy Charter Treaty*, 2006, p. 172; *CME Czech Republic B.V. (The Netherlands) v. The Czech Republic*,

view the lawfulness of an expropriation on a continuum, we might appreciate the inherent value in the international human rights approach to compensation: "The [Convention] does not, however, guarantee a right to full compensation in all circumstances, since legitimate objectives of 'public interest' may call for less than reimbursement of the full market value."[407]

Third, it is true that "the general practice in international arbitration is that, as submitted by the Claimants, successful party under an award should recover its legal costs."[408] Under the UNCITRAL Rules, only if there is "absolute 'success'"[409] by one party in light of "the circumstances of the case," might the total cost be transferred to the losing party.[410] Egregious expropriation-related governmental measures (at the inception of the facts or during the continuation of the proceedings) as well as acts of frivolous actions, fraud or deception in investment-making or government proceedings may move the ball to the other side of the scrimmage. Another possibility lies in expropriatory measures adopted by the government which utterly lack a scientific basis.[411] One might find traces of behaviourally-motivated strategy in some of these judicial approaches.

UNCITRAL (2003); Wena *Hotels Ltd. v. Arab Republic of Egypt*, ICSID Case No. ARB/98/4, Award (2000); *Metalclad Corp. v. United Mexican States*, ICSID Case No. ARB(AF)/97/1, Award (2000); *Middle East Cement Shipping and Handling Co. S.A. v. Arab Republic of Egypt* (ICSID Case No. ARB/99/6), Award (2002).

[407] *J.A. Pye (Oxford) Ltd and J.A. Pye (Oxford) Land Ltd v. the United Kingdom*, Application no. 44302/02, at ¶ 54 (Grand Chamber) (2007) (citing *Papachelas v. Greece* [GC], no. 31423/96, § 48, ECHR 1999-II).

[408] *Funnekotter and others v. Zimbabwe*, ICSID CASE NO. ARB/05/6, Final Award (2009), at ¶ 147.

[409] *S.D. Myers, Inc. v. Government of Canada*, UNCITRAL, Final Award (concerning the apportionment of costs between the Disputing Parties), December 30, 2002, at ¶ 18 ("The only benchmarks, in terms of 'success', are (a) the results on the various liability issues and (b) the difference between the amounts claimed by [the claimant] and the amount ultimately awarded."). It is not entirely clear what degree of difference(s) crosses the transfer-of-costs line.

[410] *Id.*, at ¶ 19 (The claimant, for instance, might not be able to recover from the defendant if the claimant "was not successful on all of the positions it advanced in the liability phase of the arbitration," even though "it did establish liability.").

[411] R. Moloo & J. Jacinto, *Environmental and Health Regulation*, *supra*, at 30 ("While investors can reasonably expect regulation based on scientific evidence showing legitimate health or environmental concerns, they cannot be said to reasonably expect regulations lacking a scientific basis and supported only by political pressures.").

In fact, "taking into account the situation in Zimbabwe in 2001/2002" (referring to chaos, nationalisations and lack of protection for property or persons of investors)[412] an arbitral tribunal in 2009 did mandate that "the fees and expenses of the Tribunal and charges of ICSID will be borne by the Respondent, who will reimburse the Claimants of the sums advanced by them in this respect."[413] This is no small award, for even the fee of a *single* arbitrator typically exceeds $150,000. An argument could be made that the tribunal was forcing Zimbabwe's hand to clean up its future behaviour concerning security, protection and rights of investors. Depending on who is consulted, the tribunal's decision had the effect of being majestically or intrusively "political" even though it accomplished what it had to in terms of following proper judicial form and etiquette.

Another important example comes from the frivolous-action context. When "the initiation and pursuit of this arbitration is an abuse of the international investment protection regime under the BIT and, consequently, of the ICSID Convention" itself, it frivolously "force[s]" the respondent "to go through the process."[414] In such circumstances, the sovereign "should not be penalized by having to pay for its defense," and accordingly all arbitration costs might be imposed on the claimant.[415]

Not only is it a penalty for this investor, it is also a signal of deterrence to other potential "chancers." Lastly, fraud and deception constitute so fundamental a break from the higher traditions of international law and so substantial a threat to the survival of any international law regime that, in

---

[412] *Funnekotter and others*, *supra,* at ¶¶ 83, 103-106.

[413] *Id.*, at ¶ 147.

[414] *Phoenix Action, Ltd. v. The Czech Republic*, ICSID Case No. ARB/06/5, Final Award (2009), at ¶¶ 151-52. One possible approach, tacitly planted here, is that the burden of legal costs is higher on the claimant because it is, after all, the claimant who submits the request for arbitration. However, the burden should re-equalise if and when the government files a counter-claim (*burden of legal cost-shifting thesis*).

[415] *Id.* ("[U]sing its discretionary power, the Tribunal concludes that the Claimant is to bear all ICSID costs (the fees and expenses of the Members of the Tribunal and of the ICSID Secretariat, excluding the lodging fee) which are estimated to USD 356,000.00. As a consequence, the Claimant is to pay to the Respondent USD 196,000.00. The Tribunal further finds that the Respondent's legal fees and expenses are not unreasonable having regard to the course of these proceedings and that, therefore, the Claimant is to bear such costs in the amount of CZK 21,417,199.13.").

addition to customary law, tribunals will find a way to construe IIA's penalise fraudulent behaviour both of claimants and of sovereigns.[416]

This overall emerging doctrine does not necessarily favour the State or the claimant, the developing country or the developed one. It might turn out to be the case that empirically some actors are at more of an advantage on this issue than others are but this will be as much as result of the character of the disputes as of any inherent slant or bias attributable to the cases. Over the next several decades, these developments will come into their own.

[416] See, *e.g.*, *Plama Consortium Limited v. Bulgaria*, ICSID Case No. ARB/03/24, Award, August 27, 2008, at ¶¶ 143-144 (" … the Tribunal has decided that the investment was obtained by deceitful conduct that is in violation with Bulgarian law … It would also be contrary to the basic notion of international public policy – that a contract obtained through wrongful means (fraudulent misrepresentation) should not (sic) be enforced by a tribunal … The Tribunal finds that Claimant's conduct is contrary to the principle of good faith which is part not only of Bulgarian law … but also of international law …").

CHAPTER SEVEN

FUTURE BATTLEGROUNDS: DIALOGUE AND DEBATES IN THE PIPELINE

We have until now considered the clash between sovereignty and private interests before international tribunals. This debate represents the synthesis of countless variables, perceptions, justifications and motivations that are recounted in this book. Its contentious optic has been property rights, which is considered high-stakes because of the imminent and risky zero-sum game it puts into motion. We have together laboured to understand each sub-topic through a variety of angles and have analysed the follow-up legal strategies.

Four key points about expropriation are summarised for the stakeholders. First, expropriation is much more than just another cog in the wheel of international law because of the risks and rewards it carries for the affluent corporation and the penurious peasant alike.[1] Therein lies the key to its economic universality, transcending class and tax brackets. Second, expropriation is also geographically universal and thus shorthand for a widely-applicable litmus test. The oft-competing cross-currents of politics, trade, investment, public *versus* private interests are the determinants of this calculus. International tribunals do not somehow run on autopilot whereby a multi-linear regression might generate the appropriate result for the tribunal to render. Whether through "rationalisation that glosses over the tensions, arbitrariness, contingencies, and contradictions running

---

[1] Even if the "language of the law" is generally a "vulgar tongue," then the language of expropriation law is an urgent and important tongue. See A. de Tocqueville, DEMOCRACY IN AMERICA 12 (1945 ed.) (meaning that "'the whole people' was accustomed to discoursing in legal terms," see D. L. Horowitz, *Decreeing Organizational Change: Judicial Supervision of Public Institutions*, 32 DUKE L. J. 1265, 1266 (1983)).

through legal practice"[2] or cautious reasoning, international tribunals make their deductions.

Third, various analogies, First Principles, parallel reasoning, premises, appreciation of the consequences (both the pragmatic and the theoretical), and the ever-important assumptions inform this calculus. It is here that the transfers of knowledge and cross-pollination can be most fecund. There are significant ways that international arbitration, human rights and dispute settlement bodies might learn from one another, avoid one another's pitfalls, and teach emerging international law systems both positive lessons and negative admonitions. Fourth and lastly, international law is not a staid and sedentary system of rules and networks. It is engaged in a constant, dynamic project of introspection and self-improvement. Whether or not a proposed or percolating innovation in this field is to survive will depend on how deviations from the *status quo* are treated.[3] As many domestic courts of last resort maintain an open mind regarding *stare decisis*, international law too might maintain this receptiveness.

While there is some dispute as to whether the process of investment attraction results in a race to the bottom, it is perfectly clear that the race to the top for each international tribunal has legitimacy as its prize. Each institution is really in a race with itself and its game should involve cooperation with other international organs. Above all, the institutions wish to avoid existential futility, a form of death prior to their "natural" cessation of jurisprudential life. An international tribunal, and perhaps domestic ones as well, die in two ways, either of which is sufficient to deprive the tribunal of force and meaning: (*i*) No longer having its decisions obeyed by the parties and entities actually bound by the decisions; and (*ii*) No longer being able to persuade other tribunals or other political actors to do the same.[4]

---

[2] See F. Zarbiyev, *Judicial Activism in International Law—A Conceptual Framework for Analysis*, J. OF INTERNATIONAL DISPUTE SETTLEMENT, (2012), 1, 25.

[3] See S. Katzenstein, *International Adjudication and Custom Breaking by Domestic Courts*, *supra*, at 672-73 ("The legality of the deviation is determined by how other states respond—whether they decide to accept the proposed break with [customary international law] or to adhere to the existing rules. At its heart, then, the evolutionary process of [customary international law] requires not only a break from custom but also a period of uncertainty during which other states decide whether to follow course.").

[4] These actors are not mere myth-makers. They are entities who give the tribunal their confidence that the tribunal is doing its mortal best to be an effective embodiment of the rule of law.

Those who appreciate T.S. Eliot's 1925 poem *The Hollow Men* — "The supplication of a dead man's hand/Under the twinkle of a fading star" or "Between the potency/And the existence/Between the essence/And the descent/Falls the Shadow . . . This is the way the world ends/Not with a bang but a whimper" — might also appreciate, poignantly, this point. International tribunals often survive nominally after having been robbed of (or having lost over ill-gambled stakes) its ultimate capital of legitimacy. Experience teaches that the line between rigid ideology and idealistic principles is a thin one, if a separation there even exists. Pragmatism, though not necessarily the stuff of which folk songs are written, is nevertheless the stuff of which judicial statespersons are made. Nor has tact ever been considered to be disconnected from principles. Tact, moreover, is essential to the earning and keeping of tribunal legitimacy. For an international tribunal, the oxygen of legitimacy is a complex one but it is indispensable all the same.

A cooperative model respecting other international fora transcending subject-matter or specialisation is a superior method of approaching the situation. This book concludes by enumerating and justifying which future changes to look out for and what comes next. In short, this Chapter concerns the battlegrounds where the next several episodes — both skirmishes and full-scale warfare — will be fought out. The Chapter also summarises certain lessons and forewarnings that the author hopes will prove to be more than merely Sisyphean.

Future of the Debates

This Chapter consolidates and re-emphasises four themes: (*i*) aims and capabilities of the institutions; (*ii*) precedent, consistency and the network of cases influencing each other; (*iii*) limitations such as exhaustion, backlog, and bottleneck, that affect the outcomes as well as the future direction; and (*iv*) the subliminal, subtextual, subliminal role played by attribution and causation. This Chapter also collates the coming developments on which the international community should keep an eye.

The tribunal-types analysed in this book retain separate agendas and methods. Some, like trade and investments and inter-governmental dispute settlement bodies, are quintessentially problem-solving and pragmatic above most other concerns. Their ultimate aim is to avoid adverse diplomatic and political spats. While it is true that the best sometimes comes out of (and can come *only* out of) a marketplace of competing ideas, if not outright dissonance, that marketplace requires a baseline of stability and predictability in order to function. Other international courts, such international human rights tribunals, emphasise fidelity to the individual's dignity and property as key to their own legitimacy and survival.

Chapter I (INTRODUCTION) noted that the exhaustion of local remedies, non-discrimination (MFN and NT) and the other substantive standards (FET and MST) were selected as the prisms by which to assess these three institutions. These standards are the most crucial portals allowing or blocking a plaintiff's claim and, in exhaustion's case, postponing and sometimes even precluding a claim. They are common to the three institutions (in large part).

State responsibility divides up the world of rules into primary and secondary rules. To help with our analysis, the structure of this book uses the same breakdown. However, some things elude easy classification: the political and institutional objectives of the three systems fall clearly into neither camp. The same is true of attribution and causation principles. Yet the objectives play a significant role in answering why various prototypes of international tribunals interpret key international law principles in their own ways and how they apply the attribution and causation reasoning.

The other trans-substantive factor that only sometimes rears its head is sovereignty. Particularly, what should happen in cases where there is sovereignty-*versus*-sovereignty friction (such as the GATT/WTO *U.S. – Shrimp* dispute analysed in Chapters V (NON-DISCRIMINATION) and VI (OTHER SUBSTANTIVE STANDARDS))? The contagiousness of transboundary harm is where the question becomes difficult. Where each nation has the right to protect itself makes the question particular difficult and invites *ad-hoc* analysis as the least evil, or at least the least unworkable, course of action. Only a fact-specific, if not necessarily subjective, inquiry ("totality of the circumstances" perhaps) can determine if the treatment was unlawful. In Chapter V (NON-DISCRIMINATION), we analyse how sovereignty manifests itself in the consent issue.

The powerful role of case-law is also important if we are to understand the expropriation question. Case-law and consistency are not important for their own sakes: On the one hand, it exists to generate legitimacy and predictability and, on the other hand, obsolete case-law erodes legitimacy.[5] One helpful, though not full-proof, safeguard against the latter is cross-pollination. This book has noted that cross-pollination with respected international institutions is statistically high in NAFTA—deriving principles from the other IIA's and the IUCT (but rarely from international human rights tribunals, and rarely still *vice versa*)—in order to preserve

[5] B. N. Cardozo, THE NATURE OF THE JUDICIAL PROCESS 142-43 (1921).

systemic legitimacy. This may have gone a long way in preserving the IIA tribunals' legitimacy even though the finer details of their decisions occasionally contradict each other. This is less problematic for international human rights tribunals and the IUCT which, in effect, have the last word within their respective systems.

One proposal currently floating out there, based on the "*obligation de moyens*" or "best effort" principle, states firmly that international tribunals "have an obligation to consider previous decisions rendered" across international dispute settlement but "have no duty to look at previous decisions unless those previous decisions are pleaded by the parties."[6] In other words, international arbiters are disincentivised from recognising or derecognising legal doctrines *en passant*. The problem with this blunderbuss approach is that sometimes prior cases not addressed by the parties are still relevant. There would, in fact, have been a more conservative way to accomplish this end, by stating simply that international tribunals have no such obligation unless those previous decisions are pleaded by the parties *and* they are, by and large, the exclusive paths to giving the case that outcome.

Procedurally, this book covers the exhaustion of local remedies. What often are not officially recognised are the all-critical attribution, causation, and burden of proof principles. Also less recognised is the important role played by *force majeure* and passing on obligations to successor States (applicable to international human rights tribunals and the IUCT but could easily be relevant to a future IIA tribunal as a predicate question whose resolution is necessary for the question property before the IIA tribunal to be decided). These principles inform the systems' non-discrimination and other substantive standards jurisprudence.

The rules and standards used there, including the relative weights given to the components of each test, make a significant difference. Through the sequential method of case-law-building, international tribunals will need to decide which factors are *necessary* if a claim is to succeed and which are *sufficient* for the same, rather than lumping together several factors without any further guidance.

There is an important difference between situations where an international tribunal exercises prudential discretion to *not* interfere in a serious diplomatic, military or political dispute and when the tribunal exists for that very purpose. Chapters V and VI have highlighted the

---

[6] C. Kessedjian, "*Res Judicata*: What Investment Arbitration Can Learn from the 2006 ILA Resolution on International Commercial Arbitration" *in* R. P. Alford and Catherine A. Rogers, eds., THE FUTURE OF INVESTMENT ARBITRATION, *supra,* at 409.

tipping point for judicial restraint. The line is hard to delineate, especially in emergency or *force majeure* cases.

On the substantive front, important findings include the ECtHR's non-discrimination test that guards against official bias towards domestic populations; the different attribution tests calculated to account for the IUCT's retroactive, *force majeure* imperatives; the causation and burdens of proof standards that differ about disparate *intent* with disparate *effect* (with the IUCT using less strict standards to find expropriation); and the big-picture task of deciding what constitutes a "substantive" violation such as FET or MST.

The book frequently combines the tests and rationales in order to make it actually workable and effective. Questions remain about how to weigh the different components and sub-parts of the various tests. Still, we can already see that sovereignty figures into the equation again and is sometimes balanced with the aims and purposes of the tribunals. This balancing decides the level of scrutiny that issues such as intent, reliance and proportionality concerning some act or measure of expropriation is given. We also see a distinct trend, in both non-discrimination and FET and MST analyses (Chapters V and VI): move towards adopting the international human rights system's and specifically the ECtHR's *James* proportionality test.

The new frontier may well turn out to be procedure. Chapter IV (EXHAUSTION OF LOCAL REMEDIES AND CONTINUOUS NATIONALITY) analyses exhaustion in detail. There is the continuing dispute about whether an alleged violation is properly certified as a domestic law and/or contract claim or an international law violation. This dispute transcends the procedural into the substantive, and *vice versa*. Chapter IV has explained that this classification can make all the difference as far as technical and merits reviewability before international tribunals are concerned. Chapter IV also focuses on shareholder and continuous nationality principles in order to highlight their evolution.

Procedure, substance, and between-the-lines causation and attribution reasoning all merge at several points in expropriation analysis. This makes a determinative difference as to how strictly the international tribunal elects to scrutinise the respective positions; how intrusively and independently it weighs the evidence; whether it exercises judicial restraint and does not exceed the narrowest ground(s) in disposing of a case; if it assesses the internal coherence of the expropriation in light of the State's purported goals (to see if the State's position is self-contradictory); whether, in situations where state responsibility is in doubt, the State is free of liability if its legislation on the books had proscribed or limited the expropriation; and the circumstances in which the international tribunal defers to the highest domestic court's interpretation of what domestic law says.

Unresolved structural, procedural and developmental issues, which I hope are points of knowledge transfer, which will determine what happens to this area are flagged in this book: whether the "Hobbesian security compensation" argument as a rationale will gain force as a justification behind the consent theory and therefore strengthen the latter (Chapter I); what future exists for the "3+2 Institutional Guardians" proposal and whether it will even prove to be effective (Chapter II – INSTITUTIONS AS PRISMS); where lies the burden of proof in *de facto* agency and instrumentality cases where the State countenances the violation or tacitly encourages the perpetrators (mainly through non-intervention) (Chapter III: ATTRIBUTION AND CAUSATION); how Professor Brownlie's "national economic disaster" test will be applied and whether it will become a peremptory norm in IIA tribunals and property rights regimes (Chapter III); whether an official condemnation in domestic law of the expulsion or expropriation (whatever the conduct of the parastatals or instrumentalities) can make the State non-liable (Chapter III); if "collective investment funds," "trusts" or "associations" fall within the general reading of the operative term "investor" (Chapter III); whether interference with the day-to-day operations of an investment are to be considered *quasi-de jure* expropriations as opposed to regulatory expropriations, thus recalibrating the burden of proof (Chapter III); whether it will be customary law that IIA's and indeed any instrument whose exclusive purpose, at least ostensibly, is to promote capital flow and encourage FDI are assumed not to have extended coverage to non-business assets (Chapter III); how, given silence or ambiguity in the international instruments, various international tribunal types will construe the coverage question(s) attending debt securities and loans (Chapter III); whether IIA tribunals will give "denial of benefits" clauses customary, default status in international law (Chapter III); how the "bellwether briefs" and model BIT's signalling behaviour in the IIA sphere will interact with similar developments in the international human rights sphere (Chapter III); whether domestic law has any role in guiding an international tribunal's interpretation of the treaty (Chapter III); whether the burden of proof rests on the State in cases where it is not clear if the investment has been undertaken in compliance with the host State's laws and what factors aid in this determination (Chapter III); how tribunals might decide whether the debts and obligations of predecessor regimes pass on to successor regimes (Chapter III); how a tribunal is to weigh the sector-specific realities of a commercial enterprise in order to decide on expropriation (Chapters III, V, and VI); the *Yukos* question of whether the lack of effective remedies constitutes a violation in itself (Chapter IV); the relevance of a private contract on a public law claim and where the domestic vis-à-vis international tribunal line of demarcation lies (Chapter III and Chapter IV); at which point "control" becomes determinative of the expropriation question and at which point a diminution in value becomes "substantial" (Chapters III and VI: OTHER SUBSTANTIVE STANDARDS); whether it is legitimate for a tribunal to engage with the merits in order to decide a threshold jurisdictional or procedural question, or the converse—to redefine the merits in order to slide in through the backdoor what the procedural requirements do not clearly address (Chapter IV); how to decide if a claimant must invoke a discretionary remedy before submitting the claim in international court (Chapter IV); if a tribunal can adjust jurisdiction and merits to deal with extra-legal considerations like backlog and bottleneck or should this be resolved only by the parties and the arbitral system (Chapter IV); what will happen of "partial equivalents" for the exhaustion doctrine such as fixed time-limits, local-courts-first requirements and fork-in-the-road provisions (Chapter IV); how international tribunals will respond to the nationality question and whether, as the appropriate test, they will prefer the place of incorporation or the corporate *siège social* (Chapter IV); whether the minority investor need have at least a certain proportion in stake before qualifying for protection (Chapter IV); if treaty-shopping diminishes the force and authority of the rule of law and how it can be mitigated (Chapter IV); whether the potential for opting out of IIA's by developing countries will become so overwhelming as to virtually require the presence of "special and differentiated treatment" for them (Chapter VI); whether the various sovereigns' challenges to mass claims will succeed in the fullness of time as well as whether the *amicus* process will expand in the practice of international law (Chapter VI); whether IIA will adopt, by norm or codification, certain transparency (or at least anti-opacity) principles for evidentiary scrutiny from the international human rights arena (Chapter VI); and whether this book's *burden of legal cost-shifting thesis* will gain traction in the coming decades (Chapter VI).

Several issues remain unresolved on the substantive plane (or on a mixed substantive-procedural plane): Whether "the principle that international treaties must be interpreted autonomously, i.e., not in accordance with the domestic legal orders of the contracting State parties involved" (as Judge Brower put it in *Renta*)[7] will have staying power and

---

[7] *Renta*, *supra*, at ¶ 28 (Separate opinion of Judge Charles Brower).

whether it will also apply to facts proffered by the sovereign state (Chapter III); whether the yawning divide between the prevailing mode of interpretation (text) ever return to the intentionalist approach, and the associated implications (Chapter V); whether the elements *sina qua non* as well as those sufficient to prove intent highlighted in this book will be followed by international tribunals (Chapter V); whether vestiges of class-based systemic inequality can be undone by imposing special burdens on innocent third-party individuals in order to level the proverbial playing field (Chapter V); if there are narrowly-tailored means for the tribunal to assure itself that the State is not trying evade liability in the discrimination context by using the "decoy" strategy (Chapter V); how the "necessity" test should operate in international tribunals and whether a less-restrictive or least-restrictive should be used (Chapter V); the *Feldman-S. D. Myers* differences on whether a "rational justification" by the State is enough (Chapter V); the *Maffezini*-MFN problem about the actionability of third-party MFN clauses and its implications for the consent question (Chapter V); whether and how claimants may invert the "public interest" rationale and argue that this interest is actually *enhanced* by the investor's or owner's behaviour (Chapter V); what costs are imposed on claimants and States by State (not tribunal) reinterpretations that upset the previous understanding and how a tribunal can distinguish a reinterpretation from a novel addition (Chapter V); how "creeping expropriations" will be evaluated and what such an expropriation entails (Chapter V); what implications the differences between international trade law and IIA will have (Chapter V); how the "likeness" analysis functions in effect, given the international human rights courts' preference for the pro-weaker party interpretation given by the ECtHR in *Pine Valley* (Chapter V); whether the "class of one" theory of discrimination is winnable as a non-discrimination claim (Chapter V); what the implications and relevance of the State's "Achilles Heel" strategy in the "class of one" theory context might be, as per the intent issue (Chapter V); whether the expropriation versus treasury policy distinction might be adopted in precluding relief for claims beyond non-discrimination (Chapter V); how the intent *versus* effects, reliance, and proportionality tests inform future tribunals and what trends emerge (Chapter VI – *Other Substantive Standards*); whether an international tribunal may consider the internal coherence of an expropriatory measure, viz. whether the expropriation achieves the State's own purported objectives, in deciding whether it violates an international law instrument (Chapters V and VI); how the NAFTA-IIA structures can adapt to *force majeure* and other emergency situations (Chapters IV, V, and VI); how scientific and other esoteric evidence should be analysed and whether the tribunals should evaluate it independently of the parties' experts (Chapter VI); whether voter discontentment and community pressure is, without more, a legitimate public aim that satisfies the first prong of the proportionality test (Chapter VI); whether and to what extent the international tribunal must defer to the State's view of its own "public interest" or even its "sustainable development" objectives (Chapter VI); how the tension between "sustainable development" and the interests of the investor community will be resolved and whether "sustainable development" ever will become a peremptory norm in international law (Chapter VI); whether international tribunals might find international wrongs if the sovereign imposed draconian means to meet its objectives without first attempting less drastic methods (Chapter VI); whether IIA tribunals will apply, extend or modify the "legitimate expectations" principle in order to limit retroactively imposed burdens, even in the exercise of the State's core sovereignty (Chapter VI); whether the beneficial effect on the whole society is significantly relevant or whether international tribunals will eventually form a consensus around the *TECMED-Santa Elena* path (Chapter VI); what will become of the "Be Careful What You Seek" cautionary note concerning the property rights-human rights paradox (Chapter VI); what evolutions will befall the prominence given to certain nations' "bellwether briefs" and the economic and political factors that will inform this calculus (Chapters III-VI); whether there will be a substantial transformation in the determinants of a compound-interest determination (including egregious misconduct, fraud, deception and frivolous action) (Chapter VI); whether the Direct-Evidence-of-*Scienter*, Symptomatic-Effects, and Typical-Practices strategies will gain momentum and what this might mean (Chapter VI); whether the *Funnekotter* approach of taking context into account to assess costs and damages will be judicially acknowledged as connected with the "moral damages" principle and thus place either or both on firmer footing (Chapter VI); whether and to what extent the reserve-to-capital ratio requirements might contravene customary law or an IIA (Chapter VI); and, finally, whether *LG&E Energy* tribunal's "permanence" test will be adopted by other international tribunals, especially the ECtHR (Chapter VI).

Some of these dilemmas are technical and they might sound nothing like animated cries of property protection and sovereignty. But each has the potential to drive a gaping hole through whole bodies of jurisprudence. We have thus returned to the earlier debate about primary and secondary rights. We can now deduce, with a book's worth of evidence from our institutions, that just because a question does not deal with the substantive nub of the issue does not mean that its impact is any less. The debate is consequential for the outcomes in a high volume of cases.

The Role of Dialogue in Preserving the Legitimacy of International Law

This right-remedy gap[8] in international law is automatically (or so often) mired in sovereignty questions, and actually realising this theoretical right hangs in the balance. The consent issue and the pro- and anti-*Maffezini* positions (from Chapter V: *Non-Discrimination*) connected to consent are a constant reminder.

However, this grand debate has no binary answer; its case-by-case answer depends on the specific "consent in writing" clause of the ICSID Convention or the New York Convention, as Chapter V also shows. This book highlights them partly because others have not, and the issues need percolating in the political, scholarly and arbitral stratospheres.

The book stresses upon a cooperative model, with the legitimacy and the accountability shared between the tribunals *and* the legislative and drafting processes both for international law and for domestic expropriation laws. The tri-partite requirements of the Brunnée and Toope "interactional model," articulated in Chapter III (ATTRIBUTION AND CAUSATION) and applied in later chapters, inform this perspective. Empirical scholarship on this front is woefully lacking, probably because the diplomatically- and politically-fraught international negotiations are not like the relatively transparent debates in domestic Diets, Parliaments and Congresses.[9] "Transparent" does not necessarily mean "reliable," often due to conveniently planted and at the time largely unnoticed

---

[8] The term was coined by Professor John Jeffries in his article *The Right-Remedy Gap in Constitutional Law*, 109 YALE L. J. 1425 (1999) (this gap helps develop legal doctrine because it cuts down on the costs and moral hazards of change, thus not discouraging judges and arbitrators from expanding on the holding at issue or issuing other, future expansionary decisions); L. Bergkamp, LIABILITY AND ENVIRONMENT: PRIVATE AND PUBLIC LAW ASPECTS OF CIVIL LIABILITY FOR ENVIRONMENTAL HARM IN AN INTERNATIONAL CONTEXT 357-8 (Martin Nijhoff Publishers, 2001).

[9] See M. Malik, *Recent Developments in International Investment Agreements: Negotiations and Dispute*, IV Annual Forum for Developing Country Investment Negotiators Background Papers, New Delhi, October 27-29, 2010, *available at* <www.iisd.org/pdf/2011/dci_2010_recent_developments_iias.pdf> (last accessed October 2, 2011), and sources cited therein.

speeches and positions in signing statements of intent.[10] Still, this is a good starting point (subject to credibility impeachment).

Chief Justice of the United States John Marshall's famous saying—"The people have made the constitution and they can unmake it"[11]—is apt. This international law percolation works in a bottom-up, rather than top-down, fashion. Domestic actors keep the international tribunals alive in order to organise a proliferating and potentially out-of-control dispute resolution network encompassing IIAs, human rights courts, dispute settlement tribunals, and other arbitral bodies. This is keenly important when the arbitrators and judges are duty-bound to pronounce an unpalatable but legally required result.

This network is confounded by the fact that public interest activists, advocates and claimants sometimes do not know which idea from which international (and sometimes domestic) tribunal is influencing the judges. This causes fragmentation in international law. As we saw at the end of the last chapter, activists and parties might be able to forewarn international tribunals about the logical endpoint of a particular doctrine (such as the *TECMED-Starrett-Tippetts-Metalclad-Santa Elena* tendency towards a "sole effects" test) *if* they know the tribunal's leaning. Legitimacy-affirming dialogue among the political brokers, the international tribunals and the citizenry is key here.[12]

Certainly there are the reinterpretations and add-ons enacted by signatory States to flesh out the specific, contextual meaning of the text. But even before it gets to that stage, there are ideas bubbling up in the political sphere that need to be heard. Less final and more embryonic than these reinterpretations are the political concerns, solutions and ideas, and they should be addressed by the international tribunals.

The tribunals need not agree with these concerns but only engage with them proactively. This exercise is not for its own sake. Rather, these ideas come from the citizens and negotiators who, at the end of the day, decide if the tribunals stay or go. To be sure, they have their reasons and constraints, their incentives and disincentives—some of which might make their decision inevitable or prohibitively costly. Nonetheless, Consent is back on the table. The international system depends on the political actors and their say-so. They have their own incentives to stay in the system, and clarity, predictability and dependability are just some of the reasons. Their

---

[10] S. D. Franck, *Rationalizing Costs in Investment Treaty Arbitration,* 88 WASH. U. L. REV. 769, 844 (2011) [S. D. Franck, *Rationalizing Costs in ITA*].

[11] See *Cohens v. Virginia*, 19 U.S. 264, 389 (1821).

[12] S. D. Franck, *Rationalizing Costs in ITA, supra*, at 772, n. 7.